KT-496-322

THE
TEDDY BEAR
ENCYCLOPEDIA

THE
TEDDY BEAR
ENCYCLOPEDIA

PAULINE COCKRILL

FOREWORD BY PAUL AND ROSEMARY VOLPP

PHOTOGRAPHY BY PETER ANDERSON AND JIM COIT

DORLING KINDERSLEY

LONDON • NEW YORK • STUTTGART

A DORLING KINDERSLEY BOOK

PROJECT EDITOR Irene Lyford
PROJECT ART EDITOR Peter Cross

EDITOR HelenTownsend
DESIGNER Deborah Myatt

MANAGING EDITOR Mary-Clare Jerram
MANAGING ART EDITOR Gill Della Casa

PRODUCTION Helen Creeke

First published in Great Britain in 1993
by Dorling Kindersley Limited, 9 Henrietta Street,
London WC2E 8PS
Reprinted 1993

COPYRIGHT © 1993
DORLING KINDERSLEY LIMITED, LONDON

Text copyright © 1993 Pauline Cockrill
Foreword copyright © 1993 Paul and Rosemary Volpp

All rights reserved. No part of this publication may
be reproduced, stored in a retrieval system, or
transmitted in any form or by any means, electronic,
mechanical, photocopying, recording or otherwise,
without the prior written permission of the
copyright owner.

A CIP catalogue record for this book is available
from the British Library.

ISBN 0-7513-0046-2

Computer page make-up by The Cooling Brown
Partnership, London
Text film output by The Right Type, London
Reproduced by Colourscan, Singapore
Printed and bound by Arnoldo Mondadori
Editore, Italy

CONTENTS

6 • Foreword by
Paul & Rosemary Volpp

•8•
INTRODUCTION

•14•
THE CATALOGUE

16 • Steiff: 1902–05
18 • Steiff: 1905–World War I
20 • Steiff: 1903–World War I
22 • Steiff: 1908–World War I
24 • Ideal: 1903–World War I
26 • US: c.1907–14
28 • Great Britain:
1908–c.1920
30 • Germany: 1920s–30s
32 • Bing: 1909–32
34 • Bing: c.1910–32
36 • Steiff: 1920s–30s

38 • STEIFF: IN THE BEGINNING...

40 • Schuco: 1920s–30s
42 • Schuco: 1920s–30s
44 • Helvetic: mid-1920s
46 • US: 1914–20s
48 • France: 1920s–30s

50 • J.K. Farnell: 1920s–30s
52 • Chad Valley: 1920s–30s
54 • Chad Valley: 1920s–30s
56 • Chiltern: 1920s–40s
58 • Joy-Toys: 1920s–60s
60 • Merrythought: 1930s
62 • Chad Valley: 1938–50s
64 • Chad Valley: 1930s–40s

66 • MERRYTHOUGHT MAGIC

68 • Merrythought: 1930s
70 • UK: 1930s–50s
72 • Dean's : 1920s–50s
74 • Knickerbocker:
1920–30s
76 • Knickerbocker: post-
World War II
78 • Japan: 1945–90s
80 • Australia: 1930s–60s
82 • Character: 1945–83
84 • Gund: 1930s–60s
86 • Ideal: 1930s–50s
88 • Merrythought: 1940s–50s
90 • J.K. Farnell: 1945–68
92 • Pedigree: 1937–50s

94 • THE HERMANN DYNASTY

96 • Gebrüder Hermann:
1948–c.1970
98 • Hermann & Co:
1940s–60s

100 • Steiff: 1940s–early1960s

102 • Dean's: 1950s

104 • Chad Valley: 1950s–60s

106 • Chiltern: post-World War II–1950s

108 • Chiltern: c.1958–early 1960s

110 • Steiff: 1950s

112 Schuco: 1949–76

114 • Germany: post-1945

116 • Germany: post-1945

118 • Switzerland & Austria: post-1945

120 • Merrythought: 1940s–60s

122 • Wendy Boston: 1945–76

124 • UK: post-World War II–c.1970

126 • Dean's c.1960–80

128 • Steiff: 1960s–90s

130 • Chad Valley: 1960–78

132 • Pedigree: 1960s–80s

134 • Merrythought: 1970s–80s

136 • Australia & New Zealand: 1970–90s

138 • US: 1950s–80s

140 • US: late 1970s–80s

142 • UK: 1970s–80s

144 • House of Nisbet: 1976–89

146 • North American Bear Co: 1979–92

148 • RUSS BERRIE: MASS-PRODUCED BEARS

150 • Canterbury Bears: 1980–90s

152 • Steiff: 1980–92

154 • Gebrüder Hermann: 1980s–92

156 • Germany: 1980s–90s

158 • Ireland: 1938–79

160 • Merrythought: 1982–92

162 • Dean's: 1980s–90s

164 • France: post-1945

166 • Europe: 1930s–80s

168 • Worldwide Expansion: post-1945

170 • Mass-market Collectables: 1980s–90s

•172•
BEAR ARTISTS

•188•
ARCTOPHILY: BEAR COLLECTING

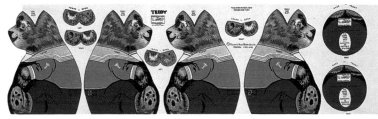

•202•
BEAR CARE & REPAIR

204 • Restoring Traditional-style Bears

210 • Caring for Modern Bears

212 • Preventive Care and Grooming

214 • Display and Storage

•215•
THE TEDDY BEAR DIRECTORY

216 • Teddy Bear Time Chart

220 • Factory Histories

230 • Useful Addresses

234 • Glossary

236 • Index

239 • Acknowledgments

FOREWORD

PAUL AND ROSEMARY VOLPP

WHAT A PRIVILEGE AND PLEASURE to introduce you to another beautiful Dorling Kindersley book written by best-selling author Pauline Cockrill. If you are already acquainted with *The Ultimate Teddy Bear Book*, and with the *The Little Books of Traditional Bears*, *of Celebrity Bears*, and *of Bear Care*, you will know that you are holding a feast of reading and viewing in your hands.

Our introduction to the teddy-bear world happened over a decade ago, in an enchanting store called The Teddy Bear Station in Yorba Linda, California. We were browsing, just killing time until a restaurant opened, when Rosemary was captivated by a blue bear in an aviator suit looking down from a shelf. The sales lady came over and said, "If you like that bear, you'd better take it now. It's the last one in southern California, and there won't be any more." Rosemary replied that that was very interesting, but she wasn't a bear collector. Famous last words! A friend who accompanied us to dinner kept teasing Rosemary that she would regret not buying the bear for the rest of her life, until she got so excited that she went back to the store between the main course and dessert and bought her. She was a North American Bear Company Amelia Bearhart. Although her original price was under $40.00, Amelias now sell for over $1,000.00 (*see p.146*).

Paul caught bear fever, too, and then we were off and running to every bear store we could find. That was the beginning of a hobby that has taken the two of us all over the world. In a remarkably short time, Amelia became part of a collection of about 5,000 teddy bears, of every description imaginable. We often say we don't know whether we are bragging or complaining when we admit to the size of our collection. But one thing is certain: the bears have led us to meet some unforgettable people, and this is a bonus of collecting. We have happy memories of having been twice in Minneapolis at the Teddy Tribune Convention, and

Very important bear
Amelia Bearhart launched the North American Bear Company's V.I.B. (Very Important Bear) range of costumed teddy characters with punning names (see pp.146–47).

Bear-happy author
Teddy-bear historian and author Pauline Cockrill signs a copy of The Ultimate Teddy Bear Book, watched by Paul and Rosemary Volpp's world-famous Steiff bear "Happy".

enjoying the company of Mr. Peter Bull, the British actor and author, who has been credited with revitalizing the teddy-bear phenomenon. Sadly, Peter died in May 1984, but the world is still enjoying the legacy of his remarkable contribution. In our own home, we have Peter's bear "Delicatessen" – or "Aloysius" as he is known in the British TV series *Brideshead Revisited* (*see p.147*).

Along with our bear "Happy" (*see p.37*), we were invited to take part in a week-long, fund-raising effort in England by Action Research – an event rather similar to our March of Dimes in the United States. During the week, we had the pleasure of spending an evening with Michael Bond, the creator of that marvellous character Paddington Bear, and we also experienced the thrill of being presented to Her Royal Highness, Princess Margaret. Today's collectors are drawn from every age group and from every corner of the globe. We recently received a letter from a ten-year-old collector in South Africa, and in our files we have copies of three doctoral dissertations on teddy bears sent to us by Ph.D. researchers. At the same time, bears and related items have become a part of almost every avenue of commerce.

One for the album
Paul and Rosemary Volpp, who have one of the largest collections of teddy bears in the world, shown here with their Steiff bear "Happy"; together they have raised large sums of money for charity.

Peter Bull once confessed that he was somewhat confused by the "sudden and quite sensational" popularity of the teddy bear. Unlike the majority of toys and dolls – the novelties that come and go along with the latest children's crazes – teddies seem to be with us permanently. But what is the reason for their triumphant survival? We agree with Peter Bull who tried to explain the phenomenon, saying, "The mystique lies in the faces of the bears themselves." It is true; every teddy is, indeed, unique. Therefore, it is with the greatest of pleasure that we urge you on to read this book: look at the bears' faces; enjoy their faces. Don't you agree? The enchantment and the mystique will last forever!

First choice
"Lindy", a 1909, golden mohair-plush Steiff, was the first traditional bear in the Volpps' collection.

Rosemary Volpp

Paul E Volpp

Introduction

FROM POLITICAL MASCOT TO TREASURED TOY AND WORK OF ART

From wild carnivore to much-loved children's toy may seem an unlikely leap for a bear to make. However, from the late nineteenth century, bears (or "bruins") were common in the nursery, both as characters in books and as playthings. Performing bears were well known in Europe and North America, travelling around with their itinerant trainers. These bears were imitated by French toy manufacturers, such as Décamps or Martin, whose clockwork models could dance, growl, or drink from bottles. At the same time, German, Swiss, and Russian toy-makers were producing carved, wooden bears.

Teddy-bear ancestor
Soft-toy bears, sometimes set on cast-iron wheels (above), and popular from the late nineteenth century, were made in Germany before World War I.

The teddy bear's immediate ancestor was the realistic soft-toy bear on all fours, produced in Germany from the late nineteenth century. Already world leaders in all aspects of the toy industry, from porcelain dolls, wooden animals and printed games, to tin boats and trains, Germany soon became the leading manufacturer of soft toys as well. For these toys, they used mohair plush – a new fabric that had been developed to resemble real fur, woven from mohair, the wool of angora goats. Reinhold Schulte founded his Duisberg weaving mill in 1901, importing spun mohair from the north of England – hence the descriptive term "Yorkshire cloth".

In 1901, Theodore Roosevelt (nicknamed "Teddy") became President of the United States. In November 1902, he embarked on a four-day hunting expedition in Mississippi, during which he refused to shoot a bear that had been cornered for him. The incident prompted a cartoon by Clifford K. Berryman which appeared in the *Washington Post* on 16 November 1902; the title of the cartoon, "Drawing the Line at Mississippi", also referred to a boundary dispute which the President had set out to resolve.

THE TEDDY CRAZE BEGINS

Soon after Berryman's cartoon appeared, Morris Michtom, a Russian emigré, displayed a plush bear, made by his wife Rose and labelled "Teddy's Bear", in the window of his New York store. It was an instant success. The wholesalers Butler Brothers eventually bought the Michtom's entire stock and, helped by the backing of Butler Brothers, Mitchom established the Ideal Novelty and Toy Company, reputed to be the first US teddy-bear manufacturer (*see pp.24–25*).

As interest in the teddy was developing in the United States, a German company founded by Margarete Steiff (*see pp.38–39*) to make felt clothes and toys, was making plush toys and developing a

Theodore Roosevelt (1858–1919)
Dressed (left) as a pioneer in hunting attire, Roosevelt loved the outdoor life.

"Drawing the Line..."
The original Berryman cartoon (below) from the Washington Post *of 16 November 1902.*

Billy Possum
The plush opossum (above), named after US president William Taft, was intended to rival the teddy bear. Steiff made a version from 1909 until 1914 and, in the US, H. Fisher & Co., Hahn & Amberg, and Harman Manufacturing Co. also made versions.

jointed bear-doll. Although these were unpopular at first, Hermann Berg of the New York wholesalers George Borgfeldt & Co. – prompted by the "Teddy" mania sweeping the US – bought 3,000 of these bear-dolls at the March 1903 Leipzig Toy Fair. Over the next five years, the Steiff business expanded dramatically.

US RIVALS STEIFF

The height of the teddy craze coincided with Roosevelt's second administration (1905–09). Several shortlived American companies were formed to compete with Steiff, producing teddy-related novelties (see pp.26–27). In 1906, the US toy trade catalogue *Playthings* first referred to "Teddy's Bears" and this was soon abbreviated to "Teddy Bear".

1905 Steiff bear
The example (above) is typical of the early, realistic Steiff teddies.

Steiff factory
Steiff was founded in 1893 as The Felt Toy Factory (below).

In 1908, an enterprising American asked the Karl Hofmann company, in the Sonneberg-Neustadt area of Germany, to make teddy bears, thereby launching a cottage industry largely devoted to US exports. This later evolved into various successful businesses, including the Hermann factories (see pp.94–95). It is said that in the same year, J.K. Farnell & Co. produced the first British teddy bear on the advice of German exporters, Eisenmann & Co. Prompted by the increased competition, manufacturers turned to novelty bears:

musical bears, whistling bears, half-bear/half-doll models, and the ingenious, clockwork bears of Gebrüder Bing.

Bear wardrobe
Produced for a US department store c.1906, this Steiff bear's possessions (above) include denim overalls and a knitted one-piece swimsuit, as well as a case of toys complete with skipping rope, train, and American football.

CHARACTER BEARS

Probably conceived as a bear-doll for boys, the design of the teddy-bear was ideal for dressing-up. Teddies in masculine costume began to appear, influenced by Seymour Eaton's poems about the Roosevelt Bears. From 1907, Kahn & Mosshacher of New York and Steiff produced outfits embroidered with "Teddy B" or "Teddy G", while D.W. Shoyer & Co. produced knitted sweaters and hats for bears. Women's magazines published patterns for teddy outfits.

In 1909, Roosevelt lost the election to William Taft, and new mascots were made, trying, unsuccessfully, to overthrow Teddy's Bear. One was Billy Possum, a reference to Taft's love of "possum and 'taters" (once served to him at a banquet in Georgia). The popular, but shortlived, Billiken also dates from 1909; other rivals included W.J. Terry's Billy Owlett, a patriotically dressed owl, which the manufacturer predicted "may challenge the supremacy of the teddy bear". But the confidence was unfounded – and the teddy bear still reigns supreme.

Electric-eye bear
From 1907, novelties abounded; the bulbs in this bear's eyes light up when its chest is squeezed (above).

EFFECTS OF WORLD WAR I

In 1913, German toy output was six times that of Great Britain. However, following the outbreak of World War I, the importation of German goods into Great Britain was designated an "act of treason" (according to a 1914 British trade journal), so launching Britain's own soft-toy industry. W.J. Terry, J.K. Farnell, and the British United Toy Manufacturing Co. were already making teddies, and other toy firms seized the opportunity to begin production. Dean's Rag Book Co. Ltd. (who had produced printed, cloth, cut-out "Knockabout" teddy bears in 1908) and Johnson Brothers of Birmingham, makers of "Chad Valley" board-games, are two such examples.

Several shortlived soft-toy firms were established, such as the Wholesale Toy Company, the Worthing Toy Factory, and the South Wales Toy Manufacturing Co., as well as pioneers W.H. Jones and the Teddy Toy Company. Many novelties were introduced, such as the British Doll and Novelty Company's Teddy Bear Exerciser, with expandable arms, or Isaac & Company's Isa spring-leg teddy bear. Also popular were uniformed mascots such as Harwin's Ally Bears (see p.29); Dean's printed Bear of Russia, Germany Crusher; the London Toy Company's Ivan the Russian Tommy; and Britannia Toy Works' Cossack.

From 1919, France also developed its teddy-bear industry and the companies Thiennot, Pintel, and F.A.D.A.P. were formed (see pp.48–49). In Australia, Charles Jensen patented a jointed bear in 1916, and the first commercially made Australian teddy bears were produced by Joy-Toys of Victoria (see pp.58–59) in the 1920s.

THE EVOLUTION OF THE BRITISH TEDDY

The 1920s and 1930s were the boom years for British teddy-bear manufacturers, with old-established firms, such as Farnell, Chad Valley, and Dean's, and new firms like H. G. Stone and Merrythought, becoming world leaders. The teddy bear acquired a new look: previously, the traditional stuffing was wood-wool – fine, wood shavings used as packing material for china etc., known in the United States by its nineteenth-century name "excelsior". Pieces of cork and horsehair were also used sometimes as stuffing. Now manufacturers turned to the lighter, softer, and more hygienic kapok – a fine cottonlike material, harvested from the seed-pod of the tropical tree *Ceiba pentandra*, and originally used as a stuffing for cushions and life-jackets. British manufacturers, in particular, preferred it as it could be purchased cheaply from within the Empire. The Teddy Toy Company patented its kapok-stuffed

1920s J.K. Farnell

The golden mohair bear (above) was made by J.K. Farnell, one of Britain's first teddy-bear manufacturers. The bear has five "webbed" claws on its paws with two dots behind, a distinctive Farnell feature.

Final grooming

Young girls working in a British teddy-bear factory during World War I (below); while the girls groom finished bears with large, scrubbing brushes, a pile of legs and arms lies on the floor awaiting assembly.

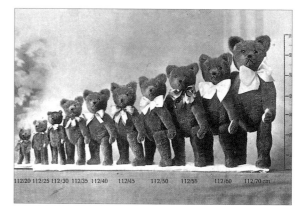

Teddy parade

The 1920s catalogue page (above) of the Sonneberg-based company Max Hermann (later Hermann-Spielwaren), shows their 112 range in 10 sizes. The design was reproduced as their 1990 German Unification Bear.

Stuffing funnels

Tin funnels (above), used in German factories to prevent the plush fraying while bears are being stuffed with wood-wool, are still in use today.

Softanlite bears in 1920, followed by Chad Valley's Aerolite (*see p.52*), and W.J. Terry's Ahsolite bears. Boot buttons, made of moulded, compressed wood pulp, were traditionally used for teddy bears' eyes, but after the war the blown-glass type of eye used by taxidermists came into favour.

Artificial-silk plush (woven from a fibre made from reconstituted wood pulp, or other form of cellulose) became a popular alternative; it first appeared in Britain in 1929 on Farnell's Silkalite and Chiltern's Silky Bear, in several fashionable colours.

1930s Chad Valley
The bear (above) *has a horizontally stitched nose, and the typical, Chad Valley red, embroidered label.*

Final details
A Peacock range bear is fitted with eyes at Chad Valley's factory in the 1930s (above).

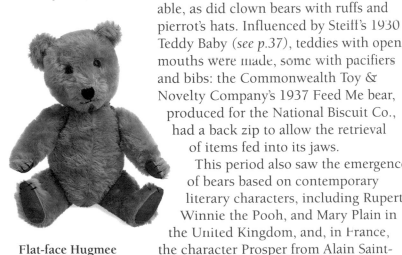

Sheepskin bear
1940s Australian bear (above) *with leather pads, "sub" stuffing, and unjointed neck.*

NOVELTY AND LITERARY BEARS
Mass-produced teddy bears, with rod-jointed, straight bodies and limbs, became increasingly popular. Novelties included the famous Yes/No bears made by Schuco (*see pp.42–43*); the London-based Wholesale Toy Company's 1921 Blinka rolling-eyed bears, which were similar to Gebrüder Süssenguth's Peter (*see p.31*); Swiss squeeze-type musical bears; and Gross & Schild's 1926 Bruno the Talking Bear of 1926, which emitted a growl from its mouth.

Tipped mohair plush became fashionable, as did clown bears with ruffs and pierrot's hats. Influenced by Steiff's 1930 Teddy Baby (*see p.37*), teddies with open mouths were made, some with pacifiers and bibs: the Commonwealth Toy & Novelty Company's 1937 Feed Me bear, produced for the National Biscuit Co., had a back zip to allow the retrieval of items fed into its jaws.

This period also saw the emergence of bears based on contemporary literary characters, including Rupert, Winnie the Pooh, and Mary Plain in the United Kingdom, and, in France, the character Prosper from Alain Saint-Ogan's 1933 comic strip.

In 1936, New York dress designer Ruth Harkness brought the first giant panda to the West; specimens were subsequently given to Chicago and London Zoos, resulting in the onset of an apparently relentless craze for panda-teddies.

AT WAR AGAIN
Hitler's rise to power in 1933, and the resulting world war, had a dramatic effect on industry. From 1939, toy production was severely reduced to give priority to munitions and uniforms. Raw materials required for making teddy bears, such as cloth, card, and metal, were rationed. "Sub" (textile industrial waste) was substituted for kapok stuffing. In the UK, leathercloth or oilcloth (a painted woven fabric with tradenames such as "Rexine" and "Duxeen", and made in Manchester) replaced the previously preferred pad fabrics of felt and velveteen.

Many children suffered the traumas of wartime evacuation, often with only their teddies for comfort. Poignant stories abound: in Austria, for example, a child's precious teddy bear was given to farmers in exchange for food, and in Croatia it is reported that a mother hid her jewellery in her daughter's Steiff bear.

Teddy gas-mask
The cover of the British child's gas-mask (above) *is decorated with a fully featured, mohair teddy head and felt clothes.*

Flat-face Hugmee
In the 1940s, Chiltern redesigned its Hugmee range (above) *to use less mohair plush.*

Jester Bear
Made by Beverly Port, doll-maker and pioneer bear artist, this porcelain-faced bear (left) is an early example of bear artistry incorporating doll- and soft-toy-making techniques. Beverly's bear-making workshops created a huge following on the West Coast of America. Her daughter and son are also bear artists.

latter was considered to be the perfect filling, until its capacity to disintegrate and its potentially toxic fume emission were later discovered. With the introduction of tougher legislation on toy safety, all teddy bears, by the late-1960s, were fitted with safe, locked-in, plastic eyes.

WIDENING HORIZONS

Just as books and radio influenced the early teddy-bear manufacturers, so too did television and cinema from the early 1960s. TV and film bear characters appeared in various related merchandise; literary heroes such as Paddington were reproduced later, in the 1970s and 1980s.

The declining birth rate, and the rise of cheap imports from East Asia during the late 1960s and 1970s, caused the demise of several leading soft-toy companies, such as Schuco, J.K. Farnell, Chiltern, Chad Valley, and Wendy Boston.

New US manufacturers, such as Dakin, Russ Berrie, and Applause, launched the trend to manufacture in countries, such as Korea, Taiwan, China, the Philippines, and Haiti where production costs were cheaper. The advent of the microchip in the 1980s opened up a whole new world of novelties: Teddy Ruxpin, with moving facial features synchronized with a taped story, and Musical Tubby Bear, of Dandee Imports, whose plastic heart flashes in time to the 14 electronically produced, popular lullabies, were two examples.

No Frills Bear
This unusual, printed calico bear, was produced in Korea in 1985 for US manufacturer R. Dakin & Co.

Bear Ritz
The 100% natural mink bear (above), made in 1983, is the work of Californian bear artists Charlotte Holst and Shawn Frey.

POST-WAR PRODUCTION

The aftermath of World War II resulted in several German companies moving from the Russian to the US Zone. At the same time, new firms were established, such as Clemens in Germany, and Fechter and Berg in Austria. In the UK, sheepskin continued to be popular during the years of rationing and beyond, with manufacturers using descriptive tradenames such as "Lamkin" and "Cuddlam".

Synthetic fibres, such as nylon, were increasingly employed in the teddy-bear industry after the war. Patented by Du Pont or Monsanto in the US, by Courtaulds in the UK, or by the Farben Bayer companies in Germany, these synthetic materials included Orlon, Acrilan, Dacron, Courtelle, and Dralon. Moulded vinyl muzzles first appeared in the early 1950s; later, rubber or plastic noses were used. 1955 heralded the introduction of the first fully washable, unjointed teddy bear produced by Wendy Boston in the UK, using the company's patented, safe, screw-in eyes and foam rubber stuffing. The

THE RISE OF BEAR ARTISTRY

In the meantime, the concept of bear artistry was emerging amongst dollmakers in the US; Beverly Port introduced her Theodore B. Bear at the 1974 International Doll Makers' Convention in Reno, Nevada, while Carol-Lynn Rössel Waugh was producing porcelain bears in Maine. In the early days, other dollmakers such as the UK's Carol Ann Stanton and Anne Keane from Australia. produced porcelain-headed bears. In 1981, an article in the

Flexible knees
This little girl bear (below), by Florida artist Donna Claustre, has "ball-and-socket" knee joints allowing human-like flexibility.

"Sewn in Haiti"
A typical post-1970s label (above).

Teddies' picnic
Typical 1960s, fully washable, Wendy Boston bears with patented, safe, screw-in eyes (above).

US magazine *Doll Reader* used the term "bear artist", and in 1984 Carol-Lynn Rössel Waugh published *Teddy Bear Artists: Romance of Making and Collecting Bears*.

During the 1980s, bear artistry developed throughout the UK, closely followed by Australia. By the late 1980s, other European countries had joined the movement, including Elke Kraus and Rotrau Ilisch in Germany. The Netherlands boasts many artists, and has hosted an annual bear artist convention since 1991. Bear artistry is now thriving in many far-flung places: Victoria Marsden in the Outer Hebrides of Scotland; Amy Shukuya in Hawaii; Margaret York in Australia's Alice Springs; Shelly Armstrong-Plaunt in Canada's Yukon Territory; and Eunice Beaton in Durban, in the Republic of South Africa. There is also a burgeoning movement in Japan.

FANTASY AND NOSTALGIA
Two major styles have emerged within bear artistry; the first stems from its origins in dollmaking, with the teddy as a vehicle for fantasy, recreating past historical and literary figures, or in the guise of other creatures. The second responds to the steady demand for old bears, and businesses have emerged that reproduce old-style teddies in antique fabrics or "distressed" mohair. Many bear-artists' bears are specifically designated "not for children" because their construction does not comply with the current safety regulations; others are exhibited as "soft sculpture" in art galleries – such as Kimberlee Port's Christmas Tree Bear in New York, and the Hanton's Edwardian Bears *(see p.185)* in Wellington, New Zealand.

LIMITED-EDITIONS AND REPLICAS
With the growth of arctophily in the 1980s, many firms turned to producing special limited-edition teddy bears; some older companies followed Steiff's example and produced limited-edition replicas of past models. Other manufacturers created dressed, adult-orientated collectables, such as the North American Bear Company's VIB series *(see pp.146–47)*, or Gabrielle Designs' Henry and Caroline series, and the Lakeland Bears, in the UK.

The introduction of the prestigious Golden Teddy and TOBY awards has done much to encourage and inspire quality in the design of teddy bears amongst both bear artists and manufacturers.

Christmas Tree Bear
Barbara McConnell's musical bear (above) has battery-operated lights inside the green, mohair-plush body.

Original and replica
The c.1904 rod-jointed Steiff bear (below, left) is shown alongside Bärle, the company's 1992 replica of a similarly jointed bear (below, right).

1992 replica "Alpha"
Bears Paw Collectables of Leicester, England, made this replica (above) of a Farnell "Alpha" bear.

1960s KNICKERBOCKER
JOY OF A TOY PRINTED LABEL

C.1956–57 MERRYTHOUGHT
PRINTED LABEL

1970s DEAN'S CHILDSPLAY
TOYS PRINTED LABEL

Dean's Childsplay Toys Lt
RYE, SUSSEX
CONFORMS TO BRITISH STANDARD BS 344
USA REG. No. PA380 & MASS 101
MANUFACTURED IN "ALL NEW MATERIAL"
MADE IN ENGLAND

HERMANN
Teddy ®
ORIGINAL
1980s–90s GEBRÜDER HERMANN
EMBROIDERED LABEL

1925–30s FARNELL ALPHA TOY
EMBROIDERED LABEL

1980s HOUSE OF NISBET
EMBROIDERED LABEL

1964–70s ACTON TOYCRAFT
TWYFORD PRINTED LABEL

1946–71 PEDIGREE SOFT TOYS
(BELFAST) PRINTED LABEL

1945–67 CHILTERN PRINTED
LABEL

JOY-TOYS
MADE IN AUSTRALIA
1930s–40s JOY-TOYS
EMBROIDERED LABEL

1980s GUND EMBROIDERED
LABEL

Pre-1914 Steiff
Even if it did not have
its "button in ear"
trademark (see p.21),
this teddy would still
be clearly identifiable
as a pre-World War I
Steiff bear, every
feature helping to
confirm its origins.

1950s Steiff
The hole in the left ear
indicates the position of
the former trademark.

1950s SCHUCO
PLASTIC CHEST-TAG

1980s LENCI
EMBROIDERED LABEL

1930s CHAD
VALLEY CELLULOID
ON METAL BUTTON

1980s DORIS & TERRY
MICHAUD CARROUSEL
PRINTED LABEL

1980s APPLAUSE
PRINTED LABEL

1930s CHAD VALLEY
EMBROIDERED LABEL

1980s DAKIN
EMBROIDERED LABEL

1960s Knickerbocker
The soft-stuffed, nylon-plush body, safe, spangle-effect plastic eyes, and printed, New York label determine the age of this bear.

POST-1986 STEIFF
METAL BUTTON AND
PRINTED EAR-TAG

C.1990 ROMSEY BEAR COMPANY
EMBROIDERED LABEL

1991 CANTERBURY BEARS
EMBROIDERED LABEL

1980s REAL
SOFT TOYS
PRINTED CARD
SWING-TAG

UK bear artist
Liz Carless achieved novelty appeal with this toddler bear, which contains a unique, internal frame that allows realistic positioning of the limbs.

THE CATALOGUE

THE MAJOR TASK FOR teddy-bear collectors, and for many owners of old or unlabelled teddy bears, is to establish the pedigree of their bears. This catalogue will help you in your research. It is set out chronologically, with each double-page spread representing either a manufacturer or a trend within a country during a certain period in the history of the teddy bear. The work of bear artists is featured at the end of the catalogue, where the teddies are grouped according to the artists' nationality.

I have chosen five representative bears for each spread, and describe each of these fully, with their key features clearly annotated. Wherever possible, I have selected bears with their original trademarks intact as these provide the most positive form of identification. When trying to identify a bear, always check for traces of a trademark – it may be hidden between limb and body, for example. Even a few, remaining, coloured threads from a tattered label are useful for comparing with the photographs of labels illustrated in the catalogue. A hole in the ear, or a faded area on a foot-pad, will also provide evidence of the former presence of a trademark.

Remember that wear and tear or repair-work can alter a bear considerably, and you should keep this in mind when trying to establish a pedigree. Anecdotes by the original or previous owners will also provide clues. Review all the relevant factors in the context of the information provided in the *Encyclopedia* and you will then be well on the way to establishing the identity of your bear.

Steiff: 1902–05

EXPERIMENTAL PERIOD; INTRODUCTION OF "BUTTON IN EAR"

I n 1902, Richard Steiff began experimenting to invent a satisfactory, flexible jointing system. He devised a series of simple, string-jointed animals, one of which was the brown *Bär 55 PB* – so called because it was 55cm (22in) high (seated), made of *Plusch* (plush), and *Beweglich* (movable). The bear was in a crate of toys sent to New York in February 1903, but was initially unsuccessful. A month later, however, US wholesalers Geo. Borgfeldt & Co. ordered 3,000 at the Leipzig Spring Fair. Steiff patented four designs, culminating in the rod-jointed *Bär 28 PB*. Made for only one year, it is now highly prized.

1904–05 ROD JOINTED; ELEPHANT LOGO

Richard Steiff's bear evolved further in 1904: a card-disc and string-jointed *Bär 35 PB* was registered on 5 March, and a double-wire-jointed bear was registered later that year, on 6 December. The teddy bear illustrated is rod-jointed like *Bär 28 PB* (registered 8 June 1905), but is larger. The rodded bears were given a new trademark in November 1904 – a nickel-plated button, with Steiff's elephant and S-shaped trunk logo.

Height: 50cm (20in)

Embossed button

Nose/mouth: the replacement shield-shaped nose and Y-shaped mouth are stitched in thick, black, embroidery thread.

Fur: the fur is beige mohair plush.

Pads/claws: the beige, felt pads are replacements; five brown claws are stitched across the plush.

Ears: the small, rounded ears are sewn across the facial seams.

Eyes: the eyes are probably replacement (but authentic) black boot-buttons.

Muzzle: the plush on the thin, elongated muzzle is worn.

BEAR PROFILE

In profile, you can clearly see the typical characteristics of early Steiff bears: the elongated, pointed muzzle; the hump; the rounded lower back; the large feet; and the long arms, which extend beyond the legs when the bear is seated.

Feet: the oval feet are typically large and narrow.

slightly cupped ears, sewn into facial seam

long, pointed, shaved muzzle

elongated arms

thick, curly, white mohair plush

original black, boot-button eyes

replacement embroidered nose

cream, felt pads in mint condition

replacement black claws

large, thin, oval feet

c.1903–04 WHITE; RODDED

Height: 38cm (15in)

This rodded bear, with an elephant button, is probably a prototype – this colour does not appear on any known production bear. Its crooked, cinnamon-coloured, embroidered nose is a replacement; the original beige stitching for the mouth is just visible.

Embossed button

pointed, shaved muzzle

sealing-wax nose with defined nostrils, moulded to resemble real bear's nose

long, narrow limbs

beige, felt pads

remains of five claws on feet and paws

distinctive seam across top of head, only ever found in such rodded Steiff bears

beige mohair plush, worn in places; wood-wool stuffing

creased left paw (bear was designed to walk on all fours, creating gaps in stuffing)

large, narrow, oval feet

c.1903–04 WAX NOSE; RODDED

Height: 38cm (15in)

The moulded, sealing-wax nose, which is in unusually excellent condition and is particularly realistic, with well-defined nostrils, makes this rodded bear highly collectable. (Sealing wax is a mixture of shellac, rosin (natural resins), turpentine, and pigment.)

Embossed button

original black, boot-button eyes

dark stain marks position of original sealing-wax nose

shaved, pointed, protruding muzzle

elongated, curved, tapering arms

slim legs with large, narrow feet

horizontal seam across top of head

remnants of inverted-Y-shaped, brown thread, double-stitched mouth

golden mohair plush; wood-wool stuffing throughout

remains of black claws on paw

c.1903–04 GOLDEN; RODDED

Height: 45cm (18in)

The typical, elongated shape of this bear can still be discerned despite extensive repair work. Rodded bears tend to suffer sagging and splitting at the wrists because of their ability to stand on all fours. A dark stain is all that remains of the sealing-wax nose.

Embossed button

horizontal seam across top of head

original black, boot-button eyes

long, curved, tapering arms extend beyond legs

large, narrow feet

black, sealing-wax nose with realistically defined nostrils

elongated, shaved, worn muzzle

golden mohair plush

worn, beige, felt pads; five claws on paws

1905 BAR 28 PB; RODDED

Height: 40cm (16in)

Unfortunately, this bear has lost its elephant button, but it clearly resembles Richard Steiff's 28 PB model in overall shape and height. It is in relatively good condition apart from some holes in the plush and pads. It still retains its sealing-wax nose.

Embossed button

Steiff: 1905–World War I

DESIGN PERFECTED; TRIANGULAR NOSE FOR SMALL SIZES

Richard Steiff perfected his plush bear-doll, patenting the design on 12 February 1905. The new bear had card disc-joints and was made in white, and light or dark brown mohair plush (although the prototype, a 32cm (13in) example now in the Steiff archives, was grey). Known as *"Bärle"* in catalogues, its code name was *"PAB"*: *Plusch* (plush), *Angeschiebt* (disc-jointed), and *Beweglich* (movable). Steiff patented its "button in ear" trademark on 13 May 1905, replacing the embossed elephant with the word "Steiff". In 1908–09, the company introduced linen ear-tags printed with product numbers.

1909 LIGHT BROWN MOHAIR

Seven sizes of this bear were produced in 1905, and two sizes were added a year later. By 1910, the range had increased to thirteen: from 10cm (4in) to 115cm (45in). Bears under 40cm (16in) had a distinct triangular, horizontally stitched nose. The example illustrated here probably dates from 1909 when the 30cm (12in) height was introduced. The boot-button eyes indicate a pre-World War I date; other design features and the trademark remained virtually unchanged until 1950.

Height: 30cm (12in)

Embossed button

Ears: *the ears are small, cupped, and set wide apart, with the inside edges caught in the facial seams.*

Eyes: *the eyes are original, small, black boot-buttons.*

Nose/mouth: *the horizontally stitched, black nose is outlined with two stitches that converge at the base to join an inverted-Y-shaped mouth.*

Fur: *the fur is short, light brown mohair plush; the bear is stuffed with wood-wool.*

BEAR PROFILE

In profile, you can see the slightly shaved, protruding, blunted muzzle; a plump body still retaining a suggestion of a humped back; elongated arms with curved, spoon-shaped paws; and large feet with narrow ankles. Notice the trademark in the left ear.

Feet: *the thin ankles end in large, narrow feet.*

Pads: *the beige, felt pads are in perfect condition (except for a small hole in the left foot).*

Claws: *each paw and foot has four black, stitched claws.*

1908 RED MOHAIR Height: 33cm (13in)

- *small, black, boot-button eyes*
- *horizontally stitched, triangular, black nose*
- *original orange, cossack-style tunic and trousers*
- *unique rust-red mohair plush, worn in places*
- *four black claws on each paw and foot*
- *damaged beige, felt pads reveal wood-wool stuffing*

"Alfonzo" was commissioned by the Grand Duke of Russia for his daughter Princess Xenia Georgievna, and accompanied her on her visit to Buckingham Palace in London in 1914. The Russian Revolution meant that neither princess nor bear ever returned home.

Embossed button

1905 BROWN MOHAIR Height: 33cm (13in)

- *brown mohair pile*
- *original small, black, boot-button eyes*
- *triangular nose with replacement stitching*
- *protruding muzzle*
- *elongated arms and curved paws*
- *replacement woven fabric pads; originals would have been beige felt*
- *large feet*
- *five claws indicate early origins*

This bear, bought in Europe by a sea captain and taken home for his daughter in Australia, is now virtually bald and has replacement pads. The left arm sags at the wrist as the wood-wool stuffing has disintegrated – probably because the bear was regularly held by this paw.

Embossed button

c.1905 BLANK BUTTON Height: 33cm (13in)

- *horizontally stitched, triangular, black nose*
- *original black, boot-button eyes*
- *light brown mohair plush; internal squeaker*
- *long arms with curved paws*
- *hand-embroidered, black claws*
- *hole in pad reveals wood-wool stuffing*
- *replacement beige, felt pad*

Although identical in design to others illustrated here, this bear possesses the rare, early Steiff, blank button in its left ear. The trademark dates from the 1903–04 experimental days, but old stock was used for a short time after the embossed Steiff button was introduced.

Blank button

c.1910 SMALL; NO PAW PADS Height: 22cm (8½in)

- *light brown mohair plush*
- *mortar board and satchel, contemporary additions*
- *original small, black, boot-button eyes*
- *horizontally stitched, triangular nose*
- *long, straight arms end in paws with four black claws*
- *large, narrow, oval feet with beige, felt pads in perfect condition*
- *paws have no pads*

In 1909, Steiff added three smaller sizes to its range: 22cm (8½in), 18cm (7in), and 10cm (4in). In 1910, a 15cm (6in) size was added. The basic design was much the same, but the three shortest in height had straighter arms and, like this bear, had no felt pads on their paws.

Embossed button

Steiff: 1903–World War I

ALTERNATIVE NOSE DESIGN USED ON LARGER BEARS

The demand for teddies, particularly in the US, soared between 1903 and 1908, the period that the Steiff company called the *Bärenjahre* (*see p.38*), when production increased from 12,000 to about 975,000. To use materials economically, Steiff cut six complete teddy-bear heads from one length of mohair plush; a seventh head was cut in two pieces, so creating the "centre-seam" teddy bear, which is now greatly prized. By 1905, seven sizes were available; this increased to fourteen by 1910. Bears over 40cm (16in) tall had a different nose design from smaller bears – shield shaped, vertically stitched, with a felt underlay.

1905 CINNAMON; CENTRE SEAM

This is an excellent example of a teddy bear with a centre seam, which is clearly visible along the length of the long, shaven muzzle. The bear is made from shaggy, cinnamon-coloured mohair plush, a colour much prized by collectors. The original shield-shaped nose has been repaired with black wool, but you can still make out the felt underlay.

Height: 55cm (22in)

Embossed button

Ears: *the small, unstuffed, cupped ears are placed high on the head.*

Eyes: *the eyes are large, black boot-buttons.*

Muzzle: *the mohair plush on the muzzle has been clipped.*

Nose/mouth: *both the nose and the mouth have been replaced in black wool, similar to the original thread.*

Face: *the central seam indicates that this bear's head was the seventh to be cut from one length of mohair plush; the other six would have been cut in one piece.*

Fur: *the curly, cinnamon-coloured mohair plush is in mint condition; the bear is stuffed with wood-wool throughout.*

Arms: *the arms are long with brown, felt paw-pads; the remains of the black, embroidered claws are visible.*

Feet: *the feet are long and narrow, with thin ankles; originally, there would have been four claws on each foot and paw.*

BEAR PROFILE
Seen from the side, this bear demonstrates all the features of a traditional, pre-World War I Steiff teddy: a realistic, protruding, shaved muzzle; a slightly humped back; elongated arms and legs, with curved, spoon-shaped paws; and large feet with narrow ankles.

Pads: *the pads have been replaced; the originals would have been beige.*

original large, black, boot-button eyes

black, shield-shaped, vertically stitched nose with black, felt underlay visible

cinnamon-coloured mohair plush; wood-wool stuffing throughout

long, tapering, curved arms with large, spoon-shaped paws

replacement woven fabric pads

long legs with narrow ankles

c.1905 CINNAMON; CONE NOSE
Height: 70cm (28in)

Arctophiles use the term "cone nose" to describe an early experimental phase in Steiff's history when the bear's muzzle, in profile, appears more cone-shaped than on other early examples. This bear would originally have had felt pads on its feet and paws.

Embossed button

original black, boot-button eyes

shaved muzzle

double-stitched, inverted-V-shaped, smiling mouth

black, vertically stitched nose; central five stitches dropped to meet mouth

shaggy, beige mohair plush in excellent condition; wood-wool stuffing throughout

unworn beige, felt pads; four black thread claws on each paw

1908 SHAGGY, BEIGE MOHAIR
Height: 50cm (20in)

Known to date from 1908, this bear is in excellent condition. It has typical pre-World War I features, including a prominent hump, and well-defined, narrow feet with small ankles. It is the fourth largest in the range of sizes available at the time.

Embossed button

large, black, boot-button eyes

Steiff button, with raised lettering, in left ear

well-worn, pointed muzzle

vertically stitched, black thread nose

slightly worn, beige mohair plush

four black claws on paws and feet, stitched across plush

large, narrow feet; dark brown, felt underlay revealed

1909 LARGE; BEIGE MOHAIR
Height: 70cm (28in)

This bear, which arrived in the US as padding around an English family's best china, is an example of one of the larger Steiff teddy bears, making it highly collectable; the next size up (115cm/45in), is very rare. Holes in the foot-pads reveal the felt underlay.

Embossed button

original large, black, boot-button eyes

large, flat ears set on sides of head

beige nose over felt underlay; five stitches dropped to meet mouth

beige thread claws to match nose and mouth

felt pads worn and darned; red, felt underlay beneath

very long, thin feet with narrow ankles

1903–05 WIDE-EAR DESIGN
Height 63cm (25in)

Some very early Steiff bears have been found with this head design – ears wide apart and set low down on the sides of the head – indicating an experimental period for Steiff. Although this bear has lost its Steiff "button in ear", similar bears exist with the trademark intact.

Embossed button

21

Steiff: 1908–World War I

INTRODUCTION OF NOVELTY DESIGNS TO RETAIN MONOPOLY

In 1908, Steiff tried to regain its monopoly on teddy-bear manufacture by producing a number of novelties; in 1909, it added bright gold to its natural range of brown, beige, and white; and in 1912, it produced a special black bear for the British market. The Dolly bear of 1913 was produced for the US election, in red, white, and blue. Other novelties included the 1909 Roly Poly bear; the clockwork somersaulting teddy (*opposite*); and the 1913 Record Teddy (seated on a wooden-wheeled metal chassis). The latter was copied by several British manufacturers, including J.K. Farnell & Co. Ltd.

1908 *MAULKORB BÄR*

This bear was first introduced by Steiff in 1908. It wears a leather muzzle and leading-rein, inspired by the popular dancing bears that performed in the town squares of central Europe. Available in brown or white mohair plush and in ten sizes, this bear is one of the smaller examples. It is basically the same Richard Steiff design as that shown on pp.18–19, with the leather muzzle added for novelty value. Steiff made a replica of this bear in 1990.

Height: 25cm (10in)

Embossed button

Eyes: the black, boot-button eyes are original.

Nose: the triangular nose is horizontally stitched in black thread, like those of the bears on pp.18–19.

Muzzle: the muzzle, made of leather, with studs like the blank Steiff buttons, has darkened with age.

Fur/stuffing/growler: the fur is brown mohair plush; the bear is stuffed with wood-wool; there is an internal squeaker.

Feet: the large feet have replacement beige, felt pads in a colour similar to that of the originals.

BEAR PROFILE

From this angle you can see clearly the typical, pointed muzzle and accentuated limbs of this bear. The long, tapering arms with curved paws are considerably longer than the legs. The leather muzzle and the leading-rein, which would originally have ended in a loop like a dog's lead, are also visible.

Claws: four claws are embroidered, in black thread, across the mohair plush only.

black, bead eyes

raised lettering on Steiff "button in ear"; cloth label still, unusually, in place

brown thread, horizontally stitched nose; inverted-V-shaped mouth

each digit of product number on label is significant: 5 means jointed; 3 means mohair plush; 07 means sitting height of 7cm

fully jointed limbs and head

white mohair plush, highly prized by collectors

central seam along each foot; no pads

1909 MINIATURE; WHITE Height: 10cm (4in)

Originally introduced in 1909, this is an early example of the smallest bear produced by Steiff; a larger, 15cm (6in), version became available a year later. In addition to the "button in ear", the bear still carries a cloth label showing the product number – a feature introduced in 1908–09.

Embossed button/label

nose and mouth embroidered in black thread; now very worn

original black, boot-button eyes

golden mohair plush, now faded and worn; wood-wool stuffing in head and limbs

opening fastened by shoelace wound around brass hooks

replacement woven fabric pads

soft padding between mohair plush and lining of body

claws embroidered in black thread

1911 HOT-WATER BOTTLE Height: 25cm (10in)

This bear was bought in the north of England for the present owner's uncle's first birthday on 11 February 1911. It is a rare find, for only 90 examples were made during the years of production, 1907–14. Its padded body would originally have housed a tin for hot water.

Embossed button

triangular, horizontally stitched nose, as used on all traditional bears up to 40cm (16in) in height

black, boot-button eyes

golden mohair plush (only colour in which this bear was produced)

beige, felt pads

c.1910 PANTOM BÄR Height: 40cm (16in)

This bear was produced, as part of a marionette range, from 1910 to 1918 in two sizes, 35cm (14in) and 40cm (16in); only 6,268 were manufactured. The range was developed by Albert Schlopsnies, an East Prussian artist who worked as a freelance designer for Steiff.

Embossed button

nose horizontally stitched in black thread

Steiff button in left ear

right arm acts as key for clockwork mechanism; when rotated, bear tips forward and turns somersaults

celluloid high collar added by present owner

light brown mohair plush

beige, felt pads in mint condition

c.1915 PURZEL BÄR Height: 26cm (10½in)

Introduced in 1909 in various colours and sizes, this teddy bear has a clockwork mechanism developed by Richard Steiff's brother, Hugo, a trained engineer. From 1911 to 1915, Steiff was involved in a legal battle with Bing who produced a similar toy (see p.35).

Embossed button

Ideal: 1903–World War I

BIRTH OF TEDDY'S BEAR AND FIRST US MANUFACTURER

The story of the original teddy bear, hand-sewn by Rose Michtom and sold as Teddy's Bear at her husband Morris's New York novelty and stationery store, is now legendary (*see pp.8–9*). In 1903, the Michtoms – having sold their entire stock of bears to the wholesale firm Butler Brothers, who then guaranteed their credit with the plush-producing mills – established the Ideal Novelty and Toy Company. The company moved to larger premises in 1907, and a year later its first advertisement appeared in the US trade journal *Playthings*, in which they claimed to be "the largest bear manufacturers in the country".

c.1905 LARGE; GOLDEN MOHAIR

Early Ideal bears were not labelled and can be identified only by their general shape and by certain design details. (One of the first teddies produced by the company was presented to the Smithsonian Insitute, Washington DC, in 1964, and is a useful reference.) These pre-World War I bears typically have triangular heads and pointed foot-pads.

Height: 49cm (19½in)

Nose: *the black nose is horizontally stitched across the junction of the muzzle seams.*

Arms: *the long, tapering arms, like those on early Steiffs, have spoon-shaped, curved paws with beige, felt pads.*

Legs: *the thighs are slightly rounded, with ankle definition; the feet have rounded heels and distinct, pointed toes.*

Ears: *the large ears are sewn from just inside the facial seams, down the sides of the head.*

Eyes: *shiny, black, boot-button eyes were in general use during this period.*

Face: *this is a classic, triangular, Ideal face shape.*

BEAR PROFILE
This bear exhibits several, classic Ideal features: the wedge-shaped muzzle; the plump, humped-back torso; the long, curved, tapering arms; and the unique, pointed, oval toes.

Claws: *there are five claws on the feet, and four on the paws.*

Fur/stuffing: *the short, golden mohair plush is typical of early Ideal bears; the stuffing is wood-wool.*

black, boot-
button eyes,
sewn just inside
facial seams

large ears, placed
wide apart and low
on sides of head

long arms tapering
to curved paws

rust-coloured,
triangular, broad-
cloth nose may be
repair work

short, beige
mohair plush;
wood-wool
stuffing
throughout

feet rounder
than usual
Ideal style;
pads
reinforced
with card

four beige claws on
paws; five on feet

c.1904 BEIGE MOHAIR

Height: 43cm (17in)

This bear is said to be one of the early prototypes produced by Ideal, and is known to have belonged to its previous owner from 1904. Although the feet are not typically Ideal, the bear exhibits the characteristic, triangular Ideal head with large ears set low down on the sides. Early American bears often had broadcloth noses like the one on this example.

small, black,
boot-button eyes

ears wide apart;
left ear has bogus
Steiff button

black, triangular,
horizontally
stitched nose

beige mohair
plush; stuffed
with wood-wool
throughout

five black,
slightly con-
verging claws
on paws and feet

beige, felt pads on
slightly pointed feet

1904–05 SMALL; BEIGE MOHAIR

Height: 28cm (11in)

This bear demonstrates many classic Ideal features: a triangular face with a broad forehead; large ears set wide apart; elongated, curved arms; and, in particular, distinct, egg-shaped feet. However, a Steiff button has been fraudulently placed in the left ear – presumably before early Ideal bears, such as this, had gained popularity or high prices in the marketplace.

blue, glass
eyes with
black pupils

ears set
wide apart, on
corners of head

distinctly triangular
face with broad
forehead

black, triangular,
horizontally
stitched nose

three black
claws on
each paw
and foot

long, curved
arms with
beige, felt pads

slightly
pointed feet
with beige,
felt pads

c.1914 GLASS EYES

Height: 40cm (16in)

Glass eyes became common on Ideal bears after World War I; before the war, Ideal – like most other teddy-bear manufacturers – used boot-button eyes. This bear, with its attractive and unusual blue, glass eyes, also exhibits a slightly more slender torso and shorter arms than the earlier Ideal bears, offering a preview of the new, slimmer designs of the 1920s.

slightly cupped
ears, sewn
down sides of
head from
facial seams

black, boot-button
eyes with white,
painted rims

very worn, short,
tan mohair plush

black, triangular,
horizontally stitched
nose, with border
stitches along two
diagonal edges

long,
curved
arms

five black
claws on
paws and
feet

beige, felt pads on
pointed feet

1904–12 CARTOON-STYLE EYES

Height: 30cm (12in)

With its characteristic Ideal face and feet, this bear has rare, painted, white-rimmed, black, boot-button eyes, possibly intended to imitate Clifford T. Berryman's *Washington Post* cartoon bear. Ideal teddies of an unusual 15cm (6in) size, with similar but more "googly" eyes, were handed out during Roosevelt's 1904 election campaign.

US: c.1907–14

SHORT-LIVED FIRMS; TRADITIONAL AND NOVELTY DESIGNS

Theodore Roosevelt's second term in office (1905–09) saw the teddy-bear craze at its peak, with the establishment of numerous manufacturers. These included the American Doll and Toy Manufacturing Co. and the Miller Manufacturing Co. Many non-toy-making companies began to make teddy bears as well at this time: in 1907 the Fast Black Skirt Company's Electric Bright Eye and Hahn & Amberg's cork-filled teddy bears came on the market. Other novelties included Harman's 1908 Teddy Bear Purse and the Dreamland Doll Company's topsy-turvy, half-teddy/half-doll of 1905–08.

---

c.1910–15 POSSIBLY STRAUSS

Although the glass eyes may indicate a later date, this example is reminiscent of illustrations of bears by Strauss (reputedly the Toy King of New York) seen in trade journals. Known principally for his 1907 Self-Whistling Bear, whose mechanism was activated by tipping the bear upside down, Strauss also produced a clockwork musical bear, which was wound up at the back.

Height: 43cm (17in)

Ears: *the fairly large ears are set wide apart, on the corners of the triangular head.*

Eyes: *the reddish brown paint on the backs of the clear, glass eyes has partially worn off.*

Nose: *the wide, black nose is vertically stitched, bordered by horizontal stitches; a few stitches are dropped in the centre to meet the wide, smiling mouth.*

Fur/stuffing: *shaggy, tan mohair plush; the bear is stuffed mainly with wood-wool, with some kapok in the head, body, and paws.*

Pads: *the beige, felt pads are in good condition.*

Claws: *there are five black, almost converging claws on paws and feet.*

Feet: *the large, oval feet narrow towards the "heels".*

BEAR PROFILE
Like many early American bears, this example has very long arms, a protruding muzzle, and large feet – all an attempt to copy the Steiff look. At this angle, however, you can see the unusual, squared shoulders, unshaven muzzle, and the wedge-shaped, more American-style head.

brown and black, glass eyes; the left eye is a replacement

small, rounded ears, set wide apart on head

inverted-Y-shaped, smiling mouth

rectangular, black, vertically stitched nose, with horizontal borders

shaggy, golden mohair plush

long, tapering arms, curving into long, spoon-shaped paws

well-worn, beige, felt pads

large, narrow, oval feet

five claws on paws and feet

c.1907 Bruin Manufacturing Co.   Height: 35cm (14in)

A few, tell-tale strands of red and gold thread left in the seam of the right foot confirm that this bear was made by the Bruin Manufacturing Co., a short-lived firm based at 497 Broome Street, New York. Early advertisements described their trademark "BMC" as being stamped on the foot; the later, woven, label was probably preferred for its permanence.

triangular face with expansive forehead

large, flat ears, set on corners of head, across facial seams

black, vertically stitched, triangular nose; inverted-V-shaped mouth

brown, glass eyes with black pupils

beige mohair plush

wide, squared-off shoulders; arms taper to curved paws

Aetna trademark, with oval outline, stamped on right foot

large, oval feet with beige, felt pads, reinforced with card

insect damage pinholes on left foot

c.1907 Aetna Toy Animal Co.   Height: 50cm (20in)

Aetna bears (formerly known as Keystone Bears) featured largely in early trade journals, but appear to have been produced for only a short period. It is rare to find an example such as this with some of the blue, stamped name remaining on the right foot. Aetna also made an unusual bear, with a two-colour body, a wide, pinked collar, and a dunce's cap.

ears set wide apart on corners of head

triangular face with wide forehead

rectangular, black, vertically stitched nose; horizontal stitch along bottom edge

black, boot-button eyes

wide, square shoulders with long, tapering arms, curved at paws

four short claws on each paw and foot-pad

woven label stitched across foot

beige, felt pads in good condition

c.1907 Bruin Manufacturing Co.   Height: 33cm (13in)

A rare find, this bear retains its original trademark – a silky, blue and red, woven label with the letters "BMC" in gold thread. Bruin claimed that their bears contained "imported voices" – referring to the growler mechanisms imported from Germany.

Woven label

small, black, boot-button eyes, set close together; glass eyes have been found on similar bears

typical wide, rectangular, horizontally stitched, black nose

mouth opens and closes to show two small, white teeth

orange-gold, short-pile mohair plush; wood-wool stuffing throughout

three black claws on each paw and foot, stitched across mohair plush

feet small compared to those of other US bears of period

beige, felt pads, worn in places

1907 Columbia Teddy Bear Mfrs.   Height: 45cm (18in)

When the stomach is squeezed, a string mechanism opens the mouth of this Laughing Roosevelt Bear, revealing two pointed teeth made of white glass. When closed, the teeth rest in holes inside the wooden upper jaw. The manufacturers, based at 145–49 Center Street, New York, also made traditional, jointed, mohair-plush teddy bears.

Great Britain: 1908–c.1920

BIRTH OF BRITISH SOFT-TOY INDUSTRY; FIRST BRITISH BEARS

The teddy-bear craze reached Britain around 1908, fuelled perhaps by the fact that the country had its own "Teddy", Edward VII. Most teddy bears available in the early years were German, though made from mohair spun in English mills. A few soft-toy manufacturers existed, such as W.J. Terry and Dean's Rag Book Company, but it is J.K. Farnell & Co. that take the credit for making the first British, jointed, plush teddy bear, in 1908. World War I had a significant effect on the manufacture of teddy bears in Great Britain, many new factories being established as a result of the ban on German imports.

1912 BRITISH PROTOTYPE

Although imitating the German teddy-bear design to a large extent, British manufacturers tended to shorten the limbs – a characteristic that was to become truly British by the 1930s. They also preferred glass, and sometimes metal, eyes to the traditional boot-buttons used by German manufacturers during this period.

Height: 48cm (19in)

Ears: the fabric is gathered and pushed into the facial seams – usually the mark of a cheaper bear.

Eyes: the painted, metal eyes are stuck into the face like carpet tacks.

Nose/mouth: a few horizontal stitches suggest the nose; the mouth is an inverted Y shape.

Limbs: the limbs, particularly the arms, are very short.

Pads: the beige, felt pads are pear-shaped; the bear's right foot-pad is a replacement.

Fur: the short-pile mohair plush is golden in colour.

BEAR PROFILE

This bear clearly illustrates the short limbs, the long, thin body, and the absence of a hump that were all distinguishing features of British bears at this time. However, the pointed muzzle still follows the German style.

Claws: some remains of the original black, thread claws are visible on the feet and paws.

golden mohair plush

boot-button eyes

shaved muzzle

fully jointed head and limbs

khaki, felt, British army officer's uniform

pale peach, felt pads on paws and feet

four claws on each paw and foot

1916 ALLY BEAR; HARWIN & CO.   Height: 29cm (11½in)

This teddy bear was designed by Dorothy Harwin of the north London firm Harwin & Co. (est. 1914) as part of its World War I series of mascots, dressed in uniforms of the Allied Forces. It is similar in design to Steiff bears; interestingly, Harwin's sales manager, Fred Taylor, had previously been a travelling salesman for the German company.

large ears, flat on sides of head

unusual vertical centre-seam meets horizontal seam halfway down face

vertically stitched, square-shaped nose

wide, smiling, embroidered mouth; small, pink tongue below

bulbous, opaque, brown, glass eyes; black pupils sewn in

blue, felt trousers with red, felt patch; webbing braces

pink and white checked shirt

very worn, light brown mohair plush

1915 MASTER TEDDY; CHILTERN   Height: 20cm (8in)

Manufactured at the Chiltern Toy Works in Chesham, Bucks. (later H.G. Stone & Co. Ltd.), Master Teddy was available in five sizes. His googly eyes are typical of the period, and mimic the popular animal caricatures of the day.

Card chest-tag

large, glass eyes with painted backs

semi-circular ears on corners of head

long limbs copy German examples

long, silky, blond mohair plush

woven cloth pads, favoured by some British manufacturers

long, curved, tapering arms

claws may be repair work

C.1913 WILLIAM J. TERRY   Height: 40cm (16in)

It is thought that this bear was made by William J. Terry of east London (one of the forerunners of the British soft toy industry) because of its resemblance to a photograph of similar bears for sale in the London department store Whiteleys. The bear's straight, tubular body and unusual hump make it unique. The growler is no longer working.

two new ears made by cutting one remaining original ear in half

large, clear, glass eyes with brown, painted backs

shaved muzzle

black, vertically stitched, shield-shaped nose; central stitches dropped to meet inverted-V-shaped mouth

light brown, brushed cotton pads with card reinforcement

front final seam, as on Steiff bears

golden mohair plush

C.1920 WEBBED CLAW   Height: 46cm (18½in)

This bear has the typical paws associated with several of the early, British teddy-bear manufacturers, including W.J. Terry, J.K. Farnell, and, much later, Merrythought. The paws are stuffed with kapok, whereas wood-wool has been used elsewhere. The five, black claws are linked by four, short, horizontal stitches over the pads only.

Germany: 1920s–30s

HERMANN FAMILY AND OTHER NEUSTADT/SONNEBERG COMPANIES

The teddy-bear industry in the Neustadt/ Sonneberg area of Germany, the traditional toy-making region, began in 1907–08 in response to the US demand for bears, and in direct competition with Steiff. By 1930, the industry was fully developed: Artur, Bernhard, and Max, sons of Johann Hermann (*see pp.94–95*) founded three major factories during this period, and even established doll companies, such as Gebrüder Süssenguth and Ernst Liebermann, turned to making bears. The bears of this region often had inset, contrasting muzzles, a style that endured after World War II (*see pp.114–115*).

1933 MAX HERMANN

This example, part of a group of dressed bears made for a large toy show held in Sonneberg in 1933, is in perfect condition, as it has been kept in the Sonneberg Toy Museum ever since. The bear is shown standing, as originally displayed, based on a photograph of a tableau that had paired teddies positioned as if dancing around a maypole. The original triangular swing-tag is the rare, earliest known trademark, featuring a bear and running dog with the words "Maheso" (from the first two letters of the words, Max Hermann Sonneberg) and "Erzeugnis" (product).

Height: 18cm (7in)

Printed label

Hat: *the traditional German hat has a turned-up brim and "feather" trim.*

Eyes: *the eyes are original black, boot-buttons.*

Nose/mouth: *the shield-shaped nose is horizontally stitched in light brown embroidery thread; the mouth is an inverted Y shape.*

Claws: *the claws are stitched in dark brown embroidery thread. There are three on each paw and foot.*

Shorts: *this bear wears a crocheted version of the traditional* lederhosen.

Fur/stuffing: *the fur is white, artificial-silk plush; the bear is stuffed with wood-wool.*

BEAR PROFILE

In profile you can see the elongated features typical of traditional bears; these include the protruding, pointed muzzle, the long, curved arms, spoon-shaped paws, and large feet. A silver-coloured metal button, clearly visible on the shoulder, is one end of the simple rod joint connecting the arms; the same system is used on the legs.

Pads: *the pads are made from a distinctive red felt.*

Limbs: *the limbs and head are fully jointed.*

hollow, moulded composition head

"googly" glass eyes set in eye sockets and attached to tongue

painted, moulded composition teeth with movable, pink tongue

black, painted, moulded composition nose

fully jointed limbs and head

thread on centre of chest marks position of original trademark

curved, tapering arms with slightly hooked paws

blond-tipped, dark brown mohair plush; wood-wool stuffing

beige, felt pads in mint condition

1925 GEBRÜDER SÜSSENGUTH

Height: 35cm (14in)

This rare model originally came with a chest-tag reading: "'Peter' *Ges Gesch*" (legally protected); with the number Nr 895257. The "googly" glass eyes and moulded composition tongue move from side to side when the head is turned. Existing "Peters" are mostly in mint condition: it is likely that the toy was too frightening for children and was never sold.

sewn-in, amber, glass eyes with black pupils

distinctive ears

slightly shaggy, brown-tipped blond mohair; wood-wool stuffing; internal voice box

horizontally stitched, shield-shaped, black nose; inverted-Y-shaped mouth

remains of black, stitched claws on paws and feet

replacement pads; originals would have been felt

1925–29 MAX HERMANN

Height: 30cm (12in)

Max Hermann founded his company in 1920 at the Hermann family home in the village of Neufang, then moved to nearby Sonneberg in 1923. A friend of Max's wife Hilde bought this unmarked bear from the Sonneberg factory as a present for her daughter, Elfriede Müller, born in 1922. The bear remains in the daughter's possession at her Coburg home.

slightly shaggy, brown-tipped, blond mohair on blond woven backing; wood-wool stuffing

horizontally stitched, oval, black nose; inverted-Y-shaped mouth

fully jointed limbs and head

replacement beige, felt pad on left paw

curved, tapering paws

relatively straight legs with small, narrow, oval feet

1927 BERNHARD HERMANN

Height 35cm (14in)

This brown-tipped blond, mohair-plush bear, typical of the era, hails from the Gebrüder Hermann archives. It was made at Bernhard Hermann's factory in Sonneberg, where he had been based since 1920. The original swing-tag would have read: "*Marke Beha Teddy Bürgt Für Qualität*" (Beha mark guaranteed for quality). A replica of this design was made in 1986.

horizontally stitched, triangular, black nose; inverted-Y-shaped mouth

large, flat ears

inset muzzle of clipped, contrasting, pale golden plush

short-pile, beige mohair plush; wood-wool stuffing

three black, stitched claws

original beige, felt pads

holes in foot-pad reveal wood-wool

1930s BERNHARD HERMANN

Height: 50cm (20in)

This bear has an inset muzzle of clipped, golden mohair plush, and slender limbs – a style adopted since the 1920s. The 1950s label, although historically incorrect, was recently added by the company to this archive sample to indicate its origins.

Printed tag

Bing: 1909–32

TRADITIONAL DESIGN; BUTTON DISPUTE WITH STEIFF

G ebrüder Bing, a Nuremberg-based tinware company, turned to toymaking in the 1880s, and quickly established a reputation for its fine-quality, mechanical tin toys. Bing then set out to challenge Steiff's monopoly on teddy bears by introducing teddies into its programme in the early 1900s.

Originally, Bing copied Steiff's overall design, differing only in small details; for example, by attaching a metal arrow to the right ear of its bears. Steiff's objection to this, however, led to Bing fixing a button (at first incised, later painted) to the left side of the bears; this was subsequently moved to the right arm.

c.1911 BUTTON UNDER ARM

Early Bing teddy bears had a metal arrow trademark clipped to the right ear. This was replaced in 1909, as a result of Steiff's protests, by a metal button fixed under the arm – permitted provided the word "button" was not used in the trademark. The "GBN" incised on the metal button is identical to that painted on the original, metal, arrow trademark.

Height: 53cm (21in)

Incised metal button

Ears: *the ears are set wide apart.*

Eyes: *boot-button eyes were used before World War I.*

Nose: *the black, triangular nose is vertically stitched; smaller Bing bears had horizontally stitched, triangular noses.*

Fur/stuffing/growler: *the mohair plush is dark chocolate-brown (Bing used similar natural colours to Steiff). This bear is stuffed throughout with wood-wool, and has a tilt growler.*

Arms: *the long arms end in curved, Steiff-like paws.*

Feet: *the large feet are similar to those of Steiff bears.*

BEAR PROFILE
You can see more easily, in profile, this bear's pointed muzzle, hump back, and extremely long arms – all features that Bing borrowed from Steiff. The metal trademark button is clearly visible under the bear's left arm.

Pads: *the original felt pads have been replaced by leather ones.*

black, vertically stitched nose

replacement brown, plastic eyes

orange painted, metal button trademark

replacement beige, felt pads

closely shaved, mohair-plush muzzle

long, silky, silver-tipped mohair plush

EARLY 1920S BUTTON ON THE ARM
Height: 58cm (23in)

This bear carries the later 1919–32 Bing metal button, painted orange, with the letters "BW" (standing for *Bing Werke*) in black. The button is attached to the right arm. The lettering on the buttons of pre-1919 bears read "GBN" (for Gebrüder Bing Nuremberg).

Painted button

typical post-World War I glass eyes

vertically stitched nose over felt

long, shaved muzzle

final seam at front

shaggy, gold mohair plush on dark brown, woven backing

repaired felt pads

1919–32 ELONGATED DESIGN
Height: 59cm (23½in)

Experts generally agree that the use of shaggy mohair plush, coupled with more elongated features, such as a pointed muzzle and a wide, smiling mouth, are characteristics of post-World War I Bing bears. Although this example has no surviving trademark, its resemblance to the bear (*left*) suggests that it was made by Bing between 1919 and 1932.

vertically stitched nose, similar to those of large, Steiff bears

boot-button eyes

final seam at front (a feature also found on early Steiff and J.K. Farnell bears)

long arms, longer than legs, a feature of early bears

long, narrow feet

felt pads

c.1910 ALL-IN-ONE EARS
Height: 48cm (19in)

Some early Bing bears, bearing the silver-coloured button with incised "GBN" diamond design, have been found with the head and ears cut all-in-one: the ear is formed by folding the extension of mohair plush forward, and over-sewing the edges into the inside of the ear. This bear has no button, but the all-in-one ears indicate its manufacturing origins.

small ears and wide forehead, typical of Bing bears from this period

boot-button eyes

vertically stitched nose with border stitches

final front seam, a common Bing feature

very long arms

replacement woven cotton paw-pads

replacement felt under worn areas of foot-pads

c.1910 BUTTON UNDER ARM
Height: 50cm (20in)

Like Steiff, Bing used beige thread for the embroidered features on light-coloured, mohair-plush bears. The nose design in this example is typical of that used by Bing for larger bears. The silver-coloured button, with incised "GBN" diamond design, is under the left arm.

Incised metal button

Gebrüder Bing: c.1910–32

ADDITION OF CLOCKWORK MECHANISMS TO TEDDY-BEAR RANGE

Gebrüder Bing, already established as the world's largest mechanical tin-toy maker, soon introduced clockwork mechanisms into its teddy bears, with a wind-up key at the side or front. Later bears, such as the somersaulting and skating bears, were dressed in felt outfits. Bing bears usually had a metal arrow (pre-World War I), a silver "GBN" button (*Gebrüder Bing Nürnberg*, pre-1919), or a red "BW" button (*Bing Werke*, post-1920). Some had a red, metal button with "DRPa div DRGM" (*Deutsches Reichs Patent/Deutsches Reichs Gebrauchmuster*). The company went into receivership in 1932.

c.1910 MOVING HEAD

A key to activate the clockwork mechanism inside this bear's body is concealed under its right arm. The mechanism moves the bear's head from side to side. Bing produced similar 28cm (11in) and 50cm (20in) bears of brown and white mohair plush. A pre-1919, silver-coloured, incised metal button, with "GBN" inside the diamond pattern, is located under the left arm, and the letters "DRPa" and "DRGM" are incised around the metal keyhole.

Height: 40cm (16in)

Incised metal button

Nose/mouth: *the vertically stitched, shield-shaped, black nose, with double stitch borders, is a typical Bing design. It has five long, central stitches extending down to meet an inverted-V-shaped mouth.*

Fur: *the fur is light brown mohair plush. The bear is stuffed with wood-wool. A clockwork mechanism inside the body controls the movement of the head.*

Legs: *the legs are rounded at the thighs, tapering to narrow ankles, with large, slender, oval feet.*

Pads: *the beige, felt pads are worn. The new felt and oversewing are visible on the left foot.*

Eyes: *the eyes are original black, boot buttons.*

BEAR PROFILE

At this angle, you can see that the bear follows the traditional early Bing design with its protruding but blunt muzzle, slight hump, elongated arms extending beyond the legs, narrow ankles, and large feet. The patching on the left paw-pad is clear, and the key is visible under the right arm.

Arms: *the very long arms curve upwards at the paws.*

small ears set wide apart on head

small, black, bead eyes

horizontally stitched, triangular, black nose; inverted-Y-shaped mouth

pink, rayon ribbon hides thick neck

straight left arm

metal rod joints protruding from paw

curved right arm

jointed legs

short, bristly, golden mohair plush

roller-skates made from thin, tin strips with small wheel at each end

1912 ROLLER-SKATING BEAR

Height: 20cm (8in)

When you wind up the key under the left arm, this bear lurches back and forth while the curved arm moves up and down. There is a metal arrow in the right ear. Other examples of this bear have an added orange "patent" button near the keyhole.

Metal arrow

horizontally stitched, triangular, black nose with border stitches; inverted-Y-shaped mouth

very long, tapering arms with internal metal rods ending in hooks

beige, felt pads

original wooden frame with chains

original black, boot-button eyes

dark cinnamon-coloured mohair plush; wood-wool stuffing; internal clockwork mechanism

traditional narrow ankles and large feet

C.1910 SOMERSAULTING BEAR

Height: 33cm (13in)

Steiff claimed that this bear copied their 1909 "Purzel-Bär"; the resulting lawsuit continued from 1911 to 1915, during which time Bing continued to produce their bear who turns somersaults after his arms have been rotated a few times. Some examples with the red, "patent" button exist, as well as a later example dressed in felt clothes.

brass key in keyhole under right arm

blue, plaited, wool collar; mother-of-pearl button a later addition

unjointed head

small, black, boot-button eyes

small, horizontally stitched, triangular nose with border stitches; metal ring through nose

beige, felt pads; four black claws

worn, short-pile, dark cinnamon-coloured mohair plush; stuffed with wood-wool

C.1913 MOVING ARMS

Height: 18cm (7in)

This small bear, made of dark cinnamon-coloured mohair plush (much favoured by Bing) can stand on all fours, as here, or sit upright. When wound up, the front legs move back and forth. It has a red-painted metal button under its left front arm.

Metal button

small, cupped ears

horizontally stitched, triangular, black nose with border stitches; inverted-Y-shaped mouth

small, black, boot-button eyes

curved right arm with internal rod protruding from paw

fixed head

straight left arm

short-pile, dark cinnamon-coloured mohair plush; wood-wool stuffing

jointed legs with small feet

tin ball made in two halves, containing clockwork mechanism with key

C.1913 FOOTBALLER BEAR

Height: 20cm (8in)

When wound up, the mechanism inside the ball makes it turn. The wheeled bear, joined to the ball by a rod protruding from its slightly curved arm, follows as if pushing it. The trademark is a red, painted, "patent" button, printed with "DRPa div DRGM".

Metal button

Steiff: 1920s–30s

TRADITIONAL AND NOVELTY BEARS; INTRODUCTION OF GLASS EYES

During World War I, the Steiff factory was turned over to making war supplies, and in the post-war period, when materials were rationed, teddies were made from reconstituted wood fibre. The 1920s saw a different style of Steiff teddy emerge, with glass eyes and kapok stuffing, and the introduction of new colours of plush. Teddy Clown arrived in 1926, followed by Teddybu, dressed in a felt waistcoat. In 1928, a squeeze-type musical teddy was made. Unique designs included Petsy, Teddy-Baby, and Dicky. In 1938, after the arrival of the first pandas in Western zoos, Steiff introduced their Panda-Bear.

1921 MEDIUM; WHITE

This is a beautiful example of a white Steiff bear, its colour and condition making it very collectable. The glass eyes and partial kapok stuffing date it to post-1920, when these features became part of the Steiff Original Teddy design. The white label indicates a pre-1926 date. The shield-shaped nose is vertically stitched; smaller bears in the range had triangular, horizontally stitched noses.

Height: 38cm (15in)

Embossed button

Nose: *the shield-shaped, vertically stitched nose is embroidered in brown thread, typically used on white bears.*

Arms: *the long, curved, tapering arms are similar in style to those of earlier Steiffs.*

Fur/stuffing: *the white, shaggy mohair plush makes this bear rare; the stuffing is a mixture of wood-wool and kapok, with wood-wool only in the head.*

Trademark: *the remains of a white, linen label, used until 1926, is still attached behind the Steiff button.*

Ears: *the large, rounded ears are positioned wide apart.*

Eyes: *the small, glass eyes with brown, painted backs are common on Steiff bears.*

BEAR PROFILE
This bear still retains the features of earlier Steiff designs: elongated arms, large feet with narrow ankles, a long, protruding muzzle, and a humped back. The plumpness in the body, caused by the use of kapok as well as wood-wool for stuffing, is a new feature.

Claws: *four brown claws are sewn over the plush, on the paws and feet.*

Feet: *the feet are large with narrow ankles.*

large ears, with
internal wire
armature, are
fully "poseable"

bulbous, blue,
glass eyes with
black pupils, sewn
in on wire shanks

remains of red
thread nose
and mouth

pointed muzzle
with unusual,
central seam
down front
of head

shaggy, "dual"
mohair plush

sweater is
not original

1927–28 BLUE-EYED PETSY   Height: 34cm (13½in)

This is the more unusual and collectable of the two
Petsy designs; the other one has brown eyes and a
black, embroidered nose. Produced in ten sizes, the
design was also available as a glove puppet, and on a
wheeled chassis, as part of the Record series.

Embossed button

large, brown,
vertically stitched,
shield-shaped nose,
over brown felt
underlay; central
stitches dropped

large, clear, glass
eyes with brown,
painted backs and
black pupils, sewn
in on wire shanks

shaggy, white
mohair plush;
internal tilt-
growler

long, narrow
feet with
beige, felt
pads,
reinforced
with card;
narrow
ankles

four brown
claws on paws
and feet

EARLY 1920s LARGE, WHITE   Height: 73cm (29in)

This bear is a larger version of the example opposite
but, unlike the smaller bear, it has beige, felt pads and
the foot-pads have card reinforcements. It has a slightly
corroded "button in ear" trademark with the remains of
a white linen tag, which effectively dates it to pre-1926.

Embossed button

large, rounded
ears set wide
apart on sides
of head

large, clear glass
eyes, with brown,
painted backs

brown, vertically
stitched, shield-
shaped nose

"dual" or
"tipped" plush,
popular in the
1920s, created by
brushing surface
of mohair with
darker dye

long,
tapering
arms with
curved
paws

large feet with
narrow pads

c.1926 "DUAL" MOHAIR PLUSH   Height: 60cm (24in)

This bear is cited in *The Guinness Book of Records* as the
most expensive teddy bear ever bought at auction. It was
sold at Sotheby's in 1989 for £55,000. Once thought to be
unique, one or two bears with the same "dual" mohair
plush and large eyes have since been found.

Embossed button

small, stiff ears;
right ear has
collapsed with age

brown, glass eyes with
black pupils, set into
muzzle seam

clipped, mohair
plush muzzle;
brown, vertically
stitched nose

open, flesh-
coloured, felt
palate

card-tag design
dates from
1928–50

blue, leatherette
collar, fastened
at back with
metal button;
card tag and
bell attached

peach-coloured
cotton plush;
internal
squeaker

four brown
claws on paws
and feet

large, flat, pink,
cotton pads,
reinforced
with card

1930 TEDDY BABY   Height: 30cm (12in)

Steiff's successful Teddy Baby series was designed
in 1929 and marketed the following year. The bear
was produced in different sizes, materials, and colours,
always with the **large**, flat feet and curved "begging"
arms. It remained popular well into the 1950s.

Embossed button

Steiff: In the Beginning...

THE STORY OF STEIFF AND THE "BUTTON IN EAR" TEDDY BEAR

Margarete Steiff was born on 24 July 1847 in Giengen, southern Germany. Although she was confined to a wheelchair as a result of polio contracted in infancy, she bought herself a sewing-machine and proceeded to earn her living as a seamstress. In 1877, Margarete established the Felt Mail Order Co., making felt clothing, and by 1880 she was also selling stuffed felt toy animals, adapted from patterns in magazines. With the help of her brother Fritz, Margarete's toy-making enterprise flourished and, in March 1893, the business became the Felt Toy Company. Margarete assembled all the samples herself, and extended the range to include toy animals in velvet, burlap, and even in real fur, all stuffed with wood-wool. She registered patents, appointed a travelling salesman, and, by 1897, was employing 10 factory workers and 30 home workers.

Margarete Steiff (1847–1909)
Despite her handicap, Margarete Steiff (above) founded the company whose name is now synonymous with teddy bears.

Richard Steiff, Margarete's nephew and the second of her brother Fritz's six sons, joined the business in 1897 after graduating from Art School in Stuttgart. He devoted himself to soft-toy design and manufacture, using sketches he had made earlier at Stuttgart Zoo and Hagenbeckschen Animal Circus. Richard's unique, string-jointed *Bär 55 PB* caught the attention of Hermann Berg, of the New York wholealers George Borgfeldt & Company, and at the Leipzig Fair in March 1903, Berg ordered 3,000 of these bears, so beginning Steiff's teddy-bear industry. In the following year, both Margarete and Richard were awarded gold medals at the World Fair in St. Louis, Missouri, USA, and the company itself gained the Grand Prix award. By the end of the year, Steiff had sold 12,000 teddy bears. Richard Steiff registered his disc-jointed teddy-bear design on 12 February 1905.

THE BÄRENJAHRE
On 6 July 1906, the Felt Toy Factory was renamed Margarete Steiff GmbH, with Margarete as owner, and her three

1903–04 Bärle
This rare, rod-jointed bear (left), with its long muzzle and sealing-wax nose, dates from Richard Steiff's experimental period.

nephews as managing directors. At this point, 400 people, with another 1,800 homeworkers, were employed to meet the almost insatiable demand – mainly from the US – for teddy bears. The company refers to this period, 1903–08, as the *Bärenjahre* (Bear Years); in 1907 alone, for example, Steiff manufactured 975,000 bears, a record that the company has still not surpassed.

Richard Steiff drew up the plans for a new factory in 1902: the east wing was completed in 1903, the west wing in 1905, and the north wing in 1908. The later work was overseen largely by Richard's brother, Hugo, who had studied engineering in Mannheim.

FRESH HORIZONS
From early on, Steiff sought to develop overseas markets; Paul ran a New York showroom during his year's visit to the city in 1902 and, in 1911, Otto founded

Steiff factory
The iron and glass buildings, seen in 1912 (left) and in the 1980s (below), are renowned for their modernistic design that pre-dated the later Bauhaus movement.

Metal buttons
The first Steiff button, in 1904, was blank, then with an elephant logo; "Steiff", with stylized final "F", was used from 1905–06; a blank button was used from 1948–50; and raised, cursive script from the 1950s.

Factory workers
Women did most of the work, from cutting out or stuffing (above), to adding details such as the nose and mouth.

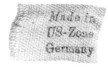

Labels
Steiff used side-seam labels (top) in 1947–53, when the factory was in the US Occupied Zone. Printed linen tags (middle) were used in 1960–72, and folded tags (bottom) from 1980.

Steiff Frères in Paris. By 1913, there were Steiff agents all over the world. In 1910, a young Prussian artist, Albert Schlopsnies, joined Steiff as a designer; he introduced elaborate displays – scenes from everyday life, staged with Steiff dolls and animals – which were set up in shop windows, exhibitions, and trade fairs. These became one of Steiff's unique specialities.

THE WAR YEARS AND BEYOND
During World War I, Steiff's toy production decreased to a minimum: the three company directors went into the army, materials such as felt, which was used for military uniforms, were in short supply, borders were closed preventing trade, and the factory was turned over mainly to the manufacture of war supplies such as gas masks, feed bags for horses, ammunition, and aeroplane parts.

For a short period after the war, Steiff made teddies from reconstituted nettle plant, as mohair plush was still unavailable. By the early 1920s, however, despite Richard's emigration to the US as the New York representative, the company was back on its feet, helped by the introduction of the conveyer-belt system, which speeded up production considerably. In 1927, Ernst, the youngest Steiff brother, joined the company. The decade following Hitler's rise to power in 1933 was difficult for the Steiff factory; toy production finally ceased in 1943, and the factory reverted to manufacturing munitions. At the

1953 Jackie-Baby
The 50th anniversary of the first Steiff teddy bear was celebrated with this bear cub (left).

Richard Steiff and prototype teddy
This 1909 photograph (right) shows Richard Steiff holding his prototype teddy, which remained virtually unchanged until 1950. Richard died in Michigan in 1939, having gone to the US in 1923 as Steiff's New York representative.

end of World War II, Giengen was occupied by American troops who stormed the factory in the hope of finding souvenirs to send home. However, all the samples and archives had been safely packed away and stored.

BACK IN BUSINESS
In October, 1945, Steiff manufactured a few toys for American troops, and started exporting again in January 1947. Low-quality plush had to be used at first, often in conjunction with blank tin buttons. The company resumed its high profile during the 1950s, when the workforce increased from 550 to 2,000, but in the 1970s, Steiff, like other soft-toy manufacturers, suffered from the competition of cheap imports from East Asia, and from the decrease in the birthrate in the West.

BEARS FOR COLLECTORS
The teddy-bear renaissance of the late 1970s in the US prompted Steiff to start producing limited-edition replicas of archive samples, heralding a period of renewed growth. Today, production methods continue on traditional lines, although some processes have been modernized (bears are now usually machine-stuffed). Collectors' bears however, are still stuffed by hand, using the traditional spiked stick and mallet.

Anniversary replica
In 1983, Steiff created a replica of Richard Steiff's 1905 design to mark the 100th anniversary of Margarete Steiff's first soft toy. The original is made of an unusual grey mohair plush, which was used only for the prototype. The example (below) has been signed on the right foot by Hans Otto Steiff, with "1983" on the left.

Schuco: 1920s–30s

SCHUCO MINIATURES AND NOVELTIES

I n 1912, Heinrich Müller, a former employee of Gebrüder Bing, founded Schreyer & Co. (usually known as Schuco) with his partner, Heinrich Schreyer, in Nuremberg. After World War I, when both men were conscripted, Schreyer left the firm and Müller took on a new business partner, Adolf Kahn. Since the company's inception, the registered trademark had been a little, tumbling man clasping his feet. In 1921, "Schuco" was officially added to this logo. Müller concentrated primarily on ingenious novelties, many of which were clockwork, including a uniformed marching bear and a bear with a football.

1927 PICCOLO; *PUDER-BÄR* (COMPACT BEAR)

In 1924, Schuco introduced its 9cm–15cm (3½in–6in) Piccolo series of miniature, jointed, mohair-plush toy animals, including teddy bears, in various colours. In 1925, the company produced a small teddy bear with sparkling, diamond-like eyes. In 1927, Schuco made this novelty bear – designed to fit into a lady's handbag – containing a mirror, compact, lipstick, and powder puff.

Height: 9cm (3½in)

Nose/mouth: *a few horizontal stitches of black thread form the narrow, rectangular nose, ending in an inverted-Y-shaped mouth.*

Ears: *the ears are small half-circles, stiffened with card inside.*

Eyes: *the eyes are painted, black, metal beads.*

Lipstick: *the metal tube still contains its red lipstick.*

Fur: *the bear is constructed of a unique internal metal frame, covered in lilac-coloured, short-pile mohair plush.*

Limbs: *the short, straight limbs do not have pads or claws.*

BEAR PROFILE
In profile, you can clearly see the typical Schuco features: the straight back and limbs, and the triangular, blunted muzzle that projects straight out from the forehead.

Compact: *the bear's torso contains a hinged compact, with powder on one side and a mirror on the other.*

painted, black, metal bead eyes

semi-circular ears stiffened with card

horizontally stitched, black, narrow, rectangular nose with inverted-Y-shaped mouth

original green, rayon, ribbon bow, now faded

short-pile, golden mohair plush

cream, felt pads

internal metal frame

c.1924 PICCOLO; MINIATURE Height: 6cm (2¼in)

Schuco intended the tiniest jointed bears to be given away free of charge, as a publicity gimmick, but they resulted in the Piccolo series. Pre-1930 examples had felt paws and feet attached to the ends of the internal metal frame, which is made up of various sections shaped by stamping and bending machines. The external jointing system used thin, metal rods.

painted, black, metal eyes

horizontally stitched, black, rectangular nose; long, vertical stitch leads to inverted-Y-shaped mouth

short-pile golden mohair, on head only

metal body frame covered by felt jacket and trousers; black, felt buttons

metal rod projects from clockwork mechanism, allowing wind-up by key

when wound up, arms go over head; legs follow arms

black, painted paws and feet are continuation of metal frame

c.1920–30s TUMBLING BEAR Height: 10cm (4in)

This miniature bear with a patented, internal metal frame, tumbles when the clockwork mechanism is wound up. Schuco also manufactured an unclothed example with a blunter muzzle, which continued to be made after World War II until 1965. The firm made larger, non-mechanical tumbling bears from 1920, including one on a metal trapeze.

painted, black, metal eyes

ears, reinforced with card, inserted into head-seam

glass bottle inserted into hollow body; hollow head conceals top of bottle

short-pile, golden mohair plush

straight arms with no pads or claws

limbs jointed with patented Schuco external metal pin method

straight legs with small feet

1920s PICCOLO; PERFUME BOTTLE Height: 13cm (5in)

Part of a series, this bear contains a corked, glass, perfume bottle designed for ladies' handbags. Contemporary advertisements also describe versions containing jam. It was available in two other sizes, 9cm (3½in) and 11cm (4¼in) and also as a brooch, with a safety-pin on the back. A prototype of a similar bear containing a cigarette lighter exists in the Schuco archive.

painted, black, metal eyes

mouth has short, metal nozzle with central hole for perfume spray

short, stubby, unjointed legs and arms sewn onto corners of fat, round body, containing bellows

short-pile, golden mohair plush (red example also exists)

round, metal, screw cap between legs gives access to perfume container

1920s MINIATURE ATOMIZER BEAR Height: 10cm (4in)

This little bear sprays perfume from its mouth when the flattened body is pressed. The bottle could be filled by unscrewing the round, metal cap at the base of the torso. By squeezing the internal bellows, the liquid is forced up a tube to the small, metal nozzle in the face. Its ingenious design reflects the excellence of Schuco craftsmanship.

Schuco: 1920s–30s

INTRODUCTION OF SCHUCO PATENTED YES/NO BEARS

I n 1921, Schreyer and Company's famous patented Yes/No bears appeared for the first time at the Leipzig Spring Toy Fair in Germany. Their heads could be turned from left to right, as well as nodded up and down, by moving the tail, which acted as a lever connected to a metal rod running up through the body to a ball-and-socket neck joint. The bears, with disc-jointed limbs and silk bows, were available in six sizes, from 25cm to 60cm (10in to 24in), in short, shaggy, and extra-shaggy mohair plush. The two larger sizes had tilt-growlers, whereas the rest contained squeakers.

1930s PICCOLO; YES/NO BEAR

This Yes/No bear is part of the Piccolo series of miniature bears, and is very similar in design to the perfume bear and the miniature compact bear *(see pp.40–41)*, although it is a fraction larger. Another example exists that was once attached to a tiny piano stool and which, when its head was moved back and forth using the tail lever, would appear to play a miniature piano.

Height: 13cm (5in)

Ears: *the large ears are pushed into holes across the head.*

Eyes: *unlike early Piccolo bears, this model has tiny, brown, glass eyes, with black pupils.*

Mouth: *the mouth is a black, inverted V shape.*

Nose: *the narrow, rectangular, black nose is horizontally stitched.*

Arms: *the arms are straight with no pads or claws.*

Fur: *the short-pile mohair-plush is golden coloured.*

Legs: *the straight legs end in little feet.*

BEAR PROFILE

At this angle, you can clearly see the similarities to the Schuco miniature compact bear *(see p.40)*, in the straight limbs and back, and the pointed muzzle. The tail, which is used to operate the head movement, is also clearly visible; the mohair covering has come adrift and reveals the wire loop beneath – a form of construction that is used on all sizes.

large, slightly
cupped ears

vertically stitched,
square nose with
inverted-Y-shaped
mouth

shaved muzzle
reveals woven
backing beneath

soft, shaggy, honey-
coloured mohair
plush in excellent
condition; wood-
wool stuffing

beige, felt pads
on paws and
feet; black,
embroidered
claws

large, oval feet

1930s YES/NO BEAR
Height: 53cm (21in)

One of the larger Yes/No bears, this example is made of soft, shaggy,
honey-coloured mohair plush and has translucent brown and black, glass
eyes with unusual opaque white surrounds. The bear's eyes, and its
chubby arms and legs with big feet, suggest its later date – the earlier
1920s examples have long, tapering limbs, and black, boot-button eyes.

silk hat in perfect
condition, except
for faded rosettes

brown, glass
eyes with large,
black pupils

vertically stitched,
square-shaped
nose on shaved
muzzle; inverted-
Y-shaped mouth

silk ruff

shaggy, beige
mohair plush
in excellent
condition;
wood-wool
stuffing
throughout

beige, felt
pads in mint
condition

1930s YES/NO CLOWN
Height: 50cm (20in)

This rare bear is similar to the previous example (left) but has more usual
brown, glass eyes, and wears a cream, silk, pierrot's hat and ruff trimmed
with frills and pink rosettes – a popular costume for teddy bears of this
period. It has large, stiffened feet and its paws are turned down, features
that anticipate the later Tricky post-war series (see p.112).

glass rims of eyes
painted, mustard colour
on backs; maroon
pupils; white surrounds

vertically
stitched,
oval nose

open mouth
lined with felt, with
separate felt tongue

original pale
blue, silk bow

pale pink, velveteen
pads; airbrushed
heels, toes, and
paw tips

beige wool
plush; wood-
wool stuffing;
plush-covered
metal tail

1930s BABY-BÄR
Height: 35cm (14in)

This is probably the largest of the four sizes of Baby Bear
design, which ranged from 20cm to 35cm (8in to 14in).
Made of shaggy, beige wool plush, with unusual side-
glancing eyes, open mouth, and a squeaker, it wears
either a silk bow, or a bib with a feeding bottle.

Card tag

narrow, oval nose
horizontally stitched in
black thread; inverted-
Y-shaped mouth

red, felt, pill-box hat
with leather chin strap

clear, glass eyes with
brown, painted backs
and black pupils

leather bag
and strap

red, felt jacket
with yellow braid
trimming and
black, felt buttons

black, felt trousers

long paws and feet,
with three black
claws; woven,
cream, fabric pads

feet, paws, head
and tail of golden
mohair plush

c.1923 MESSENGER-BÄR
Height: 36cm (14½in)

The second of three sizes of this Bellhop bear, produced
from 1921, its arms contain bent, metal rods and its feet
are stiffened with card. Earlier models had black, boot-
button eyes. This bear has a squeaker; the larger size
had a tilt-growler but smaller sizes were voiceless.

Card tag

Helvetic: mid-1920s

SWISS-MADE, SQUEEZE-TYPE, MUSICAL-BOX TEDDIES

Experts have identified a range of unmarked bears – produced *c.*1925 and containing squeeze-type musical boxes – as the work of the Helvetic Company. A 1928 issue of the US trade journal *Toy World* reported that the Helvetic Company held the exclusive manufacturing rights to teddy bears containing such mechanisms, but it is not known whether Helvetic was a US company importing the mechanisms from Switzerland, or a Swiss company exporting musical teddies. The name Helvetic is derived from *Helvetia*, the Latin name for Switzerland, where the clockwork musical box was invented.

*c.*1925 SHAGGY, BLOND/PINK MOHAIR

This bear possesses typical Helvetic features: large, glass eyes; distinctive, pear-shaped feet; and four black claws embroidered very close together at the ends of the paws. At the base of the right ear, you can just detect the original pastel pink, woven backing. Blue, gold, and green were other colours favoured by this manufacturer. The wide torso stores the music-box cylinder and comb mechanism which, for this large bear, has 32 teeth.

Height: 48cm (19in)

Ears: *the large ears are sewn across the facial seams.*

Eyes: *the large, brown eyes have a thick, white backing that renders them opaque.*

Nose: *the triangular, vertically stitched, black nose is very similar to those of early Steiff designs.*

Muzzle: *the protruding muzzle, with a long, pointed tip, is completely shaved.*

Arms: *the curved arms, tapering from wide shoulders to very narrow paws, are longer than the legs.*

Fur: *the woven backing of the blond, shaggy mohair plush, was originally pink, but this is now faded; the bear is stuffed with wood-wool throughout.*

Claws: *four black claws are embroidered very close together, across the plush, in a typical Helvetic design.*

BEAR PROFILE

From the side, you can clearly see this bear's narrow, pointed muzzle projecting from the shaggy mohair plush. The unusual curved, narrow paws and compact claw markings are also more evident at this angle, as are the bulbous, over-sized eyes, the expansive chest, and the strange, angular, humped back.

Feet: *the large feet have distinctive, narrow, pear-shaped pads, squared off at the toes.*

large eyes set wide apart, typical of Helvetic bears

large, round ears, sewn across facial seams

wide torso, containing bellows-operated musical box

worn nose repaired with vertical stitches; mouth missing

replacement dark brown, felt pads, oversewn in place

curved, thin, tapering paws; remains of black claws at ends

large, narrow, pear-shaped feet

*c.*1925 SHAGGY, BLOND/BLUE MOHAIR   Height: 38cm (15in)

This bald and badly stained bear was originally a stunning blue, a popular colour with the Helvetic Company; tinges of blue are still visible in areas of the body protected from light. The brown, glass eyes are fused onto a slightly smaller, white glass backing (creating the darker rim), each with an integral shank that is pushed into the head and glued in place.

large, brown, glass eyes with dark, outer rims

beige, felt hat, reinforced with card; two pink pompoms

narrow, pointed, slightly up-turned muzzle

small, black, horizontally stitched, triangular nose; inverted-Y-shaped mouth

two layers of rayon gathered into ruff

narrow, up-turned paws, with beige, felt pads

four black claws on each paw and foot

beige, felt pads repaired with new felt on right foot

large, narrow feet, slightly pear-shaped and squared off at ends

*c.*1925 BLOND/GREEN MOHAIR   Height: 38cm (15in)

Although in near-perfect condition, the original green, woven backing on this bear's fur has faded to yellow (the original colour is still visible beneath the pierrot's hat). The blond mohair pile is very short, but this bear possesses all other major Helvetic attributes. The woven, rayon ruff appears orange but is actually made up of pink and yellow threads.

large, rounded ears, sewn over facial seams

replacement translucent, amber, glass eyes; originals would have been larger

triangular, black, horizontally stitched nose; inverted-Y-shaped mouth

pointed, shaved, protruding muzzle

replacement cream, felt pads, oversewn around edges

large, pear-shaped feet

*c.*1925 BLOND/BLUE MOHAIR   Height: 30cm (12in)

Much of the long pile has worn away from the original blue backing, especially above the region of the musical box. The latter consists of a toothed cylinder and comb and a coiled spring, all enclosed in a round, wooden and oilcloth container. When the spring is pressed, it activates a lever, which turns the cylinder, causing the comb to strike the teeth.

large, rounded, slightly cupped ears, sewn over facial seams

replacement black, boot-button eyes

triangular nose at tip of muzzle; slightly lop-sided, inverted-Y-shaped mouth

wide chest contains round musical box

beige, felt pads; damaged left paw reveals wood-wool stuffing

beige, felt pads damaged by insects and wear and tear

large, narrow feet

*c.*1925 GOLDEN SHAGGY MOHAIR   Height: 30cm (12in)

Little of the original long pile remains on this bear's head or body, and this emphasizes its classic, Helvetic features: the narrow, pointed, slightly up-turned muzzle with horizontally stitched nose, and the curved, tapering arms, with slender paws and four-claw arrangement. Most Helvetic bears are between 30cm (12in) and 38cm (15in) high.

US: 1914–20s

CHEAP QUALITY "STICK" BEARS; TRADITIONAL AND NOVELTY

D uring the early craze in the United States (*c*.1907), the American teddy bear acquired realistic bear features, such as an elongated muzzle, long limbs, and a hump, copying the example set by Steiff and other German manufacturers. From the end of World War I onwards, however, inferior quality, US-made teddy bears were developed. Now known in American arctophilic circles as "US stick bears", because of their reduced features, these bears were produced for the masses by many small, now-forgotten, soft-toy factories. Unfortunately, these companies did not attach labels to their products.

1920s SMALL; SHORT, GOLDEN MOHAIR

This small bear demonstrates all the features of a typical "stick" bear, both in shape – with its oversized head, elongated muzzle, puny body, noticeable hump, and short, stiff limbs – and in the overall quality of the materials and the workmanship. The mohair plush, for example, has a sparse pile, indicating its inferior quality.

Height: 28cm (11in)

Ears: *the mohair-plush ears are gathered and pushed into the seam openings at the back of the head – the mark of a cheap bear.*

Eyes: *the boot-button eyes are sewn inside the two facial seams.*

Mouth: *the vertical stitch of the inverted-Y-shaped mouth is slightly awry, giving the bear a comical expression.*

Nose: *the small, elongated, triangular nose, embroidered in black, horizontal stitches across the end of the muzzle where the facial seams meet, is a typical feature of early American bears.*

Limbs: *the arms and legs are fully jointed.*

Arms: *the short, stubby, slightly curved arms taper towards the paws. The pads extend almost halfway up the arm.*

Legs: *the legs are different lengths, demonstrating poor workmanship.*

Pads: *the beige, woven cloth pads are badly stained, especially on the right paw.*

Claws: *three short, black claws are embroidered at the end of each limb.*

BEAR PROFILE

At this angle you can see the bear's "stick-like" features quite clearly: the large head with a flattened muzzle; the upright, narrow body; the short, slightly curved arms; and the thin, sausage-like legs with only the merest indication of feet.

Fur: *the bristly, golden mohair plush is very worn, especially on the chest where the squeaker has been pressed frequently.*

Foot-pads: *the legs end in small, circular pads.*

1920s ORANGE, BRISTLY MOHAIR   Height: 48cm (19in)

nose and mouth embroidered in black thread

small, rounded ears, gathered and sewn into seams at back of head – typical of poor quality bear

pointed paws stick out almost at right angles to arm

three black claws sewn across plush to edges of pads

small, rounded feet with three black claws

straight legs

This bear is made from short, bristly mohair plush (sometimes known as "sealskin" in the trade because of its texture), consisting of sparse, golden pile on an orange, woven backing. Although the body and legs are stick-like, the bear has a traditional, pronounced muzzle and slightly upturned, strangely curved arms, which are almost S-shaped.

1920s BEIGE MOHAIR; CLOTH NOSE   Height: 58cm (23in)

large, flat, floppy ears oversewn across corners of almost square head

small eyes sewn into facial seams

short, beige mohair plush, worn in places, particularly to right of chest

inverted-Y-shaped mouth, embroidered in black thread, gives glum expression

slightly curved arms

straight legs

small, tear-shaped pads

This bear has a particularly large head with a wide forehead, a typical feature of early American bears. The black, woven broadcloth nose, sewn onto the end of the muzzle between the two facial seams, is another characteristic of early bears made in the United States. The slightly asymmetrical shape of the nose indicates a teddy bear of poor quality.

1927 US "STICK" BEAR   Height: 55cm (22in)

small, rounded ears, gathered at base and badly sewn onto head; left ear has been attached too close to left eye

spherical head, with upturned, slightly pointed muzzle

small, embroidered, black nose at junction of facial seams, on tip of muzzle

inverted-V-shaped mouth, often found on cheap bears

brown, cloth pads on straight paws

sausage-shaped body has no shoulders, so arms seem to be attached halfway down body

Virtually shapeless when lying flat, this teddy bear's limbs are straight, sausage-like appendages attached, by traditional disc joints, to a similarly straight, humpless body. Both the body and the limbs are cut as almost identical oblong shapes – an easier, and therefore cheaper, procedure than that required to make the more curved, traditional design.

1917 THE NATIONAL BEAR   Height: 45cm (18in)

triangular nose of faded, black broadcloth stitched onto end of muzzle

miniature electric light bulbs connected to battery inside body, and held in place by compact wood-wool

leatherette collar around neck

body made from sections of red, blue, and white, cheap quality plush; stuffed with wood-wool throughout

short, almost straight arms, jointed to body

off-white, felt pads

unjointed legs made of same piece of fabric as body

This unusual "electric-eye" bear of patriotic red, white, and blue plush, was manufactured by the American Made Stuffed Toy Company of New York. Made in three sizes: 40cm (16in), 45cm (18in), and 55cm (22in), it retailed at $1, $1.50, and $2. This type of bear, with stiff neck and legs, was also made in traditional gold mohair plush, with electric eyes.

France: 1920s–30s

BIRTH OF FRENCH SOFT-TOY INDUSTRY; ROD-JOINTED BEARS

Although already renowned for its mechanical bears, France did import teddy bears from Germany during the early years of the craze. However, the 1914–18 war and the resulting border closures led to the establishment of a French teddy-bear industry. Generally of lower quality than their German counterparts, French bears were often made of short, bristly mohair or of coloured rayon plush. Manufacturers often employed cheaper methods of attaching eyes and ears (they pushed them into holes in the sides of the head, for example), as well as an unsophisticated, exterior jointing system.

1920s M. PINTEL FILS & CIE.

This Paris firm manufactured a range of soft toys, including animals, caricatures, and dolls. In the early 1920s, its lines were displayed in the London showrooms of Messrs. Ellis & Amiet. Pintel also manufactured mechanical bears including, later on, a dressed bear on a clockwork tricycle. The logo on the button trademark, showing two embracing bears, copied an illustration from pre-World War I Steiff catalogues. Pintel Fils always marked their bears with a chest-button.

Height: 38cm (15in)

Brass-plated button

Eyes: *the small, clear, glass eyes, with remains of paint on the backs, are sewn into the face on wire shanks.*

Nose: *this is a typical Pintel nose, vertically stitched in black thread, with the two outer stitches dropped.*

Arms: *the long, thin, tapering arms end in small, narrow paws with three claws on each; they are jointed in the traditional way using card discs.*

Fur/stuffing/squeaker: *the short, cinnamon-coloured, mohair-plush body is stuffed throughout with wood-wool. An oval squeaker in the body is still in working condition.*

Feet: *the feet are relatively large with thin, Steiff-like ankles.*

BEAR PROFILE

The side view demonstrates how slender and elongated this bear is in comparison with the more rounded German and British bears of the same period. There is the merest indication of a hump, and the muzzle is not very pronounced. The limbs are relatively long, with narrow ankles and slightly curved, pointed paws.

Claws: *the claws are stitched, in black thread, across both the plush and the pads.*

Pads: *the brown felt on the foot-pads is different from that on the paws, indicating that one set is a replacement.*

black, boot-
button eyes

card tag
attached with
metal button

vertically
stitched,
cinnamon-
coloured nose

faded pink
artificial-silk
plush, in very
good condition

long, slender body
fully jointed in
traditional
manner

beige, felt
pads on
paws and
feet; no
claws

long, slim,
tapering legs

big feet and
narrow ankles

1930s F.A.D.A.P.
Height: 43cm (17in)

This bear was made by a company based in Divonne-les-Bains, near the Swiss border. The Steiff-like button in the left ear indicates the company name in raised lettering, and the card tag behind is reminiscent of Steiff's 1928–50 circular chest-tags.

Embossed
button

light golden
mohair plush,
slightly shaved
around muzzle

clear, glass eyes
with traces of
paint on backs,
sewn into face
with knot at back

traditionally
jointed head;
fairly inflexible

black, vertically
stitched, rectangular
nose

original
price-tag

long, thin
torso

curved arms
tapering to
thin paws

beige, woven
twill pads

straight legs

1920s ROD-JOINTED
Height: 38cm (15in)

This bear is a typical example of the inferior-quality teddy bears produced in France in the 1920s. The work is not of a high standard – for example, the left ear is slightly larger than the right, and the jointing system is fairly crude. Thin, metal rods run through the body and into the arms and legs, where they emerge and form a final loop on the outside of each limb.

small, black, boot-
button eyes, sewn
into face

vertically stitched,
black, rectangular nose

slightly shaved
muzzle, pointing
upwards

short, straight
arms; no pads

pale golden
mohair plush

straight legs
with pointed
feet; no pads

original
price-tag

1920s STIFF NECK; ROD-JOINTED
Height: 25cm (10in)

A smaller version of the rod-jointed bear (above right), this example shares similar characteristics, determined largely by economy measures. It is also rod-jointed, with the loop of wire visible at the top of each limb; the neck is unjointed, as the head and body have been cut, all-in-one, from the same piece of fabric. The facial features are asymmetrical.

large, cupped
ears, set over
facial seams

black, horizontally
stitched, rectangular
nose; small, vertical
stitch in centre dropped
to meet inverted-V-
shaped mouth

original
faded blue
rayon
ribbon, tied
in bow

three black claws
on hands

blue artificial-
silk plush;
wood-wool
stuffing
throughout

white, felt
pads slightly
discoloured;
otherwise in
good condition

1920s BLUE ARTIFICIAL-SILK PLUSH
Height: 43cm (17in)

This tall, slender bear demonstrates several features typical of French bears of the inter-war period. Artificial-silk (rayon) plush became popular, and the French seem to have favoured it in pastel shades. Boot-button eyes were used in France well into the 1920s and 1930s, although other countries had, by then, turned wholly to glass eyes.

J.K. Farnell: 1920s–30s

ALPHA BEARS AND OTHER TRADITIONAL NOVELTY RANGES

Henry and Agnes Farnell, whose earlier family business made small textile items, established a soft-toy firm in their Acton home in west London after the death of their father, John Kirby Farnell, in 1897. J.K. Farnell made its name with the Alpha trademark after World War I, building a factory and becoming a private limited company in 1921. By the end of the decade, the company had showrooms in London, Paris, and New York. Despite a fire that destroyed the factory in 1934, J.K. Farnell was operating again the following year with new lines and billing itself as the "world's premier soft-toy manufacturers".

1930s ALPHA BEAR; LARGE

Farnell's famous Alpha Bear range, made with Yorkshire mohair, was first advertised in trade journals in the early 1920s. Farnell introduced a swing-tag with the words "Alpha Make" in 1925; a permanent embroidered label was used until *c.*1945. The inspiration for Winnie the Pooh was probably an Alpha Bear, bought by A.A. Milne's wife in 1921.

Height: 55cm (22in)

Embroidered label

Ears: *the slightly cupped ears are sewn over the facial seams.*

Eyes: *the amber, glass eyes with black pupils may be replacements.*

Mouth: *the inverted-Y-shaped mouth is possibly a replacement.*

Nose: *the wide, vertically stitched, rectangular nose is a typical Farnell design.*

Fur/stuffing: *the fur is high-quality, golden mohair plush; the head is stuffed with wood-wool, the body with a mixture of kapok and wood-wool, and the limbs with kapok.*

Arms: *the very long arms have curved, tapering, spoon-like paws.*

Legs: *the legs taper to narrow ankles, with large, slender, oval feet.*

Final seam: *the final, central chest-seam is a typical Farnell feature that copies the style of Steiff and Bing.*

BEAR PROFILE

This J.K. Farnell bear clearly resembles its early Steiff counterpart, with a realistic, protruding muzzle, a humped back, long, tapering arms with upward curving, spoon-shaped paws, and legs with rounded thighs, narrow ankles, and large, slender feet.

Trademark: *the embroidered label is stitched to the left foot-pad.*

amber, glass eyes with black pupils

wide, rectangular, embroidered, black nose of typical Farnell design

embroidered trademark, machine-stitched to foot-pad

cupped ears, sewn across facial seams

inverted-Y-shaped, single-stitched mouth

curly, golden mohair plush; kapok stuffing; internal squeaker

final, central chest-seam

long, thin, Rexine pads

1930s GOLDEN MOHAIR; SMALL   Height: 34cm (13½in)

This bear is possibly one of Farnell's cheap Unicorn range launched in 1931, which included Cuddle Bear in four sizes and colours. It has Rexine pads, without any claws, and its foot-label has the alternative wording "A Farnell Alpha Toy".

A FARNELL ALPHA TOY MADE IN ENGLAND

Embroidered label

---

cinnamon-tipped, white mohair plush; wood-wool and kapok stuffing in head; kapok in body; internal squeaker

long arms with spoon-shaped paws; cream, felt pads

large, brown, glass eyes with black pupils

wide, black, vertically stitched nose, with black, felt underlay

five black claws stitched over plush and pad

thick thighs; large, slender feet

embroidered label

C.1926 ALPHA BEAR; "DUAL" MOHAIR   Height: 65cm (26in)

As one of the earliest British teddy-bear manufacturers, J.K. Farnell rivalled Steiff, with many similarities between their designs. This bear, with its curly mohair plush and large, glass eyes, is reminiscent of the 1926 Steiff (*see p.37, bottom left*).

FARNELL'S ALPHA TOYS MADE IN ENGLAND

Embroidered label

---

white, artificial-silk plush; kapok stuffing with wood-wool in muzzle

original card swing-tag with company name and address

pale pink, velour jacket with powder-blue, felt edging

pink, artificial-silk feet

clear, glass eyes with blue, painted backs

black, vertically stitched nose; inverted-Y-shaped, single-stitched mouth

unjointed limbs in permanent seated position

base of body reinforced with card on which internal music box rests

C.1937 MUSICAL BEAR   Height: 30cm (12in)

In 1937, J.K. Farnell advertised a range containing the Swiss-made Thorens "Stop and Go" musical movement (Farnell held the sole rights). This example is made of artificial-silk plush, a fabric Farnell introduced with their 1929 Silkalite teddy bear.

Embroidered label

---

small, cupped ears

vertically stitched, black, oblong nose with few stitches extending to meet inverted-Y-shaped mouth

short, tapering arms

small, slender, oval feet

black, felt, circular eyes

short, white, woollen plush on woven backing; stuffed with kapok; wood-wool in head

pale peach, felt pads

embroidered trademark

1930s WHITE WOOL; SMALL   Height: 23cm (9in)

This wool-plush bear with felt eyes may be part of Farnell's Alpac range of alpaca toys for babies. Introduced in 1935, the range included pink, blue, gold, and white teddy bears. By that time, bears in a wide choice of quality and colour were available.

FARNELL'S ALPHA TOYS MADE IN ENGLAND

Embroidered label

Chad Valley: 1920s–30s

EARLY TRADITIONAL BEARS; BUTTON AND LABEL TRADEMARKS

The first Chad Valley traditional, jointed, plush teddy bears were manufactured in 1915–16, following the ban on German imports into Britain. "Chad Valley" was the trademark of Johnson Brothers who made stationery and board games at their works in Harborne, Birmingham. By 1920, the company had so expanded that soft-toy production was moved to a separate factory, the Wrekin Toy Works in Wellington, Shropshire; the business became known as The Chad Valley Co. Ltd. The teddy bears of the 1920s–30s were marked by a printed, celluloid-covered, metal button and/or a woven label.

1923–26 AEROLITE BUTTON

The early years were an experimental period for Chad Valley; some bears have been found with a stuffing of cork chippings and others with wire jointing. From 1920 onwards, Chad Valley used kapok stuffing; the company's 1923–26 Aerolite trademark refers to the soft, light nature of this material.

Height: 40cm (16in)

Aerolite button

Ears: *the large, flat ears are set on the sides of the head.*

Eyes: *the amber, glass eyes, with black pupils, are stitched into place on wire shanks.*

Nose: *the triangular nose is vertically stitched, with some horizontal stitches along the top.*

Fur: *the long, silky, golden mohair plush is clipped on the muzzle, and quite worn in places.*

Arms: *the arms are long and curved, with velveteen pads.*

Feet: *the large feet have oval, brown, velveteen pads.*

BEAR PROFILE
The protruding, rounded forehead and prominent, clipped muzzle, along with the less accentuated hump, shorter limbs, and smaller feet, illustrate the new, developing shape of the British teddy bear.

Pads: *there are five claws on each foot and four on the paws.*

flat, triangular head

large ears sewn over facial seams

large, triangular nose; smiling, inverted-Y-shaped mouth

clear, glass eyes with remains of brown paint on right eye; sewn in place and fastened off at back of head

pale golden mohair plush; shaved muzzle

beige, brushed-cotton pads

foot-pads reinforced with card

C.1920s BUTTON UNDER CHIN   Height: 73cm (29in)

Chad Valley generally placed its trademark button on the bear's right ear, but buttons are occasionally found on a bear's upper chest, as here, or on the upper back. Problems with Steiff's patent "button in ear" may have prompted these alterations.

Celluloid button

typical 1920s–30s triangular nose; vertical stitching with horizontal stitches across top

celluloid missing from button; metal corroded

shaved muzzle

glass eyes on wire shanks, sewn in and finished off at back

original felt pad; the others are replacements

unusual, wine-coloured mohair plush on brown woven backing

1930s WINE-COLOURED PLUSH   Height: 53cm (21in)

From 1930 until the 1940s Chad Valley attached a white woven label with red lettering to each of its bears. This was in addition to the celluloid-covered metal button, and was machine-stitched onto the foot-pad, or to the leg on smaller bears.

Embroidered label

amber, glass eyes on wire shanks, sewn and glued in position

large, flat ears set across top and sides of head

long, curly, golden mohair plush; largely kapok-stuffed

vertically stitched nose with horizontal stitch across top; shaved muzzle

long, curved, tapering arms

brown, brushed-cotton pads

foot-pads reinforced with card

C.1930 BUTTON IN EAR   Height: 43cm (17in)

The most common Chad Valley buttons are those with this wording, printed in black on a celluloid-covered metal stud. All Chad Valley buttons are larger than the early Steiff buttons. The nose is typical of those of Chad Valley bears produced during this period.

Celluloid button

shaved muzzle, with wood-wool stuffing

replacement glass eyes; left eye larger than right

golden mohair plush; kapok stuffing in body and limbs; hardboard joints

brushed-cotton pads on paws and feet

foot-pads reinforced with card (card in right foot broken)

thick thighs

C.1920s BUTTON IN EAR   Height: 73cm (29in)

This is yet another form of the Chad Valley trademark, with different wording and print colour, indicating an experimental phase in the company's history. This very large bear is stuffed with kapok, apart from the muzzle which contains wood-wool.

Celluloid button

Chad Valley: 1920s–30s

TRADITIONAL BEARS WITH ALTERNATIVE NOSE DESIGNS

C had Valley expanded rapidly throughout the 1920s and 1930s, taking over five companies, including Isaacs & Co. and Peacock & Co. (*see pp.70–71*). By the early 1930s, the company was advertising bears in fourteen sizes, including three that were available either "hard or soft stuffed". By the end of the decade, however, only kapok was being used. During this period, also, nose designs were modified: the rectangular, horizontally stitched nose and the triangular, vertically stitched nose developed into the thickly bound, oval shape that is now often referred to as the "typical Chad Valley nose".

*c.*1930 HORIZONTAL NOSE

Although similar in body shape to others of the period, this bear has the horizontal nose design usually associated with the Magna series (*p.55, bottom right*). Its short, bristly mohair plush also suggests it belonged to the "A" range, one of five different qualities of fur used by Chad Valley in the early years. The bear is entirely stuffed with wood-wool, which the company continued to offer as an alternative to kapok.

Height: 25cm (10in)   Embroidered label

Button: *the metal button in the right ear is corroded.*

Ears: *the large, flat, slightly cupped ears are sewn over the facial seams.*

Eyes: *the clear, glass eyes, painted bright cinnamon on the backs, may be replacements.*

Nose: *the horizontally stitched nose is reminiscent of those of Peacock bears of the period (see pp.70–71).*

Muzzle: *narrow in shape, but prominent, the muzzle is completely shaved, revealing the woven fabric.*

Fur: *the short, slightly bristly mohair plush is of inferior quality. The bear is stuffed with wood-wool throughout, and has a tilt-growler.*

Pads: *the nutmeg-brown, felt pads have been extensively repaired with a different shade of brown felt. There are no claws.*

Feet: *the pads on the large, rounded feet are reinforced with thick card.*

Trademark: *the red and white label is machine-stitched to the left foot-pad.*

BEAR PROFILE

This teddy still demonstrates some characteristics usually associated with early, traditional-style teddy bears: a slight hint of a humped back; relatively long, curved arms; and large feet. An endearing feature is the smiling, embroidered mouth, which spans the width of the distinct, protruding, shaved muzzle.

flat, relatively large ears, sewn over facial seams

small, translucent, amber, glass eyes, sewn in on wire shanks

shaggy, light golden mohair plush; kapok stuffing

slightly protruding, shaved muzzle

short, straight, jointed arms; no pads

short, straight, jointed legs

feet only slightly indicated

1930s SMALL; WIDE, BOUND NOSE
Height: 20cm (8in)

This little bear has the button trademark fixed into its upper back. Although the smallest in the traditional range, it still demonstrates many archetypal Chad Valley characteristics, such as the thickly bound, vertically stitched, oval nose with horizontally stitched borders.

Celluloid button

typical Chad Valley nose, vertically stitched with horizontal stitch across upper edge; inverted-Y-shaped mouth

large, translucent, amber, glass eyes, sewn into face and finished off at back of head

muzzle almost completely shaved, revealing woven backing

bright yellow, felt pads, with card reinforcement

four claws on left paw; only two remain on right paw

five claws on feet: one along central seam and two on each side

1930s TRIANGULAR NOSE
Height: 53cm (21in)

The soft, silky, bright yellow mohair plush on this bear is different from that of the bear opposite, and shows the range of quality offered by Chad Valley. This design was produced in white and in wine-coloured mohair as well as in artificial-silk plush.

Embroidered label

Chad Valley button in right ear

amber, glass eyes, on wire shanks, sewn into face and fastened off at back of head

black, vertically stitched, wide, bound nose, with horizontal stitch across upper edge

three black, embroidered claws on paws and feet, barely visible through plush

embroidered label stitched onto foot-pad

1930s SHAGGY, DARK BROWN MOHAIR
Height: 30cm (12in)

With its tightly bound nose, this bear demonstrates yet another quality of mohair plush available in the Chad Valley range, as well as an alternative colour to the usual gold. Its mint condition, light brown, appealing face, and surviving trademarks make it highly collectable.

Celluloid button

narrow, rectangular nose consists of several horizontal stitches; inverted-Y-shaped mouth

brown, glass eyes with black pupils, set rather wide apart

muzzle of same plush as body, not shaved as in other Chad Valley designs

light golden mohair plush

mid-brown, brushed-cotton pads; paw-pads repaired with new fabric

c.1930 MAGNA SERIES
Height: 38cm (15in)

This bear dates from around 1930 and possesses the unusual, blue and white Magna label, as well as the horizontally stitched nose generally associated with it. "Harborne" refers to the part of Birmingham where Chad Valley had its main toy factory.

Embroidered label

Chiltern: 1920s–40s

DEVELOPMENT OF FAMOUS CHILTERN HUGMEE RANGE

L eon Rees inherited the Chiltern Toy Works from his father-in-law, Josef Eisenmann, in 1919. In 1920, he collaborated with Harry Stone, formerly of J.K. Farnell, to form H.G. Stone and Co., which became one of the foremost British soft-toy manufacturers of the time. The trademark "Chiltern Toys" referred to the company's location in Chesham, in the Chiltern Hills. Bears were made there until 1940 when the factory was turned over to war work. One of Chiltern's earliest teddy bears was Baby Bruin, the Bear Cub, of 1922. In 1937, the Wagmee series – similar to Schuco's Yes/No bear – was introduced.

LATE 1920s HUGMEE; "DUAL" PLUSH

The mainstay of the company's soft-toy business was the Hugmee teddy bear which began to appear in trade journals in 1923. Permanent, cloth Chiltern labels did not appear until the 1940s; earlier bears would have possessed an orange, circular, card chest-tag, with the words "Chiltern Toys Trademark/Made in England".

Height: 58cm (23in)

Fur/stuffing/squeaker: *"dual" mohair plush was popular in the 1920s – this example has dark roots with blond tipping although the reverse was also used. There is wood-wool stuffing in the head and around the squeaker, and kapok in the limbs and body.*

SQUEAKER
The squeaker, which no longer works, is oval with a double reed (a reed at the end of each cardboard pipe) and oilcloth bellows that are now torn. The spring is rusty.

Eyes: *the clear, glass eyes are sewn in, with a final diagonal stitch at the back of the head – a typical Chiltern trait.*

Nose: *the oblong nose is vertically stitched with raised outer stitches, typical of the Hugmee range.*

BEAR PROFILE
At this angle you can see the typical Hugmee features of this period – long arms with spoon-like paws, thick thighs with large feet, an extended muzzle, and an embroidered nose with raised outer stitches.

Claws: *there are four converging claws on the paws, and five on the feet.*

Pads: *the beige, velveteen foot-pads are reinforced with card.*

white mohair plush; kapok stuffing, with wood-wool in head and around squeaker

original large, clear glass eyes with black pupils; sewn in and tied with knot at back of head

remains of typical, pre-war Hugmee nose and mouth

curved arms with spoon-shaped paws; same size as legs

four black claws over plush on each foot and paw

beige, velveteen pads; foot-pads reinforced with card

drumstick-shaped legs; fat thighs, narrow ankles, and large feet

1938 HUGMEE; WHITE MOHAIR   Height: 58cm (23in)

This bear has all the pre-war Hugmee features: the shaved, pointed muzzle; the distinct nose design, with two extended outer stitches; the remains of a typical, wide smile; long, curved arms; and "drumstick" legs with velveteen pads. Only 1,000 of these unusual white, mohair-plush teddies, advertised in Hamleys' 1938 catalogue, were made.

glass eyes

shaved muzzle

wide, enigmatic smile

oblong nose with outer stitches extended upwards

long arms

spoon-like hands with velveteen pads

large feet; pads reinforced with card

thick "drumstick" thighs

c.1930 GOLD MOHAIR   Height: 65cm (26in)

Although this particular bear is unmarked, it has many characteristics of the early Hugmee bears. This design was also available in other colours, including pink and blue, and a rare white. Hugmee bears were usually fitted with a squeaker, and originally had a chest tag reading "I Growl"; some early Hugmees contained squeeze-type musical boxes.

reddish brown, glass eyes

shield-shaped nose

indentation around waist caused by wearing elasticated trousers

golden mohair plush

small, pointed feet with Rexine pads and four claws in two-by-two arrangement

Rexine pads are typically British feature of period

1940s HUGMEE; FLAT FACE   Height: 50cm (20in)

During World War II and the years of rationing that followed, a new-look Hugmee evolved. Due to the lack of materials available, a pattern was designed that required less fabric, and so the Hugmee bear acquired a shortened muzzle and mouth, giving it a glum expression. The absence of claws on the paws was another economy measure.

translucent, reddish brown, glass eyes; sewn in and finished off at back of head

almost circular ears with inner edge caught into facial seam

shield-shaped nose embroidered in black thread

pink artificial-silk plush on woven backing

four black claws across pads and plush in two-by-two arrangement

small feet with beige, velveteen pads in perfect condition; four claws across pads and plush

1940s ARTIFICIAL SILK; MUSICAL   Height: 40cm (16in)

The Chiltern Silky Bear of 1929 was Chad Valley's first artificial-silk teddy bear. The bear illustrated (a flat-face, glum design similar to the previous bear) contains a key-operated, wind-up musical box in the small of the back, which plays Brahms' *Lullaby*. The bear is stuffed throughout with a light, soft cotton waste, known in the trade as "sub".

Joy-Toys: 1920s–60s

BIRTH OF FIRST AUSTRALIAN SOFT-TOY MANUFACTURER

J oy-Toys was founded in the 1920s by Mr. and Mrs. Gerald Kirby of South Yarra, Victoria, and was probably the first Australian commercial teddy-bear manufacturer. Before this, teddies were imported from Europe or they were home-made. After the Kirbys' departure to London in 1937 to form the soft-toy company, G.L. Kirby Ltd., Joy-Toys expanded under the leadership of Maurice Court, gaining the sole Australian franchise for Walt Disney characters and opening a factory at Whangarei, New Zealand. In 1966, the firm was bought out by the British-owned company, Cyclops, and ceased business in the 1970s.

LATE 1920s–30s FULLY JOINTED

Pre-World War II Joy-Toys bears are made of mohair plush with wood-wool stuffing and have a distinctive nose shape, which imitates the Chiltern design (*see pp.56–57*) of the same period. Chiltern's Hugmee range was exported to Australia from Britain around 1930, according to advertisements in Grace Brothers department-store catalogues, and it is possible that Joy-Toys based its bears' nose design on that of the Hugmee bears.

Height: 50cm (20in)

Embroidered label

Ears: *the ears are set wide apart at the back of the head and sewn across the facial seams.*

Eyes: *made of translucent, amber glass, the eyes are sewn into the face on wire shanks.*

Nose: *two stitches extend upwards from the vertically stitched, black nose.*

Mouth: *the inverted-T-shaped mouth is stitched in black.*

Arms: *the arms are short and fixed high on the body, giving the impression that the bear has no neck; the paws are tapered and curved.*

Body: *the body is long and thin.*

Fur/stuffing: *the fur is shaggy, golden mohair plush, worn in places, exposing the woven backing beneath; the bear is stuffed with wood-wool throughout.*

Pads: *the beige coating on the original Rexine pads is worn away, revealing the off-white, woven backing.*

Legs: *the legs are short and straight; they are slightly wider at the thighs.*

BEAR PROFILE

This bear borrows many characteristics from the typical British bears of the period, with its relatively short limbs and curved paws, plump thighs and small feet, and its straight back. The protruding muzzle projects straight out from the bear's forehead; the long, outer stitch of the distinctive nose is clearly visible.

Feet: *the feet are short and stumpy; there are no claws.*

Trademark: *an embroidered cloth label is stitched onto the left foot-pad.*

unusual glass eyes with painted, amber backs and black pupils, set wide apart

flat ears, set wide apart across facial seams, at back of head

no neck joint

vertically stitched, square, black nose; inverted-T-shaped mouth

short, coarse, golden mohair plush

short, curved, tapering arms with wide shoulders

short, stumpy, oval feet

beige, felt pads with no claws

1940s SQUARE NOSE
Height: 38cm (15in)

Perhaps as a result of wartime shortages, this bear is made from short, coarse mohair plush and has no neck joint, a feature that was to become a characteristic of Joy-Toys and other Australian bears. The nose design is a simple square shape.

Embroidered label

brown, glass eyes with black pupils sewn in on long, wire shanks

unusual triangular nose

vertical stitch is all that remains of mouth

worn, shaggy, blond mohair plush; kapok or "sub" stuffing

fur worn away by frequent use of squeaker

short, tapering arms end in pointed paws

short, straight legs with pointed feet

1940s–50s SEMI-JOINTED; NO PADS
Height: 25cm (10in)

This small, well-worn, shaggy, blond mohair-plush bear has no neck joint. The body and head are all-in-one, being cut from the same piece of fabric. Like many small bears, it lacks foot-pads. A label is machine-stitched to the heel.

Embroidered label

translucent, blue, glass eyes with black pupils sewn in on wire shanks

flat ears, set wide apart, sewn across facial seams

vertically stitched, square, black nose; inverted-T-shaped mouth

short, outstretched, unjointed arms with no pads

pale pink synthetic plush on knitted backing

feet consist of semi-circular tops and large, oval soles of same plush as body

straight, unjointed legs

c.1960 UNJOINTED; MOULDED FILLING
Height: 30cm (12in)

This unjointed bear has a complete foam-rubber filling, moulded into a bear shape, and then inserted via the back-seam into the outer covering of pale pink synthetic plush. It has a German-made, clear vinyl, concertina squeaker.

Printed label

vertically stitched, square, brown nose; inverted-T-shaped mouth

large, amber and black, glass eyes

stiff neck

jointed limbs

brown, velveteen pads

bright golden synthetic plush; foam-rubber stuffing

1960s SEMI-JOINTED; FOAM FILLING
Height: 38cm (15in)

The Joy-Toys shape did not generally change during the late 1950s and 60s. The square nose design and large, glass eyes continued to be used, and the body was semi-jointed with the characteristic stiff neck. However new synthetic fabrics were used for plush and filling, and the printed label was folded and often sewn into the leg- or pad-seam.

Merrythought: 1930s

EARLY DEVELOPMENT OF TWO TRADITIONAL BRITISH DESIGNS

I n 1930, W.G. Holmes and G.H. Laxton opened a soft-toy factory in a building originally leased from the Coalbrookdale Company, in Ironbridge, Shropshire, *(see pp.66–67)*. They registered their trademark Merrythought (a 17th-century English word meaning wishbone, and a symbol of good luck) that same year. In 1931, they produced their first catalogue, advertising two golden mohair teddy-bear designs: the Magnet range, which was designed, in four sizes, to "attract" the cheaper end of the market; and the Merrythought range, which evolved later into their key pattern, the M line.

EARLY 1930s TRADITIONAL DESIGN

This early design combines features associated with Chad Valley (printed, celluloid-covered, metal, button trademark, and large, flat ears) and J.K. Farnell (webbed claw markings). This may be because the new directors of Merrythought, C.J. Rendle and H.C. Janisch, had previously worked for these two well-established, soft-toy firms. Most Merrythought bears were made from golden mohair plush, but a dark-brown-tipped, biscuit-coloured, mohair-plush bear was produced from 1936 to 1938.

Height: 58cm (23in)

Celluloid/metal button

Button: *the printed, celluloid button, with wishbone trademark, was used during the 1930s; it is fixed to this bear's left ear.*

Eyes: *the amber, glass eyes, sewn into the face on wire shanks, are set wide apart and low down.*

Nose: *the outer two stitches of the vertically stitched nose are dropped; the mouth is an inverted Y shape.*

Fur/stuffing: *the fur is golden mohair plush; the bear is stuffed with a wood-wool and kapok mixture, apart from the limbs, which are stuffed with kapok.*

Claws: *the webbed claws on the paws, typical of early Merrythought bears, consist of four stitches across each felt pad, with the inner ends joined by horizontal stitches.*

Legs: *the fully jointed legs end in small, rounded feet; the fat thighs are typical of British bears of this period.*

Pads: *the deep orange, felt pads complement the golden mohair plush.*

Trademark: *the embroidered label, machine-stitched to the right foot, dates the bear to pre-World War II; Merrythought later used printed labels.*

BEAR PROFILE
The nose formation, clearly visible at this angle, and consisting of two, dropped, outer stitches, is typical of the early Merrythought design. The protruding, shaven muzzle emulates the traditional, realistic, Steiff design.

large, flat ears, sewn across the facial seams

completely shaved, protruding muzzle

webbed claws on paws

label machine-stitched to foot-pad

large, amber, glass eyes with black pupils, set wide apart

shaggy, blond mohair plush; wood-wool stuffing in muzzle, kapok elsewhere

four claws across plush only

beige, felt pads

EARLY 1930s SHAGGY MOHAIR

Height: 50cm (20in)

Early Merrythought bears were made in varying grades of plush. This example is made from a luxurious, long-pile mohair plush. The original golden colour has faded with time, but you can still see it inside the ears and around the joints.

MERRYTHOUGHT HYGIENIC TOYS MADE IN ENGLAND

Embroidered label

---

high forehead

completely shaved, protruding muzzle

dark brown, short wool plush; kapok stuffing, with wood-wool in muzzle and around squeaker

typical spoon-shaped paws

large, flat ears sewn over facial seams; printed, celluloid-covered, metal button in left ear

typical vertically stitched, rectangular nose with dropped outer stitches

felt pads, originally dark brown, now faded and worn; no claws remain

thick thighs

1930s DARK BROWN, SHORT PILE

Height: 48cm (19in)

This bear is similar to other 1930s Merrythought bears, but is made from a shorter pile, soft wool plush in an unusual chocolate-brown colour. The webbed claws have disappeared, but unfaded areas on the paw-pads indicate their original position.

MERRYTHOUGHT HYGIENIC TOYS MADE IN ENGLAND

Embroidered label

---

nose and mouth have been repaired but follow original design: dropped outer stitches on nose; inverted-Y-shaped mouth

four webbed claws on paws; three straight claws on feet

amber, glass eyes with black pupils, sewn in and finished off at back of head

golden mohair plush; wood-wool stuffing in muzzle and head, wood-wool/kapok mix in body, kapok in limbs

1930s GOLDEN MOHAIR

Height: 45cm (18in)

The shaved muzzle, high forehead, large, flat ears, webbed claws, and thick thighs are all typical features of a 1930s Merrythought bear. The pads, however, are made from dark brown velveteen, rather than from the more usual felt.

MERRYTHOUGHT HYGIENIC TOYS MADE IN ENGLAND

Embroidered label

---

rectangular, vertically stitched nose, without dropped outer stitches; inverted-Y-shaped, double-stitched mouth

slender torso; curved arms with thin paws

beige, woven-twill pads; five claws on paws; four on feet, across plush only

bulbous, brown and black, glass eyes

golden mohair plush, slightly worn on chest

short legs with slightly stumpy feet

woven label machine-stitched to left foot-pad

EARLY 1930s ALTERNATIVE DESIGN

Height: 50cm (20in)

This design was also available in eight fashionable shades of artificial-silk plush: "Salmon", "Ciel", "Myosotis", "Iris", "Canary", "Crimson", "Copper-glow", and "Jade". It still has its celluloid-covered, metal button on the back, behind the left arm joint.

MERRYTHOUGHT HYGIENIC TOYS MADE IN ENGLAND

Embroidered label

Chad Valley: 1938–50s

ROYAL WARRANT LABEL; TRADITIONAL TEDDY BEARS

By the end of the 1930s, The Chad Valley Company was recognized as one of the world's leading toy manufacturers. It had expanded greatly and, in 1938, was granted the British Royal Warrant of Appointment. From that time, all of the firm's toys carried a label with the declaration "Toymakers to Her Majesty the Queen", referring to Queen Elizabeth, the wife of the monarch, King George VI. The wording changed in 1953 with the coronation of the present Queen Elizabeth II, when "the Queen" became "the Queen Mother" – a detail that is helpful when trying to date Chad Valley bears.

1938–52 LARGE; GOLDEN MOHAIR

The basic, traditional teddy-bear design did not change greatly during this period. The nose shape, however, developed from the typical triangular form of the 1920s and 1930s to a tightly bound, wide, rectangular shape. Rexine, a treated buckram, became a popular fabric for the paw- and foot-pads, replacing the flannelette and velveteen that were previously preferred.

Height: 73cm (29in)

Printed label

Ears: *the large, flat ears, sewn across the top and sides of the head, are typical of Chad Valley bears.*

Eyes: *the large, reddish brown, translucent, glass eyes are sewn in on wire shanks.*

Nose: *the wide, rectangular nose is composed of closely bound, vertical, black stitches, with horizontal stitches across the top edge, as on the company's earlier, triangular nose design.*

Trademark: *the blue, printed label is sewn into the chest seam.*

Fur/stuffing: *the particularly beautiful, golden mohair plush is in mint condition, with no worn patches. The bear is stuffed with kapok.*

Feet: *the feet are long and narrow.*

BEAR PROFILE
This side view shows the typical emerging British bear shape, with its straight back, flattened muzzle, and particularly wide thighs. The arms are extremely long and curved at the paws. Notice the Royal Warrant label on the left foot.

Pads: *the Rexine pads are slightly worn, revealing the woven backing fabric. There are no claws.*

1938–52 BLUE MOHAIR

Height: 35cm (14in)

typical Chad Valley flat ears sewn across facial seams

brown, glass eyes sewn off at back of head

black, bound nose

blue mohair plush, with soft stuffing

printed label sewn into chest-seam

pre-1953 Royal Warrant label sewn onto foot-pad

blue, felt pads

Chad Valley was well known for its colourful bears, and blue was a popular choice. This bear lacks the round plumpness of earlier Chad Valley teddies – a result of the war-time rationing that reduced the materials available for making teddy bears.

Printed label

POST-1953 SHAGGY, GOLDEN MOHAIR

Height: 44cm (17½in)

reddish brown, translucent, glass eyes

large, flat ears

shaved muzzle; wood-wool stuffing in head

wide, bound nose is characteristic of this period

shaggy, golden mohair; kapok stuffing in body and limbs

dark brown, suede-like, Rexine pads

The Royal Warrant label, both pre- and post-coronation, was usually square (but sometimes oblong), with the Royal Warrant, coat-of-arms, and company name printed in blue. The label was usually zigzag-stitched onto the bear's foot.

Printed label

POST-1953 WHITE WOOL

Height: 34cm (13½in)

slightly flattened muzzle; wood-wool stuffing in head

sewn-in glass eyes

wide, bound nose

printed label sewn into right side-seam

white wool plush, with soft stuffing in body and limbs

Queen Mother Royal Warrant label sewn onto right foot

soft, light brown, Rexine pads; cracks reveal woven backing beneath

This bear shares many of its Chad Valley characteristics with the earlier, golden bear (opposite), although it is made of a cheaper plush. The Rexine pads are light brown, to complement the colour of the wool plush.

Printed label

1940s LARGE; GOLDEN MOHAIR

Height: 107cm (42in)

large, soft ears in excellent condition

large, wide head

original, amber and black, glass eyes

compact, vertical stitching on nose

shiny, brown, leather-like, Rexine pads on paws and feet; no claws indicated

short arms compared to those of German bears

good quality, golden mohair plush

This exceptionally large bear has hardboard-reinforced foot-pads. A printed label is sewn into a side-seam, the usual positioning, although Chad Valley labels are often found in the chest-seam or near the leg joint.

Printed label

Chad Valley: 1930s–40s

NOVELTIES; INTRODUCTION OF ALTERNATIVE PLUSH FABRICS

The Chad Valley Company produced a number of novelty items, beginning with its 1926 Rainbow Tubby Bear, with ruff and pierrot's hat. Its most popular novelty in the 1930s was Cubby Bear, which was made of brown and fawn alpaca plush and available in three sizes. This endearing bear was possibly the Chad Valley equivalent of Merrythought's Bingie (*see pp.68–69*). Cubby's baby brother Sonny Bear was made from biscuit-coloured plush and wore a bib. In 1934, Chad Valley produced Winnie the Pooh and various other A.A. Milne characters, popularized by the BBC radio's *Children's Hour* programme.

1930s BLUE; MUSICAL

Blue was a popular colour for British teddy bears from the late 1930s to the early 1950s. The squeeze-type musical mechanism found in this bear was one favoured by British manufacturers such as Chiltern and Chad Valley from the mid-1920s to the early 1930s, when it was superseded by the key-wound, clockwork variety.

Height: 55cm (22in)

Embroidered label

Muzzle: *the protruding, shaved muzzle is stuffed with wood-wool.*

Fur/stuffing/musical mechanism: *the curly, blue mohair plush is badly worn in places, especially in the centre of the chest above the squeeze-type musical mechanism. The body and limbs are stuffed with a mixture of wood-wool and kapok.*

Pads: *the light brown, felt pads were originally reinforced with card; (now missing from the right foot-pad).*

Label: *the red and white label is sewn onto the left foot-pad.*

Trademark: *the celluloid button in the left ear has the wording: "Chad Valley British Hygienic Toys".*

Eyes: *the large eyes are made of glass.*

Nose: *the triangular nose is typical of the period.*

BEAR PROFILE

The side view illustrates the larger feet, fatter thighs, and shorter arms of the British teddy bear compared to German bears, as well as clearly showing the protruding, shaven muzzle.

amber and black, glass eyes may be replacements

large, cupped ears

shaved muzzle, stuffed with wood-wool

black, vertically stitched nose with two horizontal stitches across top

original golden-coloured artificial silk, now dirty

original golden, felt foot-pads repaired with woven fabric

paw-pads repaired with beige kid leather; three claws on left paw

five claws on each foot

c.1930 GOLDEN ARTIFICIAL SILK

Height: 33cm (13in)

The main British manufacturers began making artificial-silk plush teddy bears in 1929. Chad Valley used a variety of colours, usually with felt pads in a matching colour. Originally this bear was a pale golden colour, but it is now discoloured.

HYGIENIC TOYS MADE IN ENGLAND BY CHAD VALLEY C? LTD

Embroidered label

---

amber and black, glass eyes

small ears sewn across facial seams

original pink, vertically stitched nose with horizontal stitch across top

shaved muzzle

soft, short-pile alpaca plush in cream and brown

short arms with replacement beige, felt pads

brown, artificial-silk pompoms on central seam

fully jointed limbs

c.1945 CLOWN BEAR

Height: 28cm (11in)

This soft alpaca plush teddy bear was illustrated on the front cover of a toy-trade journal in 1945. It is stuffed with kapok, except for the muzzle, which is stuffed with wood-wool. There is a red and white, embroidered label on each foot-pad.

HYGIENIC TOYS MADE IN ENGLAND BY CHAD VALLEY C? LTD

Embroidered label

---

black, horizontally stitched nose with inverted-Y-shaped mouth

tiny, glass eyes with brown-painted backs; sewn in with knot at back of head

dark brown, felt ears

beige, alpaca plush

fully jointed limbs; head unjointed

flattened, shaved muzzle

Baby

dark brown, felt foot-pads

blue, felt jacket and yellow, felt waistcoat

c.1938 THREE BEARS

Height: 10cm (4in)/baby 7cm (3in)

These three little bears, a mother, father, and baby, were advertised in a 1938 catalogue as the "Bears' Tea Party", complete with a wooden table and three chairs. Baby Bear holds a handkerchief to his eyes, crying as in the story of *The Three Bears*.

HYGIENIC TOYS MADE IN ENGLAND BY CHAD VALLEY C? LTD

Embroidered label

---

small, flat ears sewn across facial seams

fully jointed head and limbs

small, amber and black, glass eyes, sewn in at back

white sheepskin; soft stuffed apart from head, which is quite solid

black, vertically stitched, oblong nose

long legs with well-defined feet

black, leather pads

1940s WHITE SHEEPSKIN

Height: 28cm (11in)

This bear was probably made during the war years when mohair plush was difficult to purchase. As is traditional with sheepskin teddies, it has black, leather pads. The blue label of the 1940s–50s period is sewn to the inside of the right leg.

HYGIENIC TOYS MADE IN ENGLAND BY CHAD VALLEY C? LTD

Printed label

Merrythought Magic

I n 1919, W.G. Holmes and G.H. Laxton opened a small spinning mill in Yorkshire to weave yarns from raw mohair imported from countries such as Turkey and South Africa. During the 1920s, the partnership bought Dyson Hall and Co. Ltd., a mohair-plush weaving factory in Huddersfield. Seeking an outlet for their plush fabric, they decided to establish a soft-toy factory: Merrythought Ltd. was founded in 1930. The following year they leased one of the buildings belonging to the Coalbrookdale Co. in Ironbridge, Shropshire, on the banks of the River Severn.

1989 CHEST-TAG

Once known as "Little Switzerland", with hamlets nestling on the banks of the River Severn, the area around Ironbridge is also referred to as the "cradle of the Industrial Revolution" as it was here, in 1709, that Abraham Darby first smelted iron ore with coke. The first iron bridge, built in 1779 by Abraham Darby III, is about one kilometre (half a mile) away from the Merrythought factory, and its shape is echoed in the design of the word

the pre-World War II bears. C.J. Rendle, a former Chad Valley manager, was hired to take charge of production. The company also employed H.C. Janisch, a sales manager at J.K. Farnell, to run the sales operation at the company's London showroom at 113 Holborn. With 20 workers, Rendle began manufacturing in temporary premises in September 1930, moving into the permanent factory in February 1931. The area had excellent transport facilities, with the two main railway lines a short distance away.

Main factory
The main factory at Ironbridge, built in 1898, is guarded by two life-size "London Bears". Merrythought leased the factory in 1931–56 then bought it. The gates carry the word "Merrythought".

A GROWING BUSINESS

In early 1931 the company rented larger factory space from the iron foundry, the main workshop then measuring 40x16m (135x52ft). It also employed more people: by 1932, numbers had risen to nearly 200. An article in a trade magazine of the same year reported that Merry-thought possessed an ideal work space for toy production, describing the factory as being extremely light, unobstructed by pillars or columns, with two rows of roof lights on each side of the pitch of the roof, and large windows along one wall. At one end there were benches of power-driven sewing-machines, operated by a large, light-oil engine; by the end of 1932, electric motors were installed, with a special feed line run by West Midlands Electrical Commission. Outside, there were sheds for the storage of packing

1932 Factory floor
In the 1930s, the workers and the supervisors (centre left, standing) wore neat uniforms. The work area (above) is still used today for soft-toy production.

"Merrythought" on the company's labels. The reasoning behind the "Merrythought" name is now unknown, although it is derived from the old English word for wishbone, the forked bone in birds that is traditionally a symbol of good luck. It was registered as the company's trademark in 1930 and illustrated on buttons marking

Traditional methods
An employee hand-sews the nose of a 60th anniversary bear; two modern "M" bears sit in the background. Much of the work is still done traditionally.

Early catalogues
Catalogues from the Merrythought archives.

1931 catalogue
An illustration of the early Magnet and Merrythought lines.

PRE-WORLD WAR II, EMBROIDERED, WOVEN LABEL

c.1945–c.1956, PRINTED, WOVEN LABEL

c.1957–91, PRINTED, WOVEN LABEL

1992–PRESENT, EMBROIDERED, WOVEN LABEL

1931 BINGIE

cases and crates, bales of wood-wool, and huge sacks of kapok.

Manufacture began with cutting out the plush, followed by sewing the pieces together; the bears were then stuffed, assembled, and finished off (adding features and ribbons, etc.). The bears were then packed in boxes and sent to the stock rooms.

Florence Atwood, the chief designer employed from 1930 until her death in 1949, was deaf and had learned her trade at the Deaf and Dumb School in Manchester. She created bears from her own designs and also transformed the work of other artists, such as Lawson Wood's caricatured orang utan, Gran'pop. She designed Merrythought's first panda bear, following the panda cub Ming's arrival at London Zoo in 1939.

By 1935, the company had acquired 3,865 square metres (41,600 square feet) of work space, making it the largest soft-toy factory in the United Kingdom.

WORLD WAR II
During World War II, the British Admiralty and the Ministry of Aircraft Production took over the Merrythought factory to produce maps and to store plywood. Merrythought continued to manufacture a few toys at temporary premises in near-by Wellington, however, later undertaking Government contracts for the production of gaberdine and velour items. Toy production was reinstated at Ironbridge in 1946, although flooding of the Severn that year destroyed all pre-war samples and much of the company's supplies.

Following C.J. Rendle's death in April 1949, B.T. (Trayton) Holmes, son of the founder, W.G. Holmes, joined the company. In 1952, he employed Jimmy Matthews, now Sales Director, to boost sales after the lean post-war years. The following year, the designer Jean Barber joined the company and in October 1955 she created the popular Cheeky (*see pp.120–21*). Barber was succeeded by various designers after 1965; Jackie Harper took over from 1967–69. The post-war era saw the introduction of new, synthetic fabrics, such as nylon and Dralon, many coming from East Asia. The company also acquired new machinery: in 1955, a stuffing machine using compressed air was introduced from the US, and hydraulic press cutters were later installed.

The 1970s saw major changes in personnel. In 1970, Jacqueline Revitt, now the Design Director, joined the company; the present Managing Director, Oliver Holmes, Trayton's son, joined two years later.

LIMITED EDITIONS AND REPLICAS
In 1982, the company introduced a traditional range of limited-edition mohair teddy bears for import by Tide-Rider Inc. of New York. In 1986, Merrythought provided a giant bear, ordered by H.R.H. Prince Edward, to ride in a royal coach at his brother Prince Andrew's wedding. Also in 1986, the publication of John Axe's history, *The Magic of Merrythought*, inspired the manufacture of the first replica – the Magnet bear (*see p.161*) – followed by Bingie (*see p.68*), Mr Whoppit (*see p.121*), and a reproduction of the Bing bear "Gatti" (*see p.193*).

In 1988, Merrythought opened a shop and museum next to the factory, run by the Ironbridge Gorge Museum Trust. In 1992, the company's high quality workmanship was acknowledged with a TOBY award for its character bear Master Mischief.

Diamond jubilee
Merrythought launched a limited edition of 2,500 bears for its 60th anniversary in June 1990.

1984 catalogue
This features the Champagne Luxury Bear (see p.135).

Limited editions
Since the 1980s, the company has turned its attention to the collectors' market, introducing special commissions and replicas. This unique greenish blue, pure mohair-plush bear was made in 1983. Its foot is signed by Chairman, Trayton Holmes.

Merrythought: 1930s

BINGIE FAMILY SERIES AND OTHER PRE-WAR NOVELTIES

Soon after its foundation, Merrythought began making novelty teddy bears. The company made several soft alpaca bear-cub ranges ideal for young children, such as the very early Tumpy, and the later Chubby Bear of the mid-1930s; both are reminiscent of Chad Valley's Cubby Bear (*see p.105*).

Bobby Bruin (*opposite*) and Teddy Doofings were a new departure. The latter, available in brown, blue, pink, and green plush, with sleeping eyes, was Mickey-Mouse-like and fully "poseable". The Bingie family – introduced at the firm's outset, and available throughout the 1930s – was especially popular.

1931 BINGIE

Part of a family of novelty teddies made from 1931–38, Bingie represents a sitting bear cub with soft kapok filling and unjointed legs. It was made in seven sizes, with two extra-small sizes for babies, known as Baby Bingie. This bear possesses a rare example of Merrythought's earliest label, used only in the first year of production, omitting the words "Hygienic Toys".

Height: 35cm (14in)

Embroidered label

Arms: *the short, stocky arms end in rust-coloured, felt pads with brown, double-stitched claws over the plush and pads.*

Legs: *the short, stocky, unjointed legs are designed so that the bear adopts a sitting position.*

Feet: *the feet are particularly long and large. The rust-coloured, felt pads are wider at the heels and toes, with four claws, double-stitched in brown thread to match the nose and mouth.*

Ears: *the ears are lined with white, artificial-silk plush.*

Eyes: *the large, amber, glass eyes are positioned low on the face.*

BEAR PROFILE
From this angle you can see the pronounced muzzle, which is constructed from a separate piece of clipped plush. The large head, rounded back, and huge feet are all features reminiscent of a real bear cub.

Trademark: *the woven label is attached to the inside of the left foot.*

Fur: *the brown-tipped, cream, shaggy mohair plush is now worn in places. Bingie is stuffed with kapok, and with fine wood-wool in the feet.*

1936 BOBBY BRUIN   Height: 65cm (26in)

bulbous, dark brownish black eyes

ears placed wide apart on sides of head

unusual bend at elbow

unusual, round, felt paws, machine-stitched onto arms

very stiff, card-reinforced foot-pads, allowing bear to stand up; internal metal rods end in rings around outer edges of feet

legs cut all-in-one with body

woven label stitched to left foot-pad

Said to be "designed from nature", according to a 1936 catalogue, this large bear had patent "movie" joints – thin, metal rods in his legs to enable him to pose in various positions. He was available in three sizes, of which this was the largest.

Embroidered label

c.1933–38 BINGIE GUARDSMAN   Height: 50cm (20in)

ears lined with artificial-silk plush

black, mohair-plush busby

dropped outer stitches on nose – a Merrythought design feature

celluloid button in left ear

red, felt jacket, now faded and worn

three, brown claws across pads and plush

faded, cinnamon-coloured, tipped mohair plush on head, paws, and fronts of arms

worn, knitted socks, without toes; original shoes missing

black, felt trousers

Bingie, dressed in a Grenadier Guardsman's uniform, was first introduced in 1933. The original, cinnamon-tipped mohair plush has faded to a dirty white. The parts of the body under the clothes are made of flesh-coloured brushed cotton.

Embroidered label

1938 DUTCH TEDDY   Height: 30cm (12in)

only the head is jointed

flat ears

amber and black, glass eyes

brown, vertically stitched nose with inverted-Y-shaped mouth

pale pink, corduroy trousers, now discoloured with age

beige mohair plush; kapok stuffing in body and limbs, and wood-wool elsewhere

card-reinforced feet with three claws over plush and pads

cream, tear-shaped paw-pads, machine stitched around edge

Merrythought introduced eight sizes of Dutch Teddy in 1938, all wearing wide, Dutch-style, all-in-one trousers with patch pockets. Dutch motifs were particularly popular in toys, games, and childhood ephemera during the 1930s.

Embroidered label

1931 BARE BINGIES   Height: 38/50cm (15/20in)

inset muzzle, similar to those of Bingie and the guardsman

slightly bulbous, brown, glass eyes

typical Merrythought nose with dropped outer stitches

flesh-coloured, brushed-cotton body and limbs

three claws on pads

stiffened foot-pads, with woven trademark stitched in place

The dressed Bingie family series was introduced in 1933 and included a girl, a boy, a sailor, a guardsman, a Highlander, and a ski girl. These two bears show the flesh-coloured, brushed-cotton bodies and limbs found beneath the clothes.

Embroidered label

UK: 1930s–50s

MINOR BRITISH COMPANIES; UNMARKED, LOWER QUALITY EXAMPLES

S everal minor soft-toy manufacturers were in operation in the UK during the 1930s, many founded during World War I, but later forced into liquidation during the lean years of the late 1930s to the early 1950s. For example, W.H. Jones, a pioneering British soft-toy manufacturer, established in 1914, went into liquidation in 1937. The Teddy Toy Company, also established at the outbreak of World War I, became famous for its Softanlite teddies of the 1920s and 1930s, but eventually wound up business in 1951. Many manufacturers did not attach permanent trademarks, making identification difficult.

1930s PEACOCK & CO. LTD.

Several teddy bears with the Peacock trademark have come to light, all dating from around the 1930s; they have horizontally stitched noses similar to those of Chad Valley's Magna Series bears. Chad Valley bought Peacock & Co. in 1931, and we now know that this well-established manufacturer produced a range of bears with the new label.

Height: 68cm (27in)

Embroidered label

Ears: *the large, flat, slightly cupped ears are sewn over the facial seams – a typical feature of Chad Valley bears.*

Eyes: *the amber, glass eyes are sewn into the face and fastened off at the back of the head.*

Nose: *the black, horizontally stitched, rectangular nose is similar to that of the bear on p.54 and of the Magna Series bear on p.55.*

Head/muzzle: *the large, square head has a narrow, pointed muzzle, which is almost completely shaved.*

Fur: *the fur is golden mohair plush.*

Pads: *the spoon-shaped paws and long, narrow, oval feet have beige, felt pads.*

Claws: *the four claws are widely spaced around the foot, similar to those of Chad Valley examples. There are no claws on the paws.*

BEAR PROFILE

This bear's long, pointed, shaved muzzle, the elongated, curved arms, and drumstick legs are clearly visible from this angle. These features, together with the large chest and thin hips, are similar to those of Chad Valley bears from the 1920s–30s (see pp.52–55).

Trademark: *the red and white colour scheme is the same as that used by Chad Valley for their 1930s labels.*

golden, artificial-silk plush; Swiss-style musical box within; brass ring at back for winding up

brown, glass eyes on wire shanks, sewn into head

vertically stitched, square nose with two stitches dropped to make inverted-Y-shaped mouth

pink, felt pads and thin, tapering paws

1930s–40s EALONTOYS; MUSICAL   Height: 38cm (15in)

"Ealontoys" was the trademark (registered in 1926) of the East London Toy Factory Ltd., originally the East London Federation Toy Factory, established in 1914 by Sylvia Pankhurst. Its other novelties included a teddy-bear hot-water-bottle cover.

Printed label

square, vertically stitched nose and long, inverted-V-shaped mouth, both features of Ealontoys bears

small, brown, glass eyes with black pupils sewn into face on wire shanks

shaggy, golden mohair plush

nightshirt not original

pointed paws; no pads

pink, felt pads on feet

*c.***1940s** EALONTOYS; MOHAIR   Height: 30cm (12in)

In 1948 the East London Toy Factory Ltd. changed its name to Ealontoys Ltd., but still operated from the same premises. A 1950 advertisement described the company as "The Teddy Bear People" but, sadly, they went out of business in the early 1950s.

Printed label

black, vertically stitched, long, slender nose; mouth indicated by curved line

brown, glass eyes with black pupils, set low down

low-grade, blue artificial-silk plush; wood-wool stuffing throughout

light brown Rexine pads, slightly cracked to reveal woven fabric beneath; no claws

short, stumpy arms

short, stocky feet

LATE 1930s ARTIFICIAL SILK   Height: 70cm (28in)

This teddy bear is typical of the many cheap bears manufactured in Britain and sold in chain stores from the 1930s. It was made from cheap-quality, artificial-silk plush with Rexine pads. This design – with its large head and jutting-out chin – carried on into the 1950s, making such teddy bears difficult to date precisely. Blue was a popular colour at this time.

short, golden orange mohair plush; wood-wool stuffing in head and around squeaker, with kapok elsewhere

amber, glass eyes with black pupils, sewn into face on wire shanks

relatively straight arms and legs, similar to those of Magna Series bears

woven fabric pads, similar to those used on Magna Series bears

three long, black claws on feet

1930s PEACOCK; ALTERNATIVE LABEL   Height: 53cm (21in)

This bear, made by Chad Valley for Peacock & Co., is reminiscent of the Magna Series bear on p.55. The label features Peacock's original trademark – an open-tailed peacock. The significance of the word "Stores" is unknown.

Embroidered label

Dean's: 1920s–50s

DEVELOPMENT OF TRADITIONAL BRITISH BEAR; TWO FACTORY MOVES

Dean's produced their first catalogued teddy bears at their Elephant and Castle factory in London in 1915, although the company may have been making bears for other firms prior to this. By 1922–23 Dean's had registered its tradename "A1 Toys", observed in catalogues as triangular, card swing-tags. The bears came in three grades of plush, stuffed with wood-wool, and with either a squeaker or growler. From 1937–55 Dean's teddies were made at the new, purpose-built factory at Merton, Surrey, but few were produced during World War II, when the factory concentrated on producing war materials.

1930 LARGE; GOLDEN MOHAIR

This bear carries the printed cloth label that Dean's used on its soft toys from the 1920s until 1955. The company's trademark – a bulldog and a terrier fighting over a rag book, designed by artist Stanley Berkley and referring to the durability of Dean's toys – would have featured on the original card swing-tag. This logo formed part of a huge sign that was erected, in 1922, over the entrance to the factory in south-east London, and became something of a local landmark.

Height: 65cm (26in)   Printed label

Fur/stuffing: *the fur is golden mohair plush; the bear is stuffed with wood-wool in the head, a mixture of wood-wool and kapok in the body, and with kapok in the limbs.*

Claws: *three traditional-style claws are embroidered across the plush on the paws and feet.*

Feet: *the pads of the large, oval feet are reinforced with beige felt, visible under the worn velveteen.*

Trademark: *the label is machine-stitched at each narrow end, across the width of the pad, a feature of Deans' bears.*

Ears: *the large, flat ears are sewn in an L shape with the inner edges caught into the facial seams.*

Eyes: *the brown, glass eyes are sewn in place on wire shanks.*

Back: *there is a slight hump on the back.*

Nose: *the oval, black nose is vertically stitched where the seams meet at the end of the muzzle.*

BEAR PROFILE

This particularly large bear demonstrates many typical characteristics of the British teddy of the period, such as the short, thick-set, curved arms, and the stocky legs and feet.

Pads: *the brown, velveteen pads are very worn, with little pile left.*

brown, plastic eyes with black pupils, sewn into face and finished off at back of head; may be replacements

flat ears, sewn in L shape, with inner edges caught into facial seams

black, oblong, vertically stitched nose, with inverted-T-shaped mouth

attractive, golden mohair plush; backing slightly darker than pile

label stitched to pad at narrow ends

pink, felt pads; other pink fabric used to repair paws

three black claws across plush

1930S MOHAIR; WOOD-WOOL STUFFING Height: 40cm (16in)

The bear's shape and wood-wool stuffing indicate pre-World War II origins. By 1931, artificial-silk plush was preferred by Dean's; there was no mohair in the 1935 range, but gold, pink, and blue mohair plush was reintroduced in 1936.

Printed label

ears placed towards back of head; inner edges sewn into facial seam

expansive forehead with plastic eyes placed wide apart, set into facial seams

only one vertical, black stitch remains of original mouth

golden mohair plush; soft-stuffed, except for wood-wool around tilt-growler

remains of black, embroidered claws on paws and feet

well worn, dark brown, velveteen pads

long, narrow feet and paws

MID-1950S PLASTIC EYES Height: 44cm (17½in)

The sewn-in plastic eyes (fastened off at the back of the head with a horizontal stitch) confirm this bear's age. The dark stain on the muzzle-tip suggests that the bear may originally have had a typical Dean's, sewn-on, moulded rubber nose.

Printed label

large ears with inner edges caught into facial seams

brown and black, plastic eyes, with integral short shank, sewn into face

very worn, golden mohair plush

small, square, vertically stitched nose; inverted-Y-shaped mouth with left half missing

short, curved arms with pointed paws

cotton-waste stuffing evident

three black claws remain on right foot

pink, felt pads, repaired by darning

MID-1950S "SUB" STUFFING Height: 35cm (14in)

This bear is almost bald and is bursting at the seams, so you can see clearly the cotton-waste stuffing. Known in the industry as "sub" (substitute), it was an alternative to kapok, which was in short supply in the post-war years.

Printed label

sewn-in, clear, glass eyes with black pupils are probably replacements

cupped ears, set over facial seams

shaggy golden mohair plush, bald in places

unusual black, shield-shaped, vertically stitched nose in V shape, meets inverted-V-shaped mouth

long, slender body with arms set low down

replacement brown, woven fabric pads; reinforced with card

five black claws on paws and feet

long, narrow feet

EARLY 1920S GOLDEN MOHAIR Height: 37cm (14½in)

Although much repair work has been carried out on this bear's essential features, its slender shape and wood-wool filling match illustrations of early A1 bears. The pads are replacements, but the label is from the original pad.

Printed label

Knickerbocker: 1920–30s

TRADITIONAL MOHAIR PLUSH; POINTED MUZZLE DESIGN

The Knickerbocker Toy Company was first established in Albany, New York during the mid-nineteenth century, producing typical educational toys of the period, such as lithographed alphabet blocks. The unusual name "Knickerbocker" was derived from the traditional nickname for New York inhabitants, a reference to the original Dutch settlers' baggy breeches. A 1980 Knickerbocker label states that the company had been making soft toys for more than half a century. Certainly today the earliest bears attributable to Knickerbocker date from the 1920s when permanent labels were introduced.

c.1935–36 CINNAMON MOHAIR

Although not in possession of a trade-mark, this bear demonstrates many characteristics typical of American bears; it also resembles other Knickerbocker bears of the period. It can be accurately dated, as it is known to have been one of two identical bears belonging to twin boys; the other bear is still in existence, but has unfortunately lost its eyes. The crayoned "L" on the foot-pads helped the brothers to identify their teddies.

Height: 45cm (18in)

Ears: *the large, slightly cupped ears are typical of those of Knickerbocker bears in size and shape.*

Eyes: *the translucent, amber, glass eyes, with black pupils, are sewn in on wire shanks.*

Mouth: *the black, inverted-V-shaped mouth is almost entirely worn away.*

Nose: *the narrow, rectangular nose is vertically stitched in black thread across the muzzle seam.*

Paws: *the paws are long, curved, and tapering.*

Fur/stuffing/squeaker: *the mohair plush is a rich, cinnamon colour, much favoured by US manufacturers. The bear is soft-stuffed throughout. There is an internal squeaker.*

Pads: *the discoloured pads are made of tan velveteen, a fabric typically used by Knickerbocker.*

Feet: *the large, oval feet are slightly pointed, with no claws.*

BEAR PROFILE

From the side, you can see clearly the shape of the head, with its shaved, elongated, but blunt muzzle. Although the curved, tapering arms and large feet, with narrow ankles, follow the traditional teddy-bear design, the thin, straight body and lack of hump is typical of American bears of the interwar period.

large, rounded, cupped ears, sewn across facial seams

broad, Knicker-bocker head; pointed muzzle, with fur slightly worn at tip

black, vertically stitched, narrow, oval nose (typical Knickerbocker shape)

translucent, amber, glass eyes with black pupils, set wide apart

low-set shoulders (typical Knicker-bocker feature)

silky, shaggy, cinnamon-coloured mohair plush; kapok stuffing in body and limbs; wood-wool in head; internal squeaker

long paws

large, oval feet; replacement felt pads

1933 CINNAMON MOHAIR
Height: 55cm (22in)

This teddy was given to its present owner for Christmas 1933 and was later a favourite toy of her son, until attacked by an English setter who chewed the nose and removed the head! Thanks to early photographs, it was possible to restore the bear to almost its original state. The owner recalls that a white label was removed from the centre front body-seam.

translucent, amber, glass eyes with black pupils, sewn in on wire shanks

cupped ears; slightly smaller than usual Knicker-bocker ears

long, oval, black, vertically stitched nose; inverted-Y-shaped mouth

long, silky, white mohair plush; wood-wool stuffing in head; kapok elsewhere

inset, clipped muzzle

paws curve upwards from wrist, and widen slightly

white, velveteen pads; no claws

long, oval feet

LATE 1930s INSET MUZZLE; MUSICAL
Height: 35cm (14in)

This bear has a slightly pointed muzzle, like those of the other bears illustrated here, but it is cut from a separate piece of slightly clipped plush – a typical Knickerbocker design feature that is believed to have been introduced by the late 1930s. The internal musical box, wound up by a key in the lower back, plays the waltz from *The Merry Widow*.

slightly worn, white mohair plush; wood-wool stuffing in head; kapok elsewhere

large, cupped ears, sewn across facial seams

realistic, black, moulded metal nose, with two nostrils

translucent, pale amber, glass eyes, with black pupils, sewn in on wire shanks

mark in centre front body-seam indicates position of original cloth label

black, embroidered, inverted-V-shaped mouth

almost straight arms

white, felt pads on paws and feet; no claws

small, oval feet

LATE 1920s WHITE; METAL NOSE
Height: 30cm (12in)

Although unmarked, this bear demonstrates several typical Knicker-bocker features of the period: a flat face; a straight, slender back; ears positioned straight across the head; and arms set low. It also possesses an unusual, moulded metal nose, heavier than tin, and possibly with some iron content, judging by the rust stains around the muzzle.

translucent, brown, glass eyes with black pupils, sewn in on wire shanks

head and limbs jointed, possibly with hardboard

rectangular, black, vertically stitched nose; black, inverted-Y-shaped mouth

shaggy mohair plush, worn or clipped on muzzle; wood-wool stuffing in head; kapok elsewhere

stiff button-up collar not original

long, curved, tapering arms; shoulders set low down

long paws

tan, felt pads; no claws

large, oval feet

c.1930 DARK BROWN; LARGE EARS
Height: 50cm (20in)

This bear, made of rich, dark brown mohair plush, has the typical, broad, triangular head of pre-war Knickerbocker bears, with a pointed muzzle, widely spaced eyes, narrow, rectangular nose, and, most particularly, large, rounded ears sewn across the facial seams. The tan felt pads suggest a slightly earlier date than that of other bears shown with velveteen pads.

Knickerbocker: post-World War II

TRADITIONAL DESIGN WITH INSET MUZZLE, AND NOVELTIES

The post-war, Knickerbocker traditional design was typified by the inset, rounded muzzle of clipped plush, chubby body, and round head with high forehead, although still retaining the large ears seen on some pre-war bears. As well as beginning to use synthetic fabrics at this time, the company also adopted "spangle" eyes – of glass, and later of plastic – as well as felt noses and tongues. Knickerbocker's pre-war "Animals of Distinction" logo was joined by the new registered "Joy of a Toy" trademark in the 1950s. The company regained the license for making "Smokey Bear" from Ideal from the 1960s until the late 1970s.

1940s SHAGGY, WHITE MOHAIR

Many examples of white Knickerbocker bears have been found, suggesting that this was a popular colour. This bear is made of a particularly luxurious, shaggy-pile mohair plush that is still in mint condition, and has a typical shaved, rounded muzzle. The satinized cloth label shows a figure standing inside a lucky horseshoe with the words "Made under sanitary laws", indicating the hygienic nature of the plush and stuffing.

Height: 38cm (15in)

Printed label

Ears: *the large ears are sewn across the facial seams.*

Eyes: *the dark amber, glass eyes, with black pupils, are sewn in on wire shanks.*

Nose/mouth: *the black, oval nose is vertically stitched across the horizontal muzzle seam; the mouth is an inverted Y shape.*

Muzzle: *the inset, rounded, blunt muzzle is made of the same mohair plush as the body, but clipped short to appear bristly.*

Fur/stuffing: *the good quality, white mohair plush is shaggy and slightly curly. The length of pile and the woven backing can be seen on the right ear. The body and limbs are stuffed with kapok and the head with wood-wool.*

Pads: *the white, velveteen pads are in mint condition.*

BEAR PROFILE
From this angle, you can see clearly the typical Knickerbocker shape of this bear's rounded, flattened muzzle. Unlike those of earlier examples, the arms and legs are of similar length; the latter are particularly straight, with little ankle definition. The printed label, placed (unusually for Knickerbocker) under the left arm, is clearly visible.

Feet: *the slightly squared-off, oval feet have no claws.*

large, cupped ears

large, amber, glass eyes with black pupils, set wide apart; sewn in on wire shanks

inset, protruding, rounded muzzle of brown, short-pile mohair plush

dark brown, vertically stitched, oval nose; inverted-Y-shaped mouth

slightly curved, tapering arms

tan, velveteen pads

shaggy, long-pile, dark brown mohair plush on woven backing

large, squared-off, oval feet; no claws

1950s SHAGGY, BROWN MOHAIR
Height: 43cm (17in)

This bear demonstrates many Knickerbocker characteristics, including the large, broad head and the shape and fabric of the pads. The printed label features the company's new "Joy of a Toy" trademark, registered in the 1950s.

Printed label

amber, glass, "spangle" eyes

very large ears with golden, velveteen lining

brown, vertically stitched nose; wide, smiling mouth

inset, rounded, pale golden, velveteen muzzle

wide, rounded body, with low-set shoulders

dark brown woollen plush; wood-wool stuffing in head; kapok elsewhere

curved arms

wide thighs; narrow ankles

pale golden, velveteen pads

large, oval feet

1950s "BAT" EARS; "SPANGLE" EYES
Height: 50cm (20in)

Although this particular bear is unmarked, it possesses several, typical Knickerbocker features, such as the glass "spangle" eyes and "bat" ears – so-called because of their large, flat design. The general shape of the bear, and particularly its expansive, almost oval, head, and the contrasting muzzle, anticipates the company's Teddy Kuddles of the 1960s.

painted facial features

top edge painted brown to represent locks of hair

inset, moulded vinyl face, with slightly protruding muzzle

unjointed, curved arms with no pads

cinnamon-coloured, synthetic plush on woven backing

legs jut out at right angles to body, in permanent sitting position

slight indication of feet; no pads

c.1955 VINYL CHARACTER FACE
Height: 32cm (12½in)

This unusual bear is characteristic of both its era and its country of origin – vinyl-faced bears were being produced by other US companies at this time (see pp.85; 86). Its unjointed body and cinnamon-coloured, synthetic plush are also typical. Only a fragment remains of the original white cloth label, printed in navy-blue, which is sewn into the left side-seam.

good quality, soft, bright golden mohair plush

large, rounded ears; inner edges sewn into facial seams

amber, glass eyes with black pupils

large, rounded head with expansive forehead

black, vertically stitched nose – rounder than usual Knickerbocker shape

inset, clipped muzzle of same plush as body

narrow, pointed, oval paws

pale golden, velveteen pads with no claws

squared-off, oval feet

1940s BRIGHT GOLDEN MOHAIR
Height: 50cm (20in)

This cuddly bear, with its rounded head, inset muzzle, and chubby limbs, is stuffed with kapok. It still has its printed label sewn into the front central seam. The glass eyes may be replacements – the originals are likely to have been larger.

Printed label

Japan: 1945–90s

The Japanese had produced moulded, bisque and celluloid teddy bears from the 1920s; the post-war era saw Japan leading the technological field (from 1945 to 1950 the "Made in Japan" label changed to "Made in Occupied Japan"). From *c.*1950 to 1970 Japanese manufacturers produced clockwork and battery-operated tin bears. They also made traditional teddies with mechanical devices, such as the Kamar Toy Company's Dear Heart with a battery-operated "beating" heart. In the 1980s, Tokyo's First Corporation described itself as Japan's premier supplier of quality stuffed animals to the world.

1940s KAMAR TOY COMPANY

This bear's distinctive, airbrushed paw design has been attributed to the Kamar Toy Company, although airbrushing was common among other Japanese firms. This bear is typical of those made by Japanese manufacturers at the time, being made of synthetic plush, with "sliced-in" ears, a stiff neck, and rod jointing. Some contained musical boxes, while a unique example from *c.*1960, marked "Jestia/Made in Japan", accommodated a radio, with a tuning dial on the chest.

Height: 70cm (28in)

Nose/mouth: *the design of the nose and mouth is typically Japanese: the nose is vertically stitched in black, cotton thread made up of several strands; the mouth is an inverted Y shape.*

Limbs: *the jointed arms have fat shoulders and taper to small, curved, squared-off paws; the legs and head are also jointed.*

Fur/stuffing: *the fur is white, nylon plush on a woven backing, now discoloured; the bear is stuffed with wood-wool.*

Feet: *the feet are small and rounded.*

Ears: *the fabric is gathered at the base and pushed into a hole in the head, in a cheap method known as "sliced-in ears".*

Eyes: *the eyes are clear glass, with orange, painted backs and black pupils.*

Muzzle: *the inset, white, velveteen muzzle is now discoloured with age.*

BEAR PROFILE

From this angle, you can see this bear's rounded, "drumstick" arms and legs. The hole in the shoulder indicates where the round piece of plush, which disguises the end of the external wire and washer jointing system, has come away. The large left ear, with its internal wire frame missing, has come away slightly from the head opening, revealing some original white plush.

Pads/claws: *the pads are made from yellow, woven velveteen with black, painted claws.*

vertically stitched, narrow, oblong nose, with inverted-V-shaped mouth

large, cloth ears stiffened with wire and pushed into holes at top of head

large, reddish brown glass eyes with black pupils

pink, nylon plush on knitted backing

inset, pale golden, velveteen muzzle

four short claws embroidered in black thread across seam

large feet reinforced with thick card; black, embroidered/ airbrushed claws

pale golden, velveteen pads

inset, white, nylon-plush feet

1940s EMBROIDERED/AIRBRUSHED PAWS   Height: 38cm (15in)

Of a similar design to the bear (opposite), this example is in near-mint condition, with its original rayon ribbon and bell intact. Black claws are embroidered close together on the narrow paws; the claws are airbrushed onto the foot-pads, and embroidered over the pads and plush. The knitted backing of the nylon plush indicates a post-war date.

small, black, plastic, button eyes

hole for plastic nose

muzzle and fronts of ears in cream, flannel-like fabric

round, red, woven fabric mouth, secured with glue

head, shoulders, arms, and backs of ears in brown-beige nylon plush on knitted backing

glued-on, brown, woven fabric buttons

tin book printed with coloured pictures of farm animals with names in English

internal frame of moulded tin, in two sections

red, woven fabric overalls glued onto body

feet printed to resemble shiny brogues

1950s CLOCKWORK READING BEAR   Height: 16cm (6½in)

This unjointed, standing bear appears to read the book it holds. When wound up with a key in its back, the clockwork mechanism moves the right arm up and down. The magnet under the right hand attracts the metal page, causing it to flip back and forth. This is a simple, inexpensive toy; later Japanese battery-operated tin bears were often more complex.

soft, brown, acrylic plush; soft-stuffed throughout

two pieces of contrasting plush make up ears

large, bulbous, black, safe, plastic eyes

stylized, triangular, dark brown, safe, moulded, plastic nose

Japanese wording on swing-tag translates "Merry-go-round Dreams"

unjointed, short, stubby arms; no pads

short, thick legs with white, acrylic-plush foot-pads

1980s UNJOINTED; SYNTHETIC   Height: 23cm (9in)

This is a typical example of the safe, cuddly, unjointed bears made by Japanese manufacturers from the 1970s to the 1990s. It has locked-in, plastic eyes and nose, and wears a sewn-on outfit of a brown, gingham, short-sleeved shirt with a white collar, and brown, corduroy trousers. A stubby, brown plush tail protrudes from a hole at the back of the trousers.

contrasting plush ears sewn side-by-side on top of large, bulbous head with high forehead

large, black, safe, plastic eyes

stylized, black, safe, moulded, plastic nose

inset, protruding, white, vinyl muzzle

pink, nylon plush on woven backing; stuffed with wood-wool

stiff, unjointed neck; plastic limb joints show on outside of body

short, stubby arms; no pads or claws

1960s PINK NYLON   Height: 29cm (11½in)

This bear, with its expansive forehead, is a later version of the lower-quality, rod-jointed Japanese bears (above left and opposite). Made of pink, nylon plush with an inset, white, vinyl muzzle, it has plastic rods that allow the limbs to move up and down – the ends of the rods are visible at the shoulders and thighs. Like the earlier bears, the head is not jointed.

Australia: 1930s–60s

DEVELOPMENT OF AUSTRALIAN-MADE TRADITIONAL BEAR

S everal Australian soft-toy manufacturers were established in the 1930s, but the scarcity of traditional materials limited teddy production during World War II. Sheepskin bears with leather or suede pads and noses date from this period, when the stiff-necked Australian bear (without a neck joint) was developed, saving on card and metal (see p.11). Some new companies emerged in the 1950s, such as Parker Toys of Brunswick, Victoria, and Barton Waugh Pty. Ltd. of Hurstville, New South Wales, but by the 1970s, many established firms had gone out of business, unable to compete with cheap imports from East Asia.

c.1960 JAKAS SOFT TOYS

This fully-jointed bear, produced by Jakas, is the precursor of the machine-washable Australian teddy bear. Joe and Marion Stanford, an English couple, first established the Melbourne-based company in 1954. They later manufactured unjointed bears similar in construction to Wendy Boston's in the UK. The printed, satinized label includes the instructions "Wash in Lux", just as Wendy Boston's bears of a similar vintage had recommended the detergent "Persil".

Height: 70cm (28in)

JAKAS TOYS

Printed label

Ears: *the large, flat, slightly cupped ears are sewn across the facial seams.*

Eyes: *the translucent, brown, glass eyes with black pupils are sewn into the plush.*

Nose/mouth: *the square, black nose is vertically stitched; the smiling, single-stitched mouth is an inverted T shape.*

Fur/stuffing: *the fur is a blend of beige wool and synthetic plush on a woven backing; the stuffing is granulated foam-rubber.*

Bow: *the pink satin bow is a later addition.*

Arms: *the arms, short in comparison to the legs, end with slightly curved paws.*

Pads: *the long, clawless pads are made from woven, beige fabric.*

Feet: *the feet are large and stumpy.*

Label: *the satinized label is machine-stitched to the foot-pad.*

BEAR PROFILE

This bear has traditional features with its protruding, blunted muzzle and humped, rounded back. It is fully jointed, in contrast to the later unjointed, flat-faced bears that are more commonly associated with Jakas (see p.136). The long, thin legs have unusually narrow thighs, and the arms are positioned towards the front, accentuating the hump.

Legs: *the legs are thin with narrow thighs.*

brown, glass eyes
with black pupils

typical Emil
nose with two
outer, raised
stitches

shiny, Rexine
pads, slightly
cracked
revealing
woven backing
beneath

golden mohair
plush; wood-wool
stuffing in head,
and kapok
elsewhere

LATE 1930S–40S EMIL TOYS

Height: 58cm (23in)

Emil Toys made teddy bears from the 1930s to the 1970s. Although this example possesses no label, it does have the typical black, square nose and shiny, Rexine pads. The white, cloth labels were usually stitched into a seam and had "Emil Toys" written in script, with a bear sitting, clutching the upright of the capital "E", and "Made in Australia" printed in blue.

flat ears sewn
across facial seams

amber and black,
plastic eyes

golden mohair
plush, stuffed with
solid, shaped pieces
of foam-rubber

black, felt nose
and embroidered
mouth

fully jointed
limbs and
head

fawn, vinyl pads in
very good condition

1950S VERNA TOYS

Height: 75cm (30in)

This firm was established in Victoria by Eve Barnett in 1941, but after 1948 it made teddy bears under the ownership of Arthur Eaton. Black, felt noses were a particular feature of the bears. Embroidered labels were replaced by printed labels in the 1980s.

VERNA
CE IN AUSTRALIA

Embroidered label

slightly cupped ears with
inner edges caught into
facial seams

round, moulded,
hard rubber nose;
black, embroidered,
inverted-Y-shaped
mouth

sewn-in, brown, glass
eyes with black pupils

golden mohair
plush; cotton
wadding stuffing in
body, wood-wool
in head; internal
musical box

black, Rexine
pads, cracked
revealing
woven backing
beneath

typical, pointed
Lindee feet

C.1960 LINDEE TOYS

Height: 53cm (21in)

This Sydney-based company manufactured teddy bears from 1944 to 1976. Its white, satinized label, with an outline of a reclining deer and the red print lettering "Lindee Toys" and "Made in Australia" beneath, was usually found in a foot-pad seam. This bear has a hard rubber nose and contains a musical box that plays Brahms' *Lullaby*.

brown, glass eyes
with black pupils

vertically stitched,
triangular, black
nose with inverted-
Y-shaped, smiling
mouth

well-worn golden
mohair plush

swivel-jointed,
short arms

cream,
vinyl pads

1950S BERLEX TOYS

Height: 55cm (22in)

This Melbourne company produced bears from the 1930s to the 1970s. The bear shown here has a distinctive triangular nose and cream-coloured, vinyl paws, typical of Berlex bears. Labels have either "Berlex", in script, with "Melbourne" beneath and "Made in Australia" on the reverse, or simply "Berlex Melbourne" printed in capital letters.

Character: 1945-83

DEVELOPMENT OF TRADITIONAL AND UNJOINTED DESIGN BEARS

Two New Yorkers, Caesar Mangiapani and Jack Levy, established the Character Novelty Co. in 1932, at 14 South Main Street, Norwalk, Connecticut. The business really began to develop after World War II, when it started to produce a wide range of soft toy animals, including teddy bears. The toys were designed by Caesar Mangiapani, and his partner managed the sales side of the business. The company sold to all the major department stores, including Bloomingdales, and had a showroom in New York. Jack Levy retired in about 1960, but the business continued until 1983, when Caesar Mangiapani died.

c.1949 BLACK, BUTTON-ON-FELT EYES

This fully jointed bear demonstrates several, typical Character features, including the large, flattened, black, boot-button-style eyes sewn into the head over slightly larger circles of white felt, as well as the printed, cloth tag sewn into the seam of the left ear. Although the label is very frayed, the word "Character" is legible on one side, and "Content/mohair/cotton" on the reverse. Bears of a similar design were made with glass eyes and a red, felt tongue.

Height: 48cm (19in)

Ears: *the large, flat ears are sewn in at an angle, with the top edges caught in the facial seams.*

Trademark: *the remains of the Character cloth tag is protruding from the left ear-seam.*

Eyes: *the large, black, button eyes are sewn into the head, with white, felt circles behind.*

Muzzle: *the slightly protruding, blunt muzzle has been shaved.*

Nose/mouth: *the black, horizontally stitched, narrow, oblong nose is sewn across the end of the muzzle where the facial seams meet; the wide, smiling mouth is made up of two curved, horizontal stitches.*

Paws: *the long, curved, tapering paws end in pale beige, felt pads; there are no claws.*

Body: *the stout, rounded chest narrows at the hips, with arms set low down, giving the impression of a thick neck (a typical Character feature on this type of bear).*

Fur/stuffing: *the bright golden, slightly shaggy mohair plush, is very worn in places; the body is stuffed with wood-wool; the limbs and head with soft stuffing.*

Feet: *the large, oval feet have no claws.*

BEAR PROFILE

From this angle, you can see the typically high forehead and slightly protruding, shaved muzzle, the wide, flat ears with Character tag, and the round, solid-looking body. The arms are curved and tapering in the traditional manner, but they are shorter than the straight, thickset legs, which end in large, chunky feet.

small, rounded, black, button eyes on white, felt circles; sewn in and set low down

high forehead; head unjointed

top edges of ears caught into facial seams

inverted-T-shaped mouth with small, red, felt tongue

black, vertically stitched, narrow, oblong nose

cream, felt pads; curved, pointed paws

arms wired from paw to paw, through body

oval feet with no claws

swivel-jointed legs

1950s SMALL; WIRED ARMS

Height: 15cm (6in)

This bear has swivel-jointed legs, but the short, curved arms have a length of wire running through from paw to paw, enabling both arms to move simultaneously. The black, button-on-felt eyes and the red tongue are both typical Character features.

DESIGNED BY Character

Printed label

large, round head with flattened muzzle and extensive forehead

large, flat ears; back section made of body plush; lined with rust-brown felt

round, red, felt tongue

triangular, black, felt nose

unjointed, square body

long, curly, brown nylon plush with white flecks

short, stubby limbs with rounded ends; no pads or claws

c.1960–70 NYLON

Height: 48cm (19in)

The safe, plastic eyes, nylon plush, and synthetic foam stuffing of this unjointed bear indicate a probable 1960–70 date. The large, orange and black, spangle-effect eyes were also used by rivals, Knickerbocker, at the same time.

DESIGNED BY Character

Printed label

typically high, extensive forehead with eyes set low down towards beginning of pointed muzzle

large ears, with inner edge caught into facial seam

folded, printed, cloth ear-tag sewn into left ear-seam

white, mohair plush; soft stuffing

three long, black claws across plush and felt

pale peach, felt pads

c.1955–60 WHITE MOHAIR; JOINTED

Height: 43cm (17in)

This fully jointed bear still retains the remnants of its typical Character, red, felt tongue. The clear, glass eyes, with painted backs of brown enamel, are less typical. The ear-tag mentions "rubber contents" – probably a granulated, foam-rubber stuffing.

Printed label

large, flat ears; inner edges caught in facial seams; printed, cloth ear-tag attached to left ear

large, brown eyes with black pupils

narrow, black, vertically stitched nose; inverted-Y-shaped mouth

original yellow, satin bow

square body with short, stubby limbs

pads are made of same plush as body; no claws

LATE 1940–50s TIMME; UNJOINTED

Height: 20cm (8in)

This bear is made of a new fabric, containing some mohair, which was invented for children's toys after World War II, and carries the trademark Timme. The bear is unjointed and floppy, and originally wore a card swing-tag describing the new plush.

CHARACTER NOVELTY CO., INC. So. Norwalk, Conn.

Printed label

Gund: 1930s–60s

TRADITIONAL AND UNJOINTED DESIGNS

German emigrant Adolph Gund established Gund Manufacturing Co. in Norwalk, Connecticut in 1898, moving to New York City in the early 1900s. The firm produced novelties, including soft toys, and added teddy bears in 1906. Jacob Swedlin, a Russian emigré and Adolph Gund's aide, bought the firm after Gund retired in 1925. He was responsible for the firm's expansion and procured the license to produce Walt Disney characters. Until 1971, the factory was sited in Brooklyn, and the offices in New York City, moving to Edison, New Jersey in 1973. Today, some of Gund's teddies are made in East Asia.

c.1948 TEDDIGUND

This fully jointed, good-quality mohair-plush bear follows the traditional design. The capital "G" on its label mimics a rabbit's head; this label was first used c.1948. After World War II the firm introduced new lines that broke away from traditional design, including unjointed teddies made from modern synthetic materials, such as their 1940s–1950s Dreamies series. These culminated in Gund's revolutionary ultra-soft toys of the 1970s–1980s made of multifilament, modacrylic fibres.

Height: 38cm (15in)

Printed label

Ears: *the ears are large and slightly cupped, with their inner edges caught into the facial seams.*

Eyes: *the amber, glass eyes have black pupils.*

Nose/mouth: *the black, shield-shaped nose is vertically stitched; the inverted-T-shaped mouth forms a smile.*

Muzzle: *the inset, protruding muzzle, originally of short-pile mohair plush, is now very worn, revealing the discoloured, white, woven backing.*

Fur: *the golden mohair plush is in very good condition.*

Stuffing: *the kapok stuffing is visible through the worn foot-pads.*

BEAR PROFILE

In profile, you can see all the main characteristics of a traditional teddy bear: the large head; the pointed, clipped, mohair-plush muzzle (now very worn); tapering, curved arms with spoon-shaped paws; relatively long legs with large feet; and a very slightly humped back.

Pads: *the white, felt pads are worn, particularly on the feet.*

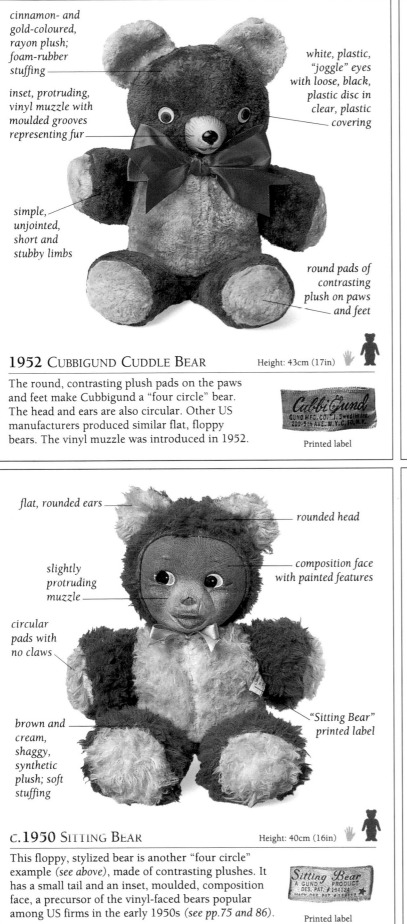

cinnamon- and gold-coloured, rayon plush; foam-rubber stuffing

inset, protruding, vinyl muzzle with moulded grooves representing fur

white, plastic, "joggle" eyes with loose, black, plastic disc in clear, plastic covering

simple, unjointed, short and stubby limbs

round pads of contrasting plush on paws and feet

1952 CUBBIGUND CUDDLE BEAR

Height: 43cm (17in)

The round, contrasting plush pads on the paws and feet make Cubbigund a "four circle" bear. The head and ears are also circular. Other US manufacturers produced similar flat, floppy bears. The vinyl muzzle was introduced in 1952.

Printed label

horizontally stitched, narrow, rectangular, black nose, and inverted-Y-shaped mouth

small, amber glass eyes with black pupils

unjointed arms wired for posing

white, twill fabric hands, with thumbs indicated

removable waistcoat of mustard-coloured leatherette with studded black trim

white, twill fabric legs beneath leatherette "chaps"; kapok stuffing throughout

tartan, cotton fabric shirt; red and white polka-dot kerchief around neck

1940s COWBOY

Height: 30cm (12in)

Cinnamon-coloured, artificial-silk (rayon) plush was popular with US firms from the late 1930s to the 1950s, and is therefore a good indicator of this unmarked bear's origins. Gund produced unjointed, dressed bears and rabbits during this time, with plush heads and bodies formed by the clothes. Paper tags stating "A Gund Animal" exist on similar soft toys.

flat, rounded ears

rounded head

slightly protruding muzzle

composition face with painted features

circular pads with no claws

brown and cream, shaggy, synthetic plush; soft stuffing

"Sitting Bear" printed label

c.1950 SITTING BEAR

Height: 40cm (16in)

This floppy, stylized bear is another "four circle" example (*see above*), made of contrasting plushes. It has a small tail and an inset, moulded, composition face, a precursor of the vinyl-faced bears popular among US firms in the early 1950s (*see pp.75 and 86*).

Printed label

rounded ears of black plush

clamped-in, plastic, "joggle" eyes

inset, white, woven fabric muzzle

vertically stitched, square, black nose with inverted-V-shaped mouth

black and white, rayon plush

"four-circle" paw- and foot-pads

1947 JUMBO CUDDLE PANDA

Height: 69cm (27½in)

Su-Lin, the West's first giant panda, arrived in the US in 1936, and was sent to Brookfield Zoo, Chicago, a year later. In 1938, New York Zoo obtained its first panda, Pandora, inspiring many US soft-toy manufacturers to produce panda teddy-bears. Like many panda toys, this example is simply a teddy-bear design manufactured in black and white plush.

Ideal: 1930s–50s

JOINTED AND UNJOINTED; INTRODUCTION OF SYNTHETIC FABRICS

In the years before World War II, Ideal bears differed little from their earlier designs and they were not permanently marked, so dating and positive identification can be difficult for collectors. Ideal's founder Morris Michtom died in 1938 but, under the leadership of his son Benjamin, the post-war era was a highly productive one, with the introduction of new designs and materials, a permanent trademark, as well as the new name of Ideal Toy Corporation. The company was granted the licence for the first Smokey Bear soft toy (promoting the US Forest Fire Prevention Campaign), which was introduced in 1953.

*c.*1950s VINYL CHARACTER FACE

Bears with soft, moulded vinyl faces were introduced by Ideal and other US companies (*see p.77*) in the early 1950s, but not all of these had realistic, moulded paws and feet like this example. The "spangle" eyes are typical of this type of bear, although some were equipped with "sleeping" dolls' eyelids. The remains of the label reads: "It's Ideal". Some of these vinyl-faced bears have been found with a tag reading: "Ideal, recommended by Miss Francis' Ding Dong School".

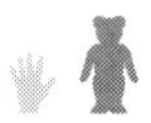

Height: 30cm (12in)

Printed label

***Ears:** the large, floppy ears, made in two sections of contrasting plush, are sewn into the facial seams.*

***Eyes:** the "spangle" amber eyes with brown pupils are made of plastic.*

***Face:** the soft, pink, moulded vinyl face is inset into the plush head; facial features are painted on.*

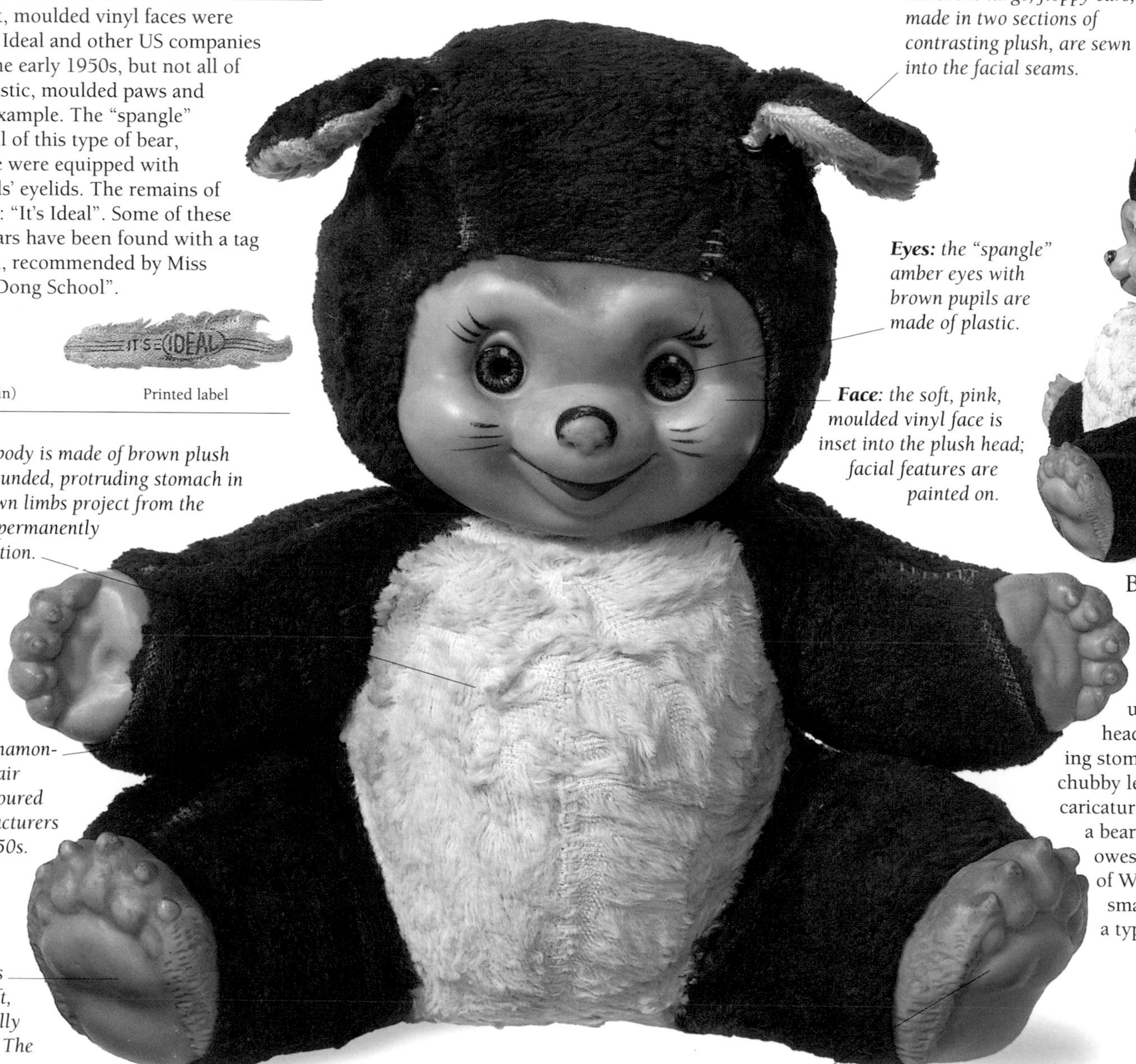

***Body:** the body is made of brown plush with the rounded, protruding stomach in white; brown limbs project from the body, in a permanently seated position.*

***Fur:** dark cinnamon-coloured mohair plush was favoured by US manufacturers during the 1950s.*

***Paws:** the paws are made of soft, pink, realistically moulded vinyl. The slightly cupped paws have five fingers, each with a tiny finger nail.*

***Feet:** the top surface of each soft, pink, vinyl foot is moulded to resemble fur, with five claws pointing upwards, and realistic moulded foot-pads beneath.*

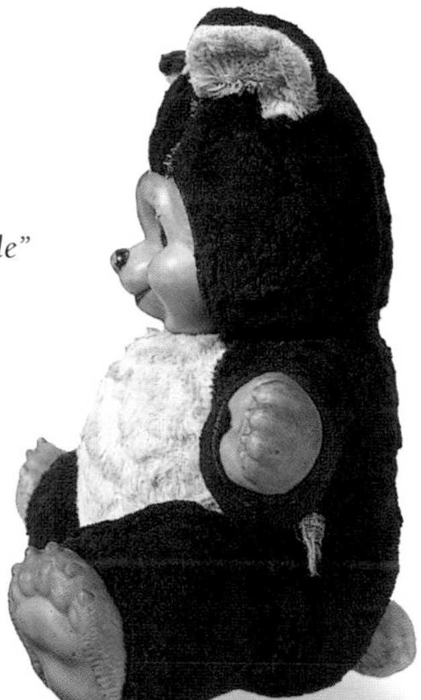

BEAR PROFILE

From this angle you can see the rounded, squat features, particularly the large head, pug nose, bulging stomach, and short, chubby legs, of a design that caricatures the attributes of a bear cub, and probably owes much to the work of Walt Disney. The small, stubby tail is a typical feature.

large, cupped ears
at corners of
triangular head

fully jointed
head and limbs

white, embroidered,
horizontal stitches
form nose

unusual small,
yellow, glass
eyes with black
pupils, sewn in

black mohair
plush on woven
backing; limbs re-
covered with grey
fabric

long, slender
torso

remains of white,
felt pads visible
on left paw; wood-
wool stuffing

long, thin limbs
with no feet,
typical of US
"stick" bears

c.1930 BLACK MOHAIR   Height: 65cm (26in)

Although unmarked, as was typical of pre-World War II Ideal bears, this example has many characteristics associated with Ideal, particularly its large, triangular head. The slender body and limbs, however, suggest a date during the interwar period. Of rare black mohair, this bear is quite a collector's item, despite much wear and tear and partial restoration.

rounded head
stuffed with
wood-wool

black, glass eyes

round, hard,
moulded
resin nose

original ribbon
bow around neck

short,
curved
arms

long, cinnamon-
coloured mohair
plush; kapok
stuffing in body
and limbs

straight,
stubby legs;
no pads

1940s SMALL; UNJOINTED   Height: 25cm (10in)

This small, unjointed bear, with large ears on a rounded head, is made of cinnamon-coloured mohair plush, a colour popular with US manufacturers at this time. In mint condition, the bear possesses a rare, printed, circus-wagon card swing-tag.

AN IDEAL
Ultrafine
ANIMAL

Card swing-tag

large, swivel-
jointed head

large, slightly
cupped ears

round, hard,
moulded
resin nose

brown, glass
eyes with
black pupils

cinnamon-coloured
mohair plush

small, round,
protruding muzzle
of clipped mohair

straight,
unjointed
legs with
small feet;
no pads

curved,
tapering
arms with
no pads;
unjointed

1940s MEDIUM; UNJOINTED   Height: 38cm (15in)

This is a larger version of the previous example, the design being available in a range of sizes. Made of a similar, cinnamon-coloured mohair plush, it also has unjointed arms and legs, although the large, rounded head is swivel-jointed in the traditional way.

AN IDEAL
Ultrafine
ANIMAL

Card swing-tag

brown, glass eyes
with black pupils

small, rounded
muzzle of shaved
mohair

hard, moulded
plastic nose

curved, tapering
arms; fully jointed
limbs and head

cinnamon-red
mohair plush in
mint condition

felt pads in
perfect condition;
no claws

small feet

1940s LARGE; JOINTED   Height: 43cm (17in)

This fully jointed, cinnamon-red bear with felt pads was also available in a smaller size. It possesses its original card swing-tag, shaped like a circus wagon with "Ideal Novelty & Toy Co. (Stuffed Toy Division) Long Island City NY" printed in small lettering.

AN IDEAL
Ultrafine
ANIMAL

Card swing-tag

Merrythought: 1940s–50s

POST-WAR TRADITIONAL BEARS AND REDESIGNED LABEL

D uring World War II, Merrythought made few bears, as the Ironbridge factory was taken over by the British Admiralty for map-making and storage purposes. A room in nearby Wellington was rented for toy production, but eventually all work turned to the war effort (*see pp.66–67*). The traditional bear design remained unaltered after the war, except for the effects of rationing on the quality and quantity of fabric. The button trademark was phased out, but the foot-label was still used, with the words printed on instead of being embroidered, as before the war; in 1957, "Ironbridge, Shrops." replaced "Hygienic Toys".

1940s ORANGE MOHAIR

This uniquely coloured, bright orange bear is typical of its era: Merrythought produced teddies in "burnished bronze" mohair plush from 1939, and introduced "amber" mohair plush to its range in 1947–48. Despite extensive repairs to its felt paw-pads, this bear still possesses its printed, foot-label with the earlier wording, "Hygienic Toys", which dates it to the period soon after World War II. In 1957 the wording on the label was changed to "Ironbridge, Shrops." (*see opposite, bottom left*).

Height: 55cm (22in)   Printed label

Ears: *the large, slightly cupped ears are centred over the facial seams.*

Eyes: *the translucent, amber, glass eyes, on wire shanks, are sewn into the face.*

Nose: *the outer stitches of the rectangular, vertically stitched nose are dropped.*

BEAR PROFILE
The basic Merrythought design changed little between the 1930s and the post-war period, and so this bear shares many characteristics with the example on p.60. It has the same, relatively long, curved arms, straight back, fat thighs, and large feet; the muzzle is still closely shaven, although it protrudes less than on the earlier bear.

Fur/stuffing: *orange mohair plush; the bear is stuffed with kapok in the body and limbs, and with wood-wool in the head and around the squeaker.*

Claws: *four black claws are sewn across the plush.*

Paw-pads: *the paw-pads are shaped so that the straight end of the felt is cut on a diagonal – a feature often seen on early Merrythought bears.*

Foot-pads: *replacement dark brown, felt pads have been sewn over the originals; a "window" has been cut in the new felt to reveal the label on the original, left foot-pad. Only three claws remain on the left foot.*

closely shaved, slightly protruding muzzle

translucent, amber, glass eyes, with black pupils, on wire stalks

brown, vertically stitched, square nose with outer dropped stitches

inverted-Y-shaped, double-stitched mouth

beige, twill pads

short, blond mohair plush; kapok stuffing throughout, with wood-wool in muzzle and around squeaker

1940s SHORT, GOLDEN MOHAIR Height: 38cm (15in)

Both the printed label and the less rounded features of this bear suggest that it was made during the period when material were rationed. The claws on the paws (three stitches across the tips of the pads) are noticeably curtailed.

MERRYTHOUGHT HYGIENIC TOYS MADE IN ENGLAND

Printed label

expansive forehead, typical of Merrythought bears

large, flat ears, sewn across facial seams

closely shaved, protruding muzzle

amber, glass eyes with black pupils, sewn in, wide-apart, on wire shanks

vertically stitched, rectangular nose

red, felt paw-pads

blue, felt pads to match legs; three straight claws on each foot

four, "webbed" claws on each paw

1953 CORONATION BEAR Height: 38cm (15in)

This bear has all the classic Merrythought features, although it lacks a label. Made in red, white, and blue mohair plush, it was produced to commemorate the coronation of Queen Elizabeth II. According to trade catalogues, similar, patriotic teddies, made of artificial-silk plush, were designed in 1937 by J.K. Farnell for the coronation of King Edward VIII.

small, amber, glass eyes with black pupils, sewn into face

large, rounded ears sewn flat across corners of head

black, vertically stitched, rectangular nose, with one horizontal stitch across top edge

fixed head, with no neck joint

single-stitched, Y-shaped mouth

straight legs with small, pointed feet

straight arms; no paw-pads

traditional, card disc-joints in limbs

LATE 1950s SMALL; GOLDEN MOHAIR Height: 23cm (9in)

Until the mid-1950s, the minimum size in the traditional range was 30cm (12in), but a smaller size was introduced in 1955–56. This bear has jointed limbs, but the head is fixed. The label, with new wording, is sewn into the back seam.

MERRYTHOUGHT IRONBRIDGE, SHROPS. MADE IN ENGLAND

Printed label

translucent, orange, glass eyes, with black pupils, sewn in

relatively large, flat ears, sewn across corners of head

single-stitched, inverted-Y-shaped mouth

black, vertically stitched, square nose; horizontal stitch along upper edge

pink, artificial-silk plush; wood-wool stuffing

pointed paws with no pads or claws

short, slightly curved arms

short, straight legs; small feet with pointed toes

fully jointed limbs

c.1955–56 SMALL; PINK, ARTIFICIAL SILK Height: 23cm (9in)

Merrythought first introduced a small, traditional bear in artificial-silk plush in 1954. This example, along with a "twin", was bought as a Christmas present from Harrods c.1955–56. The label, with old wording, is sewn along the bear's back.

MERRYTHOUGHT HYGIENIC TOYS MADE IN ENGLAND

Printed label

J.K. Farnell: 1945–68

TRADITIONAL AND NOVELTY BRITISH BEARS; REDESIGNED LABEL

The embroidered Farnell label was replaced, after World War II, by a printed, satinized label, with "Alpha" in a shield shape – a shape also used for swing-tags at this time. Although Alpha teddy bears remained Farnell's major line, the company also advertised La Vogue nightdress cases, and, in 1960, it registered Mother Goose as the trade-name for a range of washable soft toys. In 1959, the head office and some production was transferred to Hastings, Sussex; in 1964 the lease for the Acton Alpha Works terminated and all production was then moved to Hastings. The business was sold in 1968.

MID-1960s GOLDEN MOHAIR

This appealing, small bear possesses the last label used by J.K. Farnell & Co. Ltd. before the company ceased production in 1968. Slightly frayed, the satinized label is printed in the same colours as the earlier shield label (*see opposite*) but reads: "This is a Farnell Quality Soft Toy; Made in Hastings, England", with no mention of their original tradename Alpha. The safe, plastic eyes also indicate an early 1960s date; these came into general use from the mid-1960s because of the new toy safety laws.

Height: 33cm (13in) Printed label

Ears: *the flat ears are sewn centrally across the facial seams.*

Eyes: *the amber and black, safe, plastic, lock-in eyes are set low down, giving the forehead a large, expansive look.*

Muzzle: *the fur on the protruding muzzle is worn.*

Nose/mouth: *the square, black nose is vertically stitched; the mouth is a double-stitched, inverted T shape.*

Fur/stuffing/squeaker: *the fur is golden mohair plush; the bear is stuffed with soft stuffing, probably kapok or "sub" (see p.205). The squeaker feels like the plastic, concertina type.*

Limbs: *the arms and legs are short and stubby.*

Pads: *the Rexine pads are quite worn, revealing the woven fabric beneath.*

Trademark: *the satinized, printed label is sewn into the left side-seam.*

BEAR PROFILE
At this angle, you can see the thin, straight body, and the short, stubby arms and legs, ending in slightly rounded feet. The ears are sewn centrally across the facial seams and down the sides of the relatively large head; the eyes are positioned low, in line with the appealing, pert, protruding muzzle.

Feet: *the feet are slightly rounded.*

white mohair plush; wood-wool stuffing in head; kapok elsewhere

original amber and black, glass eyes, sewn in

short, flattened muzzle, typical of British bears

shield-shaped, vertically stitched nose; central stitches extended to meet mouth

fully jointed, short, stubby limbs; no feet

slightly damaged, pale blue, felt pads; no claws

label machine-stitched across right foot-pad

1940s WHITE MOHAIR; SHIELD LABEL   Height: 33cm (13in)

This small, white, mohair-plush bear has a pale cinnamon-coloured nose and mouth, typical of white Farnell bears of this era. The shortened muzzle and stubby limbs suggest that the bear was made during, or just after, World War II.

Printed label

large, slightly cupped ears, sewn over facial seams

brown, glass eyes with black pupils

golden mohair plush; wood-wool stuffing in head; soft stuffing elsewhere

square, black, vertically stitched nose; mouth missing

bear in permanently seated position

slightly worn, brown, Rexine pads

short, straight, unjointed legs

1950s NIGHTDRESS CASE   Height: 50cm (20in)

Farnell started making nightdress cases in the 1930s, but this example has the later, shield label stitched to its leg. The bear, with unjointed limbs and swivel head, contains a flexible, internal wire frame and a pink, quilted, rayon lining.

Printed label

small ears, set low down on sides of head, and caught into side-seams

orange, knitted, bobble hat and scarf (may not be original)

flattened muzzle and large, bulbous forehead – typical Toffee shape

amber, glass eyes with black pupils, sewn in with knot at back of head; set low down and wide apart

golden mohair plush; wood-wool stuffing in head; kapok elsewhere

square, black, vertically stitched nose; inverted-T-shaped mouth

worn, brown, Rexine pads; no claws

short, stumpy limbs

1960 TOFFEE; RADIO CHARACTER   Height: 25cm (10in)

Toffee is a character from the 1950s BBC radio programme *Listen with Mother*. The company first advertised an undressed version in 1960 – this outfit may be a later addition. Chad Valley also produced a version, in 1953 (*see p.104*).

Printed label

dark amber, glass eyes with black pupils, sewn in on wire shanks

large, cupped ears, centred over facial seams

square muzzle

black, vertically stitched, oblong nose

black, double-stitched, inverted-Y-shaped mouth; long, vertical stitch meets nose

dense, short-pile, white mohair plush; soft stuffed throughout

spoon-shaped paws with no claws

large, oval feet; narrow ankles

c.1960–64 WHITE MOHAIR; RED PADS   Height: 48cm (19in)

This bear resembles later, red-padded examples by Acton Playcraft Ltd. (*see p.125*), suggesting that the latter company used Farnell designs after they moved into the Alpha works in 1964. Although the label has been cut short, "Farnell" is still legible.

Printed label

Pedigree: 1937–50s

TRADITIONAL BRITISH BEARS FROM MERTON AND BELFAST FACTORIES

Pedigree Soft Toys Ltd. was a subsidiary of Lines Bros., the largest toy manufacturer in the world in the 1930s–50s; it originally operated from Lines' Triang Works in Merton, Surrey. The first catalogue offering Pedigree Soft Toys was produced in 1937, although the tradename had been used since the early 1930s for Lines' pram range. Soft and chassis toys continued to be made in Merton until the 1950s when production was transferred to the company's Castlereagh factory in Belfast, N. Ireland. Pedigree bears were also made in factories around the world including one in Auckland, New Zealand.

c.1955 "MADE IN IRELAND" LABEL

This bear demonstrates one of the two Pedigree teddy-bear designs that existed during this period (see also opposite, bottom left). The front of the face has a vertical, central seam with a second seam running horizontally across the top of the head. The ears, with the edges folded over, are sewn into this horizontal seam. The printed label is attached at the top of the back seam. The plush is described in Pedigree catalogues as "super quality 'London Gold' mohair plush".

Height: 45cm (18in)

Printed label

Ears: the entire ear, with the inner edge folded over, is sewn into the seam across the top of the head.

Eyes: these are early examples of the plastic, lock-in type of eye.

Nose: the square, black nose is vertically stitched.

Ribbon: the red ribbon is not the original, but the bear would have left the factory with a similar bow around its neck.

Fur/stuffing/squeaker: The fur is golden mohair plush; the bear is stuffed with wood-wool in the head and body, and with kapok in the limbs. There is an internal squeaker.

BEAR PROFILE

This bear's classic Pedigree, bulbous head has little muzzle definition; the eyes are set low down towards the nose, creating a large, rounded forehead. The straight body, arms, and legs, which make the bear more doll-like than bear-like, are also typical of Pedigree teddy bears.

Pads: the beige, velveteen pads are well worn, showing the woven backing beneath. There are no claws.

Feet: the little feet have round pads, a feature of this particular Pedigree design.

typical Pedigree,
amber and black,
two-part, plastic eyes

inner edges of ears
folded and sewn
into horizontal
head-seam

small piece of
stiffened black
felt cupped
over muzzle
to represent
nose (may be
repair work)

straight arms with
pointed paws, a
Pedigree feature

straight legs with
small, round feet

dirty, well-
worn, beige,
velveteen pads;
no claws

1950s "MADE IN ENGLAND" LABEL   Height: 33cm (13in)

Although the label sewn into the back seam is
almost unreadable, it is just possible to make out
the letters "Eng" of England as opposed to "Ire" of
Ireland, effectively dating the bear to the period
before all production was moved to Belfast.

Printed label

---

high forehead

inner edges
of ears folded
inwards, and
caught into
horizontal
seam

square, black,
vertically stitched
nose with inverted-
T-shaped mouth

golden mohair
plush; wood-
wool stuffing
in body and
muzzle, kapok
in limbs and
rest of head

short, slightly
curved arms

straight legs
with small feet
and round pads;
no claws

EARLY 1950s GLASS EYES   Height: 45cm (18in)

Although this bear has no label, its rounded head, with centre seams
and a horizontal seam running from ear to ear, make it almost identical
in design to the model on p.92. However, it has amber, glass eyes, with
black pupils, sewn into the face and tied off at the back, suggesting that
it was made slightly earlier, before plastic, lock-in eyes became the norm.

---

realistic, black,
moulded plastic nose

typical Pedigree, two-
part, safe, plastic eyes
with opaque, black
pupil forming shank

typical Pedigree,
black, single-
stitch, inverted-
T-shaped mouth

bow-tie is not
original (bear
would have left
factory with
ribbon bow)

golden mohair
plush; wood-wool
stuffing around
tilt-growler and
muzzle; kapok
elsewhere

LATE 1950s PLASTIC NOSE   Height: 54cm (21½in)

This example demonstrates Pedigree's second teddy-bear design of the
period. The bear has a central, triangular section inserted into the head
pattern to create a more protruding and traditional muzzle shape. Similar
bears with plastic noses were advertised in the mid-1950s, including an
example in coloured silk plush with a squeaker in each leg.

---

large ears with inner
edges folded over and
caught in horizontal
head seam

two-part, amber
and black, safe,
plastic eyes, with
centre forming
integral shank

black, moulded
plastic, slightly
off-centre nose;
inverted-T-
shaped mouth

short, straight
arms with slightly
pointed paws;
swivel-jointed

golden mohair
plush; soft
stuffing
throughout,
except for
wood-wool
around
squeaker

short, straight,
stumpy legs
with little foot
definition

LATE 1950s PLASTIC NOSE; STIFF NECK   Height: 30cm (12in)

According to a 1950s catalogue, this was the smallest bear in Pedigree's
centre-seam range, described as "number 014: teddy bear with squeak".
It is identical to the other centre-seam examples represented here, except
for the addition of a moulded plastic nose, indicating a later date, and its
fixed head, which was cut, all-in-one, from the same fabric as the body.

The Hermann Dynasty

THREE GENERATIONS OF TEDDY-BEAR MANUFACTURERS

Two German soft-toy factories bearing the Hermann name are currently in production, both producing highly collectable teddy bears: Gebrüder Hermann GmbH & Co. KG and Hermann-Spielwaren GmbH. The present owners of these family firms are distant cousins, descended from Johann Hermann, a Sonneberg toymaker, and moved to their present factories in the West following World War II. German reunification on 3 October 1990 made access to the family records possible, enabling a complete picture of the Hermann dynasty and its place in the teddy-bear story to emerge.

Johann Hermann (1854–1919) founded a toy business *c.*1907 in Neufang, near Sonneberg, at that time the worldwide centre of the toy industry. Johann specialized in children's miniature wooden fiddles, but was also a "jobber", buying toys from home-workers to sell at markets. He and his wife Rosalie Suffa (1867–1933) had six children who all became involved in teddy-bear manufacture, a fast-growing industry in this part of Germany. Johann's second son, Artur (1894–1989), worked for Neufang teddy-bear manufacturer, Ernst Siegel. He married Siegel's daughter, Viktoria, and left the company to start his own business with his elder sister, Adelheid (1891–1939) and young brother, Max (1899–1955) in the attic room of their father's house. Max left school at the age of 14 to help his family make teddy bears.

Family portrait
The 1910 photograph (above) shows Johann and Rosalie Hermann with their children, who created the first Hermann teddy bears.

Max Hermann factory
Stuffing soft toys at the Sonneberg factory in the 1930s (above).

THE FIRST HERMANN BEAR
According to family letters, the first Hermann bear was made here on 24 October 1913, when the business was operating as Johann Hermann Spielwarenfabrik. Johann sold the bears locally and to the large Sonneberg jobbers, such as Lindner, Gebrüder Fleischmann, and Escher & Son, who exported them to Britain and the United States. At the start of World War I, Artur was drafted into the army. Max and Adelheid continued the business until 1917 when Max, too, went to war.

NAME CHANGES
In 1919, Johann Hermann died; Artur moved to Sonneberg to start his own firm, called Artur Hermann, but by 1929 he had renamed it "J.Hermann Nachf. Inh. Artur Hermann" (meaning Johann Hermann follower, owned by Artur Hermann). Artur recognized that the key to his success lay in his father's reputation. His trademark was a walking teddy bear leading a bear on all fours, carrying a monkey, and later a crown with "Rex" on the rim. Artur moved from Sonneberg to Munich in 1940, selling up to the Anker Plush Toy Company (*see p.114*) in 1954, and founding the toy shop Teddy: Haus des Kindes (House of the Child).

Adelheid, co-creator of the first Hermann teddy bear, married Neufang-born Hermann Baumann. They had four children, including Franz (born 1919). In 1946, he founded his own small arts and crafts toy factory (Kunstgewerbliches Spielzeug) in Flensburg. He returned home to Rodach in 1951 and, with his old friend Franz Kienel, founded the plush toy company, Baumann & Kienel OHG, today known as Baumann & Kienel KG trading under the tradename "Baki" (*see p.116*).

Bears in the attic
Artur, Adelheid, and Max made their first teddy in the attic of their father's Neufang house (above). From 1920 to 1923, Max operated his own business from there.

Sonneberg, 1930
The small boy (above, centre) is Max's son Rolf-Gerhard who later helped his father to run the business, taking over after his death. Rolf-Gerhard now heads Hermann-Spielwaren GmbH.

Bear in *lederhosen*
The little bear (above) is one of a set of Max Hermann bears made for a Sonneberg toy exhibition in 1933. The bears were originally arranged as if dancing around a maypole.

Traditional, jointed range
Hermann & Co. developed a range of teddies in both mohair and Dralon plush in the 1950s and 60s (left).

ORIGINS OF HERMANN-SPIELWAREN

After World War I, Max Hermann remained in Neufang, founding his own firm in 1920 at the family home. In 1923, he moved to Sonneberg with his wife Hilde Stammberger (1898–1985) and their son Rolf-Gerhard (born 1922). He used the trademark "Maheso", derived from the first two letters of the words "Max Hermann Sonneberg", and later added a teddy-bear and the running-dog logo. In 1947, Rolf-Gerhard joined the firm. Two years later, father and son founded Hermann & Co. KG, in Coburg, in the US Occupied Zone, about 15km (9 miles) east of Soviet-occupied Sonneberg. On 22 February 1953, fearing the emerging Communist regime in East Germany, Max and his family fled across the border to Coburg where they relocated Max Hermann Sonneberg. When Max died in 1955, Rolf-Gerhard took over the firm, still operating in Coburg. The firm became a public limited company, Hermann-Spielwaren GmbH, in 1979. Until her death in 1992, Rolf-Gerhard's wife, Dora-Margot designed many of the bears which have won awards in Germany and the US. In 1992 they were nominated for a TOBY award. Rolf-Gerhard and his daughter Dr Ursula Hermann now run the company.

Modern techniques
Workers inserting joints (above) at the Hermann-Spielwaren factory in Coburg.

Green triangle
The running teddy and dog logo (above) was used by Max Hermann and his descendents.

Replica of 1929 design
Hermann-Spielwaren won a gold medal in the 1992 "Eurodoll" contest for this bear.

Late 1920s bear
The mohair bear (left), typical of its time, was produced by Bernhard Hermann's company, and would have borne the trademark "Beha Quality Germany". From 1930 to 1939, this wording was changed to "Marke Beha Teddy bürgt für Qualität".

GEBRÜDER HERMANN

In 1912, Johann Hermann's eldest son Bernhard (1888–1959) married Ida Jäger. After World War I, they moved to Sonneberg, where Bernhard founded his own small business specializing in teddies and dolls. Factory workers made the better quality mohair-plush bears, while local piece-workers made the cheaper models. Bernhard and Ida had four sons, all of whom helped in the business: Hellmut (1909–85), Artur (1912–90), Werner (born 1917), and Horst (1920–37). When Sonneberg came under Russian occupation after the war, Bernhard sent Werner to establish a factory in the US Zone. For over two years, Werner cycled back and forth from Sonneberg to Hirschaid, carrying machinery and tools, to set up a workshop in an abandoned bicycle factory. Finally, in 1953, both family and production were relocated in Hirschaid, with Hellmut, Artur, and Werner as partners and trading as Gebrüder Hermann KG. Following Bernhard's death in 1959, Artur became business manager with Hellmut the director of operations, and Werner responsible for design and production. Today, the firm is run by Hellmut's daughter Isabella, Werner's daughter Marion, and Artur's daughters Margit and Traudel.

Family group
Bernhard Hermann in 1929 (above, centre) with his wife Ida and their sons (from left to right) Horst, Artur, Hellmut and Werner.

New wording on tags
The wording (above) has been in use since 1952.

1986 Celebration bear
This bear (below) celebrated the foundation of Bernhard Hermann's business.

Gebrüder Hermann: 1948 – c. 1970

TRADITIONAL AND NOVELTY BEARS; NEW POST-WAR FACTORY

After World War II, when Sonneberg became part of the Soviet Occupied Zone of Germany, Bernhard Hermann, fearing the communist regime, sent his son Werner to the small town of Hirschaid, in the American Occupied Zone, to set up a new factory there. By 1951, the whole family had been relocated and the business, owned by the three brothers, became known as Gebrüder Hermann KG. Hellmut was director of operations, Artur was business manager, and Werner was product manager and designer. The company thrived, reproducing traditional designs and introducing novelty ranges.

1960s INSET MUZZLE

This bear shares characteristics with pre-World War II Gebrüder Hermann bears, retaining the traditional long, curved arms and paws, and the typical inset muzzle of contrasting, short-pile mohair plush. Other German manufacturers followed this design, so possession of a trademark is the only guarantee of a bear's origination. This bear still has its swing-tag, attached by a gold cord to the original green, ribbon bow. Hermann used green and gold, printed, paper swing-tags from 1952 until the 1970s, when the company introduced red and gold paper, or red, plastic tags.

Height: 43cm (17in)

Printed paper swing-tag

Muzzle: *the protruding muzzle is made up of three separate pieces of clipped, short, dense, beige, mohair plush.*

Eyes: *the small, amber, glass eyes with black pupils, are sewn in on wire shanks and fastened off at the back of the neck.*

Nose: *the oval, black nose is horizontally stitched.*

Fur/stuffing/growler: *the mohair plush is nutmeg coloured, with a woven backing, and contains a few darker brown strands; the stuffing is wood-wool throughout; there is an internal tilt-growler.*

Paws: *the long, square-ended paws have cream, felt pads, with three black, embroidered claws on each.*

BEAR PROFILE

The pointed muzzle, clearly visible here, is made of clipped, golden mohair plush of a lighter shade than the plush used for the body. The arms are distinctive, the long, slender, square-ended paws ending with an upward curve. The straight legs are relatively short, with small, oval feet.

Trademark: *the front and reverse of the circular swing-tag are identical.*

Feet: *the narrow, oval feet have cream, felt pads with three black, embroidered claws.*

short, golden mohair plush; length of pile clearly seen on tops of ears

small, amber, glass eyes with black pupils, set wide apart; sewn into face on wire shanks

three black, embroidered claws across tips of paws

short, stubby, curved arms

pointed feet with central seam along length; no pads

fabric label sewn into left side-seam

POST-1953 MINIATURE

Height: 13cm (5in)

This tiny, fully jointed bear was produced in Gebrüder Hermann's Hirshaid factory. The wording on the green, fabric label, which is sewn into the left side-seam, indicates a date of manufacture following the division of Germany into the Democratic and Federal Republics.

Printed label

shaggy, dark brown, Zotty mohair plush with blond-tipped shaggy pile; wood-wool stuffing in head; soft stuffed elsewhere

short, clipped, beige mohair muzzle

vertically stitched, brown, embroidered nose with two outer stitches dropped

inverted-Y-shaped mouth along top edge of peach, felt, open mouth, with pink, air-brushed, tongue

downward-curved arms with tear-shaped paws

large, slim, oval feet with three black claws on each

peach, felt pads

1960s ZOTTY TYPE

Height: 29cm (11½in)

Several German manufacturers imitated the Zotty design first created by Steiff in 1951, and examples are hard to differentiate if, as in this case, no trademark exists. The main distinguishing Gebrüder Hermann features are the lack of a chest plate, and the embroidered nose with two outer, dropped stitches – the Steiff bears had shield-shaped noses.

brown, glass eyes with black pupils

short, clipped muzzle of lighter mohair plush; open mouth lined with peach felt

shaggy, Zotty mohair on dark, woven backing; internal squeaker

three brown, embroidered claws on each paw

curved arms in begging attitude

1950s ZOTTY TYPE

Height: 25cm (10in)

This is an earlier version of the Zotty type than the previous example. It has a typical 1950s circular, metal tag. The essential Gebrüder Hermann, dropped, outer stitches on the nose, and the inverted-Y-shaped mouth are missing, having been damaged by wear and tear.

Metal tag

brown, glass eyes with black pupils one a replacement

short, golden plush ears, set over facial seams

black, oval, horizontally stitched nose; inverted-Y-shaped mouth

shaggy, honey-coloured mohair plush; internal tilt-growler

oval feet; pads repaired with woven fabric

curved, slender paws; pads repaired with woven fabric

1940s–50s SHAGGY, HONEY MOHAIR

Height: 55cm (22in)

This bear shows much wear and tear, and its colour has faded, with a richer, golden-coloured plush visible in the joint areas, where it is protected from light. There is no trademark, and the inset muzzle is uncharacteristic of Hermann bears. However, evidence in the Gebrüder Hermann factory archives confirms its pedigree.

Hermann & Co: 1940s–60s

TRADITIONAL INSET MUZZLE AND NOVELTIES

In 1947, Max Hermann's son, Rolf-Gerhard, joined the family business, which then took on the name, Max Hermann & Sohn. In 1949, they founded the subsidiary company, Hermann & Co. KG, in Coburg, Bavaria, in what was then the US Occupied Zone of Germany, about 15km (9 miles)

from Sonneberg. Fearing the Communist regime, they moved Max Hermann & Sohn and the family home to Coburg in 1953, joining Hermann & Co. KG there. Max died in 1955, leaving the business in the hands of Rolf and his wife, Dora-Margot. The company eventually became known as Hermann-Spielwaren.

LATE 1960s TALKING BEAR

This bear carries a square, red printed on cream, card swing-tag bearing the running dog and teddy-bear motif. The motif was first used c.1933 but here it has new wording. The colour and shape of the tag are unusual as this company's work is usually identified by a green triangle. This label was used only on Hermann Sprech-Bären (talking bears), which could "speak" 11 phrases when a cord was pulled activating the internal mechanism.

Height: 48cm (19in)   Printed tag

Nose/mouth: the black, shield-shaped nose is horizontally stitched; the inverted-Y-shaped, single-stitched mouth forms a glum expression. An open-mouth version was also made.

Eyes: the brown, glass eyes have black pupils.

Arms: the arms are placed high on the body, so that the bear appears to have wide shoulders and no neck.

Body: the body and limbs of this bear are particularly slender.

Claws: there are three black, embroidered claws on each paw and foot.

BEAR PROFILE

You can see here this bear's inset muzzle of contrasting plush, and the ring on the end of the speaker-mechanism cord protruding from the back of the neck. Its slender body, curved arms tapering to pointed paws, and thin, tubular legs with minimal feet, distinguish it as a 1950s–1960s Hermann & Co. bear.

Pads: the small, oval pads are made from pale golden, short-pile mohair plush.

Fur/stuffing/speaker: the fur is golden mohair plush; the bear is stuffed with wood-wool; an internal speaker mechanism is activated by a cord.

horizontally stitched, triangular, black nose with outer vertical stitches; inverted-Y-shaped mouth

brown, glass eyes with black pupils

inset muzzle of shorter pile, cream mohair plush

arms attached high up on body

triangular, metal chest-tag

three black, stitched claws

shaggy, brown-tipped, cream mohair plush; wood-wool stuffing

beige, felt pads

1948–52 BROWN-TIPPED MOHAIR   Height: 80cm (31½in)

This brown-tipped mohair-plush bear with inset, contrasting muzzle and ears was manufactured by Hermann & Co., Coburg. Although it resembles those produced by Gebruder Hermann, the triangular "Hermann Plüschtiere" tag confirms its origins.

Printed tag

---

brown, glass eyes with black pupils

horizontally stitched, thin, lozenge-shaped, black nose

inverted-Y-shaped mouth with glum expression

rounded shoulders

printed, green card trade-mark in metal surround

short, curved, tapering arms with large paws

straight legs with minimal foot definition

golden mohair plush; wood-wool stuffing

beige, felt pads

slender, straight body

c.1960 GOLDEN MOHAIR   Height: 48cm (19in)

This bear with high shoulders, inset muzzle, and small feet possesses its original triangular, metal tag. The label design was introduced in the early 1950s; from the mid-1950s to the early 1960s the words "Hermann Plüschtiere" were incised on the back.

Printed tag

---

horizontally stitched, lozenge-shaped, black nose

brown, glass eyes with black pupils

shaggy, brown Dralon plush; wood-wool-stuffed head; soft-stuffed body; internal squeaker

open mouth with peach-coloured, felt palate and airbrushed tongue

original lilac, satin, ribbon bow

green and gold, scalloped, circular, chest-tag

c.1960 ZOTTY-TYPE   Height: 25cm (10in)

This bear, produced when the firm was known as Hermann & Co. KG, resembles Steiff's Zotty. It carries a large label indicating, on the reverse, that it is made of Dralon. Throughout the 1960s, only soft-stuffed, Dralon toys bore this tag.

Printed tag

---

horizontally stitched, lozenge-shaped, black nose; inverted-Y-shaped mouth

amber, glass eyes with black pupils

green and white patterned ruff around neck

golden, artificial-silk plush, in perfect condition

fully jointed with Yes/No mechanism; small tail operates head movement

pink, felt pads

three black, stitched claws across plush

narrow, oval-shaped feet

1948–52 YES/NO BEAR   Height: 26cm (10½in)

This Yes/No bear, with original price and product number tag, was produced by Max Hermann & Sohn in Sonneberg and then sold to Hermann & Co. KG in Coburg. The two firms operated simultaneously in Sonneberg and Coburg between 1948 and 1953, when the family left East Germany, unable to return until the 1990 reunification.

Steiff: 1940s – early 1960s

POST-WAR, REDESIGNED, TRADITIONAL ORIGINAL TEDDY

R aw materials became increasingly difficult to obtain from 1939, and in 1943 Steiff ceased toy production, becoming a munitions factory for the rest of World War II. After the war, the firm made small quantities of bears, often from low-quality fabrics. Steiff remodelled their Original Teddy

design in 1950; the new version had shorter limbs and was available in 23cm (9in) and 35cm (14in) sizes, in caramel-coloured and dark brown mohair. A year later, the range increased to ten sizes and included white and beige mohair plush. The bears also carried newly designed buttons and printed card chest-tags.

c.1950 NEW ORIGINAL TEDDY DESIGN

Although its original "button in ear" trade-mark is missing, this bear still possesses the printed, cloth label sewn into its right side-seam, which was used by Steiff from 1947–53, following World War II and the subsequent division of Germany into separate military zones. The new Original Teddy design saw the end of the typical, horizontally stitched, triangular nose previously used on smaller Steiff bears; the shield-shaped nose now applied to the whole range.

Height: 35cm (14in)

Printed label

Eyes: *the eyes are brown glass, with black pupils. They are sewn into the face.*

Nose/mouth: *the nose is shield shaped and vertically stitched in brown (a feature of most white bears). The mouth is an inverted V shape.*

Fur: *the short, white mohair plush is discoloured, but is otherwise in good condition.*

Paws: *the ends of the paws are squarer than those of earlier bears.*

Claws: *four claws on each foot and paw are stitched in brown.*

Pads: *the foot-pads are made of cream felt, and are in perfect condition.*

BEAR PROFILE

The slightly shorter, blunter muzzle, and significantly less elongated limbs, are features of the Original Teddy's new design. The arms, however, are still longer than the legs, so retaining the traditional teddy-bear shape. Notice how the curved, spoon-like paws of its predecessor (see pp.18–19) are replaced by a squarer version.

Feet: *the feet are long and narrow.*

horizontally stitched, triangular, black nose; inverted-Y-shaped mouth

discoloured, pale golden, cotton plush

clear, glass eyes, with flaking, painted, brown backs, sewn into face

off-white, cloth pads (felt was unobtainable after the war)

elegant clothing added by previous owner

four black claws stitched on each foot and paw

large, narrow, oval feet

c.1949 BLANK BUTTON
Height: 33cm (13in)

Produced in the post-war years, when materials were scarce, this bear is made of low-quality cotton plush; it has a blank, tin-plate button, typical of the period. A blue-painted, blank button, and one embossed with "Steiff", in capital letters, were also used at this time.

Blank button

small, brown and black, glass eyes sewn in on wire shanks

small ears, sewn over facial seams; button and remains of original tag in left ear

fur slightly worn on muzzle

shield-shaped, vertically stitched, brown nose; inverted-V-shaped mouth

square-ended paws with four stitched claws

beige, felt pads in good condition

short, beige mohair plush

1950s ORIGINAL TEDDY; BEIGE
Height: 35cm (14in)

This bear exemplifies the remodelled Original Teddy pattern that was to remain in circulation until the introduction of the 1966 design (see p.128). It retains its button with "Steiff" in raised, cursive script, a design that was used from 1952/53 until 1977.

Embossed button

brown, glass eyes with black pupils, sewn into face

original yellow, printed ear-tag records product number 5318, 03

straight arms slightly longer than legs; no paw-pads; four claws stitched in black

short, dark brown mohair plush; wood-wool stuffing throughout; internal squeaker

long, narrow feet with beige, felt pads

STEIFF · ORIGINAL MARKE
Original Teddy

1950s ORIGINAL TEDDY; BROWN
Height: 18cm (7in)

This is an example of one of the smaller Original Teddy designs. Like its pre-war predecessors, it has straighter arms than the larger bears and lacks felt paw-pads. Its card chest-tag features the redesigned bear's head, first introduced in 1950.

Embossed button

brown, glass eyes with black pupils; originally sewn in, but right eye glued by repairer

shield-shaped, vertically stitched, brown nose; inverted-V-shaped mouth

curly, blond mohair plush on beige, cloth backing

long, slightly curved arms

wood-wool stuffing sagging near top of shoulder

holes in beige, felt pads reveal wood-wool stuffing

square-ended paws with four brown claws

1950s ORIGINAL TEDDY; CURLY
Height: 53cm (21in)

This bear possesses the unmistakable shape and features of a post-war Original Teddy and although it does not display a Steiff button, a small hole in the ear indicates its Giengen factory origins. Plastic eyes replaced glass eyes in early 1960s models.

Embossed button

Dean's: 1950s

BRITISH POST-WAR NOVELTIES; MOVE FROM MERTON TO RYE FACTORY

The first Dean's catalogue after World War II appeared in 1949, offering a much reduced range due to the shortage of raw materials. However the company, with a reorganized sales force, was soon back on its feet. A further boost to business was provided by the birth of London Zoo's first polar bear cub Brumas in 1949, generating great demand for white bears. In 1952 a new assistant designer, Sylvia R. Willgoss, joined Dean's and introduced many novel designs. She succeeded Richard Ellett as head designer in 1956 when the company moved from Merton, Surrey, to new premises in Rye, Sussex.

MID-1950s TRU-TO-LIFE

This black, North American bear was available in three sizes. It has realistic, pink, moulded rubber paws and foot-pads, with five claws on each. A white version (a polar bear) was first advertised in trade catalogues in 1955. Sylvia Wilgoss designed these unjointed bears to sit, stand upright, or walk on all fours, aided by a collar and chain lead, which have been found on similar examples.

Height: 48cm (19in)

Printed label

Ears: *the large, rounded ears are set wide apart on the sides of the head.*

Eyes: *the brown, glass eyes are placed inside rubber sockets, cut into the rubber face mask.*

Nose: *the large, black, moulded rubber nose and mouth protrude through the end of the muzzle.*

Muzzle: *the white, acrylic plush muzzle contrasts with the black mohair plush of the body.*

Arms: *the long, unjointed, soft-filled arms are particularly floppy because of the lack of stuffing at the shoulders.*

Fur/growler: *the fur is black, shaggy, acrylic plush; the bear is stuffed with wood-wool and kapok, and has a tilt-growler.*

Legs: *the unjointed legs are stuffed with wood-wool and sewn to the front of the body, giving a permanent sitting position.*

Paws: *the foot-pads and paws are made of pink rubber moulded into five claws, some of which have been bent and damaged.*

BEAR PROFILE

Notice how life-like this teddy is with its pointed muzzle and outlined, slightly curled, bottom lip. The back is rounded, the limbs are long and floppy, and the feet are splayed outwards in the typical fashion of a real seated bear.

wide-apart, amber, glass eyes with black pupils, sewn in, with knot at back of head

large, flat ears sewn to sides of head

black, horizontally stitched, triangular nose; inverted-T-shaped mouth

original pink, rayon ribbon tied in bow around neck

straight, stubby arms and legs; no pads or claws

blue wool plush; wood-wool stuffing in muzzle, soft stuffing elsewhere

EARLY 1950S WOOL

Height: 14cm (5½in)

Bought in a bankruptcy sale, this tiny, unjointed bear still carries its original, circular, card swing-tag – a lucky find for any collector. It was probably designed as a baby's plaything, although the glass eyes would not pass today's toy safety standards.

Printed label

---

wide-apart, amber, glass eyes with black pupils, sewn in, with knot at back of head

small, cupped ears, with inner edges caught into facial seams

black, vertically stitched, rectangular nose; inverted-T-shaped mouth

original yellow ribbon tied in bow; original card tag with pre-1956 Merton address

short, light brown wool plush (probably alpaca) on woven backing

short, straight arms

short, straight legs with small feet

pale peach, felt pads in perfect condition; no claws

EARLY 1950S SEATED; WIRE JOINTING

Height: 20cm (8in)

Although this small bear is not jointed in the traditional fashion, an internal wire frame enables the limbs to move up and down in unison, as well as to bend in a variety of poses. The printed fabric label is sewn into the back of the neck.

Printed label

---

ears placed wide apart, with inner edges caught into facial seams

brown, plastic eyes with integral shank, sewn into face and fastened off at back

head and paws of golden mohair plush

rectangular, black, vertically stitched nose; inverted-T-shaped mouth

blue, velvet shirt with three, orange, plastic buttons

red, velvet, jodhpur-style trousers

original, card swing-tag with Merton address: reverse reads "Velvet Bear T272/1"

blue, velvet shoes

MID-1950S VELVET BEAR

Height: 35cm (14in)

Under the designer Richard Ellett, Dean's was renowned for its velvet toys. Unjointed bears with all-in-one clothes were made from the 1930s, but remained popular in the years following World War II, when traditional materials were still scarce.

Printed label

---

small ears with inner edges caught into facial seams

brown, plastic eyes with short, integral, plastic shanks, sewn into face and fastened off at back of head

pointed muzzle

black, vertically stitched, rectangular nose

upward-stretching arms

soft, white, woollen plush (possibly alpaca), on woven backing

MID-1950S WHITE; GLOVE-PUPPET

Height: 25cm (10in)

All the major soft-toy manufacturers made teddy-bear glove-puppets. This white, woollen-plush example may have been produced as a result of the British post-1949 Brumas craze. The printed label is stitched across the lower back of the glove.

Printed label

Chad Valley: 1950s–60s

NOVELTIES, AND DEVELOPMENTS IN TRADITIONAL DESIGN

Post-war advances in the plastics industry had their effect on teddy bears. During the 1950s, Chad Valley gradually replaced glass eyes with plastic ones and produced some teddy bears with realistic, moulded plastic noses. The company also began to introduce nylon and other synthetic fabrics into its range, although the basic bear design remained the same. Radio had influenced the toy industry since the early days, but in the 1950s Chad Valley obtained the sole rights to manufacture Harry Corbett's mischievous Sooty glove puppet, which featured in a popular children's television programme from 1952.

1953 TOFFEE

Toffee was a character from the 1950s–60s BBC children's radio programme *Listen with Mother*. Jane Alan later published a book of stories about his adventures with a little girl called Lulupet. Here, Toffee wears his original red hat and scarf. J.K. Farnell also made a Toffee teddy bear (without clothes) in the 1960s *(see p.91)*.

Height: 25cm (10in)

Printed label

Ears: *the typical Chad Valley, large, flat ears are set on the sides of the head.*

Eyes: *the amber and black, glass eyes are sewn in place.*

Nose: *this is a typical Chad Valley bound nose, with black vertical stitches.*

Fur: *the dark beige mohair plush is quite long, but worn in places.*

Trademark: *the Queen Mother Royal Warrant label is zigzag-stitched onto the right foot-pad. The bear would also originally have had a card tag with "Toffee, the Teddy with a Personality" printed in red and blue.*

BEAR PROFILE

In profile, the most noticeable feature is the particularly high, domed forehead and the flat muzzle. The arms are very short, with Rexine pads. The legs are also short and quite fat with small feet. The red, knitted, woollen hat with a pompom is sewn onto the back of the head.

Pads: *the Rexine pads are worn. The left pad is torn, revealing the wood-wool stuffing that is used throughout.*

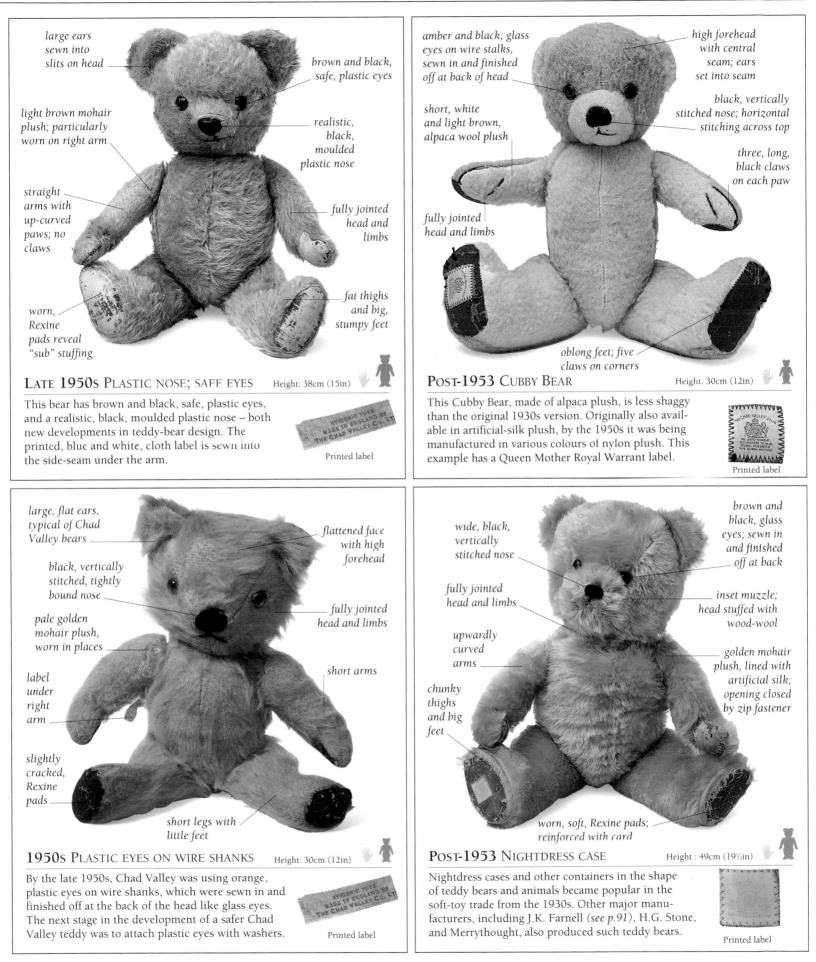

large ears
sewn into
slits on head

brown and black,
safe, plastic eyes

light brown mohair
plush; particularly
worn on right arm

realistic,
black,
moulded
plastic nose

straight
arms with
up-curved
paws; no
claws

fully jointed
head and
limbs

worn,
Rexine
pads reveal
"sub" stuffing

fat thighs
and big,
stumpy feet

LATE 1950s PLASTIC NOSE; SAFE EYES
Height: 38cm (15in)

This bear has brown and black, safe, plastic eyes, and a realistic, black, moulded plastic nose – both new developments in teddy-bear design. The printed, blue and white, cloth label is sewn into the side-seam under the arm.

Printed label

amber and black, glass
eyes on wire stalks,
sewn in and finished
off at back of head

high forehead
with central
seam; ears
set into seam

short, white
and light brown,
alpaca wool plush

black, vertically
stitched nose; horizontal
stitching across top

three, long,
black claws
on each paw

fully jointed
head and limbs

oblong feet; five
claws on corners

POST-1953 CUBBY BEAR
Height: 30cm (12in)

This Cubby Bear, made of alpaca plush, is less shaggy than the original 1930s version. Originally also available in artificial-silk plush, by the 1950s it was being manufactured in various colours of nylon plush. This example has a Queen Mother Royal Warrant label.

Printed label

large, flat ears,
typical of Chad
Valley bears

flattened face
with high
forehead

black, vertically
stitched, tightly
bound nose

pale golden
mohair plush,
worn in places

fully jointed
head and limbs

label
under
right
arm

short arms

slightly
cracked,
Rexine
pads

short legs with
little feet

1950s PLASTIC EYES ON WIRE SHANKS
Height: 30cm (12in)

By the late 1950s, Chad Valley was using orange, plastic eyes on wire shanks, which were sewn in and finished off at the back of the head like glass eyes. The next stage in the development of a safer Chad Valley teddy was to attach plastic eyes with washers.

Printed label

wide, black,
vertically
stitched nose

brown and
black, glass
eyes; sewn in
and finished
off at back

fully jointed
head and limbs

inset muzzle;
head stuffed with
wood-wool

upwardly
curved
arms

golden mohair
plush, lined with
artificial silk;
opening closed
by zip fastener

chunky
thighs
and big
feet

worn, soft, Rexine pads;
reinforced with card

POST-1953 NIGHTDRESS CASE
Height : 49cm (19½in)

Nightdress cases and other containers in the shape of teddy bears and animals became popular in the soft-toy trade from the 1930s. Other major manufacturers, including J.K. Farnell (see p.91), H.G. Stone, and Merrythought, also produced such teddy bears.

Printed label

Chiltern: post-World War II – 1950s

POST-WAR CHILTERN HUGMEE AND NOVELTY TEDDY BEARS

Towards the end of World War II, it became clear that H.G. Stone's factories in Tottenham, north London, and Chesham, Bucks., would never be able to meet the demand for Chiltern toys, and so in 1945 the company obtained a site near Pontypool, in south Wales, to build a new and larger factory with modern facilities. The company set up a school to train young girls and women in soft-toy production techniques in readiness for the factory's opening in 1947. The new factory was extended on several occasions during the highly productive, post-war period, when up to 300 workers were employed.

1956–57 HUGMEE; CHILTERN LABEL

H.G. Stone continued to make Hugmee bears during the 1950s, with little change to the original pre-war design; the company used good quality mohair plush, and velveteen pads reinforced with card on the feet. For the first time, however, they used a new, permanent, printed label.

Height: 53cm (21in)

Printed label

Eyes: *the reddish brown, translucent, glass eyes with black pupils are sewn in on wire shanks, and finished off with a diagonal stitch at the back of the head.*

Nose: *the shield-shaped nose is similar to those of the flat-face Hugmees (see p.57).*

Fur/stuffing: *this light golden, mohair-plush bear is stuffed with kapok in the body and limbs; wood-wool is used in the head and around the squeaker.*

BEAR PROFILE

This bear shares many similarities with the earlier Hugmee design *(see pp.56–57)*: thick thighs, large, slightly pointed feet, extended muzzle, and relatively long arms.

Trademark: *the new, printed label is attached to the right foot-pad.*

Pads: *the light rust-coloured, velveteen pads, are reinforced with thin card; the feet have five claws, whereas the paws have four.*

small, L-shaped ears, caught into facial seams

brown and black, glass eyes, sewn in place

light golden mohair plush; soft stuffing in body and limbs, with wood-wool in head and around squeaker and joints

triangular, black, vertically stitched nose

rust-coloured, velveteen pads with four claws over pads and plush

four claws on each foot

1950s HUGMEE; MEDIUM   Height: 35cm (14in)

The Hugmee range came in various sizes; this is a smaller version of the large Hugmee (*opposite*). This bear no longer possesses a trademark, but the discoloured area on the right foot-pad indicates where the original, printed label was attached.

CHILTERN HYGIENIC TOYS MADE IN ENGLAND

Printed label

amber and black, glass eyes, sewn in and finished off at back of head

short-clipped mohair plush on fronts of ears

black, shield-shaped, vertically stitched nose

separate section of clipped mohair plush forms muzzle

beige mohair plush; wood-wool and kapok stuffing in body and limbs; wood-wool in head

dark brown, shiny, Rexine pads

foot-pads reinforced with card

1953 TING-A-LING BRUIN BEAR   Height: 29cm (11½in)

This fully jointed teddy bear contains a mechanism (now inoperative) that was common in 1950s toys – a cardboard tube fitted with an internal metal ring of metal teeth arranged around its inner circumference. A metal clapper suspended from the top of the tube strikes each tooth when the toy is shaken or tipped up, making the teddy bear tinkle musically.

ears sewn into facial seams and into darts down sides of head

typical Chiltern, reddish brown, glass eyes, sewn in and finished off with knot at top of head

paws stuffed with wood-wool

wide, vertically stitched, black nose

golden mohair plush; head stuffed with wood-wool; finger-space inside head lined with green Rexine

unusual red on white, printed label, sewn into hem inside base of glove

1950s GLOVE PUPPET   Height: 20cm (8in)

Teddy-bear glove puppets have been made since before World War I, but in the 1950s all the major British soft-toy manufacturers, including Dean's (*see p.103*), J.K. Farnell, H.G. Stone, and Chad Valley, produced their own versions.

CHILTERN HYGIENIC TOYS MADE IN ENGLAND

Printed label

vertically stitched, oblong nose; inverted-Y-shaped mouth

woven fabric, pill-box hat, originally blue but now faded

brown, glass eyes

all-in-one, long-sleeved blue mohair plush "sweater"

artificial-silk plush stuffed with wood-wool and kapok

pads on feet only

LATE 1930s–50s SKATER   Height: 40cm (16in)

This artificial-silk-plush bear, with all-in-one, long-sleeved, blue, mohair-plush sweater, originally had a white, mohair-plush muff to match the hood. The model was illustrated in a 1937 toy-trade journal but is known to have been made after World War II as well. This bear is unmarked, but others exist with a printed Chiltern label on the foot.

Chiltern: c.1958–early 1960s

INTRODUCTION OF MOULDED PLASTIC NOSE AND WASHABLE TEDDY BEARS

T he company H.G. Stone first used moulded plastic noses on its Chiltern bears in about 1958. Originally sewn on, the noses were later locked-in with washers, in keeping with the new safety regulations. Many of the older Chiltern lines, such as the Hugmee range, were then given plastic noses for a new look. In about 1960, a sleeping bear was introduced, with plastic nose; black, felt, closed eyelids; and a bell in each ear. Washable teddy bears became available in 1964, the year that H.G. Stone & Co. Ltd. became part of the Dunbee-Combex group, makers of vinyl and rubber toys.

EARLY 1960S HUGMEE; MOHAIR

This bear has a moulded plastic, dog-like nose, although some Hugmees were still being produced with the shield-shaped, vertically stitched nose. There is no surviving trademark on this bear, but other, similar bears have been found with Chiltern labels sewn into their side-seams. It would have left the factory with a card swing-tag, like the one on p.109 (*bottom left*), and a ribbon bow.

Height 68cm (27in)

Fur/stuffing/squeaker: *the light golden mohair plush, with specks of dark hair, is commonly used on Chiltern Hugmees; here it is in excellent condition. The teddy bear is soft-stuffed throughout except for wood-wool in the head and around the squeaker.*

Pads: *the rust-coloured, velveteen, tear-shaped foot-pads are reinforced with thin card, which has become slightly misshapen with wear. There are five claws on the feet (only four remain on the left), sewn across the plush up to the seam.*

Ears: *the floppy, dog-like ears are sewn into darts down the sides of the head and then caught into the facial seams.*

Eyes: *the reddish brown, translucent, glass eyes, with black pupils, are sewn into the head.*

BEAR PROFILE

At this angle you can see the bear's dog-like ears, which flop to the sides of its head. Despite the modern addition of a plastic nose, it still retains many of the classic Hugmee features, with the long, pointed muzzle, long, curved arms, fat thighs, and shaped, card-reinforced pads.

Claws: *the four claws, sewn across the paw-pads, are typical of Chiltern bears from this era.*

inner ears lined with clipped, white mohair plush

amber and black, safe, plastic, lock-in eyes

swivel-jointed head; unjointed limbs

clipped, white mohair plush muzzle

mainly silver-tipped, grey mohair plush; white mohair plush on chest and fronts of arms

bear stands in half-seated position

creamy beige, velveteen pads; foot-pads reinforced with card

tops of feet made from separate sections of fabric; no claws

*C.*1958 MUSICAL BRUIN BEAR

Height: 29cm (11½in)

H.G. Stone produced a similar standing bear in the early 1950s, but this example's realistic, plastic nose dates it to a later period. When wound up by a key at the back of the bear, the musical box plays *Brahms' Lullaby*, and the head moves from side to side.

CHILTERN HYGIENIC TOYS MADE IN ENGLAND

Printed label

realistic, moulded plastic nose; only vertical stitch remains of original, inverted-Y-shaped mouth

brown, plastic eyes with black pupils and integral plastic shank; sewn in and fastened off at back of head

looped, gold cord across chest represents ring-master costume

artificial-silk plush in range of colours; soft stuffed; unjointed

red-painted, metal tricycle with rubber tyres, handlebars, and pedals

*C.*1958 BEAR ON A TRICYCLE

Height: 28cm (11in)

This was the first bear designed by Pam Howells, *née* Williams, (*see p.180*) when she joined H.G. Stone & Co. as assistant designer. She based the bear on a character from the Disney cartoon *Dumbo*. The tricycle was created by a colleague, Basil Rogers.

CHILTERN HYGIENIC TOYS MADE IN ENGLAND

Printed label

amber and black, safe, plastic, lock-in eyes

black, realistic, moulded plastic, safe, lock-in nose

inverted-Y-shaped, double-stitched mouth

fully jointed, short, pointed arms

beige, velveteen pads (fabric favoured for Chiltern bears from 1920s); no claws

short legs with small, tear-shaped feet

EARLY 1960s MUSICAL

Height: 34cm (13½in)

This golden, mohair-plush bear, with its moulded plastic nose, still possesses its original swing-tag. The reverse of the tag reads: "To play a tune just turn my key and listen to the melody." Like the example on p.57, it plays *Brahms' Lullaby*.

Printed card tag

unusual, blue, glass eyes with black pupils, sewn in and knotted at back of head

realistic, black, moulded plastic nose, pushed into muzzle; no washer

mainly silver-tipped, grey mohair plush; white mohair plush on chest, face, and fronts of ears

rounded, pale blue, velveteen pads

*C.*1958 UNJOINTED; PLASTIC NOSE

Height: 25cm (10in)

Pam Howells (*née* Williams) designed this bear when plastic noses were first introduced. With its unjointed, short, stubby limbs, it exemplified a break with tradition. Similar bears, composed entirely of nylon plush and stuffed with "Fairy Foam" (one-piece foam filling), were made in the early 1960s as part of the Washable Chiltern Toy series.

Steiff: 1950s

NEW NOVELTY BEARS; MODIFIED EARLIER DESIGNS

I n the 1950s, Steiff introduced several "new-look" teddies into its programme, though some still followed pre-World War II designs. The Jubilee celebrations of the first Steiff teddy bear in 1953 heralded not only Jackie-Baby but also Nimrod-Bear, dressed in a hunting suit, available in four different colours of felt, and carrying a wooden rifle. Steiff made a new 30cm (12in) Teddy-Baby and used the same head design on its 1950s Teddyli, which had a soft fabric body, dangling, unstuffed arms, and stiff legs. Some had rubber bodies but, due to the perishable nature of this material, few survive intact.

1953 JACKIE-BABY

Jackie-Baby, representing an endearing bear cub, was produced to celebrate the 50th anniversary of the first Steiff teddy bear, and was made until 1955. This particular example was the largest of the three sizes available (18cm/7in; 25cm/10in; and 35cm/14in). The navel and embroidered nose design are features unique to this bear. Steiff produced replicas of Jackie-Baby, also in three sizes, in 1986, 1989, and 1990. The bear has a new-style 1950s Steiff button, with raised, cursive lettering, in the left ear, and a printed label in the side-seam reading "US Zone Germany", only used from 1947–53.

Height: 35cm (14in)

Embossed button

Nose: the shield-shaped nose is vertically stitched, with central stitches dropped, and a single, pink, horizontal stitch across the upper, central part.

Arms: the relatively long arms are straighter than on previous examples, to represent the squat features of a bear cub.

Feet: the large feet have beige, felt pads with no claws.

Navel: the small, dark area representing the navel is a unique feature of Jackie-Baby.

Ears: the ears are large and rounded.

Eyes: the brown, glass eyes on wire shanks are sewn in, wide apart, along the top edge of the muzzle.

BEAR PROFILE
At this angle you can see how Jackie-Baby differs from the traditional, Steiff teddy-bear design: he has a straight back, short, stubby legs with large thighs, and squared-off paws. However, he still retains the distinctive, large, protruding muzzle.

Legs: the legs are short and stubby with fat thighs and large, ovoid feet.

dark brown,
vertically stitched,
shield-shaped
nose; central
stitches dropped to
meet inverted-V-
shaped mouth

small, brown,
glass eyes with
black pupils, sewn
in on wire shanks

light brown mohair
plush on back, limbs,
head, and tail; cream
mohair plush on
front of body

fully
jointed,
short
limbs

beige, felt
pads, in very
good condition

originally
four claws
on each
paw

1955 BABY-BEAR

Height: 25cm (10in)

The mohair-covered, metal, U-shaped tail activates the
head movement via an internal mechanism similar to
that of the Schuco Yes/No bear, although the head and
neck are joined in this version. This is the larger of the
two sizes available; 3,539 examples were made in all.

Embossed button

typical Steiff,
triangular nose,
horizontally stitched
with border stitching;
inverted-Y-shaped
mouth in brown
thread

black, glass bead
eyes, sewn in

fully jointed (Steiff
later produced a
range of unjointed,
miniature bears)

straight arms,
slightly wider
at shoulders;
no pads

legs have fat
thighs and
clearly defined,
large feet, no
pads and no
claws

attractive,
apricot-
coloured
mohair
plush

1950s–70s MINIATURE

Height: 10cm (4in)

The first miniature Steiff teddy bears were produced
in 1909, but have changed little over the years. Often
it is only the different buttons, labels, and chest-tags
that can help to date them. (Schuco miniatures are
distinguished by their straight legs and little feet.)

Embossed button

typical Steiff,
shield-shaped,
dark brown,
vertically
stitched nose

clipped, light
brown, mohair-
plush muzzle

open mouth reveals
felt palate, painted
tongue, and brown
painted lips

blond, shaggy
mohair plush on
dark brown, woven
backing, gives
two-tone effect

peach-
coloured,
mohair-
plush
chest
plate

short, fat legs
and large feet;
peach-coloured,
felt pads

1950s ZOTTY

Height: 35cm (14in)

First introduced in 1951, Zotty has remained a firm
favourite until the present day. The name is derived
from the German word *zottig* (shaggy) referring to its
unique fur. Other manufacturers copied the style but
only Steiff bears have the peach-coloured chest plates.

Embossed button

brown circles of felt, sewn
on with two diagonal
stitches in pink thread,
to represent closed eyes

shaggy, blond mohair plush on
dark brown, woven backing, the
typical Zotty fabric

spreadeagled,
unjointed limbs

clipped,
mohair-plush
muzzle, and
open mouth
with peach-
coloured, felt
palate

brown, shield-shaped nose
like that of Zotty (left)

1950s SLEEPING ZOTTY

Length: 20cm (8in)

Steiff made Zotty in a lying-down position as well as
in six sizes, from 17cm (7in) to 50cm (20in), in the
standing pose. The sleeping bear is made of the same,
shaggy, dark-backed, blond mohair plush, with open
mouth and clipped muzzle, but with felt "eyelids".

Embossed button

Schuco: 1949–76

POST-WAR NOVELTIES: CLOCKWORK, FLEXIBLE, TALKING BEARS

Post-war production recommenced at Schreyer and Company's Schuco plant (see pp.40–43) around 1949. New, novelty lines included the clockwork Rolly Bear (1954) wearing roller skates, and the Dancing Bear (1956–62) who turned in circles while throwing a ball up and down. When Heinrich Müller died in 1958, his son, Werner, took over alongside manager, Alexander Girz. In the 1960s, the Bigo Bello series was introduced; this included Parlo, the talking bear, (speaking German, French, or Italian) with a pull-cord mechanism (1963). Schuco was bought by Dunbee-Combex-Marx in 1976.

c.1950 TRICKY

The earlier Yes/No bear (see pp.42–43) was reintroduced after World War II as Tricky, and displayed a ribbon bow and plastic medallion that read on the reverse: "Made in US Zone Germany", indicating its pre-1953 production. Tricky was produced in seven sizes, in blond, hazelnut, or reddish brown mohair plush, and with a growler mechanism. Two sizes were available with Swiss musical boxes incorporated, and Tricky pandas were also made.

Height: 33cm (13in)   Plastic medallion

Fur/stuffing: *the mohair plush is hazelnut coloured; the stuffing is wood-wool throughout. (This size was also available in blond mohair plush.) Four sizes were available with soft, kapok stuffing, and the 14cm (5½in) size had a metal, internal frame.*

Claws: *three black claws are sewn across the plush on each paw and foot.*

Pads: *the beige, felt pads are in perfect condition.*

Eyes: *the large, brown, glass eyes, with black pupils, are sewn in.*

Nose: *the black, vertically stitched nose is shield shaped; some late-1950s examples have been found with moulded, plastic noses.*

BEAR PROFILE

Tricky's short tail which, like that of its predecessor (see p.42), acts as a lever for operating head movement, is clearly visible. This later bear also has flat, stiffened feet, but the legs are longer and thinner than earlier, often chubby-thighed examples. The unusual, begging arms, with their very broad paws, are typical of the post-war Yes/No bears.

Feet: *the oval feet, wider at the toes and with card-reinforced pads, are a typical Schuco design.*

clear, glass eyes, painted brown on backs; black pupils sewn in

small, slightly cupped ears, centred over facial seams

black, vertically stitched, square nose

open mouth with beige, felt palate; airbrushed tongue

oatmeal-coloured mohair plush; internal squeaker

squared-off paws, with beige, felt pads; four claws across plush

squared-off feet; five claws on right foot, four on left, sewn across plush

flexible, internal wire armature allows limbs to be bent into various positions

1960S BRUMMI; BIGO BELLO SERIES
Height: 23cm (9in)

This is the smallest in a range of open-mouthed, mohair-plush bears advertised as Brummi (from *brummen* – to growl like a bear). A similar design, Urso, was produced in Dralon. Both were part of the Bigo Bello series of fully "poseable" bears.

Printed label

convex, plastic, "googly" eyes

horizontal seam across top of head

open mouth; black, felt lower jaw, with smaller piece of beige felt glued on top

black, triangular, moulded plastic nose

light golden, short mohair plush; white, cotton torso beneath clothes; soft stuffing

red, brushed-nylon shirt tucked into black shorts

square, beige, felt pads on paws

flexible, internal wire armature allows body to be fully "poseable"

long, white socks sewn onto legs

LATE 1960S GERMAN SOCCER PLAYER
Height: 34cm (13½in)

One of a range of bears dressed in the coloured strips of German soccer teams, this bear has lost its black and white plastic boots, and the paper emblem on the shirt has been partly removed. Originally, it would have possessed a triangular, card tag reading "Hegi" – a Schuco range named after Herta Girz, who became a director in the late 1950s.

small, cupped ears sewn just behind horizontal head-seam; hard, internal "mask" structures head shape

large, white and black, plastic, convex, button eyes give wide-eyed look

small, rounded, black, plastic, nose

pale peach brushed-nylon on lower half of face

brown, cotton, smiling mouth

mushroom-coloured mohair plush with soft stuffing; internal wire frame allows body to be bent into various poses

three black claws stitched across plush on hands and feet

1960S PUZZI; BIGO BELLO SERIES
Height: 23cm (9in)

This unusual little bear was available in one size, although the design was reused in a larger 42cm (16½in) size for one of the Bigo Bello talking bears, described in catalogues as "*Jungbär*". The original triangular, white-edged, red, card tag with the words "Original Schuco Bigo Bello DRGM", and a ribbon bow, has been removed from the chest.

golden mohair plush over internal, metal frame

black, metal, bead eyes with white, painted, metal surrounds

black, metal, bead eyes

red, celluloid tongue

black, metal, bead nose with white, painted, metal mouth

jointed limbs

straight legs with small feet

1954 JANUS; TWO-FACED
Height: 9cm (3½in)

These little bears show the two faces of a unique novelty whose head can be "swapped" using a knob at the base of the torso. They share many characteristics with other miniature bears in Schuco's Piccolo series, which was reproduced, from the 1950s until the 1970s, in a fractionally larger size, and was advertised as "Original Schuco Talisman".

Germany: post-1945

SIMILAR TRADITIONAL STYLES; INTRODUCTION OF TAGGING

Many manufacturers operated in the Neustadt area after World War II (*see pp.30–31*). Some, like the two Hermann factories, had recently arrived from nearby Sonneberg following Russian occupation. Post-war designs did not change much from those of the pre-war period: many firms used similar patterns with narrow bodies, straight legs, small feet, and inset muzzles. By this time, however, several firms had introduced labels to their products to aid identification and recognition. The labels varied in form, and included triangular tags, scalloped, circular tags, chest-buttons, and oblong, metal, foot-tags.

c.1960 ANKER PLÜSCHSPIELWARENFABRIK

Anker was a Munich-based company. In 1954, it bought Artur Hermann's soft-toy company, J. Hermann Nachf. Inh. Artur Hermann (*see pp.94–5*), a firm that had moved from Sonneberg to Munich in 1940. Anker's trademark – an anchor (*Anker*) superimposed on a lion – is printed on a metallic paper tag similar to those used by both Hermann companies after the war. The side with the logo is blue with silver, and the reverse is silver, with the words *"Anker Plüschtiere aus München"* printed in blue. Anker ceased business during the 1970s.

Height: 47cm (18½in)　　　Printed tag

Ears: *the flat, slightly padded ears are sewn across the facial seams.*

Eyes: *the brown, glass eyes have black pupils.*

Nose/mouth: *the oval, black nose is horizontally stitched; the mouth is a double-stitched, inverted Y shape.*

BEAR PROFILE

In profile, you can see the inset, elongated, pointed muzzle of contrasting short-pile plush, a feature of bears made by Hermann and other German manufacturers. The bear has a straight body with no hump on the back; thin, slightly curved arms; slender, tubular legs; and small feet.

Muzzle: *the inset, beige, short-pile, mohair plush muzzle is elongated and pointed.*

Body seam: *the front, central seam is interrupted by the knot of the chest-tag. The final seam is at the back.*

Fur/stuffing/growler: *the curly, synthetic plush has a shiny appearance; the stuffing is wood-wool; there is a tilt growler.*

Foot-pads: *the circular foot-pads are in good condition, except for insect holes in the right pad.*

Trademark: *the front of the blue and silver, paper chest-tag is printed with an anchor superimposed on a lion.*

amber, glass eyes with black pupils, on wire shanks

inset, pointed, short-pile, beige, wool-plush muzzle

long, curved arms with spoon-shaped paws and peach-coloured, felt pads

straight legs with little foot definition

black, horizontally stitched, shield-like, nose; inverted-Y-shaped, single-stitched mouth

original green, rayon, ribbon bow, now faded, tied around neck

dark brown-tipped, beige mohair plush; wood-wool stuffing

tear-shaped foot-pads

c.1960 EM Toy and Doll Co.
Height: 38cm (15in)

This EM Toy and Doll Co. bear demonstrates the typical Sonneberg/Neustadt design, with its inset muzzle of contrasting plush. The scalloped, metallic, blue and silver swing-tag has a stylized "EM" with "the sign of quality" written in German.

Printed tag

black, safe, plastic eyes

black, horizontally stitched, triangular, nose; inverted-Y-shaped mouth

certificate of authenticity tied around neck

curly, rose-tinted, beige plush; internal tilt growler

plastic chest-tag embossed with outline of dressed cat

tan, felt foot-pads; "Kessel" signature with limited-edition number

1985 Althans
Height: 40cm (16in)

Karl Althans, a Sonneberg teddy-bear company dating from the 1920s, moved to Birkig in the US Zone of Germany after World War II, and formed a new firm, Althans KG, in 1949. The present manager, Günther Kessel, introduced limited-edition bears.

Plastic tag

small, flat ears sewn across facial seams

brown, plastic eyes with black pupils, sewn in on integral short, round shanks

typical "Grisly" oversized head

beige, felt paw-pads

black, horizontally stitched, lozenge-shaped nose; inverted-Y-shaped mouth

original blue, rayon bow

feet with no pads

red mohair plush (one of 11 available colours)

c.1983 Grisly Spielwaren
Height: 18cm (7in)

Karl Unfrecht founded this company in 1954; his two children took it over after his death in 1980. Pre-1964 bears had inset muzzles and metal chest buttons with a "Grisly" logo. The company's small, coloured bears proved popular exports for the US collectors' market.

Printed tag

inset muzzle of short pile, pale golden mohair plush

black, horizontally stitched, triangular nose; inverted-Y-shaped mouth

beige mohair plush; wood-wool stuffing

unusual body made up of one front and two back pieces

slightly cupped ears sewn over facial seams

brown, glass eyes with black pupils on wire shanks

pale peach-coloured, felt pads; three black claws stitched across plush

c.1959–60 Hans Clemens
Height: 40cm (16in)

Clemens founded his company in 1949. The first teddy bears were made, with his sister's help, from army blankets. This bear has the triangular, metal chest-tag introduced in 1957. It was replaced by plastic in 1963, but reintroduced in 1968, and it is still used today.

Printed tag

Germany: post-1945

ZOTTY LOOK-ALIKES; SYNTHETIC MATERIALS

Certain German manufacturers borrowed ideas from Steiff's novelty lines of the 1950s, such as the popular Zotty range (see p.111). Both of the Hermann factories (see pp.96–99) and Clemens produced their own Zotty bears, while other firms hinted at the Zotty design by combining shaggy fur and an open mouth with inset muzzle. The traditional teddy remained popular, while incorporating modern materials and safety measures. Cheaper East-Asian imports forced some firms, such as Petz and Eli, to close during the 1970s; others, such as Heunec, assembled some of their bears outside of Germany to cut costs.

1980s BAUMANN & KIENEL

Franz Baumann, the son of Adelheid Hermann (see pp.94–95), and an old friend, Franz Kienel, formed this company in 1951. Its tradename, "Baki", is derived from the two founders' names. Classic designs, such as this example, as well as souvenir Berliner bears, are all traditionally made by hand, as indicated by the embroidered cloth seam-label, at their original factory at Rodach near Coburg. Franz Baumann and his partner's son, Walter, presently manage the company.

Height: 30cm (12in)

Embroidered label

Nose/mouth: the black, triangular nose is horizontally stitched; the mouth is an inverted Y shape.

Bow: the original cream-coloured, ribbon bow is tied around the neck.

Trademark: there is a circular, card chest-tag printed with a scalloped edge seal design resembling the Hermann chest-tag.

Fur/stuffing: the fur is short-pile, golden mohair plush; the bear is stuffed throughout with compact soft stuffing.

Pads/claws: the paw-pads are made from beige felt; three black claws are stitched across the plush.

Ears: the inner edges of the ears are caught into the facial seams and sewn down the sides of the head.

Eyes: the large, safe, plastic eyes are brown with black pupils.

BEAR PROFILE

Notice how this bear follows the traditional design with its protruding muzzle, but with some features reduced: it has a shapeless, narrow body; almost straight limbs of equal length; and the legs have only slight indications of small stubby feet. The embroidered cloth label, sewn into the seam in the lower back, is clearly visible.

Feet: the feet are small and oval.

discoloured, white mohair plush; wood-wool stuffing

amber, glass eyes with black pupils

inset, short, clipped, white, mohair-plush muzzle

vertically stitched, black nose extends down to open mouth with felt palate and painted tongue

short, plush pads; inner edge ends in Zotty-style point

large, oval, cream, plush foot-pads; three large, airbrushed claws

unusual mauve tipping

c.1960 HUGO KOCH

Height: 30cm (12in)

Hugo Koch's logo, seen on the tag, depicts a bear wearing a chef's hat and holding a spoon (Koch is German for cook). This bear's design loosely follows Steiff's Zotty (see p.111) and the earlier Teddy Baby (see p.37) with its shaggy, tipped plush, open mouth, and "begging" paws.

Printed tag

amber, plastic, button-like eyes

large, narrow, flat ears sewn down sides of head

small, rounded, brown, vertically stitched nose across point of muzzle; no mouth

pointed muzzle, shaved to reveal woven backing and central seam

short, tubular arms with no pads or claws

printed, red trademark on gold paper tag tied with yellow cord around neck

all-in-one legs and body; small feet allow bear to stand up; no pads or claws

brown, shaggy, synthetic plush; one-piece foam rubber body

1981 KÄTHE KRUSE PUPPEN

Height: 30cm (12in)

Käthe Kruse was renowned for her 1920s–1930s life-like dolls. After World War II, her family firm moved from the East to Donauworth in West Germany. Her daughter, Johanna, introduced teddies to the new production programme (Modell Hanne Kruse) in 1967.

Printed tag

black, horizontally stitched, narrow, oblong nose; inverted Y-shaped, single-stitched mouth

large, flat ears, slotted into head

translucent, amber, glass eyes with black pupils

brown mohair plush; wood-wool stuffing; internal tilt-growler

button made of milk glass with indented red symbol

beige, felt paw-pads

body made of single piece of fabric

c.1950s PETZ COMPANY

Height: 56cm (22½in)

This Neustadt-based company made soft toys and traditional teddy bears for German department stores until 1974. Marked with glass chest buttons, those produced just after World War II also bore cloth tags reading "Original Petz US Zone".

Glass button

black, safe, plastic, button eyes

cupped ears

traditional protruding muzzle

black, horizontally stitched, triangular nose; inverted-V-shaped mouth

brown, short-pile mohair plush; soft-stuffed throughout

red, plastic trademark with gold, embossed lettering

curved, tapering arms

dark brown, felt pads; no claws

large feet

1983 ALTHANS

Height: 43cm (17in)

This classic design bear with a humped back and safe, plastic, button eyes carries the "Albico" trademark, used by Althans (see p.115) from the early 1950s to the 1980s. "Albico" is derived from the first two letter of Althans, Birkig, and Coburg.

Embossed tag

Switzerland & Austria: post-1945

FIRMS BASED IN ZÜRICH AND GRAZ

Since the 1920s, Switzerland has exported its famed musical mechanisms to the United States, United Kingdom, and Germany, for use in teddy bears. The Swiss did not generally make teddy bears themselves, although the company MCZ Schweizer Plüschtierchen (meaning little Swiss plush animals) operated after World War II. A number of Austrian teddy-bear manufacturers, including Schwika, Fechter, and Schenker, based in Graz, and SAF in Mittendorf, also existed in the post-war era. The Berg company in Fieberbrunn is currently the largest teddy-bear manufacturer in Austria.

1950s MUTZLI

Early MCZ bears carried metal, chest or ear buttons; the button featured the company logo, a white teddy-bear glove-puppet and the tradename "Mutzli" (Swiss-German for little bear). MCZ probably stands for "Mutzli Company Zürich". This Swiss firm, based in Zürich, also produced bears dressed as little girls, boys, and cooks, as well as floppy, unjointed bears (including one with a rattle in each paw).

Height: 34cm (13½in)

Printed button

Nose/mouth: *the vertically stitched, oblong, black nose is typical of Mutzli bears; the mouth is an inverted Y shape, with only a short, vertical stitch.*

Chest: *a horizontal stitch across the centre of the chest probably indicates the position of the original swing-tag.*

Claws: *three black claws extend across the mohair plush on each foot and paw.*

Fur: *the fur is short-pile, pale beige mohair plush; the bear is stuffed with wood-wool.*

Ears: *the small, cupped ears are centred over the facial seams.*

Eyes: *the eyes are brown glass with black pupils.*

Trademark: *the printed, metal button is secured to the chest.*

BEAR PROFILE

Notice how this bear's slightly blunted muzzle occupies most of its face. It has a slight hump on its back, limbs of equal length, tapering arms, and small, oval-shaped feet.

Limbs: *the limbs are fully jointed, with arms and legs of equal length.*

Pads: *the foot-pads and left paw-pad have been repaired with pale peach-coloured felt, matching the original pads.*

pale yellow, short-pile, mohair plush; compact, synthetic fibre stuffing

small ears, sewn across facial seams

brown, glass eyes with black pupils

typical expansive forehead with small, flattened muzzle

short, slightly curved arms

dark brown, vertically stitched, round nose; wide, inverted-Y-shaped mouth

short legs

1980S BERG   Height: 14cm (5½in)

Berg made its first bears from army blankets after World War II, and began using plush in 1951. A cloth label with "Berg", and occasionally "Made in Austria", was sewn into the ear or body. *Tiere mit Herz* ("animals with heart") eventually became Berg's trademark. The red metal heart is attached to the chest. Sometimes fabric labels were also used.

large, flat ears

label with brown, embroidered bear motif

reddish orange, glass eyes with black pupils

black, outlined top lip; felt palate with red, felt tongue

black, vertically stitched, shield-shaped nose

shaggy, light golden mohair plush; wood-wool stuffing; tilt-growler

oval feet

beige, felt pads with no claws

1950S–1960S FECHTER   Height: 55cm (22in)

Wilhelm and Berta Fechter started as a small, cottage industry in Graz, Austria, after World War II. They opened a factory in 1948, but ceased business in 1978. This typical Fechter bear came from unsold warehouse stock brought to California in 1983.

Embroidered label

reddish brown, glass eyes with black pupils, sewn-in

inset muzzle of short-pile, beige mohair plush

brown, vertically stitched, shield-shaped nose

peach-coloured, felt palate with red, felt tongue; lips outlined with black paint

light brown mohair plush; wood-wool stuffing

arms curve downwards in Steiff Teddy Baby fashion (see p.37)

narrow ankles and large, slender, oval feet

peach-coloured, felt pads; no claws

1950S–1960S SCHWIKA   Height: 25cm (10in)

Like Fechter, Schwika was based in Graz, Austria, and its bears (distinguished by an embossed, round, metal button attached to the left ear with a red cord) were similar in design to Fechter's bears. The curved, slender wrists are typical of this Zotty-like model.

Embossed button

cupped ears sewn across facial seams

brown, glass eyes with black pupils

black, vertically stitched, square nose; inverted-V-shaped mouth

protruding muzzle

brown mohair plush; soft-stuffed limbs; wood-wool elsewhere

original green, rayon, ribbon

mint condition, beige, felt pads

fully jointed limbs and head

1982 MUTZLI   Height: 33cm (13in)

Only 600 of these Jubilee Bears were made, of which 150 were exported to the US. The card chest-tag, with bear motif, and the basic Mutzli bear design, changed little from the 1950s, although in later years Felpa AG of Aarau, Switzerland produced the bears.

Printed tag

Merrythought: 1940s–60s

CHEEKY DESIGN AND OTHER POST-WAR NOVELTY BEARS

The Cheeky design was so named during the 1956 British Toy Fair because of the bear's wide smile. The "bell in ear" concept was later borrowed by other manufacturers as well as being used again by Merrythought in its Pastel Bear of 1957, a soft-stuffed and unjointed, artificial-silk plush bear.

Merrythought reused the Cheeky design in different plushes and again, in 1962, with an open mouth. From the late 1950s on, the company also produced many soft toys based on television or movie cartoon characters – Sooty, a British TV glove puppet appeared in 1960, and Disney's Winnie the Pooh in 1966.

1966–68 MR. TWISTY CHEEKY

Mr. and Mrs. Twisty Cheeky formed part of a range of comical, dressed, standing toys that was heralded, in 1965, by Mr. and Mrs. Twisty Bear, who could be "twisted" into different positions with the aid of an internal wire frame. Mr. Twisty Cheeky, illustrated here, is the smaller of the two sizes that were manufactured. He wears removable red dungarees with braces, which are fastened at the back with Velcro. His partner, Mrs. Twisty Cheeky, wore a skirt and pinafore.

Height: 28cm (11in)

Printed label

Fur: only the head is made of golden mohair plush.

Eyes: the safe, plastic, orange-coloured eyes have black pupils.

Nose and mouth: the nose is a tall, rectangular shape, vertically stitched in black; two curved stitches form the wide Cheeky smile.

Paws: the white, woven fabric paws have well-defined thumbs.

Collar: the white, felt collar is original; the original ribbon bow-tie is missing.

Dungarees: the red, woven fabric, now very faded, would have been bright red originally. There is a blue patch on the left knee.

Feet: the very large, clown-like feet are made of dark brown, woven fabric.

Muzzle: the typical Cheeky muzzle, made of pale golden velveteen, is a protruding, oval shape.

Body: the body is made from sky-blue woven fabric. The internal wire frame allows the body and limbs to be twisted into various positions.

BEAR PROFILE

From this angle you can see clearly the bear's bulbous head, with large ears positioned low down. The pert muzzle and wide smile are important features of the Cheeky design, as are the pot-belly and the long, flat feet.

unique domed head

large ears with metal bell sewn inside

safe, lock-in, plastic eyes

inset, golden, velveteen muzzle

tightly bound, black, vertically stitched nose at tip of muzzle; wide smile formed by four long stitches

curly, honey-coloured nylon plush

unusual large, circular pads; four claws across seams

brown, felt pads with five claws across seams

c.1960 CHEEKY; NYLON PLUSH

Height: 38cm (15in)

The Cheeky registered design, with its unique domed head and large, flat ears, each containing a bell, first appeared in the 1957 catalogue. It was originally produced in artificial-silk plush or golden mohair plush; nylon plush was also used from 1960.

MERRYTHOUGHT IRONBRIDGE.SHROPS. MADE IN ENGLAND REGᴰ DESIGN

Printed label

Mohican-style scalp lock of long, silvery grey mohair plush

clear, glass eyes, painted white on back; sewn in on wire shanks

discoloured, white mohair plush on chest and insides of ears; brown elsewhere

beige, velveteen muzzle, of similar design to that of Cheeky

slightly S-shaped arms

oval, beige, felt pads

beige, velveteen feet; beige, felt pads

1949–56 PUNKINHEAD

Height: 42cm (16½in)

Cheeky existed in a different form in Canada, as the mascot for Eaton's department store in Toronto. He became the hero of several storybooks, as well as the leader of the annual Santa Claus parade. A replica Ancestor of Cheeky appeared in 1986.

MERRYTHOUGHT HYGIENIC TOYS MADE IN ENGLAND

Printed label

amber, glass eyes with black pupils, sewn in on wire shanks

large, pointed ears with blue, felt linings

bluebird motif added by Donald Campbell, who named all his vehicles "Bluebird"

black, vertically stitched nose

original red, felt coat with pocket; fastened with two white buttons

all-in-one body, arms, and legs; bulbous thighs

blue, felt feet

1956–57 MR WHOPPIT

Height: 23cm (9in)

This bear represents one of three characters from *Robin* comic produced as soft toys in the mid-1950s. He belonged to world land and water speed record-maker, Donald Campbell. The kapok filling allowed the bear to float to the surface of Coniston Water, England, after Donald Campbell's fatal record attempt in 1967. Merrythought made a replica in 1992.

flat, white, plastic eyes; painted, black pupils with white "glints"; eyelashes drawn in above eyes

beige, velveteen, heart-shaped face, with inset muzzle of same material

wide, smiling, W-shaped mouth, drawn in on this factory sample

wide, black, vertically stitched nose, with outer stitches dropped

original pink ribbon bow

round, felt pads, machine-stitched in place

jointed arms and head

faded, golden mohair plush

shoe-shaped, beige, velveteen feet; brown, felt pads reinforced with card; three claws drawn in

1962–63 PETER BEAR

Height: 34cm (13½in)

This very rare, caricatured bear with unjointed legs (the one shown here is a factory sample) was produced briefly, in one size only, and has the same wide smile as Punkinhead and Cheeky. The "googly" eyes give him an endearing expression.

MERRYTHOUGHT IRONBRIDGE.SHROPS. MADE IN ENGLAND

Printed label

Wendy Boston: 1945-76

DEVELOPMENT OF FIRST FULLY WASHABLE TEDDY BEAR

Ken and Wendy Williams (*née* Boston) started their pioneering, soft-toy business in south Wales after World War II and moved to larger premises, at Crickhowell and Abergavenny, in 1948. As Wendy Boston (Crickhowell) Ltd., they invented the safe, screw-locked, plastic eye and then, in 1954, the first washable teddy bear, which revolutionized the soft-toy industry. A decade later, as Wendy Boston Playsafe Toys Ltd., they were producing over a quarter of the UK's total, soft-toy exports. In 1968, they were taken over by Denys Fisher Toys (subsequently Palitoy and General Mills), but the factory closed in 1976.

c.1963 LARGE; NYLON

During the early 1960s, Wendy Boston produced this unjointed, foam-filled bear in 19 sizes – from 23cm (9in) to 1.83m (6ft) – mostly in white, gold, honey, and honey-tipped, brown nylon plush. It was first shown on British television in 1955, being put through a mangle. Hoover awarded the bear a "certificate of washability". The large ears, cut all-in-one with the head, were designed to be pegged to a washing line without strain.

Claws: *three black claws across short-pile plush of paw-pads.*

Height: 55cm (22in)   Printed label

Pads: *the short-pile, nylon-plush pads at the end of the stocky legs are oval in shape.*

Eyes: *each screw-locked eye has an outer ring of amber-coloured plastic; a black, nylon screw and bolt form the pupil.*

Nose: *the black, tightly bound, nose is vertically stitched.*

BEAR PROFILE

This typical Wendy Boston, unjointed bear, made of soft, shaggy nylon plush, inspires a small child's affection, with the slightly curved arms stretching out to demand a hug; the straight, legs have no ankle or foot definition.

Fur/stuffing: *the fur is shaggy, honey-coloured nylon plush; the bear is stuffed throughout with granulated foam-rubber – a material originally prized for its washability and lightness, but which later proved to be a fire hazard, as it gives off toxic fumes when alight.*

amber-coloured, safe, plastic eyes with small, black pupils; attached by screw-on nut at back of eye

black, vertically stitched, rectangular nose with inverted-T-shaped mouth

curved, unjointed arms, projecting outwards

clipped, short-pile mohair plush on muzzle

three claws on pads

slightly discoloured, white mohair plush

printed label sewn into leg seam

short-pile, clipped, mohair-plush pads

c.1955 WHITE MOHAIR

Height: 36cm (14½in)

This unjointed bear is one of Wendy Boston's earlier bears made from mohair plush supplied by Norton (Weaving) Ltd. of Yorkshire. In 1987, House of Nisbet produced a replica of a golden, mohair-plush Wendy Boston bear that once belonged to Peter Bull.

Printed label

---

ears cut all-in-one with head

small, three-part, Wendy Boston patent, safe, plastic eyes

inset, rounded, blunt muzzle of white, short-pile nylon plush

black, vertically stitched, rectangular nose; inverted-Y-shaped mouth

three black claws stitched over paw seams

short-pile, pink, nylon plush; foam-rubber stuffing

legs in permanent sitting position

c.1955 SMALL; NYLON

Height: 24cm (9½in)

One of the smallest Wendy Boston bears of this period, the design was available in white, gold, honey, blue, and pink. The label reads "Wash in lukewarm suds" (some specify "Persil" – a washing-powder whose maker endorsed Wendy Boston bears).

Printed label

---

three-part, Wendy Boston patent, safe, plastic eyes

golden yellow, nylon-plush head, feet, and paws

small, rounded, yellow, plush paws; no claws

inset, rounded, blunt muzzle

outstretched, pink, brushed-nylon arms

red, fringed trim at neck and waist (later additions)

tartan trousers and red, brushed-nylon top form body; granulated foam-rubber stuffing

pointed, "realistic" feet

1960 DRESSED, ALL-IN-ONE TEDDY

Height: 30cm (12in)

Wendy Boston made dressed soft toys from the early 1950s. Its costume formed the body; the paws and head were of plush. This example wears Royal Stewart tartan, Dutch-style trousers. The red, fringed trim at neck and waist are later additions.

Printed label

---

dark beige nylon plush

separate, traditional-style ears

small, black, vertically stitched, rectangular nose

white, nylon-plush, inset muzzle

curved, outstretched, unjointed arms

slightly defined feet, unlike completely straight legs of original Wendy Boston bears

white, nylon-plush pads

1972 MUSICAL; NYLON

Height: 33cm (13in)

This bear was produced after the takeover by Denys Fisher Toys. Its safe, plastic eyes are not the typical Wendy Boston, three-part type. The musical box, which plays *The Teddy Bears' Picnic*, is inside the head; a key projects from the back of the head.

Printed label

UK: post-World War II – c.1970

BRITISH INDUSTRY STRUGGLES; SHEEPSKIN AND TRADITIONAL

Several new companies were established in the UK after World War II. Due to the rationing of traditional mohair at the time, these companies made teddy bears of sheepskin, a material that remained popular until the 1960s. The economic climate in Britain during the 1970s forced the demise of many newly formed traditional teddy-bear manufacturers: Gwentoys Ltd. (established in 1965) was taken over by Dean's in 1972; Acton Toycraft Ltd. (established in 1964) closed in the 1970s; and Real Soft Toys (established in 1969) was later taken over by Lefray Ltd., another post-war firm.

1965–72 GWENTOYS LTD.

The general shape of this teddy bear is reminiscent of the Chiltern Hugmee range manufactured in the late 1950s and early 1960s. It also shares such features as nose design, velveteen pads, and seam-label design and positioning. The similarities are not surprising since Gwentoys Ltd., based in Pontypool, was formed by three former managers of the Chiltern factory, also located in Pontypool, following the latter's takeover by the Dunbee-Combex group. "Gwentoys" is derived from Gwent, the old Welsh name for Monmouthshire (recently renamed Gwent), the county in which Pontypool is situated .

Height: 58cm (23in)   Printed label

HYGIENIC TOYS MADE IN ENGLAND BY GWENTOYS LTD.

Nose: *the black, squarish nose, vertically stitched across the junction of the facial seams, is Chiltern-like. The mouth is an inverted Y shape.*

Fur/stuffing/squeaker: *the fur is golden mohair plush, soft-stuffed except for the muzzle, which is stuffed with wood-wool. The bear has a tilt- squeaker.*

Pads: *the beige, velveteen pads are in perfect condition except for a few stains on the right foot. There are no claws.*

Ears: *the large, flat ears are sewn across the facial seams.*

Eyes: *the amber and black, safe, plastic eyes are fixed into the facial seams with washers.*

BEAR PROFILE

This bear's straight head and gently rounded muzzle is evocative of the earlier, flat-faced Hugmees. At this angle, you can see how the bear exemplifies archetypal features of the British 1960s bear with its shorter limbs, small, rounded feet, and lack of claws. The blue on white, printed label is sewn into the side-seam under the left arm.

orange and black, plastic eyes

area around eyes, ears, and mouth trimmed with electric clippers

cinnamon-coloured, dyed sheepskin

straight legs with dark brown, sheepskin pads

only two black knots remain of original, vertically stitched, Tinka-Bell square nose

swivel-jointed, short, curved arms

label sewn into foot-pad seam

1964 PLUMMER, WANDLESS & CO.   Height: 43cm (17in)

This is one of 70,000 sheepskin teddy bears produced annually by this Worthing-based firm during the mid-1960s. It was available in eight sizes and was exported worldwide. The company, which was founded in 1946, was sold in 1972.

A Tinka-Bell PRODUCT

Printed label

realistic, black, moulded plastic nose, locked in with washer

original blue, satin ribbon

soft, dense, golden lambskin; musical box plays Brahms' Lullaby

cheap, orange, translucent, plastic eyes on wire shanks; pupils painted black behind

triangular head with upturned muzzle moves from side to side when musical box plays

short, straight arms and legs with small feet

C.1957 LECO TOYS (WEST END) LTD.   Height: 33cm (13in)

This bear was one of a 1957 range of animated musical items produced by Leco Toys, a London company established by Ludwig and Martha Levy. The company moved to larger premises in 1965, but ceased business in the early 1970s.

MUSICAL LECO

Printed card swing-tag

large, flat ears sewn into horizontal dart across facial seams

black, vertically stitched, square nose, with inverted-Y-shaped mouth

short, golden mohair plush; cotton "sub" stuffing

black "pupils" are an optical illusion – created by hollow space on integral shank of plastic eye

short arms with chocolate-brown velveteen pads

fat thighs and stubby feet; no claws

MID-1960S LEFRAY LTD.   Height: 40cm (16in)

Throughout the 1960s, Lefray Ltd. (established in 1948) was based in St Albans, Hertfordshire; this bear was probably made shortly before the company's move to Aberbeeg, Gwent, in south Wales, where it is still operating.

LEFRAY ENGLAND TOYS ENGLAND

Printed label

black, tightly bound, vertically stitched oblong nose with black, felt underlay

soft, cream, Rexine pads, cracked to reveal woven backing; no claws

large, translucent, orange, plastic eyes with black pupils, on wire shanks, sewn into face and knotted at back

curly, white wool and, possibly, synthetic mix plush

large, narrow feet; thick thighs

1960S ACTON TOYCRAFT LTD.   Height: 63cm (25in)

In 1964, J.K. Farnell split into two operations, Acton Toycraft taking over the company's works in Acton, west London, and trading as "Twyford". Several light-coloured Twyford bears have been found with red, felt pads, also used by Farnell.

A TWYFORD PRODUCT MADE IN ENGLAND ACTON TOYCRAFT LONDON

Printed label

Dean's: c.1960-80

TRADITIONAL AND UNJOINTED BEARS MADE BY SUBSIDIARIES

T he 1960s and 1970s was an era of change for Dean's Rag Book Company Ltd. Its main production continued at the factory in Rye, Sussex, which was extended in 1961. The company used the Childsplay Toys trademark until 1965, when Childsplay Ltd. (one of two divisions formed in the 1950s, the other being Merton Toys Ltd.) became Dean's Childsplay Toys Ltd. From that time, the familiar fighting dogs logo was dropped from the label. In 1974, two years after the buyout of Gwentoys, some production moved from Rye to Pontypool in south Wales. The Rye plant eventually closed in 1980.

c.1980 DEAN'S/GWENTOY GROUP

Dean's continued Gwentoy's line of teddy bears after buying out the company in 1972 (see p.124),with the label indicating the use of both the Pontypool and the Rye factories. This branch of the Dean's/Gwentoy Group specialized in the cheaper end of the market, supplying bears wholesale for chainstores and the mail-order trade. Although this bear is traditionally styled with jointed arms and legs, the stiff, unjointed neck denotes a cheaper toy.

Height: 31cm (12½in)　　　　　Printed label

Ears: *the cupped ears are positioned towards the back of the head, caught into the facial seams, and sewn down the sides of the head.*

Eyes: *the brown and black, safe, plastic, lock-in eyes are set on the outer edges of the facial seams.*

Nose/mouth: *the black, vertically stitched, shield-shaped nose and inverted-V-shaped, single-stitched mouth are joined by a tiny, vertical stitch.*

Bow: *the red, nylon bow is original.*

BEAR PROFILE
This is a simplified version of the Gwentoys example shown previously (see p.124). The limbs are shorter, however, and the head is less Chiltern-like and more typical of a Dean's design, with the rounded muzzle projecting almost at right angles to the face. The short limbs, small, rounded feet, and lack of claws, are typical features of 1960s British bears.

Trademark: *the printed, cloth label is sewn into the left side-seam, just above the leg joint.*

Fur: *the short-pile, golden mohair plush is in perfect condition; the bear is filled with soft, synthetic wadding.*

Pads: *the pads are made from dark brown, brushed, knitted, synthetic fabric; there are no claws.*

brown, plastic eyes
with black pupils
and integral shanks,
sewn into face

large, flat ears sewn
across facial seams

replacement wide,
black, embroidered,
inverted-V-shaped
mouth

fat shoulders;
slightly curved
arms with tapering
paws and remains
of pink claws

golden mohair
plush; soft stuffing,
probably "sub";
wood-wool around
internal squeaker

replacement
beige, felt pads;
original woven
fabric beneath

short, fat
legs
and
stumpy
feet

all-in-one ears, made
from same fabric as
heart-shaped head

square, black,
vertically stitched
nose and inverted-Y-
shaped mouth

brown and black,
safe, plastic eyes

inset, egg-
shaped muzzle
with central dart,
made from same
fabric as pads

rust-coloured,
knitted, brushed-
nylon pads

straight, stick-like feet

c.1960 CHILDSPLAY TOYS
Height: 38cm (15in)

This bear's moulded, soft rubber nose, a feature
from the mid-1950s, and usually sewn on, has been
glued, perhaps by a repairer. The Childsplay Toys
label, sewn inside the right arm joint, was first used
in 1956, after Dean's move to Rye in Sussex.

Printed label

LATE 1960S DEAN'S CHILDSPLAY TOYS
Height: 28cm (11in)

In 1965, Dean's produced an unjointed, Bri-Nylon
plush bear in four large sizes. In the 1960s and
70s Dean's increasingly used synthetic fabrics,
such as the curly, brown plush and the brushed-
nylon pads and muzzle illustrated here.

Printed label

large, cupped
ears, cut from
two different
cloths; set wide
apart

large, black,
bulbous, safe,
plastic, eyes

inset, wool-like,
short, synthetic-
plush muzzle

square, black nose,
vertically stitched and
sewn centrally across
muzzle seam

triangular,
white chest
plate

limbs and
rounded body
cut all-in-one

large, wide
feet with three
black claws
tightly sewn
across plush,
giving quilted effect

shaggy, golden
nylon plush

black, vertically
stitched, shield-
shaped nose

brown and
black, safe,
plastic eyes

double-stitched,
inverted-Y-shaped
mouth

short, tan
mohair plush;
soft stuffing,
probably
synthetic,
with wood-
wool in muzzle

dark brown,
brushed, knitted,
synthetic pads;
no claws

c.1972 DEAN'S CHILDSPLAY TOYS
Height: 79cm (31in)

This large Super Bear attempts to resemble a real
"spectacled" bear, with its paler chest plate and
eye markings, instead of following the traditional
jointed teddy-bear design. The printed card tag
gives instructions to dry clean.

Printed label

c.1980 DEAN'S/GWENTOY GROUP
Height: 33cm (13in)

This bear has a small, round bell in its left ear,
a feature often used by manufacturers after the
appearance of Merrythought's Cheeky (see p.120).
Dean's used this label on bears from 1972–82, sewn
into the left side-seam, and on other toys until 1986.

Printed label

Steiff: 1960s–90s

NEW TRADITIONAL AND UNJOINTED BEARS; SYNTHETIC FABRICS

Steiff developed a number of designs at this time, notably in the soft-filled, unjointed range of teddies. Zooby of 1964 was an unjointed, standing bear with felt claws, whereas Tapsy was less menacing, with her airbrushed, smiling face and short, sleeveless dress. In 1975,

Steiff revived the ever-popular Zotty with a new Minky Zotty in a mink-like synthetic plush. During this time, manufacturers increasingly used man-made fabrics for the outer skin, and foam-rubber for the filling. They used airbrushing techniques, with non-toxic paints, for defining delicate facial features.

1966–90s ORIGINAL TEDDY

This is the Original Teddy design which was first introduced in 1966. A revised version of the bear was launched in 1992. The design represents a complete change for Steiff, with its inset, heart-shaped muzzle of clipped mohair plush. Although this particular example is made from honey-coloured mohair plush, the design is also available in beige, caramel, and chocolate-brown and, as always, comes in numerous sizes. This bear carries a post-1972 card chest-tag and a post-1982 woven label in the ear, attached by an incised, cursive "button in ear".

Height: 35cm (14in)   Incised button and label

Muzzle: *the unusual, heart-shaped muzzle, made from clipped mohair plush, matches the body plush.*

Nose: *the brown, shield-shaped nose is vertically stitched; the inverted-V-shaped mouth has a rather gruff expression.*

Arms: *the arms are tapered and curve upwards at the paws.*

Chest-tag: *the Steiff card tag is secured to the chest.*

Fur: *the long mohair plush is honey coloured; the stuffing is synthetic.*

Legs: *the legs are shorter than those of the early Steiff bears; the feet are large.*

BEAR PROFILE

In profile, this bear's unusual, heart-shaped, inset muzzle, which protrudes in the traditional manner, is clearly seen. The relatively long arms are slightly curved, like those of the old bears. However, the legs are short and stubby, although the feet are large. Unlike the early Steiffs, the back is almost completely straight.

Pads: *the pads are made from golden Dralon, a brushed, synthetic fabric.*

1980s COSY TEDDY Height: 35cm (14in)

safe, plastic, lock-in eyes with airbrushed, brown "tear" falling from base of eye

"button in ear" with 1980s yellow product label behind

mouth represented by single, airbrushed, brown dot

brown, shield-shaped, vertically stitched nose

oatmeal-coloured, plush chest plate and muzzle

brown plush body, head, and limbs

card chest tag with bear's name

part-synthetic plush is 70% acrylic and 30% cotton

light brown plush pads

This is a simplified version of a bear that first appeared in Steiff's programme in the 1960s, when it was much more Zotty-like in design. This bear is unjointed, and the mouth is represented by a single, airbrushed, brown dot.

Incised button and label

1967 LULLY Height: 20cm (8in)

nutmeg-brown plush head, muzzle, and limbs; clipped muzzle

small, silver-coloured button with incised, cursive "Steiff"; typical 1967–77, stiff, yellow, linen tag

typical, shield-shaped, vertically stitched nose

felt, open mouth with airbrushed tongue and lips

original blue ribbon

shaggy, honey-gold plush on paws and feet

white, plush chest plate

unjointed bear in standing position

wool and cotton mix plush; soft-stuffed

This unjointed baby bear was made in a small size, to be a perfect comforter for a young child. Its name is from the German *einlullen*, meaning to lull a restless infant. Lully is made from several different colours of wool/cotton plush.

Incised button and label

1980 MOLLY-TEDDY Height: 55cm (22in)

black, soft, plastic, leather-like nose, folded and padded to appear realistic

Steiff "button in ear" and cloth product label

large, black, safe, plastic, button eyes

inverted-Y-shaped mouth, airbrushed in black with single, red dot representing tongue

clipped muzzle and pads

white, plush chest plate

pale, honey-coloured, 70% acrylic and 25% cotton plush

This bear's name (*mollig* is German for "cosy" or "plump") describes it well, as it is very soft and floppy, and was designed as the perfect cuddly toy for a small child. Steiff produced a similar Molly-Bear, which lies flat on its stomach.

Incised button and label

1960s DRALON PETSY Height: 30cm (12in)

brown, plastic eyes with black pupils; sewn in and finished off at back of head

small button with incised, cursive "Steiff"; stiff, yellow, linen label behind

light brown, Dralon plush; wood-wool stuffing in muzzle and head

brown, vertically stitched, oval nose

fully jointed

pale peach, brushed Dralon pads

Steiff first introduced the new-style Petsy in 1961. It was made of Dralon (a new, German-invented, synthetic fabric), and its body was filled with foam-rubber. A 1984 Petsy was the first, fully jointed, machine-washable Steiff teddy bear.

Incised button and label

Chad Valley: 1960-78

TRADITIONAL AND UNJOINTED BRITISH BEARS: CHILTERN/CHAD VALLEY TAKEOVER

In 1960, when it celebrated its centenary, Chad Valley was operating seven factories and employing over 1,000 workers. After Chiltern Toys became a subsidiary in 1967, it became the largest manufacturer of soft toys in the UK. The 1970s recession, however, led to the closure of the Wrekin Works at Wellington, leaving Pontypool as the company's only surviving soft-toy plant. In 1978, Chad Valley was taken over by Palitoy, later to be bought by US-owned Kenner Parker. The tradename was bought in 1988 by Woolworths, who introduced a new range of Chad Valley soft toys, made in East Asia.

C.1960 SUPER; MOHAIR BLEND

1960s Chad Valley catalogues advertised four ranges of traditionally jointed bears: De-Luxe in London Gold mohair plush; Super in honey or gold blended mohair plush; Popular in gold blended mohair plush; and Nylon in white and, later, lemon plush with red paws. The firm also produced musical and talking teddy bears at this time.

Height: 58cm (23in)

HYGIENIC TOYS
MADE IN ENGLAND BY
THE CHAD VALLEY CO. Lt

Printed label

Head: the head is filled with wood-wool stuffing.

Eyes: the orange and black, plastic eyes, on wire shanks, are sewn into the face, and knotted at the back of the head.

Nose/mouth: the wide, bound, vertically stitched nose is characteristic of many Chad Valley bears; two straight, black stitches form the mouth.

Fur: the honey-coloured fur is a blend of nylon and mohair plush, on a woven backing. The mixture has a less silky finish than pure mohair.

Body/limbs: the body and limbs are stuffed with "sub"; the limbs are fully jointed.

Trademark: the remains of the original square, Royal Warrant label are visible on the right foot-pad.

BEAR PROFILE
This large bear clearly shows many typical Chad Valley features: the distinctive head has a slightly protruding muzzle, a wide, bound nose, and large, flat ears sewn centrally across the facial seams. The back is straight with wide shoulders and curved, tapering arms, which are the same length as the legs. The fat thighs and large feet are also typical.

Pads: the Rexine on the foot- and paw-pads has worn away to reveal the woven fabric beneath.

reddish brown, safe, plastic eyes with black pupils

moulded, black, safe, plastic nose

original nylon ribbon bow

"honey-pot" attached to paws with Velcro

dark brown, brushed-nylon pads

inner edge of ear folded and sewn into facial seam; rest of ear sewn into dart down side of head

single stitch, inverted-Y-shaped mouth

golden nylon plush on knitted backing

unjointed limbs in permanent, sitting position

c.1967–77 UNJOINTED; NYLON
Height: 25cm (10in)

This unjointed bear, with legs in a permanent sitting position, holds a honey-pot made of soft-stuffed, brushed-nylon fabric, attached to the paws with Velcro. The label in the left side-seam indicates that the bear was made after the Chiltern takeover in 1967.

Printed label

ears sewn across head; inner edge begins at facial seams

inset, shaved, mohair muzzle

golden mohair plush, body filled with soft stuffing, possibly "sub"

unjointed legs in permanent, sitting position

round, bulbous head with high forehead

brown, safe, plastic eyes with black pupils

moulded, black, safe, plastic nose; no mouth

outstretched arms fixed in position

beige, knitted, synthetic pads; no claws

c.1967–77 UNJOINTED; MOHAIR
Height: 39cm (15½in)

Although unjointed like the bear (left), this example is made from good quality, golden mohair plush with random dark strands, as seen in Chiltern's Hugmee bears (see pp.108-09), indicating its Pontypool origins. The label is sewn into the top of the left leg-seam.

Printed label

ears and head made from single piece of fabric; head stuffed with wood-wool

inset, slightly protruding muzzle; inverted-Y-shaped mouth

red, white, and blue artificial-silk plush (back of bear is blue)

pale blue, safe, plastic eyes with black pupils date bear to early 1960s

unusual triangular, black, felt nose

all-in-one body, arms, and legs

EARLY 1960s ARTIFICIAL SILK
Height: 58cm (23in)

This patriotic bear of red, white, and blue artificial-silk plush is unjointed; the body and legs are cut from one piece of fabric. Chad Valley also produced a cheaper range of unjointed, flame-resistant, acrylic plush bears and pandas, under the tradename "Acme".

Printed label

brown, safe, plastic eyes with black pupils

vertically stitched, black nose; single horizontal stitch across top

original orange ribbon bow

high-quality, golden mohair plush; body filled with synthetic waste stuffing; internal red, plastic, concertina-style squeaker

small, pointed, tear-shaped feet with brown, synthetic pads; no claws

1977 JOINTED; MOHAIR
Height: 30cm (12in)

Chad Valley manufactured this classic mohair-plush bear shortly before the takeover by Palitoy; it would have been made at the Pontypool works. It has a slight resemblance to earlier Chad Valley bears, but has lost the typical wide, bound nose.

Printed card-tag

Pedigree: 1960s–80s

WASHABLE, SYNTHETIC MATERIALS; NEW CANTERBURY LABEL

I n the 1960s, Pedigree factories in Northern Ireland and New Zealand were making teddy bears. This period saw an increase in the use of washable, synthetic materials, such as nylon plushes and foam-rubber stuffing. Pedigree later introduced novelties, such as the battery-operated Simon the Walking Bear and a talking Rupert Bear. In 1966, when the Lines Brothers group reorganized into Rovex Tri-ang Ltd., Pedigree – a subsidiary of Lines Brothers – moved all its soft-toy production to Canterbury, England. Dunbee-Combex-Marx took over Lines in 1972. Pedigree ceased business in 1988.

EARLY 1960S NYLON; UNJOINTED

Once pictured in a small girl's arms on the front cover of a 1961 catalogue, this cream-coloured, nylon plush bear with foam-rubber stuffing is fully washable. It is almost identical to the Wendy Boston design (see pp.122–23), with its outstretched arms, all-in-one ears and head, and safe, lock-in, plastic eyes. However, the remains of a Pedigree label sewn into the neck-seam verifies its origins.

Height: 35cm (14in)   Printed label

Ears: *the ears, cut all-in-one with the rest of the bear, are simple projections of the head.*

Eyes: *the safe, plastic eyes closely follow the Wendy Boston design; they have a central, opaque, black pupil fused onto a translucent, amber surround.*

Nose: *this bear's vertically stitched, oblong, black nose has lost a few stitches on the left.*

Mouth: *the typical Pedigree mouth is a double-stitched, inverted T shape.*

BEAR PROFILE

The similarity between this Pedigree bear and the Wendy Boston design is evident in the flattened, rounded muzzle; the ears extending from the large head; the straight back; and in the tubular legs, which are sewn at right angles to the body so that the bear is in a permanent sitting position.

Arms: *the unjointed, slightly curved arms project from the sides of the body.*

Claws: *unusually for Pedigree bears, there are three double-stitched, black claws on each paw.*

Fur: *the slightly shaggy, cream-coloured nylon plush is on a woven backing.*

Legs: *the unjointed legs are made from straight tubes of plush; no feet are discernible.*

large, bulbous head

large, slightly cupped ears

translucent, pale orange and black, safe, plastic eyes

inset muzzle

vertically stitched, oblong, black nose, with inverted-T-shaped mouth

bright yellow, Bri-Nylon plush on woven backing; foam-rubber stuffing

short, curved outstretched arms sewn onto body

disc-jointed legs

clipped plush pads

1960s BRI-NYLON; SEMI-JOINTED   Height: 48cm (19in)

In 1960, "Bri" was registered as a trademark by the British Nylon Spinners Ltd. (part of ICI) of Ponty-pool, Monmouthshire. Pedigree was one of several teddy-bear manufacturers who began using Bri-Nylon products extensively during this decade.

Printed label

translucent orange and black, safe, plastic eyes

large ears with inner edges folded over; sewn into slit in fabric

inset, shaved muzzle

small, vertically stitched, black nose; embroidered, open, smiling mouth

red, felt tongue

shaggy, brown-tipped, beige nylon plush; internal tilt-growler

dark brown, velveteen pads in perfect condition

1960s SHAGGY NYLON; JOINTED   Height: 39cm (15½in)

Although similar to the bear (left) with its large, head and muzzle, this example is fully jointed with wood-wool stuffing in the body and a red, felt tongue. Other versions have three-colour, layered glass eyes, and plush muzzles with open mouths.

Printed label

large, narrow ears, sewn flat across facial seams

brown, safe, plastic eyes

black, safe, moulded plastic nose on inset, clipped, nylon plush muzzle

golden, flame-resistant, nylon plush on knitted backing; internal tilt-growler

black, inverted-T-shaped, mouth

jointed legs and arms of equal length

irregularly shaped, oval feet with no claws

dark brown, synthetic velvet pads

1975 CANTERBURY LABEL   Height: 40cm (16in)

This bear has the new label, designed after Pedigree moved its soft-toy production to Canterbury, England. Ann Wood, designer at the Belfast factory, first introduced the inset muzzle to Pedigree teddy bears in about 1960.

Printed label

white, short-pile nylon plush; soft stuffed throughout

ears made of separate pieces of plush, sewn down sides of head

vertically stitched, square, black nose; inverted-Y-shaped mouth

fused, amber and black, safe, plastic eyes

unjointed, short, straight arms; no pads or claws

straight legs with no feet, pads, or claws

1960s WHITE NYLON; UNJOINTED   Height: 34cm (13½in)

This bear follows the style of earlier Pedigree bears (see pp.92–93) with its bulbous head and fused amber and black, safe, plastic eyes. However, it is made of a synthetic plush and is unjointed, with short, stubby limbs projecting out from the body.

Printed label

Merrythought: 1970s–80s

MODERN "M" DESIGN; TRADITIONAL BEARS AND NOVELTIES

During this period, the traditional, golden mohair "M" teddy (*see p.60*) continued to be made, but additional colours were also introduced. Updating of the design began in 1983 with the Aristocrat Bear, was available in seven sizes, with shaved muzzle, and dropped outer stitch nose design.

Merrythought's popular Cheeky design was reintroduced during the 1970s, and was available in both mohair and synthetic plush. In 1972–73, the London Bears, dressed as Guardsman, Policeman, Beefeater, or Highlander, were introduced; the 45cm (18in) Beefeater and Guardsman bears were reinstated in 1985.

1976 SMALL; TRADITIONAL "M" DESIGN

From 1965 until the present, Merrythought has manufactured a series of traditional, jointed teddy bears in "London Gold" mohair plush, available in nine sizes. This is the smallest size, first added to the range in 1975. In the catalogues, its code name was "GM/10" – "G" refers to the colour (gold); "M" to the style; and "10" to the height in inches. This teddy bear is stuffed with kapok, and with wood-wool in the muzzle.

Height: 25cm (10in)

Printed label

Ears: the large, flat ears are centred over the facial seams.

Eyes: the amber and black, plastic eyes are of the safe, lock-in type.

Nose: the rounded, square nose is vertically stitched in black, with a few horizontal stitches across the top edge – a design introduced in the 1950s.

Ribbon: the red ribbon, tied in a bow around the neck, is original.

Fur: the mohair plush is a colour known in the trade as "London Gold".

Arms: the short, tapering arms end in upward-curving paws with no claws.

Legs: the short, stubby legs end in barely distinguishable small feet; the limbs are fully jointed.

Feet: the oval feet are irregularly shaped, with no claws.

Pads: the pads are made of brown, knitted, synthetic fabric.

BEAR PROFILE
Compare this to the earlier Merrythought bear (*see p.88*), and notice how the design has developed: the muzzle is less protruding; the limbs are shorter and of equal length; the feet are ill-defined; the back is straight.

large, flat ears, sewn across facial seams

brown and black, safe, plastic eyes

brown, knitted, synthetic pads; no claws

tightly bound, black, vertically stitched nose with two horizontal stitches across top

thin body; fully jointed head and limbs

slightly curved, tapering paws

"London Gold" mohair plush; soft-stuffing; wood-wool in muzzle

irregularly shaped, oval feet

1970s MEDIUM; "M" DESIGN
Height: 40cm (16in)

Nine sizes were available in this design, ranging from 35cm to 101cm (14in to 40in), from 1965 onwards, with the addition of the 25cm (10in) and 30cm (12in) sizes from 1981. A 122cm (48in) model was made from 1971 to 1981, and again in 1984.

Printed label

ears set further down sides of head than on "M" design

brown and black, safe, plastic eyes

inverted-Y-shaped, double-stitched mouth

original cream satin bow

new 1980s design, printed chest-tag with Union Jack

nutmeg-coloured, soft, short-pile, synthetic plush; soft stuffing throughout

beige, soft, short-pile, synthetic plush pads

1986 "AR" DESIGN; PLASTIC NOSE
Height: 44cm (17½in)

The "AR" was a new design of traditional, jointed bear, first introduced for the 1986 catalogue. This example is made from nutmeg-coloured synthetic plush, but the design was produced in various colours, always with a moulded, plastic nose.

Printed label

large, flat ears, sewn across facial seams

large head with flat, rounded muzzle and high forehead

black, vertically stitched nose, with horizontal stitches across top, similar to Chad Valley design

brown and black, safe, plastic eyes

arms same length as legs, with slightly curved paws

soft, off-white, synthetic plush on woven backing; soft stuffed throughout

thin body

stubby feet

orange, velveteen pads

1980s "LM" DESIGN
Height: 45cm (18in)

This "Champagne Luxury Bear", an "M" design in a new plush, was first introduced in 1982; two years later it became available in seven sizes. An earlier 1970s range of bears was made in a similar material, described as "champagne mink plush".

Printed label

large, flat, slightly cupped ears, sewn centrally across facial seams

orange and black, safe, plastic eyes

brown, synthetic plush; wood-wool stuffing in muzzle; soft stuffing elsewhere

black, vertically stitched nose, with few horizontal stitches across top; inverted-Y-shaped, double-stitched mouth

slightly curved arms, same length as legs

fully jointed limbs and head

brown, knitted, brushed-nylon pads

small, stubby feet

1974–75 "NY" DESIGN; SYNTHETIC
Height: 39cm (15½in)

In 1974–75, a series of brown bears was produced in six sizes, from 35cm to 122cm (14in to 48in). This example is very threadbare, with much of the pile worn away. It follows the basic "M" design, with large, rounded head, slim body, and short limbs.

Printed label

Australia & New Zealand: 1970–90s

COMPETITION FROM EAST ASIA; GROWTH OF COLLECTORS' BEARS

I n the 1970s, several manufacturers based in Australia (see pp.80–81) and New Zealand – for example, Luvme Toys and Pedigree of Auckland – were forced out of business by cheaper East Asian imports. New Australian firms, including Teddy & Friends, Tomfoolery, and C.A.Toys, emerged, designing the bears themselves, but having them assembled in China or Korea. Jakas remained one of the few firms to make all-Australian bears in the 1980s and 1990s. Smaller firms, such as Sheepskin Products Ltd., Harrisons Textiles, and Robin Rive's Robbity Bob, also appeared, some targeting the collectors' market.

1978 JAKAS SOFT TOYS

This unjointed, synthetic, blue bear with its long, floppy legs is a typical 1970s Jakas design, although some of their bears did have stiff legs. Australia's longest-running children's TV programme *Playschool* featured a similar model. Wendy McDonald, the company's owner since 1989, introduced a limited-edition, synthetic, jointed range in 1991 to meet the growing demand from the collectors' market. She marketed a similar mohair-plush range the following year.

Height: 34cm (13½in)   Embroidered label

Eyes: *the small, blue, safe, plastic eyes have black pupils.*

Head/muzzle: *the head is round with a high forehead and flat muzzle.*

Nose/mouth: *the black, shield-shaped nose is vertically stitched; the inverted-T-shaped mouth is single stitched.*

Arms/claws: *the short, straight arms have no paw-pads, but three black, embroidered claws are stitched across the plush.*

Body: *the body, arms, and legs are made from one piece of plush fabric.*

Fur/stuffing: *the fur is blue nylon plush; the bear is stuffed with foam-rubber pieces.*

Label: *the Jakas Toys embroidered label is stitched to the inside of the right leg.*

BEAR PROFILE

Notice how this typical Jakas design resembles the similarly constructed, British Wendy Boston bears (see pp.122–23). Its rounded head, flattened muzzle, small, squarish body, stubby arms, and long legs (unstuffed at the point where they project out from the torso) all resemble the British manufacturer's design.

Legs: *the legs are long and straight; the feet are small and rounded with no pads or claws.*

black, safe, plastic eyes

large ears, sewn to back of head

inset muzzle of short-pile plush in contrasting colour

brown, vertically stitched, square nose

large, dark brown, short-pile plush pads

soft, shaggy, synthetic plush; soft, synthetic stuffing

printed, cloth label sewn into right foot seam

1989 HARRISONS TEXTILES
Height: 107cm (42in)

Adam was manufactured by Clive and Precille Harrison at their Auckland-based firm (established 1977), exclusively for the US store, Bear Hunt. They sold Harrisons Textiles in 1989, and resumed trading as Bear with Us in 1992.

Printed label

amber, safe, plastic eyes with black pupils

cupped ears, lined with suede

pure New Zealand lambswool, dyed, clipped, and finished by hand; wood-wool stuffing

black, safe, moulded, plastic nose

straight, stumpy legs; hardly distinguishable feet

circular, suede pads

1986 SHEEPSKIN PRODUCTS
Height: 40cm (16in)

This bear, made of pale, golden-dyed lambswool, is also a nightdress case. Valda McCombe, the designer, founded her Auckland business with husband Peter in 1981. Together, they produce the widest range of sheepskin toys in the world.

Printed label

amber, safe, plastic eyes with black pupils

nose consists of twisted piece of brown suede

original peach-coloured, satin, ribbon bow

short, straight arms with pointed paws

soft, dyed, golden-brown New Zealand sheepskin; soft-stuffed throughout

"Lambskin Products" printed label

short, straight, stumpy legs

1982 MAXWELL HAY
Height: 30cm (12in)

Maxwell Hay founded his family-run, sheepskin firm in 1964 in Mount Albert, a suburb of Auckland. The firm made mainly soft toys, adding teddies from 1976 to 1982. Only materials from New Zealand are used on this unjointed bear.

Printed label

amber, safe, plastic eyes with black pupils

large, square head with ears positioned at each corner

inset, rounded muzzle

black, safe, plastic, moulded nose; mouth indicated with black stitches

unjointed, L-shaped arms, with pointed paws and three black claws

bright yellow nylon plush; soft stuffed throughout

straight legs with small, slightly pointed feet

1970s MALROB CUDDLE TOYS
Height: 32cm (12½in)

This yellow, nylon, plush bear has a satinized label with kangaroo logo secured to the base of its left foot. Malrob Cuddle Toys (established in Brisbane, in 1961), specialized in unjointed synthetic bears. The company ceased operations in 1985.

Printed label

US: 1950s–80s

SAFE, SOFT, AND SYNTHETIC BEARS MADE IN EAST ASIA

In the late 1950s and early 1960s, several new companies were formed in the United States: R. Dakin & Co. (1955); California Stuffed Toys (1959); Russ Berrie & Co. (1963); and Princess Soft Toys (1965). They set a trend by manufacturing their bears in East Asia where labour costs were much cheaper. Many old-established firms still flourished, such as the Mary Meyer Corporation and Gund, who introduced its innovative Luv-me-Bear in the early 1970s. However, the 1980s saw the demise of Knickerbocker, Character, and Ideal, whose teddy-bear range was discontinued after the takeover by CBS Inc.

EARLY 1960s KNICKERBOCKER TOYS

The spangle-effect, safe, plastic eyes, with lines radiating around the irises, are typical of bears made by the Knickerbocker Toy Co. Inc. during this period. The New York label immediately dates this bear to the early 1960s, because the company had moved to new premises in Middlesex, New Jersey by the latter half of the decade. Knickerbocker also produced a similar, fully-jointed, white plush bear with red, felt paws and three jingle bells down the central body-seam. Their unjointed "floppy" bears of the 1960s and 1970s, including the Kuddles range, possessed inset muzzles like the one shown here.

Height: 35cm (14in)   Printed label

Eyes: the large, amber, safe, plastic eyes have radiating lines around the irises, a Knickerbocker feature.

Muzzle: the muzzle is made from the same honey-coloured velveteen as the pads.

Nose/mouth: *a vertically stitched, triangular, black nose leads onto a smiling, inverted-Y-shaped mouth.*

Fur/stuffing: *the fur is a slightly curly, golden nylon plush. The bear is stuffed with cotton and "Ico" (a material similar to "sub" or cotton waste).*

Pads: *the pads are made from honey-coloured velveteen. There are no claws.*

BEAR PROFILE

This bear retains a relatively traditional shape with its long, curved arms and protruding muzzle, although its legs are short and stumpy. Notice the "Animals of Distinction" label stitched into the side-seam; prior to the 1950s the label was sewn into the front-seam.

round, bulbous head, with no distinct muzzle

long, narrow ears sewn to sides of head

triangular, engraved, leather swing-tag

brown, safe, plastic eyes

raglan-style seams join arms to body

vertically stitched, triangular, brown, wool nose, with inverted-T-shaped mouth

matching scarf and socks in red and cream wool

short, white, wool pile on knitted, polyester backing

1982 R. DAKIN & CO.

Height: 53cm (21in)

Woolie Bear is also available in golden plush wearing a green and beige scarf and socks. Smaller examples called Wee Woolie Bear were made wearing only a scarf. The legs are in a permanent seated pose, but its head is swivel jointed.

DAKIN

Printed label

ears set wide apart on sides of expansive forehead

bulbous, black, safe, plastic eyes with airbrushed eyelashes

oval, white plush muzzle with black, triangular, air-brushed nose

pale grey, soft acrylic plush; very soft, synthetic stuffing

pale grey, short-pile plush pads

1983 APPLAUSE INC.

Height: 48cm (19in)

Wallace Berrie bought the Applause Company, a division of Knickerbocker Toys, in 1982; the whole business was later renamed Applause Inc. The Avanti line, first introduced by Wallace Berrie, was continued by Applause, in a smaller range of colours and sizes.

Embroidered label

slightly cupped ears set wide apart at back of head

inset, oval muzzle of white acrylic plush; airbrushed nose and mouth

large, black, safe eyes with airbrushed black eyelashes

tan acrylic plush; very soft, synthetic stuffing

light tan, acrylic plush pads

1982 WALLACE BERRIE & CO.

Height: 70cm (28in)

The Avanti range was designed by Riccardo Chiavetta of Jocky srl, Rome. Wallace Berrie acquired the world marketing rights in 1982. Extremely cuddly, the bears are reminiscent of those made by Aux Nations for whom Chiavetta had worked previously.

Embroidered label

embossed, plastic disc

amber and black, safe, plastic eyes

stylized, triangular, black, safe, plastic nose

open, smiling mouth lined with black felt, overlaid with pink, felt tongue

off-white, short-pile, synthetic plush pads (match ear linings)

1986 RUSS BERRIE & CO

Height: 38cm (15in)

Snuggle was produced by Russ Berrie under license from the international company, Lever Bros., who used the bear to advertise a fabric conditioner of the same name. The bear's name varied worldwide according to national variations in the product name.

Snuggle

Woven label

US: late 1970s-80s

MASS MARKET, SPECIAL EDITION, COLLECTORS' BEARS

From the late 1970s, many US teddy-bear firms began to make special editions, sometimes limited to a few thousand, for the burgeoning collectors' market, in addition to their standard ranges of toys. Gund, for example, introduced its Collectors Classics range in 1979, and its annual Gundy limited-edition series from 1983. Bears were made to mark special occasions, such as the anniversary of the firm. In 1988, for example, both California Stuffed Toys and Determined Productions Inc. produced bears representing the first Ideal bear, in celebration of the 85th anniversary of the birth of the teddy bear.

1984 WALLACE BERRIE

Wallace Berrie & Co. produced this Valentine Bear of pure white plush in 1984 as a special collectors' limited edition of 6,000. It is an Avanti bear, characterized by an unjointed, cuddly body, soft acrylic plush, and soft stuffing (see p.139), and is identical to other Jockline-designed Avanti bears, except that it wears a bright red, satin ribbon around its neck and has a unique red and white printed label that displays the bear's edition number: 0113.

Height: 40cm (16in)   Printed label

Ears: *the large, slightly cupped ears are set wide apart, with the insides airbrushed.*

Eyes: *the large, rounded, black, safe, plastic eyes have airbrushed "sockets".*

Nose: *as on many Avanti designs, the black, triangular nose is airbrushed, with smudged edges.*

BEAR PROFILE
You can clearly see here the classic rounded profile of an Avanti bear, with features typical of the range: a moderately protruding muzzle, a slight pot-belly, and straight, stubby, unjointed legs and arms. The bear has a large bulbous head, with eyes set low down to produce a deep forehead, and large ears.

Ribbon: *the red, satin, ribbon is tied in a bow around*

Pads: *the rounded pads at the end of the arms and feet are made from the same plush as the rest of the bear, but clipped short.*

Fur/stuffing: *the soft, shaggy fur is pure white, acrylic plush; the bear is stuffed with soft, synthetic, probably polyester, wadding throughout.*

Limbs/feet: *the arms and legs are short and stubby; the feet are large and chubby.*

black, vertically stitched, shield-shaped nose; inverted-T-shaped mouth

large, brown and black, safe, plastic eyes

inset, rounded, blunt muzzle of white, short-pile, synthetic plush

light brown, acrylic plush; soft, nylon fibre stuffing

fabric patch with "The Original Ideal Teddy Bear"

white, synthetic plush pads stencilled with pad markings

1978 IDEAL TOY CORPORATION

Height: 40cm (16in)

This collectors' edition bear was created to celebrate the 75th anniversary of the Ideal Toy Company, which claims to have produced the original teddy in 1903. Although this bear has lost its label, those found on other examples record the registration number, Hollis New York address, assembly in Haiti, and that the bear can be machine-washed and tumble-dried.

round, black, safe, lock-in, plastic eyes

black, vertically stitched, triangular nose; inverted-Y-shaped mouth

soft, white, acrylic plush; soft, synthetic stuffing

round, bronze-like chest-tag; incised, black lettering

three claws, sewn close together across plush

stumpy legs with large feet

white, synthetic, velvet-like pads; reinforced with card

1985 R. DAKIN

Height: 40cm (16in)

Dakin's white, special-edition Bentley Bear celebrated the firm's 30th anniversary. According to company literature, this bear "salutes our entry into the field of collectibles". Dakin later produced a limited-edition Baron Bear with a similar chest-tag.

DAKIN

Embroidered label

large, brown and black, safe, lock-in, plastic eyes

blue/grey, synthetic, brushed fabric ear lining

wide bound, vertically stitched, silvery grey nose; inverted-Y-shaped mouth

metal chest-tag embossed with "California Stuffed Toys 25th Anniversary"

blue/grey, synthetic, brushed fabric pads

1984 CALIFORNIA STUFFED TOYS

Height: 30cm (12in)

Silver Bear is the smaller of two bears celebrating the 25th anniversary of this Los Angeles-based firm and the Year of the Teddy Bear. 25,000 Silver Bears (the firm's first limited edition) were made, with a label carrying the signature of the firm's president.

25th Anniversary
Silver Bear
Limited Edition
25,000

Printed label

soft, shaggy, golden acrylic plush

fully jointed head and limbs

new, brown, crystal eyes

brown, vertically stitched, rectangular nose

narrow, beige, velveteen pads

unusual, gold-embossed, leather chest-tag

1988 GUND

Height: 38cm (15in)

Collectors Classics, such as Winston, Dickens, and Golly Golly, heralded Gund's entry into the collectors' market, followed by its 85th anniversary bear in 1983. "1898–1988" is embroidered on a seam label on this 90th Anniversary Commemorative Bear.

GUND
1898–1988

Printed tag

UK: 1970s–80s

D espite the fact that many British firms making traditional-style teddy bears closed down or were taken over in the 1970s, several new soft-toy companies were established and many of these flourished as a result of the craze for teddy-bear collecting. Little Folk began making soft toy animals in 1976, but its first teddy bear, introduced in 1980, became the company's most important product. Alresford Crafts (1970–92) also made soft toy animals originally, but later concentrated on teddies. Big Softies (est. 1978) turned to traditional teddies about 1982, and now focuses on the collectors' market.

1980s GOLDEN BEAR PRODUCTS LTD.

This company, based in Telford, Shropshire, in the same area as the Merrythought factory, was established in 1979 and is now reputed to be the largest soft-toy manufacturer in the UK. It concentrates on making soft and cuddly, often unjointed, teddy bears for the mass market. They all meet British, toy safety standards, with their lock-in eyes and nose, and flame-resistant materials. As well as having a printed fabric label, the bear has a red, rosette-shaped, card swing-tag, with a golden teddy bear in the centre.

Height: 29cm (11½in)   Printed label

Ears: *the ears are lined with short-pile fabric; the backs are made from the same plush as the body.*

Head: *the large, rounded head has a high, slightly projecting forehead.*

Muzzle: *the small, inset, protruding muzzle is made of golden, short-pile, synthetic plush.*

Fur: *the light brown, shaggy, synthetic plush is flame-resistant.*

Arms: *the short, slightly curved arms have pointed paws.*

Pads: *the pads are made of short-pile, synthetic plush.*

Legs: *the legs are short, straight, and stumpy with round pads.*

BEAR PROFILE
At this angle, you can see the bear's large, bulbous head and the contrasting, fabric ears that match the slightly projecting muzzle. The muzzle is sewn, at an angle, down the sides of the head. Notice, too, the large, rounded tail.

unusual ears with felt inner lining and top-stitched edges

realistic, black, moulded plastic nose, locked in with washer

mid-grey, acrylic plush

shaved plush on muzzle reveals contrasting, darker grey base

dark brown, suede pads; reinforced with hardboard so bear can stand

c.1982 LITTLE FOLK; LARGE; GREY
Height: 68cm (27in)

This bear was designed by Graham McBride, who made Little Folk soft toys in Devon with partner Maggie Breedon. They generally used acrylic plushes, but chose mohair for an early design and for later, limited-edition, collectors' bears.

Golden medallion

large, flat ears, sewn across facial seams

narrow, shield-shaped, vertically stitched, black nose

straight, unjointed limbs; no pads on paws

small feet with white, plush pads

safe, plastic, lock-in eyes

white, plush, inset muzzle

washable, flame-resistant, grey acrylic plush; stuffed with polyester stuffing

original triangular, card chest-tag

c.1982 ALRESFORD CRAFTS LTD.
Height: 53cm (21in)

Although the bear shown is unjointed, this company from Hampshire also produced traditionally jointed, as well as dressed bears, which were exported all over the world. They were designed by Margaret Jones, who founded the business with her husband John.

Printed label

large ears with inner edges sewn into facial seams

triangular, vertically stitched, brown, wool nose

light brown, suede pads

large, safe, plastic eyes

dark beige, synthetic plush, inset, pointed muzzle

soft, cream-coloured, synthetic plush; soft, synthetic stuffing

EARLY 1980s BIG SOFTIES
Height: 60cm (24in)

This is an early, synthetic plush example from Valerie and Fred Lyle's business in Yorkshire. The company is better known for its traditional mohair-plush bears, such as Edward in Transit (see p.196); it is currently introducing limited-edition bears for collectors.

BIG SOFTIES
Surface Washable

Printed label

lock-in, safe, plastic eyes, set wide apart

black, shield-shaped, vertically stitched nose; inverted-Y-shaped mouth

dark brown, short-pile, synthetic pads

large, flat ears sewn across facial seams

large, unjointed head with expansive forehead

small, rounded, inset muzzle

short-pile, golden, nylon-plush fur, with soft, synthetic stuffing throughout

c.1986 MULHOLLAND & BAILIE LTD.
Height: 81cm (32in)

After Pedigree's move to Canterbury in 1971, former manager James Mulholland set up his own business in Belfast, where this bear was made. Similar to later Pedigree designs, its satinized Nylena label is sewn into the left seam at the back of the head.

A Nylena

Printed label

House of Nisbet: 1976–89

PETER BULL-INSPIRED BEARS AND COLLECTORS' BEARS

In 1975, Jack Wilson acquired Peggy Nisbet Ltd., a company specializing in portrait dolls. He renamed the firm, House of Nisbet Ltd., and introduced its Childhood Classics traditional teddy bears. Peggy Nisbet's daughter, Alison (who later married Jack Wilson) designed the range. The firm was known for its limited-edition character bears. In 1979, Nisbet invited British arctophile Peter Bull to collaborate on the creation of a Bully Bear range. Nisbet reproduced his bear, "Delicatessen", in 1987, using distressed mohair, a material that Jack Wilson helped to invent. Dakin UK bought House of Nisbet in 1989.

1981 BULLY BEAR

This limited-edition bear was the initial result of collaboration between Peter Bull and the House of Nisbet. It became the central character in six books written by Bull, and inspired various other versions of the bear: the smaller Young Bully and Bully Minor; special editions Captain Bully, Harrods Bully and Tribute Bully Bear (made after Bull's death, wearing a replica of his famous sweater); and Woolly Bully in scarf and hat.

Height: 45cm (18in)

Printed label

Ears: *the large, flat, narrow ears are sewn across the facial seams.*

Eyes: *the safe, plastic, amber eyes have black pupils.*

BEAR PROFILE

Bully Bear, based on Peter Bull's 1907 US bear "Delicatessen", has typical, early American bear features: humped back, triangular head, pointed muzzle, long limbs, and tapering arms.

Nose/mouth: *the black, vertically stitched, square nose has a few stitches in the centre extending down to meet the mouth.*

Fur/stuffing: *the golden mohair and wool plush has a cotton backing; the stuffing is a soft, synthetic material.*

Paw-pads: *the pads are made from synthetic velvet and have two black claws sewn across them.*

Foot-pads: *three black claws are stitched across the foot-pads.*

Trademark: *the embroidered label, stitched across the foot-pad, shows two bears holding a shield inscribed with "NCC" (Nisbet Childhood Classics).*

large, flat, narrow ears

black, vertically stitched, shield-shaped nose; inverted-Y-shaped, single-stitched mouth

inset muzzle

large, yellow bow-tie

beige, synthetic velvet pads

floppy, yellow and black gingham, peaked cap

red-brown, safe, plastic eyes

brown, synthetic plush; soft, synthetic stuffing

dark green, corduroy bag

1984 ZODIAC BEAR
Height: 35cm (14in)

Peter Bull, a devotee of astrology, and co-owner of London tearooms, "Zodiac: the Astrological Emporium", wrote 12 books in the Zodiac Bear series. Nisbet recreated each of the characters (Tunbridge, shown here, is one) and published the books.

Printed label

distressed, beige mohair plush; soft-stuffed throughout

inverted-Y-shaped mouth

three claws on paws

pale peach-coloured felt pads

black, vertically stitched, oblong nose

fully jointed limbs

four claws stitched across plush

label with limited-editon number

1988 YES/NO BEAR
Height: 28cm (11in)

This bear, inspired by Fritz Ferschl, forms part of the Nisbet Celebrity Collection, introduced in 1987, to honour bear-makers and arctophiles. Ferschl was a Schuco toolmaker from 1945; he later renovated Schuco toys and wrote a book on the company.

Embroidered label

flat ears sewn across facial seams

black, safe, plastic eyes

white, leather pads

golden mohair plush

maroon, fine woollen scarf

black, vertically stitched, oval nose; inverted-Y-shaped mouth

badge sewn on left side of chest

printed label under left arm, with shield and limited-edition number on reverse

1987 BODY LANGUAGE BEAR
Height: 30cm (13in)

This fully "poseable" bear came in three different plushes, with eyelets on the base of the feet that fit into a metal stand. Jack Wilson's signature appears on a leather strip on the back of the right leg; only 5,000 of these signed bears were made.

Printed label

red and blue fabric rosebud

brown, vertically stitched nose; inverted-Y-shaped mouth

blue, satin bow-tie

pale blue, synthetic velvet pads

blue and black, safe, plastic eyes

red and white, striped jerkin with blue trim

white wool plush

embroidered label on left foot-pad

1987 THE ANYTHING BEAR
Height: 23cm (9in)

This bear was inspired by Rosemary Volpp, and named for her grandson Jess whose wish was to be an "Anything Man", doing anything to make people happy. This Signature Edition series honours other collectors and authors, such as Linda Mullins.

Embroidered label

North American Bear Co: 1979–92

PERSONALITY BEARS, SOME COSTUMED, FOR COLLECTORS

T he North American Bear Company was founded by New Yorker, Barbara Isenberg, following the creation of Albert the Running Bear – the hero of three books that Barbara co-wrote. The Very Important Bear series is based on historical, literary, and Hollywood characters; each is given a punning name – hence the phrase "The ones with the puns". Apart from bears such as Oatmeal and Ruggles, most are clothed, including the very popular VanderBear family. The bears are created by plush designers and Barbara Isenberg; and the bears' costumes are designed by Odl and Katya Bauer.

1980–83 AMELIA BEARHART

Inspired by the 1930s American aviator, Amelia Earhart, this was the first bear in the Very Important Bear series, introduced in 1980. It is a second edition, and is dressed in a beige suit; the first version wore a magenta suit. Four new Very Important Bears are produced annually and are later "retired" so that only twelve different styles are available each year. Others in the series include Scarlett O'Beara, Bearb Ruth, Cyrano de Beargerac, Bear Trek: Mr. Spock, and Hans Christian Anbearsen: The Snow Queen.

Height: 50cm (20in)

©1979 ALL RIGHTS RESERVED
NORTH AMERICAN
BEAR CO., INC.
CHICAGO, ILLINOIS
NOT RECOMMENDED FOR
CHILDREN UNDER 3 YRS. OLD

Printed label

Flying helmet: *the soft, leather-like, plastic helmet allows the ears to emerge through openings in the corners.*

Flying goggles: *the turquoise, plastic goggles enclose the small, round, black, safe, plastic eyes.*

Nose: *the rounded, black, plastic nose is a safe, lock-in type.*

Aviator's scarf: *the scarf is made of a cream, silk-like fabric.*

Flying suit: *the beige, cotton suit has a zip fastener down the front, and is elasticated at the waist and ankles.*

Fur/stuffing: *the soft, synthetic, velour fabric is always used for the Very Important Bears series; the bear is filled with mixed, synthetic stuffing.*

BEAR PROFILE
The distinctive, large, protruding, dome-shaped muzzle is similar to that of other examples in the Very Important Bear series, and is constructed from a separate section of the brushed-nylon fur fabric.

black, safe,
plastic eyes

horizontally stitched,
black, wool nose

Aloysius's own
hairbrush

curly, soft,
synthetic fur on
knitted backing;
soft, synthetic
stuffing

brown,
synthetic,
velvet-like
pads

fully jointed limbs and head

1991 ALOYSIUS
Height: 53cm (21in)

The North American Bear Company produced the original, unjointed Aloysius in 1984, inspired by the popular TV serial *Brideshead Revisited*. The House of Nisbet also made a replica but since it did not own the copyright it called its bear Delicatessen.

ALOYSIUS® #4011
From Brideshead Revisited
© 1981 NORTH AMERICAN BEAR CO. INC.
Chicago, IL 312/329-0020
All Rights Reserved

Printed label

ears emerge through
traditional Dutch
head-dress

black, safe,
plastic eyes

fully jointed
head and limbs

pale golden,
soft, acrylic
plush

red and
green, felt
tulip

black,
hand-
stitched
claws

hand-
carved,
wooden
Dutch clogs

1980s MUFFY: DUTCH TREAT
Height: 18cm (7in)

Muffy, the smallest member of the VanderBear family – Alice, Cornelius, Fuzzy, and Fluffy – was introduced in 1984, wearing a white christening gown. She now has an extensive collection of special outfits, including this Dutch costume.

MUFFY® Dutch Treat™ # 4327/4328
MUFFY COLLECTION
Valentine/Easter 1992
Costume by Gail Bauer
Made in Korea
Not recommended for children under
three years due to small parts & trim.

Printed label

golden,
synthetic plush

black, safe,
plastic, bead
eyes, set close
together

large, triangular,
black, velour nose

beige,
synthetic
pads on
large feet

red, knitted,
Hug scarf

HUG

1983 TED MENTEN'S HUG
Height: 70cm (28in)

This bear is based on a cartoon character in the *World According to Hug* by Ted Menten, New York bear artist, writer, and collector. The arms seem to have been put on backwards, but this is how Hug is illustrated. A Junior Hug was also produced.

HUG © ™
FROM "WORLD ACCORDING TO HUG"
ALL RIGHTS RESERVED
© 1983 TED MENTEN

Printed label

brown acrylic
plush; soft,
polyester stuffing

ears poke
through
opening

black, safe,
plastic eyes

black,
embroidered
nose

blue, tricot fabric
jogging suit with
removable trousers

white,
fabric
trainers
with laces

1978–82 ALBERT THE RUNNING BEAR
Height: 48cm (19in)

Adventures of Albert the Running Bear was published by Houghton Mifflin on Good Bear Day (October 27th) 1982. Now retired, Albert was produced in a choice of outfits by the North American Bear Company, which also made smaller version.

RUNNING BEAR ™ ©
NORTH AMERICAN BEAR CO. INC
645 NORTH MICHIGAN AVENUE
CHICAGO, IL. 60611
312-943-1055

Printed label

Russ Berrie: Mass-produced Bears

MODERN BEARS FROM EAST ASIAN FACTORIES; SOLD WORLDWIDE

Russ Berrie and Company Inc. manufacture and distribute the world's largest range of "impulse gift" products, including soft toys, mugs, figurines, greetings cards and posters, candles, and dolls. Now a world-wide organization, with sales topping $400,000,000, the company has been a leader in the soft-toy industry since the late 1970s, selling to over 95,000 international retailers in a variety of locations such as shopping-malls, airports, hospitals, and college campuses, and as far apart as Africa, the Middle East, India, Russia, Iceland, Europe, North America, and Australasia.

Russ trademark
On teddy bears, the trademark (above) with its butterfly motif (registered in the 1960s) is often found on a plastic, embossed medallion attached to the ear.

In 1963, Russell Berrie, then a manufacturer's representative and now the president of this world-famous organization, founded a business selling novelty merchandise in Palisades Park, a suburb of New York City. Using a converted garage as a warehouse and his home as an office, he worked each day from 6.00 a.m. to 10.00 p.m. calling on retailers, packing orders, and completing paperwork. Early on, Russell created a character named Fuzzy Wuzzy that proved particularly successful; he later added the Bupkis and Sillisculpts figurines to the range.

A MODERN ORGANIZATION

Through Russell's flexibility, and his total commitment to his customers, the company achieved rapid sales growth and worldwide distribution, and, in 1982, Russ Berrie and Co. was recognized by *INC* business magazine as one of the 500 fastest-growing, privately owned firms in the US. The company went public in March 1984.

Staff at Russ Berrie's headquarters in Oakland, New Jersey are responsible for product research, design, and development; marketing and advertising; finance, accounting, and the budgets; and administrative and executive functions. The company's Market Research Department studies trends in the rapidly changing gift industry, working closely with Product Development to maintain an ongoing supply of new products. Each of these is thoroughly market-tested to ensure consumer appeal.

The company is divided into two divisions that together market more than 10,000 seasonal and everyday products: the Gift division markets figurines and troll products, picture-frames, stationery, greetings cards, and mugs; the Plush 'n' Stuff division markets stuffed animals and other "soft" products, including teddy bears, and fabric dolls. There was a third division, Expression Centre, marketing items such as keyrings and pins with printed maxims, but this amalgamated with the Gift division at the beginning of the 1990s.

WORLDWIDE ACTIVITIES

Russ Berrie employs 2,600 people worldwide, including more than 800 sales representatives, executives and managers; and over 350 employees in the offices in Hong Kong, Korea, Taiwan, Thailand, and Indonesia. There are four regional distribution centres throughout the US, as well as a subsidiary company, Amram's, in Canada. Russ Berrie (UK) Ltd., based in Southampton, not only distributes throughout Europe, but also has

New Jersey HQ
Russ Berrie's corporate headquarters at 111 Bauer Drive, Oakland, New Jersey (above), where all the company's worldwide activities are coordinated.

Teddy-bear leprechauns
Ceramic teddy-bear leprechauns (above), made especially for St. Patrick's Day, 1988. Figurines are an important part of Russ Berrie's Gift division.

Ready for shipping
The toys are carefully packed and boxed (below) for shipping, with not too many in each container, to prevent squashing.

Equal stuffing
Workers in a Chinese factory (above) weigh wads of polyester fibre to ensure that each teddy is stuffed with the same amount of filling.

Safety check
Each teddy is passed over a metal detector (above) to ensure that no needles have been left in the fabric.

Product Development and Market Research offices, which develop ideas to match European as opposed to American trends. Russ Berrie & Company (Australia) Pty. Ltd. is a wholly owned, Australian business based in Kirrawee, New South Wales. It carries many Russ items, with the addition of koalas and kangaroos designed and manufactured specifically for the Australian market. It is one of the largest manufacturers of such soft toys in Australia. Each distribution centre is staffed by management, sales force, order processing, customer service, and packing departments. Russ is very much a sales-driven company, which lives by the motto: "Nothing happens until the sale is made", and close links are developed between representatives and retailers. Training programmes help to keep Russ sales personnel among the most knowledgeable in their field.

An art and design department exists at the Hong Kong Tri Russ office, which also deals with world export. Staff are employed in other East Asian offices to find suitable factories to manufacture

Russ's soft toys – these are generally either in Korea or China. However, because of increasing expense in recent years, Korea has been replaced by Indonesia as a manufacturing base. The factories can range from small, family businesses to large concerns. Russ's teddy bears are made under the highest quality control. No animal skins or products are used, and all materials are non-allergenic, surface washable, and meet worldwide safety laws.

LUV PETS, CARESS, AND YOMIKO
Russ has produced three special brands of soft toy: Luv Pets, Caress, and Yomiko. Today their most popular line is the Caress product which has come to symbolize the firm because of its excellent quality, softness, cuteness, and reasonable price range. Their most well-known bears Brittany, Benjamin, and Gregory (see p.170) are all made from an increasingly popular, synthetic, curly, long-pile plush.

AUSTRALIAN BEARS
In February 1993, Russ (Australia) launched two teddy bears – Barton and Deacon – as part of an independent, Australian-made, quality range under the name "Koala Families", which proved instantly popular with the collectors' market. They were unique for Russ, whose bears are usually made in Chinese factories; and unique for Australia, where the majority of commercially made teddy bears are also East Asian imports.

Gregory
Gregory is one of Russ's most popular 1990s teddies (above). Made from curly, long-pile synthetic plush, he is a modification of an original design by US bear artist, Carol-Lynn Rössel Waugh – a new departure for the company, which normally employs its own designers.

The three bears
Three mugs (above) marketed by Russ's Gift division in 1988, and sold in a boxed set.

Final inspection
Each bear is checked (left) to make sure that it is firmly sewn, that the face is satisfactory, and that the product matches the master sample supplied by the company.

Snuggle Bear
This 1986 bear (left) featured in a world-wide promotion for Lever Brothers' fabric conditioner. The name of the bear varied according to the product name in different countries.

Canterbury Bears: 1980~90s

TRADITIONAL COLLECTORS' BEARS BY A BRITISH FAMILY BUSINESS

John Blackburn established Canterbury Bears with his daughter Kerstin in 1980, at their home in Westbere, Kent. His wife Maude and children Mark and Victoria later joined the firm which moved to its present workshop in Littlebourne, a village outside Canterbury, in 1984. Canterbury Bears are fully jointed, and are made of natural or top quality synthetic fabrics; they come in a Classic or Special range, which expands each year. They often have unusual features, such as partially shaved faces or unique claws. The firm introduced special commissions, limited editions, and replicas in the later 1980s.

1989 CLASSIC RANGE

Louise is the largest of seven sizes in Canterbury Bears' Classic range which extends in size from 15cm (6in) to 68cm (27in). The firm also makes a similar, golden mohair-plush model called Gregory. In 1987, the Mayor of Canterbury granted the firm the privilege of using the historic city's Coat of Arms on its labels, as seen on the card tag around this bear's neck.

Height: 69cm (27in)

Tag: inside the card tag is printed "My name is Louise", along with the Blackburns' signature.

Bow: the pink, satin ribbon bow is original.

Fur/stuffing: the fur is soft, white mohair plush; the bear is stuffed with soft, polyester fibre.

Pads: the clawless pads are made of pale grey suede, a favourite choice of Canterbury Bears.

Ears: the large, flat ears are sewn across the facial seams.

Eyes: the brown, safe, plastic eyes have black pupils.

Nose/mouth: the black, vertically stitched nose is oval; the mouth is an inverted Y shape.

BEAR PROFILE
You can see here the slightly protruding muzzle; the thick, curved arms; the large feet, and the large, flat ears.

Legs: the legs are swivel-jointed, as are the arms.

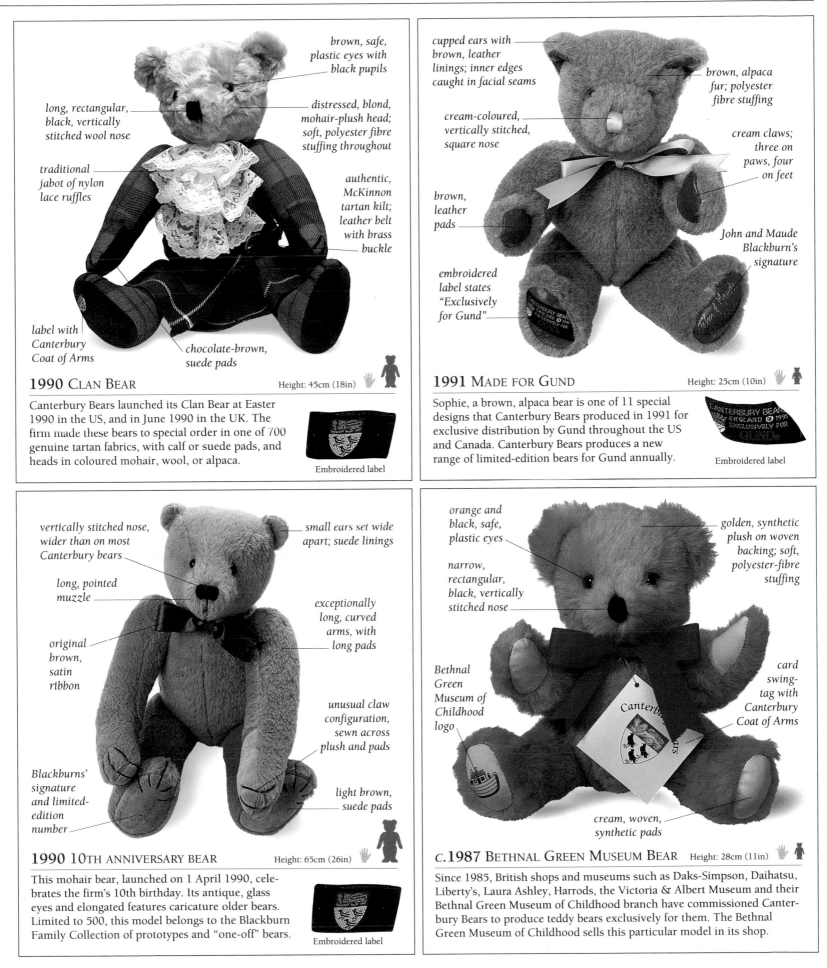

brown, safe, plastic eyes with black pupils

long, rectangular, black, vertically stitched wool nose

distressed, blond, mohair-plush head; soft, polyester fibre stuffing throughout

traditional jabot of nylon lace ruffles

authentic, McKinnon tartan kilt; leather belt with brass buckle

label with Canterbury Coat of Arms

chocolate-brown, suede pads

1990 CLAN BEAR   Height: 45cm (18in)

Canterbury Bears launched its Clan Bear at Easter 1990 in the US, and in June 1990 in the UK. The firm made these bears to special order in one of 700 genuine tartan fabrics, with calf or suede pads, and heads in coloured mohair, wool, or alpaca.

Embroidered label

cupped ears with brown, leather linings; inner edges caught in facial seams

cream-coloured, vertically stitched, square nose

brown, alpaca fur; polyester fibre stuffing

cream claws; three on paws, four on feet

brown, leather pads

embroidered label states "Exclusively for Gund"

John and Maude Blackburn's signature

1991 MADE FOR GUND   Height: 25cm (10in)

Sophie, a brown, alpaca bear is one of 11 special designs that Canterbury Bears produced in 1991 for exclusive distribution by Gund throughout the US and Canada. Canterbury Bears produces a new range of limited-edition bears for Gund annually.

Embroidered label

vertically stitched nose, wider than on most Canterbury bears

small ears set wide apart; suede linings

long, pointed muzzle

exceptionally long, curved arms, with long pads

original brown, satin ribbon

unusual claw configuration, sewn across plush and pads

Blackburns' signature and limited-edition number

light brown, suede pads

1990 10TH ANNIVERSARY BEAR   Height: 65cm (26in)

This mohair bear, launched on 1 April 1990, celebrates the firm's 10th birthday. Its antique, glass eyes and elongated features caricature older bears. Limited to 500, this model belongs to the Blackburn Family Collection of prototypes and "one-off" bears.

Embroidered label

orange and black, safe, plastic eyes

golden, synthetic plush on woven backing; soft, polyester-fibre stuffing

narrow, rectangular, black, vertically stitched nose

Bethnal Green Museum of Childhood logo

card swing-tag with Canterbury Coat of Arms

cream, woven, synthetic pads

c.1987 BETHNAL GREEN MUSEUM BEAR   Height: 28cm (11in)

Since 1985, British shops and museums such as Daks-Simpson, Daihatsu, Liberty's, Laura Ashley, Harrods, the Victoria & Albert Museum and their Bethnal Green Museum of Childhood branch have commissioned Canterbury Bears to produce teddy bears exclusively for them. The Bethnal Green Museum of Childhood sells this particular model in its shop.

Steiff: 1980–92

REPLICAS FOR COLLECTORS; SPECIAL COMMISSIONS

I n 1980, a limited-edition replica of the 1905 Original Teddy was produced to celebrate the centenary of Steiff's earliest soft toy, initiating an annual programme of reproductions of archive samples (often in limited editions). Other trends followed: copies of one-off celebrity bears, such as "Alfonzo" (*see p.19*) and "Happy" (*see p.37*); editions exclusive to certain countries; special collectors' items, such as the Goldilocks and the Three Bears sets; and a miniature historical series. Special commissions, beginning with the 1970s Olympic mascot, Waldi, have also been produced for museums and shops.

1987–88 TEDDY ROSE REPLICA

Steiff originally made 5,000 Teddy Rose bears in 1925–30. In 1987–88 the company issued a limited edition of 10,000 replicas, distributed worldwide. Each bear came in a presentation box with a certificate guaranteeing authenticity. A smaller 25cm (10in) version was produced in a limited edition of 8,000 in 1990, and a 20cm (8in) Record Teddy Rose, part of Steiff's Museum Collection, was introduced in 1992. The white ear-tag, as opposed to a yellow tag, indicates that the bear is one of a limited edition.

Height: 40cm (16in)

Incised button

Trademark: *the white ear-tag, attached with the cursive Steiff button, indicates that this bear is one of a limited edition.*

Nose/mouth: *the nose is a brown, vertically stitched, shield shape; a few central stitches drop to meet the inverted-V-shaped mouth.*

Fur/stuffing/growler: *the fur is pale pink, shaggy mohair plush; the stuffing is wood-wool throughout. This bear has an internal tilt-growler.*

Arms: *the traditional, curved, tapering arms are longer than the legs.*

Pads: *the pads are made from pale pink felt with brown, embroidered claws over the plush.*

BEAR PROFILE
In profile, you can see this bear's distinctive face, imitating the earlier design, with an endearing smile embroidered along the length of the long, slightly upturned, shaved muzzle.

Feet: *the feet are large, narrow, and oval in shape.*

vertically stitched, pink nose, unusual for its dropped stitches in centre and at outer edges

large, wired ears

blue eyes

brown-tipped blond, "dual" plush (popular in mid-1920s)

inverted-V-shaped mouth

red claws

printed card chest-tag

long arms

large feet with beige, felt pads

1989–90 PETSY REPLICA   Height: 50cm (20in)

This is a reproduction of the unusual 1927 "dual" plush mohair bear with blue eyes and large, wired ears (*see p.37*). The white, printed ear-tag indicates that this bear is one of a limited edition; its card chest-tag copies those used on 1928–50 bears.

Incised button

black, safe, plastic eyes, imitating original boot-buttons

"button in ear" with printed ear-tag

long, distressed, golden mohair plush

black, safe, moulded plastic nose, reproducing the original sealing-wax nose

very long, curved arms

printed, card chest-tag

long, narrow, oval-shaped, beige, felt pads

black claws across mohair plush

1991 *BÄR 35 PB* REPLICA   Height: 50cm (20in)

This limited-edition bear of 6,000 pieces with unique card-disc and string jointing copies the 1904 bear that represented the design between the now lost "55 PB" and the rod-jointed "28 PB" (*see pp.16–17*). It won the TOBY Design Concept of the Year Award in 1991.

Incised button

black, safe, plastic, replica boot-button eyes

"button in ear" with embroidered ear-tag

black, vertically stitched nose, with dropped central and outer stitches

golden wool and cotton plush; soft, polyester stuffing

long, curved arms with spoon-shaped paws

beige, felt pads

1984 MR. CINNAMON BEAR   Height: 40cm (16in)

Based on the 1903 *Bärle* (*see pp.38–39*), this bear represented the central character in the 1907 children's story by US author Sara Tawney Lefferts, which was reprinted in 1984. The story describes how a little girl tries to make her toys accept the new German bear.

Incised button

comical face with open mouth, felt palate, and brown, outlined lips, unique to Dicky

"button in ear" with printed ear-tag

vertically stitched, shield-shaped nose, airbrushed above and below

pale golden, mohair plush with inset muzzle of short-pile mohair plush

outfit of felt lederhosen, checked shirt, and green tie

curved paws, unique to Dicky design, with black claws

flat feet with reinforced soles

1989 DICKY REPLICA   Height: 30cm (12in)

This replica of the 1930 Dicky was specially produced for the New York store, F.A.O. Schwartz, to celebrate the reopening of San Francisco's Golden Gate Bridge in 1989. Many reputable stores, including Harrods and Hamleys, now sell their own "house" Steiff bears.

Incised button

Gebrüder Hermann: 1980s–92

UNJOINTED BEARS; COLLECTORS' SPECIAL EDITIONS AND REPLICAS

F ollowing the retirement of the original three Hermann brothers (*see pp.96–97*), the 1980s saw this company under the management of their daughters (*see p.95*). Although still producing teddy bears for children, the business began to expand into the field of adult collectables. In 1984, Model 63 was produced, replicating the classic first Gebrüder Hermann teddy bear. Other replicas and special limited editions followed, including Bernhard Bear (named after the original founder). Special commissions included three 91cm (36in) bears made for the store P. & E. Rubin, each in a limited edition of ten.

c.1983 UNJOINTED; SYNTHETIC

This unjointed bear, made of soft, shaggy, rust-coloured, synthetic plush on a knitted backing (denoting a lower-quality material), is soft-stuffed throughout with polyester fibre. Designed as a child's toy, it has safe, plastic eyes and a safe, stylized black, plastic nose. Apart from the metallic, green and golden, paper swing-tag, the bear also possesses a printed, green on white, cloth label, which reads: "Hermann Teddy Original", sewn into the right side-seam.

Height: 38cm (15in)

Card swing-tag

Ears: *the slightly cupped ears are set wide apart.*

Eyes: *the large, brown and black, safe, plastic eyes are set into the facial seams.*

Nose: *the stylized, black, moulded, plastic, oval nose is locked in with a washer.*

Ribbon: *the red, ribbon bow is original.*

Fur/stuffing: *the shaggy, rust-coloured, synthetic plush has a knitted backing; the bear is stuffed with soft, polyester fibre.*

Pads: *the pads are made from pale golden, brushed, knitted, synthetic fabric.*

Feet: *the large, narrow, oval feet are traditional in shape.*

BEAR PROFILE
This bear has the distinctive features of the safe teddy of the post-war period: a large, bulbous head, large ears, short arms, straight back, and long legs with large feet.

cupped ears, sewn across facial seams

black, horizontally stitched, oval nose; inverted-Y-shaped mouth

original ribbon around neck, printed with teddy bears in romper suits

three black claws on feet and paws

brown and black, plastic eyes, sewn in

inset, clipped mohair-plush muzzle

pure golden mohair plush on cotton backing; wood-wool stuffing; internal tilt-growler

cream, felt, oblong foot-pads

1991 REPLICA OF SONNEBERG *BÄR* Height: 50cm (20in)

One of a limited edition of 4,000, this bear reproduced a 1922 design, produced when Bernhard Hermann's company operated from Sonneberg. The toy horse pictured on the information card refers to Sonneberg's long tradition of making wooden toys.

HERMANN Teddy ORIGINAL

Embroidered label

unusual pink, vertically stitched, shield-shaped nose, with inverted-Y-shaped mouth

black fur, composed of 53% wool and 47% cotton; wood-wool stuffing; internal tilt-growler

white, safe, plastic eyes with black, cartoon-style pupils

original red ribbon bow around neck

fully jointed limbs and head

1982 FUDDO Height: 40cm (16in)

This unusual black bear represents American Sally Bowen's story-book character Fuddo. As well as a special, signed, black label, the bear has the usual green, printed, Hermann label sewn into the arm-seam, and a red, plastic seal attached to the chest.

FROM THE BOOK BY Sally Bowen ©1982

Printed label

brown and black, safe, plastic eyes

black, vertically stitched, shield-shaped nose; inverted-Y-shaped mouth

red, plastic seal attached to chest

large, narrow, oval feet

ears sewn across facial seams

wool plush on cotton backing

inset muzzle with swelling on left-hand side indicating toothache

Bear With Us label (limited edition No. 76)

beige, brushed, synthetic, knitted fabric pads

C.1983 PAYNE, THE TOOTHACHE BEAR Height: 30cm (12in)

Specially commissioned by the Los Angeles bear store Bear With Us, this limited-edition "Toothache Bear" wears a scarf around his swollen muzzle, and carries a plastic tooth on a chain. In 1992, the Austrian company Berg produced a similar bear.

PAYNE© THE ORIGINAL "TOOTHACHE BEAR"®

Printed label

black, vertically stitched, shield-shaped nose

golden, short-pile mohair plush; soft, polyester-fibre stuffing; internal tilt-growler

original ribbon bow in colours of German flag

traditional long, curved arms

cream, felt paw-pads and left foot-pad

three black claws on each paw and foot

1990 GERMAN UNIFICATION BEAR Height: 43cm (17in)

This limited edition bear, No. 642 of 4,000, was manufactured to celebrate the reunification of East and West Germany on 3 October 1990. The right foot-pad is made up of stripes of black, red, and yellow felt, to represent the German flag.

HERMANN Teddy ORIGINAL

Embroidered label

Germany: 1980s–90s

TRADITIONAL RANGE INCLUDING LIMITED EDITIONS AND REPLICAS

Since the 1980s, many German firms have been making bears specifically aimed at collectors. These are either traditional (sometimes limited-edition designs) or replicas of their own or other firms' earlier lines. In 1992 Hermann-Spielwaren, for example, introduced a limited-edition replica of a teddy made in 1910 by the old Sonneberg firm, Leven. This commemorated the return of Leven to its rightful owners, Dora-Margot Hermann and her sister, after German reunification. Firms are also making bears to celebrate national and international events, such as Sigikid's 1993 United Europe bear.

1990 HERMANN-SPIELWAREN JUBILEE BEAR

This bear, part of Hermann-Spielwaren's *Jubiläumsbären*, is a reproduction of Max Hermann's 1920s 111 series. It was made to celebrate the firm's 70th anniversary and heralded its entry into the market of collectables. Hermann-Spielwaren introduced a number of limited editions appealing to the European market, such as *Berlin Deutsche Hauptstadt-Bär*, (meaning Berlin German capital city bear), and the US collectors' market with American Cheerleader Bears, for example.

Height: 20cm (8in)   Printed tag

Ears: *the small, narrow, flat ears are sewn across the facial seams.*

Eyes: *the brown, safe, plastic eyes have black pupils.*

Nose/mouth: *the nose is horizontally stitched; the mouth is an inverted Y shape.*

BEAR PROFILE
This bear's traditional features include an elongated, protruding muzzle; long limbs of similar length; curved, tapering arms; and small, defined feet.

Trademark: *the folded, printed label is sewn into the right arm-seam.*

Chest-tag: *the green and gold card tag is attached to the chest with gold-coloured thread.*

Fur/stuffing: *the fur is short, golden mohair plush; the bear is stuffed with wood-wool throughout.*

Limbs: *the curved, tapering arms are the same length as the legs.*

Pads: *the pads are made from a shorter pile plush than that used for the rest of the bear.*

1991 HERMANN-SPIELWAREN; REPLICA Height: 39cm (15¼in)

fully jointed head and limbs

black, horizontally stitched, shield-shaped nose; inverted-Y-shaped, single-stitched mouth

"Old German Teddy Bear" and limited-edition number

large, cupped ears

brown, glass eyes with black pupils

dark brown-tipped beige mohair plush; wood-wool stuffing

tapering arms with spoon-shaped paws

oval, beige, felt pads

Hermann-Spielwaren produced two replicas of Old German Teddy Bear, a design featured in the 1929 Max Hermann Sonneberg factory catalogue. The replicas of bear 115 *(above)* and bear 113 (golden mohair) were both sold as limited editions of 3,000.

Original Hermann design Made in Germany

Printed label

1992 SIGIKID; MIRO COLLECTION Height: 20cm (8in)

translucent, amber, glass eyes with black pupils

round, black, vertically stitched nose; inverted-Y-shaped mouth

beige, felt pads; three black, stitched claws

short-pile, golden mohair plush

ears with beige, felt linings

"Certificate of Authenticity"

small, narrow, oval-shaped feet

In 1992, Sigikid introduced replicas of Hamiro designs, a Czech firm confiscated by the Communist government. "Made in CSFR" on the label indicates that this bear was made at the new Miro factory, established by the original founder's son.

sigikid MIRO Limited Edition

Embroidered label

1980s CLEMENS; TRADITIONAL Height: 50cm (20in)

fully jointed head and limbs

amber and black, safe, plastic eyes

apricot-coloured, synthetic plush on knitted backing; soft-stuffed; internal tilt growler

black, vertically stitched, shield-shaped nose; inverted-Y-shaped mouth

printed, mauve chest-tag with Clemens logo

During the 1980s, Clemens produced a range of traditional, jointed bears in a variety of plushes, including miniatures and dressed models. The firm introduced a Collectors' Range in 1992, with a camel-coloured woollen bear, to celebrate their 40th anniversary.

CLEMENS SPIELTIERE

Printed label

1992 HEIKE-BÄR; SCHUCO REPLICA Height: 7cm (2¾in)

small ears

inverted-Y-shaped, black, single-stitched mouth with small, red, felt tongue

short-pile, bright golden mohair plush

black bead eyes

two black, horizontal stitches form nose

straight limbs with no pads

This tiny bear, made by Karl Bär with equipment bought from the receiver handling Schuco's bankruptcy in 1977, copies Schuco's original design *(see p.41)*. The tradename is composed of Bär's wife's name, Heike, and their surname, Bär.

Heike-Bär 100% Mohair Handmade W.Germany

Printed label

Ireland: 1938-79

SUBSIDIZED TOY INDUSTRY AND TRADITIONAL STYLE BEARS

Irish manufacturers, such as Philip Sher's Hibernian Novelty Company in Dublin, had been making soft toys since the World War I period. In 1938, an Irish government department, the *Gaeltacht* Services Division (the Board of *Gaeltarra Eireann* from 1957), established a subsidized toy industry, operating three factories. (*Gaeltarra Eireann* means "Irish produce".) The toys were marketed from Dublin until 1969, when the head offices moved to County Galway. Because Ireland remained neutral during World War II, exports of Irish soft toys rose dramatically at this time to meet overseas demand.

1964 "REPUBLIC OF IRELAND" LABEL

This traditional, disc-jointed bear was made by Tara Toys, the soft-toy section of the Irish Government-funded toy industry, at their Elly Bay factory in County Mayo. In 1969, production was transferred to Crolly, County Donegal, under a new company called Soltoys Ltd., which eventually ceased business in 1979. Traditional bears like this are typical, but they also produced novelties such as Freddie the Laughing Bear and the musical bear, Tara the Tuneful Teddy.

Height: 50cm (20in)

Embroidered label

Eyes: *the amber, glass eyes with black pupils are sewn into the face on wire shanks.*

Nose/mouth: *the vertically stitched, black nose is shield-shaped; the mouth is a double-stitched, inverted Y shape.*

Fur/growler: *the pale golden mohair plush has faded from orange-yellow and is slightly worn in places. The bear has a tilt-growler.*

Pads: *the pads are made from chocolate-brown felt.*

Feet: *the oval feet have no claws.*

Label: *the original embroidered label is sewn into the foot-pad seam.*

BEAR PROFILE

In profile this bear demonstrates clearly several typical features of the post-World War II Irish teddy: its pointed, protruding muzzle, high forehead, and large, flat ears. The curved arms are the same length as the legs, and taper to a sharp point at the paws. The feet are distinctively rounded and stubby.

unjointed head

brown, glass eyes with black pupils

glued-on, triangular, black nose

double-stitched, inverted-Y-shaped, black mouth

golden mohair plush

short, slightly curved arms

two printed, card chest-tags

straight legs and small feet with oval pads

red, embroidered foot-label

brown, suedette pads with no claws

1960s TARA TOYS; FELT NOSE

Height: 30cm (12in)

This bear possesses its original foot label and two printed, card swing-tags. The reverse of the tri-angular tag reads, "Hi! Little Girl...Ho! Little Boy/ I want to be your Plushy Toy!/I'd like to have you hold me tight/And go to bed with you each night!"

Embroidered label

---

wide, shallow ears, sewn across facial seams

high forehead with horizontal seam across top of head

amber, glass eyes with black pupils, sewn into face on wire shanks

horizontally stitched, shield-shaped, black nose with inverted-Y-shaped mouth

golden mohair plush; soft-stuffing in limbs; wood-wool and soft stuffing elsewhere

short, curved, pointed arms

short, stubby legs with fat feet

rust-red, felt pads

red, embroidered foot label

1938–49 "MADE IN EIRE" LABEL

Height: 40cm (16in)

From 1937 until 1949, when Ireland left the British Commonwealth and became a Republic, the country was known as Éire (the Gaelic word for Ireland, used in their 1937 constitution). Labels with this wording therefore date a bear to the 1938–49 period.

Embroidered label

---

large ears sewn across facial seams

vertically stitched, triangular, black nose with single, long stitch extending from each top corner

amber and black, plastic eyes sewn into head on wire shanks

dark golden mohair plush; wood-wool stuffing in head; wood-wool and kapok mix elsewhere

tapering arms

replacement corduroy pads, originally Rexine

small, stumpy feet

c.1957 TARA TOYS; UNIQUE NOSE

Height: 56cm (22½in)

Although unmarked, this bear's shape, and particularly its unique nose design, resembles that of bears seen in trade journal advertisements for the *Gaeltarra Eireann*. Bears were designed for the *Gaeltacht* by former Sonneberg toy designer, Hans Weberpals, from 1950 until 1965, when he left to start his own factory, Celtic Toys, in County Cork.

---

flat ears, sewn across facial seams

small, pale orange, glass eyes with black pupils

inset, rounded muzzle with T-shaped seam extending across nose and down chin

worn, horizontally stitched, triangular, black nose; black, embroidered mouth almost worn away

short, tapering arms with unusual pointed paws

stubby feet with brown, felt pads

white cotton plush; stuffed with wood-wool; internal squeaker

c.1947 ERRIS TOYS; COTTON PLUSH

Height: 33cm (13in)

Teddy bears made at Elly Bay bore the "Erris Toys" trademark until c.1953, then changed to "Tara Toys". This rare Gaelic label "*Bréagáin Iorruis; Déantús Na Gaeltachta*" means "Erris Toys; Made in the *Gaeltacht*". The cotton plush is typical of the era.

Embroidered label

Merrythought: 1982-92

COLLECTOR BEARS; REPLICAS AND SPECIAL COMMISSIONS

In 1982, Merrythought introduced a range of limited-edition teddies for import into the US by Tide-Rider Inc. of Baldwin, New York – a partnership that continues today. Novelties included a green/blue, traditional-style teddy bear and the 1984 Seasonal Bear series, in which each bear represented either Spring, Summer, Autumn, or Winter. In 1992, Merrythought introduced Mr and Miss Mischief, depicting naughty "children". By 1986–87, replicas of Punkinhead and the Magnet bear were in production followed, in 1992, by replicas of Mr Whoppit, Bingie, and *Titanic* survivor Gatti.

1983 EDWARDIAN BEAR

This bear's name refers to its "antique-look" design, with a long muzzle and limbs and humped back, emulating bears of the Edwardian period of British history (1901–10). As indicated on the printed label sewn into the left side-seam, this particular example is No. 493 of a limited edition of 1000. It was the second design in the Tide-Rider collectors' series; the first was the golden mohair-plush Anniversary Bear, with slightly rounder features and a black, embroidered nose.

Height: 50cm (20in)

Printed label

Fur: *the pure mohair plush is described as "Old Gold", possibly because it resembles the colour of old teddies.*

Claws: *four brown, webbed claws are embroidered across each felt pad.*

Label: *the label, with wording used since the late 1950s, is machine-stitched onto the foot-pad.*

Nose: *with its wide shape, vertical stitching, and dropped, central stitch meeting a wide, inverted-Y-shaped mouth, the nose is modelled on those of pre-World War I Steiff and Bing bears.*

Muzzle: *the elongated muzzle has been shaved down to bristly stubble, revealing the woven cloth backing beneath.*

BEAR PROFILE

In profile, you can clearly see this bear's humped back and extremely long, curved arms – features that were typical of teddy bears at the beginning of the century, before Merrythought's foundation.

Swing-tag: *this printed, card tag guarantees that the pile is made from pure mohair, and illustrates its source – an angora goat.*

Pads: *the beige, felt pads are spoon-shaped on the paws and slightly pointed on the large, narrow feet.*

horizontally stitched, rectangular nose; slightly smiling, inverted-Y-shaped mouth

black, plastic, replica boot-button eyes

protruding, shaved muzzle

original floral ribbon

pointed, shaved, mohair-plush paws

slim torso, narrowing at chest

finest mohair and silk plush; soft-stuffed body and limbs; wood-wool head

two black, diagonal stitches, forming V-shaped claws, on each pad

1992 TOUCH OF SILK
Height: 45cm (18in)

Shown in the International Collectors' Catalogue in 1992, this bear's unusual arms and pads depart from the traditional style. It was designed by Jacqueline Revitt, Merrythought's design director since the 1970s, and carries the 1990s wishbone label.

Embroidered label

---

brown and black, safe, plastic eyes

shaved muzzle stuffed with wood-wool

black, vertically stitched nose, with dropped outer stitches

green, Harrods ribbon

short, golden mohair plush; soft, polyester stuffing

dark brown pads of soft synthetic, Dralon-type fabric

four black, webbed claws on paws, three straight claws on feet

green label with gold lettering, exclusive to Harrods

1986 HARRODS BEAR
Height: 30cm (12in)

During the 1980s, Merrythought produced various bears, such as this one, for Harrods – the large, London department store. These included a standing bear dressed in the green, Harrods' commissionaire's livery. The green and gold label is exclusive to Harrods.

Embroidered label

---

large, black, safe, plastic eyes, resembling boot-buttons

black, vertically stitched nose with dropped outer stitches

mauve-tipped, beige mohair plush on beige woven backing; soft, polyester stuffing

original mauve, satin ribbon around neck

printed foot label with 1957–80s wording

beige, synthetic fabric pads

1990 LAVENDER; MAGNET REPLICA
Height: 19cm (7½in)

This reproduction of the 1930s Magnet design is made from mauve-tipped, beige, "dual" mohair plush, and is impregnated with lavender perfume. It is one of several scented bears produced by Merrythought. Others included Rose Petal and Peach Blossom.

Printed label

---

beige-tipped, mushroom-coloured mohair plush; soft, polyester stuffing

swivel-jointed head; bear in permanently seated position

black, shield-shaped nose

inset muzzle of darker plush, stuffed with wood-wool

red ribbon around neck and on right arm

hand-made accordion with poker-work decoration and mother-of-pearl keys

short, dark, plush pads, with airbrushed paws and feet

1992 BIRTHDAY BEAR
Height: 39cm (15½in)

Since 1984, Karin Heller, a German doll designer, has sold a range of teddy bears, manufactured by Merrythought, in Germany. This bear is one of four, 500-piece, limited-edition bears produced in 1992, dressed by Karin in clothes suited to the German market.

Printed label

Dean's: 1980s~90s

In 1981, Dean's launched into collectables with a limited-edition series of three bears inspired by Norman Rockwell illustrations. Aiming at the US market, the company also made a nightshirt-clad Porridge Bear, based on a 1909 illustration by Jessie Willcox Smith. In 1983, Dean's produced a limited-edition, 80th anniversary bear, and in 1984, it collaborated with Donna Harrison and Dottie Ayers of the Baltimore shop, The Calico Teddy, to make Teddy B and Teddy G to their design. In 1986, Dean's was taken over by the toy and gift importers Plaintalk, forming The Dean's Company (1903) Ltd.

1987 TRADITIONAL DESIGN

This traditional, fully jointed teddy bear was originally marketed with a printed calico drawstring bag. The bear has a red on white embroidered label in the left side-seam, designed after the takeover by Plaintalk in 1986. Rationalization forced the firm into voluntary liquidation, but the newly appointed director, Neil Miller, bought out the firm and commenced trading as a new company on 7 March 1988.

Height: 48cm (19in)

Embroidered label

Ears: *the small, flat ears are sewn into the vertical seams down the sides of the head.*

Eyes: *the safe, plastic eyes are amber-coloured with black pupils.*

Mouth: *the wide, smiling mouth curves upwards.*

Nose: *the black, shield-shaped nose is vertically stitched.*

Bow: *the red, ribbon bow is original.*

Fur/stuffing: *the fur is "London Gold" mohair plush on a woven, woollen backing; the bear is stuffed with polyurethane foam granules.*

Arms: *the arms are the same length as the legs, and end in curved, tapering paws.*

Feet: *the feet are large and rounded, and have brown, synthetic-velvet pads.*

BEAR PROFILE
In profile, you can see the smiling mouth embroidered onto the inset, blunt, protruding muzzle. The large, rounded head is made up of four pieces of plush; the ears are set into the side-seams. The bear has short arms, unusual squared-off shoulders, and small, tapering paws.

brown, safe, plastic eyes with black pupils

large, flat ears sewn across facial seams

light brown mohair plush; soft stuffing; internal tilt-growler

vertically stitched, shield-shaped, black nose; inverted-Y-shaped mouth

long, curved arms

original brown, orange, and red silk bow

foot label with "fighting dogs" logo

brown, suedette pads with no claws

1991 DEAN'S RAG BOOK CO. LTD.

Height: 43cm (17in)

The old Dean's Rag Book Co. name was dropped during the Plaintalk takeover, but Neil Miller purchased the trading rights and logo in 1990. In 1991, the company launched a new range of limited-edition bears, using the old "fighting dogs" logo.

Printed label

---

reddish brown, safe, plastic eyes with black pupils

realistic, black, safe, moulded plastic nose

black, inverted-T-shaped, smiling mouth

original red, nylon, ribbon bow

golden mohair plush; soft-stuffed except for wood-wool in head; internal tilt-growler

curved, tapering arms

small, tapering feet

dark brown, brushed-nylon pads

C.1984 DEAN'S CHILDSPLAY TOYS

Height: 40cm (16in)

From 1982 to 1986, Dean's employed a new green embroidered label (retaining the name Dean's Childsplay Toys), for use only on teddy bears. The label, which was sewn into a side-seam, was used on bears in both the general and the collectors' ranges.

Embroidered label

---

black, safe, plastic, button eyes

vertically stitched, shield-shaped, black nose; inverted-T-shaped mouth

original red, velvet bow-tie

champagne-coloured, "distressed" mohair plush; wood-wool stuffing in head; foam stuffing elsewhere

brown, Dralon pads; three black claws across mohair plush

foot label with "fighting dogs" logo

1991 LIMITED-EDITION REPLICA

Height: 43cm (17in)

Dean's launched a series of replicas in 1991; this bear is based on a 1940s design by sales manager, Jack Crane, father of the present sales director, Michael Crane. The label reads "Made in Great Britain"; pre-1956 labels read "Made in England".

Printed label

---

bulbous head with high forehead and central seam

large, slightly cupped ears

large, round, black, safe, plastic eyes

vertically stitched, narrow, rectangular, black nose with inverted-Y-shaped mouth

golden woollen plush, made in Britain, as indicated on card chest-tag

original red ribbon

thick, curved arms; no pads or claws

stubby feet; no pads or claws

BRITISH WOOL

1985 NORMAN ROCKWELL SERIES III

Height: 30cm (12in)

The last in a limited-edition series, based on Rockwell bears featured on *Saturday Evening Post* front covers, this bear is based on one in his painting "Election Day" (1948). 1,000 bears were made with Republican ribbons; another 1,000 with Democratic ribbons.

Embroidered label

France: post-1945

NEW COMPANIES PRODUCING CUDDLY, UNJOINTED BEARS

Some French companies founded before World War II, such as Pintel and A.L.F.A. (producing popular, dressed teddy bears from 1936), continued after 1945, but using synthetic materials. Several new companies were also established during the 1950s and 1960s, such as Anima (1947), Boulgom (1954), and Nounours (1963). They all used the new, foam-rubber filling that revolutionized the soft-toy industry. Though some manufacturers failed during the 1970s and 1980s, several were bought by Nounours who, by the 1990s, was responsible for 80 per cent of all French soft-toy exports.

c.1980s BOULGOM

M. Frenay founded Boulgom at Oullins in 1954. In 1964, the company moved to Chaponost, near Lyon, where the factory is still situated. Boulgom was one of the first soft-toy manufacturers to produce washable bears with foam-rubber stuffing. The company expanded considerably during the 1970s, buying Anima in 1972, but went bankrupt in 1990. It is now part of the well-known French manufacturing group, Alain Thirion, along with the other toy manufacturers, Joustra and Vulli.

Height: 23cm (9in)   Printed label

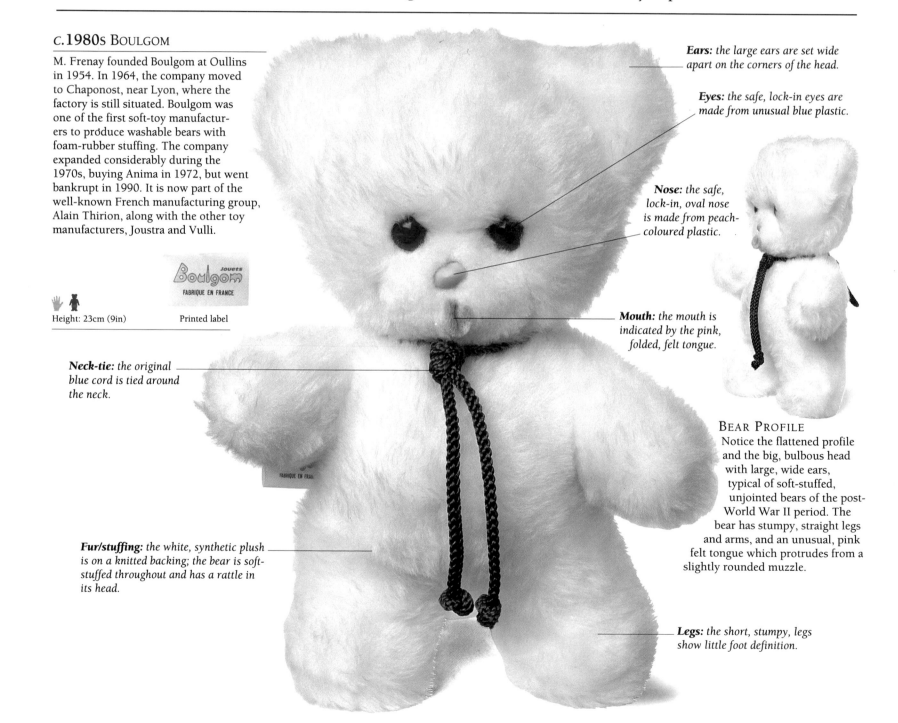

Ears: *the large ears are set wide apart on the corners of the head.*

Eyes: *the safe, lock-in eyes are made from unusual blue plastic.*

Nose: *the safe, lock-in, oval nose is made from peach-coloured plastic.*

Mouth: *the mouth is indicated by the pink, folded, felt tongue.*

Neck-tie: *the original blue cord is tied around the neck.*

Fur/stuffing: *the white, synthetic plush is on a knitted backing; the bear is soft-stuffed throughout and has a rattle in its head.*

BEAR PROFILE
Notice the flattened profile and the big, bulbous head with large, wide ears, typical of soft-stuffed, unjointed bears of the post-World War II period. The bear has stumpy, straight legs and arms, and an unusual, pink felt tongue which protrudes from a slightly rounded muzzle.

Legs: *the short, stumpy, legs show little foot definition.*

1980s NOUNOURS

Height: 71cm (28in)

black, safe, plastic eyes

black, leather-like, vinyl nose

muzzle seams form mouth

short, unjointed arms

brown, shaggy, synthetic plush; soft-stuffed throughout

"Nounours", a colloquial French term for "teddy", is derived from *un ours* (a bear). Jacky Dubois established the firm in 1963, which eventually became the Brittany-based Nounours Group, with factories in France, Italy, Tunisia, and Mauritius.

Printed label

C.1983 LES CRÉATIONS ANIMA

Height: 45cm (18in)

large, flat ears set wide apart

black, safe, locked-in, plastic eyes

hard, padded, suede nose

printed card chest-tag with French flag, paw-print, and Anima's logo

shaggy, honey-coloured plush; soft-stuffed

Suzanne Vangelder established Anima in Paris in 1947 and, in 1972, after becoming a subsidiary of Boulgom, it moved to Chaponost. Gund bought the firm in 1992. Special sewing machines, used in the fur-coat trade, are used on their teddy bears.

Printed tag

C.1988 AUX NATIONS

Height: 55cm (22in)

shorter pile, plush muzzle

brown and black, safe, glass eyes

realistic black, leather nose

folded leather strip creates realistic mouth

long, dark brown nylon plush; soft-stuffed throughout

embroidered, label sewn to top of left hip

Inspired by Annaud's film *The Bear*, Frédérique Quentin designed Kodiak Bear for Aux Nations. (Another French company produced the official licenced product.) Established in the 1960s, Aux Nations became part of Nounours in 1975.

Embroidered label

C.1980 AJENA

Height: 39cm (15½in)

large, round, brown, safe, plastic eyes

inset muzzle

safe, oval, velvet-covered nose

circular, printed card tag attached to right paw

synthetic fabric shirt

leather badge printed with name "Léon"

light brown, synthetic, short-pile plush on woven backing; soft, polyester-fibre stuffing

large feet; no claws

This bear, named Léon, was bought in the large Paris store Printemps about 1980. In 1989, Ajena, a company based in Le Lude, near Tours, was bought by Nounours, who retained the tradename. The firm now produces a cheaper quality Ajena range that is distributed to French supermarkets and made at Nounours' factories in Tunisia and Mauritius.

Europe: 1930s–80s

EASTERN EUROPE; MEDITERRANEAN; SCANDINAVIA; BENELUX

From the interwar years until its nationalization in 1948, Czechoslovakia had a thriving teddy-bear industry. In 1938, Hamiro was the second largest European soft-toy manufacturer and, from 1925 until 1948, Wilhelmine Walter made Kersa bears at Lobositz, then in Bohemia. Poland also was a major exporter of teddy bears from the 1950s. Lenci introduced teddies to Italy in 1931 (Three Bears, with open mouths and bibs); GZB made similar examples, and Trudi and Jocky have produced bears in more recent years. A few teddies originate from Spain, such as G. Fali's Osito, a *c.*1959 googly-eyed baby bear.

*c.*1960 POLAND

Although unmarked, this bear shares many characteristics with the few existing bears that still retain their "Made in Poland" paper labels – the latter either stuck to the foot-pad or in the form of a swing-tag. Dating from the 1950s to the 1960s, these bears were produced with traditional embroidered facial features as well as with leather noses and felt tongues as seen here. The most popular colour was golden, but white, grey, and brown examples were also made in a range of sizes.

Height: 38cm (15in)

Ears: *the flat, narrow ears are sewn across the facial seams.*

Eyes: *the clear, glass eyes, painted amber on the backs, are sewn in on wire shanks.*

Mouth: *only part of the original semi-circular, red, felt tongue remains.*

Nose: *the nose consists of a narrow piece of brown leather, with the ends curled under tightly to form the "nostrils"; it is secured to the end of the muzzle with fuse wire.*

Fur/stuffing: *the short, curly, golden cotton plush is typical of Polish bears. The bear is solidly stuffed with wood-wool – another typical feature.*

Limbs: *the limbs are fully jointed, with thin, plywood discs connected by metal rods across the body at the shoulders and thighs; this is a cheap method of jointing that makes the arms or legs move back and forth simultaneously.*

BEAR PROFILE

From the side you can see the solid shape of this bear. The wide head, with its very square muzzle and thick neck, is set on a body that is deeper than it is wide; the short, curved arms end in tapering paws, and the slightly longer legs, with "drumstick" thighs, narrow at the ankles and end in rounded, stubby feet.

Pads: *the pads, typical of those of Polish bears, are made from the reverse of the plush, revealing the pale yellow (now discoloured and stained) woven fabric. The lack of claws is also typical.*

large, triangular head with all-in-one ears

smooth, triangular, safe, moulded plastic nose; no mouth

inset, pointed muzzle

short, stubby, unjointed arms; no pads or claws

"Certificate of Origin No. 998089"

large, brown and black, safe, plastic eyes

original chain around neck, to mimic dancing bears of Europe

soft synthetic plush

short, unjointed legs with large, rounded feet, slightly splayed out from body

1980s LENCI
Height: 40cm (16in)

This soft-stuffed, unjointed, wide-hipped bear is typical of the Italian firm Lenci's modern work. World-famous for its 1920s dolls with moulded felt heads, Lenci's tradename is derived from the Latin motto: "To Play Is Our Constant Work".

Lenci TORINO

Embroidered label

amber and black, plastic eyes, sewn in

original red, satin ribbon around neck

dyed, golden-brown lambskin; soft, Styrofoam stuffing

fully jointed limbs and head

large, natural lambskin ears

narrow, shield-shaped, dark brown, vertically stitched nose; mouth represented by two horizontal stitches beneath nose

brown, suede pads on feet and paws; no claws

large, oval feet

1980s AB MERIMEX
Height: 43cm (17in)

This lambskin and suede bear is typical of Ab Merimex, the most well-known Swedish teddy-bear manufacturer, founded after World War II by refugee Emil Grünfelt. Originally based in Mälmo, the company has since moved production to Portugal.

Card swing-tag

large, flat ears sewn across corners of head

large head, with flattened muzzle

safe, black, moulded plastic, realistic nose with nostrils; no mouth

unjointed arms and legs; no pads; no feet

amber and black, safe, plastic eyes

narrow, red ribbon around neck

shaggy, cream-coloured, synthetic plush; soft stuffing

c.1973 FLUFFIES
Height: 43cm (17in)

This is a typical example of the synthetic, unjointed, 1970s bears made by this Belgian company. According to the Benelux Association of Toy Manufacturers, there are no longer any teddy-bear manufacturers in either Belgium or the Netherlands.

Fluffies MADE IN BELGIUM

Embroidered label

small, flat ears sewn on sides of head; lined with contrasting white, rayon plush

small, bulbous, dark turquoise-green, plastic eyes with black pupils, glued in place

short, stumpy, fully jointed legs and arms; no pads or claws; slight foot definition

large, rounded head with centre seam

black, moulded plastic nose, glued to end of muzzle

original yellow ribbon bow

silky, beige rayon plush on knitted backing; soft stuffed

1960s POLAND
Height: 33cm (13in)

The printed tag indicates that this bear was made at the Bajka Toymaking Co-operative Works in Lublin, south-east of Warsaw. "Bajka" means "fairy-tale" or "story", the logo being a blonde girl. In the mid-1960s, 15 toy-making co-operatives existed in Poland.

Printed paper tag

Worldwide Expansion: post-1945

EXPORT AND HOME-MARKET TRADE BY ISRAEL, CANADA, CHINA & SOUTH AFRICA

After World War II, teddy-bear manufacture was no longer restricted to Europe and the US. Many countries, including China, Israel, and Brazil, began making cheap-quality bears largely for the export market to the UK, US, and Australia. Canada, too, established several soft-toy companies during the 1950s, such as Ganz Brothers and Mighty Star Ltd. who, by the 1990s, also produced a range of collectors' bears to meet the demand at home and abroad. In South Africa, teddy bears are manufactured primarily for the home market, such as those produced by Prima Toys' Durban-based factory.

1980 TOYLAND

Israeli-produced teddy bears have been exported to various countries, including the United Kingdom, the United States, and Australia, since the 1960s. Some, like this shaggy, brown and beige Toyland bear, give the manufacturer's name, as well as the sitting poodle logo, on the label which is sewn into the left side-seam; others simply have "Made in Israel". Toyland Ltd. is a division of Caesarea, whose headquarters are based in Glenoit, Indiana.

Height: 40cm (16in)

Printed label

Ears: *two large pieces of contrasting plush, sewn centrally across the facial seams, make up the ears.*

Eyes: *the brown, safe, plastic eyes have black pupils.*

Nose: *the safe, stylized nose is made from black, moulded plastic.*

Muzzle: *the inset, protruding muzzle is made from two pieces of pale golden, synthetic, velvet-like fabric.*

Bow: *the original red, ribbon bow is tied around the neck.*

Arms: *the curved arms end in tapering paws.*

Fur/stuffing: *the fur is shaggy, brown and beige, synthetic plush with contrasting beige plush on the muzzle and pads; the stuffing is shredded polyurethane.*

BEAR PROFILE

In profile, you can see this bear's unusually constructed, protruding, two-piece, inset muzzle, as well as the large, two-piece ears sewn down the sides of the head. The slightly curved arms are shorter than the legs, which have clearly defined ankles; the feet are small and rounded.

Legs: *the legs are short and drumstick-shaped; the feet are small.*

sewn-on peaked cap and overalls of navy blue and white, striped cotton fabric

dark brown, synthetic plush head, ears, paws, and feet

realistic, black, safe, moulded plastic nose

large, amber, safe, plastic eyes with black pupils

inset, light brown, synthetic plush muzzle

folded, card swing-tag with English and French wording

red, synthetic plush body stuffed with non-allergenic foam chips

woven "CN Rail" badge

1984 CUDDLY TOYS LTD.

Height: 40cm (16in)

Oscar (the nickname for railway engineers in Montreal) is the mascot for the Canadian National Railways and was designed by Dalyce Feir of Mara's Stuffed Animals for their associated firm Cuddly Toys Ltd., which specializes in the distribution of corporation mascots. All their bears are designed and produced in Canada with Canadian raw materials.

unjointed head with inset, pale golden, synthetic plush muzzle

green, velour hat with black band, always worn by Yogi in cartoons

large, round, black nose

large, oval, plastic eyes with black pupils

wide, black, embroidered mouth; airbrushed whiskers

brown, synthetic plush; stuffed with mixture of cellulose fibre, shredded plastic, and synthetic foam beads

illustrated card swing tag with "Characters by Mighty Star"

1980 MIGHTY STAR

Height: 40cm (16in)

Yogi Bear, named after US baseball player, Yogi Berra, gained fame in the 1960s after appearing in US television programmes by Hanna Barbera. He featured in a film in 1964, and has inspired many children's toys, including this Canadian-made bear.

© 1980
HANNA-BARBERA PRODUCTIONS, INC.
BY/PAR
MIGHTY STAR

Printed label

brown and black, safe, plastic eyes

large, cupped ears sewn from facial seams down sides and towards back of head

dark brown, square, synthetic fabric nose; black, inverted-Y-shaped, single-stitched mouth

short-pile, golden synthetic plush on woven backing; soft stuffed

dark brown, synthetic fabric pads with three black, stitched claws

foil rosette with "SDF Shanghai Dolls Factory"

1980s SHANGHAI DOLLS FACTORY

Height: 38cm (15in)

Teddy bears have changed little since they were first exported from mainland China after World War II, although safe, plastic eyes have replaced glass eyes. The Shanghai Dolls Factory is one of China's main teddy-bear manufacturers.

Printed tag

large, cupped ears with inner edges caught into facial seams

modacrylic, high pile, knitted fabric; polyester-fibre stuffing

black, triangular, moulded nose; black, double-stitched mouth

short, stumpy legs; pads of dark brown plush

tag with instructions, "Cool gentle wash in machine; brush when dry"

cloth label sewn into leg-seam

1992 BUNJY TOYS

Height: 25cm (10in)

Honey Bear (above) was made by South African firm Bunjy Toys, founded by Eve Mayhew in 1980. The firm moved to larger premises in Estcourt, Natal, in 1982, to meet growing demand. Their soft-toys are made from imported and South African materials.

BUNJY TOYS c.c.
ESTCOURT
MADE IN
SOUTH
AFRICA

Embroidered label

Mass-market Collectables: 1980s-90s

MASS-PRODUCED, ARTIST-DESIGNED BEARS FOR COLLECTORS

The growth of arctophily prompted an alliance of bear artists and manufacturers to produce mass-market, limited-edition collectables. The US company Applause heralded this approach by introducing Robert Raikes' bears to its range in 1985. From 1987, the House of Nisbet in Britain reproduced the designs of well-known US artists, including Carol-Lynn Rössel Waugh, Beverly Port, Ted Menten, Dee Hockenberry, and April Whitcomb. By 1990, other companies in the UK, US, and Germany had followed suit. Limited editions could number as many as 10,000 when produced by major manufacturers.

1991 CAROL-LYNN RÖSSEL WAUGH

Carol-Lynn Rössel Waugh designed Gregory, named after her brother, for the New York company Effanbee in 1989. The company was later bought by Russ Berrie, who first introduced Gregory in 1991 along with Eureka, designed by US bear artist Linda Spiegel Lohre. The original Gregory was 35cm (14in) high and jointed; the manufacturers later developed this smaller, unjointed design.

Height: 23cm (9in)   Embroidered label

Eyes: *the black, safe, plastic eyes resemble boot-buttons.*

Muzzle: *the plush on the protruding muzzle is clipped.*

Nose/mouth: *the square, brown nose is vertically stitched; the mouth is an inverted Y shape.*

Bow: *the maroon, satin, ribbon bow is original.*

Arms: *the elongated arms are the same length as the legs, and have spoon-shaped paws.*

Fur: *the fur is shaggy, curly, golden synthetic plush; the stuffing is a soft, polyester fiberfill.*

Feet/pads: *the oval feet have brown, synthetic, velvet-like fabric pads and no claws.*

BEAR PROFILE

It is difficult to distinguish the arms, legs, and body, or the positioning of the ears on the sides of the head, on this shaggy bear. However, you can see the protruding muzzle, and the short, stubby tail. Notice that the arms are as long as the legs.

1986 ROBERT RAIKES　　Height: 45cm (18in)

brown plastic eyes; pupil formed by hole drilled into wood behind

light brown acrylic plush

mouth described as "pouty face"

hand-carved face

carved, button-like nose

fully jointed limbs and body

sailor's jacket with brass buttons

carved feet with defined toes

Robert Raikes, a professional wood sculptor during the 1970s, began carving dolls, and then, in 1982, teddy bears; these were known as "Woody Bears" and later "Raikes Originals". He signed a contract with the US company Applause, which has been producing his bears since 1985. This sailor bear, Christopher, has unique carved wooden head and paws.

1992 JOYCE ANN HAUGHEY　　Height: 38cm (15in)

horizontally stitched, oval nose and inverted-Y-shaped mouth

black, safe, plastic eyes, resembling boot-buttons

golden mohair plush; stuffed with plastic pellets and polyester fiberfill

long, tapering arms with upward curving paws

fully jointed body and limbs

long, slightly bent legs

red, plastic chest-tag

During the 1980s, Werner Hermann and his niece Traudel Mischner, designed Gebrüder Hermann's bears. Then, in 1992, Hermann introduced bears designed by US bear artists Joyce Ann Haughey and Jenny Krantz for the collector's market. Robin Hood (*above*), one of a limited edition of 2,000, was nominated for a TOBY award in 1992.

1990 CATHIE HANNA　　Height: 50cm (20in)

charcoal-grey acrylic plush; polyester fiberfill stuffing

large, flat ears lined with blue suede

square, black, vertically stitched nose; inverted-Y-shaped mouth

original spectacles

blue, suede pads; three black claws stitched over plush

limited-edition number on right foot-pad

large, oval feet

fully jointed limbs

Ohio-based artist, Cathie Hanna, designed this Grandmother Brompton bear and her grand-daughter Abbey (a white bear); she also wrote a story about Abbey, whose photograph is in Grandmother Brompton's silver locket. Canterbury Bears (*see pp.150–51*), whose work is normally designed by John and Maude Blackburn, manufactured these bears.

1990 BONITA WARRINGTON　　Height: 35cm (14in)

black, vertically stitched, shield-shaped nose; inverted-Y-shaped, single-stitched mouth

safe, black, button eyes

brown acrylic fur

printed wooden trademark tied around neck

blue denim overalls with large side pockets

suede pads with four black, embroidered claws

large feet

Bonita began to make bears in 1983, inspired by a reproduction, antique teddy bear. She later successfully exhibited her work at the San Jose convention, and turned to full-time bear-making at her California home. C. Owen, shown here, came in three sizes in a limited edition of 5,000, and was one of her first designs produced by Applause.

Bear Artists

INDIVIDUAL CREATIONS FROM AROUND THE WORLD

Bear artistry has spread throughout the world since it began on the West Coast of the US in the early 1970s. Many other countries are now renowned for the work of their bear artists, including the UK, Germany, France, the Netherlands, New Zealand, Australia, and Canada. It is not possible to include an example of the work of every bear artist, as there are now hundreds worldwide, but a selection of work, covering a range of nationalities and design trends, is illustrated on the following pages.

A bear artist is someone who both designs and hand-makes a bear, thereby producing an original work. Some artists are helped by family and friends, and a few, with the growing demand for their work, have enlarged their businesses and employed cutters, machinists, or stuffers. The artist, however, generally hand-finishes each bear, giving the final personal touches. Arctophiles often question whether this can be counted as true artistry; it is perhaps comparable to great painters of the past who have had the help of artisans to mix colours and transfer designs to canvas. Bear artists usually produce limited editions in small numbers, up to 25; those with extra workers make more. The value and unique character of each bear is ensured by limiting the numbers produced.

Bear artists frequently use decorative printed or embroidered labels as trademarks. The artist's signature and the edition number often appear on the label or the foot-pad, while some individualized symbols appear on other parts of the body. Some bear artists sell their bears from home; others market them in specialist shops or at conventions. Several bear artists even design bears for production by major manufacturers on a much larger scale (see pp.170–71).

brown synthetic plush

black, replica boot-button eyes

silver-painted medallion with embossed standing bear

black, horizontally stitched, triangular nose

cream, felt paw-pads; four embroidered claws

blue, synthetic plush body with musical box inside

*c.*1980s BEVERLY PORT   Height: 40cm (16in)

antique, black, boot-button eyes

three-piece head with shaved, pointed muzzle

black, horizontally stitched, narrow, oval nose; small, inverted-T-shaped mouth

golden mohair plush; polyester fiberfill stuffing

beige, ultrasuede pads

pear-shaped torso

*c.*1988 STEVE SCHUTT   Height: 35cm (14in)

Beverly Port, from Retsil, Washington State, is considered to be the first recorded, professional bear artist. Originally a porcelain doll-maker, Port turned to teddy bears in 1974. She has won many awards for her innovative work, some of which has been exhibited in art galleries. Her children, Kimberlee and John Paul, are also bear artists.

Steve, an art teacher from Clarion, Iowa, has been involved in puppetry for 17 years. He began making bears for the collectors' market in 1980, and later became a bear artist under the tradename "Bear-'s'-ence". Steve has won prestigious awards for his work; Tyler and Pawpet are shown here. Since 1983, his assistant Barbara Smith has cut and sewn for him.

black, horizontally stitched, triangular nose; inverted-T-shaped mouth

black, replica boot-button eyes

red velour plush

black claws stitched across plush

gold-coloured, metal heart fixed onto plush

spoon-shaped, black velour pads

traditional large feet and narrow ankles

1984 K. AND H. CALVIN   Height: 45cm (18in)

Karin Calvin first made bears with friends in 1979, then formed a partnership with Howard in 1982. Their Ballard Baines Bear Company takes its name from a bear Karin bought. They made this bear for the 1984 Great Western Teddy Bear Show.

BALLARD BAINES Bear Company (c) Bellevue, Wash.

Printed label

---

bonnet decorated with rosebuds and ribbon

replica boot-button eyes

pink, woollen plush

black, horizontally stitched, triangular nose; inverted-T-shaped mouth

salmon-pink cotton dress with white polka dots

felt cub

cream, felt pads

broderie Anglaise apron

1983 LINDSAY PURPUS   Height: 33cm (13in)

Cheryl Lindsay and Joanne Purpus of California, created Purpusly Prairie (above); she is dressed in early nineteenth-century, American pioneer clothing, with a wide-brimmed bonnet, and carries a bear cub made of felt.

Lindsay Purpus

Printed label

---

black, boot-button eyes with single, diagonally embroidered eyebrow

brown, vertically stitched, shield-shaped nose with inverted-Y-shaped, single-stitched mouth

shaggy, cinnamon-coloured mohair plush

chocolate-brown, velvet pads

four dark brown, embroidered claws

painted, white ceramic heart pendant

1989 C-L. RÖSSEL WAUGH   Height: 38cm (15in)

Carol-Lynn Rössel Waugh, of Winthrop, Maine, the creator of PJs (above), was one of the first US bear artists and writers on the subject of bear artistry. She began making porcelain and latex teddies in 1975, and mohair bears from 1985 onwards.

Handwritten label

---

black, blown-glass eyes

black, vertically stitched, triangular nose; inverted-Y-shaped mouth

shaved, pointed muzzle

medium grey, German mohair plush; polyester fiberfill stuffing

curved paws with grey, felt paw-pads

long, fully jointed legs; large feet

1983 CHESTER FREEMAN   Height: 25cm (10in)

This bear artist, a former chaplain, began making teddy bears in 1982. In 1983, he formed Baskets and Bears, a mail-order firm, with basket-maker John McGuire. They work in an 1820 Federal row house in Geneva, New York State.

A HAND-MADE ORIGINAL

Printed label

brown, vertically stitched, shield-shaped nose

cameo brooch with bear's head

polka-dot apron with rick-rack braid

beige mohair plush

collarless shirt with vertical stripes

denim overalls and dark jacket

three-pronged pitchfork

thumb indicated on paws

four brown claws stitched to each paw and foot

1990 BARBARA CONLEY

Height: 48cm (19in)

At a teddy-bear convention in Clarion, Iowa, in 1990, bear artists were asked for their interpretation of Grant Wood's "American Gothic" painting, which depicts an elderly couple in front of their mid-western home. The winning entry, by Barbara Conley, of San Jose, California, was exact in detail, down to the wife's brooch and the husband's spectacles.

toy rifle with wooden stock, metal barrel, cork "bullet", and leather sling

hunter's fringed, soft leather shirt

eyes set inside shaved area of face

fake, racoon-skin hat

large, rounded, shaved muzzle

1985 BARBARA SIXBY

Height: 48cm (19in)

This Californian bear artist recreated the 18th-century, American frontiersman Daniel Boone in 1985. Boone, a skilful hunter, reputedly wore a fringed, hunting shirt that reached down to his knees. Only two of these bears were made.

ZÜCKER BEARS
SAN RAMON, CA.

Printed label

hand-made, mohair-yarn curls

lollipop refers to famous Shirley Temple song, On the Good Ship Lollipop

baked, moulded, black nose

black, embroidered mouth with broad smile

beige, synthetic plush; kapok stuffing

red, polka-dot cotton dress with pleated ruff

1983 BEV MILLER LANDSTRA

Height: 20cm (8in)

This artist from Veneta, Oregon, first made teddies for her son in 1963. As well as Shirley Teddy, shown here, Bev is renowned for her sets of personality bears from 1983, including Stan and Ollie, The Marx Bears, and T.R. Bear.

Shirley Teddy

Printed label

wide-brimmed, straw hat

plastic, replica, boot-button eyes

head tilts to one side with endearing expression

grey plush

baggy, blue, denim overalls

large, flat ears sewn to sides of head

black, embroidered nose and mouth

small, wooden catapult protruding from left pocket

1984 DORIS KING

Height: 33cm (13in)

This bear pays homage to American literary hero, Huckleberry Finn, and is described by the artist as "a picture of innocence". Second in The Pre Loved Ted series, he is dressed in denim overalls and straw hat. The bear was created in 1984, as a limited edition of 75, only a year after Doris, from Sacramento, California, made her first teddy bear.

head opens to reveal lipstick

bright, cerise-pink, synthetic, velvet-like fabric

cotton lace ruff and pink ribbon around neck

black, embroidered, triangular nose with smiling mouth beneath

pink, felt pads with four tiny, black claws

black, bead eyes

jointed arms and legs

1984 SARA PHILLIPS   Height: 2.5cm (1in)

These tiny bears, made in 1984, conceal a perfume bottle and compact respectively; they emulate the intriguing designs of similar, miniature bears made by Schuco in the 1920s and 30s. Sara, from Westminster, Maryland, began making copies of miniature antique bears in 1981 for a tiny teddy-bear shop she was opening. She also creates her own designs.

tiny, black, horzontally stitched, oval nose

inset, slightly protruding, cream, felt face; eyes sewn in near seam

wide, smiling mouth in style of Steiff's Dicky

fully jointed limbs and head

short-pile, good quality, golden mohair plush

cream, felt feet, with four long, black claws

1988 E. FUJITA-GAMBLE   Height: 7.5cm (3in)

Flaine is a physical education teacher in Washington State, but she has been making teddy bears, particularly miniatures, in her spare time since 1979, and selling them at shows in the US. A keen teddy-bear collector, Flaine likes to base her creations on antique bears: this tiny bear is a replica of Steiff's 1930 Dicky. Her husband pins and cuts out the pieces.

red ribbon bow

small, black, bead eyes

fully jointed head and limbs

red, felt jacket and pill-box hat trimmed with gold braid

black, embroidered claws

light brown plush

large, narrow feet

c.1984 SUSAN L. KRUSE   Height:15cm (6in)

Baby Bear Hop, created in 1984, copies Bing and Schuco Bell Hop teddies from the 1920s. This Californian bear artist taught herself with Margaret Hutching's *Teddy Bears and How to Make Them* when expecting her first child.

Printed card tag

shaved muzzle

golden mohair plush

inverted-Y-shaped, smiling mouth

horizontally-stitched, black, rectangular nose

large, narrow, spoon-like paws

baggy, knitted cardigan

large, oval feet

light gold, synthetic fabric pads

1985 D. & T. MICHAUD   Height: 45cm (18in)

The Professor is a replica of an antique US bear, from Doris and Terry Michaud's Carrousel Museum Collection. Their first commercially manufactured bear appeared in 1980; they produce both reproductions and original designs.

CARROUSEL
505 W. Broad St.
Chesaning, Mi. 48616

Printed label

fully jointed head and limbs

shaggy, purple-maroon plush; internal tilt-growler

suede pads painted to represent paws

maroon, vertically stitched, wide, rectangular nose

traditional long limbs

curved, spoon-shaped paws

large feet

1983 LORETTA BOTTA   Height: 63cm (25in)

This 1983 "one-of-a-kind" bear, adorned with plastic imitation grapes, is called Vino: Wine Country Bear. Loretta Botta, of San Francisco, was one of the first bear artists to operate in the US, under the name Botta Bears. She ceased business in 1992.

Handwritten label

---

fully jointed head and limbs

hand-embroidered, flannel blanket comforter, with pink, ribbon bow

beige alpaca plush

black, glass bead eyes with tears embroidered in clear thread under each eye

brown, horizontally stitched, oblong nose

embroidered flower trademark

ultrasuede pads

C.1990 LYNN LUMLEY   Height: 11cm (4½in)

Born in 1921, Lynn Lumley of Carson City, Nevada, started bear-making in 1983 despite crippling arthritis, and produces her work in three small sizes: 11cm (4½in), 14cm (5½in), and 16cm (6½in). Her trademark is an embroidered flower on the left foot. She makes 250–350, limited-edition bears a year, under the label "Grandma Lynn's Teddy Bears".

---

authentic 1953 Bing Crosby ice-cream carton came with bear for storage

bear made from 1950s cashmere coat

blue, bead eyes with black, embroidered eyebrows

handmade pipe attached to mouth with wire

VALLEY FARM'S
Bing Crosby
ICE CREAM
VANILLA
ONE PINT

Bing Crosby
ICE CREAM
★ ★
"the Cream of
VANILLA

A Bear
With a Heart

1984 DIANE GARD   Height: 15cm (6in)

The Crooner is an early example of this artist's work. Diane started making bears in 1982 under the name "A Bear With a Heart"; she now designs bears with a less traditional look, including whimsical, character bears and her well-known Fashion Model Bears.

Glass heart

---

unusual oval, black nose with dropped stitches on outside and down centre

removable jacket with brass buttons

black, replica boot-button eyes

white, cotton shirt

short-pile, grey mohair plush

leather, hobnailed boots

C.1985 G. AND M. NETT   Height: 45cm (18in)

Bears by Nett is a partnership between Gary, who began bear-making in 1983 after losing his job, and his mother Margaret, a professional seamstress. They produce detailed, historical US figures, like this Civil War Union Artillery Sergeant.

Embroidered logo

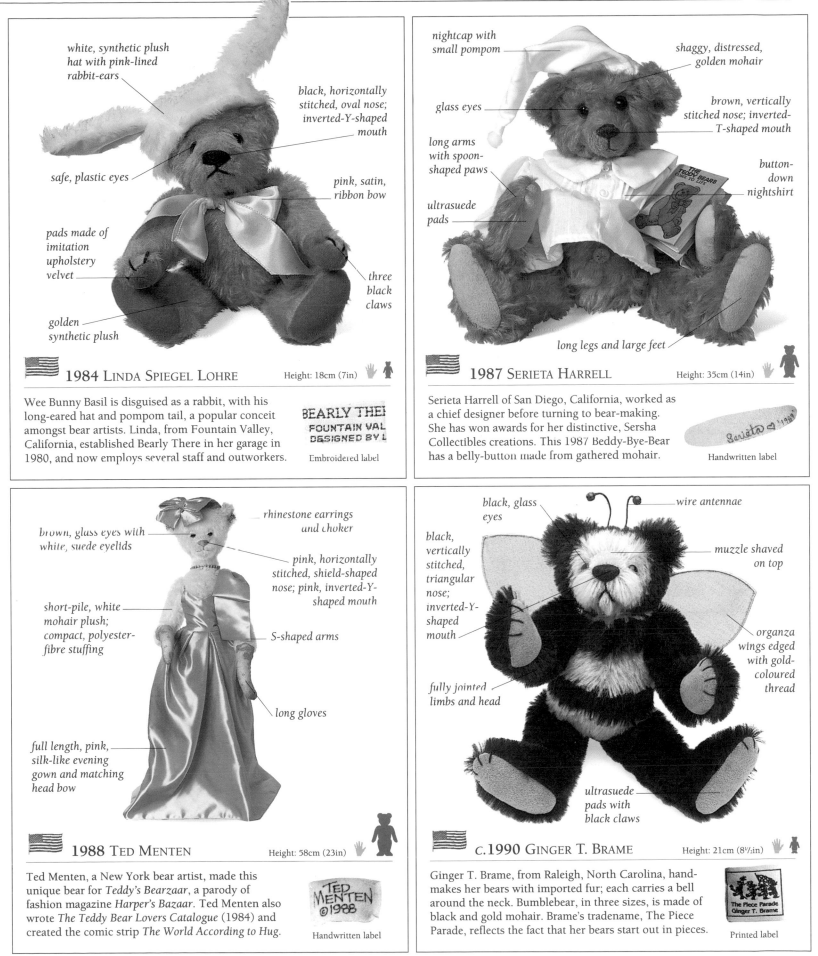

white, synthetic plush hat with pink-lined rabbit-ears

black, horizontally stitched, oval nose; inverted-Y-shaped mouth

safe, plastic eyes

pink, satin, ribbon bow

pads made of imitation upholstery velvet

three black claws

golden synthetic plush

1984 LINDA SPIEGEL LOHRE

Height: 18cm (7in)

Wee Bunny Basil is disguised as a rabbit, with his long-eared hat and pompom tail, a popular conceit amongst bear artists. Linda, from Fountain Valley, California, established Bearly There in her garage in 1980, and now employs several staff and outworkers.

BEARLY THEI FOUNTAIN VAL DESIGNED BY L

Embroidered label

nightcap with small pompom

shaggy, distressed, golden mohair

glass eyes

brown, vertically stitched nose; inverted-T-shaped mouth

long arms with spoon-shaped paws

button-down nightshirt

ultrasuede pads

long legs and large feet

1987 SERIETA HARRELL

Height: 35cm (14in)

Serieta Harrell of San Diego, California, worked as a chief designer before turning to bear-making. She has won awards for her distinctive, Sersha Collectibles creations. This 1987 Beddy-Bye-Bear has a belly-button made from gathered mohair.

Serieta ♡ 1987

Handwritten label

brown, glass eyes with white, suede eyelids

rhinestone earrings and choker

pink, horizontally stitched, shield-shaped nose; pink, inverted-Y-shaped mouth

short-pile, white mohair plush; compact, polyester-fibre stuffing

S-shaped arms

long gloves

full length, pink, silk-like evening gown and matching head bow

1988 TED MENTEN

Height: 58cm (23in)

Ted Menten, a New York bear artist, made this unique bear for *Teddy's Bearzaar*, a parody of fashion magazine *Harper's Bazaar*. Ted Menten also wrote *The Teddy Bear Lovers Catalogue* (1984) and created the comic strip *The World According to Hug*.

TED MENTEN ©1988

Handwritten label

black, glass eyes

wire antennae

muzzle shaved on top

black, vertically stitched, triangular nose; inverted-Y-shaped mouth

organza wings edged with gold-coloured thread

fully jointed limbs and head

ultrasuede pads with black claws

c.1990 GINGER T. BRAME

Height: 21cm (8½in)

Ginger T. Brame, from Raleigh, North Carolina, hand-makes her bears with imported fur; each carries a bell around the neck. Bumblebear, in three sizes, is made of black and gold mohair. Brame's tradename, The Piece Parade, reflects the fact that her bears start out in pieces.

The Piece Parade Ginger T. Brame

Printed label

brown, lead-crystal eyes with black pupils

dark brown mohair plush

suede nose with needle-sculpted nostrils

brown, suede pads

elasticated trousers

green, knitted balaclava with holes for ears

printed lapel badge reads: "Some people have one of those days. I have one of those lives."

miniature metal frying pan and fish-slice

1988 JOANNE MITCHELL   Height: 65cm (26in)

Joanne, from Houston, Texas, became a bear artist in 1984 after collecting teddy bears for years. Rusty the Bagman, pictured here, is dressed as a "hobo" with his worldly goods, including a teddy bear, in his pocket. He represents the spirit of a friend of Joanne's, a Marine, who died in action. Joanne's Paws for Peace bear won a TOBY award in 1990.

curly, shaggy, golden mohair plush; stuffed with polyester fibrefill throughout

black, shield-shaped nose; inverted-Y-shaped mouth

pale golden, felt pads; four black claws stitched across plush

polyester-stuffed head and limbs

amber and black, glass eyes

jointed, long, curved arms

jointed, long, legs with narrow ankles

very large, slender, feet

1988 CINDY MARTIN   Height: 88cm (35in)

Cindy from Fresno, California, made her first bear in 1982, inspired by antique teddies. Her bears range from miniatures to those over 122 cm(48in) high. Sailor Bear, with distinct, elongated limbs and neck, is typical of her larger creations.

YESTERBEAR SAILOR

Handwritten label

black, vertically stitched, shield-shaped nose

black, single-stitched, smiling mouth

chocolate-brown, synthetic wool plush; compact stuffing

child's, black, lace-up shoes

safe, plastic eyes

red jacket with three metal buttons and US/Canada lapel pin

white linen "dicky" shirt with black, ribbon bow-tie

brown, suede pads with no claws

1992 MARCELLA PITTANA   Height: 44cm (17½in)

Vagabond Teddy is the central character in a series of story colouring books, created by this retired, Niagara College French teacher. The books, published since 1986, were the first of their kind to appear in Canada. Marcella Pittana has a large collection of teddy bears at her Port Colborne, Ontario home and runs bear-making workshops in Canada and the US.

amber and black glass eyes

black, vertically stitched oval nose; inverted-Y-shaped, mouth

pointed muzzle

curved arms with chamois leather pads; no claws

straight legs with large feet

red, woven jacket with three brass buttons and stand-up collar

Canadian national flag on pole

extra dense, golden mohair plush; polyester fiberfill stuffing; internal tilt growler

1992 TRUDY TENEYCKE   Height: 45cm (18in)

Trudy Teneycke, from Regina, Saskatchewan, has been a bear artist since 1987 and has won several awards. Sergeant Sam Brown is one of a limited-edition of 150; he wears an approved Royal Canadian Mounted Police uniform and holds the national flag.

Trudy's Teddies

Printed tag

brown, vertically stitched
nose and inverted-Y-
shaped mouth

slightly cupped ears,
set on sides of head

pointed muzzle,
clipped between
nose and mouth

brown glass eyes
with black pupils

S-shaped arms
bent at elbows
and wrists

large, oval feet
with dark brown,
leather pads

four
brown,
stitched
claws

light brown
mohair plush

1989 JOAN RANKIN   Height: 33cm (13in)

Joan, a retired art teacher from Moose Jaw,
Saskatchewan, began making bears in 1988. She
created Baxter Brown Bear in 1989, and has
written and illustrated stories about him, soon
to be published and sold with replicas of Baxter.

Printed label

large, rounded
ears, set wide
apart

brown and black,
safe, plastic eyes

black, vertically
stitched, circular,
nose; inverted-Y-
shaped mouth

speckled
synthetic plush;
soft stuffed;
internal tilt
growler

long, curved,
tapering arms

narrow
ankles and
large feet

orange,
synthetic,
velvet-like
fabric pads
with no claws

1990 SUSAN RIXON   Height: 45cm (18in)

Susan Rixon and husband David from Berkshire have
made bears since 1979 under the label Nonsuch Soft
Toys. This bear, named after British archaeologist Sir
Mortimer Wheeler, was created to celebrate the
centenary of the excavation of Silchester, Berkshire.

Nonsuch
Mortimer
Bear ©
Limited Edition
of 200 only

Printed label

pink-brown, safe,
plastic eyes with
black pupils

vertically stitched,
square nose;
inverted-Y-
shaped, double-
stitched mouth

shaved muzzle

original bow

short-pile, cinnamon
mohair plush;
internal tilt
growler

fully
jointed
limbs

long arms;
brown,
suedette
pads with
five claws

long legs
and large feet

1990 BEDFORD BEARS   Height: 35cm (14in)

Bedford Bears makes mohair collectors' bears and a
modacrylic plush range, all designed by Eddie Owen
in Dunton, Bedfordshire. This limited-edition bear,
made for the firm's 10th anniversary, is sold
from their stall in Covent Garden, London.

Embroidered label

brown, safe, plastic
eyes with black pupils

synthetic plush on
acrylic backing; soft,
polyester stuffing;
internal tilt
growler

black, hand-embroidered
nose and mouth

suedette pads; four
black claws stitched
across each pad

leather
school
bag

cotton
poplin
shirt

grey
school
trousers

1987 SUE QUINN   Height: 38cm (15in)

Sue, who has made soft toys since the 1960s, founded Dormouse Designs
in 1978, in an old drapery in Renfrewshire, Scotland. She introduced
teddies to her range in 1982, and began making limited editions in 1986.
In 1987, inspired by her son going to school, she created Bramble School-
days and, in 1983, Sue was acclaimed British Toymaker of the Year.

felt cap with badge

muzzle, front of ears, and above eyes shaved to appear worn

black, plastic, replica boot-button eyes

blue, felt blazer with schoolboy treasures in pocket

black, wool, vertically stitched nose; inverted-V-shaped mouth

blond, distressed mohair; wood-wool stuffing in muzzle; soft stuffing elsewhere

white shirt; blue and yellow striped tie

brown, leather pads

1991 STACEY LEE TERRY　　Height: 33cm (13in)

Stacey, a full-time bear artist since 1987, who lives in Winslow, Bucks., produced this teddy in 1991. It is based on Theo, a schoolboy bear character drawn by British teddy-bear illustrator Prue Theobald, and was produced in a limited edition of 250.

Embroidered label

black, plastic, replica boot-button eyes

black, vertically stitched nose

original, red, printed cravat

elongated, very slender muzzle

narrow, beige, velvet-like pads; three black claws across plush and pad

alpaca plush, popular in 1930s

1987 BRIAN BEACOCK　　Height: 40cm (16in)

Brian Beacock, bear artist, collector, and restorer, designed this caricature of the classic old teddy bear for Joan Bland of Asquiths (the first exclusive teddy-bear shop in the UK) in 1987. It was produced by Big Softies (*see p.143*) in three colours and sizes. Although this is a manufactured sample, Brian's artistry is well known on both sides of the Atlantic.

safe, plastic, replica boot-button eyes

hat trimmed with fabric roses

brown, vertically stitched nose with dropped centre and outer stitches; inverted-Y-shaped mouth

protruding, shaved muzzle

shaggy, golden mohair plush

cotton lace collar

long legs with large feet

brown, velvet pads; four, webbed claws on paws and feet

1991 PAM HOWELLS　　Height: 43cm (17in)

Pam was a designer at Chiltern's factory in Pontypool from 1957–67, but she has been making her own soft toys since 1972. This mother bear is part of a tableau called Feeding the Ducks, made in 1991.

Embroidered label

wide, rectangular, vertically stitched nose; long muzzle

black, safe, plastic, replica boot-button eyes

Welsh woven fabric bow-tie

carved, wooden, Welsh love-spoon

very long arms with curved, spoon-shaped paws

distressed golden mohair plush

large, narrow feet

beige, felt pads

1991 SUE SCHOEN　　Height: 34cm (13½in)

Dewi hails from the workshop of Sue Schoen, whose Welsh business name "Bocs Teganau" means "toy box". Sue has been making bears since 1986, producing standard and limited-edition ranges, many with Welsh names.

Printed label

elongated
muzzle

small, folded ears, lying
flat at back of head

black, vertically
stitched, oval nose

flat, black, plastic
eyes, resembling
flat, metal studs of
early British bears

long, tapering
arms with
curved paws

original scarf
around neck

four, black
claws on
paws and
feet

light brown,
suede pads

narrow ankles
with large,
slender feet

1985 NAOMI LAIGHT   Height: 33cm (13in)

This bear was made for a Save the Children
charity auction in 1985 using a khaki,
chenille-like, short plush. Naomi has been
making limited-edition, collectors' teddy
bears from her home since the early 1980s.

A Naomi Laight
COLLECTORS BEAR

Embroidered label

clipped mohair
plush on muzzle

black, glass,
boot-button eyes

vertically stitched,
rectangular nose;
inverted-Y-shaped mouth

long, curly, grey-gold
mohair plush; stuffed
with compact wood-
wool throughout

arms much
longer than legs,
with upward-
curving paws

beige, felt
pads;
four
claws
on paws
and feet

fully
jointed

1992 A. & W. MULLANEY   Height: 60cm (24in)

Alistair was made in 1992 by Alan and Wendy
Mullaney from their home in the Scottish Highlands.
They started designing and making bears in 1989,
and their original range consisted of six sizes and
three colours. They produce eight bears in a week.

*Atlantic
Bears*

Printed label

German black,
blown-glass eyes

blue, satin ribbon
tied around head

shaved, protruding
muzzle

long limbs with
internal, American
Loc-Line system,
allowing range
of poses

black, vertically
stitched, triangular
nose

polka-dot,
synthetic
dress

typical
American
toddler's black,
plastic shoes

1991 LIZ CARLESS   Height: 63cm (25in)

Named after her creator, Elizabeth Anne was a
special commission for the Cotswold Teddy Bear
Museum in 1991. Liz used to live in both Florida
and London, hence her business name Transatlantic
Teddies. She has been making bears since 1987.

This bear has been
designed and
hand made by
the artist
Liz Carless
Lillibet
TRANSATLANTIC
TEDDIES

Printed label

black, vertically
stitched, triangular
nose

black, safe,
plastic, replica
boot-button eyes

original, blue
ribbon bow

mohair dyed red
in Nottingham,
especially for
Romsey Bears

traditional body
shape with
curved arms

big feet
with
maroon
pads; name
machine-
embroidered
on right pad

"1991" and
limited
edition
number
"19"
embroidered
on left pad

1991 ROMSEY BEAR CO.   Height: 40cm (16in)

Li.Bear.A.Ted is the second of three, limited-
edition bears produced in 1990, 1991, and 1992
to commemorate the liberation of the Channel
Islands in 1945. The company is named after
Romsey, Hampshire, where the bears are made.

CE   ROMS EY BEAR CO.
COLLE CTORS BEARS
SO51 7RF

Embroidered label

1992 MADDIE JANES — Height: 32cm (12½in)

- distressed, shaggy mohair plush; soft, polyester stuffing
- black, boot-button eyes, handmade by artist
- long, curved arms
- beige, felt pads
- vertically stitched, oblong nose; inverted-V-shaped mouth
- darned patch on left foot gives worn appearance
- oval feet with four brown, stitched claws

Cobweb, one of a limited edition of 12, is the work of Maddie Janes from Shropshire, England, who began making teddies in 1991. The bear's body is filled with polyurethane pellets to give a sagging, "antique" feel. The handwritten label displays the bear artist's name.

Handwritten label

1992 DEBORAH CANHAM — Height: 6cm (2½in)

- small, black, bead eyes
- beige, suede pads with three black claws
- short, golden mohair plush on head, hands, and lower legs; soft-stuffed throughout
- green, felt lower body and thighs
- navy blue, felt hat
- horizontally stitched nose; inverted-Y-shaped mouth

This Devon-based artist designs and makes tiny, jointed bears. Her largest bear is 7cm (3in). Punch and Judy, the dressed character bears illustrated here, are special, limited editions based on a traditional French Punch and Judy design. In 1992 Deborah was voted Bear Artist of the Year by S.M.A.L.L. (Society for Miniature Arctophiles Loving and Learning).

1991 CATHERINE M. WHILE — Height: 9cm (3½in)

- brown, vertically stitched nose; inverted-Y-shaped mouth
- slightly clipped, white, mohair plush muzzle
- lace ruff with satin rosebud
- shaggy, pink mohair plush
- sewn-in, black, bead eyes
- fully jointed limbs and body
- lilac, leather pads

Catherine M. While produced her first tiny bear in 1989 from her home in Chesterfield, Derbyshire, England, inspired by a newly acquired, limited-edition Raikes bear. She made Hyacinth (*above*) in 1991. Her mother helps to cut and hand-sew the bears, her father helping to stuff them. The creations are sold under the label, Chasing Rainbows.

1991 ANITA OLIVER — Height: 6cm (2½in)

- black, embroidered eyes
- hand-knitted, Fair Isle sweater
- long, curved arms
- fully jointed limbs and head
- long legs and large feet
- black, horizontally stitched nose; inverted-V-shaped mouth
- very soft, short-pile, golden, bonded fabric; kapok stuffing
- golden, synthetic-velvet pads

Boris Bear, one of a limited editon of 200, came in a hand-marbled paper box. He is a typical example from Anita Oliver, one of the earliest British miniature-bear artists. She made her first small teddy in 1980, after a career in graphic design and publishing, though making soft toys and dolls was her hobby. Her bears are sold in Europe and the United States.

1992 IRENE MOORE — Height: 35cm (14in)

black, safe, plastic eyes

black, oblong nose; inverted-Y-shaped mouth

brown, felt pads with three black claws stitched across plush

distressed golden mohair plush; polyester stuffing throughout

pointed, clipped muzzle stuffed with wood-wool

hand-knitted, red scarf

long, fully jointed, limbs

Oscar, one of a limited edition of 25, is the creation of the first bear artist to emerge from Northern Ireland. Irene Moore began making traditional bears in 1991, and named her business, Pinecroft Bears, after her County Down home.

NECROFT BEARS'' ditional Teddy Bears in Newtownards, Co. Down. BT23 3RJ/149

Printed label

1991 JOAN HANNA — Height: 34cm (13½in)

safe, black, replica boot-button eyes

golden, distressed mohair; stuffed with soft, polyester fiberfill

black, vertically stitched, shield-shaped nose; inverted-Y-shaped mouth

long, curved arms

narrow ankles and large feet

brown, velveteen pads with four black claws

Joan, from County Cork, is believed to be the first bear artist from the Republic of Ireland. She made soft toys in her teens, and formed Craft-T-Bears in 1990. Joan works alone, with some family help at busy times. Tufty is one of her traditional range.

Craf Made in C NOT FOR U

Printed label

1992 JONETTE STABBERT — Height: 28cm (11in)

shaved, pointed muzzle

four stitches form W-shaped mouth

fully jointed limbs

paws curved at right angles to arms; no pads

low-set ears

small, amber, glass eyes with black pupils

velour nose

cinnamon-coloured synthetic plush

straight legs with beige, felt pads reinforced with card

Honey Bear was made by the first Dutch bear artist, US-born Jonette Stabbert. With a background in art and design, she was one of the world's leading cloth doll artists until she turned to bear-making in about 1983, with the tradename "Poppette Bears".

Poppette Bears AMSTERDAM

Embroidered label

1991 JANE HUMME — Height: 13cm (5in)

black bead eyes over red felt

wide, inverted-Y-shaped, double-stitched mouth

long, curved arms

beige, felt pads

slightly cupped ears

nose stitched in thick, black thread

distressed, black mohair plush; soft stuffing

fully jointed limbs and head

narrow ankles and large feet

Jane Humme, from Bodegraven in the Netherlands, began making traditional bears in 1989. This tiny reproduction of a 1912 Steiff black bear is the only replica Jane has made. Too small for a label, Jane embroidered her initials in red under its arm.

HANDMADE BY Jane Hu

Embroidered label

clear, glass eyes with black pupils and hand-painted backs

ears lined with 1940s red, silk-velvet; sewn across facial seams

pale gold, medium-pile mohair plush; wood-wool stuffing

red, embroidered, Y-shaped nose

fully jointed limbs

long, slightly curved arms and tapering paws

leather tag with inscription "Les Ours de Marcelle"

large, oval feet with red, silk-velvet pads

1992 MARCELLE GOFFIN   Height: 34cm (13½in)

Rouen-based Marcelle Goffin specializes in copies of old French bears. Tintin is a 1990s replica of a 1940s teddy that was originally made from woollen blanket fabric. Marcelle has formed a club "Teddy's Patch" with fellow artist, Marylou Jouet.

Ours de Collection
Embroidered label

sewn-in, antique, black, boot-buttons eyes

wide head stuffed with wood-wool

inverted-T-shaped, single-stitched mouth

semi-circular nose hand-embroidered in black thread

short-pile, cotton and rayon plush; stuffed with kapok

three long, black, stitched claws

dark beige, felt pads

long, slender feet

slim legs; narrow ankles

1991 ALINE COUSIN   Height: 26cm (10½in)

Aline Cousin has made limited-edition, collector bears from Noisy le Grand, outside Paris, since December 1990. She uses old and new mohair, cotton, wool, and rayon plush fabrics, and favours traditional designs, such Napoleon, shown here.

Aline Cousin's Teddies
Embroidered label

black, vertically stitched, oval nose

flat ears sewn across facial seams

pointed muzzle

antique, black, boot-button eyes

patchwork of printed cotton fabrics; wood-wool stuffing

inverted-Y-shaped, double-stitched mouth

printed, card label

curved, tapering arms

three black claws

large thighs, narrow ankles, and large, oval feet

1992 MARYLOU JOUET   Height: 28cm (11in)

This special Christmas bear, called Patchnours, is made from 150 pieces of American fabric. Marylou Jouet (her surname means toy in French), from Rennes, Brittany, is a member of the Paris Patchwork Association. She has been teaching quilting since 1984. She also makes traditional mohair-plush bears, dressed and in miniature.

black, plastic button eyes

large, flat ears

black, triangular nose; inverted-T-shaped mouth

hand-made, woollen felt; wool stuffing

felt bag contains card with bear's details

short, stumpy, bulbous legs

1988 DAWN NICHOLL   Height: 30cm (12in)

Dawn Nicholl, from Whangarei, North Island, New Zealand, has experimented with art forms to produce her distinctively designed bears, made of hand-made, pure New Zealand wool felt. She made Mr. Oz E. Bound for the 1988 Australian World Expo.

Embroidered label

small, black, safe, plastic eyes

small, slightly cupped ears set on sides of head

black, vertically stitched, shield-shaped nose

inverted-V-shaped mouth

printed swing-tag

long, curved arms extend beyond legs; spoon-shaped paws

beige, suede pads with no claws

large, oval feet

short-pile mohair plush; stuffed with cotton fibre waste

1991 J. AND M. WALTON   Height: 34cm (13½in)

Halifax was designed by the Waltons of Upper Hutt, New Zealand. Part-time bear artists since 1989, Judy is also a registered nurse, and her husband Michael is a dentist. They are members of the Antipodean Bear Makers Co-op and the British Toymakers' Guild.

Printed label

---

amber and black, translucent, glass eyes; white opaque glass beneath

oblong, black nose with inverted-Y-shaped mouth

cinnamon-coloured mohair plush; soft-stuffed

black and gold, heart-shaped card; black ribbon with brass bell

slightly curved arms

brown, leather pads

long, oval feet; no claws

1992 JANIS HARRIS   Height: 35cm (14in)

Originally a doll-maker, Janis Harris has also made limited-edition and one-off bears from her home in Auckland since 1985. Baby Bobby has unusual glass "googly" eyes but follows the traditional design preferred by this award-winning artist.

ALMOST SOUTH POLE BEARS
MADE IN NEW ZEALAND BY JANIS HARRIS

Embroidered label

---

brimmed hat

head of long-pile, grey mohair on golden plush base

large, flat ears, sewn to sides of head

black, safe, plastic, button eyes

black, vertically stitched, triangular nose

double-stitched, inverted-Y-shaped mouth

golden synthetic plush fur; Dacron polyester stuffing

striped, button-down shirt with stand-up collar and cuffs

pale beige, suede paw-pads

baggy, tweed trousers with elasticated waist

black, leather-like boots

1992 FRANCES MCLEARY   Height: 53cm (21in)

Frances McLeary created the gardener Garmonsway as part of her Colonial Character collection, with the help of her husband, Bill, at their farm "Braidwood", Frankton, on the North Island. Frances holds several New Zealand bear-making awards.

Braidwood Bear

Printed tag

---

hand-dyed, cotton-bucked mohair, mixed fibre flock stuffing

small, slightly cupped ears

hand-tinted, dark brown, safe, plastic eyes with black pupils

black, oblong nose

inverted-Y-shaped, double-stitched mouth

shaved, pointed muzzle

arms longer than legs, with long curved paws

double-stitched, felt pads

card tags

long, slender, oval feet

1992 ALLIE AND NIGEL HANTON   Height: 30cm (12in)

Thaddeus was made by the Hantons, trained artists and teachers who turned to bear-making in 1989. Each limited-edition bear is made to order at their Wellington home studio, and based on traditional designs from the Edwardian era (1901–10).

Printed label

felt, bushman's hat

safe, plastic eyes

leather waistcoat

suede thong around neck

golden, synthetic plush; Dacron stuffing; internal growler

leather belt

cream, suede pads

plastic knife

toy, rubber crocodile

denim jeans

1989 PAT LOVELOCK   Height: 45cm (18in)

This 1989 Crocodile Dunbear was inspired by actor Paul Hogan's character "Crocodile Dundee" in the film of the same name. From Rosebud, Victoria, Pat Lovelock has been a bear artist since 1984 and has won awards in Australia for her Pat L. Original Bears.

An Original by Pat L.

Printed label

---

black, horizontally stitched, shield-shaped nose; inverted-T-shaped, smiling mouth

artist's, red, felt beret

unusual red and black, glass eyes

large, red, ribbon bow around neck

wooden palette with real paint brush

grey, felt pads on feet

grey, synthetic plush

1985 MARJORY FAINGES   Height: 28cm (11in)

Rembearandt, dressed as an artist, is an early example of Marjory Fainges' work. Most of her bears are now limited editions, sold under the trade-name "Miffi", which is derived from her initials. From Everton Park, Queensland, Marjory is well known throughout Australia and the US as an artist, restorer, collector, teacher of bear-making, and author.

---

brown and black, safe, plastic eyes

wide-brimmed, straw hat

beige, synthetic plush; polyester stuffing

black, shield-shaped nose; inverted-T-shaped mouth

long, curved arms with elongated, spoon-shaped paws

beige, felt pads

long legs with narrow ankles and slender, oval feet

striped dungarees printed with bears

1987 GERRY WARLOW   Height: 40cm (16in)

Gerry first made bears in 1983, and Edgar is an early example of her work; her more recent bears are made of mohair plush. Gerry works from her home in Rosewood, Queensland, Australia, under the name Gerry's Teddy and Craft Designs.

Gerry's

Printed label

German, golden mohair plush

German, black, glass eyes

brown, vertically stitched, narrow, rectangular nose; inverted-Y-shaped mouth

original blue and maroon, satin bow

long, curved arms

relatively large feet; narrow ankles

light brown, suede pads; three brown claws stitched across plush

1992 JENNIFER LAING   Height: 20cm (8in)

This Sydney artist has made traditional bears since 1990, following her appointment as manager of *The Teddy Bear Shop* in Neutral Bay, New South Wales. Jennifer's bears are all hand-stitched. She is a member of the Antipodean Bear Makers's Co-op.

Totally Bear

Printed tag

German, white, string mohair (unbrushed and undyed)

black, glass eyes

black, horizontally stitched, triangular nose; inverted-Y-shaped, single-stitched mouth

pointed, shaved muzzle

traditional, elongated arms with curved, spoon-shaped paws

large, slender, oval feet; narrow ankles

beige, suede pads

1991 JENNY ROUND   Height: 43cm (17in)

Jenny Round, of Round-A-Bout Bears, won Best Bear Artist Award for Ben (*above*) at the 1991 Australian Doll and Teddy Fair. She began making bears, including their joints, in 1988. She lives in New South Wales, Australia, and has a collection of 400 bears.

Printed label

---

brown and black, safe, plastic eyes

felt, bushman's hat with corks and gum leaves

"swag" (rolled-up bushman's bed)

"swagman's" red, open-necked shirt and tweed waistcoat

brown, synthetic plush

beige, leather paw-pads

wide legs; foot-pads reinforced with wood

hessian "tucker bag" (food bag)

1990 BOB WHITE   Height: 45cm (18in)

A Fine Art teacher at Tasmania's Latrobe High School, Bob White decided to make his first bear when he could not find an Australian-made example in a teddy-bear shop. His bears, made under the tradename Bob's Bears, are always masculine characters.

Printed logo

---

sewn-in, black, bead eyes

sewn-on, soft, black, oilcloth nose; black, embroidered, inverted-Y-shaped mouth

straight arms

four black, embroidered claws

golden, short-pile velveteen

beige, suedette pads

jointed limbs

wide, flat body with final side seam

1992 MARY KELLY   Height: 26cm (10¼in)

Bear-making has been Mary Kelly's hobby for years, but she only began to sell her bears commercially after opening Bear Basics in Simon's Town in 1991 – the first teddy-bear shop in South Africa. Aided by her daughter Samantha, Mary makes her bears mainly in velveteen and upholstery fabrics, as traditional plushes are expensive and not readily available.

---

sewn-in, brown and black, plastic eyes

black, leather nose

smiling mouth made with two, black stitches

AFRICA

wa me

black, leather pads

unjointed body

leather tag with "wa me" ("why me")

1990 BOTSWANA MADE   Height: 25cm (10in)

Bears like "Wa Me", shown above, are made by a woman on a farm in a Botswana village. Local women help with the decorated boxes that imitate wooden animal transit crates. The bear is crocheted in 100% wool; special loops incorporated in the stitching give the impression of shaggy, mohair plush, while the plain stitches on the muzzle create a shaved appearance.

Teddy-bear muff
Teddy muffs have always been popular; this German example (*right*) has a squeaker.

Silver nurseryware
Late 19th and early 20th century cutlery (*above and left*) decorated with bears.

Tea for two
Mother bear's skirt (*above*) is a tea-cosy; the baby is jointed.

Teddy philately
Teddies depicted on postage stamps from around the world (*left*).

First friend
Studio portraits
featuring teddies are
attractive to collect.
This 1913 photograph
(*left*) was taken in
Hackney, east London.

Feeding-bottle cover
This 1940s–50s feeding
bottle, with its ingenious
cover (*below*), was also
available in pink plush.

On the shelf
This collection of child-
hood teddies (*left*) was
gathered from members
of the design and editorial
team who worked on
this book.

ARCTOPHILY: BEAR COLLECTING

BY THE MID-1980s, teddy-bear collecting had achieved a relatively serious status as a hobby; it had also acquired a commonly accepted name, "arctophily", to describe it – the word is derived from the Greek *arctos* (bear) and *philos* (love).

The beauty of teddy-bear collecting is that it can be approached on different levels, according to individual circumstances, making it a pastime for both children and adults, of varying means. You can concentrate on antique bears, bear artists' bears, modern limited editions, or cheap, secondhand teddies. Or you can collect just anything that features teddy bears, which, again, can vary from expensive silver or china, to cheaper items, such as biscuit wrappers, postage stamps, or badges. Arctophily in its true sense, therefore, can encompass anything that is bear-related. As a collector, you can widen your boundaries to include, for example, polar bears, pandas, or even objects relating to Teddy Roosevelt, who gave teddies their name. The choice is yours.

As well as looking at the historical development of bear collecting as a hobby, this practical chapter discusses what being an arctophile entails, suggests possible types of collections and their various sources, as well as indicating how and where you can learn more about this extraordinarily fascinating and internationally popular subject.

Arctophily: Bear Collecting

A COMPREHENSIVE SURVEY OF THE HOBBY

Adults as well as children have long accepted teddy bears as mascots. Until recently, however, collecting teddy bears was a relatively unknown pastime. The English actor Peter Bull (1912–84), who is recognized as the catalyst behind the arctophily movement, not only encouraged the collecting of teddy bears as an acceptable hobby, but also introduced his philosophy of "bear awareness" in the late 1960s. Recognition of the hobby did not come of age, however, until the resurgence of teddy-bear mania in the 1980s. In 1981, Sue Arnold, in an article in the UK's *Observer* colour magazine, described Peter Bull as an "ursophile" (*urso* is Latin for bear). By the mid-1980s, the words "arctophile", "arctophilia", and "arctophily" had become accepted terminology amongst collectors of teddy bears.

Father of arctophily
Peter Bull (above) with Bully Bear, the first bear he produced with House of Nisbet.

TEDDY AMBASSADOR

When Peter Bull was sixteen, his mother gave away his childhood teddy, causing him great anguish. In the late 1960s, he realized that others experienced similar trauma, and he resolved to investigate the subject further. During an appearance on the American NBC chat-show *Today*, he asked the audience for interesting teddy-bear stories and, within a week, he had received over 2,000 letters. His research culminated in the publication of

House of Nisbet bear
This giant bear (left) is wearing Peter Bull's own sweater, which features some of his favourite sayings. The 1984 Tribute Bully wears a replica sweater.

Bear with Me (Hutchinson) in 1969. Already the author of several autobiographical books, this work marked the beginning of a career as an international ambassador for the teddy bear. He attended rallies and conventions in the United Kingdom and the United States, and collaborated with the House of Nisbet (*see pp.144–45*) on a range of limited-edition bears. His now-celebrated teddy "Aloysius" fuelled the teddy-bear renaissance of the early 1980s when he featured in the British television adaptation of Evelyn Waugh's novel *Brideshead Revisited*, later inspiring replicas by the House of Nisbet and the North American Bear Company (*see p.147*).

Peter Bull's book *A Hug of Teddy Bears* was published in 1984, the year of his death. His collection of around 250 teddy bears was bequeathed to the London Toy and Model Museum, where most of them are still displayed. However, some of the teddies were sold, including "Aloysius", who now resides at the Californian home of Paul and Rosemary Volpp.

"Hug" of bears
A collection of teddy bears is often described as a "hug". An old suitcase provides a perfect platform for this group of Gebrüder Hermann bears (above).

CARING BEARS

Collecting teddy bears is now a worldwide hobby with universal appeal. For some, it is not just a pleasure, but an investment like any other form of antique collecting. For most, however, teddies provide companionship. Their suitability for dressing up and investing with personalities, and their endearing facial expressions, has often led to teddies becoming honorary family members. As Peter Bull pointed out, there is a strong emotional attachment between a human and his or her teddy, which, from childhood days, has been his or her earliest and closest confidante.

GOOD BEARS OF THE WORLD

Inspired by such sentiments, Jim Ownby, an American, thought up the idea of "Good Bears of the World", an organization dedicated to distributing bears to sick or traumatized children, and to the elderly and infirm. Chartered in Berne, Switzerland in 1973, the organization celebrates "Good Bear Day" on 27th October, in honour of Theodore Roosevelt's birthday. Members can join individually or as "dens" – groups who raise funds to make or buy bears to give to hospitals, police departments, nursing homes, and other suitable institutions. The late Colonel Bob Henderson of Edinburgh, Scotland, introduced Good Bears of the World to the United Kingdom. There are now "dens" worldwide.

THERAPEUTIC BEARS

For several years, American police departments have used teddy bears to help children talk through traumatic experiences, and this procedure is now practised in other countries. Some hospital doctors perform "operations" on teddy bears to help to minimize pre-surgery fears

Injured bears
The bear on crutches, by Softouch Inc. (above), and Port Wine by E. Kay Peck (below), are examples of teddies designed to help children cope with disabilities.

Bear lover
Nick Bisbikis Jr. (right) and his wife Cassie have accumulated around 700 old and new collector bears since the early 1980s at their California home. Nick Bisbikis also sells Gebrüder Hermann bears, as well as Fechter bears (seen here).

among young patients. Special bears have also been made to help children overcome difficult circumstances. Muffin Enterprises' Sir Koff-a-Lot, for example, was created by two cardiovascular surgeons as a therapeutic aid for patients recovering from open-heart, thoracic, and abdominal surgery.

Teddy bears have been developed for use in schools for the deaf: Honey the Signing Bear (invented by Pat Yockey of California-based Quiet Bears) allows for hands to be slipped through the unstuffed arms as an aid for teachers of sign language. Teddies with "heart-beats" have been made to lull fretful infants to sleep. Bears frequently symbolize children's charities, often becoming fund-raisers themselves – in the United Kingdom, Pudsey represents the BBC's annual "Children in Need" campaign, and, in Australia, Bandaged Bear can be adopted to raise money for the Royal Alexandra Hospital for Children in Campertown, New South Wales.

Fundraisers
Teddy-bear dealer and writer Linda Mullins (above) organizes conventions in San Diego, California, the proceeds of which go to a local home for abused children. The gift of an early Steiff from her husband Wally in 1974 launched Linda on the road to arctophily.

A COLLECTING STRATEGY

When launching into serious arctophily, you will have to adopt a strategy tailored to your individual circumstances, considering funds and space available, as well as personal taste. You may decide to concentrate on antique teddy bears, the term "antique" in this case referring to teddies manufactured before World War I. Teddies made in the 1920s and 1930s are now reaching higher prices in the sales rooms, however, and even 1950s and 1960s bears are becoming sought-after. Alternatively, you may choose to collect by manufacturer, by country, or by specializing in a particular design.

TEDDIES PAST AND PRESENT

Within the wider area of antique teddy-bears, it may be interesting to collect bears with colourful pasts, such as those belonging to famous people, or acting as sporting mascots. However, this can also prove to be costly; "Alfonzo", an early Steiff bear made of unusual red mohair and wearing a cossack outfit, said to have been made by the nanny of its Russian princess owner (see p.19), was sold at Christie's for a record price of £12,100.

Some arctophiles specialize in limited editions produced by modern manufacturers or by bear artists, of whom there are many around the world. You may decide to concentrate on the work of one particular artist, or buy simply because

the "face fits"; or you might prefer to be guided by colour, collecting white teddy bears exclusively, for instance.

INTERNATIONAL BEARS

You can also collect bears from around the world, or those designed as souvenirs – for example, the many Berliner bears (a bear is part of Berlin's coat-of-arms), with crown and sash, usually reading "Greetings from Berlin". Of the thousands produced by firms in the Neustadt region of Germany, most of these Berliner bears are unmarked. Some major names, such as Steiff and Schuco, also produce this type of bear. Another interesting souvenir is one sold at Yellowstone Park during the late 1930s – a small bear whose tag bears a poem beginning: "I'm just a loving, hugging bear...."

MINIATURE COLLECTION

If space is likely to pose a problem, focus your attention on miniature examples, either those made by past masters of the miniscule, such as Steiff or Schuco (see pp.40–41), or concentrate on the work of the many modern bear artists (see pp.172–87) who are producing smaller and smaller bears, all perfectly formed and traditionally jointed.

Past histories
"Fritz" (above), an early Steiff, was hidden under the floor of a British Nissen hut by his original owner, a German POW.

Working bears
Harmles (below, left), a Steiff, was the pre-1914 sports mascot for the US boys' school, Kimbal Union Academy. Another Steiff (below, right) saw active duty with the London Fire Brigade during the Blitz in World War II.

Thimble size
Sandy Williams of Woodbridge, Virginia, USA, makes a range of tiny, Ultrasuede teddies, from 5cm (2in) to 2cm (¾in) size (above). The oversewn seams, have approximately 11 stitches per centimetre (28 per inch).

"Sergeant Culver"
A c.1914 American bear, "Sergeant Culver" (below, left) was the mascot for Culver Military Academy, in Logansport, Indiana.

Survivor
This early Bing (above), now at England's Ribchester Museum of Childhood, is a "good luck" charm that survived the 1912 RMS Titanic disaster – unlike its unfortunate owner, Gaspare Gatti, the First Class Catering Manager.

Cheeky collection
This group of Merrythought Cheeky teddy bears (right) includes the Cotswold Teddy Bear Museum's 1992 Bedtime Bertie (top), based on the earlier 1977 Bedtime Cheeky, but with the addition of a miniature hot-water bottle.

KEEPING RECORDS

Once the hobby of arctophily has become a serious occupation, it is as well to consider practicalities such as cataloguing, numbering systems, and photographic records. Some form of checklist or pictorial record is useful for easy reference when you are researching or sending information to other collectors, valuers, or appraisers. You can make up your own system, using lined, index cards, a simple exercise book, or by filing individually completed sheets for each bear in a ring binder. You can also store this type of information on a computer.

Whatever method or degree of sophistication you employ for your records, you must make sure that the information listed is consistent for each bear. In the case of an old, antique bear, for example, this should include: name, manufacturer, date of manufacture, exact label details, and any background history regarding provenance; purchase date, place, and price paid; plus basic information on height and materials used for fur, stuffing, eyes, pads, etc. You should also note whether the clothing is original, as well as whether the bear has a growler or squeaker in working order or otherwise.

Also describe any repairs in detail. It is useful to keep all associated ephemera such as card-tags, original photographs, and receipts with the documentation. If you have a large collection, number each bear, giving the same number to its corresponding record sheet. Numbering can be written on card, paper, or cloth tags, and tied to the bear or to its clothes.

It is advisable to take photographs of your bears not just for insurance and valuation purposes, but also to provide a useful aid when you are studying or showing off your collection. Take both front and side views of the bears, as it is useful, from the

Zotty bears
Collectors may try to acquire each size of a particular popular design, such as these various versions of Steiff's Zotty (above).

evaluator's point of view, to see the shape and size of the bear's muzzle or hump. Where possible, include written details, such as the type of stuffing or the method of attaching the eyes, as this will not be shown on a photograph.

Satisfactory documentation is essential for insurance purposes and collectors should ensure that their teddy bears are adequately covered by their household contents policies. You may discover that you can claim only the original cost of a bear, and not the present market value, so it may be advisable to arrange further cover, scheduling each article separately, with their agreed value alongside. You must retain all documentation on the bear's original price, and at the same time keep abreast of current pricing trends.

TEDDY-BEAR VALUATION

You can form a rough idea of the value of your collection from the various teddy-bear and soft-toy price guides that have been published since the 1980s. These are regularly updated and give values in US dollars, pounds sterling, and Deutschmarks. Reputable teddy-bear dealers or international auction houses such as Sotheby's, Christie's, and Phillips, with specialist departments staffed by experts who deal with teddy-bear enquiries, can also give advice on the value of a bear.

Record-breaker
Bunny Campione, who introduced teddy-bear sales to Sotheby's, holding Lot 19, the c.1926 Steiff (above) sold for the record sum of £55,000 on 19 September 1989.

Frannie Bear
The limited-edition bear (below) was created to celebrate the opening of the Teddy Bear Museum in Naples, Florida.

FACTORS TO CONSIDER

I am often asked what makes a teddy bear valuable? Of course, many childhood bears are of great sentimental value and are therefore priceless. However, if you are interested in financial gain, there are several, often closely related, criteria to take into account regarding antique bears. Bears made by those manufacturers considered to be world leaders in the soft-toy industry – for example, Steiff, Bing, and Schuco – hold greater value than others, and if a bear's button, label, or card-tag trademark is still attached, this will also instantly raise the price. Age is obviously important, too: pre-World War I bears are generally considered to be the most valuable, although 1920s–30s British bears are now increasing in price. Other factors such as rarity of design, colour, and past history can sometimes affect the value. The condition of the bear plays an important part, too: severe wear and tear, or obvious repairs, will lower the price. A 1904, 75cm (30in), white Steiff was sold for £5,280 at Sotheby's in Chester, England in 1986. Its early date, rare colour and size, and its mint condition (it had never been played with by its original owner), all contributed to the then record price.

The expression on these old teddies also helps to increase their value. The record-breaking price of £55,000 paid in 1989 for "Happy" far outstripped the £3,520 raised a year later by a similar "dual" plush Steiff with large, bulbous, glass eyes. This was due not just to the fact that prices vary, depending on who is bidding, but also because of the sweet, enigmatic expression on "Happy's" face.

Teddies at auction
Christie's (above), fine art auctioneers since 1766, was the first auction house to hold a teddy-bears-only sale. It was held on 13 December 1985 at the South Kensington branch in London.

British fine-art auctioneers Christie's, Sotheby's, and Phillips, held their first teddy-bear sales in the mid-1980s. Prices soared in a short space of time, attributed to the increasing interest in arctophily, and influenced perhaps by popular antique-appraisal shows on television. Sales are now held several times a year and collectors can subscribe to their catalogues, which are useful guides for new collectors. Attending previews and sales also provide good lessons.

Antique teddy bears can also be purchased from specialist dealers, many of whom have emerged since the early 1980s. In the United Kingdom, these include Pam Hebbs in London and Ian

Exclusively bears
In 1984, Joan Bland opened the first exclusive teddy-bear shop in the United Kingdom, in Windsor, Berkshire (above).

Archie
Designed by bear artist, Brian Beacock, Archie (above) is made exclusively for Asquiths Teddy Bear Shop.

The Calico Teddy
Donna Harrison and Dottie Ayers make exclusive bears for their shop (label, above).

Pout in Oxfordshire. In the United States, Barbara and Bob Lauver in Annville, Pennsylvania; Barbara Baldwin of Sparks, Maryland; and New York's The Rare Bear shop all sell antique teddy bears.

SHOWS AND CONVENTIONS
Some dealers, particularly in the US, organize conventions where a variety of teddy bears, from antique bears to the work of bear artists, can be purchased. Dealers Dottie Ayers and Donna Harrison organize an annual show in Baltimore, Maryland, and Linda Mullins arranges shows in San Diego, California. Numerous teddy-bear shows are now held throughout the United States, the dates of which are advertised in specialist magazines. Collectors can buy special limited-edition bears unique to a particular convention – for example, those produced by manufacturers and artists for the annual show at Disney World, Florida. The United Kingdom has followed suit, the main annual event being *Hugglets* British Teddy Bear Festival held in London on August Bank

Holiday Monday. In Australia there is Jacki Brooks' October Sydney show, which was first introduced in 1989; New Zealand held its first teddy-bear convention in Tauranga in 1992.

TEDDY-BEAR SHOPS
Shops exclusively selling teddy bears and related items have developed as demand grew. Bear in Mind Inc., of Concord, Massachusetts, was established in 1978 by Fran Lewis and a friend. They also publish a quarterly newsletter *The Arctophile* for collectors of new bears. In the United Kingdom, Asquiths was the first of this type of shop, a trend which has spread to nearly every major town.

In Australia, the first exclusive teddy-bear shop, *Teddy & Friends*, opened in Neutral Bay, New South Wales, in the early 1980s. Today, a number of stores called *The Teddy Bear Shop* can be found, in most major Australian cities. Such shops sell teddy bears aimed at the collector – limited editions and replicas, and sometimes bear artists' bears, as well as designs particular to that shop. Exclusive teddy-bear shops are now to be found worldwide, in Canada, New Zealand, South Africa, Northern Ireland, Jersey, and Hawaii. In the United States, collector bears are even sold on television shopping channels. Remember, though, that teddy bears do not have to be bought new: jumble sales, charity and junk shops, or car boot sales are sources to consider, and, if you are lucky, they can turn up a few interesting finds.

Jack's event bear
A small model of House of Nisbet's Jack's Bear (above), available only from Jack Wilson when he attended a teddy-bear event. This is the first bear he produced in distressed alpaca plush – a material that he helped to invent.

Limited editions
The three teddy bears (below) were all made as limited editions, exclusively for certain shops. Steiff made "Klein Archie" (left) and Merrythought created a special bear (right) for the 25th anniversary of Vermont's Enchanted Doll House. Sapphire (centre) was produced for the US store The Bear Tree by Canterbury Bears Ltd.

BOOKS FOR COLLECTORS

As a serious arctophile, it is important to build up a comprehensive library of books on teddy bears. The seminal works by US collectors Patricia Schoonmaker (*The Collector's History of the Teddy Bear*), Linda Mullins (*Teddy Bears: Past and Present; Volumes 1 and 2*), and Margaret Fox Mandel's series of identification guides are invaluable. Although many of the early works, for example by the Bialoskys, Ted Menten, Carol-Lynn Rössel Waugh, and the Volpps – are American, do not forget the sterling work of British authors Phillipa and Peter Waring whose *In Praise of Teddy Bears* first published in 1980, was followed by a number of teddy-bear books, notably by Pam Hebbs, Sue Pearson – and my own titles, including *The Ultimate Teddy Bear Book*.

In Australia, Romy Roeder and Jacki Brooks lead the field in teddy-bear publications. A rising number of arctophiles in other countries are also now writing books: for example Geneviève and Gérard Picot in France; Christina Björk in Sweden; and Erika Casparek-Türkkan in Germany.

Old toy-trade journals are useful sources of information about the history of teddy-bear manufacture; in England, *The Toy Trader* and *Games and Toys* can be viewed at the British Library's Colindale branch in north London. In the United States, the equivalent journal is *Playthings*, first introduced in 1903. Old manufacturers' catalogues are useful for identification purposes, but only a few companies – notably Merrythought and Steiff – maintain archives.

IDENTIFICATION KNOW-HOW

You cannot expect to find out everything by reading books, however. Try to do as much background research as possible by going to auctions and conventions, by talking to experts, and by actually handling old bears. Learn to tell the difference between mohair and artificial-silk plush, and between kapok and wood-wool stuffing (the latter is heavier and "crackles" under your fingers). Get to recognize the tell-tale signs that indicate a bear's age or origins – examine the body shape, including the length of the limbs, the muzzle, and the presence or otherwise of a hump; identify the materials used for fur, eyes, pads, and stuffing. Familiarize yourself with the particular characteristics of certain manufacturers – for example, the stitching employed on early Bing noses – and learn to spot replacement eyes. You must also be

Gyles' Bear
The Nisbet bear (above) is named after Gyles Brandreth – arctophile, founder of the Teddy Bear Museum, in Stratford-upon-Avon, British Member of Parliament, TV personality, and a man renowned for his personally designed sweaters.

Helen Sieverling
A California-based collector (right) and feature writer for the magazine Teddy Bear and Friends, *Helen Sieverling holds an early Steiff and Gebrüder Hermann's limited-edition bear, produced to commemorate her work for US publishers Hobby House Press.*

Edward in Transit
This pure mohair-plush bear (above) by Big Softies (see p.143) comes in a cardboard box with "air" holes.

All-in-one ears
Some early Bings have ears cut all-in-one with the head (below) – useful to know when identifying unmarked antique bears.

ID parade
Notice the subtle difference between an early Steiff (above left) and a Schuco (above right) miniature. The latter has a thinner, straighter body and limbs, a more pointed muzzle, and smaller feet.

aware that there are now fake antique bears on the market, sometimes with the addition of fraudulent trademarks.

Californian collector
Mrs. Sydney Charles (above) holds her childhood Knicker-bocker, "Frederic Pooh Robinson III" and an early American bear.

TEDDY-BEAR MUSEUMS

Museums are another source of bear facts. Teddy bears can usually be found in the various museums of childhood and toy museums around the world. However, the first museum devoted entirely to teddy bears was opened in Berlin in 1986, to hold Florentine Wagner's collection of around 2,000 bears. This was followed by Judy Sparrow's Bear Museum at Petersfield, Hampshire, England. Other museums soon opened in the UK: Gyles Brandreth's collection at Stratford-upon-Avon (1988); the Cotswold Teddy Bear

Florida museum
George B. Black Jr., son of founder Frannie Hayes, is director of the Teddy Bear Museum of Naples, Florida (above). Purpose-built, it is surrounded by specially commissioned bear sculptures and attractive pine woodland.

Museum at Broadway (1991); and Teddy Melrose in Scotland (1992). Dealer Ian Pout displays his collection of bears in a separate room off his shop Teddy Bears of Witney in Oxfordshire. The first teddy bear museum in the United States opened in December 1990, in Naples, Florida, based on Frannie Hayes' collection of around 1,800 bears. The curator is also building up an archive of information on bear manufacturers and artists. Doris and

Terry Michaud's museum collection of around 200 old bears can be viewed as part of their shop at Chesaning, Michigan; opening times vary, so make enquiries before a visit.

LIMITED EDITIONS

During the 1980s, a new form of collectable, the limited edition, was intro-duced by manufacturers and bear artists to meet the demand for special bears. Numbers to choose from are increasing constantly as manufacturers produce replicas of past models. On these bears, the limited-edition number is usually printed on a label sewn into the bear, sometimes with a printed, director's signature, and there is usually an authentication certificate. Smaller companies and bear artists generally hand-write their edition number, perhaps on a foot-pad or on a sewn-in label. Collectors can also get their bears signed at conventions or shops, further increasing the bear's value. Limited editions and replicas are fast becoming a high investment market, with retired VIBs *(see pp.146–47)*, Raikes Bears *(see p.171)*, and Steiff replicas *(see pp.152–53)* being sold as arctophiles continually strive to upgrade their collection. Collecting limited-edition bears is not necessarily a cheaper hobby than collecting antique teddy bears.

"Happy" inspirations
Steiff introduced a limited-edition replica (top) of the record-breaking "Happy" in 1990, followed by a smaller size the next year. In addition, House of Nisbet pro-duced Happy Inspired (above), part of their Way We Were series.

Reproducing "Happy"
Jorg Jünginger (below), Steiff's chief designer, archivist, and grand-nephew of Margarete Steiff, measuring "Happy" for the replica. No original patterns of "Happy" exist in Steiff's archives.

Mohair-plush coat
Following the 1907 teddy craze, children's coats were produced in mohair plush, and fastened with brass buttons embossed with bears. The coat (above) is a fine example of cinnamon mohair plush.

1920s sweet box
The bear-shaped lid of moulded card (above), covered in golden velveteen, has black bead eyes glued on.

BEAR MEMORABILIA

Few arctophiles can resist the temptation to include teddy-related items in their collection. Indeed, this off-shoot of the hobby can become a consuming passion in itself. Various useful books, for example Dee Hockenberry's reference and price guide *Bear Memorabilia*, have been written about this aspect of teddy-bear collecting.

Advertisements in the US trade journal *Playthings*, and in women's magazines from around 1907, show that the love of teddies is not a modern phenomenon; during the earlier craze, children's coats were made of mohair plush with brass buttons embossed with teddy bears; muffs, purses, and bags in the shape of teddies were also popular, as were infants' robes, crib covers, and pillow tops, all decorated with teddy-bear designs.

All kinds of teddy-bear containers can be found. In the catalogue section, I have already illustrated teddy-bear hot-water bottles (*p.23*), perfume and compact cases (*pp.40–41*), and nightdress-case bears (*p.91*) in traditional plush.

Sweet containers, dating from *c.*1910 were also made, one example consisting of a traditional teddy bear with a lift-off head revealing a card tube inside the neck. Other container bears include American-made, cast-iron money boxes, lithographed biscuit tins, and vinyl toothbrush holders.

SILVERWARE

Before World War I, a number of sterling silver teddy teething rings and rattles were made; the latter often had mother-of-pearl handles, and the silver, cast teddies had small bells attached to their feet or sides. These originated mainly from England, and were notably the work of Birmingham silversmiths, renowned for their production of small silver objects. The serious collector should have access to a book of hallmarks to help establish exact dates and provenances.

Other small silver items made during this period include boot-button hooks, charms, hat-pins, thimbles, pin-cushions, menu-holders, napkin-rings, egg-cups, letter-openers, and sand-shakers. Silver spoons, with the handles, and sometimes the bowls, decorated with embossed teddy bears, or realistic bears engaged in various activities (*see p.200*) are particularly popular among collectors. Examples also exist on which whole cast bears form the ends of the handles. Many have English hallmarks though several, originally designed as souvenirs, hail from the US, Switzerland, or Russia, some dating from the nineteenth century.

Brass, bronze, or pewter writing accessories, such as inkwells, pen-wipers, letter-openers, and paper weights, were also produced in the shape of, or decorated with teddy bears, and are believed usually to be of German origin.

CARVED, WOODEN ARTEFACTS

Various carved, wooden bear items – from large, bulky pieces of furniture, such as hat-stands and seats, to more delicate smoking and writing accessories, bottle-stoppers, brush-holders, and nut-crackers – are also highly collectable. Dating from the late nineteenth century to about 1914, they are often referred to as "Black Forest", since that area of Germany is traditionally renowned for its carved wooden objects. However, many also originate from either Switzerland or Russia. Reproduction bear furniture was also made by such firms as Bartholomew & Company during the 1980s.

TEA SETS AND CHINAWARE

China nurseryware and children's tea sets printed with teddy-bear images are much prized by arctophiles

Studio portrait
Photographs of children with their teddy bears, such as the "Little Lord Fauntleroy" example (above) from c.1905, are highly collectable, and are charming when framed.

Teething-ring rattle
This hollow, silver-plated, teddy-bear rattle with a bone teething-ring attached (below), was made in England c.1910.

Badges and buttons
Some arctophiles collect any bear-related items, such as the Roosevelt badges, advertising lapel pin, and brass, child's coat buttons (above).

– especially those with a teddy bears' picnic theme. The Three Bears motif was popular even before the teddy was invented and can be found on pre-1903 babies' plates. Many items, sadly, are unmarked, but some have been found to come from Stoke-on-Trent, the home of English pottery, while others were made in Germany or Japan. Other popular ceramic items include bisque (unglazed porcelain) bears or figurines of children holding teddy bears, as well as jugs, honey-pots, salt and pepper sets, and toothpick holders made to resemble teddy bears.

TEDDY ROOSEVELT COLLECTION

Some arctophiles collect items relating to Teddy Roosevelt: books written by the statesman or about him; campaign items *(see p.200)*; commemorative pins, medals *(left)*, china and moulded glass plates. Various versions of "Teddy and the Bear" – small, cheaply made, china toothpick-holders showing a bear and the President crouched down beside a tree stump – are now highly collectable. A 53-piece set of carved, wooden figures, including the President, entitled "Teddy's Adventures in Africa" by the US doll manufacturers Schoenhut is much sought-after. Dating from 1909, it is an expensive set, especially if complete. Some arctophiles also collect Clifford K. Berryman cartoons, either in newspapers or originals, although the latter are expensive. Roosevelt devotees can visit Harvard College Library, where some memorabilia is housed, or his birthplace in New York City, which is now a museum.

TEDDY STORYBOOKS

Arctophiles often start collecting teddy-bear storybooks, of which there are thousands. Some of the early examples, such as Frederick L. Cavally's *Mother Goose's Teddy Bear*, published by the Bobbs Merrill Company of Indianapolis in 1907, are rare. You could specialize, for example, in versions of *The Three Bears* or famous bear character books such as Pooh, Rupert dressed in checked trousers and scarf, and Paddington from "deepest, darkest Peru". First-edition Pooh books (published by E.P. Dutton in the United States and by Methuen in the United Kingdom) are highly collectable. For those with healthy bank balances, original Shepard drawings occasionally turn up at auction. Other printed Pooh ephemera includes early 1930s board-games, produced by Parker Bros. in the US, or the English Teddy Toy Company.

Rupert annuals illustrated by Alfred Bestall, first published in 1936, are fiercely collected; other Rupert memorabilia includes the rare 1920s Dutch *Bruintje Beer* (Brown Bear) postcard series. Paddington items are numerous.

It may also be fun to include in a collection books and other printed ephemera produced in a variety of foreign languages. After 1906, the Roosevelt Bears, based on stories by Seymour Eaton appeared printed on a variety of items, including postcard sets, china plates and jugs, and toys.

Handkerchief sachet
Well-known for her cloth dolls and mascots, Norah Wellings designed this bear sachet (above) in the 1930s at her factory in Wellington, Shropshire, England.

Sporting bear
The motif (below) was very popular from c.1910 to the 1930s, and can be found on many pieces of china, of varying quality, originating from England, Czechoslovakia, Germany, and Japan.

Teddy postcard
Teddies often feature on stationery (above).

Silverware
The early 20th-century silver mug and spoon (above) are embossed with an attractive teddy-bear design.

POSTCARDS AND OTHER EPHEMERA

Collecting teddy-bear postcards is a popular branch of arctophily, which has many themes. You might choose to concentrate on cards celebrating Christmas and Easter; souvenirs; photographs; or humorous cards, such as the renowned "Mary and her Little Bear Behind" series.

Paper teddy-bear "dolls" date back to around 1907, and are still

Steiff tableau
Collectors prize early Steiff postcards (above), always with the "Knopf im Ohr" trademark.

made today, along with reproductions of some early examples. Paper scraps (printed, embossed, shaped pictures that were collected, particularly during the Victorian and Edwardian periods, in scrap albums) have been produced over the years, featuring bears or teddies, and are now sought-after by arctophiles.

Stamps and photographs are another interesting area for collection, as is teddy-bear ephemera such as booklets, magazine or newspaper cuttings, metal lapel pins, jars, boxes advertising all kinds of products such as Teddy Bear Bread and Bear Brand Hosiery; or the various consumer offers, such as the 1926 printed, cloth, cut-out "Three Bears" series made for Kelloggs.

Warming plate
A child's c.1920 china warming-plate with metal base (above).

Given that 400 songs were registered between 1907 and 1911 with titles including the words "teddy" or "teddy bear", there are plenty of music scores to collect – many with attractive covers. There are also recorded songs, such as *The Teddy Bear's Picnic*.

MODERN TRENDS

Do not feel you have to specialize in antique bear memorabilia. Plenty of contemporary teddy-bear items are available, from clothing and jewellery, to paintings and ornaments. A growing number of illustrators around the world are producing paintings or drawings of teddy bears, either in book form, or for adorning the walls. Prue Theobalds and Jane Hissey in the United Kingdom, and Rosalie Upton in Australia are three such contemporary artists.

Figurines are increasingly popular: "The Cherished Teddies Collection" by Hamilton Gifts Ltd. of California (limited editions based on illustrations by artist Priscilla Hillman), or Peter and Frances Fagan's "Colour Box Miniature Teddy Bears", introduced in 1988, and based on real teddies in their collection in Lauder, Berwickshire, Scotland. The latter now boasts a thriving Collectors' Club.

Few areas are untouched by teddy-bear mania: there are teddy car alarms, and teddy telephones; and even a computer which, with a few accessories, can be turned into a teddy-bear shape.

TEDDY MAGAZINES

Arctophily is a sociable hobby; collectors worldwide are linked by a variety of magazines and clubs. "Good Bears of the World" (*see p.191*) issues a quarterly journal, *Bear Tracks*, from its base in Ohio, with news updates on "dens" around the world, and forthcoming conventions, as well as articles and letters.

In the United States, magazines such as *Teddy Bear and Friends*, *The Teddy Tribune*, and *The Teddy Bear Review*, which

Vote-catcher
Worn on the lapel by Roosevelt supporters during the 1904 Presidential election campaign, this 7.5cm (3in) bear with paper paws and sealing-wax nose (above) is now much sought-after.

Billy the Buccaneer
The limited-edition bear (above) was made especially for the Robert Raikes Collectors' Club convention.

were introduced during the 1980s, are essential reading for dedicated arctophiles. In the United Kingdom, Glenn and Irene Jackman, who originally produced teddy-bear kits as well as a bear-making manual under the name *Hugglets*, went on to publish the *UK Teddy Bear Guide* in 1988, a booklet listing essential contacts, including bear artists, manufacturers, material suppliers, shops, and museums. In 1990 they published *The Teddy Bear Magazine*. In the same year, another British magazine, *The Teddy Bear Times*, was launched; this is also distributed in Canada and the United States.

For Antipodean readers, the *Australian Doll Digest* was first published in 1985 by Jacki Brooks. This incorporated a section called "Bear Facts", which went on to become a separate magazine, *Bear Facts Review*, in 1991. In the Netherlands, where arctophily is a growing passion, the magazine *Beer Bericht* (Bear News) was launched in Amsterdam.

CLUB NETWORK

The number of clubs is growing throughout the world, not only of the Good Bears of the World variety, but also the type run by specialist teddy-bear shops, in order to inform arctophiles of what products are currently available.

Manufacturers, such as Steiff and Canterbury Bears, have their own clubs. In the United States, Robert Raikes (*see p.171*) runs a collectors' club from his home in Mount Shasta, California; he organizes an annual convention where he signs collectors' bears.

There are also clubs organized by collectors who wish to meet regularly and exchange news and ideas, although most also engage in philanthropic activities. In the United States, many have been inspired by the work of the Californian-based B.E.A.R. (Bear Enthusiasts' All 'Round Collectors Club Inc.), founded in 1983.

In the United Kingdom, *Hugglets* officially launched the British Teddy Bear Association in 1991, issuing their regular newsletter *Bearings* to keep members informed of new bears and shops, as well as linking clubs and individual collectors.

Clubs are forming in other parts of Europe, including the *Berenfanclub* in the Netherlands and *Club Francais de L'Ours Ancien*, and Teddy's Patch: *Le Club des Amis de l'Ours*, in France.

Collectors and organized groups of bear lovers also exist in Canada, Australia, New Zealand, and South Africa, and there is now an International League of Teddy Bear Clubs that attempts to unite all the clubs. It looks as if the hobby of arctophily is definitely here to stay.

Bear press
Teddy-bear collectors' magazines are now published in Europe, the US, and Australia, including: (below, left) Beer Bericht (Bear News) launched in Amsterdam in 1991, and (below, right) Hugglets Teddy Bear Magazine launched in Brighton, UK in 1990.

Convention bear
The bear (above) was created as a limited edition of one by Doris and Terry Michaud, for auction at the 1983 Teddy Tribune convention.

Club/magazine bears
Jamie (below, left) was made in 1988 by Irene Jackman of Hugglets, a bear-making business turned publisher. The bear (below, centre) was issued in the UK by Teddy Bear Times. The second Good Bears of the World bear (below, right) was made by Dakin.

1930s J.K. Farnell collectable
The worn teddy (*right*), with make-shift trouser-button eyes, could be more suitably restored using glass eyes from the same period.

1930s Victim of childhood
The wood-wool stuffing in the limbs of this bald and blind old bear (*right*) has turned to powder and settled in the paws and feet, leaving the tops of the arms and legs empty.

Replacement plush
Look for plush from old soft toys or clothing to patch a teddy or to make replacement parts.

Traditional joints
Use new card discs, washers, and pins to replace old joints.

Split seams
Repair split seams with strong cotton thread, in an appropriate colour.

1930s Swiss musical boxes
These typical Swiss musical boxes no longer work, but it is possible to buy modern, Japanese replacements.

Threadbare bear
This ailing 1930s bear needs a complete over-haul, including a surface wash, fumigation, extra stuffing and a new ear.

Wash-day disaster
Card disc-joints will not survive submersion in water.

1950s Mohair bear
Attractive outfits protect worn areas or disguise imperfections; detached pads and lost stuffing should be replaced.

Early Steiff bear
Despite fur loss, pad damage, and potential loss of stuffing, this bear still has its original, boot-button eyes.

Metal joint pins
Cotter pins and nails, used to secure disc joints, can suffer from rust or metal fatigue.

Dislocated arm
You have to repair broken joints from inside the body and limbs; this involves opening the final seam.

BEAR CARE AND REPAIR

TEDDY BEARS ARE MADE from a variety of fabrics and stuffings and, like all textiles, they are affected by a number of potentially destructive factors. Dust, light, humidity, and pests, as well as children and dogs, can cause damage to your precious teddy bear.

Many teddy-bear hygiene products are now on the market: moth-repellents, shampoo, dust covers, and even vanity sets. However, basic care procedures, as discussed on the following pages, are simple, using readily available household products.

The development of arctophily has led to the emergence of the professional teddy-bear restorer; teddy-bear "clinics" and "trauma centres" – once a minor offshoot of the dolls' hospital – are now a burgeoning, worldwide phenomenon. For major repairs, only entrust your valuable teddy bear to a recommended, reputable restorer who is skilled in sewing and understands the construction and history of the teddy bear. Avoid using glue in repair-work; the superficial effect may seem satisfactory, but glue is fundamentally detrimental.

With patience, a steady hand, and an understanding of teddy-bear construction, you can do many minor repairs on your teddy bear at home; the clearly illustrated, step-by-step instructions on the following pages will help you in the task.

Restoring Traditional-style Bears

Dismantling and Reassembly; Repair and Renovation

Traditional-style teddy bears are those most likely to need restoration and repair, and you must carry out such work carefully and sensitively if the original charm and character of the bear is to be preserved. This is especially true of valuable old bears, which may be best entrusted to a professional repairer. The step-by-step overhaul of an old teddy bear shown on the following pages illustrates how traditional-style bears are constructed, which will give you the confidence to dismantle a bear that needs repairing. Washing the fabric of an old bear by immersion in water is not generally recommended, but it is necessary to dismantle a traditionally made bear in the way shown if you want to repair or replace joints, or to add extra stuffing.

Bear to be restored
This 1930s Merrythought bear, with its button trademark still intact, is showing signs of advanced deterioration: the left ear is loose; the original eyes are lost; the body is sagging; and the original pads have been covered in inappropriate fabric.

head droops due to loss of stuffing around neck joint

unravelled threads on nose and mouth

mohair plush discoloured, stained, and badly worn

worn, circular area on chest indicates presence of squeaker

body sags due to disintegration and loss of stuffing

original pads covered by inappropriate fabric

BUGBEARS!
Teddies suffer from the effects of light, dust, damp, and pests. Before repairing, look out for signs of insect life, such as larvae casings. If you find any bugs, seal the bear in a plastic bag with flea powder or moth balls, and leave overnight.

Professional bear-repairer's toolbox
Basic equipment – thread, needles, scissors, pliers – is easy to obtain. Joints, eyes, cotter pins, and washers, as well as plush and felt, are available from specialist handicraft shops.

DISMANTLE

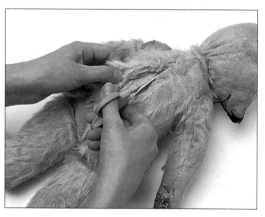

1 **Unpick main seam.** With sharp scissors, carefully cut a few stitches on the main seam (the final seam, usually at the back of the body, hand-sewn after the bear is stuffed); gently unpick the hand-sewn stitches.

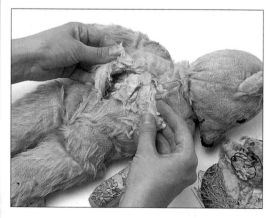

2 **Unstuff body.** Remove stuffing and reserve for re-use. Gently feel for the voice box, which may be in pieces; remove for later renovation. This bear is filled with kapok; wood-wool around the oval squeaker prevents kapok clogging the reed.

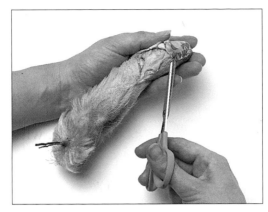

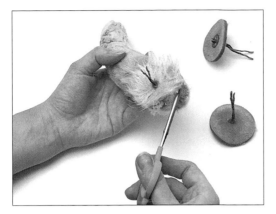

3 **Detach limbs.** Holding arm joint inside body casing, straighten curled prongs of cotter pin with pliers; slide disc over pin; remove arm. Repeat for other limbs. The head has already been removed in this way.

4 **Unpick replacement pads.** With sharp scissors, carefully unpick stitches attaching replacement fabric, to reveal original pads beneath. Take care not to destroy any remnants of the original manufacturer's label.

5 **Remove limb joints.** Unpick final, hand-sewn seam around the top of the limb. Pull back opening to remove card disc-joint and straightened cotter pin. Repeat process for remaining limbs.

Plushes for restoration work
Use old or new plush, matched to the original, to patch a teddy or to make a replacement limb or ear.

Dismantled bear
A traditional teddy, dismantled to show its components: head, disc-joints, limbs, unstuffed body casing, and broken squeaker.

wood-wool now is hard to find; old, cheap toys may yield enough to pack around a squeaker

cotton plush, a natural fabric with a woven backing, is cheaper than mohair plush .

disc-joints and washers, removed from body; cotter pins formerly attached head and limbs to body

woven, short-pile mohair plush (left) and distressed mohair plush (right) are expensive; look for cheaper offcuts

real sheepskin is difficult to work with, but synthetic sheepskin is a good alternative

mixture of wood-wool and "sub", used during World War II

kapok is a natural, soft, hygienic stuffing,

shaggy, mohair plush can be clipped and brushed to create a short, denser pile

an old piece of plush, cut from a discarded soft toy, is useful for patching old teddies with worn fur

squeaker needs new oilcloth to hold two card ovals together

original pads covered with inappropriate fabric; look for traces of claws and original label when removing

"sub" (textile waste) stuffing

Traditional stuffings
Kapok replaced wood-wool as a stuffing for teddies in the 1920s. "Sub" provided an alternative stuffing material during and after World War II.

WASH AND DRY

You should never immerse old, jointed teddies in water: metal parts, such as cotter pins and washers, will rust, and mould will develop if you do not dry the bear properly. Some materials, including kapok and artificial silk, react badly to water, causing staining. I have removed the joints and stuffing from this bear, leaving only the mohair-plush casings to be washed. Take care, as the delicate fibres could disintegrate further during washing.

white, cotton towel is absorbent and avoids colour bleeding

use hair dryer, on coolest temperature and lowest speed, held 30cm (12in) away from fabric, to hasten drying process

when dry, fluff up pile with nylon comb

soft-bristled brush

use soft toothbrush on stubborn stains

a washing-up bowl is ideal for washing teddy-bear fabric

dissolved in water, baby shampoo makes a gentle lather for washing delicate old fabrics

Wash mohair plush
Squeeze gently in a solution of mild shampoo and warm water; rinse well; fabric conditioner in last rinse removes odours and softens fabric.

Drying
Gently squeeze out excess water; towel-dry; leave in airing cupboard or blow dry.

MEND THE PAW-PADS

black felt

brown felt

rust-coloured velveteen

mustard-coloured velveteen

woven cotton

Rexine

fine, sharp needles

artist's brushes for applying acrylic paint

Pad repair kit
Pads on old teddy bears often need repair or replacement. Keep scraps of felt, velveteen, and suede, and a selection of threads and needles. You can fake Rexine by painting closely woven cotton with brown acrylic paint.

strong, synthetic thread

cotton thread

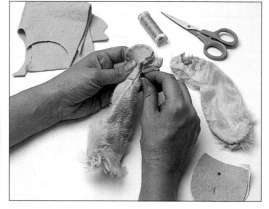

6 **Replace pads.** Match new material to original pads. Here, I used cream felt, but bears of a similar age may require velveteen or woven-cotton pads. Make a paper template, slightly larger than the pad, and cut new pads from the felt. Fold under excess felt, matching the pad size, and tack in place, over the original pads. With synthetic thread and fine needle, oversew pads into place with tiny stitches. Repeat for second paw and feet.

FIX THE HEAD

wood-wool stuffing
for muzzle

kapok stuffing

wooden knitting
needle useful for
pushing stuffing
firmly into position

7 Restuff head. Insert a little wood-wool into the muzzle and fill the rest of the head with kapok. Reuse original stuffing material if it is in good condition. Pack stuffing firmly, but do not overstuff.

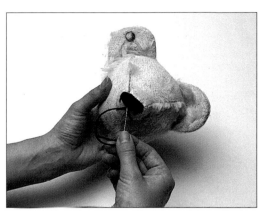

10 Stitch nose and mouth. Remove remnants of old features, noting stitch pattern. Restitch with black embroidery thread, following previous needle holes.

8 Fit neck joint. Place new disc, with washer and cotter pin (or reuse old ones if sound) inside neck opening, with pin pointing upwards. With needle and strong thread, tack around opening, near top edge.

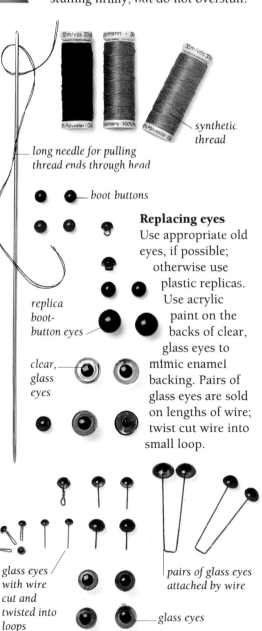

synthetic
thread

long needle for pulling
thread ends through head

boot buttons

Replacing eyes
Use appropriate old eyes, if possible; otherwise use plastic replicas. Use acrylic paint on the backs of clear, glass eyes to mimic enamel backing. Pairs of glass eyes are sold on lengths of wire; twist cut wire into small loop.

replica
boot-
button eyes

clear,
glass
eyes

glass eyes
with wire
cut and
twisted into
loops

pairs of glass eyes
attached by wire

glass eyes

11 Insert new eyes. Select appropriate new eyes, in this case glass eyes on wire shanks. Fasten strong, doubled thread to wire shank; with long needle, position eye and bring thread out through back of head.

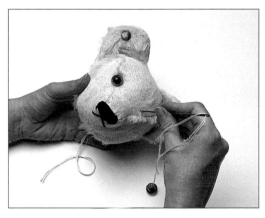

9 Close neck opening. Grasping head securely in palm of hand, pull tacking thread tightly so that fabric gathers tightly around cotter pin. Finish off, bringing needle out at back or side of head.

12 Fasten off eyes. Firmly pull loose threads from eyes outwards at back of head. Fasten off threads securely, tying together with several knots; cut off excess thread, or sew back into head.

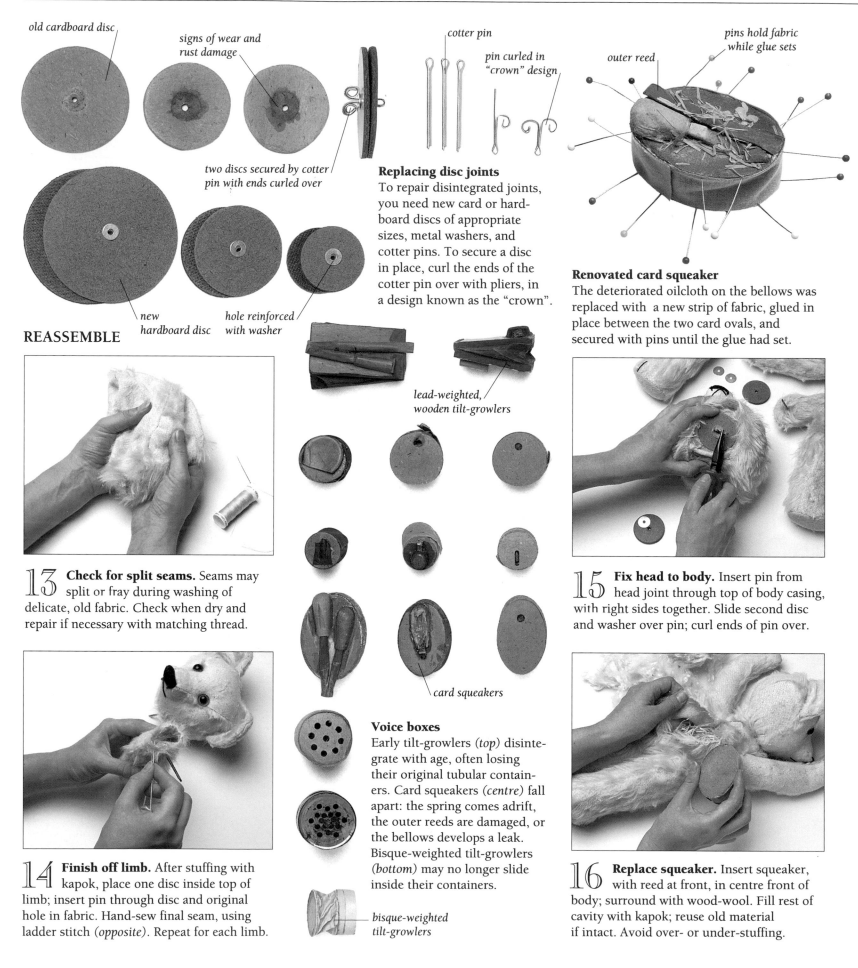

old cardboard disc

signs of wear and rust damage

cotter pin

pin curled in "crown" design

pins hold fabric while glue sets

outer reed

two discs secured by cotter pin with ends curled over

Replacing disc joints
To repair disintegrated joints, you need new card or hardboard discs of appropriate sizes, metal washers, and cotter pins. To secure a disc in place, curl the ends of the cotter pin over with pliers, in a design known as the "crown".

Renovated card squeaker
The deteriorated oilcloth on the bellows was replaced with a new strip of fabric, glued in place between the two card ovals, and secured with pins until the glue had set.

new hardboard disc

hole reinforced with washer

REASSEMBLE

13 **Check for split seams.** Seams may split or fray during washing of delicate, old fabric. Check when dry and repair if necessary with matching thread.

lead-weighted, wooden tilt-growlers

15 **Fix head to body.** Insert pin from head joint through top of body casing, with right sides together. Slide second disc and washer over pin; curl ends of pin over.

14 **Finish off limb.** After stuffing with kapok, place one disc inside top of limb; insert pin through disc and original hole in fabric. Hand-sew final seam, using ladder stitch (*opposite*). Repeat for each limb.

card squeakers

Voice boxes
Early tilt-growlers (*top*) disintegrate with age, often losing their original tubular containers. Card squeakers (*centre*) fall apart: the spring comes adrift, the outer reeds are damaged, or the bellows develops a leak. Bisque-weighted tilt-growlers (*bottom*) may no longer slide inside their containers.

bisque-weighted tilt-growlers

16 **Replace squeaker.** Insert squeaker, with reed at front, in centre front of body; surround with wood-wool. Fill rest of cavity with kapok; reuse old material if intact. Avoid over- or under-stuffing.

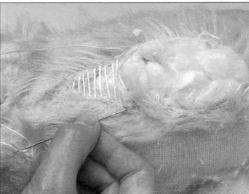

17 **Ladder-stitch final seam.** Use ladder-stitch to close final seams on limbs and body; pull thread tight to finish off.

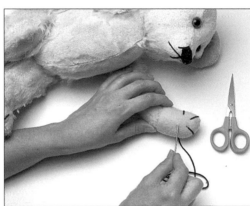

18 **Stitch claws.** With thread matched to originals, stitch claws, following original or classic design – in this case, the Merrythought, webbed-claw design.

Claw materials

Embroidery silk is ideal for replacing missing claws. Match colour of originals or, if none remains, use appropriate colour.

embroidery silks

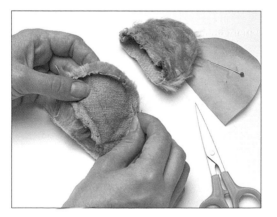

Renovated bear

Clean, upright, and with new facial features and paws, this bear has been restored to something of his former glory. The restorer should, of course, renovate with caution and sensitivity, to avoid destroying a much-loved teddy's unique charm.

head firmly stuffed

webbed claw design on paws

three black claws on each foot

new, cream felt pads

original plush very worn, revealing woven backing

SPLIT EAR TECHNIQUE

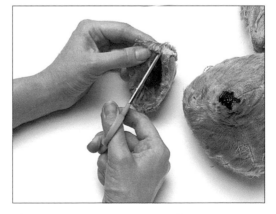

1 **Remove ear.** One ear is often missing from teddies with ears sewn across the head, and not caught into seams. Carefully remove the remaining ear. Unpick the seam and gently ease the two flat ear pieces apart.

2 **Make new ear.** Using original ear as a template, cut two new ear pieces from matching plush. With right sides facing, place one old ear piece against a new piece; back-stitch together. Repeat for other ear.

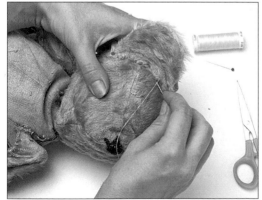

3 **Sew ears onto head.** Turn the two new ears right sides out; carefully pin into position, centring across facial seams, with original plush to the front. Oversew in place, with tiny stitches, along the front and back.

Caring for Modern Bears

WASHING AND GROOMING UNJOINTED, SYNTHETIC BEARS

The introduction, in 1955, of the unjointed, machine-washable teddy bear revolutionized the soft-toy industry. Made from synthetic fur and filling, and with safe, plastic eyes, the new teddy could be washed and dried, and quickly re-united with its young owner. However, not all syn-thetic bears are fully immers-able: foam-rubber-filled bears are happy to be bathed, but some other man-made materials react badly to water. Pay close attention to washing instructions on seam labels, particularly when these indicate "surface washable only". On these pages we illustrate the components of a modern teddy bear, and show you how to keep it in optimum condition, including the recommendation that hand-washing and natural drying methods will prolong teddy's life.

washer locks in plastic nose

Synthetic bear
This nylon-plush bear, stuffed with granulated foam rubber, shows signs of wear: the pile is grubby, matted, and worn, revealing the knitted backing. Use synth-etic thread to repair seams.

worn plush revealing knitted backing, indicates a cheaper quality bear

integral shank

Moulded, plastic noses
Modern, moulded plastic noses come in realistic and stylized designs; a metal washer pushed over the shank holds the nose in position.

strong, polyester thread

plastic joint

Plastic joints
Available in different sizes, each joint consists of a disc with integral shank, a second disc, and a smaller washer.

two plastic discs and washer

modern, plastic eye

teeth of metal washer locks eye in place

SAFE EYES

Manufacturers introduced safe eyes during the 1950s and they quickly became a requirement under toy-safety laws. Teddy bears today undergo rigorous testing to ensure that eyes are irremovable. If you plan to give your old teddy to a child as a toy, replace the original sewn-in eyes with safe, lock-in replacements.

safe, replica, boot-button eye

Modern, plastic eyes
Available in a variety of sizes and colours, the eyes are locked securely in place with a washer.

metal washer

Inserting a safe, lock-in, plastic eye
Insert shank through fabric; push toothed washer over shank to secure eye in place. To insert new eye in teddy, first remove stuffing from head to allow access to back of fabric.

WASH A SYNTHETIC TEDDY

1 Wash bear. Immerse the bear in a bowl of warm water with a little baby shampoo added, and gently scrub the stained areas with a stiff, natural-bristled brush.

2 Dry outside. Place the bear in a muslin bag pegged to the clothesline. Do not hang the bear on the line by its ear.

3 Groom bear. When completely dry, brush bear firmly with a teasel brush; the fine, wire "bristles" will separate and fluff-up the matted fibres of the plush.

Pad fabrics

After World War II, synthetic materials, such as Ultrasuede and Dralon, replaced cotton and velveteen as the most commonly used pad fabrics. Unjointed, synthetic teddy bears often have pads made from contrasting plush.

synthetic plush

Ultrasuede

Rexine

woven cotton fabric

velveteen

felt

Modern voice boxes

Modern tilt growlers and squeakers are usually made of plastic. Most modern musical boxes are made in Japan.

flat, plastic squeaker

tilt growler in plastic container

musical box

tilt growler

plastic, concertina squeakers

Synthetic fabrics

Nylon (first commercially produced in 1938), and other synthetic materials such as Orlon, Dralon, Acrilan, and Courtelle, have all been woven into plush for teddy bears. Cheaper synthetic plushes have a knitted backing.

synthetic plush fabric

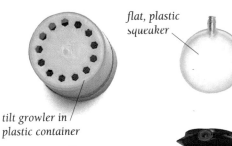

Dralon

synthetic plush on knitted backing

Post-World War II stuffing

Foam-rubber became popular because it was light and washable; waste from synthetic fabric mills was used in a similar way to "sub" (see p.205); polyester wadding is now widely used.

polyester wadding

granulated foam-rubber

foam-rubber and polystyrene pellet mix

wood-wool

low-grade synthetic waste

Preventive Care and Grooming

DEBUGGING, VACUUMING, SURFACE-CLEANING, AND PATCHING

The teddy-bear lover must consider the many hazards, including direct sunlight and dust, that can damage his collection. Teddy-bear fur attracts the larvae of the carpet beetle and the clothes moth, which feed on natural woollen fibres. New pinpricks in the felt pads can indicate that furniture beetle larvae are attacking the wood-wool stuffing. Even animal fleas will thrive in long pile.

Systematic checks, regular dusting, and prompt action are vital if such infestations are to be prevented. But cleaning must be done with caution: chemical dry-cleaning should never be considered, for example, and no traditional, jointed bear should ever be immersed in water. Only surface-washing is advisable for mohair, and must be followed by thorough drying. A bran bath is a useful method of drawing grease from bear fur.

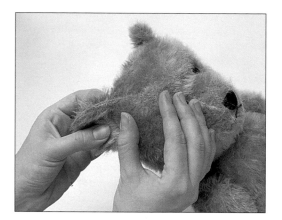

1 Check for bugs. You must regularly check your bears, particularly old ones, for bugs. Systematically part the pile, looking for signs of infestation; pay particular attention to ear and joint crevices. If you find any bugs, treat with the appropriate insecticide.

Larva in plush
Papery casings indicate the presence of carpet beetle larvae. Immediately fumigate the bear and check entire collection.

carpet beetle larva

Fumigation
Place an infested teddy overnight in a sealed, plastic bag with moth-balls or flea-powder. Treat all newly acquired, old teddies likewise.

infested teddy bear

plastic bags

moth balls

2 Vacuum fur. Bears collect dust, which ultimately damages the fur as well as detracts from the appearance. Clean regularly with a vacuum-cleaner; if using a powerful, full-size cleaner, cover the end of the nozzle with fine gauze for a gentler suction.

A FAMILY HEIRLOOM

"Jessica" is a very special bear; her bald, sagging, well-patched body represents many childhood memories for the author – including the games of doctors and nurses during which "Jessica" was the willing patient, as the lovingly stitched "operation wound" testifies. "Jessica" is an example of a bear whose priceless charm would be destroyed by restoration. This is also true of bears like the Blitz survivor (*p.192*) with his scorched feet or the well-worn Aloyius (*p.190*), who would lose not only their unique appeal but also their value, if signs of their colourful pasts were eradicated.

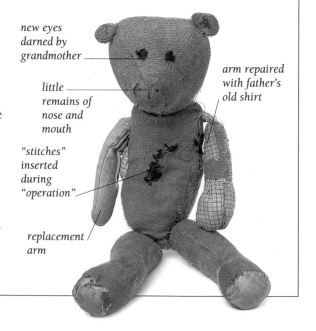

new eyes darned by grandmother

little remains of nose and mouth

"stitches" inserted during "operation"

replacement arm

arm repaired with father's old shirt

HOW TO PATCH

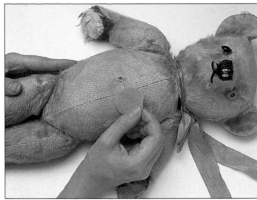

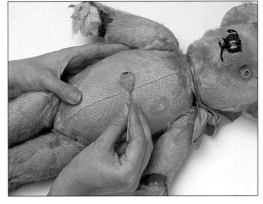

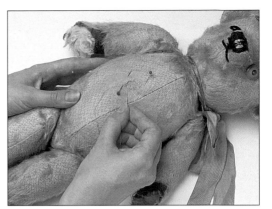

1 **Match fabric.** Choose plush to match colour and pile. For a bald bear, reverse plush, with woven backing uppermost. Cut the patch a little larger than the hole.

2 **Fit patch.** Fold the patch around a darning-needle, and push it into the hole. Flatten and manoeuvre gently into position, with the weave matching.

3 **Stitch patch in place.** Pin the patch securely in position. Oversew the edges of the hole to the new patch. Finish off and lose the end of the thread inside the body.

GIVE A BRAN BATH

1 **Rub in bran.** Fill a clean, plastic bag with bran (available from health-food or pet shops). Place the teddy bear in the bag and rub the bran liberally into the fur.

2 **Brush out.** When you have drenched the teddy with bran, brush it out with a stiff, natural-bristled brush. Use a damp cotton bud to wipe any dust from the eyes.

SURFACE WASH AND DRY

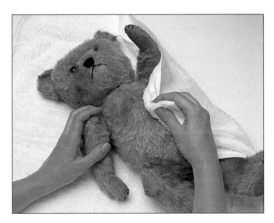

1 **Surface wash.** Fill a bowl with warm water and mild shampoo; whisk to create a lather. Dab lather onto the fur with a wad of cotton; wipe over the surface of the fur.

2 **Towel dry.** Rinse the surface with clean water; pat bear dry with a white towel. Leave to dry naturally, avoiding sunlight.

3 **Groom.** When dry, use a metal comb or a natural-bristled brush to fluff up the pile. Brush downwards for a smooth effect, or upwards to give the plush more volume.

Blow-dry
If you are in a hurry, use a hair dryer, but be careful. Set it to the coolest temperature and the slowest speed, and hold it at least 30cm (12in) away from the bear.

Display and Storage

SHOWING OFF AND PRESERVING YOUR COLLECTION

Teddy bears must be treated with care and respect if they are to survive, so do consider their security and well-being when planning a display. Fragile old teddies, in particular, will deteriorate rapidly if constantly handled and exposed to dust, direct sunlight, and insects. Glass display cases, such as nineteenth-century glass domes or – for large collections – wall cabinets with glass doors, are ideal for showing off and protecting your teddy bears. You will need to check them regularly for insects, though. Remember that dressing bears can help to protect them from the damaging effects of dust and sunlight.

Effects of sunlight
These old bears demonstrate the damage that is caused by excessive sunlight. The 1920s musical bear (*right*) was originally bright green, but only traces of the colour are now visible in joint crevices. The 1930s Bingie Guardsman (*right, centre*) is now a dirty grey except for a patch on his head, where the original, bright cinnamon colour has been protected by the bear's hat.

green mohair visible at edges of neck joint

original colour seen when hat is removed

faded patches on red felt jacket

Protection
An elderly, balding Steiff is protected by his "Little Lord Fauntleroy" suit, which also helps to hide any imperfections.

Bear display
A display of teddy bears and related memorabilia (*above*) arranged on shelves at the Volpps' home. An antique tricycle supports a large Steiff bear.

BOXED BEAR
When your collection has outgrown all available display space, you may need to pack and store some teddy bears. Plastic bags are not recommended, except for short periods, as moisture can build up inside, encouraging mould.
Calico bags, clean brown paper tied with string, or cardboard boxes in which the teddy bear is first wrapped in white, acid-free, tissue paper are ideal (a shoe-box is perfect for a small bear). Add mothballs, anti-moth, drawer lining-paper, cedar-wood shavings, or cloves in order to help prevent insect damage. Store the teddy bear away from damp, dust, and extremes of temperature.

THE TEDDY BEAR DIRECTORY

THE INTRODUCTION to this Encyclopedia (*pp.8–13*) gives an overall survey of the history of the teddy bear; the teddy's development is examined more closely in The Catalogue (*pp.14–187*), and the practicalities of collecting are reviewed in the chapters on Arctophily: Bear Collecting (*pp.188–201*) and Bear Care and Repair (*pp.202–215*). Here, the Teddy Bear Directory consolidates essential reference information in the Teddy Bear Time Chart, Factory Histories, Useful Addresses, and Glossary, which arctophiles, both amateur and professional, will find invaluable.

The Time Chart plots the history of the teddy bear, setting it chronologically against the world events that so influenced its evolution; while the Factory Histories give concise accounts of each of the main teddy-bear manufacturers. An exhaustive list of Useful Addresses gathered from around the world, provides you with information that will help you develop this absorbing hobby: addresses of museums, specialist shops, clubs, and magazines, all devoted to the teddy bear. Delve into this Directory and you will discover the extent to which arctophily has developed and gained international stature in the world of serious collecting.

Teddy Bear Time Chart

A CONCISE HISTORY OF THE TEDDY BEAR

Bears are known to have figured in western culture as far back as Neanderthal man's bear-worshipping rituals, and have also featured widely in stories and legends. In Greek mythology, Zeus's lover, Callisto, was transformed into a she-bear by jealous queen Hera, while another bear, "Mishka", has been part of Russian folklore since the twelfth century. "Bruin", a popular name for bears, was first used in Caxton's 1481 translation of *Reynard the Fox*. Bears have been hunted for their fur and for use in home remedies, as well as being captured and trained to dance or to take part in the "sport" of bear-baiting.

Children's playthings often reflect life, and so it was natural that bears should feature widely as the toy industry developed in the nineteenth century. They did so in the work of German toy-makers, and in the creations of the Russian co-operatives which, from the 1890s, produced small, carved, wooden bears in Bogorodskoye. The French firms Roullet et Décamps and Martin, based in Paris, made many ingenious mechanical tin and fur bears during this period. Bears at this time were usually depicted on all-fours or standing up on their back legs, unlike today's seated teddy.

NURSERY BEARS

Though wild bears no longer roamed the British Isles by the late nineteenth century, bears were known to British children, familiar with the performing bears that came to Britain from mainland Europe (an 1890s photograph shows a muzzled bear with its trainers in a London school playground). The original *Three Bears* story was first written down in 1831, and the soft-toy makers W.J. Terry and J.K. Farnell (later major teddy-bear manufacturers) were established by 1890 and 1897.

Bears have always played a key part in North American heritage and by the late nineteenth century, they were appearing in children's stories. The standard version of *The Three Bears*, featuring Goldilocks, was published in 1888. In the 1890s, Joel Chandler Harris's *Uncle Remus* books with the Br'er Bear character appeared. Patterns for soft toys, including bears, were also regularly seen in women's magazines.

SOFT-TOY INDUSTRIES

Until the outbreak of World War I in 1914, Germany was the toy-making capital of the world. Particular regions specialized in certains products; for example, tin toys were made in Nuremberg, and doll and wooden toy manufacture was centred around Sonneberg. By the late nineteenth century, several major toy manufacturers were established. Margarete Steiff (*see pp.38–39*) had added soft toys to her felt-clothing business by 1880 and bears became part of her range in 1892; these were later developed by her nephew Richard Steiff.

Reinhold Schulte opened a mohair-weaving factory in Duisberg in 1901 to supply soft-toy manufacturers with plush; mills in northern England provided the mohair for the plush.

PRESIDENTIAL INFLUENCE

Although many children's nurseries were already equipped with toys modelled on the wild bear, it was the 26th President of the United States, Theodore ("Teddy") Roosevelt (born 27 October 1858) who precipitated a movement in which bears became a model for the world's favourite toy, and one of the most endearing phenomena of the twentieth century.

WORLD WAR I

1902–03 | 1904–05 | 1906–07 | 1908–09 | 1910–14 | 1915–20

1902

12 November: Theodore Roosevelt leaves for Smedes, Mississippi, for four-day hunt; he fails to bag a bear.

16 November: Clifford J. Berryman's cartoon in the *Washington Post* shows Roosevelt refusing to shoot a bear cub (the cartoon title "Drawing the Line" refers to Roosevelt's attempt to settle a boundary dispute between Louisiana and Mississippi, the main reason for his visit to the southern states).

Inspired by Clifford J. Berryman cartoon, Russian emigrés Morris and Rose Michtom make "Teddy's Bear" to sell in their Brooklyn stationery and novelty store.

1903

February: Steiff sends shipment of soft toys to Paul Steiff in New York, including *Bär 55 PB*; it is not successful.

March: *Bär 55PB* shown at Leipzig Toy Fair; Hermann Berg of New York wholesalers Geo. Borgfeldt & Co. orders 3,000.

July: Steiff registers jointed bear pattern. Richard Steiff continues to experiment with methods of jointing.

August: Henry Samuel Dean establishes Dean's Rag Book Co. in London.

Morris Michtom establishes Ideal Novelty & Toy Co., becoming first US teddy-bear manufacturer, with backing of wholesalers Butler Bros.

1903–08: Steiff factory expands three times in period known by the company as the "Bärenjahre".

1904

February: last entry of *Bär 55 PB* on Steiff's price list.

March: Steiff registers new improved *Bär 35 PB*, with string jointing. Franz Steiff conceives "button in ear" trademark; blank buttons introduced.

November: Steiff introduces elephant button.

December: Steiff patents improved, double-wired, jointed design; "button in ear" trademark registered in US.

By end of year, Steiff introduces rod-jointed *Bär 28 PB* to range; total of 12,000 bears produced during year.

1905

February: Steiff registers *Bär 35 PAB*, first disc-jointed, now standard, teddy-bear design.

May: Steiff's "button in ear" trademark officially confirmed.

June: Steiff patents rod-jointed bear *Bär 28 PB*.

August: *Bär 35 PAB* first features in Steiff's price list as "*Bärle*", with elephant button.

1905–06: Seymour Eaton's Roosevelt Bears poems first copyrighted, appearing in US newspapers, and, from 1906, appear in series of books; soon followed by dressed bears made by Steiff and US manufacturers, Kahn & Mossbacher and D.W. Shoyer & Co.

1905–09: US President Theodore Roosevelt's second term of office coincides with height of teddy-bear craze.

1906

May: US toy trade journal *Playthings* first uses term "Teddy's Bear".

July: Steiff becomes private limited company.

October: term "Teddy Bear" first used in *Playthings*.

November: Charles Sackman and Martha Borchardt file individual patents for teddy-bear designs in New York.

1906–07: many short-lived manufacturers set up in US, producing teddy bears; often using imported German mohair and growlers – eg. Aetna, Bruin, Hecla, Columbia, Miller, Harman. As competition grows, Steiff and other manufacturers create novelty bears.

1907

February: term "teddy bears" first used in Seymour Eaton's poem *The Roosevelt Bears Abroad*, published in *The Sunday Oregonian*, Portland.

Mr. Cinnamon Bear by Sara Tourney Lefferts published in US.

Steiff produces 975,000 bears – the company's still unbeaten record.

US composer, John W. Bratton writes *The Teddy Bear's Picnic*.

The Teddy Bears, first moving picture featuring teddy bears, made by US Thomas A. Edison Co.

First teddy comic strip, *Little Johnny and the Teddy Bears*, appears in *Judge* magazine.

1907–11: 400 songs registered with "teddy" or "teddy bear" in title.

1908

US businessman asks Karl Hofmann company in Neustadt area of Germany to produce teddies for US market, launching Neustadt teddy-bear industry.

German exporters Eisenmann suggests to English firm J.K. Farnell that it makes its own teddy bears, launching British industry.

Tilt-growler first mentioned in Steiff's catalogues; glass eyes first used by Steiff for British market.

William Taft elected US President: various mascots created to rival teddy bear – eg. Billy Possum (Steiff and US manufacturers); Billiken (Horsmann in US).

Dean's Rag Book & Co. produces teddy bear as part of printed, cloth Knockabout Toys series, and teddy-bear rag book.

First lawsuits between Steiff and German companies such as Wilhelm Strunz and Gebrüder Bing over "button in ear" trademark.

1909

9 May: Margarete Steiff dies, aged 61.

Teddy Bright Eyes published, one of first British teddy-bear stories.

Steiff introduces golden mohair to previous range of light brown, dark brown, and white bears.

1909–12: Heinrich Schreyer works for Nuremberg firm, Gebrüder Bing.

1910–13: Steiff appoints agents and opens warehouses in New York, Sydney, and in several European countries.

1912

Steiff introduces special black bear for British market with boot-button eyes over orange felt.

Heinrich Muller and Henrich Schreyer establish Schreyer & Co. in Nuremberg.

Steiff introduces red, white, and blue Dolly-Bär for US election.

1913

October: first Hermann bear produced by Artur, Adelheid, and Max Hermann in Neufang, near Sonneberg.

Steiff introduces Record Teddy on wheeled chassis, later copied by British manufacturers – eg. British United Toy Manufacturing Co.

1914–15: soft-toy industries established in Great Britain as German imports are banned.

East London Federation Toy Factory founded by Sylvia Pankhurst; Wm. H. Jones establishes soft-toy firm as unable to get work as agent for German doll manufacturers; Teddy Toy Company founded by B.C. Hope and Abe Simmonds; Harwin & Co. founded, assisted by former Steiff sales agent.

1914–18: World War I disrupts production in Germany as men called up for military service; factories used for war work – Steiff factory makes armaments and aeroplane parts; borders closed preventing export; Margarete Steiff Frères, Paris agents, closed.

1915–16: Dean's and Chad Valley produce first jointed, mohair teddies.

British firms make patriotic bears: eg. Dean's The Bear of Russia, Germany's Crusher; Harwin's Ally Bear.

1919

Thiennot, one of first French manufacturers, established.

Josef Eisenmann dies, leaving Chiltern Toy Works to Leon Rees.

Bobby Bear appears in *Daily Herald*, first comic-strip bear in British newspaper.

1919–21: Steiff produces bears from reconstituted nettle plant because of shortage of plush.

1920

February: London's Teddy Toy Company patents "Softanlite" kapok stuffing; copied by other UK firms during early 1920s: Terry's "Absolite"; Chad Valley's "Aerolite" bears.

November: Mary Tourtel's Rupert Bear first introduced in UK newspaper *Daily Express*.

Chad Valley moves soft-toy production from Birmingham to Wellington, Shropshire.

Harry Stone and Leon Rees establish H.G. Stone, to produce Chiltern soft toys.

Thiennot wins bronze medal for teddy design at Lépine competition.

1920s–30s: ban on toy imports from Germany and imposition of import duty lead UK firms to supply UK and foreign markets: eg. Chad Valley, J.K. Farnell, H.G. Stone, Merrythought, and Dean's.

WORLD WAR II

1921–29

1921
J.K. Farnell registered as private limited company; Alpha Works built, and tradename "Alpha" used.

A.A. Milne's wife buys bear (possibly Alpha) from Harrods for son Christopher Robin's first birthday.

Steiff introduces glass eyes and kapok stuffing; Hugo Steiff introduces conveyor-belt system.

Schreyer & Co. registers trademark "Schuco" and patents Yes/No bears.

First Rupert Bear merchandise produced.

1923
First Chiltern Hugmee bears advertised.

1925–28: "Dual" plush mohair popular; novelties such as Gebrüder Süssenguth's open mouth/rolling-eyed Peter; Gross & Schild's talking Bruno; and Swiss squeeze-type musical bears introduced.

1926
October: *Winnie the Pooh* published by Methuen.

Teddies wearing pierrots' hats and ruffs (Steiff's Clown-bear; Chad Valley's Tubby Bear) become popular.

1929
Wall Street crash and economic depression leads to production of low-quality teddy bears such as US "stick" bears.

Artificial-silk-plush bears such as J.K. Farnell's Silkalite bear (March) and Chiltern's Silky Teddy (July) first advertised.

J.K. Farnell opens showrooms in New York and Paris.

1930–37

1930
Steiff launches unique and influential Teddy Baby and Dicky designs.

Merrythought Ltd. established in Ironbridge, Shropshire.

Mary Plain by Gwynaed Rae published (character later produced as soft toy by J.K. Farnell).

Lyrics added to *The Teddy Bears' Picnic* by Jimmy Kennedy in UK.

1930–35: Winnie the Pooh toys and games made in UK by Chad Valley and Teddy Toy Co; in US by Parker Brothers and F.W. Woolnough.

1930s: novelty teddies become popular – eg. Schuco's miniatures; nightdress cases and other sachets by UK firms.

1933
Hitler comes to power; rise of National Socialist Party affects German toy industry: Ernst and Hugo Steiff removed from office because of Jewish sympathies. Adolf Kahn, a Jew, leaves Schuco for England.

1935
US patent application filed for nylon, invented by W.H. Carothers.

1937
British Lines Bros., then largest toy manufacturer in world, launches Pedigree Soft Toys.

Coronation of British monarch George VI, following Edward VIII's abdication, inspires production of patriotic red, white, and blue bears.

Chicago Zoo receives first giant panda in West, launching panda-bear industry.

1938–44

1938
Chad Valley awarded Royal Warrant, by appointment to HM The Queen Elizabeth (consort of George VI).

First commercial use of US invention, nylon.

1939
Outbreak of World War II forces many European soft-toy factories to close or turn to war work.

Late 1930s–50s: teddy bears in all-in-one clothes popular, saving on plush.

1940–45: raw materials in short supply, resulting in reduced output and economy measures, such as use of alternative fabrics; new designs with shorter limbs and muzzles; unjointed necks.

Magazines publish knitting patterns for bears, using unravelled wool.

Teddy-bear firms turn to essential war-work; eg. Dean's makes life-jackets; Chad Valley makes children's clothing; Merrythought produces military uniform accessories. In Germany, Steiff makes munitions and Schuco telephone equipment.

Some factories, including Schuco and J.K. Farnell suffer air-raid damage.

1941
Polyester invented by J.R. Whinfield and J.T. Dickson in UK.

1944
Smokey the Bear becomes symbol of US Forest Fire Prevention Campaign.

1945–50

1945
World War II ends. Germany partitioned into four military zones.

1945–51: post-war rationing results in few toys being available.

Cottage industries in Germany, Austria, and UK make teddies from any available materials; sheepskin remains alternative to mohair. "Sub" (textile waste) provides alternative to kapok stuffing.

Nylon and rayon plush commonly used for teddies from post-war period.

1947–48: companies once based in Sonneberg now in Soviet-occupied zone of Germany. Fearing communist regime, many move to US zone, forming new companies. Additional "Made in US Zone" labels sewn on bears.

1948
Wendy Boston patents first screw-in safe eye.

1950–53: first commercial use of synthetic fibres, such as Terylene, Dacron, Orlon, Dralon, and Acrilan.

1950s: rise of Japan as industrial empire; influx of Japanese clockwork, and later battery-operated, bears forces demise of German companies that previously led mechanical tin-toy market.

1950s–60s: synthetic plush and stuffing (eg. Polyester) becomes popular for teddy bears.

1951–57

1951
Steiff introduces innovative Zotty design.

1952
Introduction of vinyl muzzles, particularly by US manufacturers, such as Gund and Ideal.

British glove-puppet Sooty first appears on TV; Chad Valley gains exclusive rights to produce Sooty toy.

1953
Germany divided into Democratic and Federal Republics; "US Zone" labels change to "Made in the Federal Republic of Germany".

Coronation of Queen Elizabeth II prompts production of patriotic bears. Wording on Chad Valley's Royal Warrant label changes from "Queen Elizabeth" to "Queen Mother".

First Smokey Bear produced by Ideal for US Forest Fire Prevention Campaign.

Toffee (BBC Radio *Listen with Mother* story character) produced by Chad Valley.

1954
Wendy Boston test-markets first fully washable, nylon plush, safe-eyed, foam-rubber-stuffed teddy bear in UK.

1955
Wendy Boston's bear launched on BBC TV with demonstration of its washability. Boulgom in France launches similar bear. Other manufacturers follow suit.

1957
Merrythought introduces Cheeky with bell in ear; other British manufacturers copy this feature.

1958–63

1958
Michael Bond's *A Bear called Paddington* first published in UK.

British Standards Institution (B.S.I.) proposes test methods for flammability of soft-toy fabrics.

1959
Wendy Boston introduces new safety eye with nylon screw and bolt. Safe, vinyl noses begin to be used.

1960
Trademark "Bri-Nylon" registered by British Nylon Spinners; Bri-Nylon teddies produced by Dean's and Pedigree.

J.K. Farnell & Co. produces its version of Toffee (BBC Radio *Listen with Mother* character).

Early 1960s: Yogi Bear first features on TV shows, produced in US by Hanna Barbera.

Australian TV character Humphrey B. Bear first produced as soft toy by L.J. Sterne of Melbourne.

Winnie the Pooh cartoon character created by Walt Disney Studios inspires new Pooh merchandise.

First talking teddies, with miniature records activated by pull-cords.

1961
B.S.I. issues first toy standard on flammability of pile fabrics.

Hoover awards Wendy Boston bears Certificate of Washability.

1962
Teddy Edward by Patrick and Molly Mathews published in UK.

1963
Teddy Bear comic launched in UK.

1964–72

1964
Margaret Hutchings publishes *Teddy Bears and How to Make Them.*

Theodore Roosevelt's grandson presents early Ideal teddy bear to Smithsonian Institute, Washington, D.C.

c.1965
All-in-one foam bodies introduced.

1967
Mr. Whoppit, Donald Campbell's Merrythought teddy-bear mascot, survives Campbell's fatal attempt to beat world water-speed record on Coniston Water, England.

1968
B.S.I. recommends that rayon materials used for soft toys be treated with flame-resistant solution, and that eyes be attached in such a way that they cannot be gripped by fingernails or teeth.

1969
Peter Bull's *Bear with Me* published.

Early 1970s: US doll artists begin to produce teddy bears as art objects.

1970s: many leading soft-toy firms, especially old-established UK firms, go out of business as a result of recession and drop in birth-rate. Many firms move production to East Asia to cut costs.

1971
US-invented, synthetic Ultrasuede first used; becomes popular for teddy-bear pads and miniature teddies.

1972
Paddington Bear first produced as soft toy in UK by Gabrielle Designs.

1973–80

1973
Good Bears of the World launched in Switzerland, by James T. Ownby.

1974
Beverly Port shows first artist bear in Reno, Nevada, at International Dollmakers Convention.

1975
Eden Toys gains world rights to manufacture Paddington Bear.

Carol-Lynn Rössel Waugh in Maine makes fully jointed, porcelain artist bears with moulded-on clothing.

1978
Bear in Mind mail-order company established in Concord, Massachusetts.

1979
International Year of the Child marked by teddy-bear events, including one in UK hosted by Marquis of Bath; similar rallies in Australia and New Zealand follow.

Collectors' bears and limited editions popular; Gund launches Collectors' Classics series.

B.S.I. updates toy safety standards on eyes, noses, and flammability.

1980
Steiff introduces first replicas; North American Bear Company launches VIB range; Dakin produces Mishka bear, mascot of Moscow Olympic Games.

The Teddy Bear Catalogue: Prices, Care & Repair, Lore, by Peggy and Alan Bialosky, published in US.

In Praise of Teddy Bears by Philippa and Peter Waring published in UK.

1981–84

1981
Peter Bull's teddy bear "Delicatessen" changes name by deed poll to "Aloysius" after starring in *Brideshead Revisited.*

House of Nisbet launches Bully Bear range.

The Collector's History of the Teddy Bear, by Patricia Schoonmaker, published in US.

Term "bear artist" first coined in US *Doll Reader* article. Bear artistry grows in US and UK.

1982
Merrythought introduces special-edition collector bears.

1983
October: Bunny Campione introduces teddy bears to Sotheby's collectors' auctions.

Teddy Bear and Friends magazine for teddy-bear collectors launched in US by Hobby House Press.

Bear Enthusiasts All Round Collectors Club Inc. (B.E.A.R.) launched in California.

1984
Peter Bull dies, aged 72.

Joan Bland opens Asquiths in Windsor, Berkshire, first exclusive UK teddy-bear shop.

Teddy Bear Artists: Romance of Making and Collecting Bears by Carol-Lynn Rössel Waugh published in US.

Steiff produces Petsy, its first fully washable, soft-stuffed, fully jointed teddy bear.

Gebrüder Hermann introduces special-edition collector bears.

1985–88

1985
May: First teddy bear (Steiff *c.*1905–10) to fetch over £1,000 at Sotheby's, London.

December: Christie's of London holds first teddy-bears-only sale.

Dakin produces Mike Young's Super Ted character after success of cartoon series on US TV.

1985 designated International Year of the Teddy Bear by Good Bears of the World.

American Teddy Bear Artists Guild founded by Rowbear Lohman.

1986
World's first teddy-bear museum opens in Berlin.

Launch of *Teddy Bear Review* in US.

Teddy Bears Past and Present Vol. 1 by Linda Mullins, published in US.

House of Nisbet's Jack Wilson invents process for "distressing" mohair.

1987
Golden Teddy Awards launched by *Teddy Bear Review.*

Big Softies produces Tough Ted, Simon Bond's storybook character.

1988
Teddyberendag, first teddy-bear event in the Netherlands, held at Amsterdam's Artis Zoo.

"Loc-Line" articulation introduced to bear artistry in US by Jeff Trager of Beaver Valley.

Gyles Brandreth's Teddy Bear Museum opens at Stratford-upon-Avon.

1989–90

1989
"Happy", a *c.*1926 Steiff bear, enters *Guinness Book of Records* after fetching record-breaking £55,000 at Sotheby's.

Reunification of Germany allows Hermann family to return to Sonneberg to research family history.

Australia's major teddy-bear show first held in Sydney.

Button in Ear, official Steiff history by Jürgen and Marianne Cieslik, published.

B.S.I. updates safety standards regarding soft toys; British Toy and Hobby Manufacturers Association introduces Lion Mark indicating toys manufactured to UK safety standards

1990
East European firms, formerly confiscated by communists, handed back to descendents of original owners. Replicas of old patterns reproduced, eg. Leven by Hermann-Spielwaren; Hamiro by Sigikid.

UK Hugglets *Teddy Bear Magazine* and Ashdown Publishing's *Teddy Bear Times* launched.

Mary Holden of Only Natural produces Bill Bear, first teddy in UK for the chemically sensitive, with "EVE" environmental safety symbol.

Growing numbers of European bear artists, especially in Germany, France, and Holland.

Teddy Bear and Friends introduces TOBY awards.

CE mark introduced in UK to indicate toys meet EEC safety standards.

1991–93

1991
Teddy-bear museums open in US and UK. First bear-artist festival held in the Netherlands.

Dorling Kindersley publishes *The Ultimate Teddy Bear Book*, No.1 best-seller in UK.

Dean's launches limited-edition replica range.

Jakas introduces limited-edition range and replica of *Playschool's* "Big Ted".

British Teddy Bear Association launched.

Bear Facts Review launched in Australia, and *Beer Bericht* in the Netherlands.

1992
Steiff Collectors' Club formed, with special limited-editions for members only.

Limited-edition Columbus Bear by Hermann-Spielwaren celebrates 500th anniversary of founding of America.

Hermann-Spielwaren produces Europa Bear.

First New Zealand bear show held in Tauranga.

Berg launches 500 piece limited-edition replica 1952 teddy.

Clemens produces "40 Jahre Clemens-Bären".

Merrythought reproduces "Gatti" to mark 80th anniversary of Titanic disaster.

1992–93: Thiennot launches 100 piece limited-edition 1920 replica teddy.

1993
Sigikid's United Europe bear marks founding of common market.

Factory Histories

A DIRECTORY OF TEDDY-BEAR MANUFACTURERS, PAST AND PRESENT

The factory histories on the following pages were compiled from a wide variety of sources and include, in alphabetical order, all the main teddy-bear manufacturers, past and present, the majority of which feature in this encyclopedia. Each entry includes, wherever possible, the date of found-ation and closure, as well as a brief outline of import-ant events in the history of the factory. Where the company is still in operation, their current address is given at the end of the entry. In some cases, firms have been cross-referenced by their tradename when the latter is more well known than the company name.

Acton Toycraft Ltd. *(see also J.K. Farnell & Co. Ltd.)*
1964 1 October, registered as new private company No. 821,432; directors W.E. Hunt and F.W. Hase. Part of J.K. Farnell, it leases former Farnell factory, the Alpha Works in Uxbridge Road, Acton, west London, after Farnell's move to Hastings. Factory, adjacent to Twyford Avenue, west London, renamed Twyford Works.
Mid-1970s Ceases operations.
Trademark: "A Twyford Product".

Aetna Toy Animal Co.
*c.*1906 Manufactures teddy bears in New York (adver-tisements describe Aetna bear as "formerly the Keystone Bear"). Wholesalers, George Borgfeldt & Co. sole selling agents. Later becomes Aetna Doll and Toy Co.
1919 E.I. Horsmann Co. of New York buys firm
Trademark: "Aetna" in oval outline, on right foot.

Ajena
1965 Founded by Bernard Meffray in Luché-Pringé.
1989 Nounours group buys company. Produces lower quality range to distribute to chainstores; bears made at Nounours factories in Tunisia and Mauritius.
Luché-Pringé, BP 9, 72800, Le Lude, France.

Albico *(see Althans KG)*

A.L.F.A. (Article de Luxe Fabrication Artisanale)
1930s Founded in Paris.
1936 Company produces first teddy bear – unjointed, dressed as little boy or girl, with all-in-one clothes.
Post-1945 Creates first jointed teddy bears.
1960s Dressed bear design, in synthetic fabrics.
*c.*1970s Ceases business.
Trademark: "ALFA" printed on left sole.

Alresford Crafts Ltd.
1970 Established by John and Margaret Jones at The Town Mill, Alresford, Hampshire, England. Margaret Jones designs soft toys; originally includes only one teddy but, due to demand, bears become main product.
1980s At height of success, employs 100 staff, exporting world-wide, with US warehouse.
1991 John Jones dies.
1992 Margaret Jones continues business until year end.

Althans KG
1920s Althans family begins making teddy bears in Sonneberg, Thüringia, Germany.
1945 Soviets occupy area. Karl Althans escapes from Soviet zone to village of Birkig eight kilometres (five miles) away in US zone; marries Else Kessel and becomes farmer; works on in-laws' farm.
1949 Karl and Else Althans form part-time teddy-bear business in farmhouse, cycling with rucksacks of bears to sell at markets in nearby towns of Neustadt, Coburg, and Lichtenfels. Gradually convert farmhouse to teddy-bear-making. Later firm employs over 100 workers in two factories. Has showroom above old pig-pens.
Early 1950s Tradename: "Albico" (derived from Althans Birkig Coburg).
Early 1980s Tradename: "Althans/Quality you can feel".
Mid-1980s Company introduces limited-edition collectors' teddy bears.
1988 Introduces "Althans Club" trademark for separate range of products manufactured in East Asia under Althans' design and quality control.
1990s Karl Althans' brother-in-law Günther Kessel now manages this family-owned business, and signs feet of limited-edition teddy bears
Horber Straße 4, 8632 Neustadt-Birkig, Germany.

Les Créations Anima
1947 Established in Paris by Suzanne Vangelder.
1972 Company is sold to M. Frenay of Boulgom; head office moves to Chaponost, near Lyon.
1990 The Alain Thirion group buys Boulgom, including the Anima range.
1992 American company Gund buys Anima.
1993 Anima moves to new premises in St Genis Laval.
Parc des Aqueducs, Chemin Favier, 69230 St Genis Laval, France.

Anker Plüschspielwarenfabrik GmbH
*c.*1953 Founded in München-Pasing (part of Munich) by Herr Bäumler, designer of plush animals.
1954 Firm buys soft-toy company belonging to Artur Hermann (son of Johann Hermann), known as J. Hermann Nachf. Inf. Artur Hermann, also located in München-Pasing. Based at Karl-Hromadnik-Straße 3.
Early 1960s Makes plush glove-puppets and animals, including popular donkey Mufti, and range of traditional mohair and Dralon teddy bears; standing bears with chains through noses; open mouth Zotty-like bears; and comical short-legged bear with large paws called Drolly.
1976 Unsuccessful collaboration with Hegi (part of Schuco in Nuremberg).
1977 Ceases business.
Trademark: an anchor superimposed on a lion.

Applause Inc.
1981 Wallace Berrie sells his firm, Wallace Berrie & Co., to Larry Elins and Harris Toibb.
1982 Acquires Applause Company from Knickerbocker Toys; gains marketing rights to Italian Jockline's Avanti line of soft toys.
1985 Introduces teddy bears designed by Robert Raikes.
1986 Changes name to Applause, becoming one of largest manufacturers in the gift industry, producing ceramic items, greetings cards, and other novelty items.

1988 Good Company division of Applause produces Robert Raikes bears.
1989 The Applause and Good Company divisions merge to become Applause Inc.
1991 Introduces bears designed by Bonita Warrington.
6101 Variel Avenue, PO Box 4183, Woodland Hills, California, 91365-4183 USA.
(see also Wallace Berrie & Co.; Knickerbocker Toy Co. Inc.)

Aux Nations
1964/65 Founded by Marc Fremont.
1975 Jacky Dubois of Nounours buys company.
1976 Awarded Oscar of Good Taste (French annual prize for toys) for Aux Nations collection.
Today soft toys are designed at Nounours headquarters in France, but made in Schio, near Venice, Italy.
c/o Nounours 35210 Chatillon en Vendelais, France.

Baki *(see Baumann & Kienel KG)*

Barton Waugh Pty. Ltd.
Post-World War II Established, operating from 7 Connells Point Road, Hurstville (a Sydney suburb), New South Wales; produces a range of fully jointed, mohair, kapok-filled bears with leatherette paws, distinct pointed feet, and triangular noses, in various sizes.
Late 1960s Ceases business.

Baumann & Kienel KG
1946 Franz Baumann, son of Hermann Baumann and Adelheid Hermann (daughter of Johann Hermann, and maker along with brothers Artur and Max of first Hermann bear), founds small arts and crafts toy company, Kunstgewerbliches Spielzeug in Flensburg.
1951 Franz founds plush toy company, Baumann & Kienel oHG (later Baumann & Kienel KG) with old friend Franz Kienel in little town of Rodach, near Coburg. Company managed today by Franz Baumann and Walter Kienel (son of original founder).
Trademark: "Baki" formed from **Ba**umann and **Ki**enel.
Coburger Straße 53, 8634, Rodach bei Coburg, Germany.

Bear With Us *(see Harrisons Textiles)*

Berg Spielwaren Tiere mit Herz GmbH
1946 Broschek family makes teddy bears from old army blankets, with army uniform buttons for eyes, and small boxes of pebbles for voices; works from Tyrolean farm-house in Fieberbrunn, Austria; trades under name Berger, the grandmother's maiden name, later shortened to Berg.
1951–52 Business expands when woven plush and glass eyes become available; "Berg" printed on cloth ear-tag becomes trademark.
1957 Trademarks become little red heart sewn into

chest and "Tiere mit Herz" ("Animals with Heart").
1966 New factory is built at Admont, in the Steiemark for assembly; toys are sent to Fieberbrunn factory for final inspection and distribution.
1992 Introduces replica limited editions.
A-6391 Fieberbrunn, Tyrol, Austria.

Berlex Toys Pty.
*c.*1930s Established in Melbourne, Australia.
*c.*1971 Based at 311 Boundary Road, Melbourne.
1970s Ceases business.
Trademark: "Berlex Melbourne" and "Made in Australia".

Russ Berrie & Co. Inc.
1963 Russ Berrie establishes business to sell novelty merchandise, including figurines, from converted garage in Palisades Park, New Jersey, USA.
Late 1970s Becomes a leader in soft-toy industry.
1984 Registered as public limited company with divisions, Gift, Plush 'N' Stuff, Expression Centre. Later reduced to first two. Headquarters in Oakland, New Jersey with distribution centres throughout world; soft toys manufactured in Korea, China, and Indonesia.
1993 First Russ teddy made in Australia under tradename "Koala Families".
111 Bauer Drive, Oakland, NJ 07436, USA.

Wallace Berrie & Co.
1964 Wallace Berrie, brother of Russ Berrie (*see Russ Berrie & Co. Inc.*) founds small firm; manufactures drugstore novelty items; slow, steady growth in first decade.
Mid-1970s Gains worldwide rights to Smurfs, creating sales phenomenon. Sells over $1 billion in retail merchandise and becomes one of leaders in licensing industry.
Late 1970s Main lines are plush toys.
1981 Firm is bought by Larry Elins and Harris Toibb.
1982 Acquires Applause Company from Knickerbocker Toys, picking up more classic licenses including Disney; gains worldwide marketing rights for Italian-designed Avanti line of soft toys.
1986 Changes name to Applause (*see Applause Inc.*).

Big Softies
1978 Family business established by Valerie and Fred Lyle, makes life-size, realistic animals, hence tradename.
1982 Firm starts making teddy bears, inspired by thesis on teddy bears' history by one of Fred's college students; teddy bears are now a major part of Big Softies' range – known as Good Companions. Also makes commissioned bears for British shops and department stores as well as collectors' limited editions.
The Old Mill House, Skipton Road, Ilkley, West Yorkshire, LS29 9RN, England.

Gebrüder Bing
1863 Company founded by brothers Ignaz and Adolph Bing in Nuremberg, to sell toys and kitchenware; later establishes own factory manufacturing tin toys – known as Nürnberger Spielwaren Fabrik Gebrüder Bing (Bing Brothers' Nuremberg Toy Factory) in Karolinestraße. Becomes renowned for mechanical trains, boats, and cars.
1880s Company has 100 employees and 120 outworkers.
1890 Establishes factory at Grünhain, Saxony.
1895 Becomes public limited company and name changes to Nürnberger Metall und Lackierwarenfabrik vorm, Bing AG (Nuremberg Metal and Enamelware Works). Adolph Bing leaves company and Ignaz Bing becomes chairman.
1908 Employees number 3,000. Catalogue proclaims Bing the "Greatest Toy Factory in the World".
1909 Legal battle with Steiff over "button in ear" trademark.
1911–15 Lawsuit with Steiff over somersaulting bear.
1909–12 Heinrich Müller (*see Schreyer & Co.*) joins firm.
*c.*1911 Bings Ltd., sole agents in Britain (part of

Eisenmann & Co. Ltd.) operate from 25 Ropemaker Street, east London; John Bing, sole representative in US, operated from 381 Fourth Avenue, New York.
1917 Agents Concentra markets Bing's complete line under various brand names.
World War I Reduces production.
1918 Ignaz Bing dies.
1919 Agents, L. Rees & Co. form in London to distribute Bing toys in Britain and Commonwealth.
1919 Ignaz Bing's son Stephen takes over as director general and name changes to Bing Werke (Bing Works).
1927 Stephen leaves firm after disagreement with board.
1932 Firm goes into receivership and departments are sold off, for example, to rival Nuremberg toy company, Karl Bub.

Les Créations Blanchet
1953 Current President Director General, Madame Blanchet, creates first teddy bear – girl bear cub in a felt dress, in Argenton-sur-Creuse in central France. Adds boy bear cub in felt pants and cotton shirt later.
1954 These two bears, made of rayon or mohair plush with wood-wool stuffing, blown glass eyes, and card disc or rod jointing, become first in range of animals marketed by Monsieur Blanchet and distributed at toy specialists and general stores.
1956 Moves to larger site in Chabenet Le Pont Chretien.
1962 Madame Blanchet joins forces with son, Michel, the present Director General, and firm becomes Ets O. Blanchet et Fils "Créations Blanchet", launching period of expansion, producing variety of soft toy animals.
1965 Trademark: a red heart with *Les Jouets qui ont un Coeur* ("The toys which have a heart").
1987 S.A. added to status.
1993 Teddy bears still central to range with new limited edition replicas of original bear cubs for collectors.
Chabenet, BP 6, 36800, Le Pont-Chretien, France.

Wendy Boston Playsafe Toys Ltd.
1941 Wendy Boston leaves London home for Crickhowell, south Wales, to avoid Blitz; makes soft toys out of pieces of unrationed material as hobby.
1945 Husband Ken Williams, returns from RAF, staying in Wales to start soft-toy business; Wendy Boston (Crickhowell) Ltd. established in small shop with staff of three.
1947 Staff increases to 16.
1948 Factory opens at Queen Street, Abergavenny, Monmouthshire, and Castle Road, Crickhowell, Brecon, with staff of 30. Firm uses mohair from Norton (Weaving) Ltd. of Yorkshire. Invents and patents safe, lock-in eyes, originally using rust-proof nuts and screws.
1952 Increases capital.
1954 Fully washable, nylon-covered, foam-filled teddy bear test-marketed
1955 Washable bear is launched on BBC TV. Fire destroys main Abergavenny factory; moves into large warehouse at 79 Queen Street. Introduces printed velvet toys.
1959 Moulded nylon introduced for eye screws and nuts; washability demonstrated at Milan Toy Fair using washing-machine with wringer.
1960 Name changes to Wendy Boston Playsafe Toys Ltd.
1962 New factory opens at Hengoed, Glamorgan; employee numbers rise to 100.
1964 Firm achieves over 25% of Great Britain's soft-toy exports, exporting mainly to Sweden, Belgium, Holland, Italy, and Australia; also exporting to US and Rhodesia.
1968 Denys Fisher Toys (Spirograph inventor) buys firm.
1976 Production ceases.
1987 Replica of Peter Bull's gold mohair-plush Wendy Boston bear produced by House of Nisbet in two sizes.

Boulgom
1954 Company founded by M. Frenay in Oullins, France; first French soft-toy manufacturer to produce

washable teddy bears stuffed with foam-rubber.
1964 Moves to Chaponost, near Lyon.
1972 Buys French soft-toy company Anima.
1990 Becomes bankrupt; Alain Thirion group, which includes toy manufacturers, Joustra and Vulli, buys firm.
Rue des Gilères, BP 91 74150 Rumilly, France.

Britannia Toy Company Ltd.
1914–15 Established, as Britannia Toy Works, by Mark Robin (originally Mark Robin & Co.). Based at 9–11 Worship Street, east London for wholesale and export.
Late 1920s Operates as private limited company at 23 Stamford Hill, north London.
Late 1930s Moves to Alliance Works, Windus Road.
Post-World War II Ceases business.

British United Toy Manufacturing Co. Ltd.
1894 Founded as James S. Renvoize Ltd., principally manufacturing lead toy soldiers.
*c.*1911 Name changes to British United Toy Manufacturing Co. Ltd. adding teddy bears and other soft toys.
1916 After different locations in north London, moves to Union Works, Carysfort Road, Stoke Newington.
1914 Ban on German toys fuels expansion. Firm claims to be "original and only British makers" of coaster toys (copying Steiff's Record Teddy of previous year); opens north London office and showroom at 114 Fore Street.
1920s Claims to be first to introduce artificial silk to British soft-toy industry; featherweight kapok-stuffed soft-toy range introduced.
1929 Registers trademark "Omega", used since World War I, as No. 494,205.
*c.*1928 Following death of founder, company managed by H. Stanley Renvoize, until his death in 1952.
Post-World War II Products restricted to supplying wholesalers and export.
Early 1980s Ceases business.

Bruin Manufacturing Co.
1907 First advertised in US trade journal *Playthings*. Based at 497 Broome Street, New York City with trademark "B.M.C." The Strobel & Wilken Co. of 591 Broadway and Frank W. Owens, 714 Broadway, are the selling agents. Manufactures range of soft-toy animals including teddy bears with imported German voices, as well as bear outfits and accessories.

Bunjy Toys
1980 Eve Mayhew starts making teddy bears as hobby; originally based in workrooms in small house in Mooi River, Natal, South Africa, with eight workers. Moves within months to small factory with 16 employees.
1982 Expansion results in relocation to larger factory in nearby Estcourt, where Bunjy Toys now employs 50 people. Produces range of bears for home market; exports pure wool examples to US.
1991 Eve Mayhew retires; sells factory to George Allison. Only South African factory making soft toys for game parks, including Kruger National Park.
210 Albert Street, Estcourt, Natal 3310, South Africa.

California Stuffed Toys
1959 Established in Los Angeles.
Early 1980s Produces character bears (Winnie the Pooh; Br'er Bear; Radar's Teddy from M.A.S.H.) and limited editions for collectors.
1984 Celebrates 25th anniversary with two limited-edition bears, signed by president Nat L. Gorman; manufactured in Korea.
1986 Trades under division name "Caltoys".
*c.*1989 Ceases business.

Canterbury Bears Ltd.
1980s Established by John Blackburn (member of Society of Industrial Artists and Designers) with

daughter Kerstin (now Managing Director) at family home in Westbere, Kent, England following commission for traditional, fully jointed teddy bear previous year. Later, wife Maude (now chairman), son Mark, and daughter Victoria assist.
1981 Firm first exhibits products at London's Earls Court Toy Fair.
1982 Awarded British Design Council approval. Establishes worldwide export trade.
1983 Wins first prize at First Great Western Teddy Bear Show and convention in San Jose, California.
1984 Moves to Littlebourne, near Canterbury, Kent.
1987 Mayor of Canterbury allows company to use city's ancient Coat of Arms on labels and corporate identity.
1990 Celebrates 10th anniversary. Produces 50,000 bears annually; exports 25%; agents in Australia and Holland.
1991 Gund becomes exclusive distributor in US and in Canada; Canterbury Bears Collector's Society founded.
The Old Coach House, Court Hill, Littlebourne, Canterbury CT3 1TY, England.

The Chad Valley Co. Ltd.
*c.*1820 Anthony Bunn Johnson founds printing and book-binding works in Lichfield Street, Birmingham, England.
1860 Johnson's sons, Joseph and Alfred, found stationery firm Messrs. Johnson Bros. in George Street, Birmingham.
1889 Joseph's son Alfred J. Johnson enters business.
1897 Joseph and son move to new factory in neighbouring village of Harborne, trading as private limited company, Johnson Bros. (Harborne) Ltd. Factory is known as Chad Valley Works, named after Chad stream nearby. Firm registers Chad Valley trademark; prints cardboard games to add to range of stationers' sundries.
1904 Joseph Johnson dies; Alfred Johnson becomes chairman and managing director, assisted by E. Dent, brothers Arthur and Harry, and brother-in-law William Riley.
Pre-World War I Simple toys added each year; range increases during war due to ban on German imports.
1915–16 Firm makes first soft toys, including teddy bear.
1916 Alfred Johnson patents soft-toy stuffing machine.
1919 Acquires Harborne Village Institute to house printing works.
1920 Opens Wrekin Toy Works, Wellington, Shropshire for soft toys; firm renamed The Chad Valley Co. Ltd.
1923 Registers "Aerolite" trademark for kapok-stuffed soft toys and dolls (used until 1926). Extends Wellington factory; buys Messrs. Isaacs & Company, Birmingham, makers of bouncing, stuffed "Isa" toys.
1928 Builds new factory at Harborne works.
1931 Buys Peacock & Co. Ltd., London, makers of wooden, kindergarten toys.
1932 Expands Harborne works.
1938 Company is granted Royal Warrant of Appointment "Toymakers to Her Majesty the Queen".
World War II Drastically cuts toy and game production; carries out government contracts for war effort; makes children's clothes at Wrekin Works.
1946 Buys A.S. Cartwright Ltd., Birmingham, makers of aluminium hollowware. Acquires Waterloo Works, Wellington for manufacture of new range of rubber toys.
1950 Becomes public limited company.
1951 Buys Hall & Lane Ltd., Birmingham, maker of metal toys.
1954 Buys Robert Bros. (Gloucester) Ltd., maker of Glevum toys and games.
1958 Buys Acme Stopper & Box Co. Ltd., Birmingham, maker of metal toys.
1960 Celebrates centenary.
1967 Acquires H.G. Stone & Co. Ltd.; some soft-toy

production moves to Chiltern's Pontypool factory.
1973–75 Restructuring of company; all but two factories close; all soft-toys are produced at Pontypool.
1978 Taken over by Leicester-based toy firm, Palitoy (later bought by US company Kenner Parker).
1988 Chainstore, Woolworths, acquires Chad Valley tradename; new range is made in East Asia.

Character Novelty Company Inc.
1932 Founded by New Yorkers Caesar Mangiapani and Jack Levy, at 14 South Main Street, Norwalk, Connecticut; Mangiapani designs and Levy operates sales; within few years moves to nearby 50–52 Day Street.
Post-1945 Business expands producing wide range of soft-toy animals; showroom in New York.
*c.*1960 Jack Levy retires, and later dies.
1983 Mangiapani dies; business ceases.
Trademark: printed cloth ear-tag.

Chiltern *(see H.G. Stone & Co. Ltd.)*

Hans Clemens GmbH
Pre-World War II Hans Clemens owns factory and wholesale shoe business in Alsace, France; loses this during war.
1948 Moves to Kirchardt/Baden and opens shop in Mannheim, Germany, selling glass, china, and gifts. Teddy bears not readily available, but with help from sister, begins making them from old, woollen, German army blankets. Later takes on more employees to meet demand.
Today Peter Clemens, son of original founder, runs firm; products include limited-edition teddy bears.
Waldstraße 34-36, D-6926 Kirchardt/Heilbronn, Germany.

Columbia Teddy Bear Manufacturers
*c.*1907 Based at 145–49 Center Street, New York City. Produces range of teddy bears made of imported German plush and voices, including Laughing Teddy Bear. Name derives from Christopher Columbus.

Commonwealth Toy & Novelty Co. Inc.
1934–35 Founded by current president, Steve Greenfield's grandfather in New York.
1937 Produces Feed Me teddy for National Biscuit Company to advertise animal crackers. Still produces novelty bears including one with back zipper revealing red/white heart-shaped bag.
27 West 23rd Street, New York, NY 10010 USA.

Cuddly Toys Ltd.
1984 Founded in Alberta, Canada, specializing in distribution of mascots for large corporations. All products designed and manufactured in Canada, using Canadian raw materials; world-wide distribution.
PO Box 3790, Spruce Grove, Alberta, T7X 3B1 Canada.

Dakin Inc.
1955 Family business importing expensive, hand-crafted shotguns from Italy and Spain, founded by Richard Y. Dakin in San Francisco.
1957 Son, Roger B. Dakin, joins firm; product diversification including bicycles, sailing skiffs, wooden products, and toys; shipment of battery-operated trains from Japan includes six velveteen, stuffed animals used as packing. Roger orders small number, which are an instant success; toys later designed at Dakin's US headquarters, as Dream Pets, officially launching company into soft-toy business.
1961 Harold A. Nizaman joins as assistant to president.
1963 Sports goods division phased out.
1964 Acquires Dardenelle Company of Lindsay, California, manufacturers of infants' plush toys, where all domestic manufacturing is now handled.

Mid-1960s Has factories in Japan, Hong Kong, Mexico.
1966 Tragic plane crash, in Baja, California, kills Mr. and Mrs. Richard Dakin, Mr. and Mrs. Roger Dakin, and four of their five children. Nizaman appointed president and chief executive officeer and other Dakin family members join board of directors along with Norman P. Canright (previously vice-president for sales and advertising).
1970 Sales expands to 35 countries; production is transferred from Japan to Korea.
1987 R. Dakin & Company becomes Dakin Inc.
1989 Acquires House of Nisbet, managed by David Potter, Managing Director for Dakin Europe/UK.
1990s Dakin Inc. has sales to over 80 countries; many international production and distribution centres with over 10,000 production workers throughout world. Company operates six marketing divisions: Gift (for gift and department stores); Fun Farm (for chain stores); Special Markets (mascots and premiums); Baby Things (infant toys and accessories); School Sales (fund-raising merchandise); Dolls (collectors' market).
PO Box 7746, San Francisco, California, 94120, USA.

Dean's Rag Book Co. Ltd.
1903 Founded on 5 August by Henry Samuel Dean to launch his rag book for children who "wear their food and eat their clothes", at Gough Square, 160a Fleet Street, east London (site of Dean & Son, established publishing house), with Harry E. Bryant managing binding department. Artist, Stanley Berkeley designs trademark depicting two dogs fighting over rag book.
1905 Introduces Knockabout toy sheets.
1908 Introduces Knockabout teddy bear and Teddy Bear Rag Book.
1912 Binding department and registered offices move to larger premises at 2–14 Newington Butts, Elephant & Castle, south-east London. Richard Ellett joins firm as company secretary, later becoming chief designer.
1915 Markets first catalogued teddy bears under Kuddlemee brand name for The British Novelty Works, a subsidiary company.
1916 Fire destroys early productions (although duplicate copies held elsewhere).
1922 Huge sign with logo is erected over works entrance. First teddy bears with Dean's logo. Registers tradename "A1 Toys" and patents "Evripoze" joints.
1924 New showroom opens at Debrett House, 29 King Street, Covent Garden, London.
1933 New showroom opens at 6 La Belle Sauvage, Ludgate Hill, east London.
1936 Building begins on factory, on site of Lord Nelson's farm, 61 High Path, Merton, south-west London.
1940 Reduces toy production; manufactures Mae Wests and bren-gun covers.
1949 Produces first post-war catalogue.
1952 Sylvia Willgoss joins firm as Richard Ellett's assistant. Company splits with marketing agents Dean & Son, operating own sales organization, hiring travelling salesmen nationwide, including Jack Crane (Dean & Son's representative since 1920) as northern representative (exhibiting products in mobile showroom pulled by Rolls Royce). London showroom moves to factory premises; introduces soft toys made solely to supply wholesalers by subsidiary, Merton Toys Ltd., with bulldog trademark.
1953 Michael Crane joins firm; joins forces with Projects (Coventry) Ltd., makers of plastic and nursery toys.
1955 Sells Merton factory.
1956 Moves to 18 Tower Street, Rye, Sussex. Subsidiary Childsplay Ltd. forms to manufacture soft toys for retail and export trade. Sylvia Willgoss becomes chief designer
1957 Richard Ellett dies.
1959 Marmet Ltd. (pram manufacturers) becomes major shareholder.

1960 New sales policy: production and dispatch continue at Rye, sales office transfers to offices of parent company Marmet (Sales) Ltd., Letchworth, Hertfordshire.
1961 Rye factory expands; new production unit established in Wimbledon (for Merton Toys).
1965 Name changes to Dean's Childsplay Toys Ltd.
1971 H.E. Bryant dies 21 October; Jack Crane dies 18 December.
1972 Company buys Gwentoys Ltd., makers of soft toys for wholesale trade, becoming Dean's/Gwentoy Group.
1974 Some production moves to Gwentoys' Pontypool factory.
1980 Rye factory closes; all production is in Pontypool.
1983 Celebrates 80th birthday; issues anniversary bear.
1986 Toy and gift importer, Plaintalk, takes over firm, funded by substantial shareholders Fine Art International plc. Becomes The Dean's Company (1903) Ltd.
1987 Neil Miller, now Managing Director, joins firm.
1988 Firm goes into voluntary liquidation; Miller buys Wendley Ltd. to achieve management buy-out and buys trading rights to Dean's name and logo; commences trading on 7 March (with wife Barbara as finance director and Michael Crane, sales director). Officially named Wendley Ltd., trading as The Dean's Company (1903).
1990 December, purchases original company Dean's Rag Book Company Ltd.
1991 New range of collectors' bears launched, including replicas of old patterns, using original Dean's Rag Book Company trademark.
1993 Centenary year; anniversary catalogue issued.
The Dean's Company (1903), Pontypool, Gwent NP4 6YY, Wales.

Ealontoys Ltd.
1914 Originally called the East London Federation Toy Factory, founded at 45 Norman Road, Bow, east London by suffragette Sylvia Pankhurst. Firm makes a variety of soft toys and dolls designed by artists from Chelsea Polytechnic including Hilda E. Jefferies.
c.1921 Name changes to the East London Toy Factory.
1924 Teddy bears first mentioned in advertisements, produced in 11 sizes in best quality plush.
1926 Tradename Ealontoys registered No. 464,617, with illustration of seated, shaggy dog beneath and "Made in England"; soon after becomes private limited company.
1935 Moves to 74–78 Bingfield Street, Kings Cross, London.
1948 Name changes to Ealontoys Ltd.
1950 Advertisement bills firm "The Teddy Bear People".
Early 1950s Ceases business.

Eisenmann & Co. Ltd.
1881 German fancy goods and toy exporters founded by brothers Josef and Gabriel Eisenmann; Josef deals with British trade at 45 Whitecross Street, London, and Gabriel with German in Fürth, Bavaria.
c.1900 Leon Rees moves to England from Germany. He is naturalized, and becomes Josef's business partner.
1908 Rees marries Josef Eisenmann's daughter Maude. First company to introduce teddy bear to Britain; said to have encouraged J.K. Farnell to manufacture teddy bears. Chiltern Works, the firm's Chesham-based toy factory, is in operation.
1912 Produces large number of fabric dolls with porcelain heads for *London Evening News*.
1913 Leon Rees registers patent for eyes for dolls, toy animals, and puppets from 46 Basinghall Street, London.
1918 Gabriel Eisenmann dies.
1919 Josef Eisenmann dies leaving Chiltern Works to son-in-law Leon Rees (*see H.G. Stone & Co.*). Company continues under Josef Eisenmann's nephew, Paul Ellison.
1931 Registers "Bobby the Bear" trademark for toy bears from 25 Ropemaker Street, London.
Post-1945 Become agents for British United Toy Manu

facturing Co., sometimes trading under "Einco".
(*see also British United Toy Manufacturing Co.*)

Eli Doll and Toy Company
1894 Company founded in Wildenhaib, village near Neustadt, Germany, by Ernst Liebermann, to manufacture bisque dolls and later plush animals.
1925 Franz Liebermann, founder's son, registers trademark "Eli", derived from father's name.
1950s Still manufacturing teddy bears, with triangular chest-tag on cord.

Emil Toys
c.1930s Established in Australia, continuing to make teddy bears and soft toys.
c.1955 based at 246 Hoddle Street, Abbotsford, Victoria.
1970s Ceases business.
Trademark: "Emil Toys" with bear sitting on base of "E", holding onto upward stroke.

Erle Teddy Bear Company
Post-World War II Established in Neustadt, Germany. Firm's name derives from founder, Erich Leistner, well-known lecturer and author of teddy-bear and doll books.
1970s Ceases business.

F.A.D.A.P.
1920 Fabrique Artistique d'Animaux en Peluche (Artistically Made Plush Animals) founded at Divonne-les-Bains, France, small town near Swiss border, with offices in Paris. Celebrated illustrator Benjamin Rabier designs first teddy bears of golden mohair with boot-button eyes, bat-shaped nose, and four claws.
Trademark: embossed metal button over printed card-tag in left ear.
c.1925 Other colours introduced, such as red, white, and blue; claws reduced to three; some bears jointed externally with wire. Certain luxury models made with glass eyes and felt pads with four claws.
1930s Firm introduces artificial silk (rayon) plush.
World War II Flannelette bears with button eyes made due to shortage of traditional materials.
1950s Mohair and rayon plush used again. In collaboration with US Ideal Toy Corporation, firm creates new range of bears with soft, moulded vinyl head, mask, or muzzle, using new process called "slush moulding".
1970s Ceases business.

J.K. Farnell & Co. Ltd.
1840 Small family business established by City of London silk merchant, John Kirby Farnell, in Notting Hill, London, to make pen-wipers, pin-cushions, and tea-cosies.
1897 Following founder's death, family moves to Acton, leasing eighteenth century house, "The Elms", where soft-toy firm is established and run by John Farnell's children, Henry Kirby and Agnes Farnell. Initially uses rabbit skins
1908 Said to have first produced teddy bears.
1921 Registered as private limited company with £10,000 capital. Firm builds new factory, Alpha Works, next to "The Elms". Employs more staff, including H.C. Janisch, sales manager throughout 1920s (joins Merrythought in 1930). Agnes Farnell designs toys with Sybil Kemp.
1925 "Alpha" (used since early 1920s) officially registered as trademark.
1926 T.B. Wright joins firm as sales representative.
1927 Firm introduces Anima wheeled toys, including a bear. Extends factory space.
1928 Agnes Farnell dies 25 January. Permanent City showroom opens at 19 New Union Street, east London.
1929 Joins forces with Louis Wolf & Co. Inc. for distribution throughout US and Canada with showroom at 215–19 Fourth Avenue, New York. Managing director

A.E. Brett-Rose makes tour of US and Canada. Société Anonyme J.K. Farnell formed at 80 Rue du Faubourg St. Denis, Paris, to sell products throughout France. Silkalite artificial-silk plush bears are introduced.
1931 Introduction of cheap Unicorn soft toys, including Cuddle Bear. G.E. Beer becomes director until 1935.
1932 J.K. Farnell and toy manufacturers, William Bailey (Birmingham) Ltd., managed by Percy V. Goodwin, join forces using one sales team.
1934 Fire destroys entire factory and stocks.
1935 New one-storey, brick, 2,137 square metres (23,000 sq. ft) factory opens, large enough to employ 300 workers. Alpha and Teddy series of bears are reintroduced. Many new lines including Che-Kee (lambswool); Alpac (alpaca) and Joy Day dolls. Moved to larger showrooms at 1 New Union Street, east London.
1937 New wing added due to increased business, particularly new patriotic lines for coronation of George VI.
1940 Factory destroyed by Blitz but later rebuilt.
1944 Henry Kirby Farnell dies.
1950s Trademark redesigned. New City showroom at Condor House, 13–14 St Paul's Churchyard, east London.
1959 Firm establishes production unit with 100 employees at 39 George Street, Hastings, Sussex, later extended to become Olympia Works. 95% of teddy bears produced here are for export. Acton is used for home market. Head office transfers to Hastings.
1960 Registered "Mother Goose" trademark for washable nylon soft-toy range.
1964 All production moves to Hastings. Subsidiary company, Acton Toycraft Ltd., takes over lease of Alpha Works, renamed Twyford Works.
1968 Farnell bought by finance company.
(*see also Acton Toycraft Ltd.*)

Fechter Co.
1946 William Fechter and wife Berta Bohn (German teddy-bear seamstress in Neustadt during 1930s) start up teddy-bear cottage industry in Graz, south-eastern Austria, originally using US-made towels.
1948 Firm moves into factory at Theodor Körner Straße 49; employs over 20 workers, uses German-made mohair.
1950 First exhibits at Vienna Toy Fair, resulting in wider recognition and continuing expansion; supplies over 200 European dealers.
1963 Buys large, glass factory at Altenmarkt 2 in Wies, south of Graz.
1973 Berta Bohn dies.
1978 Business discontinues.
1984 Antique dealer, Lisl Swinehart, of Davis, California, buys warehouse stock of Fechter soft toys in Austria, importing them to US, where firm was previously unknown.
1985 Wilhelm Fechter dies.

Felpa AG (*see MCZ*)

Gaeltarra Eireann
1938 Irish government department, *Gaeltacht* Services Division, subsidizes new industry making toys and small utility goods, to create jobs in rural areas. Operates in three factories: Elly Bay, County Mayo (soft toys); Spiddal, County Galway (lead toys); Crolly, County Donegal (dolls). Head Office at Oriel House, Westland Row, Dublin, with sole sales agent, William Girvan.
1949 Ireland is declared a Republic and labels change.
1950 Hans Weberpals (studied at College of Applied Arts, Nuremberg; designer at Sonneberg toy factory before World War II) comes to Ireland and joins toy division of *Gaeltacht* Services as Production Manager and Designer.
c.1953 Erris Toys tradename, used by Elly Bay soft-toy factory, changes to Tara Toys.

1958 Board of *Gaeltarra Eireann* takes over administration of rural industries from *Gaeltacht* Services Division; reorganization removes management from civil servants (taken over by civilians), and encourages profit-making.
1965 Foam-rubber stuffing introduced. Hans Weberpals leaves *Gaeltarra Eireann* to set up own factory, Celtic Toys, at Millstreet, County Cork with partner. Retires and goes into voluntary liquidation in 1975, but in 1978 reopens factory, assisted by Tom Burke. Present range includes cheap teddy bears, trademark: Clara Toys.
1969 *Gaeltarra Eireann* head offices transfer to Furbo, County Galway. Elly Bay factory closes and production transfers to Crolly, County Donegal, under new company, Soltoys Ltd.
1979 Soltoys Ltd. ceases business.
1980 *Udaras na Gaeltachta* (meaning "body that runs the Irish-speaking area of Ireland") forms to take over from *Gaeltarra Eireann*.

Ganz Bros. Toys
1950 Founded by brothers, Sam and Jack Ganz; manufactures, imports, and distributes variety of gift items, including soft toys. Now the largest teddy-bear manufacturer in Canada; range includes collectors' bears and licenced bears such as Rupert. Sam Ganz is chairman of the board; his son Howard is the current president.
One Pearce Road, Woodbridge, Ontario L4L 3T2, Canada.

Trudi Giocattoli spa
1948 Current President Trudi Mueller marries Antonio Patriarca and settles in Tarcento, village near Venice.
1949 Trudi makes first teddy bear on the occasion of son's birth, and founds family soft-toy business to produce a wide range of plush animals.
1990s Now employs five designers; firm exports throughout Europe and the US. Limited-edition collector bears added to range.
Trademark: circular card chest-tag "Original Trudi Hand Made".
Via Angelo Angeli 120, 33017, Tarcento (Udine), Italy.

Golden Bear Products Ltd.
1979 Established; now reputedly largest soft-toy manufacturer in UK.
*c.*1988 Takes over rights to Tough Ted from Big Softies.
Rookery Road, Wrockwardine Wood, Telford, Shropshire TF2 9DW, England.

Grisly Spielwaren GmbH & Co. KG
1954 Founded by Karl Theodor Unfrecht in family home in village of Kirchheimbolanden, near Mainz, Germany.
1964 Metal button trademark, showing needle and thread superimposed upon grizzly (German: *grisly*) bear on all-fours, replaced by paper tag with same logo.
1980 Karl dies; son Hans-Georg and daughter Hannelore Wirth take over company.
PO Box 1127, Beethovenstraße 1, 67284, Kirchheimbolanden/Rheinphalz, Germany.

Gund Inc.
1898 Gund Manufacturing Company founded in Norwalk, Connecticut, by German immigrant Adolph Gund to make belts, necklaces, novelties, and soft toys.
Early 1900s Moves to new premises in New York City.
1906 Adds teddy bears in four sizes to range.
1909 Jacob Swedlin, Russian immigrant, joins business as janitor, but after training in cutting, pattern-making, and design becomes Adolph Gund's personal assistant.
1925 Gund retires and sells business and all patents to Jacob Swedlin; Swedlin's three brothers later join him, the company becomes J. Swedlin Inc., although still

retains the Gund tradename.
1927 Manufactures mechanical jumping animals of coloured velveteen under trademark "Gee Line".
1948 Expansion after World War II helped by gaining exclusive rights to produce stuffed-animal versions of Walt Disney and, later, King Features and Hanna Barbera cartoon characters.
New trademark with rabbit faced "G".
1956 Factory moves to Brooklyn.
1973 Firm moves to Edison, New Jersey; showroom remains at 200 Fifth Avenue Toy Center, New York City.
1976 Jacob Swedlin dies.
1979 Introduces Collectors Classics range, targeting adults and collectors.
1988 Firm moves to new, larger headquarters in Edison.
1992 Becomes distributor of Canterbury Bears in US and Canada; buys French company Anima. Remains privately owned, in the hands of Jacob Swedlin's daughter Rita (secretary-treasurer and director of design), her husband Herbert Raiffe (president), and their son Bruce (vice president; director of marketing). Teddies now made in Korea.
One Runyons Lane, Edison, NJ 08817, USA.

Gwentoys Ltd.
1965 Founded by three former managers – A. Thwaites, Jack Jacobs, and R.G. Green – from old Chiltern/Stone/ Combex factory in Pontypool, south Wales. Named after Gwent, old Welsh name for Monmouthshire, county where firm is located. Offices and factory of 557 square metres (6,000 square feet) situated at Forge Road, Pontypool.
1968 Builds larger premises Pontypool Industrial Estate.
1971 Extends premises.
1972 Becomes part of Dean's Group, specializing in soft toys for supplying wholesalers and mail-order trade.
(see also Dean's Rag Book Co. Ltd.)

Hamiro
1910 Karel Pospísil establishes foundry near Rokycany, in what was Bohemia; makes lead figures and tin soldiers.
1919 Wife Miluse designs textile rabbit to boost low sales after World War I. Founds soft-toy company at old forge and employs 12 people; exhibits at European trade fairs – exports 60% of products overseas.
1930 Moves to new, larger factory in Rokycany.
1932 "Hamiro" trademark registered (*Hammerwerk* or forge; *Miluse*, Czech nickname for Emilie; *Rokycany*).
1936–38 An international business with 500 employees; second largest plush-toy manufacturer in Europe.
World War II Produces war materials: military uniforms and underwear.
1948 Company is confiscated by Czechoslovakian communist government; low quality stuffed animals continue to be made in factory but under government ownership. Karel and Miluse's son, Libor, hides firm's archive in attic.
1990 Libor Pospísil sees exhibition of German company H. Scharrer & Koch GmbH's products *(see entry)* in Prague; collaborates and establishes new Miro firm at Hamiro's old factory in Rokycany.
1992 Creates series of 1920s–30s replicas.

Harman Manufacturing Company
1907 Produces teddy bears in nine sizes from 8 West 13th Street, New York City. All have imported German voices. Includes Teddy Bear Shopper, its back containing a gold-coloured, metal-framed, silk-lined pocket with leather handles; and teddy doll.

Harrisons Textiles
1977 Founded by Clive and Precille Harrison at 143 Church Street, Otahuhu, Auckland, New Zealand to make teddy bears. Later goes into partnership with Australian company, and becomes known as

Harrisons Gifts.
1990 Sells share to US firm Milton Bradley (later Hasbro). Australian company operates from Gymea, New South Wales, with Harrisons label, but bears are made in Korea.
Trademark: printed cloth label; red heart superimposed with "Harrisons" in black script.
1992 Clive and Precille Harrison establish new teddy-bear business, Bear With Us; bears designed by Clive.
41 Budgen Street, Mt Roskill, Auckland, New Zealand.

Harwin & Co. Ltd.
1914 Established by G.W. Harwin at Eagle Works, 52 Blackstock Road, Finsbury Park, north London, to produce needlework and Dot's series of felt dolls, caricatures, and teddy bears, designed by his daughter, Dorothy Harwin. Sales manager Fred Taylor had previously worked for Steiff's British agent, Herbert E. Hughes. Notable teddies are Ally Bears in World War I allied uniforms, and Eyes Right with googly eyes in Highland dress; also reputedly making first mascots to cross Atlantic, accompanying Alcock and Brown on momentous 1919 flight.
Registered trademark: although not used on permanent label, includes intertwined letters DOTS inside double circle with words "British Made".
*c.*1930 Ceases business.

Maxwell Hay & Co. Ltd.
1964 Founded by Maxwell Hay in Auckland, New Zealand; sheepskin manufacturers making mainly soft toys, hand-dyed in the early days.
1976 Introduces teddy-bear range.
1982 Ceased production of teddy bears, but continues to make soft toys. Following Maxwell's death, his wife Nancy and their son run the business.
5/22A Willcott Street, Mt Albert, Auckland, New Zealand.

Hegi (Herta Girz & Co.) *(see Schreyer & Company)*

Heike-Bär
1985 Karl Bär, from long line of Neustadt teddy-bear makers, who had previously made Berliner bears, begins to produce replica Schuco miniature teddy-bears using patterns, tools, and equipment bought from Schuco's receiver in 1977. Trades under wife's name: "Heike-Bär".
Glashüttenweg 2, 8632, Neustadt/Coburg, Orsteil Fürth a. Berg, Germany.

Helvetic Company
1928 Cited in trade journal *Toy World* as holding exclusive rights to manufacture teddy bears with squeeze-type musical boxes. Name suggests Swiss origins, but possibly US company using imported mechanisms. In operation for short period during 1920s.

Artur Hermann
1913 Artur Hermann founds teddy-bear firm with sister Adelheid and brother Max at Neufang home, operating under father's name, Johann Hermann Spielwarenfabrik.
Post-World War I Artur Hermann moves to Sonneberg to establish own company, trading under the name Artur Hermann Plüsch-Spielwaren-Fabrik.
Late 1920s Changes name to J. Hermann Nachf. Inf. Artur Hermann.
1940 Company moves to Lackerbauerstraße 1–3, Munich.
1954 Sells to Anker plush toy firm in Munich; Artur Hermann founds Munich toy shop Teddy: Haus des Kindes.

Gebrüder Hermann KG
Post-World War I Bernhard Hermann and wife Ida Jäger move from Neufang home (where he had helped

in father Johann's toy factory, following apprenticeship in trade and business in Meiningen) to Sonneberg to found small firm trading under "Be–Ha". Makes mohair-plush teddy bears. Lower-quality examples are made by piece-workers.

1930s Bernhard and Ida's four sons, Hellmut, Artur, Werner, and Horst, help in family business.

1937 Youngest son Horst dies.

World War II Three brothers go into military service.

1948 Production starts to transfer to factory in Hirschaid, near Bamberg, Bavaria (part of the American zone); company reforms as Gebrüder Hermann KG, with the three brothers as business partners.

1952–53 Entire family and factory relocates to the West. Trademark: "Hermann Teddy Original" introduced.

1959 Bernhard Hermann dies; management passes to Artur; production and design to Werner; direction of operations to Hellmut.

1980 Hellmut retires.

1984 Firm produces first limited-edition collectors' bears.

1985 Hellmut dies; Artur and Werner continue to manage firm briefly. From the mid-1980s, Isabella Reiter, Marion Mehling, Margit Drolshagen, and Traudi Mischner (designer), daughters of the three brothers, manage the firm.

1990 Artur dies.

1992 Three bears are produced, designed by US bear artists Jenny Krantz and Joyce Ann Haughey.

Amlingstadter Straße 9, Postfach 1207, D-8606, Hirschaid, Germany.

Hermann-Spielwaren GmbH

1913 Max Hermann leaves school to help in family teddy-bear business, Johann Hermann Spielwarenfabrik, run by brother Artur and sister Adelheid at father's house in Neufang, near Sonneberg, Germany.

1920 Max founds business at Neufang family home.

1923 Moves to Sonneberg, to Wilhemstraße 17, and again within first month to larger premises at Kirchstraße 4, and later to Karlstraße 23. Trades as Max Hermann, Sonneberg, using trademark "Maheso" with bear and dog logo.

c.1930 Moves to Friedrichstraße 7a.

1933 May–October, exhibits set of dressed bears at special toy exhibition in Sonneberg.

1939–45 Reduces production.

1947 Produces first teddy bears in peacetime and exhibits at Leipzig fair; son Rolf-Gerhard joins firm, forming Max Hermann & Sohn, Sonneberg.

1949 Subsidiary company, Hermann & Co. KG, formed in Coburg, 20km (12 $^1/_2$ miles) from Sonneberg in US zone.

1951 Rolf marries Dora-Margot (Dorle) Engel, daughter of joint owner of Sonneberg toy company H. Josef Leven.

1953 February 22, family escapes to West across border at Berlin and relocates entire company in Coburg.

1955 Max dies; Rolf Hermann leads business with wife Dora-Margot responsible for design.

1968 Introduces present swing-tag.

1979 Becomes private limited company Hermann-Spielwaren GmbH.

1990 Celebrates 70th anniversary with introduction of limited editions. Reunification of Germany enables family to return to Sonneberg to research archives; Rolf's daughter and co-director Dr. Ursula Hermann compiles history of firm; Leven company (owned by communists since 1945) is officially handed back to descendent, Dora-Margot Hermann; replicas of old Leven designs made.

1992 Dora–Margot Hermann dies.

Im Grund 9–11, D-8630 Coburg-Cortendorf, Germany.

Hermann & Co. KG (see Hermann-Spielwaren GmbH)

Heunec Plusch Spielwaren Fabrik KG

1891 Hugo Heubach founds company in Sonneberg, as distributor of toys and Christmas tree decorations.

c.1945 firm moves to Neustadt/Coburg area of West Germany and changes name to Heunec (derived from Heubach/Neustadt/Coburg).

1972 becomes manufacturer of plush toys, with only two employees; expansion of buildings and staff follows. Company now employs over 1,000 workers in its three factories in Switzerland, Mauritius, and China, with administration and design department in Neustadt/Coburg, and is one of the top ten European soft-toy manufacturers. Around 1,000 items in range, particularly licensed items for TV, films, mascots for sporting events and companies, as well as range of teddy bears.

Am Moos 11, Mörikestraße 2+6, Neustadt/Coburg, Germany.

Ideal Novelty and Toy Company

1902–03 Russian emigrés, Morris Michtom and wife Rose, produce hand-made Teddy's Bears, inspired by Clifford T. Berryman *Washington Post* cartoon, for sale at their novelty and stationery store on Thompson Avenue, Brooklyn, New York. Large scale production and firm is established after wholesalers, Butler Brothers, purchase stock and support Michtom's credit with plush-producing mills.

1907 Moves to larger premises in Brownsville section, 311–317 Christopher Avenue, Brooklyn.

1912 Abraham Katz joins company as co-chairman.

1923 Michtoms' son Benjamin joins firm as co-chairman.

1938 Michtom dies and Benjamin takes over leadership.

1941 Lionel A .Weintraub joins company.

1953 Licensed to produce first "Smokey Bear" (second and third versions follow).

1962 Lionel A. Weintraub becomes president.

1968 Becomes publicly owned firm, The Ideal Toy Corporation, based in Hollis, New York, with new large factory in Newark, New Jersey and production and distribution in Japan, UK, Germany, Canada, Australia, and New Zealand; employs 4,000 people worldwide.

1978 Celebrates 75th anniversary with special issue bear.

1982 Grandson of founder, Mark Michtom sells company to CBS Toys with President Boyd Browne.

1984 Produces collectors' porcelain replica of first Ideal bear, but bears generally removed from production. Hasbro acquires some assets.

Invicta Toys Ltd.

1935 Founded by G.E. Beer and T.B. Wright (former J.K. Farnell director and sales representative, respectively), at Sunbeam Road, Park Royal Road, northwest London. Soft toys designed by Beer include teddy bears Teddy, Grizzlie, and Sammy.

Early 1950s Ceases business.

Jakas Soft Toys

1954 Founded by English couple, Joe and Marion Stanford, at Altona, a seaside suburb of Melbourne, Australia.

1956 Company is registered and moves to Blackburn, Victoria. "Jakas" derived from first and second names of Stanford family members.

c.1962 Produces Big Ted who appears on Australia's longest-running children's programme *Playschool*.

1984 Company is sold, and undergoes two further shortlived ownerships.

1989 Wendy McDonald, present owner, buys company.

1991 Moves to existing site; merges with Koala Mate, makers of fine quality soft-toy Australiania; introduces limited-edition range.

Unit 1, 85 Lewis Road, Wantirna South, Victoria 3152, Australia.

Jocky srl

Post-World War II Founded in Rome. Produces

Jockyline soft toys, including Avanti series designed by Riccardo Chiavetta.

1982 World rights bought by Applause (*see Applause Inc*).

Viale Pola 25, 00198, Rome, Italy.

W.H. Jones

1914 William Henry Jones, a German doll manufacturers' agent since early 1900s, establishes soft-toy firm at 48 Red Cross Street, east London, with six workers.

1915 Moves to large, four-floored, modern factory with large basement at 11 Charterhouse Buildings, with 14 power-driven sewing-machines and 46 workers. Opens another factory of similar size a few months later in south-east London at 60–61 Parish Lane, Penge.

c.1925 Moves to 8–10 Great Arthur Street, east London. Introduces Hugyu (kapok) and Shagylox (shaggy mohair) series of soft toys.

1928 Introduces wheeled soft toys, including bear.

1935 Registered as private limited company, W. H. Jones (Toys) Ltd.

1937 Goes into voluntary liquidation.

Joy-Toys Pty. Ltd.

1920s Reputedly Australia's first commercial teddy-bear manufacturer, established by Mr. and Mrs. Gerald Kirby in South Yarra, Victoria; financial backing from Melbourne business friends including Daryl Lindsay.

1930 Moves to larger premises.

1935 Maurice Court joins company.

1937 Court takes over; restructures firm after Kirbys' move to London, where they found G.L. Kirby Ltd.

Late 1930s Business expands, acquiring franchise for Walt Disney characters; produces set of promotional Three Bears for leading Australian manufacturers of oatmeal products, Jas. F. McKenzie Pty. Ltd. Opens another factory in Whangarei, New Zealand.

1966 Cyclops, owned by British Lines Brothers since 1950s, buys Joy-Toys. Operates from 70 Stephenson Street, Richmond, Victoria 3121.

1971 Ceases business following collapse of Lines Brothers; UK-owned Tube Investments purchases firm soon after.

1976 Maurice Court and Toltoys, a toy manufacturer, buy Sydney soft-toy company Sandman Pty. Ltd.

1979 Maurice Court sells his shares to Toltoys.

1980 Sandman Pty. Ltd. closes but Court is able to buy Joy-Toys equipment and tradename for Toltoys.

Jungle Toys

1914 Established by young girl, Miss E.M. Daniels, who worked for six months for various toymakers before setting up on own with two workers at 82 Richmond Road, Earls Court, London.

1919 Factory runs on co-operative system, employing 13–15 assistants; exports worldwide, including Australia.

1928 Registered design The Bingo Bear – a koala bear. Later includes teddy bears in range. Production continues until *c.*1950.

Kersa (see W. Walters KG)

G.L. Kirby Ltd.

1938 Established by Gerald L. Kirby (founder of Joy-Toys) at 1–3 Golden Lane, east London to produce dolls and soft toys including Australian native animals, and range of kapok-filled teddy bears called Sun Bears, made of finest plush in range of colours – green, white, sky, pink, ruby, scarlet, gold, peach, canary, lemon, cream, dark brown.

No longer in business.

Trademark: round card swing-tag with "Kirby Toys".

Knickerbocker Toy Company Inc.

1850 Established in Albany, New York State to produce toys such as lithographed alphabet blocks.

1920s Introduces teddy bears and other soft toys.

1930s–50s Becomes incorporated company.
c.1968 Moves to Middlesex, New Jersey; licensed to produce "Smokey Bear" until 1977.
1982 Wallace Berrie buys firm's Applause gift division.
1980s Ceases business.

Hugo Koch
Post-World War II Probably established by Hugo Koch.
Early 1950s Based at Bahnhofstraße 233, Pressath. Trademark: bear dressed as cook (German *Koch*) with spoon.
1970s Based in nearby Eschenbach/Opf at Pressather Straße 18; son also works for firm.
1990 Ceases business.

Käthe Kruse Puppen GmbH
1911 Käthe Kruse establishes company making unique cloth dolls with sculpted faces of painted, pressed muslin (range later includes famous life-sized, weighted *Träumerchen* used by nursery nurses and midwives).
1912 Family moves to Bad Kösen, founding workshop under Käthe Kruse's personal management.
1947 Sons, Michael and Max Kruse, move to West German city of Donauwörth, north-west of Munich, and open dollmaking workshop.
1950 Käthe Kruse leaves East Germany to join sons.
1952–53 Käthe Kruse withdraws from active management. Michael Kruse emigrates to South Africa, replaced by son-in-law Heinz Adler (married to daughter Hanne) as technical manager; Max Kruse is general manager.
1956 Käthe Kruse retires; her daughter Hanne takes over as designer; products now marked "Modell Hanne Kruse".
1958 Company is incorporated under name Käthe Kruse GmbH. 70% sold to Schildkröt (doll manufacturers); Max keeps 30% then sells his shares to Hanne and Heinz.
1967 Hanne introduces plush and terry-cloth animals, including teddy bears.
1976 Heinz and Hanne Kruse buy back Schildkröt's shares to own company outright.
1990 Hanne Kruse retires; Stephen and Andrea Christenson and family of Prince Albrecht zu Castell-Castell buy firm.
1993 Tag redesigned; red with "Modell Hanne Kruse" and description.
Alte Augsburger Straße 9, 86609, Donauwörth, Germany.
US office: 22 Westover Road, Troy, NY 12180.

Leco Toys (West End) Ltd.
c.1950 Husband and wife team Ludwig and Martha Levy start to make soft toys in small back room of house.
1955 March 8, registered as private limited company, based at 361 Edgware Road, in London's West End. Develops successful business specializing in lambskin novelty toys, including nightdress cases and animated musical items for worldwide export. Moves to 186 Campden Hill Road, Kensington.
1965 Moves to modern, one-storey factory twice size of previous premises, in Lyon Road Industrial Estate, Bletchley, Buckinghamshire.
1971 Last mention in trade directories.

Lefray Toys Ltd.
1948 Established as Lefray Ltd., originally based at 52 Golborne Road, west London.
c.1958 Moves to 14b South Hill Park, north-west London.
1960 Relocates to a new factory of over 929 square metres (10,000 square feet), enabling modern methods of manufacture and greatly increased production, at 56 Victoria Street, St. Albans, Hertfordshire.
1969 Transfers to Wales where company is still based.
1980s Takes over Real Soft Toys.
c.1990 Obtains licence to produce Rupert Bear. Today Lefray has separate Real Soft Toy range and specializes in custom-made promotional items.
Glandwr Industrial Estate, Aberbeeg, Abertillery, Gwent NP3 2XF, Wales.

Lenci srl
1919 Founded Turin, Italy. Receives worldwide recognition for pressed-felt-headed dolls, many sculpted by well-known Italian artists.
Registered trademark: *Ludus Est Nobis Constanter Industria* (Latin: "To Play Is Our Constant Work") encircles child's spinning top
1922 Trademark shortened to "Lenci".
1931 First traditional teddy bears appear in catalogue. Present-day teddy bears are unjointed, children's toys.
Via San Marino 56 bis 10137 Turin, Italy.

H. Josef Leven
1891 Hubert Josef Leven and Theodor Sprenger found Leven & Sprenger in Sonneberg, Germany, to make toys mainly for export but also for German customers.
1910 Known as H. Josef Leven; manufactures teddy bears.
1912 Employs 10 office and 150 factory workers; one of largest toy firms in Sonneberg. Exports toys worldwide.
1923 Fred Engel (joined firm in 1904 as apprentice) becomes partner and president of company. Later buys remaining shares, becoming joint owner of firm with daughters Hildegard and Dora-Margot.
Post-World War II The company is gradually expropriated from Engel family by communist government.
1951 Dora-Margot Engel marries Rolf-Gerhard Hermann (see *Hermann-Spielwaren GmbH*).
1972 Becomes wholly state-owned.
1990 Communist regime collapses; company buildings and titles officially handed back to Engel daughters.
1992 Hermann-Spielwaren introduces Leven replicas.

Lindee Toys
1944 Established in Australia.
1969 Wins "Toy of the Year".
c.1960s Based at 23–25 Daking Street, Parramatta North, New South Wales 2151.
1976 Ceases business.
Trademark: "Lindee Toys", inside outline of seated fawn and "Made in Australia".

Little Folk
1976 Founded by Graham McBride and Maggie Breedon in Devon, England to manufacture soft toy animals. Based at 700-year-old mill employing eight full time staff and 13–14 outworkers.
1980 Produces first teddy bear. Mainly uses top quality acrylic plush, although today the firm produces some limited-edition mohair bears for the collectors' market. At its height, exports worldwide, 70% going to US.
1991 Maggie Breedon dies.
1992 Firm becomes division of Possible Dreams Europe when Graham McBride forms partnership with directors of US company, Possible Dreams Ltd. of Foxboro, Massachusetts. Now also imports figurines. Produces bears for Wendy Phillips of Lakeland Bears.
3 Blackdown Park, Willand, Devon, EX15 2QH, England.

The London Toy Company
1915 Importer of Japanese lacquer and antimony ware establishes soft-toy company at Three Crowns Court, 11 Jewry Street, Aldgate, east London. Specializes in soft toys of plush, felt, and velvet, including teddy bears, for wholesale and export throughout the 1920s.

Luvme Toy Manufacturing Co.
1939 In operation in Auckland, New Zealand, making soft-bodied dolls with hard heads (import control introduced in 1938 resulted in establishment of home-based industries including toy manufacture).
1950s Makes soft toys, including teddy bears, often with Rexine paws and printed black on white cloth label reading "Luvme/Made in NZ".
1970–80s Ceases business.

Malrob Cuddle Toys
1961 Established in Brisbane, Queensland, Australia, to make unjointed bears from synthetic fabrics.
1985 Ceases operation.
Trademark: "Malrob Cuddle Toys; Made in Australia".

Max Hermann Sonneberg (see *Hermann-Spielwaren GmbH*)

Max Hermann & Sohn Sonneberg (see *Hermann-Spielwaren GmbH*)

MCZ
1950s Established in Zürich, Switzerland, using tradename "Mutzli". Company later known as Felpa AG Spielwarenexport, based in Aarau, with tradename "Felpa".
c.1990s Ceases business.

AB Merimex
c.1947 Founded in Sweden by refugee Emil Grünfelt, to make white, yellow, and brown sheepskin bears. Originally based in Malmo, St. Göransgatan 12, 21618; production moves to Portugal where bears are still made Tradename: "Amica".

Merrythought Ltd.
1919 W.G. Holmes and G.H. Laxton open spinning-mill in Oakworth, near Keighley, Yorkshire, England.
1920s Holmes and Laxton buy Dyson Hall & Co. Ltd. of Huddersfield, a mohair-plush-weaving factory.
1930 Merrythought Ltd. founded and trademark registered; leases temporary premises from Coalbrookdale Company. Hires C.J. Rendle from Chad Valley as production director; H.C. Janisch from J.K. Farnell as sales director for London showroom at 113 Holborn; and 20 workers to make soft toys.
1931 Rents larger factory space from Coalbrookdale Company. Leases two-storey building nearby (the Grand Hall) for staff social area. Produces first catalogue, with designs by Florence Atwood, designer from Chad Valley.
1932 Installs electric motors for sewing-machines. Employs more staff.
1935 Factory expands, reputed to be largest soft-toy factory in England.
1939 Produces first panda bear including special commission from London Zoo for stand-in at filming sessions.
World War II British Admiralty and Ministry of Aircraft take over factory for map-making and storage. Moves to temporary premises in Wellington.
1940–43 Company turns to war work, making textile items for armed forces and hospitals.
1946 Toy production reinstated but flooding of River Severn destroys pre-war samples and supplies.
1949 C.J. Rendle dies. Florence Atwood dies. B.T. Holmes (son of founder, W.G. Holmes) joins company.
1952 Hires Jimmy Matthews of Dean & Son Ltd. as sales agent.
1953 Designer Jean Barber, joins company (until 1965).
1955 US compressed-air stuffing machine introduced.
1956 Company buys factory premises from Coalbrookdale Company.
1967 Designer Jackie Harper joins firm (until 1969).
1970 Designer Jacqueline Revitt joins company (leaves 1977, but rejoins 1983).
1972 Oliver Holmes (son of B.T. Holmes, and grandson of W.G. Holmes) joins company.
1982 Collaborates with Tide-Rider Inc., Baldwin,

New York, to export new collectors' range to US.
1986 Publication of John Axe's company history *The Magic of Merrythought* by Hobby House Press, followed by production of first replica Magnet bear.
1988 Merrythought's shop and museum opened.
1990 Produces special, Diamond Jubilee teddy bear to celebrate 60th anniversary.
Dale End, Ironbridge, Telford, Shropshire TF8 7NJ, England.

Mary Meyer Corporation
1933 Established by Mary Meyer.
1993 Mary Meyer's son, Walter, is presently chairman of the board, and grandson, Kevin, is President and Chief Executive Officer. Offers range of collector bears, including Grandma's Bear and 60th anniversary bears. Company sells to over 15,000 retail stores.
Route 30, PO Box 275, Townsend, Vermont, 05353–0275, USA.

Mighty Star Ltd.
1959 Established in Montreal, Canada. Lines include 24K range of teddy bears, licensed characters, as well as collectors' limited editions, created by their designer, Laval Bourque. Products assembled in factories in Korea or China, then returned to Canada for stuffing, finishing, and distribution.
2250 Boulevard de Maisonneuve Est., Montreal, Quebec, H2K 2E5, Canada.

Mulholland & Bailie Ltd.
1971 James Mulholland, former manager of Pedigree's Belfast works (*see Pedigree Soft Toys Ltd.*), sets up own business with colleague, in part of Castlereagh Road, Belfast factory, to produce soft and chassis toys, under brand name "Nylena". Now retired; son runs firm.
407–09 Castlereagh Road, Belfast, Northern Ireland.

Mutzli (*see MCZ*)

House of Nisbet Ltd.
1953 Peggy Nisbet founds Peggy Nisbet Ltd; makes collector portrait dolls at her home in Weston-super-Mare, England. Later moves to larger premises.
1975 Canadian Jack Wilson becomes executive chairman. Employed by Canadian investment company, which (through UK subsidiary) acquires control of Peggy Nisbet Ltd. from Evans & Owens (Drapers) Ltd.
1976 Changes name to House of Nisbet Ltd; introduces first teddy-bear range designed by Peggy Nisbet's daughter, Alison, later Jack Wilson's wife. Based at Dunster Park, Winscombe, Avon BS25 1AG, England.
1979 Initiation of association with Peter Bull, resulting in Bully series of bears and storybooks.
1983 Reprints Peter Bull's popular *The Teddy Bear Book* as limited edition of 10,000.
1984 Publishes collectors' limited edition of Peter Bull and Pauline McMillan's *The Zodiac Bears*.
1986 Celebrates 10th anniversary of House of Nisbet with two limited-edition bears.
1987 Produces replica of Peter Bull's 1907 Delicatessen (Aloysius) to celebrate bear's 80th birthday. Invents process for distressing mohair, using a 1904 velvet-crushing machine, with Norton (Weaving) Ltd.
1989 May 4, Dakin acquires share capital and David Potter, Dakin's Europe/UK managing director, becomes Nisbet's managing director with Jack Wilson as director and honorary chairman. Jack Wilson and family now live in Florida at Calusa Lakes in Sarasota County.
Dakin Inc., PO Box 7746, San Francisco, CA 94120, USA.

North American Bear Co. Inc.
Mid-1970s New Yorker Barbara Isenberg starts company producing uniquely designed, high-quality bears.
1978 Asks fashion designer friend Odl Bauer to make bear out of old sweatshirt, which eventually evolves into Albert the Running Bear. Brother Paul Levy becomes business partner.
1979 First VIBs (Very Important Bears) appear; clothing first made in New York City toy factory and later in Massachusetts dolls' clothes factory. Parts of bears cut out in New York and sewn in Haiti, then returned to US for machine-stuffing. To further reduce costs, some production transfers completely to East Asia.
1982 Barbara goes to Korea to investigate two potential factories. *Adventures of Albert the Running Bear* by Barbara Isenberg and Susan Wolf, illustrated by Dick Gachenbach, is published by Houghton Mifflin.
1983 VanderBear family introduced.
1984 Muffy VanderBear, company's most well-known bear, introduced. Firm's design studio is in Manhattan.
Main office: 401 N Wabash, Suite 500, Chicago, Illinois, 60611, USA.

Nounours
1963 Jacky Dubois founds family business in Brittany, northern France.
1975 Nounours buys Aux Nations; becomes top of range.
1989 Buys Ajena, producing cheaper quality range to sell to chainstores. Nounours is based in a large natural park setting; some of Nounours range made there, others at Djerba factory in Tunisia and Curepipe factory on Mauritius. The Nounours group is responsible for 80% of French soft-toy exports; also produces baby accessories.
Le Roche Bidaine, 35210 Chatillon en Vendelais, France.

Parker Toys
1950s Soft toy and doll manufacturer established in Australia. Based at 390a Lygon Street, Brunswick, Victoria.
1970s Ceases business.

Peacock & Co. Ltd.
1853 Established as Peacock & Sons, London, makers of wooden kindergarten toys and games (dissected maps, puzzles, alphabet blocks, cubes, etc.).
1904 Listed as William Peacock & Co., 3 Adelaide Terrace, Dane Street, north London. Later becomes Peacock Bros., a partnership between Albert Frank and William Edward Peacock.
1918 July 29, dissolves by mutual consent when Albert is called up for military service; William Peacock registers firm as Peacock & Co. Ltd., operating from both Adelaide Terrace and 2 Prebend Street after World War I.
1931 Chad Valley purchases Peacock & Co. Ltd., moves to modern factory at 175–79 St. John Street, Clerkenwell, east London, and incorporates wooden toys into programme, while manufacturing new range of teddy bears with Peacock label at Chad Valley factory.
1939 Last mention in London trade directory, listed as A. & A. Peacock Ltd., First Avenue House, High Holborn, London.

Pedigree Soft Toys Ltd.
Mid-nineteenth century G. & J. Lines Ltd. established in London by two brothers, George and Joseph Lines, to make wooden toys and baby carriages.
1919 Joseph Lines's three sons, William, Arthur, and Walter, establish Lines Bros. Ltd. in London's Old Kent Road.
1924 Firm moves into new purpose-built factory on 11 hectares (27 acres) in Morden Road, Merton, south-west London. "Tri-ang Toys" registered as trademark, with triangular symbol representing three brothers. Produces mainly large wooden and metal toys (cars, bicycles, prams, nursery furniture, rocking horses), but reported to be also producing fur, felt, and plush toys.
c.1931 "Pedigree" registered as trademark for prams.

1937 First catalogue produced by Pedigree Soft Toys Ltd., offering "Pedigree Pets" (soft toys) and "Pedigree Dolls"; operates from Merton Tri-ang Works.
1946 Lines buys Australian-owned Joy-Toys Ltd. factory at Whangarei, North Island, New Zealand, and founds Lines Bros. (NZ) Ltd., later building large factory in Auckland suburb of Tamaki where manufactures "Made in NZ" Pedigree soft toys. Builds factory at 407–09 Castlereagh Road, Belfast (opened October by Countess Granville, wife of Governor of Northern Ireland and sister of HM the Queen Mother) for production of "Made in Ireland" Pedigree soft and chassis toys.
1950 Lines merges activities of subsidiaries, International Model Aircraft Ltd. (plastic division) and Pedigree Soft Toys, the former making and marketing both products.
1951 Lines buys Rovex Plastics Ltd., of Richmond, Surrey, building new factory for them in Margate, Kent; acquires 50% interest in Australia's Cyclops Company, forming Cyclops and Lines Bros. (Aust.) Ltd. Lines' factories in Australia and South Africa do not produce soft toys.
1955 Buys remaining 50% of Australia's Cyclops Company; all UK soft-toy production moves to Belfast.
1966 Lines-owned Cyclops buys Joy–Toys Ltd. in Victoria, Australia. Reorganization of Lines Bros. Group companies results in formation of Rovex Tri-ang Ltd. Belfast factory eventually closes and UK soft-toy production transfers to Canterbury, England.
1971 Rovex Tri-ang Ltd. collapses.
1972 Taken over by Dunbee-Combex-Marx.
1988 Canterbury factory closes; Pedigree ceases business.

Petz Company
1948 Company founded in Neustadt; name of firm derived from German colloquial word for bear. Makers of traditional mohair bears with glass button trademark until 1974, exporting to both US and rest of Europe.

M. Pintel Fils & Cie.
c.1918 Established in Paris to make soft toy animals, caricatures, dolls, and teddy bears in range of quality, length of pile, and size, as well as tumbling example.
c.1924 Firm exports to UK where exhibits at showrooms of Messrs. Ellis & Amiet, 2 Finsbury Square, London. Boot-button eyes used until 1930s when replaced with glass, with uniquely coloured, painted backs. Pre-World War II bears have very elongated, slender bodies with humped backs and felt pads. Later known as Pintel & Frères.
World War II One of brothers dies in prison; design of bears subsequently changes.
1950s Bears have very short bodies and relatively long legs; plastic noses introduced; firm also produces mechanical bears such as those on bikes or with hula-hoops.
1960s Pintel continues to use kapok and wood-wool stuffing, refusing to produce fully washable bears like those introduced by Boulgom; business declines and eventually ceases.
Trademark: Embossed brass-plated chest-button with embracing bears and "PF France".

Plummer, Wandless & Co Ltd.
1946 April 1, sheepskin soft-toy business established in West Worthing, Sussex, England, by John Plummer and Dudley Wandless with staff of one. Expands greatly over next decade.
1955 Forms subsidiary company to distribute baby linen and nursery accessories.
1957 March 29, registered as private limited company.
1958 Takes over London-based W.H. Kendal Ltd., manufacturers of children's playsuits, tents, and wigwams. Builds new factory at Station Road, East

Preston, Sussex to bring all concerns under one roof. Teddy bear – most popular item – is sold to major stores and exported overseas, particularly to Canada.
1972 Business sold to one of their agents. Tradename "Tinka-Bell", after fairy in J.M.Barrie's *Peter Pan*.

Prima Toys Pty. Ltd. (*see Speciality Manufacturers*)

Real Soft Toys
1969 Founded by R.M. Francis and son N.J. Francis, formerly of Radio Electronic Engineering where they first produced soft toys. Based at Unit 7, Sandown Road Industrial Estate, Watford, Hertfordshire, England. Range includes teddy bears made of real mink fur.
1980s Taken over by Lefray Toys (*see Lefray Toys Ltd.*)

Robbity Bob Ltd.
1972 Established by Robin Rive of Auckland, New Zealand, designing and manufacturing soft-toy collectables.
1989 Introduces antique-style, hand-made teddy bears under label "Countrylife New Zealand", including limited editions; largest bear manufacturer in New Zealand.
58 Elizabeth Knox Place, Auckland 6, New Zealand.

SAF
Post-World War II Manufacturer of teddy bears based in or near Mittendorf, Austria.
No longer in business.

H. Scharrer & Koch GmbH
1856 Trading and export company for beads and toys founded at Friedrichstraße 7, Bayreuth, Germany, by Nuremberg merchant Heinrich Scharrer. Later establishes branch offices in Venice and Gablonz (Bohemia). Scharrer's father-in-law, Christian Koch, owner of Bayreuth's Hotel Sonne joins company soon after foundation.
1872 Bruno Müller from Coburg (Scharrer's son-in-law) appointed managing director.
1900 Theodor Köhler joins as apprentice, later rounding off his commercial training during eight years in England.
1912 Köhler buys company from Müller (continues to manage company until 1930s, exporting exclusively beads; dies aged 87 in 1969).
1968 Grandchildren Sigrid and Josef Gottstein take over, introducing aesthetically pleasing wooden and soft toys for babies; new tradename: "Sigikid" derived from Mrs. Gottstein's first name and English word "kid".
1972 New factory opens at nearby village of Mistelbach for production of ladies', children's, and babies' clothing.
1977 Plush animals introduced to toy range, with independent production line developed at Fürth im Wald, for worldwide export.
1984 Vinyl dolls introduced.
1986 Wooden marionettes introduced.
1989–92 First artist doll collections introduced in vinyl, porcelain, and felt.
1991 Collectors' limited-edition plush animals first introduced; all plush animals in recyclable cotton bags.
1992 Firm first enters replica market with Miro Collection, helping to re-establish Czech firm (*see Hamiro*).
Am Wolfsgarten 8, 8581 Mistelbach, Germany.

Schenker
1952 Established by Martin Schenker at Glockenspielplatz 6, A-8010 Graz, Austria, to produce principally sheepskin soft toys.
1975 Company sold to Michael Rosen; operates from same premises until 1982 when ceases business.

Schreyer & Company
1912 November 16, founded by Heinrich Müller, former Gebrüder Bing employee, and Heinrich Schreyer,

former furniture salesman at Rohnstraße 10, Nuremberg, Germany.
1913 First advertisement appears for "Tipp-Tapp-Tiere" wheeled animals, including bear. Moves to Celtisstraße17.
1914–18 Factory closes for duration of World War I; both partners are drafted into military service.
1918 Schreyer leaves business and Müller takes on new partner, wholesaler Adolf Kahn.
1919 Firm moves to Singerstraße 26.
1921 "Schuco" abbreviation of company name, adopted as official trademark.
1929 Firm moves to larger, four-storey premises at Fürther Straße 28–32.
1936 Following Hitler's rise to power in 1933, Adolf Kahn, a Jew, leaves company.
1939 Kahn and wife move to England.
1940 Join son Eric Kahn in US.
World War II Müller recruits Alexander Girz as manager of factory which operates as war plant, making telephone equipment; bombed several times.
1946–49 Operates at quarter capacity making household hardware and toys on small scale.
1947 Adolf Kahn and son Eric establish Schuco Toy Co. Inc. in US with import rights to all Schuco products for US and Canada.
1958 June 3, Müller dies and only son Werner takes over business along with manager Alexander Girz.
1960s–70s Firm sells toys produced by division, Herta Girz & Co. with trademark "Hegi" (Mrs. Herta Girz directs production), which operates within Schuco premises at Fürther Straße 32.
1976 Collaboration between Hegi and Munich-based Anker (*see Anker Plüschspielwarenfabrik GmbH*), their toys sold by Schuco (*see Schuco*). Company under management of Klaus Albrecht.
Company is sold to leading toy manufacturers, Dunbee-Combex-Marx as unable to compete with Japanese toy industry.
Schuco trademark is sold to Georg Adam Mangold GmbH & Co. KG, Large Straße 69–75, 8510 Fürth/Bayern, Germany, which it uses for replica model cars. Replica Schuco miniature bears made by Heike-Bär (*see Heike-Bär*).

Schuco (*see Schreyer & Company*)

Schwika
Post-World War II Manufacturer of teddy bears based at Graz, Austria. No longer in business.

Shanghai Dolls Factory
Post-World War II Manufacturer making teddy bears on mainland China, bearing printed, paper rosette label with trademark "SDF". Teddy bears also exist wearing card tags that read "Shanghai Toys Factory" and give address 159 Puan Road, Shanghai.

Sheepskin Products Ltd.
1981 Founded by Peter and Valda McCombe in Auckland, New Zealand. Company produces widest range of sheepskin toys in world. All products are designed by Valda and each one is hand-clipped and finished.
66c Barrys Point Road, Takapuna, Auckland, New Zealand.

Sigikid (*see H. Scharrer & Koch GmbH*)

The South Wales Toy Manufacturing Co. Ltd.
1915 Established at 49 Salisbury Road, Cardiff, Wales, to make teddy bears, soft toys, printed calico dolls, and cloth balls for supplying wholesalers and export only. Employs French lady cutter with 11 years' experience in soft-toy-making, Mr. Gigot as manager, and Mr. Joseph Layfield as sales agent.

Trademark: "Madingland".
Ceases business during inter-war period.

Speciality Manufacturers
1951 Australian George Weir (originally soft-toy manufacturer Bunky Doo, Hurstville South, Sydney) establishes small factory, Ark Toys, at Escombe, Natal, South Africa; produces range of golden mohair jointed bears and black and white pandas, using imported mohair (from Nortons, UK), local wood-wool, imported Ceylon kapok, masonite joints with split pins, imported German glass eyes, voice-boxes, and squeakers. Moves to larger site as demand for teddies grows, but increased costs in raw materials and competition from East Asian imports forces firm to concentrate on economy range in rayon and nylon.
1970 Sold business; becomes division of Prima Toys Pty. Ltd., large toy company based in Cape Town. George
Weir remains managing director; son is later appointed a director. Teddy bears continue to be made at Pinetown, outside Durban. Cloth label has both "Prima Toys" and "Ark Toys" trademarks and "Speelgoede".
39 Richmond Road, Pinetown, 3600/PO Box 10307, Ashwood, 3605, Republic of South Africa.

Margarete Steiff GmbH
1877 Margarete Steiff opens Felt Mail Order company to make felt underskirts and children's clothes in hometown, Giengen, Germany.
1880 Introduces animal toys to range after success of little felt elephant pin-cushion she had adapted from magazine pattern.
1889 Moves to larger premises in Muehlstraße.
1893 March 3, registers business as the Felt Toy Co.
1897 Nephew Richard Steiff joins company to develop range of soft toy animals.
1902–05 Experiments with jointed bear design culminate in Bär 35 PAB (registered 12 February 1905).
1905 May 13 "button in ear" trademark registered.
1902–08 Factory expands three times to meet enormous demand for teddy bears: this time of high productivity and expansion is called the *Bärenjahre* (Bear Years).
1906 Re-registered as Margarete Steiff GmbH, private limited liability company with Margarete Steiff's nephews, Paul, Richard, and Franz-Josef as managing directors.
World War I All three brothers enlist, and factory is used for making war supplies.
*c.*1920 Conveyor-belt system is introduced.
1930s New managerial staff, hand-picked by Nazi regime, replaces some Steiff family members.
1943 Factory makes munitions for war effort.
1950 Full production and trade resume after lifting of war-time restrictions.
1953 Celebrates 50th anniversary of Steiff teddy bear.
1958 Celebrates 100th anniversary of Theodore (Teddy) Roosevelt's birth.
1965 Subsidiary branch, the Steiff Toy Company founded in Grieskirchen, Austria, to establish better export facilities.
1980 Produces first replica, heralding new successful era of expansion throughout 1980s. Opens museum and publishes an account of company's history, *Button In Ear* by Jürgen and Marianne Cieslik.
1992 Celebrates 90 years of Steiff teddy bear, and begins Steiff Collectors Club on 1 April.
Alleenstraße 2, D-7928, Giengen/Brenz, Germany.

H.G. Stone & Co. Ltd.
1919 Leon Rees inherits Chiltern Toy Works on death of his father-in-law and business partner, Josef Eisenmann of Eisenmann & Co. (*see Eisenmann & Co. Ltd.*); leaves company to lease large building at 12 New

Union Street, east London, forming L. Rees & Co., wholesaler of fancy goods, houseware, and toys, and distributor of Bing products (and later Chiltern Toys) in Britain and Commonwealth.
1920 Collaborates with Harry Stone, formerly of J.K. Farnell and forms H.G. Stone & Company, to manufacture soft toys at Chiltern Toy Works, Chesham, Buckinghamshire, moves from Bellingdon Road to larger premises at Waterside. Leon Rees responsible for marketing and sales, Harry Stone for design and manufacture.
1921 Opens second factory – Grove Works – at Grove Road, Tottenham, north London.
1923 "Chiltern Toys" tradename first appears in trade journals (registered 1924), and "Hugmee" teddy-bear range introduced.
1925 Takes over production of "Panurge Pets" of Edinburgh, large soft toys modelled from life by artist Ann Cameron Banks of Paris *Salon des Humoristes*.
1929 Firm builds new factory, Chiltern Works, Bernard Road, South Tottenham; all production transfers here from old Tottenham factory. Introduces "Silky Teddy", firm's first artificial silk plush bear.
1932 December 31, registered as private limited company.
1934 November 20, Harry Stone dies.
1940 Toy-making ceases at Chesham factory, but some toys made throughout war at London headquarters.
1945 Soft toys made at Amersham Works, Chesham, another Rees-owned wooden-toy factory.
1946 February, training school established at new factory in process of being built on five-acre site near Pontypool, Monmouthshire in Wales.
1947 New factory in operation; managed by Mr. Thwaites. London offices moved to 31–35 Wilson St., east London.
1957 Pamela Williams joins as assistant designer to Madeleine Biggs; takes over as chief designer when Madeleine is in South Africa for four to five years.
1960 Amersham Toy Works, Chesham, closes.
1963 July 23, Leon Rees dies.
1964 Both Rees and Chiltern companies taken over by Dunbee-Combex group. Chiltern Fairy Foam (one-piece, plastic, foam filling) introduced.
1967 Becomes sudsidiary of Chad Valley (*see The Chad Valley Co. Ltd.*), resulting in Chiltern/Chad Valley label.

Strauss Manufacturing Co. Inc.
1907 Described as "the Toy King", based at 395 Broadway, Dept 1, New York City. Manufactures toys, games, and musical novelties; produces novelty teddy bears during height of US teddy-bear craze.

Gebrüder Süssenguth
1894 Founded by the Süssenguth brothers in Neustadt, Bavaria, to make dolls' bodies and composition heads for German doll industry.
*c.*1925 Company manufactures unique but then unpopular "Peter" bear, introducing doll-making techniques to traditional teddy-bear design.

Tara Toys (*see Gaeltarra Eireann*)

Teddy & Friends: The Bear Essentials
Unique Australian firm that manufactures as well as wholesales and retails its teddy bears.
Firm developed from single retail store in Neutral Bay, New South Wales in early 1980s. Bears are designed by Carole Williams, and manufactured principally in Korea.
Section 3, 57 Hereford Street, Glebe, NSW 2037 Australia.

The Teddy Toy Company
1914 Established by Beresford Charles Hope and Abraham Simmonds at 45 Golden Lane and 78 Fann

Street, east London. Claims to be largest manufacturer of teddy bears in Britain during World War I.
1920 February, firm patents "Softanlite" kapok-stuffed teddy bears, first of kind in Britain. Uses circular printed card-tag: "Original 'Softanlite' Toys British Made" with letters "TT Co." intertwined.
1930 Produces Winnie the Pooh range of soft toys and board game.
Mid-1930s Moves to Nicholls Buildings, Playhouse Yard, east London; Abraham Simmonds assisted by son Harry, who later takes over management.
1937 Transfers to purpose-built factory at Oxlow Lane, Dagenham, Essex.
1939 Moves to Duke Street, Fenton, Stoke-on-Trent, Staffordshire, to avoid Blitz; produces war materials.
1943 Becomes private limited company.
1945 Becomes known as T.T. Industries Ltd.
1951 Firm goes into voluntary liquidation.

W.J. Terry
1890 William J. Terry claimed to have first established soft-toy business in Stoke Newington, north London.
1909 "Skin merchant and soft-fur-toy manufacturer", opens large, new factory at 25 Middleton Road, Hackney, making name through "Terry'er" soft toy dog, based on King Edward VII's dog, Caesar. "Terry'er" and dog with tag reading "I am Caesar" later registered as trademark.
1913 Operates from Welbury Works, 96 & 96a Lavender Grove, Hackney.
Introduces "Billy Owlett" to "challenge the supremacy of the teddy bear".
1915 Extends premises, taking adjoining building.
*c.*1919 Produces teddy bears with webbed claws.
1921 "Ahsolight" trademark, indicating kapok first used.
1924 February 3, William Terry dies; son Frederick B. Terry continues business with sales agent J. Hopkins, working from London showrooms, 93 Aldersgate Street. Ceases business by World War II.

Thiennot
1919 Founded in converted barn in Piney, near Troyes in the Champagne region of France by Émile Thiennot. Uses "Le Jouet Champenois" tradename; works for local wholesalers at first, later hiring his own representatives.
1920 Wins a bronze medal for a teddy-bear design in famous Lépine competition run by the Association of French small manufacturers and inventors.
1949 André, youngest son of Emile and Georgette Thiennot, joins firm as an apprentice for 3 years.
1957 Tradename "Le Jouet Champenois" replaced by "Création Tieno".
1959 André Thiennot takes over the management; firm subsequently expands during the 1960s.
1978 Current economic crisis results in selling off Jeux Mercier and Bondrôle enterprises. Launches TV campaign for "Sleepy" small bears with sleeping eyes.
1989 "Petitou" plush toys for babies, including pyjama cases, and "Coati" exotic animal range launched for 70th anniversary. Standard "Tieno" range continues.
1992-93 Produces 1920 replica "Emile"; limited edition of 25, in four sizes. André Thiennot is current President Director General; his son Rémy is Production Director.
BP 6, rue du Stade, 10220 Piney, France.

Tinka-Bell (*see Plummer, Wandless & Co. Ltd.*)

Twyford (*see Acton Toycraft Ltd.*)

Verna Toys
1941 Established by Eve Barnett as home-based doll-making concern; moves to large shop in Bay Street, Brighton, Victoria, Australia.
1948 Arthur Eaton buys company, introducing tradename "Verna" and teddy bears to range.
Mid-1980s Ceases business.

W. Walter KG
1925 Founded by Wilhelmine Walter in Lobositz (which was then in Bohemia) about 48 kilometres (30 miles) north of Prague. Wilhelmine originally made teddy bears and other soft toys and puppets for her daughters.
1948 Moves company to Mindelheim, Germany, producing teddy bears, cats, dwarfs, and Easter hares.
Until *c.*1956 Bears have metal tags with "Kersa" on base of feet.
*c.*1960 Teddy production ceases; company concentrates on producing range of cloth and wooden puppets. Founder's grandson, Walter Schubert, now manages firm.
Trademark: "Kersa" derived from "*Künstlerisch Erzeugte Spielsachen*" (meaning "artistically produced playthings").
Ifenstraße 7, D-8948 Mindelheim, Germany.

Norah Wellings
1927 Previously designer of soft toys for Chad Valley, established own business at Victoria Toy Works, Wellington, Shropshire, England.
Trademark: "Norah Wellings Productions" with little girl in large bonnet printed on card swing-tag, as well as permanent embroidered labels.
1929 Moves into new premises, King Street Hall, Wellington, formerly Baptist chapel and latterly local Freemasons' temple. Soon employs around 150 workers.
1935 London showrooms operate at 19 Regent Arcade House, 254 Regent Street, W1; Mr. A. Ferriday becomes sales manager.
1959 Death of Norah Welling's brother, her business partner, prompts winding-up of business the following year.

The Wholesale Toy Company
1914 Soft-toy and doll manufacturers established at 52a Blackstock Road, Finsbury Park, north London, as a result of ban on German goods during World War I.
1916 Firm introduces Hercules series of wheeled animals, including bears in five sizes.
Trademark: "Hercules Brand" with Hercules holding scroll with "W.T. Co. Toys".
1921 Patents Blinka rolling eyes for teddy bears and soft-toy animals.
Ceases business by World War II.

Worthing Toy Factory Ltd.
Post-World War I Established business at Broadwater Road (later Station Road Works), Worthing, Sussex, England.
Trademark: Humpty Dumpty Toys (Humpty Dumpty figure smoking long pipe).
Ceases business by World War II.

The Zoo Toy Company
*c.*1920 Joseph Burman, merchant previously dealing in South African goods, establishes London firm at 32–36 Whitecross Street, east London, specializing in novelty fur, felt, and plush mascots including teddy bears, but also importing other toys and games.
1926 In partnership with A J Burman.
1929 Although used previously, trademark "Fondle Toy: in every way they're safe for play" is now registered.
1931 Becomes limited company, with directors F. Burman and K.C. Groombridge (managing director since 1920s).
World War II Based at 9–11 London Lane, east London; reduces production to supply export and registered customers only.
1950s Still in production.
No longer in business.

Useful Addresses

TEDDY-BEAR MUSEUMS, SHOPS, CLUBS, AND MAGAZINES

he following international list of useful addresses includes those of specialist teddy-bear stores, museums, clubs, and magazines. The addresses are arranged by country, and each address is preceded by one of three symbols, which indicates whether it is that of a specialist teddy-bear shop 🏷️, a teddy-bear museum 🏛️, or a teddy-bear club/magazine 📓. At the end of the main country-by-country list, a separate section gives the addresses of major teddy-bear manufacturers throughout the world that are still in business. All addresses included on these pages were correct at the time of publication.

AUSTRALIA

🏷️ **Bronte's Teddy Bears & Country Wares**
137–41 Victoria Street
W. Melbourne
Victoria 3003

🏷️ **Dolls & Bears in the Attic**
129 High Street
Kew
Victoria 3101

🏷️ **Enchanted Bears**
76 Mount Eliza Way
Mount Eliza
Victoria 3930

🏷️ **Numbat Books**
PO Box 50
Frankston
Victoria 3199

🏷️ **Quaint Collectibles**
PO Bag 503
Moss Vale
NSW 2577

🏷️ **Second Childhood**
Shop 11
Claremont Court
Guydri Street
Claremont
WA 6010

🏷️ **The Teddy Bear Shop**
Shop 6
434 Hay Street
Subiaco
WA 6008

🏷️ **The Teddy Bear Shop**
28 Regent Arcade
Adelaide
SA 5000

🏷️ **The Teddy Bear Shop**
Shop 9, Double Bay Plaza
19–27 Cross Street
Double Bay
NSW 2028

🏷️ **The Teddy Bear Shop**
Shop DF12
Level One, Canberra Centre
City Walk
Canberra
ACT 2600

🏷️ **The Teddy Bear Shop**
145 Collins Street
Hobart
Tasmania 7000

🏷️ **The Teddy Bear Shop**
Shop 2
162 Military Road
Neutral Bay
NSW 2089

🏷️ **Teddy & Friends**
Shop 124a, Chatswood Chase
Chatswood
NSW 2067

🏷️ **The Twig**
4 Piccadilly Arcade
Perth
WA 6000

📓 **Bear Facts Review**
PO Box 503
Moss Vale
NSW 2577

📓 **In Teddies We Trust**
PO Box 297
Rosebery
NSW 2018

AUSTRIA

🏛️ **Spielzeugmuseum**
Bürgerspitalgasse 2
A-5020 Salzburg

BELGIUM

🏛️ **Musée du Jouet**
Rue de l'Association
2400 Brussels

🏛️ **Speelgoed Museum**
Nekkerspoel 21
2800 Mechelen

CANADA

🏷️ **Banff Bears**
2nd Floor, Banff Avenue Mall
Banff
Alberta T0L 0C0

🏷️ **Bears Galore**
396 Academy Road
Winnipeg
Manitoba R3N 0B8

🏷️ **Fascination Dolls & Teddies**
24 Queen Street East
Cambridge
Ontario N3C 2A6

🏷️ **The Historic Martin House Dolls and Bears**
46 Centre Street
Thornhill
Ontario L4J 1E9

🏷️ **The Teddy Bear Garden Limited**
557 Mount Pleasant Road
Toronto
Ontario M4S 2M5

🏷️ **Teddy Bear Magic**
138 Mill Street
Georgetown
Ontario L7G 2C1

🏷️ **The Teddy Bear's Picnic**
205–2205 Oak Bay Avenue
Victoria
British Columbia V8R 1G4

🏷️ **Teddies To Go**
1783 Hamilton Street
Regina
Saskatchewan S4P 2B4

🏷️ **Treasures and Toys**
10436 82nd Avenue
Edmonton
Alberta T6E 2A2

📓 **BC T-Bear**
7576 Humphries Crescent
Burnaby
British Columbia V3N 3E9

📓 **Bearly Ours Teddy Bear Club**
18 Welsford Gardens
313 Don Mills
Ontario M3A 2P5

📓 **Good Bears of the World**
PO Box 69548
Station K
Vancouver
British Columbia V5K 4W7

Good Bears of the World
PO Box 982
Elora
Ontario N0B 1S0

The Peterborough Teddies
1333 Sandalwood Drive
Peterborough
Ontario K9K 1Y1

Teddy Bear Collectors Association of Alberta
PO Box 3056
Sherwood Park
Alberta T8A 2A6

Teddy Bear Tymes
7 Whiteoak Drive
St. Catharines
Ontario L2M 3B3

Vancouver Island Club Ted
6441 Rodolph Road
Victoria
British Columbia V8Z 5W3

Victorian Harvester: Dolls and Teddy Bears
438 Draycott Street
Coquitlam
British Columbia V3K 5K2

FRANCE

Club Français de l'Ours
70 Rue du Docteur Sureau
93160 Noisy Le Grand

**Teddy's Patch,
Le Club des Amis de l'Ours**
34 Rue Lieu de Santé
76000 Rouen

GERMANY

Teddybären und Plüsch
Dossenheimer Landstrasse 64
6900 Heidelberg

Berni Brumm's Teddymuseum
Hauptstrasse 98
8751 Leidersbach

Deutsches Puppen – und Barenmuseum "Loreley"
Sonnegasse 8
5401 St. Goar

Spielzeugmuseum in Alten Rathaustrum
Sammlung Ivan Steiger
Marienplatz 15
8000 München 2

Margarete Steiff Museum
Alleenstrasse 2
Postfach 1560
D-7928 Giengen (Brenz)

THE NETHERLANDS

Käthe Kruse Poppenmuseum
Binnenhaven 25
1781 BK Den Helder

Speelgoedmuseum
Sint Vincentiusstraat 86
4901 GL Oosterhout

Beer Bericht/Berenfanclub
Prinzengracht 1089
1017 JH Amsterdam

NEW ZEALAND

Bear Essentials
648 Dominion Road
Balmoral
Auckland

Bears on Broadway
272 Broadway
Newmarket
Auckland

Mr. Bear's Gift Factory
Shop 28, Queen's Arcade
Queen Street
Auckland

Not Just Bears
137 Victoria Street
Christchurch

Teddy's Toy Box
565 Colombo Street
Christchurch

Bears Unlimited
PO Box 96120
Balmoral
Auckland

Teddy Bear Express Club
PO Box 31195
Ham
Christchurch

The Wellington Teddy Bear Club
34 Park Avenue
Waikanae 6454

SOUTH AFRICA

Bear Basics
The Railway Station
Simon's Town 7995

Bear Collection
Box 13091
Northmead
Benoni 1510

SWITZERLAND

Spielzeugmuseum
Baselstrasse 34
CH-4125 Richen

UNITED KINGDOM

Asquiths Teddy Bear Shop
10 George V Place
Thames Avenue
Windsor
Berkshire SI 4 1QP
(branches also in Henley-on-Thames and Eton)

Bears & Friends
32 Meeting House Lane
Brighton
East Sussex BN1 1HB

Bears-on-the-Wold
11 Talbot Court
Sheep Street
Stow-on-the-Wold
Gloucestershire GL54 1AA

Bramwell Brown's Hug Shop
21–23 Church Road
Holywood
Co. Down BT18 9BU

Collector Teddy Bears
24 Journeaux Street
St. Helier
Jersey C.I.

Dolly Land
862–64 Green Lanes
Winchmore Hill
London N21 2RS

Margaret and Gerry Grey's Teddy Bear Shop
The Old Bakery Gallery
38 Cambridge Street
Wellingborough
Northamptonshire NN8 1DW

Growlies of Glasgow
11 Springfield Woods
Ravenscourt Park
Johnstone
Strathclyde PA5 8JR

Heather's Teddys
World Famous Arcade
177 Portobello Road
London W11 2DY

Pam Hebbs
No. 5 The Annexe
Camden Passage
Islington
London N1 8EU

Lakeland Bears
2 Crag Brow
Bowness-on-Windermere
Cumbria LA23 3BX

Merrythought Ltd.
Dale End
Ironbridge
Telford
Shropshire TF8 7NJ

Paddington & Friends
1 Abbey Street
Bath
Avon BA1 1NN

Sue Pearson Antique Dolls & Teddy Bears
13½ Prince Albert Street
The Lanes
Brighton
East Sussex BN1 1HE

Pooh Corner
High Street
Hartfield
East Sussex TN7 4AE

Recollect Studios
The Old School
London Road
Sayers Common
West Sussex BN6 9HX

**Teddy Bears
of Witney**
99 High Street
Witney
Oxfordshire OX8 6LY

The Bear Museum
38 Dragon Street
Petersfield
Hampshire GU31 4JJ

**Bethnal Green Museum
of Childhood**
Cambridge Heath Road
London E2 9PA

**The Cotswold
Teddy Bear Museum**
76 High Street
Broadway
Worcester WR12 7AJ

**The London Toy &
Model Museum**
21–23 Craven Hill
London W2 3EN

Museum of Childhood
42 High Street
Edinburgh
Lothian EH1 1TG

Pollock's Toy Museum
1 Scala Street
London W1P 1LT

**Ribchester Museum
of Childhood**
Church Street
Ribchester
Lancashire PR3 3YE

Sooty's World
Windmill Manor
Leeds Road
Shipley
West Yorkshire BD18 1BP

The Teddy Bear Museum
19 Greenhill Street
Stratford-upon-Avon
Warwickshire CV37 6LF

Teddy Melrose
The High Street
Melrose
Roxburghshire TD6 9PA

**Toy & Teddy
Bear Museum**
373 Clifton Drive North
St. Annes
Lytham St. Annes
Lancashire FY8 2PA

The Wareham Bears
18 Church Street
Wareham
Dorset BH20 4NF

Bear Friends
Mount Windsor
Farnahoe
Innishannon
Co. Cork
Republic of Ireland

**Colour Box
Collectors' Club**
High Tweed Mill
King Street
Galashiels
Selkirkshire TD1 1PX

**Good Bears
of the World (UK)**
256 St. Margaret's Road
Twickenham
Middlesex TW1 1PR

**Hugglets Teddy Bear
Magazine/British Teddy Bear
Association**
PO Box 290
Brighton
East Sussex BN2 1DR

Midland Good Bears
40 Fairfax Road
Sutton Coldfield
West Midlands B75 7JX

Paddington's Action Club
Action Research
Vincent House
North Parade
Horsham
West Sussex RH12 2DA

Steiff Collectors Club (UK)
c/o Ingram Public Relations
69–71 High Street
Epsom
Surrey KT19 8DH

Teddy Bear Times
Shelley House
104 High Street
Steyning
West Sussex BN44 3RD

UNITED STATES

The Bear Care Co.
Suite 957-F, 505 S. Beverly Drive
Beverly Hills
CA 90212

The Bear-ee Patch
Suite 107
2461 San Diego Avenue
San Diego
CA 92110

Bear in Mind
53 Bradford Street
Concord
MA 01742

Bears N Things
14191 Bacon Road
Albion
NY 14411

Bears N Wares
312 Bridge Street
New Cumberland
PA 17070

The Calico Teddy
22 E. 24th Street
Baltimore
MD 21218

The Cross-eyed Bear
PO Box 630061
Miami
FL 33163

Cynthia's Country Store
11496 Pierson Road #C–1
West Palm Beach
FL 33414

Dreamland Toys
Suite G, 555 West Lambert
Brea
CA 92621

Edinburgh Imports Inc.
PO Box 722
Woodland Hills
CA 91365-0722

Grin & Bear It
20 W. Chicago Avenue
Naperville
IL 60540

**Harper
General Store**
RD 2
PO Box 512
Annville
PA 17003

Now & Then
20 Powder Horn Road
Ardsley
NY 10502

The Rare Bear
21 Mill Hill Road
Woodstock
NY 12498

**Tailor Maid Togs
for Teddy Bears**
4037 161st St. SE
Bellevue
WA 98006

The Toy Store
Franklin Park Mall
5001 Monroe Street
Toledo
OH 43623

**Aunt Len's Doll
and Toy Museum**
6 Hamilton Terrace
New York
NY 10031

**The Carrousel Shop
and Museum**
505 W. Broad Street
Chesaning
MI 48616

**Children's Museum
of Indianapolis**
PO Box 3000
Indianapolis
IN 46206

**Theodore Roosevelt
Birthplace**
28 E. 20th Street
New York
NY 10003

Ⅲ **Margaret Woodbury**
Strong Museum
1 Manhattan Square
Rochester
NY 14607

Ⅲ **Teddy Bear Castle Museum**
431 Broad Street
Nevada City
CA 95959

Ⅲ **Teddy Bear**
Museum of Naples
2511 Pine Ridge Road
Naples
FL 33942

American Teddy Bear
Artists Guild
PO Box 66823
Scotts Valley
CA 95067

Bill Boyd's Teddy Bear
Jubilee MO-Kan Teddy
Bear Society
4922 State Line
Westwood Hills
KS 66205

Good Bears of the World
PO Box 13097
Toledo
OH 43613

Robert Raikes
Collectors Club
PO Box 82
Mt. Shasta
CA 96067

Theodore Roosevelt
Association
PO Box 719
Oyster Bay
NY 11771

Teddy Bear Artists
Association
PO Box 905
Woodland Hills
CA 91365

Teddy Bear and Friends
900 Frederick St.
Cumberland
MD 21502

The Teddy Bear Review
PO Box 1239
Hanover
PA 17331

Teddy Bear Times
3150 State Line Road
Cincinnati
North Bend
OH 45052

The Teddy Tribune
254 W. Sidney Street
St. Paul
MN 55107

S.M.A.L.L. (The Society of
Miniature Arctophiles Loving
and Learning)
951 S. Copper Key Ct.
Gilbert
AZ 85234

Muffy Vanderbear Club
North American Bear Co. Inc.
401 N. Wabash
Suite 500
Chicago
IL 60611

MANUFACTURERS

Althaus KG
Horberstrasse 4
8632 Neustadt Birkig
Germany

Les Créations Anima
Parc des Acqueducs
69230 Saint Genis Laual
France

Applause Inc.
6101 Variel Avenue
PO Box 4183
Woodland Hills
CA 91367-4183
USA

Baumann & Kienel KG
Coburger Strasse 53
D-8634 Roadach
(bei Coburg)
Germany

Berg Spielwaren Tiere
mit Herz GmbH
Rosenegg 66
A-6391 Fieberbrunn
Austria

Russ Berrie & Co.
111 Bauer Drive
Oakland
NJ 07436
USA

Big Softies
Otley Mills
Ilkley Road
West Yorkshire LS21 3JP
England

Boulgom
Rue des Gilères, BP 91
74150 Rumilly
France

Bunjy Toys
PO Box 496
Estcourt 3310
Natal
Republic of South Africa

Canterbury Bears Ltd.
The Old Coach House
Court Hill
Littlebourne
Kent CT3 1XU
England

Hans Clemens GmbH
Waldstrasse 34–36
6926 Kirchardt/Heilbronn
Germany

Dakin Inc.
World Headquarters
7000 Marina Blvd.
Brisbane
CA 94005
USA

Dean's Company (1903)
Pontypool
Gwent NP4 6YY
Wales

Gabrielle Designs Ltd.
The Bear Garden
Great North Road
Adwick-le-Street
Doncaster
Yorkshire DN6 7EJ
England

Ganz Brothers Toys
One Pearce Road
Woodbridge
Ontario L4L 3T2
Canada

Golden Bear
Products Ltd.
Rookery Road
Wrockwardine Wood
Telford
Shropshire TF2 9DW
England

Grisly Spielwaren
GmbH & Co. KG
Beethoven Strasse 1
6719 Kichheimbolanden
Germany

Gund Inc.
PO Box H
Edison
NJ 08817
USA

Trudi Giocattoli spa
Via Angelo Angeli 120
33017 Tarcento (Udine)
Italy

Gebrüder Hermann KG
Postfach 1207
Amlingstadter Strasse 6
8606 Hirschaid
Germany

Hermann-Spielwaren
GmbH
Im Grund 9–11
D-8630 Coburg-Cortendorf
Germany

Heunec Plüsch
Speilwaren Fabrik KG
Strasse am Moos 11
Mörikestrasse 2 & 6
96465 Neustadt/Coburg
Germany

Jakas Soft Toys
85 Lewis Road
Wantirna
Victoria 3152
Australia

Lefray Toys Ltd./
Real Soft Toys
Glandwr Industrial Estate
Aberbeeg
Abertillery
Gwent NP3 2XF
Wales

Little Folk
3 Blackdown Park
Willand
Nr. Cullompton
Devon EX15 2QH
England

Mary Meyer Corporation
PO Box 275
Townsend
VT 05353
USA

Merrythought Ltd.
Ironbridge
Telford
Shropshire TF8 7NJ
England

Mighty Star Ltd.
2250 Boulevard de
Maisonneuve Est
Montreal
Quebec H2K 2E5
Canada

North American Bear Co.
Suite 500
401 N. Wabash
Chicago
IL 60611
USA

Nounours SA/
Aux Nations
Le Rocher Bidaine
F 35210 Chatillon en
Vendelais
France

H. Scharrer & Koch
GmbH (Sigikid)
Am Wolfsgarten 8
8581 Mistelbach
Germany

Speciality Manufacturers
39 Richmond Road
Pinetown 3600
Republic of South Africa

Margarete Steiff GmbH
Alleenstrasse 2
Postfach 1560
D-7928 Giengen
Germany

Thiennot SA
BP 6 Rue du Stade
10220 Piney
France

GLOSSARY

• **Acrilan**
US tradename for an acrylic fibre invented by the Chemstrand Corporation, Decatur, Alabama. First introduced commercially in 1952; later woven into plush fabric for use in the soft-toy industry.

• **Acrylic Plush**
Fabric woven from acrylic fibres that are synthetically produced; the chemical, acryl-onitrile makes up 85% of content. Acrylic (polymethyl methacrylate) was invented in 1934, and was developed in the post-World War II period for fibres such as Acrilan, Courtelle, Dralon and Orlon, and other products such as paints. Acrylic fibres are fine and downy, making exceptionally soft and warm fabrics such as synthetic fur.

• **Airbrushing**
Painting by means of an airbrush – a device for spraying colour over a surface using compressed air, which enables an artist to work quickly and produce an even finish. Originally called an aerograph, it was first patented in Britain by US-born Charles L. Burdick in 1893. It is used in the soft-toy industry for applying non-toxic liquid dyes.

• **Alpaca Plush**
Originally imported from Bolivia and Peru, this plush is woven from alpaca yarn, spun from the long, strong fleece of the alpaca – a small llama. Extremely soft and woolly, it was often used to make baby toys.

• **Artificial-silk Plush**
Artificial silk was the first man-made fibre, and has been produced commercially from the 1880s. It is created from regenerated cellulose (wood pulp or cotton), which is chemically dissolved to form a viscose solution, then passed through spinnerets followed by mineral acid baths to produce a fibre. Often referred to as "art silk", it was introduced to the soft-toy industry in 1929.

• **Boot Buttons**
From the 19th to early 20th century, boots and shoes were often fastened with buttons. Being readily available and usually black and globular, they made perfect eyes for early teddy bears. The buttons were made from moulded wood pulp, resembling compressed paper (like hardboard); metal hooks were pushed into the flat backs.

• **Broadcloth**
A fine, dark-coloured cloth, usually in twill weave, originally for men's suits and later used in the US for teddy-bear noses.

• **Brushed Nylon** see Nylon.

• **Buckram**
A coarse, woven fabric that is stiffened with gum or paste.

• **Burlap**
Also described as hessian, a coarse, woven textile made from jute or hemp, used for making teddy bears in the very early years.

• **Calico**
A plain white, unprinted, bleached or un-bleached cotton cloth. The name derives from Calicut, a chief trading port between India and Europe in the 16th century.

• **Celluloid**
A semi-synthetic plastic composed of cellulose nitrate and camphor, which was first patented in 1869 by brothers, John and Isaiah Hyatt, in the US. It was particularly popular in the toy industry during the 1920s and 1930s, but was later banned because of its high flammability.

• **Chamois Leather**
Originally a leather prepared from the skin of the chamois – a European goat-like antelope. The name is now applied to any soft, pliable, yellowish brown leather.

• **Composition**
Also known as "compo", this is a mixture of various substances (similar to *papier mâché*) including plaster of Paris, bran, sawdust, and glue. It was used primarily in the doll and toy industry from the mid-19th century. While wet and still plastic, it was pressed into moulds and left until it hardened, when it could be painted.

• **Cotter Pin**
Double-pronged metal pin used to fasten the disc joints into place, enabling a teddy bear's limbs and head to swivel.

• **Cotton Plush**
A cheap quality plush, popular in the soft-toy industry during and immediately after World War II, woven entirely from cotton.

• **Cotton Waste**
A refuse yarn from the manufacture of cotton introduced as a stuffing material during World War II when kapok was unavailable. Such fillings were also known as white art wool, flock, and "sub". From the 1960s, waste from synthetic fabrics was also used – the darker the colour, the lower the grade of stuffing.

• **Courtelle**
Tradename for an acrylic fibre invented by the British company Courtaulds after World War II; the fibre was woven into plush and used in the soft-toy industry.

• **Dacron**
A teddy-bear stuffing material, bearing the US Du Pont Company's tradename for a polyester fibre patented in 1953.

• **Distressed Plush**
A plush, either alpaca or mohair, specially treated to resemble antique teddy-bear fur. The distressing process was invented in 1986 by Jack Wilson of the House of Nisbet in collaboration with Norton (Weaving) Ltd. of Yorkshire, using a 1904 "carricule" or velvet-crushing machine. Distressed plushes have become popular among bear artists and manufacturers attempting to produce old-looking bears.

• **Dralon**
Tradename for an acrylic staple fibre invented by the German company Farben Bayer AG at Dormagen near Leverkusen.

Naturally a light cream colour, it is woven and dyed into plush fabrics chiefly for the upholstery industry. It proved popular in the soft-toy industry from the 1960s for both fur and pads, as it is washable.

• **Dual Plush**
Refers to plush with pile dyed two colours, also known as tipped mohair. The process of tipping mohair involves laying the plush fabric out on a flat surface, brushing the tips of the pile with a contrasting dye, and leaving to dry. Dual plush was particularly popular during the 1920s.

• **Duxeen**
An imitation leathercloth like Rexine, used by bookbinders and toymakers, patented in 1920 by the Dux Chemical Solutions Co., Bromley-by-Bow, London, and produced by Messrs. Robert Williams & Sons (Gorton) Ltd. of Gorton, Manchester.

• **Excelsior**
Mid-19th century US tradename for fine wood shavings, or wood-wool, used for stuffing upholstery etc., and later teddy bears. The Latin motto for "higher", it was often used as a trademark.

• **External Jointing**
A primitive rod jointing system in which the ends of the rods running through the body of the teddy bear are visible at the shoulders and thighs.

• **Fairy Foam**
Mid-1960s British tradename for all-in-one foam-rubber stuffing material.

• **Felt**
Densely-matted, non-woven woollen fabric, which has been subjected to heat, steam, and pressure to compact it. It is the traditional material for the foot- and paw-pads of teddy bears.

• **Fibrefill**
Polyester fibres in the form of white, light-weight wadding, used as stuffing material in modern teddy-bear manufacture. It is also known by its US tradename, Dacron.

• **Flannelette**
A woven cotton textile with open weave, made to imitate flannel; brushed to give a slight nap. Also referred to as brushed cotton, it was popular with British teddy-bear manufacturers in the 1920s and 30s.

• **Flock** see Cotton Waste.

• **Foam-rubber**
Another term for polyurethane which has had pockets of inert gas introduced during its manufacture to form a light, foam-like material used in upholstery, cushions, and for artificial sponges, as well as a stuffing material in the soft-toy industry since the 1950s. It could be moulded to fit inside the outer casing or chopped into small pieces, sometimes described as poly-urethane foam chippings/chips/granules; shredded polyurethane; granulated foam rubber; latex foam; plastic foam; or synthetic foam stuffing. Tradenames such as "Fairy Foam" in the UK and "Sani-Foam" in the US have been patented.

• **Glass Eyes**
Originally made for taxidermists, blown glass eyes originating from Britain or Germany were introduced into teddy-bear manufacture around 1908. Early examples tended to be of clear glass with opaque black pupils; the backs were painted with brown enamel paint to appear life-like. Translucent amber glass with black pupils was one of the most popular designs for teddy bears' eyes.

• **Googly Eyes**
Also described as "Goo-Goo" eyes in the doll industry, this style of large, round, and staring eye was used from the early 1900s and throughout the 1920s, copying popular caricatures on postcards or in cartoons of the day. The term refers to bulbous opaque glass eyes with askance pupils. Sewn into a bear's face, they could be turned manually to give new comic expressions; or they were set in sockets, like those of a doll, to give a rolling action.

• **Growler**
An internal voice-box activated by tilting the toy, introduced to the teddy bear c.1908. Although modernized since, the mechanism's principle remains the same: weighted bellows force air through a reed, emitting a "growl". Pre-1930s examples consisted of hinged wood and oilcloth bellows with lead weights, a metal reed (sometimes with a double reed to create a two-tone growl), and card pipes, all contained in a cardboard tube with gauze protection at each open end. In the 1930s, the slide tilt-growler was introduced, with a weight consisting of a round tablet of bisque (unglazed porcelain) with the reed enclosed, joined to spiral oilcloth bellows. Upon tilting, the mechanism slid up and down in its card, tin, or plastic, container, with a perforated speaker at one end.

• **Hardboard**
Made from wood pulp, compressed in the drying process to form a stiff, dense type of fibreboard that was used by teddy-bear manufacturers to make joints.

• **Joggle Eyes**
Introduced after World War II, these eyes consisted of flat, white, plastic rounds with a clear plastic covering, each containing a loose, small, black circle representing the pupil. The pupils move in various directions to produce comical expressions when the bear is tilted or shaken.

• **Kapok**
A stuffing material popular in the soft-toy industry during the 1920s and 1930s, and still used to some degree after World War II because of its many ideal qualities: it is light, resilient, resistent to water, buoyant, and hygienic. The name derives from the Malayan word *kápoq*, an off-white, vegetable fibre or fruit hair found in the seed pods of the tropical tree *Ceiba Pentandra*. Known since the 18th century, kapok was first imported into Europe in 1851.

· Kid Leather
Soft leather made from kid or lamb skins. It was originally employed for making gloves and shoes, but it is also used in the soft-toy industry for the production of paw-pads and foot-pads.

· Leathercloth
Imitation leather, woven or knitted fabric coated on one side with either cellulose nitrate, a vinyl such as polyvinyl chloride (PVC), or polyurethane, often embossed to simulate leather. Also known as leatherette, or by a tradename such as Rexine or Duxeen, it is used principally in the upholstery and bookbinding trade. It is also employed in the toy industry for teddies' paw-pads.

· Leatherette see Leathercloth.

· Modacrylic Plush
Woven from modacrylic fibres, similar to acrylic fibres, but with a content of only 35–85% of the chemical acrylonotrile.

· Mohair
Derived from the Arabic word muxayyar meaning "cloth of goat's hair", the term originally referred to yarn or cloth made from the fleece of the Turkish angora goat, although today it is generally a mixture of wool and cotton. In 1830, some angora goats were sent to South Africa, which is now one of the biggest mohair producers.

· Musical Movement
This term refers to the type of clockwork cylinder and comb musical mechanism invented in 1780 by Louis Favre of Switzerland. In teddy-bear manufacturing, the movements were originally encased either in squeeze-boxes, or in tin or wooden and tin boxes, activated through an external crank shaft or key. Later examples were produced in plastic boxes, sometimes activated through a pull-cord. Japanese manufacturers largely took over the Swiss monopoly of this product after World War II.

· Nylon
The first completely synthetic fibre, Nylon was invented by chemist W.H. Carothers in the laboratories of the Du Pont Company of Delaware, in the US. It was first introduced commercially in 1938, after 11 years' research. Also known as a polyamide, it is produced using amides, chemicals similar to those that make up proteins in animal fibres, derived from the petrochemical caprolactam. Nylon is tough, lightweight, and elastic, and since World War II has been used extensively in the toy industry. Brushed nylon is treated on one surface to give it a raised and soft-textured nap.

· Oilcloth
A cloth treated to render it waterproof; also a name for leathercloth.

· Orlon
US tradename for an acrylic fibre registered by the Du Pont Company in 1948, and first employed commercially in 1950. Orlon is frequently used in knitted fabrics such as imitation fur and in carpets, as well as in the soft-toy industry.

· Pile
Vertical threads which stand out from the surface of a fabric. Plush can be described as shaggy or short pile. Pile in loop form is known as "terry".

· Plastic
From the Greek word plastikos, meaning "able to be shaped", plastic is a general term describing a varied class of organic substances made up of long chains of molecules (or polymers), based on man-made chemicals (such as vinyls) or modified natural materials (such as celluloid). Under heat and pressure, they become plastic and can be cast in moulds to produce a permanent or rigid form.

· Plush
From the Latin word pilus, meaning "hair", and the old French word pluche, meaning "hairy fabric", plush is a cloth with a cut pile on one side, which is longer and less dense than velvet. It is usually woven, often by weaving two cloths together with a pile warp common to both, which is afterwards cut. Since World War II, cheaper plush made from synthetic yarns has been produced on a knitted backing.

· Polyester
A synthetic fibre that uses oil as raw material, and was invented in 1941 by J.R. Whinfield and J.T. Dickson at the Calico Printers Association in the UK. Its registered tradename in Britain is Terylene, whereas in the US it is known as Dacron. It is often mixed with natural fibres to make easily washable, woven fabrics, or to make strong sewing threads or a wadding known as fibrefill, a type of stuffing.

· Polystyrene
Developed in Germany in 1929, as one of the first synthetic plastics. Since World War II, it has been used as stuffing in the toy industry in the form of a lightweight, rigid foam, in granules, or pellets.

· Polyurethane
Describes a large class of synthetic resins and plastics first produced in 1937 and developed during World War II; it is used for making foam-rubber.

· Rayon
Term used generally since World War II for artificial silk. Since that period, modifications to equipment and chemicals used in the manufacturing process have resulted in a variety of rayons, such as viscose, acetate, and triacetate.

· Rexine
A tradename for a leathercloth or imitation leather used in upholstery and bookbinding, it was listed in the 1915 Trademarks Journal as belonging to the British Leather-cloth Manufacturing Co. Ltd. (later Rexine Ltd), Hyde, near Manchester. Rexine is formed by covering a woven cloth with several coatings of cellulose nitrate. The term is often used to describe the leather-cloth used on British and Australian bear pads from the late 1930s to early 1960s.

· Rod Jointing see External Jointing.

· Rubber
Originally commercial rubber was based on a natural substance, the milky viscous liquid or latex obtained from the tropical tree Hevea brasileinsis. During World War II, synthetic rubbers were extensively developed, and various types based on different chemicals are now produced for use in industry, including toy manufacture.

· Safe Eyes
Plastic eyes, each with an integral shank forming a screw and secured with a washer behind the plush; also referred to as "safe-lock" or "screw-lock" eyes; the recommended method of applying soft-toy eyes by toy safety standard laws worldwide.

· Satin
Originally described a silk fabric with a smooth glossy surface produced by a warp-faced weave. Now a term also used for other textiles resembling satin, but not necessarily of silk. Satinized fabric is that which has been treated to imitate satin.

· Sealing Wax
A man-made wax that was originally used for sealing documents, it was also employed in the early years of teddy manufacture, particularly in Germany, for making realistically moulded noses. Malleable when hot, it cooled to a hard finish, but was unsatisfactory as it often cracked.

· Shanks
The shaft or hook, usually of wire, protruding from the back of a glass or plastic eye, used for securing it inside the head. Later plastic eyes often had integral (all-in-one) shanks.

· "Sliced in" Ears
Term referring to a cheap method of securing ears to a teddy bear by cutting or "slicing" holes in the sides or top of the head and pushing in the gathered edge of the ear; no stitching is required.

· Slush Moulding
Also known as rotational moulding, this method of making hollow vinyl objects was used particularly for making doll and teddy-bear heads of the post-World War II era. The mould is partially filled with a powdered resin, and then heated and spun rapidly. The centrifugal force pushing the melting resin against the moulded walls holds it there as the mould cools. The resin eventually solidifies.

· Squeaker
Internal voice box, used from the earliest days of teddy-bear manufacturing, made from two rounds or ovals of card or wood held together by a strip of oilcloth to form bellows, containing a coiled spring. When squeezed, a rush of air caused the internal or external reed to vibrate producing a squeak. Any old piece of card, including photographs, was used for their manufacture. Post-World War II versions of the squeaker use the same principle, but with soft vinyl bellows that are often in the form of a concertina.

· Styrofoam
US tradename for a type of polystyrene foam that was patented in 1950 by the Dow Chemical Company, and used in the soft-toy industry as a stuffing material.

· Sub see Cotton Waste.

· Suede
Derived from Suède (French for Sweden), this originally described undressed kid leather, but now applies to other kinds of leather (such as lamb skin or cowhide) resembling kid skin. Its special finish has a napped, velvety surface which is produced by buffing the flesh side with an emery wheel.

· Suedette
A type of cotton or rayon fabric with a velvety nap, dating from 1915, designed to imitate the texture of suede.

· Swing-tag
A paper, card, metal, or plastic tag usually bearing the manufacturer's tradename and/ or bear's name, and attached by thread either around the neck or arm, or sewn into the chest (also known as a chest -tag). Often lost or removed, it is thus named to differentiate it from the more permanent fabric label, usually sewn across a pad or into a seam.

· Tipped Mohair see Dual Plush.

· Twill
A woven fabric with diagonal ridges, created by passing the weft threads over one and under two or more of the warp threads (instead of over and under in regular succession as in plain weaving).

· Ultrasuede
US tradename for a synthetic, non-woven fabric that resembles suede, first used in 1971 and patented in 1973 by Spring Mills Inc., Fort Mill, South Carolina, US.

· Velcro
Registered tradename derived from the French velours croché, meaning "hooked velvet". Describes a revolutionary fastener consisting of two woven nylon strips, one with tiny loops, the other with hooks, which can be simply pressed together or pulled apart. It was first conceived by Swiss engineer, Georges de Mestral, in 1948.

· Velour
From the French word meaning "velvet", this describes a velvet-like plush fabric, with either a woven or a knitted backing, often synthetic in recent years.

· Velvet
A woven, silk fabric with a short, dense, and smooth-piled surface.

· Velveteen
A velvet-like fabric in appearance and texture, but woven from cotton instead of silk, which makes it cheaper to produce.

· Vinyl
Refers to various plastics that contain the chemical substance vinyl. Durable and inexpensive, vinyls are used both to make rigid products (such as toys) and flexible products (such as films) as well as vinyl coatings for fabrics. The most well known, polyvinyl chloride (PVC), was the first to be manufactured commercially.

· Wood-wool
Long, fine quality, soft wood (such as birch) shavings, originally a packing material for delicate objects but also used in upholstery and taxidermy. It is the traditional stuffing material for teddy-bears. Arriving in large bales, the material must be pulled apart and stuffed manually using rods.

· Yorkshire cloth
A term sometimes used for mohair plush, because it was spun in Yorkshire in the north of England, the traditional centre of the textile industry. Angora goats' hair was imported from Turkey and South Africa to be converted into yarn. It was then woven into plush in Yorkshire, or exported to one of the German mills such as Schulte's.

INDEX

A

A1 Toys 72
AB Merimex 167
  history of 226
Acton Toycraft Ltd. 125
  history of 220
  label 14
Aerolite button **52**
Aetna Toy
  Animal Co. 27
  history of 220
Ahsolite bears 11
*A Hug of Teddy
  Bears* 190
Ajena 165
  history of 220
Albert the
  Running Bear 147
Albico 117
A.L.F.A.
  history of 220
Alſonzo 19
Alistair 181
all-in-one ears 33
Ally Bear 29
Aloysius 147
Alpha Bear:
  large 50
  "dual" mohair 51
  replica 13
Alpha Toy label 14
Alresford Crafts Ltd. 143
  history of 220
Althans 115
  history of 220
Amelia Bearheart 146
American Doll and
  Toy Manufacturing
  Company 26
American Made Stuffed
  Toy Company 47
Amram 148
Anima, Les
  Créations 165
  history of 220
Anker Plüschspiel-
  warenfabrik 114
history of 220
Anything Bear, The 145
Applause Inc. 139
  history of 220
  label 14
Archie 195
Arctophile, The 195
arctophily 189
"AR" design 135
Article de Luxe Fabrication
  Artisanale, *see A.L.F.A.*
Asquiths Teddy Bear
  Shop 195
Atwood, Florence 67
Australia:
  1930s–60 80
  and New Zealand
  1970–90s 136
Australian Doll Digest 201
Austria and Switzerland:
  post-1945 118
Aux Nations 165
  history of 220
Avanti line 139
Axe, John 67
Ayers, Dottie 195

B

Baby-Bär 43
Baby-bear 111
Baby Bobby 185
Bajka Toymaking
  Co-operative Works 167
Baki 116
Baldwin, Barbara 195
Bär:
  PB 16
  28 PB 17
  55 PB 38
  1904 35
  PB replica 153
Barber, Jean 67
Bärenjahre 38
Bärle 18, 38
Barton 149
Barton Waugh Pty. Ltd. 80
history of 220
"bat" ears 77
Bauer, Odl and Katya 146
Baumann, Hermann 94
Baumann and Kienel 116
  history of 220
Baxter Brown Bear 179
Beacock, Brian 180
bear:
  artists 172
  artistry, rise of 12
  care 203
  dismantling 204
  drying 206
  grooming 211
  identification 15
  modern 210
  patching 213
  repair 212
  restoration 204
  surface washing 213
  synthetic 210
  unjointed 210
  washing 206
bear artist convention 13
Bear Enthusiasts' All 'Round
  Collectors Club Inc. 201
Bear Facts Review 201
Bearings 201
Bear in Mind 195
Bear Memorabilia 198
Bear of Russia 12
bear on a tricycle 109
bear on crutches 191
Bear Ritz 12
Bears Paw Collectables 13
Bear Tracks 200
Bear Tree, The 195
Bear With Me 190
Beddy-Bye-Bear 177
Bedford Bears 179
Bedtime Bertie 193
Beefeater 134
Beer Bericht 201
bell in ear 120
Benjamin 149
Berenfanclub 201
Berg, Hermann 9
Berg Spielwaren
  Tiere mit Herz 119
  history of 220
Berlex Toys 81
  history of 221
Berliner bears 192
Berrie, Russ and Co. 139
  archives 148
  history of 221
Berrie, Wallace and Co.
  1982 139
  1984 140
  history of 221
Berryman, Clifford K. 199
Bestall, Alfred 199
Bethnal Green Museum
  Bear 151
Bigo Bello 112
Big Softies 143
  history of 221
Billiken 9

Billy Owlett 9
Billy Possum 8
Billy the Buccaneer 200
Bing, Gebrüder
  1909–32 32
  c.1910–32 34
  history of 221
Bingie 68
Bingie guardsman 69
Bingies, bare 69
Birthday Bear 161
Bisbikis, Nick 191
Björk, Christina 196
Black, George B. 197
Blanchet, Les Créations,
  history of 221
Bland, Joan 195
Blinka bears 11
Bobby Bruin 69
Bob's Bears 187
Bocs Teganau 180
Body Language Bear 145
boot buttons 207
  replica 210
Borgfeldt, George and
  Company 9
Boris Bear 182
Boston, Wendy:
  1945–76 122
Playsafe Toys Ltd.
  history of 221
Botswana Made 187
Botta, Loretta 176
Boulgom 164
  history of 221
Brame, Ginger T. 177
bran bath 213
Brandreth, Gyles 197
Breedon, Maggie 143
Bright Eye 26
Bri-Nylon 133
Britannia Toy Works 12
  history of 221
Brittany 149
British Doll and Novelty
  Company 12
British United Toy Manu-
  facturing Co. Ltd.
  history of 221
Brooks, Jacki 196
Bruin Manufacturing Co. 27
  history of 221
Bruintje Beer postcards 199
Brummi; Bigo Bello
  series 113
Bruno the Talking Bear 11
brushing and combing 206
bugs 212
Bull, Peter 190
Bully Bear 144
Bumblebear 177
Bunjy Toys 169
  history of 221
button
  in ear 14
  on the arm 33
  under arm 33
  under chin 53
"BW" button 33

C

Calico Teddy, The 195
California Stuffed Toys 141
  history of 221
Calvin, K. and H. 173
Campione, Bunny 194
Canham, Deborah 182
Canterbury Bears:
  1980–90s 150
  history of 222
  label 15
care and repair 212
Caress 149
Carless, Liz 181
carpet beetle 212
Carrousel label 14
cartoon-style eyes 25
Casparek-Türkkan,
  Erika 196
Cavally, Frederick L. 199
centre-seam teddy 20
Chad Valley:
  1920s–30s 52
  1930s–40s 64
  1938–50s 62
  1950s–60s 104
  1960–78 130
  button 14
  history of 222
  label 15
Champagne Luxury
  Bear 135
Character Novelty
  Company Inc:
  1945–83 82
  history of 222
character bears 9
Charles, Mrs. Sydney 197
Cheeky design 134
  c.1960; nylon plush 121
Cherished Teddies
  Collection 200
Chiavetta, Riccardo 139
Childsplay Toys 127
Chiltern:
  1920s–40s 56
  post-World War II
  –1950s 106
  c.1958–early 1960s 108
  label 14
Christie's 194
Christmas Tree Bear 13
Christopher 171
Chubby Bear 68
Clan Bear 151
Classic range,
  Canterbury 150
Claustre, Donna 12
claws:
  materials 209
  stitching 209
Clemens, Hans 115
  history of 222
  traditional 157
clockwork reading
  bear 79
clown bear 65

*Club des Amis de
  l'Ours, Le* 201
*Club Francais de l'Ours
  Ancien* 201
Cobweb 182
*Collector's History of the
  Teddy Bear, The* 196
Colour Box Miniature
  Teddy Bears 200
Columbia Teddy Bear
  Manufacturers 27
  history of 222
Commonwealth Toy and
  Novelty Company 11
  history of 222
compact bear 40
cone nose 21
Conley, Barbara 174
Coronation Bear 89
Cossack 12
Cosy Teddy 129
Cotswold Teddy Bear
  Museum 197
Cousin, Aline 184
Cowboy 85
C. Owen 171
Crocodile Dunbear 186
Cubbigund Cuddle
  Bear 85
Cubby Bear 105
Cuddly Toys Ltd. 169
  history of 222
Cyclops 58
Czechoslovakia 166

D

Dakin, R. and Co.
  1982 139
  1985 141
  history of 222
  label 15
Dancing Bear 112
Deacon 149
Dean's
  1920s–50s 72
  1950s 102
  c.1960–80 126
  1980s–90s 162
Dean's Childsplay Toys 163
  label 14
Dean's Rag Book
  Co. Ltd. 163
  history of 222
Dewi 180
Dicky 36
  replica 153
display cases 214
Dolly Bear 22
Dreamland Doll
  Company 26
drying 206
"dual" mohair plush 37
Dunbee-Combex group 108
Dutch Teddy 69
D.W. Shoyer and
  Company 9

E

Ealontoys 71
  history of 223
ear, replacing 209
Eaton, Seymour 9
  collectables 199
Edgar 186
Edwardian Bear 160
Edward in Transit 196
Eisenmann and Co. Ltd.
  history of 223
electric eye bear 9
elephant logo 16
Eli Doll and Toy Company
  history of 223
Elizabeth Anne 181
Ellett, Richard 103
Emil Toys 81
  history of 223
EM Toy and Doll Co. 115
Enchanted Doll House,
  Vermont 195
Erle Teddy Bear Company
  history of 223
Erris Toys 159
Europe: 1930s–80s 166
excelsior stuffing 12
  (see also "sub")
eyes:
  cartoon 25
  electric 9
  inserting 207
  plastic 210
  plastic, inserting 210
  replacing 207
  rolling 11
  safety 210
  "spangle" 77

F

fabric:
  matching 213
  synthetic 211
factory histories 220–29
F.A.D.A.P. 1930s 49
  history of 223
Fagan, Peter and
  Frances 200
Fainges, Marjory 186
Fali, G. 166
Farnell, J.K.
  1920s–30s 50
  1945–68 90
  history of 223
  label 14
Fast Black Skirt
  Company 26
Fechter 118
  1950s–60s 119
  history of 223
feeding-bottle cover 189
Feed Me bear 11
Felpa, see MCZ
Felt Toy Factory 38
Fieberbrunn 118
Fluffies 167
foam-rubber filling 59
footballer bear 35
France:
  1920s–30s 48

post–1945 164
Frannie Bear 194
Frederick Pooh
  Robinson III 197
Freeman, Chester 173
Frey, Shawn 12
Fritz 192
Fuddo 155
Fujita-Gamble, Elaine 175
fumigation 212

G

Gaeltarra Eireann 158
  history of 223
Games and Toys 196
Ganz Bros. Toys
  history of 224
Gard, Diane 176
Garmonsway 185
Gatti 160
Gebrüder Bing:
  c.1910—32 34
Gebrüder Hermann,
  see Hermann, Gebrüder
Gebrüder Süsenguth,
  see Süssenguth, Gebrüder
George Borgfeldt
  and Company 9
German soccer player 113
German Unification
  Bear 155
Germany:
  1920s–30s 30
  post–1945 (traditional) 114
  post–1945 (Zotty
    lookalikes) 116
  1980s–90s 156
Germany's Crusher 12
Giocattoli, Trudi 166
  history of 224
G.L. Kirby Ltd.,
  see Kirby, G.L.
glue 203
Goffin, Marcelle 184
Golden Bear
  Products Ltd. 142
  history of 224
Golden Teddy award 13
Good Bear Day 191
Good Bears of the
  World 191
Grandma Lynn's
  Teddy Bears 176
Grandmother Brompton 171
Great Britain:
  1908–c.1920 28
  minor companies:
    1930s–50s 70
  new firms: 1970s–80s 142
  post-World War II–
    c.1970 124
  evolution of bears in 12
  prototype 28
Gregory 149
  unjointed 170
Grisly Spielwaren 115
  history of 224
grooming 211
Gross and Schild 11
Guardsman 134
Gund:
  1930s–60s 84

1988 141
  history of 224
  label 14
Gwentoys Ltd. 124
  history of 224
Gyles' Bear 196
GZB 166

H

Hahn and Amberg 26
hair dryer 206
Halifax 185
Hamiro 166
  history of 224
Hanna, Cathie 171
Hanna, Joan 183
Hans Clemens,
  see Clemens, Hans
Hanton, Allie and Nigel 185
Happy 7
  replicas 197
Happy Inspired 197
Harkness, Ruth 11
Harman 26
  history of 224
Harmles 192
Harper, Jackie 67
Harrell Serieta 177
Harris, Janis 185
Harrison, Donna 195
Harrisons Textiles 137
  history of 224
Harrods bear 161
Harwin and Co. 29
  history of 224
Haughey, Joyce Ann 171
Hay, Maxwell and
  Company 137
  history of 224
Hayes, Frannie 197
head:
  fixing to body 208
  removing 205
  renovating 207
Hebbs, Pam 194
Heike-Bär:
  history of 224
  Schuco replica 157
Helvetic:
  mid-1920s 44
  history of 224
Hermann and Co.
  1940s–60s 98
Hermann, Adelheid 94
Hermann, Artur 94
  history of 224
Hermann, Bernhard 31
Hermann Dynasty 94
Hermann, Gebrüder:
  1948–c.1970 96
  1980s–92 154
  history of 225
  label 14
Hermann, Johann 94
Hermann, Max:
  1933 30
  1925–29 31
Hermann, Rolf-Gerhard 95
Hermann Spielwaren 98
  history of 225
  Jubilee Bear 156
  replica 157

Hermann, Werner 95
Heunec Plüsch Spielwaren
  Fabrik, history of 225
Hibernian Novelty Co. 158
Highlander 134
Hillman, Priscilla 200
Hissey, Jane 200
Hockenberry, Dee 198
Holst, Charlotte 12
Honey Bear
  Bunjy Toys 169
  Jonette Stabbert 183
Honey the Signing Bear 191
horizontal nose 54
hot-water bottle 23
House of Nisbet:
  1976–89 144
  history of 227
  label 14
Howells, Pam 180
Hug 147
Hugglets 195
Hugmee:
  artificial silk: musical 57
  Chiltern label 106
  "dual" plush 56
  flat face 57
  medium 107
  mohair 108
  white mohair 57
Humme, Jane 183
Hyacinth 182
hygiene products 203
Hygienic Toys 88
  label 15

I

Ideal:
  1903–World War I 24
  1930s–50s 86
  glass eyes 25
  history of 225
Ideal Toy
  Corporation 1978 141
injured bears 191
In Praise of Teddy Bears 196
International League of
  Teddy Bear Clubs 201
Invicta Toys Ltd.
  history of 225
Ireland: 1938–79 158
Isaac and Company 12
Isa spring-leg bear 12
Isenberg, Barbara 146
Ivan the Russian Tommy 12

J

Jackie-Baby 110
Jack's Bear 195
Jäger, Ida 95
Jakas Soft Toys
  c.1960 80
  1978 136
  history of 225
J.K. Farnell, see Farnell, J.K.
Janes, Maddie 182
Janus; two-faced 113
Japan: 1945–90s 78
Jester Bear 12

Jocky 166
  history of 225
Johnson Brothers 12
joint pins, metal 203
joints:
  disc, replacing 208
  plastic 210
  traditional 202
Jones, Margaret 143
Jones, W.H. 70
  history of 225
Jouet, Marylou 184
Joy of a Toy label 14
Joy-Toys:
  history of 225
  label 14
  1920s–60s 58
Jumbo Cuddle Panda 85
Jünginger, Jorg 197
Jungle Toys, history of 225

K

Kamar Toy Company 78
kapok stuffing 12
Kahn & Mossbacher 9
Karl Hofmann Company 9
Käthe Kruse Puppen 117
  history of 226
Kelly, Mary 187
Kenner Parker 130
Kersa 166
Keystone Bears 27
King, Doris 174
Kirby, G.L. Ltd. 58
  history of 225
Klein Archie 195
Knickerbocker Toys:
  1920–30s 74
  post-World War II 76
  early 1960s 138
  history of 226
  label 14
Knockabout bears 12
Koala Families 149
Koch, Hugo 117
  history of 226
Kruse, Käthe, see Käthe
  Kruse Puppen
Kruse, Susan L. 175

L

Laight, Naomi 181
Laing, Jennifer 186
Landstra, Bev Miller 174
Lauver, Barbara
  and Bob 195
La Vogue 90
Leco Toys (West End)
  Ltd. 125
  history of 226
Lefray Toys Ltd. 125
  history of 226
Lenci 167
  history of 226
  label 14
Les Créations Anima,
  see Anima, Les
  Créations
Leven, H. Josef,

history of 226
Lewis, Fran 195
Li.Bear.A.Ted. 181
Lillibet 181
limbs:
  dislocated 203
  finishing 208
  removing 205
Lindee Toys 81
  history of 226
Lindsay Purpus 173
Lindy 7
Lines Bros. 92
Little Folk 143
  history of 226
"LM" design 135
Lohre, Linda Spiegel 177
London Bears 134
London Toy Company 12
Lovelock, Pat 186
Lully 129
Lumley, Lynn 176
Luvme Toy Manufacturing
  Company, history of 226
Luv Pets 149

M

McBride, Graham 143
McConnell, Barbara 13
McLeary, Frances 185
Made for Gund 151
"Made in Eire" label 159
"Made in Ireland" label 92
Magic of Merrythought,
  The 67
Magna series 55
Magnet replica 161
Malrob Cuddle Toys 137
  history of 226
Mandel, Margaret Fox 196
Martin, Cindy 178
Mary Meyer Corporation,
  history of 227
Mary Plain 11
Mass Manufacturers:
  1980s–90s 170
Master Teddy 29
  Maulkorb Bär 22
  Max Hermann 30

Maxwell Hay 137
MCZ 118
  history of 226
"M" design:
  1970s medium 135
  1976 134
Menten, Ted 177
  Hug 147
Merimex, AB, *see AB Merimex*
Merrythought:
  1930s (traditional) 60
  1930s (Bingie series and novelties) 68
  1940s–50s 88
  1940s–60s 120
  1970s–80s 134
  1982–92 160
  archives 66
  chest-tag 66
  label 14
Messenger-Bär 43
Michaud, Doris and Terry 175
  museum 197
Michtom, Morris 8
Michtom, Rose 24
Mighty Star Ltd. 169
  history of 227
Miller Manufacturing Company 26
miniature atomizer bear 41
Minky Zotty 128
Mr. and Miss Mischief 160
Mr. Cinnamon Bear 153
Mr. Oz E. Bound 184
Mr. Twisty Cheeky 120
Mr. Whoppit 121
Mitchell, Joanne 178
modern bears, caring for 210
mohair plush, washing 206
Molly-Teddy 129
Moore, Irene 183
Mother Goose's Teddy Bear 199
Mother Goose trademark 90
Muffin Enterprises 191
Muffy: Dutch Treat 147

Mulholland and Bailie Ltd. 143
  history of 227
Mullaney, A. and W. 181
Mullins, Linda 191
musical boxes, Swiss 202
musical bear 51
Musical Bruin Bear 109
Mutzli:
  1950s 118
  1982 119

N

Napoleon 184
National Bear, The 47
National Biscuit Co. 11
Nett, G. and M. 176
New Zealand and Australia:
  1970–90s 136
Nicholl, Dawn 184
nightdress case:
  Chad Valley 105
  J.K. Farnell 91
Nimrod-Bear 110
Nisbet, *see House of Nisbet*
No Frills Bear 12
Norman Rockwell Series III 163
North American Bear Company: 1979–92 146
  history of 227
nose and mouth, repairing 207
noses, moulded plastic 210
Nounours 165
  history of 227
"NY" design 135

O

Oliver, Anita 182
Original Teddy 128
  new design 100
Oscar
  Cuddly Toys 169
  Irene Moore 183
Osito 166
Ownby, Jim 191

P

PAB 18
Paddington Bear collectables 199
pads:
  fabrics 211
  removing replacements 205
  replacing 206
Palitoy 130
Panda-bear 36
Pantom Bär 23
Parker Toys 80
  history of 227
Parlo 112
patching 213
Patchnours 184
paw-pads, repairing 206
Payne, The Toothache Bear 155
Peacock and Co. Ltd. 70
  history of 227
Pearson, Sue 196
Pedigree:
  Canterbury label 133
  glass eyes 93
  history of 227
  label 14
  1937–50s 92
  1960s–80s 132
Peter Bear 121
Petsy 36
  blue-eyed 37
  Dralon 129
  replica 153
Petz Company 117
  history of 227
Phillips 194
Phillips, Sara 175
Piccolo:
  miniature 41
  perfume bottle 41
Picot, Geneviève and Gérard 196
Pintel, M., Fils et Cie. 1920s 48
Pittana, Marcella 178
PJs 173
Plaintalk 162
Playsafe Toys, *see Boston, Wendy*
Playthings 198
Plummer, Wandless and Co. 125
  history of 227
plush:
  replacement 202
  types for restoration 205
  washing 206
  washing mohair 206
Poland:
  *c.*1960 166
  1960s 167
Porridge Bear 162
Port, Beverly 172
Port Wine 191
post-war production 12
Prosper 11
Pudsey 191
Punch and Judy 182
Punkinhead 121

Purpusly Prairie 173
Purzel Bär 23
Puzzi; Bigo Bello series 113

Q

Quiet Bears 191
Quinn, Sue 179

R

Raikes, Robert 171
Rainbow Tubby Bear 64
Rankin, Joan 179
Rare Bear Shop, The 195
R. Dakin and Co., *see Dakin, R. and Co.*
Real Soft Toys 124
  history of 228
  swing-tag 15
record-keeping 193
Record Teddy 22
Rembearandt 186
repairing, when not to 212
replacement pads, removing 205
"Republic of Ireland" label 158
Rexine, fake 206
Rixon, Susan 179
Robbity Bob Ltd., history of 228
Robin Hood 171
rod-jointed bear French 17
  Steiff 49
Roeder, Romy 196
roller-skating bear 35
Rolly Bear 112
Roly Poly bear 22
Romsey Bear Co. 181
  label 15
Roosevelt Bears 9
  collectables 199
Roosevelt, Theodore 8
  items relating to 199
Rössel Waugh, C-L. 173
Round, Jenny 187
Rovex Tri-ang Ltd. 132
Rupert 11
  collectables 199
Russ Berrie and Co., *see Berrie, Russ and Co.*
Rusty the Bagman 178

S

SAF 118
  history of 228
Sailor Bear 178
Sapphire 195
Scharrer, H. and Koch, history of 228
Schenker 118
  history of 228
Schlopsnies, Albert 39
Schoen, Sue 180
Schoonmaker, Patricia 196
Schreyer and Co. 40

history of 228
Schuco:
  1920s–30s 40
  1949–76 112
  chest-tag 14
Schulte, Reinhold 8
Schutt, Steve 172
Schwika 118
  1950s–60s 119
  history of 228
Seasonal Bear series 160
Sergeant Culver 192
Sergeant Sam Browne 178
Shanghai Dolls Factory 169
  history of 228
Sheepskin Products 137
  history of 228
short-lived US firms:
  *c.*1907–14 26
Shoyer, D.W. and Company 9
Siegel, Ernst 94
Siegel, Viktoria 94
Sieverling, Helen 196
Sigikid; Miro Collection 157
Silky Bear 57
Sir Koff-a-Lot 191
Sir Mortimer 179
Sitting Bear 85
Sixby, Barbara 174
Skater 107
Smokey Bear 86
Snuggle Bear 139
Softanlite 70
Softouch Inc. 191
somersaulting bear 35
Sonneberg Bär, replica 155
Sonny Bear 64
Sotheby's 194
South Wales Toy Manufacturing Company 12
  history of 228
"spangle" eyes:
  Knickerbocker 1950s 77
  Ideal *c.*1950s 86
Sparrow, Judy 197
Speciality Manufacturers history of 228
split seams 202
squeakers, renovating 208
Stabbert, Jonette 183
Stammberger, Hilde 95
Steiff:
  1902–05 16
  1903–World War I 20
  1905–World War I 18
  1908–World War I 22
  1920s–30s 36
  1940s–early 1960s 100
  1950s 110
  1960s–90s 128
  1980–92 152
  archives 38
  blank button 19
  button in ear 14
  ear-tag 15
  elephant logo 16
  history of 228
Steiff, Fritz 38
Steiff, Hugo 38
Steiff, Margarete 38
Steiff, Otto 38
Steiff, Richard 38
Stone, H.G. 106
  history of 228

Strauss Manufacturing Co. Inc. 26
  history of 229
  stuffing 204
  excelsior 12
  funnels 12
  kapok 12
  post-World War II 211
  traditional 205
"sub" stuffing 73
Suffa, Rosalie 94
Süssenguth, Gebrüder 31
  history of 229
Swiss musical boxes 202
Switzerland and Austria: post-1945 118
synthetic fabrics 211

T

talking bear 98
Tapsy 128
Tara Toys 159
tea-cosy bear 188
Teddigund 84
Teddy and Friends: The Bear Essentials, history of 229
Teddy and the Bear 199
Teddy B 162
teddy bear:
  chinaware 198
  collecting 189
  conventions 195
  displaying 214
  ephemera 200
  feeding-bottle cover 189
  history of 216
  leprechauns 148
  limited editions 197
  memorabilia 198
  museums 197
  muff 188
  origin 8
  origin of name 9
  philately 188
  postcards 200
  protecting 214
  shops 195
  shows 195
  silverware 188
  storybooks 199
  tea-cosy 188
  tea sets 198
  teething-ring rattle 198
  time chart 217
  valuation 194
  warming plate 200
Teddy Baby 37
Teddy Bear and Friends 201
Teddy Bear Artists: Romance of Making and Collecting Bears 13
Teddy Bear Exerciser 12
Teddy Bear Magazine, The 201
Teddy Bear Museum (Florida) 197
teddy-bear restorers 203
Teddy Bear Review 200
Teddy Bear Shop 195
Teddy Bears of Witney 197

*Teddy Bears Past and
  Present* 196
Teddy Bear Times, The 201
Teddybu 36
Teddy Clown 36
Teddy Doofings 68
Teddy G 162
teddy gas-mask 11
Teddyli 110
Teddy Melrose 197
Teddy Rose replica 152
Teddy's Adventures
  in Africa 199
Teddy's Bear 8
Teddy's Patch 201
Teddy Toy Company 70
  history of 229
Teddy Tribune, The 200
Teneycke, Trudy 178
10th Anniversary
  Bear 151
Terry, Stacey Lee 180
Terry, William J.
  *c.*1913 29
  history of 229
Thaddeus 185
Theobalds, Prue 200
therapeutic bears 191

Thiennot,
  history of 229
threadbare bear 202
Three Bears 65
Three Bears, The 216
tilt-growlers 208
Timme 83
Ting-a-Ling
  Bruin Bear 107
Tintin 184
TOBY award 13
Toffee:
  Chad Valley 104
  J.K. Farnell 91
toolbox 204
Touch of Silk 161
Toyland 168
Toy Trader, The 196
traditional-style bears,
  restoring 204
Tricky 112
Trudi, *see*
  Giocattoli, Trudi
Tru-to-Life 102
Tufty 183
Tumbling bear 41
Tumpy 68
Twyford label 14

*UK Teddy Bear
  Guide* 201
*Ultimate Teddy Bear
  Book, The* 196
Upton, Rosalie 200
US:
  short-lived firms:
  *c.*1907–14 26
  1914–20s 46
  1950s–80s 138
  late 1970s–80s 140
  stick bear 47

vacuuming 212
Vagabond Teddy 178
Velvet Bear 103
Verna Toys 81
  history of 229
Very Important Bear
  series 146
Vinyl character face:

Ideal *c.*1950s 86
Knickerbocker *c.*1955 77
voice boxes,
  modern 211
Volpp, Paul and
  Rosemary 6

Wagmee 56
Wagner, Florentine 197
Wallace Berrie and Co., *see*
  Berrie, Wallace and Co.
Walter, Wilhelmine 166
  history of 229
Walton, J. and M. 185
Wa Me 187
Waring, Phillipa and
  Peter 196
Warlow, Gerry 186
Warrington, Bonita 171
  washing 206
  disasters 202
  surface 213
wax nose 17
Way We Were

series 197
webbed claw 29
Weberpals, Hans 159
Wee Bunny Basil 177
Wee Woolie Bear 139
Wellings, Norah 199
  history of 229
Wendy Boston, *see*
  Boston, Wendy
While, Catherine M. 182
White, Bob 187
Wholesale Toy
  Company 11
Wilgoss, Sylvia R. 102
Williams, Sandy 192
Wilson, Jack 195
Winnie the Pooh 64
  collectables 199
Woolie Bear 139
Woolworths 130
World War I,
  effects of 10
World War II,
  effects of 11
Worldwide Expansion:
  post–1945 168
Worthing Toy Factory 12
  history of 229

Yes/No bear 42
  Hermann 1948–52 99
  Nisbet 1988 145
Yes/No clown 43
Yockey, Pat 191
Yogi Bear 169
Yomiko 149

Zodiac Bear 145
Zooby 128
Zoo Toy Company,
  history of 229
Zotty 111
  Minky 128
  sleeping 111
  type 97

ACKNOWLEDGMENTS

Author's Acknowledgments

I am more than grateful for the assistance, support, and advice of Rosemary and Paul Volpp, George Black, Colin and Wendy Lewis, Brian Beacock, the curatorial staff of the Bethnal Green Museum of Childhood (especially Halina Pasierbska and Caroline Goodfellow), Pam Hebbs, and Gerry and Margaret Grey, without whom this book would not have been possible.

I am indebted to the numerous arctophiles, teddy-bear manufacturers, and artists who allowed their bears to be photographed, and particularly to those who put their trust in the postal service and mailed their teddies from various corners of the globe to London. I am also grateful to those people who spared the time to help me track down bears or information for this mammoth project. To all of these listed below, I offer a huge, heartfelt "thank you": **Australia:** Jacki Brooks; Jenny Marchionni (The Camperdown Children's Hospital Fund); Nancy Evans; Marjory Fainges; Jenny Laing; Pat Lovelock; Pol McCann; Wendy McDonald (Jakas Soft Toys); Joan McPherson; Lynn Riddell-Robertson (Numbat Books); Romy Roeder; Jenny Round; Keith Schneider (Russ Berrie [Australia] Pty. Ltd.); Tomoko Sato; Carole Williams (Teddy & Friends: The Bear Essentials); Gerry Warlow; Bob White. **Austria:** Udo Broschek (Berg Tiere mit Herz GmbH); Dr. Filek-Wittinghausen (Austrian Chamber of Commerce); Kurt Klaritsch and K. Koritnik (Steiermark Chamber of Commerce). **Canada:** John Cox (Ganz Toys); Dillon Goldsmith (Mighty Star Ltd.); Marcella Pittana; Joan Rankin; Mrs. S. Stratton (Cuddly Toys Ltd.); Trudi Teneycke. **France:** Philippe Mangon (Anima); O. Blanchet (Créations Blanchet); Patricia Braunstein (Boulgom); Aline Cousin; Marcelle Goffin; Marylou Jouet; Manera J-Jacques (sarl Maxi Jouet); Christophe Couvreur (Nounours Group). **Germany:** Roland Spindler (Althans KG); Jürgen and Marianne Cieslik; Peter Clemens and Elke Untch (Hans Clemens GmbH); Margot Drolshagen and Mrs. G. Lee (Gebrüder Hermann KG); Rolf and Dr. Ursula Hermann (Hermann-Spielwaren GmbH); H. Dransfeld (Heunec Plüsch Spielwaren Fabrik KG); Marion Hohmann (Käthe Kruse Puppen GmbH); Sabine Zoller and Simone Schneider ("Sigikid", H. Scharrer & Koch GmbH); Jörg Junginger (Margarete Steiff GmbH); Klaus and Jutta Hartmann (Teddybären & Plüsch); Walter Schubert (W. Walter KG). **Republic of Ireland:** Mairead Donlevy (National Museum of Ireland); Joan Hanna; Audrey Harris; Jagoda Mansfield. **Italy:** Bibija Garella (Lenci srl); Giuseppe Patriarca (Trudi Giocattoli spa). **The Netherlands:** Dorothée Wennink (Association of Benelux Toy Manufacturers); Jane Humme; Jonette Stabbert. **New Zealand:** Peggy Armstrong; Clive and Precille Harrison (Bear with Us); Allie and Nigel Hanton; Janis Harris; Nancy Hay (Maxwell Hay & Co. Ltd.); Denise Jackson; Heather Lyell; Frances McLeary; Dawn Nicholl; Denise Parsons; Sally Pearson; Robin Rive (Robbity Bob Ltd.); Peter and Valda McCombe (Sheepskin Products Ltd.); Cathy Philips (Teddies & Treasures); Michael and Judy Walton. **Republic of South Africa:** Annwen Bates; George Allison (Bunjy Toys); Mary Kelly; Julian Pells (Prima Toys); G.A. and D.J. Weir (Speciality Manufacturers Division); Eunice Beaton (Thread Bears); Ken and Helen Wynne-Dyke. **Sweden:** Peter Pluntky; Agneta Thomson. **Switzerland:** Stephen Ernst; Stéphane Kaercher. **UK:** Margaret Jones (Alresford Crafts Ltd.); Paul Goble and Kim (Bears & Friends, Brighton); Kate Barringer; Valerie and Fred Lyle (Big Softies); Janice O'Dair (Bramwell Brown's Hug Shop); Deborah Canham; Maude and John Blackburn (Canterbury Bears Ltd.); Liz Carless; Marlene Couchman; Neil Miller and Michael Crane (The Dean's Company [1903]); Anna Dartnell; Gill Dutton; Faith Eaton Collection; Valerie (Especially Bears Shop); Mrs. Lawley (Golden Bear Products Ltd.); Katherine Grant; Jack Wilson (House of Nisbet); Pam Howells; Glenn and Irene Jackman (*Hugglets*); Staff of Imperial War Museum's Photographic Collection; Ray Jackson; Maddie Janes; Naomi Laight; Ben Lyford; Graham McBride (Little Folk); Deirdre Mackinnon; Felix Sear (Melrose Teddy Bear Museum); John Parkes and Oliver Holmes (Merrythought Ltd.); June Miller; Irene Moore; Jim Mulholland (Mulholland & Bailie Ltd.); Alan and Wendy Mullaney; Sue Nicoll; Belinda O'Brien; Anita Oliver; Eddie Owen; Ian Pout; Sue Quinn; John Radmall; Christina Revell; Sue Rixon; Pat Rush; Gwyneth Ashcroft and Curts Cooke (Russ Berrie [UK] Ltd.); Maureen and Alan Samuels; June Sanders; Sue Schoen; Ian Scott; Bunny Campione (Sotheby's); Judy and John Sparrow; Mr. and Mrs. Stubbs; C. A. Symon; Sylvia Coote (Teddy Bear Museum, Stratford-upon-Avon); Stacey Lee Terry; Rosemary Waterson; Coralie Wearing; Catherine While. **USA:** Art Husted; Alison Nielson and Julie Ruttenberg (Applause Inc.); Barbara Baldwin; Nick and Cassie Bisbikis; Loretta Botta; Ginger T. Brame; Sydney Charles; Audrey McFadden and Robyn Kutch (Dakin Inc.); Diane Gard; Shari J.K. Meltzer (Gund Inc.); Serieta Harrell; Marie Pamental (Hasbro Inc.); Dee Hockenberry; Linda Spiegel Lohre; Cindy Martin; Walter Meyer (Mary Meyer Corporation); Doris and Terry Michaud; Bev Miller; Joanne Mitchell; Linda Mullins; Barbara Isenberg and Bethany Pearlman (North American Bear Company Inc.); Russ Berrie & Company Inc; Sara Phillips; Carol-Lynn Rössel Waugh; Donna L. Saqui; Patricia Schoonmaker; Steve Schutt; Helen Sieverling; Barbara Sixby; Lisl Swinehart; Stephen Cronk (*Teddy Bear Review*); Susan Weiser; Susan Wiley.

I also wish to thank my editors, Irene and Helen, and designers Peter and Debbie for all their hard work and patience, particularly having to deal with an author 12,000 miles away; as well as photographer Peter for his tremendous skill and good humour throughout the many hours of "bear shoots".

Last but not least, I am deeply indebted to my mother Joan; my husband David; and friends Ruth Bottomley, Ruth Cornett, Janice Hunt, Ann and Jill Skinner, and Lynnet Wilson for all "bearing with me" throughout and keeping me sane. And to Medusa, who although tempted, did not chew up my text.

Publisher's Acknowledgments

DORLING KINDERSLEY WOULD LIKE TO THANK: Susie Behar, Polly Boyd, Lucinda Hawksley, Damien Moore, and Connie Novis for editorial assistance; Andrea Fair for keying-in the text; Sharon Moore for design assistance; Alastair Wardle and Adam Moore for computer support; Julia Pashley for picture research; Murdo Culver for organizing the transparencies; Michael Allaby for compiling the index; and Chris Elfes for additional photography in Australia.

PICTURE CREDITS

(Abbreviations: t=top, b=bottom, r=right, l=left, m=middle, c=centre.)

Photography by Peter Anderson: 1; 2; 3 c; 4 tr; 5 tl, bl, br; 9 br; 13 bl; **14 tr**; 15 b; 16; 17 bl; 21 tr; 23 tr; 25 br; 26; 29 tl, br; 30; 31 tr, bl, br; 33 tr, bl, br; 35 tl, bl; 37 tr; 41 tr, bl; 42; 45 tr; 49 bl, tr; 50–51 all; 53 tl, br; 54; 55 tr, bl, br; 56; 57 tl, bl; 61 tr, tl, bl; 63 tl, tr, bl; 64–65 all; 69 tl, tr, bl; 70; 71 br; 73 tl, bl, br; 74; 75 tl, tr bl; 76; 77 tl, bl; 78; 79 br; 83 tr, bl, br; 84; 85 tl, bl; 87 tl, bl, br; 88; 89 tl, br; 90; 91 tr, bl, br; 93 all; 95 tl, tr, bl; 96; 97 tr, bt 98; 99 tl, bl, br; 100–01 all; 103 tl, tr, br; 104; 105 tl, tr, br; 106; 107 tl, tr bl; 108; 109 tl, bl, br; 111 bl, br; 113 tl, tr, bl; 114; 115 tl; 117 tl, tr, bl; 118; 119 tl, tr; 121 tr, br; 123 all; 124–25 all; 126; 127 tl, tr, br; 129 br; 130; 131 tl, tr, bl; 133 tl, tr; 135 all; 136; 137 tr; 141 tl; 143 bl, br; 145 tl, tr, bl; 150; 151 tl, tr; 155 tl, br; 156; 157 tl, tr, br; 158; 159 tl, bl, br; 161 all; 163 tl, tr, bl; 164; 165 tl, bl; 166; 167 bl; 168; 169 br; 171 tr, bl; 173 bl, br; 177 bl, br; 178 tr, bl, br; 179 tl, bl; 180 tl, bl, br; 181 tr, bl, br; 182–83 all; 184 tl, tr, bl; 185 all; 186 br; 187 bl; 188 tm, m; 189 tl; 191 tl, ml, bl; 192 tl, bm, tr; 193 bl, cr, tr; 195 tr, cl; 196 tl, bl, cl; 197 tl, br, mr; 198 tl; 199 tr; 201 cl.

Photography by Jim Coit: 3 tl; 4 bl, br; 5 tr, ml; 6 ml; 7 bl; 8 r; 9 tl, tr; 10 br; 11 tr; 12 tl, mr, bl, tr, br; 13 tr, br; 14 bl; 15 tl; 17 tl, tr; 18; 19 tr; 21 tl, bl; 23 tl, bl; 24; 25 tr, bl; 27 all; 32; 33 tl; 34; 37 tl, bl; 39 bl; 40; 41 bl; 43 tl, tr; 44; 45 tl, bl, br; 46–47 all; 49 tl, br; 55 tl; 59 tl, tr; 62; 63 br; 67 tr; 71 tl, tr; 73 tr; 75 br; 77 br;

79 tl, bl; 82; 83 tl; 85 tl, br; 86; 89 bl; 91 tl; 95 br; 97 tl; 103 bl; 105 bl; 109 tr; 110; 111 tl, tr; 112; 115 tr, bl, br; 116; 117 br; 119 bl, br; 120 127 bl; 129 tl, tr, bl; 133 br; 137 tl, bl, br; 138; 139 tr, bl, br; 140; 141 tr, bl, br; 142; 143 tl, tr; 145 br; 146–47 all; 151 br; 153 all; 154; 155 bl, tr; 157 bl; 159 tr; 160; 163 br; 165 tr; 167 tl, tr, br; 169 tl, tr, bl; 172 all; 173 tl, tr; 174 all; 175 all; 176 tl, bl, br; 177 tl, tr; 178 tl; 184 br; 186 tl, tr, bl; 187 tr, br; 188 tl, tr; 189 ml; 190 bl; 192 bl, br; 194 bl; 195 tr, bl-all; 196 mr; 197; 198 bl; 199 bl; 200 bl, bm, br, tl br; 201 bl, bm, bl, tl.

Photography by Roland Kemp: 10 tl; 11 ml, br; 17 br; 19 tl, bl, br; 20; 21 br; 22; 23 br; 28; 29 br; 31 tl; 35 tr; 36; 37 br; 38 bl; 39 br; 48; 52; 53 bl; 57 tr, br; 59 bl; 60; 61 bl; 67 bl, br; 68; 69 br; 71 bl; 72; 79 br; 89 tr; 92; 97 bl; 102; 107 br; 110; 113 br; 122; 128; 139 tl; 151 bl; 152; 171 tl; 179 tr, br; 180; 188 b; 198 tr, br; 199 tl.

Additional photography: Courtesy of Asquiths of Windsor 195 tl. Courtesy of Christie's 94 tr. Courtesy of Sotheby's 194 tl. Courtesy of the Trustees of the V&A, photographed by Pip Barnard: 38 bl; 41 tl; 43 bl; 99 tl; 131 br; 133 bl; 134; 144; 162. Chris Elfes (Australia): 58; 59 br; 80–81 all. Linda Mullins 191 tr. Private collection 13 tl. Matthew Ward 170. Paul Volpp 21 bl; 87 tl; 132.
Bear Care and Repair: 202–03 main bear Peter Anderson, others Jim Coit, Roland Kemp, Matthew Ward; 204–07 Peter Anderson, Matthew Ward, Roland Kemp; 208–09 Peter Anderson, Matthew Ward; 210–11 Peter Anderson, Matthew Ward, Roland Kemp; 212–13 Peter Anderson, Matthew Ward; 214 Jim Coit, Paul Volpp, Peter Anderson, Matthew Ward.

Library usage: 8 bl Mary Evans Picture Library; 8 bc T. Roosevelt Collection/ Harvard College Library; 10 Imperial War Museum; 11 Hulton Picture Company; 190 Rex Features; 169 tr ©1992 Hanna-Barbera Productions, Inc., licensed by Copyright Promotions Ltd. – Yogi 170

Factory archive material: 38–39 Margarete Steiff GmbH; 3 bl, 66–67 Merrythought Ltd; 94–95 Hermann-Spielwaren GmbH; Gebrüder Hermann KG; 148–49 Russ Berrie & Co. Inc.

BEAR CREDITS

- MRS. BAKER 202 br.
- KATE BARRINGER 23 tr.
- BRIAN BEACOCK 5 br; 65 br; 73 bl; 83 bl; 107 bl; 129 br; 156; 161 bl; 166; 188 c; 212; 213.
- RUSS BERRIE & COMPANY INC UK 170.
- BETHNAL GREEN MUSEUM OF CHILDHOOD (V&A) 38 bl; 41 tl; 43 bl; 99 tr; 131 br; 133 bl; 134; 144; 162.
- NICK BISBIKIS JNR. 85 bl; 119 tr.
- HEATHER BISCHOFF 29 bl.
- GEORGE B. BLACK JNR. 77 bl.
- GYLES BRANDRETH 17 br; 20; 21 br; 79 tr; 102; 179 tr; 198 br.
- BUNJY TOYS 169 br.
- GINA CAMPBELL 121 bl.
- CANTERBURY BEARS 5, 151 tl, bl.
- SYDNEY R. CHARLES 25 br; 26; 75 tl, tr, bl; 38 bl; 91 br; 97 bl; 107 br; 115 tl; 117 bl.
- JOAN COCKRILL 212 br.
- PAULINE COCKRILL 57 br; 157 br; 189 tl.
- MARLENE COUCHMAN 103 tl, tr; 159 tl.
- ANNA DARTNELL 157 tr.
- GILL DELLA CASA 212 CR; 214 br.
- FAITH EATON COLLECTION 31 tl; 165 br.
- NANCY EVANS 59 bl.
- PAUL GOBLE (BEARS & FRIENDS, BRIGHTON) 13 bl.
- JO GREENE 204.
- MARGARET & GERRY GREY 56; 106; 108; 183 br; 192 tr.
- GUND INC. 85 tl, br.
- AUDREY HARRIS 159 br.
- KARIN HELLER 161 br.
- GEBRÜDER HERMANN 5 c; 31 bl, br; 95 tl; 97 br; 190 br.
- PAM HEBBS 9 br; 16; 19 bl, br; 22; 23 br; 33 bl; 36; 39 br; 42; 48; 63 tl, bl; 73 tl; 103 br; 118; 130 tr; 135 bl; 177 bl, br; 178 tr, br; 186 br; 188 c; 191 tl, cl; 198 tr.
- HERMANN-SPIELWAREN 4 c; 10 tr; 30; 31 tl; 95 tl; 99 tl, bl. br.
- RAY JACKSON 124 tl.
- LEVER BROTHERS Snuggle courtesy of Lever Brothers Company 139 br.
- COLIN & WENDY LEWIS 1; 2; 4 tl; 5 bl; 11 tr; 14 tr; 15 b; 21 tr; 29 br; 33 tr, br; 37 tr; 41 tr; 49 tr; 50 tl; 53 tl, tr, br;

54; 55 tr, bl; 57 bl; 61 tl, tr, bl; 63 tr; 64; 65 tl, tr, bl; 69 tl, tr, bl; 70; 78; 88; 89 tl; 90; 91 tr; 93 all; 96; 97 tr; 101 tr, bl, br; 105 tl, tr, bl; 107 tl, tr; 109 tl, br; 111 bl; 113 tl, tr, bl; 114; 117 tl; 124; 125 bl, br; 127 tl, tr, br; 130; 131 tl, bl; 132 tr; 135 tl; 155 tl; 163 tl; 171 tr; 180 tl, bl, br; 181 bl; 182 tl, bl, br; 192 tl; 192 cb; 193 cr, bl; 214 c; 234; 239.
- GILLIAN LISTER 11 tl.
- BEN LYFORD 136; 210.
- DEIRDRE MACKINNON 17 bl; 55 br.
- MERRYTHOUGHT LTD. 67 br; 121 tr, br.
- JUNE MILLER 123 tr, bl, br.
- CAREY MINHINNETT 104.
- BELINDA O'BRIEN 89 br.
- MRS. PEARCE 202 tr.
- IAN POUT 19 tr; 43 br; 69 br; 89 tr; 113 br.
- PRIVATE COLLECTION 35 br; 71 bl; 92, 139 tl; 152; 171 tl; 181 tl.
- JOHN RADMALL 10 tl; 51 br; 91 bl.
- CHRISTINA REVELL 109 bl.
- ROMY ROEDER 58; 59 br; 80-81.
- MR. & MRS. SAMUELS 135 tr; 143 bl; 145 tl, bl; 150; 161 tl; 163 tr, bl; 181 br; 195 cl; 196 tl; 197 cr; 199 tr; 203 bl; 214 tr.
- JUNE SANDERS 51 bl.
- FELIX SEAR 50, 73.
- KIOK SIEM 37 br.
- HELEN SIEVERLING 35 tl; 76; 77 tl; 83 br; 84; 85 tr; 87 tr, bl, br; 98; 198 tl.
- ANN SKINNER 159 bl.
- JILL SKINNER 132.
- JUDY SPARROW 10 tl; 11 br; 28; 52; 53 br; 57 tr; 60; 61 br; 67 bl; 68; 71 br; 72; 121 tl; 123 tl; 125 tr; 128; 135 br; 199 tr; 203 br; 214 tr.
- LINDA SPIEGEL LOHRE 79 br.
- MR. & MRS. STUBBS 45 tr.
- SUDBURY HALL MUSEUM OF CHILDHOOD 29 tl.
- C.A. SYMON 158
- TEDDY BEAR MUSEUM OF NAPLES, FLORIDA 74; 83 tr; 95 bl; 100; 101 tl; 117 tl; 119 tl; 126; 137 tr; 141 tl; 151 tr; 155 br; 157 tl; 164; 165 tl, bl; 167 bl; 168; 171 bl, br; 173 bl, br; 176 tr; 177 bl; 178 tr, br; 191 tl, cl.
- PAUL & ROSEMARY VOLPP 3 tl; 4 tl, bl, br; 5 tr, cl; 6; 7; 8 r; 9 tl; 10 br; 11 tr; 12 all; 13 tr, bl; 14 br; 15 tl; 17 tl, tr; 18; 19

t.r; 21 tl, bl; 23 tl, tr, bl; 24; 25 tl, tr, bl; 27 all; 32; 33 tl; 34; 37 tl, bl; 39 bl; 40, bl, br; 41 bl, br; 43 tl, tr; 44; 45 tl, bl, br; 46; 47 all; 49 tl, br; 55 tl; 59 tl, tr; 62; 63 br; 67 tr; 71 tl, tr; 73 tr; 75 br; 77 tr, br; 79 tl, bl; 82; 83 tl; 86; 87 tl; 89 tl; 91 tl; 95 tl; 97 tl; 103 bl; 105 bl; 109 tr; 110; 111 tl, tr; 112; 115 tr, bl, br; 116; 117 br; 119 bl, br; 120; 127 bl; 129 tl, tr, bl; 133 br; 137 tl, bl; 138; 139 tr, bl, br; 140; 141 tr, bl, br; 142; 143 tl, tr; 145 br; 146–47; 151 br; 153 all; 154, tr, bl; 155 bl; 157 bl; 159 tr; 160; 163 br; 165 tl, tr, br; 169 tl, tr, bl; 172 all; 173 tl, tr; 174–75 all; 176 tl, bl, br; 177 tl, tr; 178 tl; 184 br; 186 tl, tr, bl; 187 tr; 188 tl, tr; 189 c; 190 bl; 192 bl, br; 194 bl; 195 tr, br; 196 tr, cr; 197; 198 bl; 199 bl, tl; 200; 201; 202 tl; 203 c; 214 bl; 236; 237; 238.
- WALSHAW & CO. 205.
- PENELOPE WARTON 212.
- CORALIE WEARING 35 bl.
- ANNA WHITE 161 tr.
- LISA WHITE 133 tl.
- ANKIE WILD, RIBCHESTER MUSEUM OF CHILDHOOD 193 tl.
- LYNNET WILSON 122.

- BEAR ARTISTS
Deborah Canham 182 tr.
Aline Cousin-Debrowolska 184 tr.
Marcelle Goffin 184 tl.
Joan Hanna 183 tr.
Allie & Nigel Hanton 185 br.
Janis Harris 185 tr.
Marylou Jouet 184 bl.
Mary Kelly 187 bl.
Frances McLeary 185 bl.
Irene Moore 183 tl.
Alan and Wendy Mullaney 181 tr.
Eddie Owen 179 bl
Joan Rankin 179 tl.
Jenny Round 187 tl.
Jonette Stabbert 183 bl.
Trudy Teneycke 178 br
Michael & Judy Walton 185 tl.

Every effort has been made to acknowledge bear-owners and copyright-holders. Dorling Kindersley apologizes for any omissions and will be pleased to rectify such cases in future editions.

The DORLING KINDERSLEY
ENCYCLOPEDIA
of
FISHING

The DORLING KINDERSLEY
ENCYCLOPEDIA
of
FISHING

COVENT
GARDEN
BOOKS

Devised, designed, and
edited for Dorling Kindersley
by Bookbourne Limited
The Old Farmhouse
Newton, Sleaford
Lincs NG34 0DT
Editor: Ian Wood
Art Editor: Steve Leaning
Designer: Stuart John
Fish Species Illustrator:
Colin Newman

Managing Editor:
Krystyna Mayer
Managing Art Editor:
Derek Coombes
Production Controller:
Antony Heller

Contributors: Peter Gathercole,
Trevor Housby, Dennis Moss,
Bruce Vaughan, Phill Williams

First Published in Great
Britain in 1994 by
Dorling Kindersley Limited,
80 Strand,
Loudon WC2R ORL

Copyright © 1994 Dorling
Kindersley Limited, London

www.dk.com

This 2000 edition
Published by Covent
Garden Books.

All rights reserved. No part of
this publication may be
reproduced, stored in a
retrieval system, or transmitted
in any form or by any means,
electronic, mechanical,
photocopying, recording or
otherwise, without the prior
written permission of the
copyright owner.

A CIP catalogue record for
this book is available
from the British Library

ISBN 0 7513 0085 3

Typeset by Ace Filmsetting
Limited, Somerset
Reproduced by J. Film
Process, Singapore
Printed and bound in China
by L.Rex Printing Co. Ltd

CONTENTS

Foreword   6

Introduction   7

TACKLE

Basic Tackle   12
  The Rod   14
    Spinning Rods   16
    Leger Rods   18
    Float Rods   20
    Fly Rods   22
    Poles & Whips   26
    Boat Rods   28
    Shore Rods   30
    The Reel   32
    Fixed-spool Reels   34
    Closed-face Reels   38
    Baitcasting Reels   40
    Fly Reels   42
    Boat Reels   46
    Shore Reels   48
  Lines, Crimps, Beads, &
    Swivels   50
  Fly Lines & Leaders   52
  Hooks   54
  Freshwater Weights   58
  Saltwater Weights & Booms   60
Floats   62
Bite Indicators & Rod Rests   64
Landing Tackle   66
Tackle Boxes   68
Footwear   70
Vests & Jackets   72
Waterproofs   74
Hats, Gloves, & Sunglasses   76
Accessories   78

BAIT

Freshwater Naturals   82
Freshwater Processed Baits   84
Freshwater Groundbait   86
Spinners & Spoons   88
Plugs   90
Saltwater Naturals   92
Saltwater Groundbait   94
Saltwater Lures   96

THE FLY

The Naturals   100
The Artificial Fly   104
Fly Tying Equipment   106
Fly Tying Basics   108
Dry Flies   112
Wet Flies   114
Nymphs   116
Salmon & Steelhead Flies   118
Streamers & Hairwings   120

SPECIES

Anatomy — 124

FRESHWATER FISH

Black Bass — 126
Bluegill, Crappies,
  Pumpkinseed, & Sunfish — 128
Barbel, Tench, & Asp — 130
Bream, Nase, & Vimba — 132
Carp — 134
Chub, Dace, Roach, & Rudd — 136
Pike, Pickerel, &
  Muskellunge — 138
Bullhead — 140
Freshwater Catfish — 142
Bass & Murray Cod — 144
Australian Perch & Grunters — 146
Perch, Sauger, Walleye, &
  Zander — 148
Char — 150
Salmon — 152
Trout — 154
Whitefish & Grayling — 156

SALTWATER FISH

Bonefish, Bluefish, & Tarpon — 158
Eels — 160
Sea Catfish & Barracuda — 162
Amberjack & Jack — 164
Pompano, Jackmackerel, &
  Roosterfish — 166
Cobia, Snook, & Barramundi — 168
Surfperch — 170
Cod, Hake, Ling, & Burbot — 172
Billfish & Swordfish — 174
Wrasse & Dolphinfish — 176

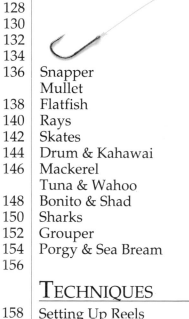

Snapper — 178
Mullet — 180
Flatfish — 182
Rays — 184
Skates — 186
Drum & Kahawai — 188
Mackerel — 190
Tuna & Wahoo — 192
Bonito & Shad — 194
Sharks — 196
Grouper — 200
Porgy & Sea Bream — 202

TECHNIQUES

Setting Up Reels — 206
Basic Knots — 208

FRESHWATER FISHING

Playing & Landing — 210
Basic Casting — 212
Lure Fishing – Spinning — 214
Lure Fishing – Spoons — 216
Lure Fishing – Plugs — 218
Legering — 220
Float Fishing — 222
Pole Fishing — 226
Trolling — 230

FLY FISHING

The Overhead Cast — 232
The Roll Cast — 234
Wet-fly Fishing — 236
Dry-fly Fishing — 238
Nymph Fishing — 240
Boat Fly Fishing — 242

SALTWATER FISHING

Inshore Fishing — 244
Offshore Fishing — 246
Wreck Fishing — 248
Surfcasting — 250
Shore Fishing — 252
Shark Fishing — 256
Big-game Fishing — 258

THE WATER

Streams & Rivers — 262
Stillwaters — 266
Shorelines — 270
Estuaries — 272
Offshore Temperate Waters — 274
Offshore Tropical Waters — 276
Conservation — 278

APPENDICES

Glossary — 280
Index — 283
Index of Scientific Names — 287
Acknowledgments & Credits — 288

FOREWORD

TREVOR HOUSBY
This book is dedicated to the memory of Trevor Housby, who died in August 1993, shortly before it was completed.
Trevor was the most knowledgeable and versatile fisherman I have ever known. During a colourful career spanning 35 years he penned over 40 books and took thousands of photographs. In addition to being a big-game specialist of international repute, with record blue marlin, blue shark, whitetip shark, white marlin, and wahoo to his credit, he gave fly fishermen the Dog Nobbler lure and was angling consultant to many tourist boards and several airlines. He was truly a giant among men, and will be sadly missed.
John Wilson, August 1993

One of the great things about fishing is that you never stop learning. What catches fish today seldom catches fish tomorrow, so to be consistently successful as an angler you must be prepared to watch, learn, and improve on your techniques at all times. You will also get more out of the sport if you are prepared to try different techniques and styles of fishing to those you already practise. Maybe you only fish a river or a sandy beach now, but as time goes by, your angling horizons will broaden and fishing that appears to be an impossibility today may become reality in the future. In addition, by exploring different aspects of the sport, you will increase your knowledge and enjoyment of it dramatically.

One of the finest ways of broadening your angling horizons is by reading – angling magazines and books contain a wealth of information just waiting to be tapped. Most, however, specialize in particular forms of angling, and to find a book that deals with every major aspect of the sport within its covers is rare. *The Dorling Kindersley Encyclopedia of Fishing* is one of those rarities, a magical volume that gives information about fish species, types of tackle, baits, techniques, in fact everything an angler could wish to know.

This is a hundred angling books rolled into one, and beautifully illustrated with photographs and accurate, full-colour artwork. Essential reading for any angler, it is a book that will spend little time on the shelf.

TREVOR HOUSBY

INTRODUCTION

The development of angling techniques and tackle is a story of continuing advance, from the early days of simple fixed-line rods to the invention of the reel, and from then to the ever-improving modern tackle and methods of using it. This book describes typical examples of the latest rods, reels, and other essential items of tackle, tells you what baits to use in freshwater and in the sea, explains the basics of fly tying, and illustrates typical examples of the major categories of artificial fly. It also describes the major freshwater and marine fish species – which are depicted in beautiful full-colour drawings – tells you how to catch them, and explains the secrets of "reading the water" to find out where the fish are.

ANCIENT SPORT
The tranquillity of freshwater angling is evoked by this old woodcut, which depicts an angler sitting at the edge of the water in the quiet early morning.

PEACOCK QUILL
Peacock quill is one of the many natural and synthetic materials that are used in the tying of artificial flies.

TACKLE

Good-quality tackle is as important to an angler as a well-tuned instrument is to a musician: the limits to your angling performance should be determined by your ability, not by any inadequacy of your tackle. This comprehensive chapter gives examples of the vast range of tackle on the market, discusses their advantages and disadvantages, and gives guidance on choosing basic outfits.

BAITS

You can have the best rods, reels, lines, and hooks in the world, but you will never catch fish unless you have good baits and know how to use them. This chapter tells you how to choose and use natural and processed baits for freshwater fishing, and how to mix and use

SEA FISHING
Saltwater anglers fish from beaches, rocks, piers, and harbour walls, and from private and charter boats. Here, anglers and crews are busy loading tackle, bait, and other supplies onto charter boats before setting off for a day's fishing.

freshwater groundbait. It describes the main types of artificial bait, including spinners, spoons, and plugs, and concludes with practical advice on the use of natural baits, groundbait, and lures in saltwater fishing. Flies, whether the natural insects or artificial patterns, are also baits, but because of their complexity they are described separately, in the following chapter.

THE FLY

Fly fishing is one of the oldest forms of angling, and is known to have been practised in Macedonia as early as the 3rd century AD. Its age, complexity, and subtlety, and the fact that fishing on many of the best salmon and trout waters is beyond the financial reach of most anglers, have given it enormous prestige. But there is no doubt that catching a good-sized fish on an artificial fly, especially a fly that you have tied yourself, is an immensely rewarding experience. This experience is now available to everyone, thanks to the extensive stocking of reservoirs and other public waters with popular gamefish species such as brown trout and rainbow trout.

This chapter describes the natural insects that form an important part of the diet of salmon, trout, bass, and other gamefish and also discusses and illustrates the different types of artificial fly, how they are tied, and how they are used.

BOAT FISHING
Fishing from a small boat, whether on a stillwater or a large river, allows you to cover water that is beyond the casting range of anglers fishing from the bank or wading in the shallow margins.

SURFCASTING
Surf beaches are often exciting and very productive fishing venues. This angler is wading in the surf of Inch Beach, in County Kerry, Ireland, a wild Atlantic beach that is noted for its excellent bass fishing.

SPECIES

There are thousands upon thousands of different fish species in the world, of which comparatively few are sought by anglers. But even this small minority of species is numbered in hundreds, and this chapter describes nearly 250 of them, from little freshwater fish such as dace and sunfish to ocean giants such as marlin and tuna. Each species is accurately illustrated in full colour to make identification easy, and the accompanying text gives details of distribution, habitat, food, and size, and suggests techniques, tackle, and bait for catching them. The basic anatomy of fish is also described, with cutaway drawings to indicate the principal internal organs and the basic skeletal structure. The main differences between bony fish and cartilaginous fish are described, and there are details of important features such as types of scale, the functions of the lateral line, and how fish "breathe" with their gills.

WILD TROUT
Wild trout, such as these fine browns, tend to be warier and wilier than their hatchery-bred cousins, and can therefore be much harder to catch.

TECHNIQUES

In general, there is no single, foolproof method of catching a particular species in a particular water at any given time, and experienced anglers need little encouragement to argue for hours over the best technique to use. However, such arguments are usually about variations on the basic techniques and tackle rigs, and you need to learn these before you can begin to modify them in the light of personal experience and preference. In this chapter, you will find concise, easy-to-follow descriptions of a wide range of angling techniques, from pole fishing to big-game fishing.

THE WATER

There is a lot more to successful angling than acquiring the right tackle and learning how to use it. The best anglers are also good naturalists, who learn the habits of fish, and study currents, tidal flows, bankside vegetation, submerged weeds, the underwater topography,

and a host of other natural and artificial underwater features that indicate where the fish are likely to be and what they will be feeding on. You can build up an enormous store of useful knowledge while you are fishing, simply by observing what is going on in and around the water, and noting how the movements and feeding habits of the fish vary with the time of day, the weather, and the light conditions. If you are a freshwater angler, studying your favourite fishing water during the closed season will help you to understand it better, and provide you with information that can be put to good use when the next season opens. This chapter gives an insight into the underwater world and its inhabitants, and tells you how to find the best fishing spots.

LURES
Fishing with artificial lures, such as plugs and spinners, is an effective and enjoyable way to catch pike, perch, bass, and other predatory species.

HANDLING FISH
Always handle fish with care, and return them promptly to the water if you are not keeping them for the table. Hold them securely but gently, and remove hooks carefully to minimize damage. When returning them, support them in the water until they have recovered their strength and are ready to swim off. Never leave discarded hooks, line, or other tackle on the bank or shore or in the water, where they will be a danger to birds and other forms of wildlife.

READING THE WATER
Experienced anglers who spend time studying the water in which they fish can read it like a map. They know where the fish are likely to be at a particular time, and can therefore usually avoid the frustration of fishing an unproductive stretch of water.

TACKLE

THE PRODUCTION OF FISHING TACKLE is one of the world's oldest industries, one that can trace its origins back to prehistoric times. The earliest known fishing implements were harpoons, and small lengths of bone, antler, stone, or shell, pointed at each end, that were concealed within bait and fished on handlines. These were in use in Asia Minor during the Middle Stone Age (*c* 12,000 to 9000 BC), and the first curved fish hooks, made of bone, appeared towards the end of that period. The first metal hooks, made of copper, were produced about 5000 BC, and since then the development of hooks has continued alongside that of metallurgy. The production of rods and reels is also an ancient craft. The Macedonians were using short rods to fish simple flies by the 3rd century AD, and the Chinese were probably using rod-and-reel combinations at around the same time.

Today, the manufacture of fishing tackle is a diverse, worldwide, and innovative industry, and its products are under continuous development. New styles and trends in angling are quickly catered for, and tackle manufacturers are among the first to exploit new alloys and composite materials. This chapter describes typical examples of the vast range of tackle now available to anglers, but these are of necessity just a small sample.

TACKLE CHOICE
Good-quality, well-balanced tackle is a pleasure to use and will improve your chances of landing a good catch.

BASIC TACKLE

When you are buying a basic outfit, always remember that having expensive tackle will not in itself guarantee that you will catch large numbers of fish. Additionally, if you are a newcomer to the sport, it is unlikely that you will be able to realize the full potential of your tackle anyway. It is far better to begin with a reliable but inexpensive outfit, and upgrade it as your angling skills develop.

SALTWATER FISHING

In shore fishing, especially from a beach, the ability to cast long distances is important, but do not be misled into thinking that distance casting with high-performance tackle catches all the fish. Many species move into very shallow water, and if a beach slopes steeply, deep, fish-holding water may be quite close to the shore and easily covered with an inexpensive, relatively soft-actioned rod. For boat work, there is no single outfit that will cover every eventuality. For example, you cannot fish uptide with a basic boat rod, and a supple-tipped uptide rod cannot cope with the rigours of wreck fishing. Buy tackle appropriate to your intended style of fishing.

Shore fishing
In general, fishing from rocks or piers calls for less casting than fishing from an open beach, so the rods used need not be quite as refined in their design. What is needed is strong, reliable tackle, for beating heavy ground and subduing large fish from positions where your freedom of movement is restricted. This means having an outfit with plenty of backbone for pulling free from snags, steering fish away from obstacles, and lifting fish from the water with the rod. Comparatively short rods, well-made reels with high gear ratios, and strong, abrasion-resistant lines form the basis of shore-fishing kit.

Beach fishing
Because most beaches slope relatively gently, the deep, fish-holding water is usually further out than is the case on a rocky shore, and there is more need to place the baits a long way out. As a result, beach fishing tackle is generally lighter and more suited to distance casting than that used for rocky-shore fishing, but it should also be strong enough to deal with mixed or broken ground. However, rods designed primarily for casting are very stiff and demand a high level of skill, so until you have acquired that skill, use softer tackle that matches your ability, and fish close in for shallow-water species.

Boat fishing
To get the most out of boat fishing, you need at least two different rods plus suitable reels. The first rod should be a 2.1 m (7 ft), 13.6 kg (30 lb) class boat rod which, although too heavy for some aspects of boat work and a shade too light for others, will cope with most situations. The second, for general uptiding, should be a 2.7 to 3 m (9 to 10 ft) rod able to cast weights of up to 227 g (8 oz). In addition to these, it is worth having a 5.4 kg (12 lb) class boat rod or a 57 to 113 g (2 to 4 oz) uptider for light inshore work, or a 22.7 kg (50 lb) class boat rod for deep water work and wreck fishing.

Big-game fishing
Big-game fishing is not a cheap pursuit, and specialist big-game tackle is expensive. However, most big-game charter boats will provide the tackle if required, and standard boat and uptiding tackle can be used when drift fishing for the smaller big-game species. Trolling requires a short, stiff rod to set the hook, and a heavy-duty reel with a smooth-acting drag mechanism (preferably a lever drag) and a large line capacity. A 13.6 to 22.7 kg (30 to 50 lb) class standup rod, with a 30- to 50-class lever drag reel, is adequate for all but the largest fish, for which 36.3 or 59 kg (80 or 130 lb) class tackle is advisable.

SHORE TACKLE
Rod: 3.4 m (11 ft) beach.
Reel: multiplier with two retrieve speeds.
Line: 9.1 to 18.1 kg (20 to 40 lb) mono.
Hooks: Mustad, in sizes from 1 to 8/0.
Terminal tackle: disposable sinkers, small bombs, drilled bullets; 13.6 to 27.2 kg (30 to 60 lb) trace mono; strong swivels; beads; standoff booms; line stops; slider floats.
Landing tackle: wherever access allows, use a gaff. When fishing a vertical drop, take a drop net.
Bait: crab, mackerel, squid, and worms.

BEACH TACKLE
Rod: 3.7 m (12 ft) beach.
Reel: multiplier or large-capacity fixed-spool.
Line: 5.4 to 8.2 kg (12 to 18 lb) mono.
Hooks: Aberdeens, in sizes 1 to 4/0.
Terminal tackle: wired and plain bombs weighing from 57 to 170 g (2 to 6 oz); shock leader mono to 31.8 kg (70 lb); 9.1 to 18.1 kg (20 to 40 lb) trace mono; oval split rings; bait clips or impact shields; swivels; beads; line stops; standoff booms.
Landing tackle: landing net or gaff.
Bait: crab, mackerel, squid, and worms.

BOAT TACKLE
Rods: a 2.1 m (7 ft), 13.6 kg (30 lb) class boat rod, and a 2.7 to 3 m (9 to 10 ft) uptide rod able to cast weights of up to 227 g (8 oz).
Reels: multipliers.
Line: 8.2 to 22.7 kg (18 to 50 lb) mono.
Hooks: Mustad or uptide, in sizes from 1 to 8/0.
Terminal tackle: selection of sinkers; 18.1 to 27.2 kg (40 to 60 lb) trace mono; strong swivels; beads; selection of standoff booms.
Landing tackle: charter boats usually provide this.
Bait: crab, mackerel, squid, worms; mackerel feathers or Hokkai lures.

BIG-GAME TACKLE
Rod: 13.6 to 22.7 kg (30 to 50 lb) class standup.
Reel: lever-drag multiplier, 30- to 50-class.
Line: 13.6 to 22.7 kg (30 to 50 lb) big game.
Hooks: forged hooks rigged with lures; wide-gape livebait hooks.
Terminal tackle: 45.4 to 91 kg (100 to 200 lb) mono and braided wire traces; crimps; link swivels.
Landing tackle: the boat will supply this.
Bait: range of suitably rigged trolling lures to suit species sought; live and dead baits caught from or supplied by the boat.

FRESHWATER FISHING

The species of fish that live in freshwater are many and various, and many different methods of catching them have been developed. Some, particularly the non-predatory species, are fished for with natural or processed baits. These baits are sometimes fished on a freeline – the most natural presentation of all – but more usually they are presented beneath a float or on a weighted line that takes them down to the river or lake bottom. Predatory species can be fished for with natural baits, but they will also take artificial baits, or lures. Lures are very effective, and they have the added advantage of being more convenient to use than natural baits. Some are designed to imitate the prey of particular species, others simply to trigger the predators' aggressive instincts, and these principles are also used in the creation of artificial fly patterns. Trout, salmon, and many other freshwater species are taken by fly fishing, which is claimed by its countless devotees to be one of the most enjoyable of all forms of angling.

Lure fishing

Lure fishing is the pursuit of predatory species by casting and retrieving artificial baits, or lures, and it is the action of the lure on the retrieve that makes it attractive to fish. When lures are fished with a multiplying reel, the technique is known as baitcasting; when a fixed-spool or spincasting reel is used, it is known as spinning. Whichever type of reel is used, its slipping clutch or drag mechanism must be smooth running, and the rod must be fitted with ceramic guides to prevent wear: several thousand casts may be made in the course of a single lure-fishing session.

Lure-fishing rods include some of the shortest used in angling, and an ultralight baitcasting rod can be as short as 1.4 m (4½ ft). These little rods are ideal for use in confined areas, for example where dense bankside vegetation and overhanging trees make casting with a long rod difficult or impossible.

Bait fishing

In freshwater, almost all fishing with natural or processed baits is done with float or leger tackle. Floats are undoubtedly the most sensitive devices there are for detecting bites, and just about every species of freshwater fish can be caught on some form of float rig.

Floats consist of two basic types: those attached to the line by the top and the bottom and designed mainly for river work, and those attached by the bottom end only, which can be used on both still and moving water.

In legering, baits are presented on the bottom of the river or lake, anchored by a weight or weights attached to the line. Although it is not as sensitive as float fishing, legering is a very good method of presenting baits to bottom-feeding fish, and it is often more effective than float fishing, for instance when fishing in swiftly flowing streams or at extreme range on large stillwaters.

Pole fishing

In pole fishing there is no reel: the line is attached to the pole tip either directly or via a length of shock-absorbing elastic. Because there is no running line, control of the terminal tackle is very precise. Fishing with a pole is one of the oldest forms of angling, and poles were in use for centuries before the reel was invented. The traditional cane pole is still around, but pole technology was revolutionized by the introduction of glass fibre poles in the 1960s. These have since been largely replaced by carbon fibre poles, either telescopic or take-apart, which are extremely light and strong, and easy to handle despite being anything up to 17 m (56 ft) in length.

Poles are always fished in conjunction with floats, and because they are most often used to catch small fish, a great variety of small and highly sensitive pole floats have been developed to show up the most delicate of bites.

Fly fishing

Many species can be taken on an artificial fly, but most freshwater fly fishing is for the members of the salmon family and for largemouth and smallmouth bass.

The main categories of artificial fly are dry flies, wet flies, and nymphs. Dry flies are fished on the surface of the water, while wet flies and nymphs are fished submerged. Dry-fly fishing is probably the most visually exciting way to catch trout and salmon, but its use is restricted to the warm months of the year, when the fish are feeding on insects at or near the surface.

The most important skill you need for successful fly fishing is an ability to cast well, and the best way to learn casting is to take lessons from a properly qualified instructor. Casting a fly is enjoyable in itself, and it is worth learning how to do it properly in a variety of styles to suit different weather and water conditions.

LURE TACKLE
Rod: 2.1 to 2.7 m (7 to 9 ft) spinning rod with a medium to stiff action.
Reel: fixed-spool or small multiplier.
Line: 3.6 to 4.54 kg (8 to 10 lb) mono.
Hooks: already on lures (usually trebles).
Terminal tackle: wire traces; swivels; anti-kink vanes; weights for fishing buoyant baits just off bottom in snaggy waters.
Landing tackle: Gye-type net, or glove for lifting out sharp-toothed species.
Bait: spinners, spoons, and plugs to suit quarry.

BAIT TACKLE
Rod: 3.7 m (12 ft) float or 3 m (10 ft) leger; or a 3.4 m (11 ft) Avon rod for both float fishing and legering.
Reel: fixed-spool.
Line: 1.36 kg (3 lb) mono for float fishing, 2.7 kg (6 lb) mono for legering.
Hooks: sizes 12 to 26 for float fishing, sizes 2 to 12 for legering.
Terminal tackle: split shot; swimfeeders and weights for legering; selection of stick, waggler, and loafer floats for float fishing.
Landing tackle: net.
Bait: maggots, casters, bread, worms, hempseed.

POLE TACKLE
Pole: carbon fibre, about 5 to 7 m (16 to 23 ft) long.
Line: mono, 227 to 340 g (8 to 12 oz) for very small fish, stronger pro rata for bigger, heavier species.
Hooks: spade-ended, in sizes 16 to 26 fine-wire for small fish, and sizes 10 to 16 medium-wire for larger fish.
Terminal tackle: bristle, bung, and quill floats; split shot; olivettes; selection of ready-made rigs.
Landing tackle: fine-mesh pan net with a long but stiff telescopic handle.
Bait: maggots, bloodworms, bread, hempseed.

FLY TACKLE
Rod: 3 m (10 ft), #6/7 medium-action fly rod.
Reel: lightweight fly reel taking a #6/7 line and 46 m (50 yds) backing.
Fly lines: floating, neutral density, medium-sinking, fast-sinking.
Leaders: 910 g to 2.27 kg (2 to 5 lb) for dry fly, 2.7 kg (6 lb) for wet fly, 3.2 to 5.4 kg (7 to 12 lb) for lures.
Landing tackle: folding or Gye-type net.
Flies: selection of dry, wet, nymph, and lure patterns to suit species sought, style of fishing, water conditions, and season.

THE ROD

Until the middle of the 19th century, rods were made of woods such as hazel, ash, hickory, and greenheart, but in the 1840s both William Blacker in England and Samuel Phillippe in Pennsylvania began fashioning rods from split cane, which is bamboo split lengthwise into strips and glued together. Split cane rods proved lighter, more flexible, and more durable than wooden rods, and cane was to remain the most popular rod material for over a hundred years. It is still used today for expensive, hand-built fly rods, but since the late 1940s its use has rapidly declined in the face of strong competition from man-made materials. Tubular steel and aluminium were its first challengers, but were quickly superseded by glass fibre, itself now eclipsed by even newer materials, including boron, Kevlar, and, most successful of all, carbon fibre (graphite).

ROD COMPONENTS

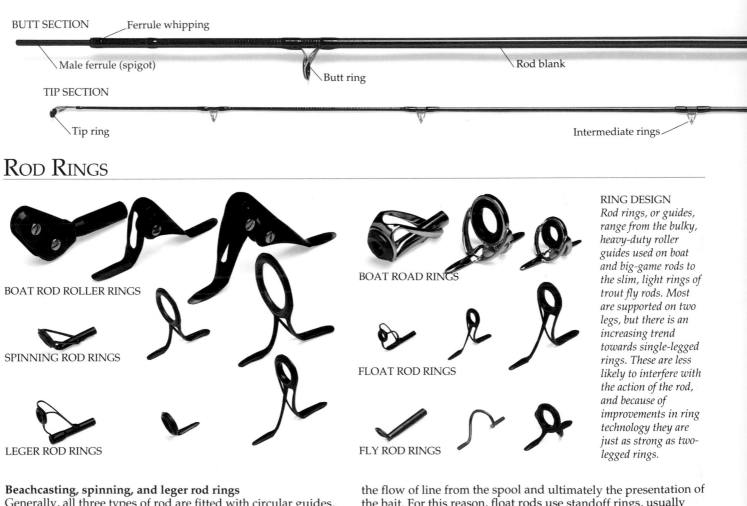

BUTT SECTION

Ferrule whipping

Male ferrule (spigot)

Butt ring

Rod blank

TIP SECTION

Tip ring

Intermediate rings

ROD RINGS

BOAT ROD ROLLER RINGS

SPINNING ROD RINGS

LEGER ROD RINGS

BOAT ROAD RINGS

FLOAT ROD RINGS

FLY ROD RINGS

RING DESIGN
Rod rings, or guides, range from the bulky, heavy-duty roller guides used on boat and big-game rods to the slim, light rings of trout fly rods. Most are supported on two legs, but there is an increasing trend towards single-legged rings. These are less likely to interfere with the action of the rod, and because of improvements in ring technology they are just as strong as two-legged rings.

Beachcasting, spinning, and leger rod rings
Generally, all three types of rod are fitted with circular guides, most of which are lined to reduce wear (of both line and guide) and friction. On standard leger rods the tip ring is often threaded to take a screw-in tip, while on rods with spliced-in quivertips the fine tip is normally ringed with lined, single-legged guides. Some boat rods sport roller rings throughout, or roller butt and tip rings with low-bridge intermediates. Rollers cut down resistance to the passage of line and minimize guide wear, particularly when wire line is being used.

Float rod rings
The most important task of float rod rings is to keep the line away from the blank. This is particularly important in wet weather, when line is all too ready to stick to the rod, inhibiting the flow of line from the spool and ultimately the presentation of the bait. For this reason, float rods use standoff rings, usually hard chrome and lined with durable, low-friction materials such as aluminium oxide or silicon carbide.

Fly rod rings
In the past, trout fly rods were always fitted with stainless steel or hard chrome guide rings: circular, bridge-type tip and butt rings, with snake intermediates – pieces of twisted wire whipped down at both ends. Snake rings are still in use today, but many rods are now fitted with ceramic-lined guides, usually two-legged butt rings (to withstand the rigours of heavy casting) plus single-legged intermediates. Light salmon rods generally have a similar guide configuration, but those for heavy-duty work usually have two-legged intermediate rings.

TIP-ACTION

MIDDLE-TO-TIP

THROUGH-ACTION

ROD ACTIONS
The action of a rod is the way in which it bends. Tip-action rods are designed for fast striking and long-distance casting, middle-to-tip-action rods for use where the ability to play big fish is more important. Through-action rods bend from tip to butt, which is useful for playing big fish at close range.

GLOSSARY OF TERMS
AFTM scale A method of classifying fly lines according to their weight and other characteristics, devised by the American Fishing Tackle ManufActurers Association (AFTMA). Fly rods are classified by the AFTM number of the line they are designed to cast (the higher the AFTM number, the heavier the line).

Blank The basic rod minus its fittings such as rings, reel seat, and ferrules.

Butt The handle section of the rod.

Line class Boat rods are classified by the breaking strain of the line with which they should be used, for example a 13.6 kg (30 lb) class rod with 13.6 kg (30 lb) line.

Reel seat Device for fixing reel to rod.

Taper The change in the diameter and wall thickness of the rod from tip to butt. The taper of a rod has a direct effect on its action.

Test curve This gives an indication of the power a rod possesses. It is the amount of force that is needed to pull the tip end of the rod around until it is at a right angle to the butt end.

Winch fitting The reel seat.

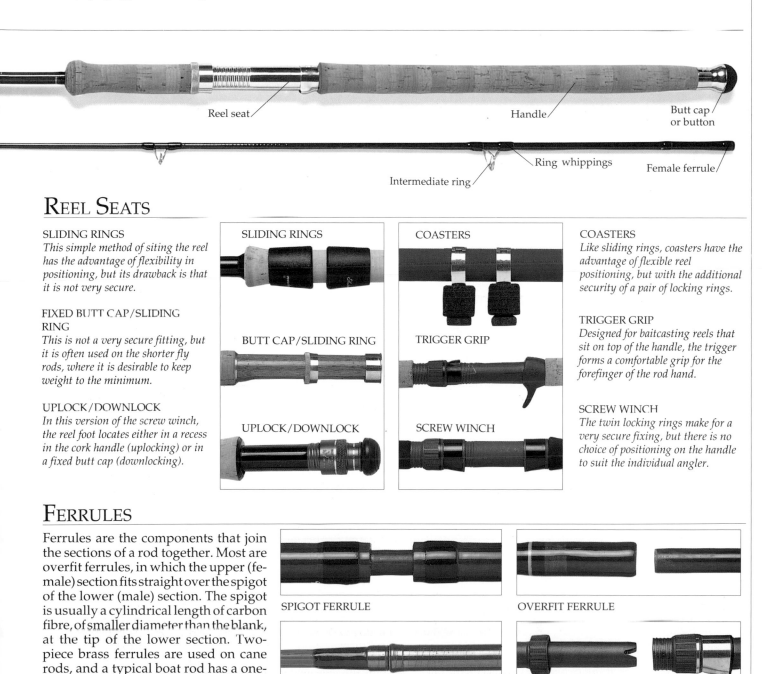

Reel seat   Handle   Butt cap or button

Intermediate ring   Ring whippings   Female ferrule

REEL SEATS

SLIDING RINGS
This simple method of siting the reel has the advantage of flexibility in positioning, but its drawback is that it is not very secure.

FIXED BUTT CAP/SLIDING RING
This is not a very secure fitting, but it is often used on the shorter fly rods, where it is desirable to keep weight to the minimum.

UPLOCK/DOWNLOCK
In this version of the screw winch, the reel foot locates either in a recess in the cork handle (uplocking) or in a fixed butt cap (downlocking).

SLIDING RINGS

BUTT CAP/SLIDING RING

UPLOCK/DOWNLOCK

COASTERS

TRIGGER GRIP

SCREW WINCH

COASTERS
Like sliding rings, coasters have the advantage of flexible reel positioning, but with the additional security of a pair of locking rings.

TRIGGER GRIP
Designed for baitcasting reels that sit on top of the handle, the trigger forms a comfortable grip for the forefinger of the rod hand.

SCREW WINCH
The twin locking rings make for a very secure fixing, but there is no choice of positioning on the handle to suit the individual angler.

FERRULES

Ferrules are the components that join the sections of a rod together. Most are overfit ferrules, in which the upper (female) section fits straight over the spigot of the lower (male) section. The spigot is usually a cylindrical length of carbon fibre, of smaller diameter than the blank, at the tip of the lower section. Two-piece brass ferrules are used on cane rods, and a typical boat rod has a one-piece blank joined to the handle by a combined ferrule and reel seat.

SPIGOT FERRULE

OVERFIT FERRULE

BRASS FERRULE

COMBINED FERRULE/REEL SEAT

SPINNING RODS

Spinning rods are designed to cast artificial lures of all types. They need to be as light as possible because they may well be in use for many hours at a time, and should be fitted with rings of the highest quality because many hundreds, if not thousands, of casts may be made during a single fishing session. For general spinning, a rod with a medium action is best. Such a rod will bend progressively from the tip into the middle section, leaving latent power nearer the handle to come into play should a big fish be hooked. Anglers specializing in fishing surface lures need a stiff, tip-actioned rod for best results, because this type will impart the most life into the lures. One-piece rods, generally under 2.1 m (7 ft) long, are often known as baitcasters. These are designed for use with a small multiplier reel sited on top of the rod rather than with a fixed-spool reel positioned below it.

SHIMANO CANIS CS80D-T
This is a 2.4 m (8 ft), two-piece rod, with a forefinger trigger on the reel seat for a secure and comfortable grip of both rod and reel. It is designed to be used in conjunction with small plugs, and is particularly suitable for salmon and steelhead fishing. The recommended lure weights for this rod are 10 to 20 g (³⁄₈ to ³⁄₄ oz), and these should be fished on 3.6 to 5.4 kg (8 to 12 lb) lines.

SHIMANO CANIS CS80D-T

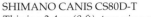

SHIMANO CONVERGENCE CV70H2

DAIWA OSPREY AWS10M

SOUTH BEND PROFESSIONAL

HARDY FAVOURITE
This 2.6 m (8½ ft) rod from the long-established Hardy Favourite range is ideal for medium spinning conditions, and equally at home with a fixed-spool reel or a light multiplier. Weighing 198 g (7 oz), it is designed to cast weights up to 35 g (1¼ oz) on 2.7 to 5.4 kg (6 to 12 lb) line.

HARDY FAVOURITE

DAIWA OSPREY AWS9S

DAIWA OSPREY AWS9S
This 2.7 m (9 ft), two-piece rod is whipped with Fuji SiC (silicon carbide) guides and used with a fixed-spool reel. It is at its best when casting artificials weighing from 7 to 30 g (¼ to 1 oz).

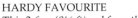

SHIMANO CONVERGENCE CV70H2
*The Convergence CV70H2 is a 2.1 m (7 ft)
baitcasting rod with a snappy action. The blank
material has a high carbon content, and the rod
is at its best when casting plugs, spoons, and
spinners in the 20 to 60 g (¾ to 2 oz) weight
range. It sports a comfortable forefinger trigger
on the reel seat, is lined throughout with hard-
wearing, three-legged Fuji guides, and is suitable
for use with 5.4 to 11.3 kg (12 to 25 lb) lines.*

DAIWA OSPREY AWS10M
*A construction process combining carbon cloth
with 24-strand amorphous metal braid and
silicon carbide whiskers produces an extremely
light rod, weighing only 283 g (10 oz), with
plenty of power. Made in two sections, this 3 m
(10 ft) rod is fitted with a forefinger trigger and
screw winch reel fitting. It is designed for use
with a multiplier reel, and for casting lures in
the 10 to 50 g (⅜ to 1¾ oz) weight range.*

SOUTH BEND PROFESSIONAL
*The South Bend Professional is a 1.7 m (5½ ft),
one-piece baitcasting rod with a medium action
and a short, but comfortable, pistol-grip handle
with forefinger trigger. The best performance of
this light, compact piece of tackle is achieved
when it is used with a small multiplier
reel filled with 4.54 to 9.1 kg (10 to 20 lb)
monofilament line and casting plugs and
spinners weighing about 7 to 20 g (¼ to ¾ oz).*

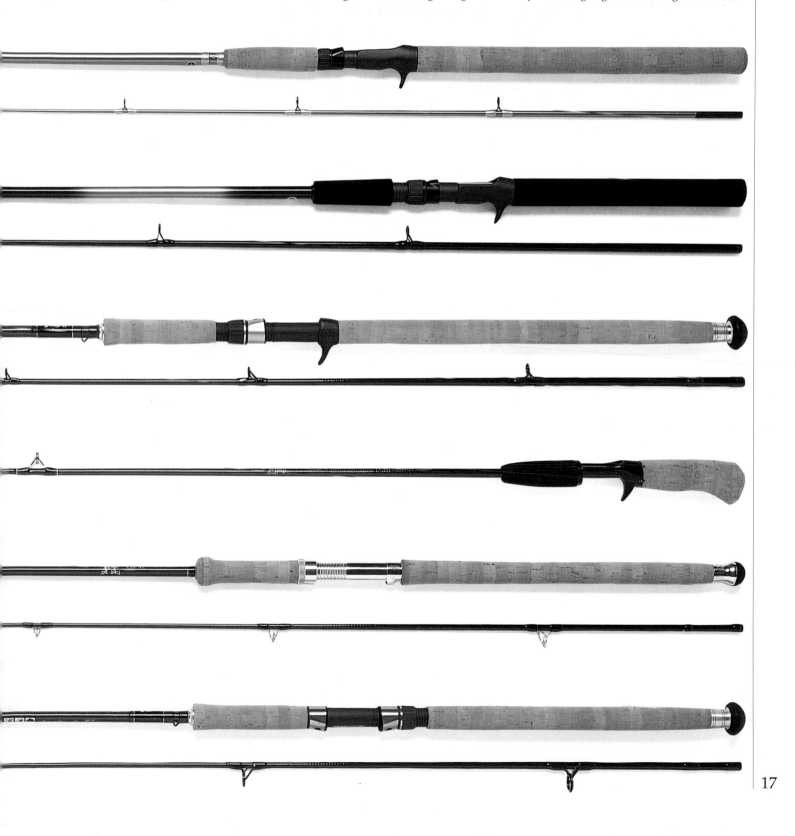

LEGER RODS

Leger rods can be separated into two basic types. The first is the standard rod, generally between 2.7 and 3 m (9 and 10 ft) in length, with a threaded tip ring to take a swingtip or quivertip but also suitable for touch legering. The action of standard rods ranges from soft to stiff. A soft action is best when a swingtip is to be used, because steady, looping casts and a progressive lifting of the rod on the strike are called for if tangling around the rod tip is to be avoided. The second leger rod type is that with a spliced-in quivertip. Although most commonly used on rivers, rods with spliced-in quivertips can be fished on stillwaters. They are particularly useful for the pursuit of shy or wary fish.

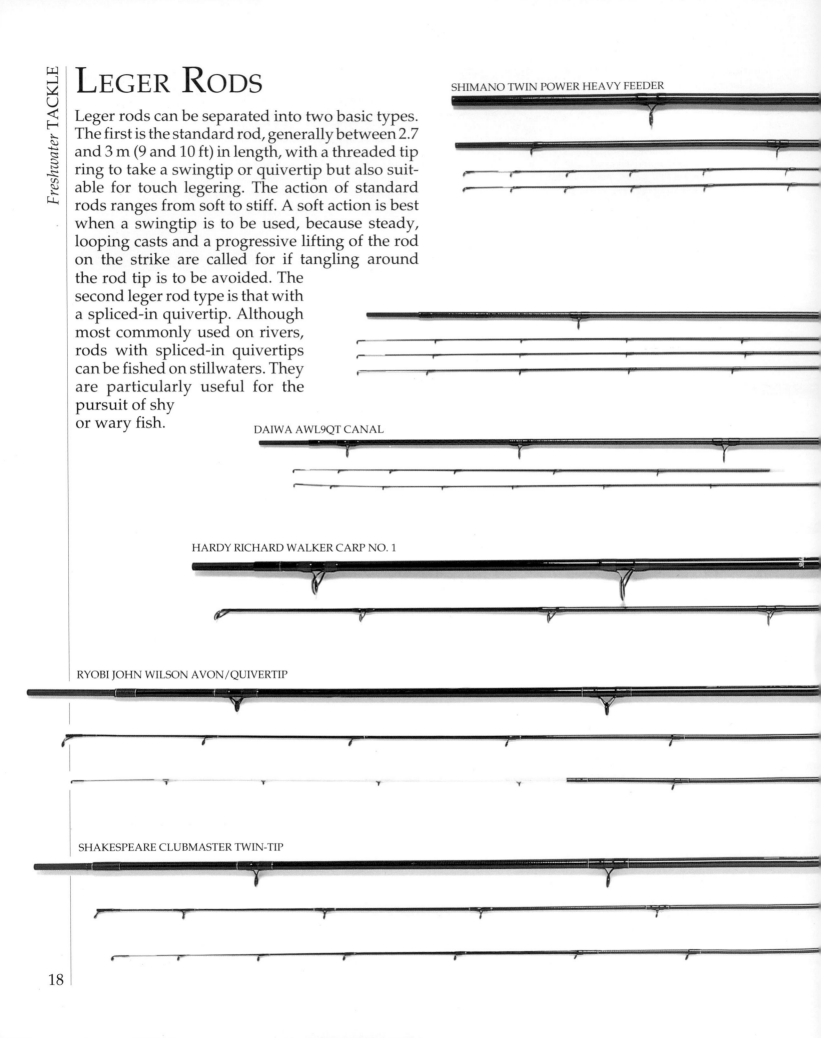

SHIMANO TWIN POWER HEAVY FEEDER

DAIWA AWL9QT CANAL

HARDY RICHARD WALKER CARP NO. 1

RYOBI JOHN WILSON AVON/QUIVERTIP

SHAKESPEARE CLUBMASTER TWIN-TIP

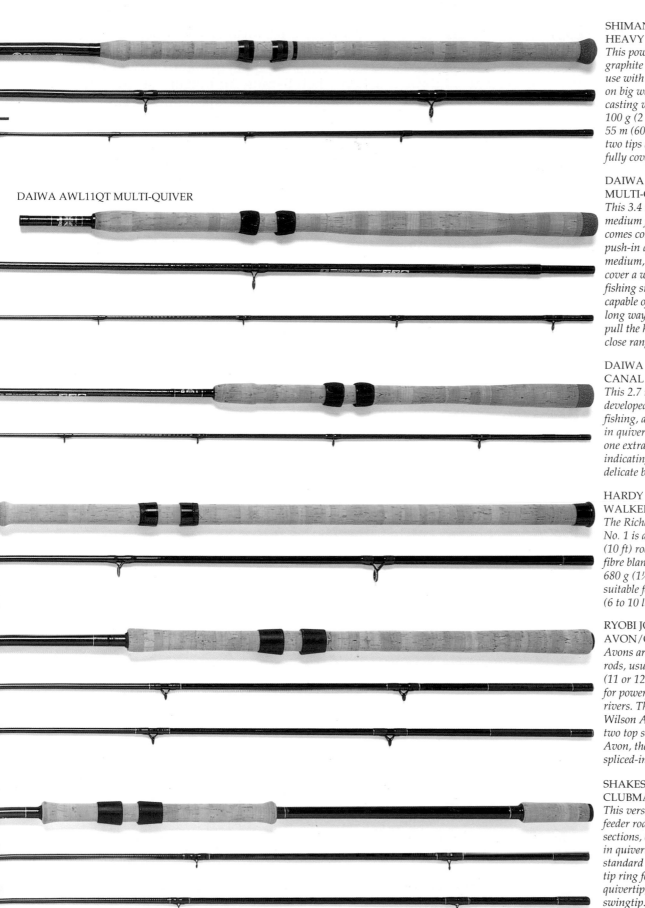

SHIMANO TWIN POWER HEAVY FEEDER
This powerful 3.7 m (12 ft) graphite rod, designed for use with heavy swimfeeders on big waters, is capable of casting weights of 60 to 100 g (2 to 3½ oz) up to 55 m (60 yds). It comes with two tips and the handle is fully covered in cork.

DAIWA AWL11QT MULTI-QUIVER

DAIWA AWL11QT MULTI-QUIVER
This 3.4 m (11 ft), light to medium feeder or bomb rod comes complete with three push-in quivertips (light, medium, and heavy) to cover a wide range of fishing situations. It is capable of casting feeders a long way, but it will not pull the hook out of a fish at close range.

DAIWA AWL9QT CANAL
This 2.7 m (9 ft) rod was developed for drain or canal fishing, and has two push-in quivertips, one soft and one extra soft, for indicating the tiniest, most delicate bites.

HARDY RICHARD WALKER CARP NO. 1
The Richard Walker Carp No. 1 is a two-piece, 3 m (10 ft) rod made on a glass fibre blank. Its test curve is 680 g (1½ lb), making it suitable for 2.7 to 4.54 kg (6 to 10 lb) lines.

RYOBI JOHN WILSON AVON/QUIVERTIP
Avons are standard leger rods, usually 3.4 or 3.7 m (11 or 12 ft) long, designed for powerful fish in fast rivers. The Ryobi John Wilson Avon/Quivertip has two top sections, one an Avon, the other with a spliced-in quivertip.

SHAKESPEARE CLUBMASTER TWIN-TIP
This versatile 3.4 m (11 ft) feeder rod has two top sections, one with a spliced-in quivertip, the other a standard top with threaded tip ring for attaching a quivertip, springtip, or swingtip. The carbon blank is fitted with lined guides to reduce wear.

19

FLOAT RODS

Most float rods (including those termed match rods) are made of carbon fibre. As a general rule, the greater the percentage of carbon there is in the blank, the better the rod will perform. Rods 3.7 to 4 m (12 to 13 ft) in length will meet most float-fishing requirements, while longer rods, of 4.3 to 4.6 m (14 to 15 ft), are better for fishing very deep swims. Even longer rods, of up to 6.1 m (20 ft) or more, are used in the "Bolognese method" of fishing (so called because it originated in Italy), which is a recent arrival on the match-fishing scene. Their benefit is seen as giving superior float control, as with a pole, but with the advantage of a running line. Select a rod with a sensitive tip action when after small fish, and one with a through action when fishing for bigger fish such as tench and small carp. Float rod handles should be no longer than about 60 cm (24 in) and around 2.2 to 2.5 cm (⅞ to 1 in) in diameter.

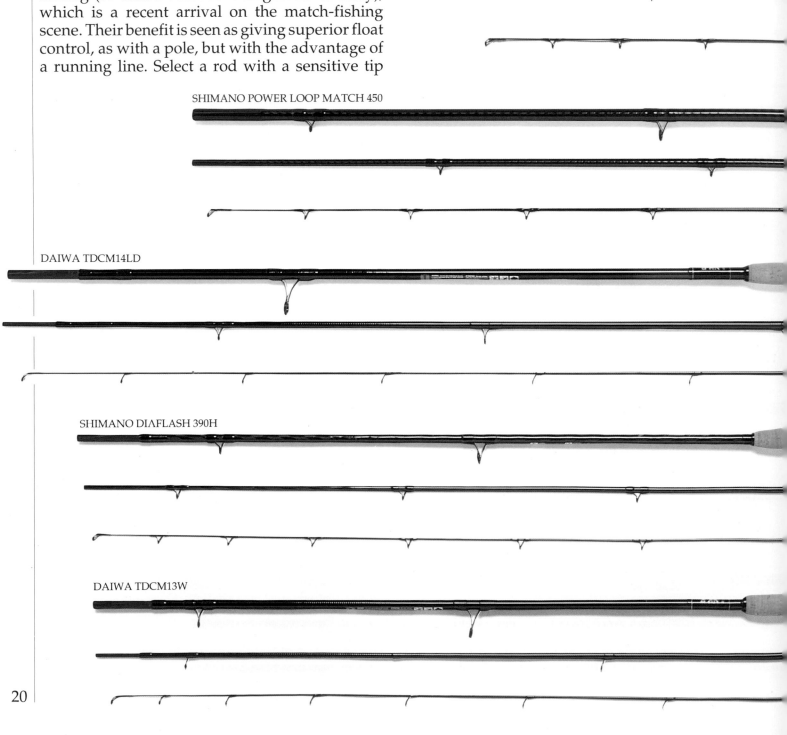

SHIMANO DIAFLASH MATCH 360

SHIMANO POWER LOOP MATCH 450

DAIWA TDCM14LD

SHIMANO DIAFLASH 390H

DAIWA TDCM13W

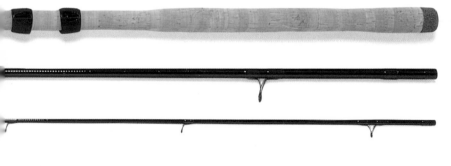

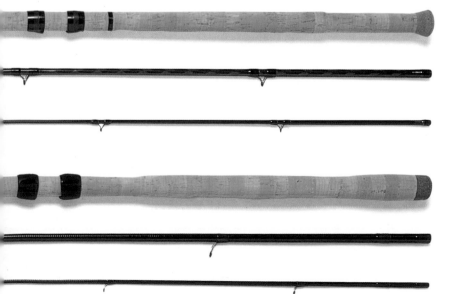

SHIMANO DIAFLASH MATCH 360

The Diaflash Match 360, a beautifully balanced 3.7 m (12 ft) match rod, is considered to be one of the better models currently available for general float work. Manufactured from high-quality carbon fibre, it is extremely light and slim and possesses a crisp action with rapid tip recovery. It is ringed throughout with Fuji guides lined with hard-wearing silicon carbide (SiC), has a slim, 60 cm (24 in) cork handle, and is suitable for both stick-float and waggler fishing.

SHIMANO POWER LOOP MATCH 450

This 4.6 m (15 ft) rod is aimed at the float angler who wants a longer rod at a competitive price. It is a versatile rod, suitable for a variety of float-fishing situations, but is especially useful for fishing at long range and in deepwater swims, where its extra length and good line pickup ability will score. Finished in an attractive reddish brown, it has a comfortable cork handle and is whipped with guides lined with hard-wearing aluminium oxide.

DAIWA TDCM14LD

This 4.3 m (14 ft) rod is designed for long-range or deepwater float fishing with 1.1 to 1.8 kg (2½ to 4 lb) reel lines and hook links down to 680 g (1½ lb). When fishing outsize wagglers at range, however, it is advisable to use a shock leader of 2.7 to 3.6 kg (6 to 8 lb) mono between the reel line and hook link. A shock leader absorbs the stress of casting heavy terminal tackle, which can break a relatively light reel line; it should be twice the length of the rod plus a few turns around the reel spool.

SHIMANO DIAFLASH 390H

The 390H is similar to the Diaflash 360 but longer, at 4 m (13 ft), and with a heavier action, and is designed for use by those anglers wishing to use stronger lines for bigger fish. It features the same lined guides and slim, short handle of the other models in the Diaflash range.

DIAWA TDCM13W

This 4 m (13 ft) rod is designed for fishing the waggler, but a spliced-tip version with more power and a stiffer top is available for stick-float fishing. Its compound taper blank produces a middle-to-tip action, and the fine, hollow tip permits rapid strikes and a crisp line pickup. It is at its best with 910 g to 1.36 kg (2 to 3 lb) reel lines of and hook links down to 454 g (1 lb).

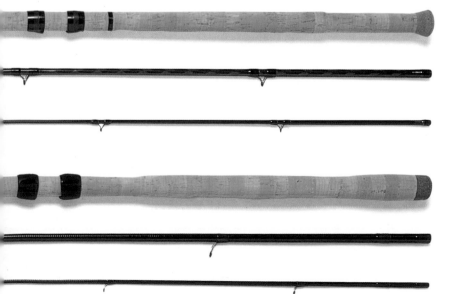

FLY RODS 1

PARTRIDGE DUNNERDALE #4

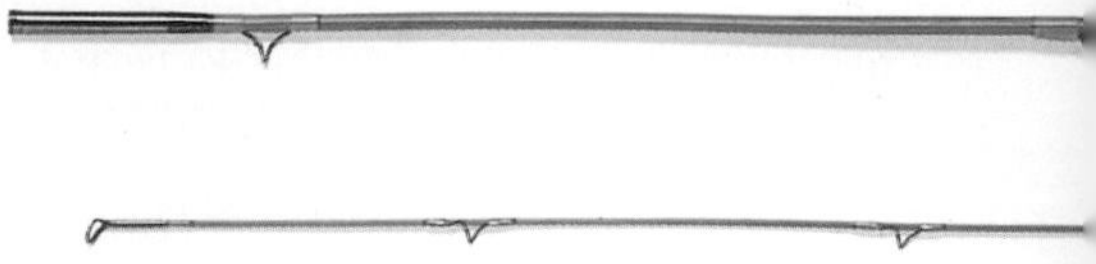

For fly fishing, it is vital to use a reel and line that match the rating of your rod, and your chosen rod should be suitable not only for the style of fishing but also for the prevailing conditions. For example, it is no use expecting a 1.8 m (6 ft) midge rod to perform properly when casting into a strong wind on a big lake. When choosing a fly rod, consider carefully what you expect from it.

ORVIS ONE-WEIGHT #1

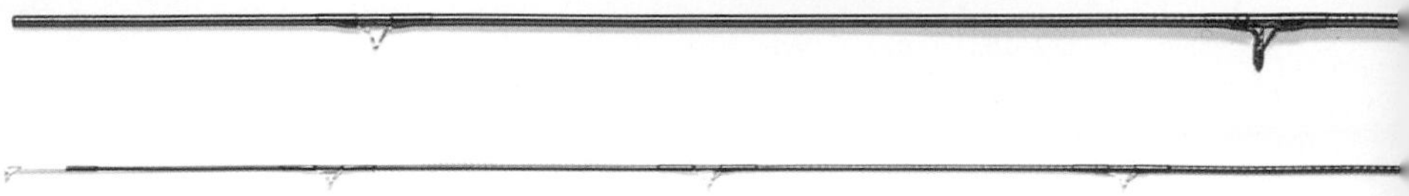

RYOBI CHALLENGE LOCH STYLE #5/7
This 3.4 m (11 ft) carbon fibre rod takes #5 to #7 lines, and is ideal for fishing from a drifting boat with floating or intermediate lines. Its length allows the angler to lift the bob fly and hold it on the surface away from the fish-scaring boat.

RYOBI CHALLENGE LOCH STYLE #5/7

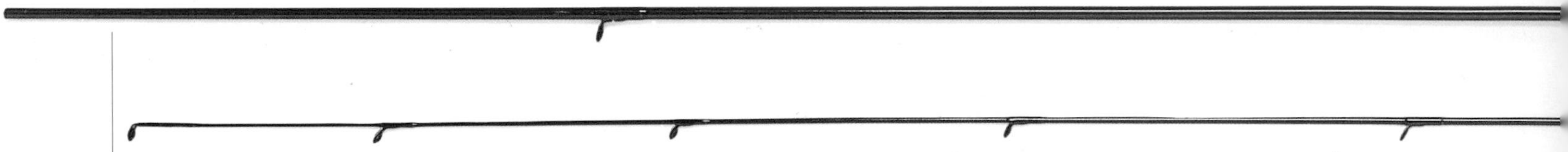

SAGE GFL 796 RPL #7
A blend of lightness and power makes this 2.9 m (9½ ft) carbon fibre rod a good all-rounder for bank fishing on large stillwaters and rivers. It is ideal for large trout, summer salmon, and steelhead. It has a ceramic butt ring, and the snake intermediates and tip ring are hard chrome.

SAGE GFL 796 RPL #7

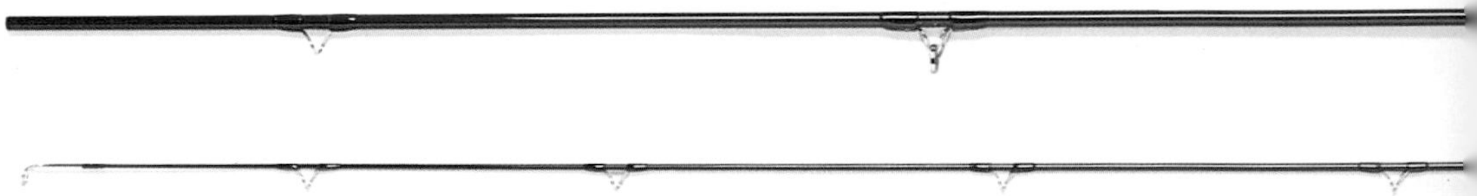

BERKLEY ACCUFLEX SERIES 1 #7/9

BERKLEY ACCUFLEX SERIES 1 #7/9
The Accuflex Series 1 is a 3.2 m (10½ ft), two-piece carbon fibre rod for #7 to #9 lines. The cork handle has an uplocking screw-winch reel seat and extended fighting butt, and the non-flash satin finish will not scare fish in bright weather. It is ideal for sunline work from a drifting boat and for species such as sea trout, summer salmon, and steelhead.

HARDY SOVEREIGN #5/6

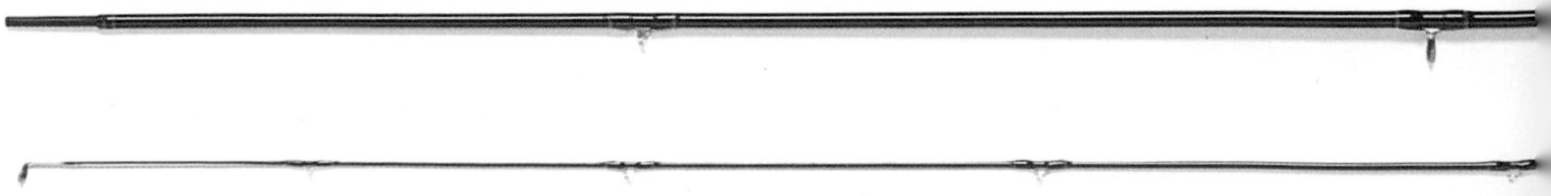

PARTRIDGE DUNNERDALE #4
This is a 1.8 m (6 ft) split cane rod with a progressive action, and matched to a #4 DT floating line it is ideal for fishing dry flies and nymphs on streams and small rivers. Cane has a slower action than carbon fibre, and projects a wider loop of line, which permits better judgement of the cast.

ORVIS ONE-WEIGHT #1
At 2.3 m (7½ ft) and weighing just 50 g (1¾ oz), this is a two-piece carbon fibre rod with a superfine grip, taking a #1 line, and is designed for fishing light lines on small rivers and streams. This is a specialist tool, not recommended for beginners or for anglers looking for a general-purpose fly rod.

HARDY SOVEREIGN #5/6
The 2.4 m (8 ft) Sovereign #5/6 is a two-piece, tip actioned carbon fibre rod, ideal for streams, medium-sized rivers, and fishing dry flies on small stillwaters. It is a good rod for mayfly fishing, and is capable of dealing with large trout.

FLY RODS 2

This selection of rods is from the heavier end of the fly-rod range. The models described may appear similar, but each is designed for a specific application and there is little overlap between them. However, they are all designed for heavy lines, and are suitable for salmon and steelhead, big trout on large stillwaters and rivers, and for saltwater fly fishing.

HARDY FAVOURITE SALMON #9

SHIMANO TWIN POWER SALMON FLY #9/11

SHIMANO TWIN POWER SALMON FLY #9/11
At 4.6 m (15 ft), this is the longest of the Twin Power salmon rods. It is fine for late-spring and summer fishing with light flies on #10 floating or intermediate lines, but lacks the power required for early-spring and backend fishing with heavy flies and sinking lines.

DAIWA AUTUMN GOLD CWF17 #11/13

DAIWA AUTUMN GOLD CWF17 #11/13
The CWF17 is a four-piece, 5.2 m (17 ft), double-handed salmon rod built on a carbon fibre blank. It is a powerful rod, which makes it very suitable for fishing in the early spring, and at the backend of the season, when heavy lines and large tube flies or Waddingtons are called for.

SAGE GFL 996 RPL #9

ORVIS RESERVOIR #8

SAGE GFL 7100 RPL #7

HARDY FAVOURITE SALMON #9

This light 3.8 m (12½ ft), double-handed carbon fibre rod, with a middle-to-tip action, is a good choice for summer salmon fishing with floating or intermediate lines. It is whipped with aluminium oxide butt and tip rings and hard chrome intermediates, and has a long handle with an uplocking reel seat.

SAGE GFL 996 RPL #9

This is a powerful 2.9 m (9½ ft), two-piece rod, weighing just 110 g (3⅞ oz). It is excellent for casting long distances with WF lines and shooting heads, and for bank fishing on large stillwaters, with big streamers and hairwings. It is a good rod for steelhead, bonefish, and salmon.

ORVIS RESERVOIR #8

The two-piece, 2.9 m (9½ ft) Orvis Reservoir #8 is a good choice of rod for bank fishing on large lakes and reservoirs, where both distance and accuracy can be very important. It is ideal for large trout, including sea trout, and for steelhead and summer salmon.

SAGE GFL 7100 RPL #7

Power, good casting ability, and light, crisp action are key features of this two-piece, 3 m (10 ft) carbon fibre rod. They make it a good all-rounder for bank and boat fishing on big lakes and reservoirs, and an excellent rod for summer steelhead on large streams.

POLES & WHIPS

Poles and whips enable the terminal tackle to be controlled with tremendous accuracy and great delicacy, and allow baits to be lowered into places to which it would be difficult, if not impossible, to cast. Instead of having a reel and running line, a pole has a fixed line attached to its tip, which is either a "flick" tip or an "elasticated" tip. On flick-tip poles, the line is tied directly to a ring or nylon loop whipped to the tip, while on elasticated-tip poles it is attached to a short length of elastic running through the tip section and anchored within the section below it. Poles can be up to 17 m (56 ft) long, and are used for tackling medium-range to distant swims; whips are very light, slim, and short poles, usually less than 6 m (20 ft) long, and used for close-in work. Poles are either telescopic or have several take-apart sections, while whips are usually telescopic.

GARBOLINO VECTRA 4.0 m (13 ft)

GARBOLINO COUNTESS 6.90 m (23 ft)

GARBOLINO SPIRIT 9.30 m (31 ft)

DANGER WARNING
Carbon fibre is an excellent conductor of electricity, so NEVER use a carbon pole or rod anywhere near overhead power lines, or during a thunderstorm. And remember, your pole or rod does not need to touch a live line for you to get a potentially fatal electric shock: electricity can arc through the air to it if it comes near a line, especially in humid or wet weather.

GARBOLINO VECTRA 4.0 m (13 ft)

The Vectra range of telescopic whips, available in 50 cm (20 in) size increments, are made of carbon fibre reinforced with Kevlar and combine strength and a fast action with delicacy and lightness: the 4.0 m (13 ft) version weighs only about 100 g (3.5 oz). Whips such as this are ideal for close-range fishing for small species such as bream, perch, and rudd, especially when fishing into difficult spots, such as gaps in weedbeds close to overhanging trees. When held supported on the forearm, they can be used comfortably for quite long periods.

GARBOLINO COUNTESS 6.90 m (23 ft)

Poles really come into their own in running water because they permit the float and bait to be held back gently. A float fished out in the flow on rod-and-reel tackle tends to lurch slightly off line each time it is checked, but this does not happen with pole presentation because the pole tip is above and just upstream of the float. The Countess 6.90 m (23 ft) pole is designed specifically for use on rivers where good bait presentation is of utmost importance. It is telescopic, with seven sections, and is made of carbon fibre and weighs just 280 g (about 10 oz).

GARBOLINO SPIRIT 9.30 m (31 ft)

In addition to offering precise control over float tackle in running water, a pole allows you to fish baits overdepth far more effectively than you can with rod and reel. This is because it gives you a very high level of control over the terminal tackle, and the more rigid the pole, the higher that level will be. In general, take-apart poles are more rigid than telescopic models, and the Spirit 9.30 m (31 ft) carbon take-apart pole is exceptionally stiff, slim, and light, weighing about 730 g (26 oz). An 11 m (36 ft) model is also available, which weighs 930 g (33 oz).

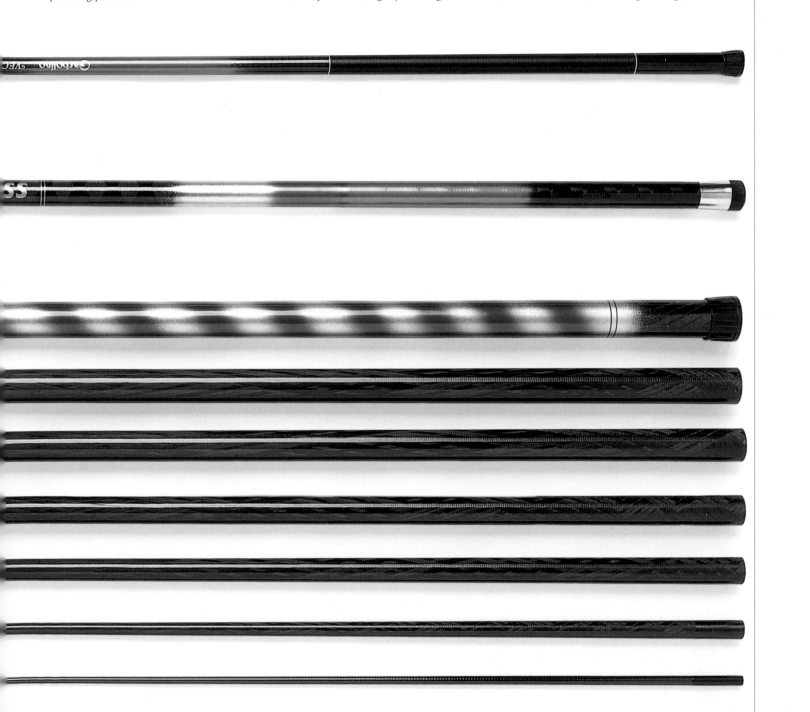

BOAT RODS

Boat fishing can be hard work for the angler and punishing for the tackle, so a boat rod needs to be tough, well-made, and able to withstand a fair amount of use. A compromise between power and flexibility is a must, however, because all power with no "give" kills the action, overwhelming small to average-sized fish, and without that vital "soft cushion" there is a risk of losing big fish. Boat rods are built to IGFA test curve ratings from 5.4 through to 54 kg (12 to 120 lb), with 9.1 kg (20 lb) and 13.6 kg (30 lb) the most popular, and they should be used with lines of the same rating. Another option is the uptide rod, which has a longer casting butt and a long, soft tip to cast the weight and play fish without risk to the obligatory light line.

CONOFLEX INTEGRA UPTIDE
Uptide rods are used from boats to cast a grip weight that holds the bait away from the scare area in shallow water. Optimum lengths are 2.7 to 3 m (9 to 10 feet). The Integra offers three tips, including an 85 g (3 oz) tip for light tide work. It also has a telescopic butt, which reduces to a more comfortable standard boat length after casting.

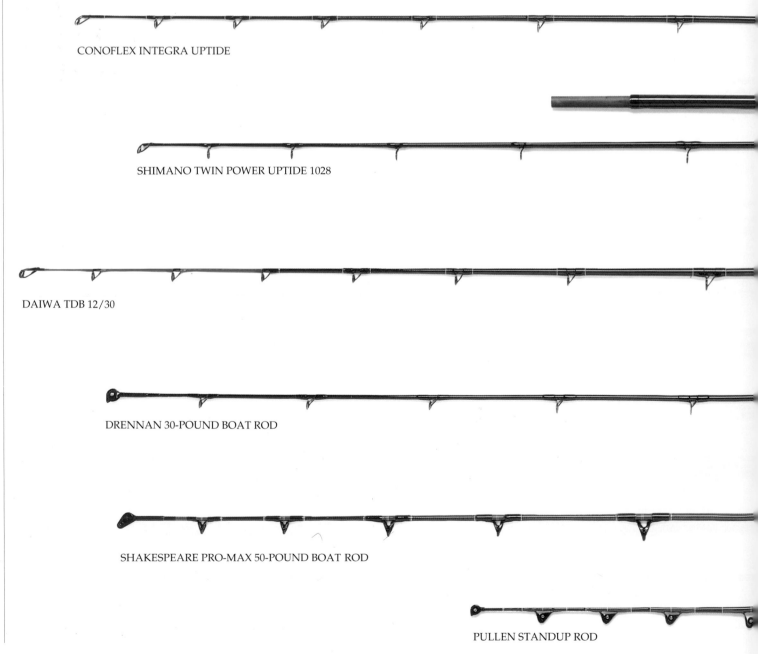

CONOFLEX INTEGRA UPTIDE

SHIMANO TWIN POWER UPTIDE 1028

DAIWA TDB 12/30

DRENNAN 30-POUND BOAT ROD

SHAKESPEARE PRO-MAX 50-POUND BOAT ROD

PULLEN STANDUP ROD

SHIMANO TWIN POWER UPTIDE 1028

The current trend with uptide rods is to make them around 3 m (10 ft) long and capable of throwing a wide range of weight sizes. In this respect, the Twin Power Uptide 1028 is without doubt a market leader. It is gentle enough to feel good handling even the smallest codling, yet has enough power to subdue a small shark.

DAIWA TDB 12/30

Rods covering a range of IGFA ratings rarely work really well, but Daiwa's Amorphous Whisker TDB 12/30 is an exception. With the right reel and line, it can be rated at 5.4, 9.1, or 13.6 kg (12, 20, or 30 lb). Some individually rated rods may well outperform it, but it is an excellent compromise rod when used with a suitably balanced reel and line combination.

DRENNAN 30-POUND BOAT ROD

Most boat fishing situations, apart from shark or heavy wreck fishing, are handled readily with a 13.6 kg (30 lb) class rod, making it the number one choice for multipurpose use. At 2.4 m (8 ft) in length, with an easy-actioned tip and power in reserve, the Drennan 30 boat rod offers across-the-board fishing pleasure.

SHAKESPEARE PRO-MAX 50-POUND

Shakespeare's 22.7 kg (50 lb) class Pro-Max is intended for the bigger end of the boat fishing range, designed to work very heavy weights and subdue large fish. Its action is stiffened by the carbon in the blank, enabling it to deliver more power at an earlier stage in the taper, and the gimballed butt offers extra leverage when used with a butt pad.

PULLEN STANDUP ROD

Standup fishing is a technique for beating big fish quickly by standing on the boat deck and using body weight as opposed to arm strength. Standup rods are short, powerful, and have roller guides, a very long butt, and a low reel position to maximize leverage. A 13.6 to 22.7 kg (30 to 50 lb) class Pullen Standup Rod would suit most situations.

SHORE RODS

Shore-rod design is probably the most complex aspect of sea-rod production. With so many tapers, lengths, materials, and layup thicknesses to choose from to get the required action, blank design has become a highly technical art. To make things worse for the designer, there is no such thing as an optimum action, length, or power rating unless related to a particular individual. Because anglers differ in casting style, stature, and strength, buying a rod thus becomes rather like buying a suit: either you have one made, or, like most people, you buy off-the-peg and ignore any minor shortcomings. The secret is to try before you buy. The rods shown here are representative of the wide range available, but your individual casting requirements may well dictate a different choice.

SHAKESPEARE INTERNATIONAL EQUALIZER CARP
The best way to enjoy float and light leger work for fish such as wrasse and bream over hospitable ground is with a carp rod, such as the International Equalizer. A length of around 3.4 m (11 ft) gives ease of casting and is good for playing a lively fish at close range, while a 910 g to 1.1 kg (2 to 2½ lb) test curve lets it know who's boss.

CENTURY LONG E-ZEE MATCH

SHAKESPEARE HURRICANE BASS MASTER
When fishing from the shore, you often need to use weights of only 57 g (2 oz) or so placed at close to medium range. In such situations, the best rod to use is one with a soft, tippy action and good reserves of mid-blank power, such as the 3.5 m (11½ ft) Hurricane Bass Master. It is a superb example of a rod that enables you to feel a hooked fish and be in tune with its every move, without losing control.

DAIWA PMB122M
The pendulum style of casting requires stiff rods, which need immense amounts of body power from the angler to wind them up to their maximum. Only anglers favouring this casting style should choose power-casting rods such as the Daiwa Powermesh Beach (PMB) range. The PMB122M is a formidable rod, designed for casting weights in the 113 to 170 g (4 to 6 oz) range, and its coaster reel grips permit fine tuning of its overall balance.

CENTURY FORMULA ONE
Rods exceeding 4 m (13 ft) in length are currently regarded as the optimum distance-casting tools, and Century has invested much effort in creating rods for this particular corner of the market. The slow taper and stiffish action of its Formula One make it a pendulum caster's rod that is a good choice for heavy-ground work with a large-capacity reel.

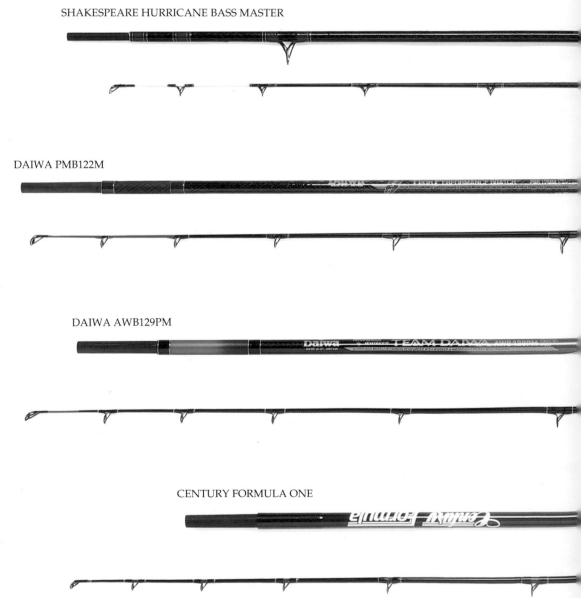

SHAKESPEARE HURRICANE BASS MASTER

DAIWA PMB122M

DAIWA AWB129PM

CENTURY FORMULA ONE

SHAKESPEARE INTERNATIONAL EQUALIZER CARP

CENTURY LONG E-ZEE MATCH
Because of its soft, tippy action, the Long E-zee Match is more of an angler's rod than a casting-tournament machine. But it is still a powerful rod and is capable, in the right hands, of throwing a 142 g (5 oz) weight a couple of hundred metres. Its light-walled blank gives it excellent sensitivity and bite detection, and it is an excellent choice of rod for the non-specialist beach angler.

DAIWA AWB129PM
Part of the Team Daiwa Amorphous Whisker range of power casting rods, this rod can handle 227 g (8 oz) weights to cope with difficult fishing conditions. The overall stiffness of the blank is moderated at the tip by the inclusion of glass fibre, which has a softening effect that enhances bite detection. This is an angler's rod designed for ultra-long-distance work, not a caster's rod that can also be used to fish.

THE REEL

The reel is primarily a line reservoir that enables the angler to fish at a greater range than is possible with a line fixed to the rod tip, which was the only method available to the earliest anglers. The reel has evolved into several different forms, with two distinct types of spool: the revolving spool and the fixed spool. The oldest and simplest form of revolving-spool reel is the centrepin, in which the line is carried on a simple flanged spool that revolves on a steel axle; this reel was once close to extinction but is now showing signs of making a comeback. Fly reels and multipliers (including baitcasters) are more complex forms of revolving-spool reel. In a fixed-spool reel, the spool does not revolve, and the line is retrieved and wound onto it by a rotating arm, called the bale arm.

ADCOCK STANTON CENTREPIN REEL
The spool of this centrepin runs on ball bearings, which give it an exceptionally smooth and sensitive action.

EVOLUTION OF THE REEL

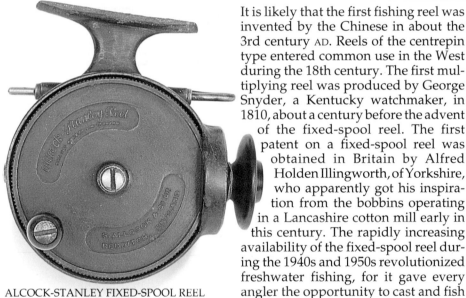

ALCOCK-STANLEY FIXED-SPOOL REEL
S. Alcock & Company produced this early fixed-spool reel in 1926.

It is likely that the first fishing reel was invented by the Chinese in about the 3rd century AD. Reels of the centrepin type entered common use in the West during the 18th century. The first multiplying reel was produced by George Snyder, a Kentucky watchmaker, in 1810, about a century before the advent of the fixed-spool reel. The first patent on a fixed-spool reel was obtained in Britain by Alfred Holden Illingworth, of Yorkshire, who apparently got his inspiration from the bobbins operating in a Lancashire cotton mill early in this century. The rapidly increasing availability of the fixed-spool reel during the 1940s and 1950s revolutionized freshwater fishing, for it gave every angler the opportunity to cast and fish at much greater range than ever before.

GLOSSARY OF TERMS

Anti-reverse A mechanism that prevents the spools of multipliers and fixed-spool reels from turning backwards and thus releasing line.
Bale arm The wire arm on a fixed-spool reel that picks up the line and guides it onto the spool.
Check or ratchet A device that varies the tension at which line is pulled from a fly reel by a running fish.
Drag/slipping clutch A mechanism on multipliers and fixed-spool reels that allows hooked fish to take line from the spool at a preset tension.
Foot The part of the reel that attaches to the rod handle.
Gear ratio The number of times the spool or bale arm of a reel rotates for each turn of the handle.
Level wind Fitted on multipliers to spread line evenly across the spool.
Line guard Found on centrepin and fly reels, this prevents line from tangling around the drum or the handle.
Rotor The part of a fixed-spool reel on which the spool sits.

TYPES OF REEL

Fly reel
The two most common types of fly reel are the single action and the multiplier. The spool of a single-action reel revolves once for each turn of the handle, while that of a multiplier makes several turns. A third type, the automatic, has a clockwork mechanism, which turns the spool when a lever is operated. Fly reel check mechanisms are either simple ratchets or more sophisticated drag systems.

Reel foot

Ventilated spool lets water drain from line

Handle

Spool release lever

Counterbalance

Exposed spool rim

Reel cage

Backplate

Drag adjuster

Spool arbor

Line guard

Multiplier/Baitcaster

A multiplier is basically a geared version of the centrepin. Multipliers are used for a wide variety of techniques, from freshwater baitcasting to surfcasting and blue-water big-game fishing. Most have a free-spool facility, which allows the spool to rotate without resistance for casting, mechanical or magnetic brakes, a drag system, and often a level-wind mechanism for even line lay. Multipliers fit on top of the rod.

Drag adjuster
Spool spindle
Reel cage
Spool release button
Sideplate
Spool "endfloat" adjuster
Handle
Reel foot
Level wind

Fixed-spool reel

This type of reel is so named because the spool does not revolve to recover line: the line is wound around it by a rotating bale arm. The spool does rotate, under tension from a slipping clutch, to give line to a running fish, and an anti-reverse system prevents the handle backwinding while the spool rotates. This reel is very versatile and, within reason, will handle most freshwater fishing except fly fishing.

Reel foot
Handle grip
Bale arm
Spool skirt
Reel stem
Bale arm roller
Handle release lever
Bale arm rotor
Anti-reverse lever
Spool release button
Spool
Rotor arm
Body casing
Drag control

Closed-face reel

This is a fixed-spool reel with an enclosed front face. The line passes through a hole in the centre of the face and is wound onto the spool by a pickup pin. The pin is freed for casting by finger pressure on the front face or on a rear-mounted button. A very efficient light-line reel, especially for float fishing, because the enclosed spool gives good line control when fishing in windy weather.

Reel foot
BELL HOUSING REMOVED
Anti-reverse
Reel stem
Bell housing
Paddle grip
Line release button
Handle
Pickup pin
Line release button
Body casing
Gear lock

Spincaster

This is a rugged version of the closed-face reel, suitable for 2.27 to 9.1 kg (5 to 20 lb) lines. Most spincasters are mounted on top of the rod but some, like the Zebco shown here, are fitted beneath it. Line is released by a pushbutton, by pressure on the front face, or by a lever (which allows "feathering" of the cast to prevent the lure from overshooting). The bell housing virtually eliminates line coil problems.

Reel foot
BELL HOUSING REMOVED
Finger brake/ line release lever
Reel stem
Drag wheel
Grip
Anti-reverse button
Handle
Back cover assembly
Bell housing
Ceramic pickup pin

33

FIXED-SPOOL REELS 1

Unlike fly reels and multiplier reels, which have revolving spools, the fixed-spool reel (or spinning reel) has a static spool, onto which line is wound by a rotating bale arm made of wire. To ensure that line is laid on evenly, the spool oscillates (moves backwards and forwards) on a rotor as the reel handle is turned. Good-sized fish, when hooked, can be prevented from breaking the line by use of the adjustable slipping clutch. This mechanism allows running or lunging fish to take line from the spool at a preset level of tension or resistance. This tension should be adjusted so that the line is released from the spool at a little below the breaking strain of the line, thus making a hooked fish fight for every inch of line it takes. On most fixed-spool reels, the reel is prevented from winding backwards when the spool is turning and giving line by an anti-reverse mechanism. On some reels this mechanism is silent, but on others a clicking noise can be heard while winding.

GENERAL-PURPOSE REELS

RYOBI PROTARGET 2000M *(right)*
The 2000M is a lightweight reel of an ideal size for both float fishing and light legering, with a high gear ratio of 6.1:1 that ensures a rapid retrieve. Its line capacity is 91 m (100 yds) of 1.36 kg (3 lb) mono, and it has three ball bearings for smooth and reliable operation.

SHIMANO AERO GTM2000 *(below)*
This high-speed reel has a gear ratio of 6.2:1 and is supplied with three spools, one deep, one shallow, and one match (ultra-shallow). Its effective line-laying system and long, tapered spool enable light baits to be cast long distances, which is ideal for situations in which a gentle presentation is vital for success.

MITCHELL EXCELLENCE 60 *(right)*
The Excellence 60 is a rear-drag version of the world-famous Mitchell 300. It comes complete with two spools, one shallow, one deep; line capacities are 91 m (100 yds) of 2.7 kg (6 lb) mono (shallow spool), and 183 m (200 yds) of 4.54 kg (10 lb) mono (deep spool).

MATCH REELS

DAIWA TD1650DF (right)
This is a top-of-the-range match/feeder reel with a long-stroke spool oscillation, giving excellent line lay and consistent casting. It has a line capacity of 200 m (220 yds) of 4.54 kg (10 lb) mono, and a gear ratio of 5.2:1.

DAIWA HARRIER AUTO 1657DM (below)
The Harrier Auto series are the only match reels available with a bale arm that can be opened by a dab of the finger then closed either the same way or automatically by a turn of the reel handle. Line capacity is 100 m (110 yds) of 910 g (2 lb) line, the gear ratio 5.4:1.

SHAKESPEARE PRESIDENT DELUXE 2510/030 (above)
This reel sports many features, including brass gears, stainless steel ball bearings, a ceramic line roller, and a long, tapered spool for easy long-distance casting with light rigs. It has a line capacity of 150 m (164 yds) of 2.7 kg (6 lb) mono, and a gear ratio of 5.2:1.

SHAKESPEARE SIGMA SLS 2500/035 (left)
The Sigma is a lightweight, carbon-bodied reel with an extended spool for improved casting performance. It has a gear ratio of 5.6:1 and is supplied with two spools, one deep, one match. The deep spool will take 240 m (262 yds) of 2.7 kg (6 lb) mono, the match 100 m (110 yds) of 1.1 kg (2½ lb) line.

35

FIXED-SPOOL REELS 2

A variety of speeds of retrieve are available in fixed-spool reels; a few reels even have two, one fast, the other slow. Most have gear ratios of between 3:1 and 4:1, which give retrieval rates of about 40 to 50 cm (15 to 20 in) of line wound onto the reel spool for each revolution of the handle. For high-speed work, such as occurs in match fishing, a reel with the rapid retrieval rate offered by a high gear ratio is best. A ratio of 6:1 will see about 75 cm (30 in) of line retrieved for every turn of the handle. A rapid retrieve is also an advantage if you want to crank lures rapidly through clear water. Whatever the gear ratio of a fixed-spool reel, it will operate at its most efficient when fully loaded with line. Half-filled spools make casting any distance difficult, because the line encounters excessive friction as it rubs against the underside and lip of the spool.

SPECIALIST REELS

SHIMANO AERO GTM3000 (left)
This high-speed reel is a perfect size for use with a swimfeeder and comes with three spools (deep, semi-deep, and shallow). Line capacity is 230 m (250 yds) of 4.54 kg (10 lb) mono (semi-deep spool), gear ratio 6.2:1.

SHIMANO BAITRUNNER AERO 3500 (above)
The Aero 3500 features a long, coned spool for greater casting distance, a gear ratio of 4.7:1, and a line capacity of 256 m (280 yds) of 4.54 kg (10 lb) mono. The lever-operated Baitrunner facility allows fish to take line without the angler having to open the bale arm, while turning the reel handle engages the preset clutch.

SHIMANO BAITRUNNER AERO GT4500 (left)
One of the most popular specialist reels in use today for long-distance fishing, the Aero GT4500 possesses all the features of the standard Aero reels plus a trio of ball bearings for a very smooth retrieve. It has a gear ratio of 4.7:1 and a line capacity of 293 m (320 yds) of 5.4 kg (12 lb) mono, and is supplied with two spools.

BROWNING 8512 (left)
This reel has a long carbon fibre spool (it is supplied with two) for medium-range specialist fishing. Its capacity is 200 m (220 yds) of 3.6 kg (8 lb) mono, and an oscillating winding mechanism on a worm shaft produces excellent line lay. The gear ratio is 4.6:1.

BROWNING 9512 (below)
The 9512 is aimed at the specialist angler fishing at medium range. It features three ball bearings for smooth and durable operation and is supplied with three spools. The gear ratio and line capacity are the same as those of the 8512.

DAIWA BR2050 (left)
Designed for medium-range fishing, this reel has a line capacity of 270 m (295 yds) of 4.54 kg (10 lb) mono. The gear ratio is 4.9:1, and the long, coned spool and even, crossover line lay permit good casting distance and accuracy.

ABU CARDINAL GOLD MAX 4 (right)
This reel, designed for close- to medium-range carp and pike fishing, has a line capacity of 210 m (230 yds) of 3.6 kg (8 lb) mono and a gear ratio of 5:1. It is fitted with five ball bearings to give reliable, super-smooth operation.

CLOSED-FACE REELS

The closed-face reel is a variant of the fixed-spool. The front of the reel is shrouded by a casing through which the line emerges, and line retrieval is by means of a pin that guides the line onto the spool. Pressing a spring-loaded button retracts the pin, leaving the line free for casting. This design eliminates the common problem associated with fine lines, which is that they blow about on windy days, constantly tangling around the reel spool, rotor, or bale arm with potentially disastrous results. They are at their best when fitted with light lines, and are used for light spinning and for match fishing.

ABU GARCIA 507 MK II GOLD MAX (*above*)
Designed for competition fishing at the highest level, the 507 Mk II contains no drag system; instead, big fish are played by backwinding the handle. The extra-wide spool and dual-geared oscillation system produces a criss-cross line lay on the retrieve, eliminating the possibility of coils of line bedding into gaps between the coils beneath them. This line bedding, a traditional problem with closed-face reels, inhibits subsequent casts and float control. The reel has a gear ratio of 3.23:1.

D.A.M. QUICK POWER CFP (*above*)
The Quick Power CFP is fitted with a disc brake, adjustable drag, and low gearing (3.5:1) to enable big fish to be played sensitively yet with power. The reel also possesses a quick-release bell (rotor) fitted with two hard-chromed steel pins for quick line pickup.

D.A.M. QUICK CFM MATCH (*right*)
Designed for match fishing, this reel features a fast retrieve (gear ratio 4.2:1) and has no drag system: fish are played by backwinding. It has two revolving, hard-chromed pickup pins for fast line take-up, and the bell has a quick-release mechanism for rapid access to the spool.

ABU GARCIA 1044 ABUMATIC *(left)*
The 1044 is very well engineered, with brass gearing (ratio 3.9:1) and a stainless steel pinion gear for smooth operation. Its drag system is designed to reduce the risk of fish hooked on light lines being lost if they suddenly surge off: winding the handle back one quarter of a turn reduces the braking power by up to 75 per cent.

DAIWA HARRIER 123M *(above)*
With its carbon fibre body and lack of drag, the Harrier 123M is extremely light in weight. It comes with two spools, and with its high gear ratio of 4.1:1 it is aimed specifically at the match angler. It is a simple reel, yet one with the right features to ensure that it is up to the demands of the open match circuit.

DAIWA HARRIER 125M *(left)*
This reel is very popular with match anglers. It has a high gear ratio (4.1:1) for rapid line retrieval, and the line is wound onto the spool in a cross-weave pattern to minimize the danger of bedding-in and subsequent poor line release. The reel comes complete with two spools, and has a rear drag control for those who prefer to play fish off the clutch rather than by backwinding.

BAITCASTING REELS

Baitcasting reels are small multipliers, designed to be both easy to use and comfortable to operate for long periods. Many are fitted with a level-wind mechanism, which spreads the retrieved line evenly across the spool, and big and hard-running fish being played are allowed to take line by an adjustable drag system. Tangles during casting (caused by the spool overrunning) have been eliminated by adjustable magnetic braking systems, which slow down the speed at which the spool rotates, and newer-generation baitcasting reels are fitted with a thumb bar to enable rapid casting. Clamping the thumb onto the spool prior to casting automatically depresses the bar, which in turn disengages the spool.

SHIMANO CALCUTTA 200 (above)
The Calcutta 200 has a one-piece, anodized aluminium body and aluminium spool, and a line capacity of 210 m (230 yds) of 3.6 kg (8 lb) mono or 110 m (120 yds) of 6.4 kg (14 lb) line. It features a recessed foot to give a low profile on the rod, ball bearings for smooth running and durability, "Quickfire" thumb bar casting system, and a hard-wearing ceramic line guide on the level-wind mechanism.

ABU GARCIA AMBASSADEUR 1022 (below)
This reel features a gear ratio of 4.7:1, a level wind, two braking systems (one mechanical, the other magnetic), and a thumb bar. The spool is released for casting by flicking the thumb bar, and re-engaged for retrieving either by turning the reel handle or by using the "flipping trigger", which permits instant striking.

SILSTAR NOVA 20 (above)
The sideplates and frame of the Nova 20 are made of a lightweight blend of carbon fibre and titanium, and the level wind is fitted with an aluminium oxide line roller to reduce line wear. The Nova also features a thumb bar to disengage the spool, a star drag, and a magnetic braking system. The gear ratio is 5:1, and the line capacity is 247 m (270 yds) of 5.4 kg (12 lb) mono or 206 m (225 yds) of 6.8 kg (15 lb) line.

RYOBI LX4 (below)
Streamlined shaping and lightweight construction make this an excellent reel to use with many of today's pencil-thin baitcasting rods. It has a line capacity of 183 m (200 yds) of 4.54 kg (10 lb) mono, and it has a level wind, a star drag, a thumb bar for rapid casting, and adjustable magnetic braking to eliminate overruns during casting.

SHIMANO BANTAM CITICA 200 (above)
The Citica has a high gear ratio (5:1) for rapid line retrieval, while trouble-free casting is aided by a magnetically controlled casting system. The line capacity is 192 m (210 yds) of 4.54 kg (10 lb) mono or 128 m (140 yds) of 6.4 kg (14 lb) line, and the weight has been kept to a minimum by the use of carbon fibre for the body and aluminium for the spool.

SHIMANO BANTAM CURADO 200 (below)
This is a reel with a very rapid rate of retrieve, having a gear ratio of 6:1. Four stainless steel ball bearings and one roller bearing ensure silky-smooth operation and long-term reliability, and line capacity is 192 m (210 yds) of 4.54 kg (10 lb) mono or 128 m (140 yds) of 6.4 kg (14 lb) line.

RYOBI LR-130 (above)
The LR-130 has a gear ratio of 4.2:1, and its line capacity is 165 m (180 yds) of 4 54 kg (10 lb) mono. Its level wind disengages for improved distance casting, and it also features a thumb bar and a handle drag, with which the spool drag setting can be altered quickly and accurately by simply turning the reel handle backwards.

FLY REELS 1

Whether you are content with a well-made, budget-priced reel or insist on a leading brand from the top end of the market, the most important thing to consider when buying a reel is how you are going to be using it. For instance, a lightweight, narrow, small-diameter, caged-drum reel will not be robust enough for large salmon, steelhead, or sea bass, or capable of holding the heavy lines required. This selection of small-capacity, single-action, geared, and disc-braked models is ideal for trout, sea trout, and small salmon on light, single-handed rods.

ORVIS BATTENKILL
5/6 7.9 cm (3⅛ in) *(right)*
This cast aluminium reel will take #5 or #6 lines plus 91 m (100 yds) backing. It has a counterbalanced spool, bronze bushings, and an exposed rim for fingertip control.

LEEDA/3M SYSTEM TWO 67L *(above)*
This aluminium alloy reel has a counterbalanced spool with an exposed rim, a stainless steel spindle, and a fully adjustable disc brake. It takes WF7F line plus 55 m (60 yds) backing.

HARDY PERFECT
7.9 cm (3⅛ in) *(below)*
First introduced in 1891 (see page 45), Hardy Perfect reels are machined to very close tolerances and the interchangeable spools are mounted on ball bearings. They are available in left- and right-hand versions.

LEEDA LC80 *(below)*
The LC80 is a light reel with a graphite outer frame and a wide, interchangeable plastic spool. It has a capacity of DT6 plus 69 m (75 yds) backing, and there is a useful line clip on the backplate to hold the loose end of the leader.

HARDY LRH LIGHTWEIGHT *(above)*
This aluminium alloy reel has an adjustable compensating check, interchangeable spools, and a caged drum, and converts to left- or right-hand wind. It is an ideal reel for all-round trout fishing, and its capacity is DT5F plus 37 m (40 yds) backing.

SHAKESPEARE SPEEDEX
8.9 cm (3½ in) *(above)*
The 2:1 gear ratio of the Speedex gives rapid line retrieval, and an adjustable drag provides resistance to running fish. It is available with narrow or wide spools; the narrow spool takes DT6F plus 23 m (25 yds) backing, the wide spool DT7F plus 69 m (75 yds) backing.

HARDY MARQUIS 2/3
6.5 cm (2⁹/₁₆ in) *(above)*
This little aluminium reel is designed for use on small streams with #2 or #3 lines. It has a reversible nickel silver lineguard, interchangeable spools, and an exposed rim, and converts to left- or right-hand wind.

ORVIS CFO 123 7.3 cm (2⅞ in) *(left)*
The CFO 123 has an exposed rim and adjustable drag, and converts to left- or right-hand wind. Its capacity is WF3F plus 46 m (50 yds) backing, and the one-sided frame permits quick spool changes.

ORVIS CFO III 7.6 cm (3 in) *(above)*
The CFO III has a similar specification to the CFO 123 but its larger size makes it more versatile, and it is popular with stillwater boat-fishing enthusiasts using short rods. Its capacity is WF6F plus 46 m (50 yds) backing.

FLY REELS 2

These reels are suitable for the heavier end of fly fishing, such as steelhead, salmon, large trout, and sea trout fishing, and for saltwater fly fishing. They are capable of holding the heavy lines and ample backing that are so necessary for large, hard-running fish, and most feature exposed rims, which are essential for controlling big fish. In addition, their large diameters allow quick line recovery and also limit line memory – the tendency of line to remain coiled when stripped from the reel – because the line is wound on in larger coils. Line memory can be a problem with small-diameter reels.

ORVIS BATTENKILL DISK 8/9
8.6 cm (3⅜ in) *(right)*
This reel is similar to the Battenkill 5/6 model (see page 42) but it is larger and has a Teflon disc drag. This drag is normally audible but it can be switched to silent running if preferred. The wide, lightweight drum reel has good capacity for its diameter, and can take WF9F plus 155 m (170 yds) backing.

HARDY OCEAN PRINCE *(below)*
The Ocean Prince is a heavy reel ideal for salmon, tarpon, and bonefish, and has a multi-plate clutch, strong, adjustable, anti-reverse drag, interchangeable spools, and exposed rim control. It converts to right- or left-hand wind and its capacity is DT10F plus 137 m (150 yds) backing.

ORVIS CFO VI 10 cm (4 in) *(above)*
This reel is similar to the CFO 123 (see page 43) but larger and with a caged drum; capacity is DT11F plus 137 m (150 yds) backing. It is ideal for steelhead and salmon, but unsuitable for bonefish or estuary sea trout because it is not designed for saltwater fishing.

LEEDA MAGNUM 140D *(below)*
The 140D is a full-cage reel with adjustable disc drag, exposed rim, counterbalanced interchangeable spools, and a capacity of DT10F plus 128 m (140 yds) backing. It is ideal for shooting-head work, steelhead, and salmon.

SHAKESPEARE PFLUEGER MEDALIST 10 cm (4 in) *(right)*
This large-capacity reel is ideal for shooting-head work and for heavy sunk-line fishing. It is often used by anglers fishing deep stillwaters with a lead-cored trolling line for fry-feeding brown and rainbow trout.

HARDY MARQUIS 8/9 MULTIPLIER 9.2 cm (3⅝ in) *(below)*
This reel is similar to the Marquis 2/3 (see page 43) but is larger and geared for rapid line retrieval; capacity WF8F plus 46 m (50 yds) backing. It is ideal for trout, sea trout, steelhead, and salmon fishing with single-handed rods.

LEEDA/3M SYSTEM TWO 1011 *(left)*
With its fully adjustable disc brake, exposed rim, and capacity of DT10 plus 100 m (110 yds) backing, this reel is ideal for large trout, sea trout, steelhead, and salmon.

HARDY PERFECT *(right)*
The Perfect was first introduced by Hardy in 1891 and then later dropped from their range. It was reintroduced during the 1970s because of the resurgence of interest created by angler/author Hugh Falkus, who professed it to be the ultimate sea trout reel. The older reels are much sought after by collectors. It is ideal for large trout, sea trout, steelhead, and salmon.

SHAKESPEARE REVOLUTIONARY CASSETTE FLY 10 cm (4 in) *(above)*
This unusual reel from Shakespeare has the line spooled onto a plastic cassette, which is then loaded onto the spool proper. Its disc brake, cageless design, and counterbalanced spool offer generous line capacity and make it a good reel for fast-running gamefish.

BOAT REELS

To cope with the rigours of boat angling, a multiplier reel must be strong and well-engineered with an adequate spool capacity for its intended use. The gearing should be precise and robust, and the drag mechanism should be smooth and reliable to minimize the risk of line breakage when you are playing a large, free-running fish. Boat reel drag mechanisms are adjusted either by turning a star-shaped knob (star drag) or by moving a lever (lever drag) – pushing the lever forward increases the drag tension, and pulling it back reduces it. The lever drag, once found only on large, expensive reels designed for big-game fishing, is now used on many smaller models. The advantage of the lever drag over the star drag is that it allows you to increase the drag tension more gradually and precisely.

SHIMANO TRITON 100G (right)
Shimano has played a large part in popularizing the lever drag outside of the big-game scene, and the drag application on the Triton 100G is wonderfully smooth and precise. This small multiplier has a carbon/titanium body and a spool capacity of 230 m (250 yds) of 7.7 kg (17 lb) mono line. It is a perfect reel for run-of-the-mill boat work, but is not suitable for uptiding because lever drag reels do not cast well.

DAIWA MILLIONAIRE II M37–2B (above)
Millionaire reels are designed primarily for surfcasting, but they are also excellent as light to medium boat reels. The M37–2B has a spool capacity of 340 m (370 yds) of 5.4 kg (12 lb) line, and its two stainless-steel ball bearings ensure smooth spool rotation under pressure and at speed. It is an ideal light uptiding reel, perfect for light-line pollack fishing, shallow-water tope, fast-moving bass, and some of the smaller pelagic gamefish such as dolphinfish.

ABU GARCIA AMBASSADEUR 10000 C (left)
This high-quality, heavy-duty reel is designed for both beach work and boat fishing, including trolling. The gear ratio of 4.2:1 is shifted down automatically to 2.5:1 when a big fish is being played and the reel is heavily loaded, giving a slower but more powerful retrieve.

ABU GARCIA AMBASSADEUR 7000 C SYNCRO (above)
A spool capacity of 230 m (250 yds) of 15.9 kg (35 lb) mono line makes this reel ideal for all light to medium work, and its centrifugal braking prevents overruns when casting heavy lures. When playing troublesome fish, you can remove up to 75 per cent of the drag simply by backwinding; full drag is reapplied automatically when the handle is cranked. Unfortunately, it comes with a level wind, but conversion kits are available.

PENN INTERNATIONAL II 30 SW (left)
Reels with two-speed retrieves help anglers beat the biggest fish on the lightest tackle. The Penn International II 30 SW features a 3.8:1 gear ratio for regular retrieval work, and 1.8:1 for when the pressure is really on. A ratio of less than 2:1 might seem too low to be useful, but when a big fish is proving difficult, using too high a ratio can result in failure. It is like riding a bicycle uphill: get the gearing right, and you will progress with relative ease.

SHAKESPEARE FULMAR 400 (right)
Lever-drag reels have rightly earned themselves the reputation of being the first choice for heavy boat-fishing work. They also have a reputation for being expensive, but the Fulmar 400, with its 3:1 gear ratio, carbon/titanium construction, aluminium spool, and capacity for 460 m (500 yds) of 22.7 kg (50 lb) mono line, is both reliable and reasonably priced. It is a perfect reel for heavy-duty wreck fishing and for middle-range gamefish work.

PENN INTERNATIONAL 50 (left)
The biggest jobs in the boat-fishing world require reels that have earned themselves the biggest reputations. On the big-game scene, that usually means Penn reels. Penn makes larger reels than the International 50 – up to 130 class – but it has the capacity, power, and quality of construction to handle almost any big fish. Its spool capacity is 550 m (600 yds) of 22.7 kg (50 lb) mono line, the gear ratio is 3:1, and its lever drag is the smoothest anyone could wish for.

47

SHORE REELS

Shore reels, like shore rods, have great demands placed upon them by the rugged nature of fishing from the shore. This has lead to much innovation in their design and manufacture, but so far it has not proved possible to combine the best features of each main type (multiplier, fixed-spool, and sidecaster) into one super-reel. The multiplier, in theory more robust and capable of casting greater distances, is not as easily mastered as the fixed-spool reel, which in its turn is better suited to light spinning and float work than the multiplier. The third option, the Alvey Sidecast, is a cross between a centrepin and a fixed-spool reel. It has some undoubted benefits but also, like the other types, has its drawbacks.

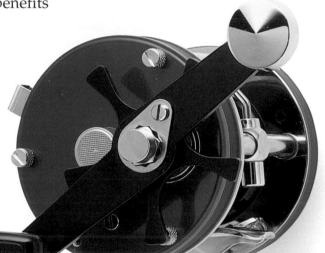

ABU GARCIA AMBASSADEUR 9000 CL *(above)*
The robust, high-capacity 9000 CL is ideal for the tougher jobs along the shore, such as fishing in heavy kelp, and for dealing with powerful fish. Good casting ability is combined with a two-speed retrieve: low for playing fish and high for skipping fast over snags.

ABU GARCIA AMBASSADEUR 7000 *(right)*
The precision of the Ambassadeur 7000 revolutionized casting and distance fishing, and its design has not changed in two decades because it has not needed to. It is still the best casting and fishing option for general shore angling.

ABU GARCIA AMBASSADEUR 6500 C SPECIAL *(left)*
The 6500 C puts proven Abu Garcia technology into arguably the smallest practical package for medium to heavy shore use. A tournament casting favourite with real angling ability.

DAIWA MILLIONAIRE TOURNAMENT 7HT *(right)*
The 7HT's 5:1 gear ratio, its lack of level wind and top bar, and its special foot to suit coaster clamps, make it a superb distance-caster's reel. It is also very good for long-range beach fishing.

ABU GARCIA CARDINAL C5 (right)
The Cardinal C5, with its skirted spool and rear drag, typifies the sort of middle-range fixed-spool reel that is so valuable for pelagic species such as bass and mullet. It is also useful for light legering over snaggy terrain.

DAIWA PM9000H (below)
A good, heavy-duty fixed-spool reel requires a skirted, coned spool; automatic and manual bale arm operation; a powerful, rear-operated drag; anti-reverse; and fast line retrieval. Such features are found on the PM9000H, which is suitable for most shore work involving long, easy casting for small to medium-sized fish.

ALVEY SIDECAST 60 A-5 (right)
An Alvey Sidecast is a type of centrepin with a two-position spool. For casting, the spool is positioned with its axle parallel to the rod, and the line spills freely over the rim as with a fixed-spool reel. On the retrieve, the spool is aligned with the rod and the line is wound on as with a standard centrepin. An Alvey casts well and offers tremendous direct power, but slow line uptake makes it less suitable for work where other reels can cope.

49

Lines, Crimps, Beads, & Swivels

Although they are small and seem insignificant, leader (or trace) lines, crimps, beads, swivels, and the like are as important as rods and reels because, along with hooks and lures, they constitute the tackle that fish come directly into contact with. Unless they perform correctly and reliably, perfect bait presentation (without which the bait, no matter how good, loses some of its appeal to fish) will be difficult, as will the successful playing and landing of a hooked fish. Similar considerations apply to the reel line, whether it be monofilament, braided fibre (such as braided Dacron), or wire. An outfit can only be as strong and reliable as its weakest link, which is often the line. Look after it and change it regularly, and always use line that is of the correct type and breaking strain (the load or weight that a line can take before it breaks) for its intended application.

Monofilament

For bait and lure fishing, monofilament nylon (mono) far outsells every other line material combined, and it is also used as backing for fly lines, which are usually made of coated Dacron (see page 52). It is cheap, reliable, the only line that can be distance cast, and a virtual must for freshwater fishing. However, there are disadvantages to consider. Different brands stretch to varying degrees. This can be helpful in cushioning violent movement from big fish, but it also cushions the bite and strike in deep water. Other drawbacks of mono are that it is weakened by knotting, its breaking strain is reduced when it is wet, and exposure to the ultraviolet light in sunlight will weaken it. In general, mono line should be changed at least once per year.

Braided Line

Once extremely popular, braided Dacron line has fallen from favour as a result of monofilament improvement and competition from wire. This is a pity, because it has useful attributes such as specified breaking strain control for IGFA line class records, excellent knot strength, and no deterioration over time. On the downside, it chafes easily, offers no cushion for bullying lively fish, and has a low breaking strain for its diameter. Its big advantage is its lack of stretch, which is vital in deep water and helpful for trotting float-fished baits (see page 223), where mono might mask the strike. Otherwise, it is used mainly for trolling, float fishing for sharks, and sea fishing in deep water with not much tide.

Wire Line

Wire line comes in three forms: single-strand stainless steel, braided or twisted multi-strand steel, and single-strand Monel (an alloy based on copper and nickel). It is an excellent choice for sea fishing in deep water where tides run particularly hard, because it does not stretch and has a high breaking strain for its diameter. This means instant bite detection at any depth, positive striking, and the ability to hold bottom with a fraction of the additional weight that is required by other lines. Its drawbacks are that it requires a narrow, deep-spooled multiplier reel without a level wind, a rod with roller guides (at least a roller tip), and a monofilament weak link at the end. It cannot be cast, hooks can be ripped out easily because it has no cushioning stretchiness, and care must be taken to avoid cut hands.

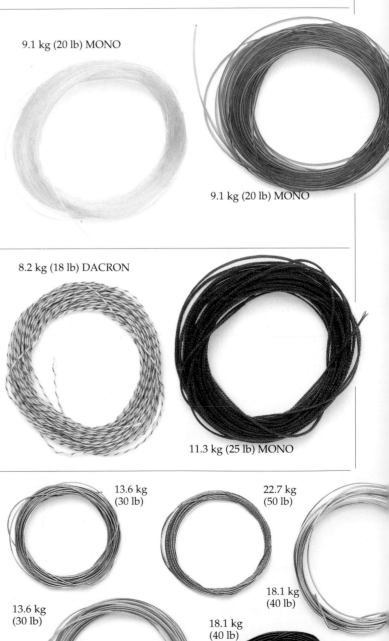

9.1 kg (20 lb) MONO

9.1 kg (20 lb) MONO

8.2 kg (18 lb) DACRON

11.3 kg (25 lb) MONO

13.6 kg (30 lb)

22.7 kg (50 lb)

13.6 kg (30 lb)

18.1 kg (40 lb)

18.1 kg (40 lb)

LEADER LINE

When fishing in freshwater for pike and other species with sharp teeth and strong jaws, a strong leader (trace) between the reel line and the hook or lure is essential. Freshwater leaders should be uncoated braided wire or, for deadbait trolling, single-strand wire. In saltwater, plain mono is adequate for small to medium-sized fish without teeth, but for large fish, or those with sharp teeth, use longliner's nylon or wire. Generally speaking, plain monos from 18.1 kg (40 lb) upwards make the best leaders for boat fishing; anything lighter tends to present the bait poorly. Use nylon of 68 kg (150 lb) for heavy wreck and reef fishing, and at least 91 kg (200 lb) nylon for giant tuna and billfish.

79 kg (175 lb)
STAINLESS STEEL

27.2 kg (60 lb)
MONO

CRIMPS & BEADS

Wire line and heavy-guage mono are joined to other lines and to swivels by means of crimps, which are small metal sleeves. For example, to fix a swivel to a wire line, a crimp is slipped over the end of the line, which is then looped through the eye of the swivel and back into the crimp. Then the crimp is squeezed tight with crimping pliers. Beads are used to protect knots from sliding booms and to act as buffers ahead of fixed stops.

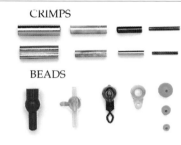

CRIMPS

BEADS

COIL CRIMP (right)
Coil crimp is springy, spiral stainless steel wire. Short lengths of it can be wound onto the line to replace stop knots and plastic stoppers that are superglued into position for fixing droppers and booms in place. They can be repositioned quickly or removed for reuse.

COIL CRIMP

SWIVELS

Every terminal rig, no matter how simple, should ideally contain at least one swivel to prevent twists in the line, and using a swivel is the perfect way to attach a leader or a dropper to the reel line. Even the best brands are cheap, so go for the quality names such as Berkley, Mustad, Drennan, and Sampo; unbranded imitations are generally unreliable and can refuse to turn under stress.

BARREL SWIVELS
Barrel swivels are the best choice for general-purpose work. Their design almost guarantees long-term reliability.

BALL-BEARING SWIVELS
These offer superb, freely rotating twist correction, which is essential for all trolling work.

THREE-WAY SWIVELS
These were once popular for linking in droppers, but standoff booms terminating in barrel swivels are now generally preferred.

CONGER HOOK SWIVEL
This is not to be trusted. The hook has a habit of coming out of the swivel head, which can also prove too weak for a big fish.

LINK SWIVELS

LINK SWIVELS
A link swivel is a swivel with a quick-release link to which the terminal tackle is attached. Several types of link are available, but they all allow easy changing of terminal tackle, either to unhook fish while continuing fishing, or to replace a kinked or damaged leader.

SAMPO SWIVELS

BIG-GAME SWIVEL
Reliable, heavy-duty ball bearing swivels, such as those made by Sampo and Berkley, are essential for the prolonged, tackle-testing battles with exceptionally large fish that are typical of big-game fishing.

51

FLY LINES & LEADERS

Most artificial flies are small and weigh next to nothing, and the casting weight needed to carry them out onto the water is provided by the fly line. The fly is joined to the fly line via a braided or solid leader, and the fly line in turn is attached to a length of braided or solid backing line. The backing provides a reserve of line for playing big, fast-running fish, and, by partly filling the reel spool, it ensures that the fly line coils are of large circumference. These big coils are less likely than small ones to tangle as they are pulled off the reel. Fly lines are made from materials such as braided nylon, braided Dacron, and PVC, and coated with a variety of polymers such as polyurethane and PTFE.

LINE COLOUR
Most floating lines are pale in colour, but sinking lines are usually produced in darker hues.

THE AFTM SYSTEM

Formulated by the American Fishing Tackle Manufacturers Association (AFTMA), this system uses a code of letters and numbers to describe the characteristics of a fly line. The first letters of the code indicate the line's profile or shape, the number that follows indicates its weight, and the last letter (or two letters) signifies its density. The number assigned to a fly line *(see right)* depends on the weight, in grains, of the first 9.1 m (30 ft) of the line, excluding any level tip. AFTM numbers are also assigned to fly rods, and the number of the line should match that of the rod with which it is used.

AFTM LINE WEIGHT NUMBERS

AFTM number	Weight in grains	Weight range
1	60	54–66
2	80	74–86
3	100	94–106
4	120	114–126
5	140	134–146
6	160	152–168
7	185	177–193
8	210	202–218
9	240	230–250
10	280	270–290
11	330	318–342
12	380	368–392
13	430	418–442
14	480	468–492

AFTM FLY LINE PROFILES

ANATOMY OF A FLY LINE (DOUBLE TAPER)

Tip — Front taper — Coating — Belly (Body) — Core — Rear taper — Tip

The fly line profiles, or tapers, in common use today are the double taper, the weight forward, and the shooting head or shooting taper. The level line, which is the same diameter throughout its length, is difficult to cast and is now seldom used. Double-taper lines are designed to present flies gently at close to medium distance and are easy to cast. Weight-forward lines are intended for medium to long-distance casting, and once the tip and belly of the line have been cast, the thin running line shoots easily through the rod rings. A well-designed weight-forward line will present a fly just as delicately as a double taper. Shooting heads consist of short lengths of fly line, backed by fine braided or flat solid monofilament which produces little resistance when pulled through the rod rings, and are used for casting prodigious distances on big stillwaters.

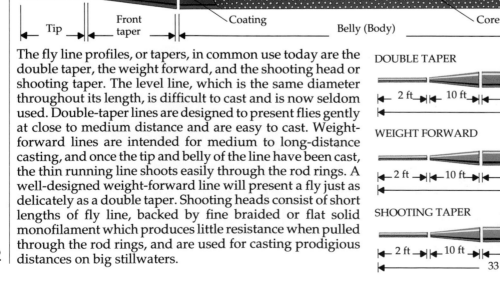

DOUBLE TAPER
2 ft — 10 ft — 66 ft / 90 ft — 10 ft — 2 ft

WEIGHT FORWARD
2 ft — 10 ft — 20 ft / 90 ft — 3 ft — 55 ft

SHOOTING TAPER
2 ft — 10 ft — 18 ft / 33 ft — Mono shooting line is attached to loop

AFTM Fly Line Symbols

In the AFTM system of fly line classification, the letters preceding the weight number (DT, WF, or SH – or sometimes L, for level line) indicate the taper of the line. The letter or letters that come after the weight number (such as F, ND, I, S, FS, and VFS) signify the density, or function, of the line, that is, whether the line floats, sinks, or has an intermediate or neutral density and thus sinks very slowly.

For example, a fly line described as DT9F is one that has a double taper, is of weight number 9, and floats, while a number 7 line with a weight-forward taper and a neutral density is described as WF7ND.

Fly Line Symbols	
DT	Double taper
WF	Weight forward
SH	Shooting head
F	Floating
ND	Neutral density
I	Intermediate
S	Sinking
FS	Fast sinking
VFS	Very fast sinking

Line Densities

Fly lines are made in a variety of densities, and the density of a line determines whether it will float or sink. Those with the lowest densities are floating lines, and those with the highest are the very fast sinkers. However, the descriptions given to individual lines are not always a reliable guide to their performance, and one manufacturer's fast-sinking line might sink at the same rate as another's very fast sinker.

To give a more accurate indication of how their sinking fly lines perform, many manufacturers publish their sinking rates. These are given in centimetres per second or inches per second, or as the depth to which the line will sink after a specified period of time. The only problem with this is that different parts of a line may sink at different speeds, and sinking rates may be influenced by many factors. For example, water temperature and wind speed (with attendant undertow) both affect the rate at which a line will sink.

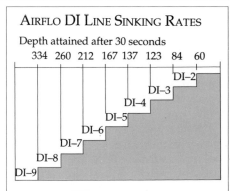

Airflo DI Line Sinking Rates

Depth attained after 30 seconds

334 260 212 167 137 123 84 60

DI–2, DI–3, DI–4, DI–5, DI–6, DI–7, DI–8, DI–9

SINKING RATES *(above)*
This is an example of a manufacturer's sinking rate data, in this case for Airflo's DI range. The depths are stated in inches.

Leaders

The leader is the length of nylon that connects the fly line to the fly. To ensure a good turnover during casting, it should taper from the fly line down, with the butt section (that closest to the fly line) being at least a third of the fly line's thickness. When surface fishing, use a long leader to put a good distance between the thick, coloured fly line and the fly. This distance is usually not so important when you are using sinking lines.

Braided leaders

These leaders are made of nylon braid that tapers continuously throughout its length and is very supple. They are produced in a range of floating and sinking versions, and because of their excellent turnover they are a great aid to good fly presentation. With some braided leaders, the butt end fits over the tip of the fly line and is held in place by a piece of silicone tubing, while others are joined to the fly line by loops. The fly is attached to a braided leader by a short length of mono called a tippet.

Monofilament leaders

Commercially made mono leaders consist either of a continuous, tapering length of nylon, or of lengths of progressively smaller diameters and lower breaking strains knotted together. The knotless leaders are stronger and less likely to pick up weed than the knotted versions, but they do have the drawback that each time the fly is changed, the tip of the leader becomes thicker. Eventually, the entire leader has to be changed or a finer tip section attached.

ROMAN MOSER
BRAIDED LEADERS

LEADER DENSITIES
The high-density braided leaders now available allow unleaded or very small flies to be fished at depth without the need for a sinking fly line.

AIRFLO
BRAIDED LEADERS

HOOKS 1

Hooks are essential if unglamorous items of tackle. Although their functions are simple, their design is often complex and subtle, and there are innumerable patterns, sizes, and finishes on the market. These have evolved in response to the requirements of the different styles and methods of fishing, the varied sizes, mouth shapes, teeth, and lips of fish, and the baits needed to tempt them. As a result, it is essential to match your choice to your intended method of fishing and the species you intend to catch when buying your hooks. In this respect, as with any other tackle purchase, the advice of a reputable dealer will prove invaluable.

HOOK CHOICE
Always use a hook large enough to cope with the fish you intend to catch.

HOOK TYPES

There are three basic types of hook, the single, the double, and the treble. The range of hooks is enormous, but without doubt the most popular type is the single in its many guises, from the small spade-end hooks used by match fishermen to the large stainless steel hooks used by big-game anglers. Double hooks are used chiefly for fly fishing, but some, such as the Whichway, are used for pike fishing. With its three points, the treble hook offers great hooking potential and is used mainly for spinning baits (plugs and spoons), pike rigs, and salmon flies (either long-shank trebles or tube flies).

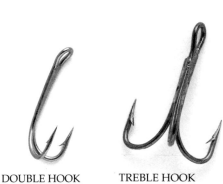

SINGLE HOOK   DOUBLE HOOK   TREBLE HOOK

PARTS OF A HOOK

The component parts of a typical hook are the eye, shank, bend, point, barb, throat, and gape (or gap). Hooks are made of high-carbon steel, usually with a corrosion-resistant finish, or of stainless steel.

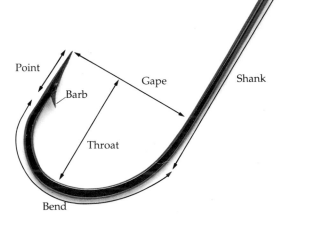

Eye

Point

Barb

Gape

Shank

Throat

Bend

HOOK SIZES

Hook sizes are denoted by numbers, but the number allocated to a particular size of hook may vary from one manufacturer to another. The smallest hook size is the 30, and, as an approximate guide, hooks from size 30 up to size 1 are used for freshwater fishing, and hooks 1/0 up to 16/0 for saltwater fishing. Japanese hooks tend to be a size smaller than European hooks, and importers compensate for this by moving the hooks down one size, so a Japanese size 6 becomes a size 8.

EUROPEAN SIZE 8
Forged heavy wire, round bend

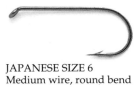

JAPANESE SIZE 6
Medium wire, round bend

JAPANESE SIZE 6
Medium wire, sproat bend

WIRE GAUGES

The diameter, or gauge, of the wire from which a hook is made depends on the hook's pattern and size, but manufacturers now offer a choice of gauges for each pattern and size of hook. Fine-wire hooks are used for light-line fishing and dry flies, and medium-wire hooks for general fishing and most wet flies. Heavy wires are used for very strong hooks for big-game fishing, freshwater fishing for large fish, and heavy flies such as salmon flies and wet flies that are required to sink rapidly through the water.

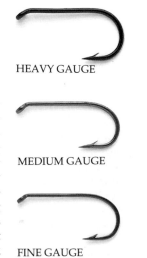

HEAVY GAUGE

MEDIUM GAUGE

FINE GAUGE

HOOK EYES

Hook eyes come in many different shapes and sizes, and some hooks have spade ends instead of eyes. Flattened shanks were once very popular for hooks tied to nylon, but the labour-intensive whipping and varnishing required is no longer commercially viable when competing with whipped spade-end hooks. Similarly, tapered ring eyes are more expensive to produce than straight-wire ring eyes and are falling out of favour with manufacturers. Straight eyes are very popular with freshwater and sea anglers for bait fishing, and the angle-eyed hooks are popular with fly anglers. When buying a hook, always check that the end of the wire used for forming the eye butts up against the shank; any hook with a gap at the eye should be discarded. A spade-end hook should have no sharp edges at the front of the spade that could cut the nylon when it is pulled tight.

RING EYE
This is a round eye formed from straight wire, and is the most popular type of eye.

TAPERED EYE
The wire is tapered where it meets the shank, giving a neat, unobtrusive eye.

SPADE END
The spade end is formed by flattening the end of the wire.

LOOPED EYE
This very strong eye is used on traditional single salmon hooks.

NEEDLE EYE
The needle eye is used on treble hooks, especially those for tube flies.

SWIVEL EYE
This is used on strong hooks for big game and large sea fish.

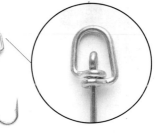

Angled eyes
Eyes are formed either straight (in line with the hook) or angled towards or away from the point. The eye of an up-eyed hook is angled away from the point for good clearance between the shank and the point. The down-eyed hook has its eye angled towards the point to give better penetration on the strike.

UP-EYED   STRAIGHT-EYED   DOWN-EYED

GUT EYES
Gut eyes, now obsolete, were formed from gut whipped to the shank before a fly was tied.

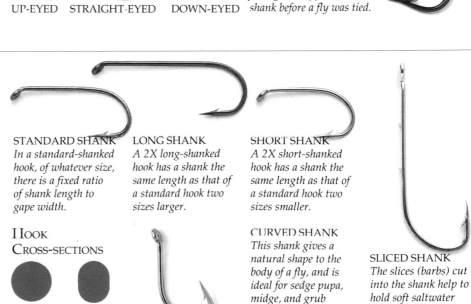

HOOK SHANKS

Hooks designed for bait fishing vary less in shape and in shank length than hooks designed for fly fishing, which have to cater for the huge number of different sizes and patterns of fly. Hooks with short or standard-length shanks are used for freshwater bait fishing, but saltwater hooks tend to have long shanks, to accommodate the larger baits used and to protect leaders from the teeth of many species of sea fish. Many large hooks, especially saltwater patterns, have forged shanks and bends. Forging involves hammering the wire of the hook, after it has been shaped, to give it a flattened cross-section. This makes the hook much stronger than one of the same size with an unforged, round cross-section.

STANDARD SHANK
In a standard-shanked hook, of whatever size, there is a fixed ratio of shank length to gape width.

LONG SHANK
A 2X long-shanked hook has a shank the same length as that of a standard hook two sizes larger.

SHORT SHANK
A 2X short-shanked hook has a shank the same length as that of a standard hook two sizes smaller.

CURVED SHANK
This shank gives a natural shape to the body of a fly, and is ideal for sedge pupa, midge, and grub patterns.

SLICED SHANK
The slices (barbs) cut into the shank help to hold soft saltwater baits firmly in place on the hook.

HOOK CROSS-SECTIONS

ROUND WIRE   FORGED WIRE

Hooks 2

Hook Bends

The shape of the bend is an important distinguishing factor between one hook pattern and another, and as with other features of hooks, such as shank length and eye, a large number of different forms have evolved over the years. The shape of a bend is largely dictated by the intended use of the hook, but in general, a smoothly rounded bend is stronger than one that is sharply angled, while angled bends allow the hook point to penetrate deeper. Some bends are at their best when used for a particular style or method of fishing, but others are more versatile. The Sproat, for example, is an ideal bend for traditional flies, emergers, and dry flies, while the round bend is suitable not only for freshwater and saltwater bait fishing but also for fly hooks.

CRYSTAL BEND
The crystal is a popular bend for freshwater bait fishing, particularly in small sizes.

ROUND BEND
Round bends are used with offset points for bait angling, straight points for fly fishing.

SPROAT
The Sproat is a good fly hook bend. The front angle is not as sharp as that of the crystal.

ABERDEEN
This is a round-bend, fine-wire sea hook with a long shank. It is a good bait hook.

LIMERICK
The Limerick is widely used for freshwater and saltwater hooks and for salmon hooks.

KENDAL ROUND
This is a slightly less rounded, more angular version of the ordinary round bend.

SHRIMP BEND
This long bend is designed for humpbacked flies such as shrimp and bug patterns.

TIEMCO
This has a slightly curved shank and a straight point, and is ideal for emerger and dry-fly patterns.

O'SHAUGNESSY
The O'Shaughnessy is a classic and very strong bend for heavy sea fish, including big-game species.

SPECIMEN BEND
A modern bend, used with an offset point, for freshwater and saltwater bait fishing.

Hook Shapes

The overall shape of a hook is its style of bend, point, shank, and eye. Freshwater bait hooks tend to have offset points with short or standard straight shanks, and are either eyed or spade end. The "weedless" hook has a spring-loaded wire guard that shields the point to prevent it snagging in weed. For saltwater bait fishing, the hooks are eyed and usually have longer shanks than those used for freshwater work. The very popular O'Shaughnessy, Kirby, and Aberdeen patterns are good examples of saltwater bait hooks. The majority of fly anglers use up-eyed or down-eyed hooks with straight points, straight shanks of various lengths, and a variety of bends.

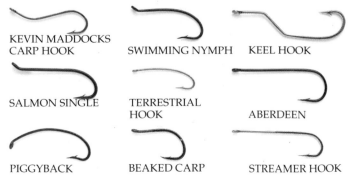

KEVIN MADDOCKS CARP HOOK SWIMMING NYMPH KEEL HOOK

SALMON SINGLE TERRESTRIAL HOOK ABERDEEN

PIGGYBACK BEAKED CARP STREAMER HOOK

HOOK POINTS

Hook points vary with the different patterns and from manufacturer to manufacturer; cut hollow and superior points, for example, are typical of the Mustad range of hooks. Most hooks have cut or knife-edge points because these are easier to mass-produce than ground points. The outer edge of the hollow point is straight, while the inner line between the point and the tip of the barb is curved. With the superior point this arrangement is reversed and the outer edge is slightly curved while the inner edge is straight. A Dublin point, found on many salmon hooks, has features of both, and the point curves away from the shank. Some of the best and strongest points, however, are the ground and chemically sharpened needle points with fine-cut barbs that are produced in Japan.

BARLESS
A point without a barb allows easy unhooking so is ideal for catch-and-release fishing.

HOLLOW POINT
This cut point is used on many of the wide range of hooks produced by Mustad of Norway.

DUBLIN
This point originated in Dublin and is used on salmon "irons" and game fishing hooks.

ARROWPOINT
The arrowpoint does not penetrate as easily as a standard barbless point, but it is claimed to hold fish better.

BEAKED
This ground, chemically sharpened point is strong, and penetrates well, because its barb is not deeply cut.

FALKUS OUTBARB
The barbs of this treble are on the outsides of the points. It has excellent fish-holding properties.

OFFSET POINTS

Hook points not only vary in shape but also are either straight or offset. To determine whether a point is straight or offset, check the alignment of the point to the shank. If the point is straight, it will be in line with the shank. An offset point will point either to the left, which is known as kirbed, or to the right, which is reversed. Straight points are ideal for fly fishing, but offset points are better for bait fishing. The most popular offset is the reversed, because most anglers are right-handed: for them, it is easier to bait a hook with a reversed point than one with a kirbed point, because the point is angled upwards when the hook is held in the right hand.

OFFSET LEFT /
KIRBED

OFFSET/RIGHT
REVERSED

HOOK FAULTS

UNFORMED EYES

POOR BRAZING

OVERCUT BARB

OVERLONG POINT

Common hook faults include unformed eyes, poor brazing, overcut barbs, poor temper, and overlong points. Most will be obvious, but poor temper may be difficult to detect. Carefully hook the point behind your thumbnail and pull the hook to open the bend. An under-tempered hook will bend out easily and not spring back when released; an overtempered hook will snap.

HOOK FINISHES

Hooks come in a variety of coloured and corrosion-resistant finishes for different styles of fishing. The traditional black japanned finish is still used on some patterns, particularly salmon hooks, but the most unobtrusive colour is bronze, and most hooks are now coated with a bronze finish. Some saltwater hooks are made of stainless steel, which is left uncoated because it is almost totally resistant to the corrosive properties of seawater. Other saltwater hooks are sometimes coloured silver so that they attract fish to the bait.

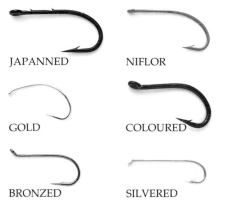

JAPANNED

NIFLOR

GOLD

COLOURED

BRONZED

SILVERED

FRESHWATER WEIGHTS

The great many sizes and designs of weight are used to perform a variety of functions, from cocking a float to anchoring a legered bait. In the past, almost all weights were made of lead, but in many countries the use of lead weights has been banned or restricted for environmental reasons. In the United Kingdom, for example, all leger weights weighing up to 28 g (1 oz) and split shot between sizes 6 and SSG (swan shot) must be made of non-toxic materials, so leger weights in the affected sizes are usually steel, zinc, or brass, and split shot is made of tungsten or heavy alloys.

CORK-BASED PLUMMET

CLIP-ON PLUMMET

PLUMMETS
These are used in float fishing to find the depth of the swim. With a cork-based plummet, the line is threaded through an eye and the hook embedded in a cork strip at the base; a clip-on plummet has spring-loaded jaws that clamp over the hook.

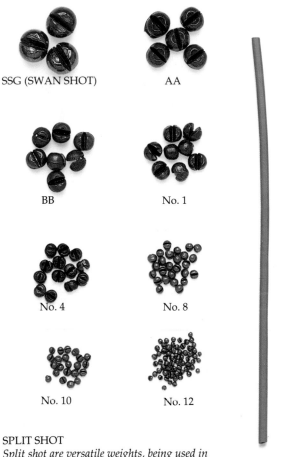

SSG (SWAN SHOT)

AA

BB

No. 1

No. 4

No. 8

No. 10

No. 12

SPLIT SHOT
Split shot are versatile weights, being used in float fishing to lock eyed floats in position, to cock floats, and to add weight to rigs. In legering, shot are used to lock larger weights in position and to weight light rigs. They are available in a range of sizes from swan shot (SSG) – so called because this size was used in shotgun cartridges when swans were the shooters' quarry – down to "dust" shot (sizes from 8 down to 12). As a rule of thumb, two split shot of any one size are roughly equal in weight to one shot of the size above (see page 222). Always use a finger and thumb, never your teeth, to close shot over the line. Never slide them along the line when altering their position: this causes abrasion and frictional heat that can damage and weaken the line. Open them up with a thumbnail and then reposition them..

TUBE SHOT
These thin, flexible tubes, made of polymer and tungsten, are less likely to snag than shot, and are a good alternative when seed baits are being used: fish often nibble at the shot instead of the bait. They are cut to length with scissors, threaded on the line, and locked in place with tiny shot.

LEADED WIRE
Like tube shot, leaded wire is a good alternative to split shot when float fishing with seed baits. To cock the float, the wire can be twisted directly around its base, or wound around a matchstick then threaded onto the line beneath the float and held in place by a small shot.

PUTTY WEIGHT
This heavy, puttylike material was an early alternative to lead shot, but its use declined when satisfactory non-lead shot was developed. It is now used mainly by carp anglers as a casting weight and to balance the weight of baits for improved presentation.

OLIVETTES
These tiny, streamlined weights originated in France, and are used in pole fishing. The smallest, the size 4/0, weighs just 0.081 g (0.003 oz); the largest, the size 12, weighs 3 g (0.106 oz).

DRILLED BULLETS
A drilled bullet is used to present a moving bait. It will roll freely through a fast-flowing swim, pulling the bait towards fish holding station in the flow.

HILLMAN
This is used in spinning to take the lure down farther in deep or swift-flowing water, and to help reduce line twist. This weight should be clipped to the eye of the swivel to which the main line tied.

BARREL
The barrel weight is designed to roll slowly along the bed of a river to present a moving bait. The line is threaded through the weight's hollow body.

COFFIN WEIGHTS

The coffin weight was designed for presenting static baits in running water. Its flattened shape and sharp edges ensure that it sits tight on the bottom, digging itself into gravel or silt. The line is threaded into a hole drilled down the centre of the weight.

DISC WEIGHTS

These flattened, almost-circular weights will keep baits static in fast-flowing swims. Being flat, a disc weight offers little resistance to the current flowing over it when it is lying on the riverbed, while its large surface area gives it a good grip on the bottom. It is attached to the rig by a swivel, which minimizes the risk of tangling during casting.

SPHERICAL BOMB

This is often used on bolt rigs. It should be attached by a short link of weak line, so that if a hooked fish runs into a snag such as thick weed, the weight will break off. Without the weak link, the reel line may break first, leaving the fish tethered to the snag and condemned to a lingering death.

ARLESEY BOMBS

These were devised by Richard Walker in the 1950s, for catching big fish at long range in deep water. The streamlined shape makes them easy to cast long distances, and their swivel attachments reduce the risk of tangling. Today, they are probably the most widely used of all leger weights, and are as suitable for quivertipping on a river as they are for fishing at long range for perch or carp. They are available in sizes ranging from 3.5 g (⅛ oz) to 113 g (4 oz), and some incorporate a screw-in swivel that allows the size of weight being used on a rig to be changed rapidly.

BUZZ BOMB (right)

The buzz bomb is a variation of the Arlesey bomb incorporating fins that reduce wobble during flight. It can be cast with consistent accuracy over distances of about 90 m (100 yds) or more.

FLAT-BOTTOMED WEIGHT

This type of weight is used mainly in carp fishing. Its flattened shape helps it to rise quickly from the bed and plane through the water when retrieved, and makes it less prone to snagging.

TROLLING WEIGHT (right)

Trolling weights can weigh up to 1.36 kg (3 lb), and are used to get the bait down quickly in deep water. They are simply lowered into the water, so a streamlined shape is not necessary.

BOTTLE WEIGHTS

This clever design allows the weight on the line to be changed quickly. A piece of silicone rubber tubing is attached to the line by a snaplock swivel, and a bottle-shaped weight is inserted into its lower end. The weight can be changed simply by pulling it out of the silicone tubing and replacing it with one that is the same size but either lighter or heavier.

WYE

Like the Hillman weight, the Wye is used in spinning to add weight to a lure and to overcome the problem of line twist produced by a revolving lure. Many anglers prefer it to the spiral weight, also used in spinning, which has a tendency to fall off the line. Its shape is not as aerodynamic as that of the spiral, but it casts well enough.

SPIRAL WEIGHT

This is used on spinning rigs to add weight and prevent line twists. It is attached to the reel line above the swivel that joins the line to the lure or leader. The line is wrapped tightly around the body of the weight (in the spiral channel) and through the spirals of wire at each end. The aerodynamic shape of the weight gives good casting distance.

59

SALTWATER WEIGHTS & BOOMS

Sea angling often involves coping with strong tidal currents, deep waters, and long casting distances. To avoid problems, make sure you have enough weight on the line to get the bait down and hold it in position, and use standoff booms to prevent traces (leaders) from tangling. In addition, you can minimize the risk of damage to baits during long-distance casting by using devices such as impact shields and bait clips.

WEIGHTS

In general, a weight or sinker is anything an angler cares to put on the end of a line to take it to the bottom. For example, shore anglers fishing heavy ground, where there is a high risk of snagging, often use cheap, expendable sinkers such as old sparkplugs instead of purpose-made weights. It is, however, usually best to use a weight that has been designed for use in the prevailing conditions and for the type of fishing intended.

STANDARD BREAKAWAY

BREAKAWAY ADAPTER

LONG-TAILED BREAKAWAY
(with clip-on lifter)

EXTENDED-NOSE
BREAKAWAY

BREAKAWAY SINKERS
The wires of a breakaway sinker dig into the seabed to anchor the bait. They are clipped against the sinker body, and on the retrieve they spring free and trail behind for a snagless return. The extended-nose and long-tailed versions give good grip at short range or in deep water, making them suitable for uptide fishing; the plastic breakaway adapter can be used in tandem with a standard breakaway for increased grip.

BOOMS

Nylon traces tend to tangle, and baits dropped from a boat often spiral as they fall, wrapping their traces around the main line. Mounting the traces on carefully spaced booms will reduce these problems. Droppers (short traces) suspended from booms spaced above the weight are good for shore fishing when large numbers of small fish are sought, because they present multiple baits in the best possible way.

BREAKAWAY BOOMS *(right)*
These booms, attached to the line by beads, are used as flying collar booms and as dropper booms. When bottom drifting, however, they can get choked with sand, which can stop them sliding.

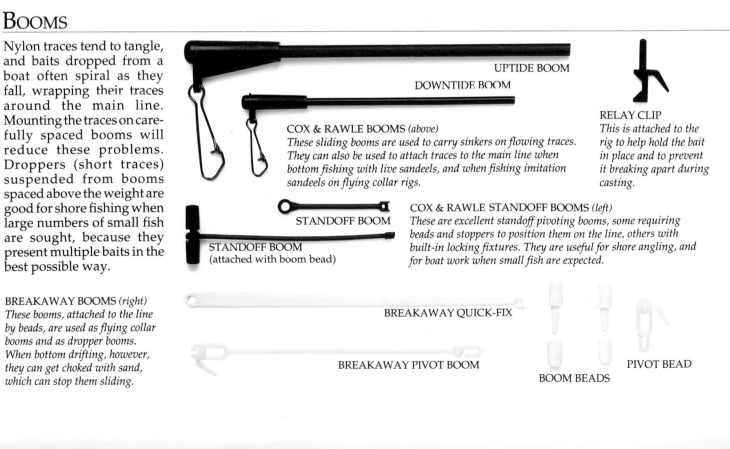

UPTIDE BOOM

DOWNTIDE BOOM

COX & RAWLE BOOMS *(above)*
These sliding booms are used to carry sinkers on flowing traces. They can also be used to attach traces to the main line when bottom fishing with live sandeels, and when fishing imitation sandeels on flying collar rigs.

RELAY CLIP
This is attached to the rig to help hold the bait in place and to prevent it breaking apart during casting.

STANDOFF BOOM

STANDOFF BOOM
(attached with boom bead)

COX & RAWLE STANDOFF BOOMS *(left)*
These are excellent standoff pivoting booms, some requiring beads and stoppers to position them on the line, others with built-in locking fixtures. They are useful for shore angling, and for boat work when small fish are expected.

BREAKAWAY QUICK-FIX

BREAKAWAY PIVOT BOOM

BOOM BEADS

PIVOT BEAD

ROUND BOMB
This is ideal for slow downrigger trolling. It can also be used for bottom fishing, but it tends to roll.

WYE
The streamlined shape of this lure-fishing weight makes it ideal for distance-casting spinners and rubber eels and for getting them down deep.

TORPEDO
Because of its flat sides, this beach sinker is less likely to roll in the current than rounded weights.

PIERCED BALL
This is used for weighting slider float tackle and for helping get large deadbaits down when freelining.

WEIGHT LIFTER
On a fast retrieve with the rod held high, this plastic vane rises in the water. This helps to lift the sinker clear of heavy snags close to your feet.

SPIRAL WEIGHT
This is designed for use with cast or trolled lures. Because the line is simply wrapped around it, its position can be altered quickly and easily. It can also be used to sink slowly trolled livebaits.

UPTIDE WEIGHT
(left)
This weight is favoured by uptiders because its long nose wires give exceptional grip in fierce currents. The wires dig into the bed to anchor the bait, but pull out easily when a fish picks it up, and they spring readily out of snags.

BELL WEIGHT
This can be used from an anchored boat, but is not the best shape for drift fishing.

BOMB
The bomb is the best shape for beating snags and tide, and good for working a constantly moving bait from the beach.

SLIDING LINK
Attaching a flowing trace to the main line by a sliding link (or a sliding boom) allows it to move without taking the sinker with it, which could cause a fish to drop the bait.

WATCH WEIGHT
This is a useful grip sinker for short-range beach work and drift fishing over banks.

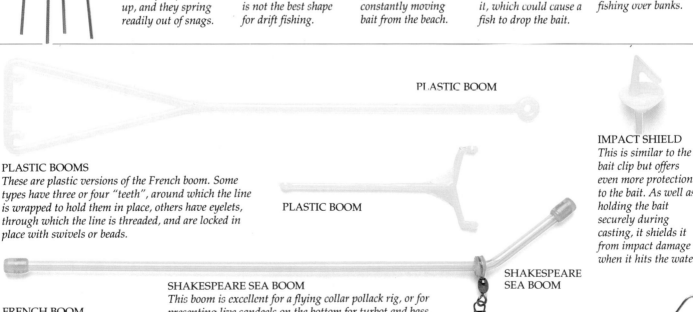

PLASTIC BOOM

PLASTIC BOOMS
These are plastic versions of the French boom. Some types have three or four "teeth", around which the line is wrapped to hold them in place, others have eyelets, through which the line is threaded, and are locked in place with swivels or beads.

PLASTIC BOOM

IMPACT SHIELD
This is similar to the bait clip but offers even more protection to the bait. As well as holding the bait securely during casting, it shields it from impact damage when it hits the water.

SHAKESPEARE SEA BOOM
This boom is excellent for a flying collar pollack rig, or for presenting live sandeels on the bottom for turbot and bass. Because it curves upward, it cannot become blocked by sand and prevented from sliding when fished on the drift.

SHAKESPEARE SEA BOOM

FRENCH BOOM
The wire French boom has been superseded to some extent by the plastic varieties, but because it is stronger for direct trace tying it is still widely used by wreck anglers for flying collar rigs.

FRENCH BOOM

FLOATS

Floats are extremely sensitive and versatile bite indicators, and much more pleasing to watch than a rod tip. Although they are available in a staggeringly wide variety of materials, shapes, sizes, and colours, all floats have been designed to perform specific tasks.

BALSAS
These floats, made entirely of balsa wood, are superior to stick floats in windy conditions and fast-flowing swims. Fish them close in and attach them top and bottom to the line. They tend to lift out of the water if held back too hard, due to the inherent buoyancy of the balsa wood.

LOAFERS
Made either from hollow plastic or balsa, loafers are very buoyant and designed to fish swift, turbulent waters. They should be attached top and bottom.

POLYWAGS   SWINGERS

POLYWAGS AND SWINGERS
These are ideal for stillwater use where ripples, rather than waves, are being created on the surface by the wind. Both patterns are fished bottom-end only, and a short distance beyond the rod tip.

DRIFTBEATERS
The ideal floats for stillwater fishing in strong winds, when there are big waves on the water. They are fished bottom-end only.

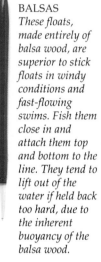

CRYSTAL AVONS

WIRE AVONS

AVONS
These floats, attached top and bottom, can present baits in quite turbulent streams and be fished at longer range than stick floats.

BIG STICK

STICK

STABLE STICK

WIRE STICK

STICKS
A stick float is at its best in smoothly flowing swims, attached top and bottom and fished close in. The upper part of the float is made of balsa.

ONIONS
These floats are designed for use in stillwaters, in all but the strongest of winds, and in swims at fairly close range (up to several rod lengths).

BLUES

GREYS

DARTS

BLUES, GREYS, AND DARTS
These are fished bottom-end only and are at their best on stillwaters and canals.

GIANTS

CANAL

INSERT

CRYSTALS
Crystals are made of clear plastic, and designed for use in clear, shallow water where wary fish might regard the arrival in the swim of a solid-coloured float as highly suspicious and a sign of danger. They are equally effective on still and slow-flowing waters.

BODIED

PEACOCKS
Quills taken from the tail feathers of peacocks make superb floats. The quills are long and straight, very light, and completely waterproof. Floats made from the thicker ends of quills are buoyant in turbulent water and easily visible at a distance, while those produced from the thinner ends will be more sensitive to delicate bites.

WAGGLERS
All wagglers are attached to the line bottom-end only, and are designed for use on stillwaters and slow- to medium-paced rivers. They are made from a variety of materials including peacock quill, sarcandas reed, plastic, and balsa.

LOADED
These floats have weighted bases. Their increased weight means that they can be cast greater distances and do not need shotted lines.

ZOOMERS
The zoomer was developed by match anglers for catching wary fish in shallow swims at long distances. It consists of a cane stem with a big balsa body and a brass stem insert at the base. It should be attached top and bottom, and is at its best in light winds on wide rivers and stillwaters.

NIGHT FLOATS
These floats are used for night fishing. They are fitted with Betalights, which are transparent tubes filled with a luminous gas. They will glow for 20 to 30 years.

POLE FLOATS
Floats for pole fishing tend to be small, often with thin bristle tops, to show up the most delicate of bites.

PIKE FLOATS
Most pike floats are built for slider fishing, being either hollow or fitted with eyes. Some, equipped with a dartlike vane above the tip, are designed to catch the wind and take the bait long distances from the bank, to predatory fish lying beyond casting range.

63

BITE INDICATORS & ROD RESTS

Bite indicators are used primarily in legering, where there is no float to indicate that a fish has taken the bait. Bites can be indicated simply by movement of the rod tip, but often this is not sensitive enough and some other form of indication is needed. This can be a swingtip, springtip, or quivertip fitted to the rod tip, or a device such as a bobbin or electronic alarm that indicates any movement of the line. Rod rests are used when it is not necessary to hold the rod all of the time, for instance when bites are expected to be infrequent, and when two rods are in use at the same time.

DROP-OFF ARM *(left)*
This was developed for pike fishing. The end with the indicator ball clips to the line and the hinged end is attached to the rear rod rest. When a bite occurs, the line pulls free and the end with the ball drops down.

BOBBINS *(right)*
A bobbin is attached to the line between the reel and the butt ring. If a fish takes the bait and moves away, the bobbin climbs towards the rod; if the fish moves towards the bank, the bobbin drops towards the ground.

BELL *(right)*
A bell clipped to the rod tip gives an audible indication of a bite. The use of bells has declined greatly, but they are occasionally used by freshwater anglers and more commonly by sea anglers fishing from beaches and piers.

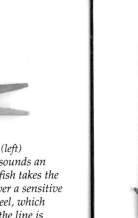

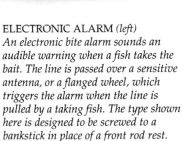

ELECTRONIC ALARM *(left)*
An electronic bite alarm sounds an audible warning when a fish takes the bait. The line is passed over a sensitive antenna, or a flanged wheel, which triggers the alarm when the line is pulled by a taking fish. The type shown here is designed to be screwed to a bankstick in place of a front rod rest.

SWINGTIP, SPRINGTIP, AND QUIVERTIP *(right)*
These screw into the threaded tip rings found on most leger rods. The swingtip hangs at an angle and indicates bites by lifting or dropping back. The springtip is similar, but has a sprung base. This holds it in line with the rod but acts like a hinge when a bite occurs, allowing the tip to swing down. A quivertip simply acts as a very sensitive extension of the rod tip.

SPRINGTIP

SWINGTIP

QUIVERTIP

MONKEY CLIMBER *(right)*
This is a bobbin that slides freely up and down a shaft pushed into the bank. It is used in the same way as an ordinary bobbin, but is much less likely to give false indications in windy conditions. When a strike is made, the line pulls out of the bobbin clip.

BANKSTICK (below)
This is a spiked metal rod with a threaded top to take a screw-on rod rest head or electronic bite alarm. Most are 60 to 90 cm (2 to 3 ft) long, but telescopic models that extend to 1.2 m (4 ft) are also available.

T-BAR (left)
T-bars double the rod-holding capacity of a pair of banksticks. Instead of screwing a rod rest head onto each bankstick, a T-bar is screwed on and a rod rest is fitted to each end of it.

ROD REST HEADS
Rod rests consist of rest heads screwed onto banksticks, and are normally used in pairs, one supporting the rod ahead of the reel, and the other supporting the rod butt. The rest heads are available in a variety of shapes and sizes to suit different angling styles.

SANDSPIKE (left)
Sandspikes, or monopods, are used by beach anglers to hold their rods upright during the often lengthy intervals between bites. They hold either one or two rods, and have sharp points that can be driven deep into the sand to provide stability.

TRIPOD (right)
Tripod rod rests, especially those with adjustable telescopic legs, are very stable. They are available with single or double rest heads, and are widely used by shore anglers fishing from shingle beaches and harbour walls.

POLE REST (above)
This type can be used either as a front rest or a rear rest. It has a V-shaped section to support the pole when it is used as a front rest, and an inverted V-section to prevent the butt from rising when it is used as the rear rest.

65

LANDING TACKLE

After being hooked and played out, a fish should be landed as quickly as possible. If it is too big to be swung to the bank or boat, or gently lifted from the water by hand, it can be landed in a net or lifted out with a tailer or gaff. Landing nets vary in size and design from the shallow, fine-meshed "pan" nets with long handles that are used to land small fish, to the large nets used by specialist anglers to engulf the biggest fish they are likely to encounter. Tailers and gaffs are used mainly for salmon and saltwater fish. A tailer is a running noose of braided wire, attached to a handle, which is slipped over the "wrist" of the fish's tail, and the gaff is a metal hook that is impaled in the body of the fish. The use of a gaff is now illegal on many waters.

STEADE-FAST TRIANGULAR SPECIMEN NET (below)
This 107 cm (42 in) landing net has two rigid arms of solid glass fibre, mounted on a nylon spreader block and connected at their tips by a nylon cord. The nylon mesh is deep, soft, and knotless, and can accommodate large fish such as specimen-sized carp, pike, and catfish.

HARDY TROUT NET (above)
The bow-shaped frame of this net folds back over the telescopic handle when not in use, but can be brought quickly into action with one hand. It is ideal for both stillwater and river trouting, and can be carried clipped to a vest.

ORVIS MADISON TROUT NET (right)
This compact net is popular with anglers who fish by wading or from float tubes, allowing the hooked fish to be brought close to hand. It has a laminated wood frame and Dacron mesh.

STEADE-FAST TRIANGULAR PAN NET (right)
This small, shallow net is designed for match fishing and general freshwater angling for small to medium-sized fish. The frame folds up for easy stowing.

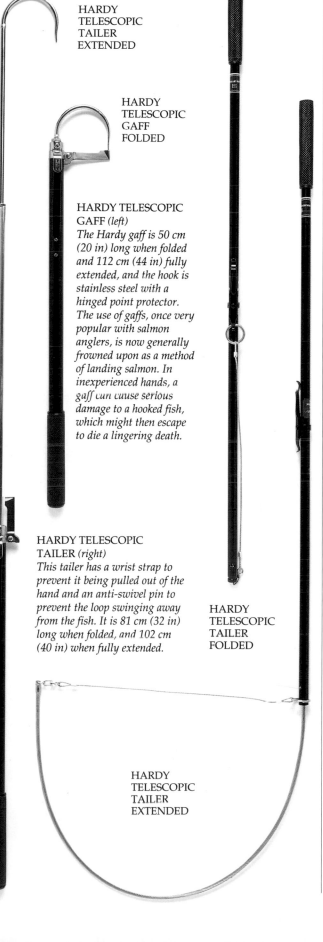

HARDY
TELESCOPIC
TAILER
EXTENDED

HARDY
TELESCOPIC
GAFF
FOLDED

**HARDY TELESCOPIC
GAFF** *(left)*
*The Hardy gaff is 50 cm
(20 in) long when folded
and 112 cm (44 in) fully
extended, and the hook is
stainless steel with a
hinged point protector.
The use of gaffs, once very
popular with salmon
anglers, is now generally
frowned upon as a method
of landing salmon. In
inexperienced hands, a
gaff can cause serious
damage to a hooked fish,
which might then escape
to die a lingering death.*

**ORVIS GYE SALMON
NET** *(above)*
*Many salmon anglers prefer to
use a net such as this, rather
than a tailer or gaff. It is big
and circular, and can hold
large salmon and sea trout, but
is easy to carry, because its
frame can be slid down the
handle when not in use.*

**HARDY TELESCOPIC
TAILER** *(right)*
*This tailer has a wrist strap to
prevent it being pulled out of the
hand and an anti-swivel pin to
prevent the loop swinging away
from the fish. It is 81 cm (32 in)
long when folded, and 102 cm
(40 in) when fully extended.*

HARDY
TELESCOPIC
TAILER
FOLDED

**STEADE-FAST
KEEPNET** *(right)*
*Keepnets are long nets,
anchored to the bank and
submerged in the water,
in which caught fish can
be retained alive until the
end of the fishing session,
when they are weighed,
measured and perhaps
photographed, then
released. This model is
available in 2.4 m and
3 m (8 ft and 10 ft)
versions, both with 45 cm
(18 in) diameter rings.*

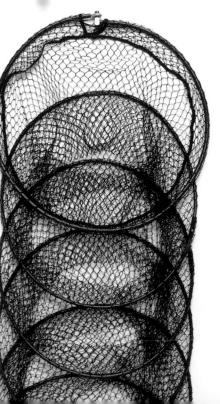

HARDY
TELESCOPIC
TAILER
EXTENDED

TACKLE BOXES

Tackle boxes fall into two broad categories: the small type, in which you can carry a selection of lures, flies, floats, or other small items when you are actually fishing, and the large, capacious type, in which you can store all your small tackle when it is not in use. Many anglers use improvised tackle boxes, adapted from containers ranging from cigar boxes to toolboxes, but in general there is no substitute for a purpose-made storage system. Wooden tackle boxes look nice, but are heavy and need to be cared for, so most anglers choose plastic or aluminium boxes, which are light, strong, and water resistant.

SEAT BOXES

These are large tackle boxes that double as seats. They are used mainly by freshwater anglers who fish with float or leger tackle and spend long periods fishing one swim. Most have two sections, one large and deep for storing bulky items such as groundbait, and one with drawers that take small items such as floats, sinkers, rigs, and hooks.

SHAKESPEARE/SNOWBEE SPECIMEN TACKLE BOX (right)

This is a good example of the cantilever type of tackle box, which offers good storage capacity, gives easy access to the contents when opened out, and is compact when closed. It is made in two-tone green plastic, and has three trays with movable dividers so that the compartment sizes can be adjusted to suit individual requirements. It is also available in one-, two-, and six-tray versions.

WOODEN FLOAT BOX (below)

Made of varnished hardwood, this simple, three-tray float box has foam strip inserts, in which you can cut slits to hold the ends of the floats.

FOX BOX (below)

This plastic fly box will hold up to 66 dry flies, and its rubberized lining will not retain moisture, which could rust their hooks. The clips are designed to hold the flies securely without crushing their delicate hackles.

RICHARD WHEATLEY FLY BOX MODEL 4607F (right)

The lid of this tough aluminium fly box is lined with closed-cell plastic foam, into which wet flies and nymphs can be hooked, and its base contains 16 dry-fly compartments with individual, spring-loaded plastic lids.

RICHARD WHEATLEY TUBE-FLY BOX (right)

Tube flies require special boxes for proper storage. Some tube-fly boxes have a row of needles over which the flies are slipped, but this one has bullet-shaped indentations to hold up to 28 of them. The loose treble hooks can be stuck into the foam lining.

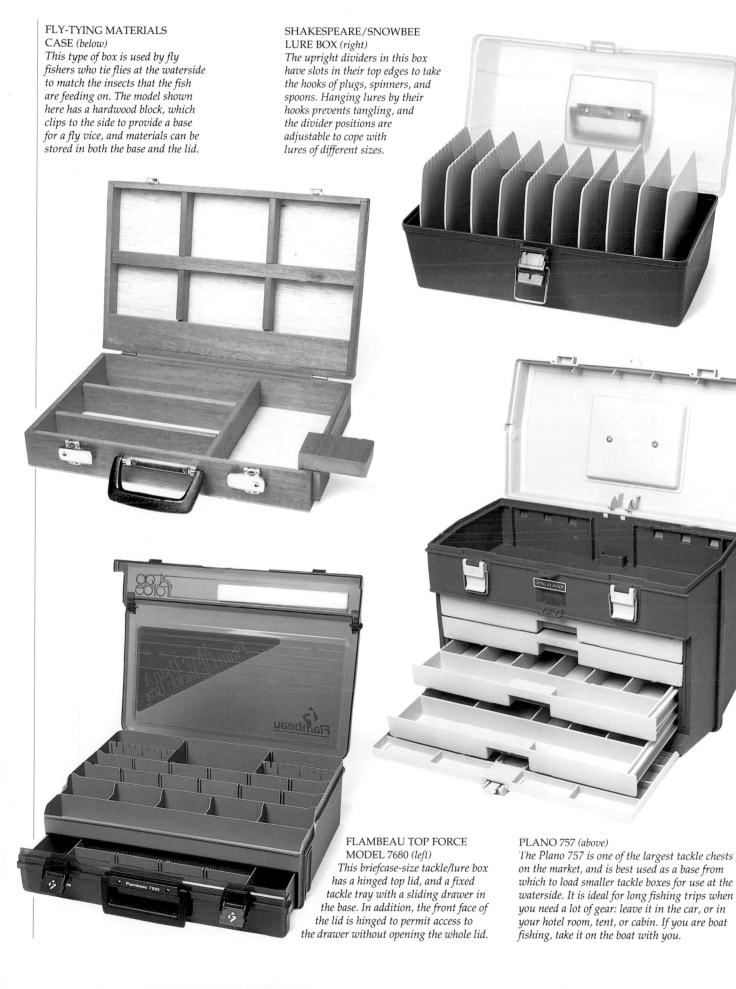

**FLY-TYING MATERIALS
CASE** (below)
*This type of box is used by fly
fishers who tie flies at the waterside
to match the insects that the fish
are feeding on. The model shown
here has a hardwood block, which
clips to the side to provide a base
for a fly vice, and materials can be
stored in both the base and the lid.*

**SHAKESPEARE/SNOWBEE
LURE BOX** (right)
*The upright dividers in this box
have slots in their top edges to take
the hooks of plugs, spinners, and
spoons. Hanging lures by their
hooks prevents tangling, and
the divider positions are
adjustable to cope with
lures of different sizes.*

**FLAMBEAU TOP FORCE
MODEL 7680** (left)
*This briefcase-size tackle/lure box
has a hinged top lid, and a fixed
tackle tray with a sliding drawer in
the base. In addition, the front face of
the lid is hinged to permit access to
the drawer without opening the whole lid.*

PLANO 757 (above)
*The Plano 757 is one of the largest tackle chests
on the market, and is best used as a base from
which to load smaller tackle boxes for use at the
waterside. It is ideal for long fishing trips when
you need a lot of gear: leave it in the car, or in
your hotel room, tent, or cabin. If you are boat
fishing, take it on the boat with you.*

FOOTWEAR

Good footwear is an essential part of any angler's equipment. Whichever type you choose, it should give a secure grip on slippery surfaces, and be both comfortable and suitable for the prevailing conditions. For example, lightweight boots are excellent during the warm summer months, but in cold winter weather you need boots with thick, insulated soles to keep your feet warm. Similarly, waders with lightweight uppers that can be folded down, transforming them into boots for walking to and from the water, are ideal for summer use. But when wading for salmon or trout in the springtime, when the water can be extremely cold, you need thick, thermally insulated waders.

TYPES OF SOLE

Felt soles
Felt soles provide the best grip of all on wet, slippery surfaces, and have the advantage of being quiet, so you can wade without scaring fish.

Studded soles
These are excellent for walking across wet grass or mud banks, but are noisy and do not give as much grip as felt soles do on slippery underwater stones.

Rubber soles
Rubber soles are usually cheaper than felt or studded soles. They give reasonably good grip on grass or mud but are less effective on rocks.

AIR-GRIP KNEE BOOTS (left)
These fully waterproof, knee-length boots are 43 cm (17 in) high and made of nylon-lined rubber. The cushioned soles provide insulation and comfort, and the top straps can be tightened for a snug fit to stop stones, leaves, and other debris from getting in.

EDINGTON WELLY-WADERS (left)
These boots have thin, lightweight wader uppers that can be folded down to below the knee when not required. They can thus be used both as waders and as boots for walking along the bank. The wader uppers should be kept away from snags such as thorns and barbed wire.

SKEE-TEX INSULATED KNEE BOOTS (above)
Insulated knee boots such as these are widely used by winter anglers who choose to sit on the bank and fish in one swim all day. The thick, insulated soles prevent cold from creeping up into the boot and chilling the feet, and because the insulation is so good, a pair of ordinary socks is sufficient to keep feet warm.

ORVIS GREEN MOUNTAIN THIGH BOOTS (above)
These rubber thigh boots have non-slip felt soles, and wader uppers made of lightweight, laminated PVC. In warm weather, the uppers can be folded down and held in clips to allow air to circulate around the legs.

**ORVIS LIGHTWEIGHT
BOOT-FOOT CHEST WADERS** (below)
These waders, made of nylon with all the seams sealed, weigh only 340 g (12 oz) and can be rolled up very small to tuck into the corner of a tackle bag until needed. They are ideal for use in warm weather, and highly resistant to punctures and abrasion.

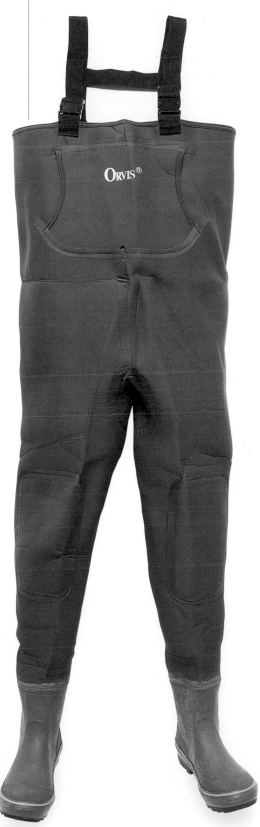

ORVIS GRAVEL GUARDS (above)
Gravel guards are fixed around the tops of ordinary boots, in effect making them higher, and prevent stones from getting inside. Stones inside boots are uncomfortable, and if they are not removed they may cut into the soles.

**ORVIS LIGHTWEIGHT
WADING SHOES** (below)
The moulded, one-piece heel and sole design of these shoes, and their felt covering, provide excellent stability when wading on slippery riverbeds. In addition, foam-padded insoles, hard toes, and padded ankle collars give good protection on rough ground.

**ORVIS GRIP STABIL-ICERS
FITTED TO BOOT**

**ORVIS GUIDEWEIGHT
STOCKING-FOOT CHEST WADERS** (above)
Being made of nylon and thick neoprene foam, these waders provide comfort and warmth even in icy waters, such as those endured by early-spring salmon anglers. They feature reinforced knees, a handwarmer pocket, and quick-release buckles, and all the seams are sealed. Unlike boot-foot waders, which are a combination of boots and waders, stocking-foot waders do not have tough soles and must be worn with wading shoes.

ORVIS GRIP STABIL-ICERS
(above)
These are fitted to the soles of boots, boot-foot waders, or wading shoes to give extra grip when walking on ice or slopes of wet grass or mud. They are also reasonably effective on slippery rocks.

VESTS & JACKETS

The great advantage of fishing vests is that an array of small but essential items of tackle can be carried in their multiple pockets. This makes them very useful in any form of angling where mobility is important, including fly fishing, lure fishing, and stalking fresh-water fish such as carp. Most vests are short, so that they do not trail on the water during wading, but longer-length designs are also available for anglers who usually fish from the bank. These keep the lower back area covered, and so in cool weather they are more comfortable to wear than short vests.

Jackets made of traditional materials, such as waxed cotton, are still available, but most are made of lightweight, waterproof, synthetic fabrics *(see page 74)*. These jackets "breathe" to prevent condensation building up inside them, need no reproofing, are fully washable, and can be rolled up and tucked away in a corner of a tackle bag, to be forgotten until the rain comes. Some have detachable linings, and can be used comfortably all year round.

WYCHWOOD FOUR SEASONS *(right)*
This multi-pocketed vest is designed for use in cool weather. It is made of a polyester/cotton mix with a fleecy lining, and is cut long to ensure that the small of the back is protected from draughts in cold winds. Its features include a rugged two-way zip that can be opened from the bottom to prevent constriction when sitting in a boat, pockets in a variety of sizes, a scissors retainer, and two landing net rings.

ORVIS SUPER TAC-L-PAK *(below)*
This vest is virtually a wearable tackle bag, with no less than 35 pockets to carry almost everything an angler might need, from a pair of scissors to a set of lightweight waterproofs. Made of a tough polyester/cotton mix, it features a yoke collar for good weight distribution, wide-cut shoulders, and oversize armholes, and it is cut short for deep wading.

STEADE-FAST BAIT SMOCK *(above)*
Designed for match fishing, the Steade-fast bait smock is light and supple for ample freedom of movement, and has adjustable, quick-release side fastenings for easy fitting and removal. There are two bait pockets, the larger sporting a rain flap to ensure that its contents remain dry in bad weather, three other pockets designed to carry a range of terminal tackle and rigs, and a loop to hold a catapult handle.

SHAKESPEARE SAFETY VEST *(below)*
This light, comfortable fly-fishing vest doubles as a buoyancy aid should a mishap occur while boat fishing or walking the bank. It can be inflated instantly by pulling a toggle to activate a replaceable carbon dioxide cartridge, and can also be inflated by mouth. It has numerous pockets, a D-ring for scissors, and a loop to carry a landing net.

MUSTO HIGHLANDS JACKET *(right)*
The Highlands jacket has a waterproof Gore-Tex liner between its polyester/cotton outer shell and its inner lining, and can be cleaned in a domestic washing machine. It has a two-way zip for comfort when sitting down, plenty of generously cut pockets, and a built-in waterproof flap to sit on. A hood and a zip-in waistcoat are available as extras.

NOMAD ⅝ RANGER *(above)*
This five-eighths-length jacket has a stretch cord and toggles at the waist, so that its weight is carried on the hips rather than the shoulders, and its sleeves are generously cut to give unrestricted movement when casting. It is machine-washable and has plenty of pockets, a permanently attached hood, two handwarmer pockets, a double storm flap, and a two-slider main zip.

HARDY WAXED WADING JACKET *(below)*
Designed primarily for use with chest waders, this waist-length jacket has generously cut sleeves for easy casting and features two breast pockets and internal pockets. It is made of waxed Egyptian cotton, with a smart tartan lining, and is fully waterproof, but like all waxed clothing it eventually needs reproofing to prevent water from seeping through it.

73

WATERPROOFS

In the past, the big drawback of most waterproof clothing was that perspiration would condense inside it, making it uncomfortable to wear. The fabrics tended to be heavy, were often difficult to clean, and required regular reproofing, often with waxes that would leave marks on car seats. These problems have been eliminated by the use of new fabrics and proofing processes, and modern waterproofs are comfortable to wear and easy to care for. The use of "breathable" fabrics, which have microscopic pores that prevent water getting in but allow water vapour to escape, has solved the condensation problem, and clothing made from these fabrics is light, washable, needs no reproofing, and does not stain car seats.

ORVIS EASY-ON-AND-OFF OVERTROUSERS (below)
These lightweight, waterproof overtrousers can be rolled up and tucked away in a pocket or bag until needed, and the zips at the bottoms of the legs allow you to put them on or take them off without removing your shoes. Made of nylon waterproofed with polyurethane, they are ideal for bank fishing on showery days and for boat fishing in choppy water. They are also thornproof, so they will protect your trousers if you are pushing through high bankside vegetation when stalking fish.

WYCHWOOD ONE-PIECE
THERMAL SUIT (above)
This light, fully waterproof, one-piece suit has a heat-retaining thermal lining, and is also breathable to prevent condensation. It has a high, protective collar and a zip-on hood, and is ideal for static fishing in cold weather.

**WYCHWOOD THERMAL
BIB & BRACE** *(below)*
*In the cooler months of the year, a cold draught
in the small of the back can be most
uncomfortable and spoil a day's fishing. A bib
and brace eliminates this problem, and when
teamed with a jacket is more versatile than a one-
piece suit. The Wychwood Thermal Bib & Brace
is made of a lightweight, thermally lined
polyester/cotton mix that has been made fully
waterproof and breathable. It has ample pocket
space and its two side zips make it easy to put on
and take off.*

MAINSTREAM SURVIVAL FLOTATION SUIT *(above)*
*This is an insulated and waterproof, but not breathable, one-piece suit
designed for use at sea. As well as providing protection from spray and the
weather, it acts as a buoyancy aid should the wearer be unfortunate enough
to fall in (but is not an alternative to a lifejacket). It is produced in a bright
red material for maximum visibility. Velcro straps at the ends of the sleeves
and legs allow wrists and ankles to be kept snug, and a simple hood,
permanently attached, folds up and tucks inside the collar.*

HATS, GLOVES, & SUNGLASSES

A suitable hat will keep your head dry in wet weather, cool in summer, and (probably most importantly) warm in winter: in cold weather, you can lose 30 per cent or more of your body heat through your head if it is not covered.

A pair of warm gloves or mittens, preferably waterproof, should always be a part of your outfit in inclement winter weather. Having cold and aching fingers can be very uncomfortable, and makes it difficult to set up your tackle and to use it properly. Gloves are also useful when handling sharp-toothed or sharp-spined fish.

Polarized sunglasses cut out reflected glare from the surface, which helps you to spot fish more easily in clear water. They can also protect your eyes from badly cast hooks – whether your own or someone else's – especially when fly fishing.

SHAKESPEARE OPTI-SHIELDS
The frames of these polarized sunglasses are shaped to provide top shade, and the tinted side panels offer extra protection from miscast flies.

ASSET NIGHT VISION GLASSES
These glasses give enhanced contrast in poor light conditions, which makes them a useful form of eye protection when fly fishing at dusk.

ASSET HALF-EYE MAGNIFIERS
Available in a range of magnification strengths, these are useful when you are performing intricate tasks such as tying on flies at the waterside.

ORVIS NEOPRENE GLOVES
Neoprene is an excellent glove material, providing both warmth and resistance to water. These neoprene gloves are nylon lined, to make them easy to take off and pull on, and have adjustable Velcro closures at the wrist to ensure a snug fit.

GUL NEOPRENE GLOVES
These gloves are designed to keep hands warm and dry in the foulest of weather. They are also supple and flexible, allowing the freedom of movement that is essential when, for example, you are tying knots or unhooking lively fish.

DAIWA SHOWERPROOF SPLIT-PALM MITTENS
The split-palm design of these fully lined mittens permits the end sections to be folded back to expose the fingers. This is useful when setting up tackle and when sensitive control is required, for instance during casting.

DAIWA THERMAL FINGERLESS MITTS
Fingerless mitts keep hands warm but leave fingers free for fiddly tasks such as controlling the line as it leaves the reel, and making up or adjusting terminal rigs. These Daiwa mitts have elasticated wrists for a snug, draught-free fit.

UP-DOWNER (left)
This lightweight hat is similar in style to those that were worn by the French Foreign Legion in North Africa, having a large visor to shade the eyes and a back-flap to cover the nape of the neck. It gives excellent sun protection in hot weather, and has become popular with American fishing guides.

SHAKESPEARE SUN VISOR
The Shakespeare sun visor has a tinted plastic peak and a lined, elasticated headband that acts as a sweatband on hot days. A sun visor leaves the top of the head exposed to any cooling breeze that might blow, but a cap is preferable in very hot weather because it shields the head from the sun.

DAIWA BASEBALL CAP (above)
This nylon cap is available in either a full cloth style or a half-mesh version that provides better ventilation for the back of the head. A large peak shields the face from the sun, and an adjustable, press-studded strap at the back ensures that the cap will fit all head sizes.

DEERSTALKER
The deerstalker is a traditional type of tweed hat, made either with a rigid rim all the way around or peaked front and back. The peaked versions usually have side flaps to cover the ears for warmth or to keep biting midges at bay.

ACCESSORIES

In addition to basic gear such as rods, reels, lines, and hooks, there are a number of items of tackle, broadly categorized as accessories, that every well-equipped angler should have. These include equipment for unhooking fish, weighing them, and dispatching and cleaning those retained for eating. Additional accessories, not described here but worth considering, include padded unhooking mats, a pair of binoculars for watching for signs of fish activity, and a compass. The last should be considered essential by any angler who wishes to explore some remote hill lake or a stream far from the beaten track, and cannot afford the luxury of a GPS (Global Positioning System) receiver.

HARDY PIN-ON RETRACTOR (below)
This contains a spring-loaded spool of cord carrying a snaplock swivel. Items such as scissors can be clipped to the swivel, where they hang out of the way until needed.

SHAKESPEARE KNOT-TYING TOOL (left)
This is useful if you do not have nimble fingers, and when cold weather makes knot-tying difficult.

HARDY POCKET THERMOMETER (right)
A thermometer helps you to find the areas of a water that are likely to be holding fish, such as cool spots in hot weather and warm ones in cold weather. Tie it to a line, lower or cast it into the water, and leave it there for a few minutes to get an accurate reading.

LUCKY TOOLS ANGLING PLIERS
Heavy-duty angling pliers such as these are essential when you are using wire line or traces. They have long handles for good leverage, their strong jaws make crimping easy, and their wirecutter blades are capable of cutting heavy wire line.

DAIWA HEADLAMP LIGHT (right)
Anglers who fish at night, such as beach anglers, find lights of this type very useful because they are worn strapped to the forehead, leaving the hands free to handle the tackle. The model shown here is powered by a battery pack that clips to your belt.

DAIWA FLEXI-LIGHT (right)
A lamp is a very useful implement to have to hand when fishing on into darkness, and this clip-on model incorporates a flexible stem that allows the light to be directed onto a specific point.

DAIWA SEA KING FILLET KNIFE (left)
Fish that are to be retained for the table should be gutted with a sharp filleting knife, such as this one, as soon after capture as possible.

HARDY PRIEST (left)
Using a priest is a humane way of dispatching fish that are to be retained for eating. The weighted head should be brought down smartly on the skull of the fish at least twice.

HARDY SPRING BALANCE (below)
Using a spring balance is a convenient method of weighing fish. This balance is calibrated in kilograms and pounds, and has a micrometer adjustment for accurate zeroing.

HARDY SCISSOR PLIERS (left)
This versatile tool has many uses, such as pinching on split shot, debarbing hooks for barbless fishing, and (using the cutting blades) cutting through monofilament and light wire.

HARDY ARTERY FORCEPS (above)
These are an excellent tool for removing hooks of about size 10 upwards, especially from sharp-toothed fish such as pike. The finer wire of smaller hooks is easily bent by forceps, and these hooks are best removed with a disgorger.

HARDY HOOK SHARPENER (left)
Hook sharpeners can improve the points of mechanically sharpened hooks, but chemically etched points to not need further sharpening.

NICAN ENTERPRISES UNI-LOADA (left)
The onerous task of loading line onto a reel is made easier if you use a line spool holder such as this. This tool is adjustable so that line spools can be aligned correctly for loading either fixed-spool or multiplier reels, and it can cope with all but the largest bulk line spools.

HUFF FISHING FLY ROD BUTT GRIP (left)
This 50 cm (20 in) aluminium spike is designed to hold your fly rod so that it does not get trodden on when you are resting or changing your terminal tackle. The rod butt sits in a cup, and a spring clip at the top of the grip holds the rod upright.

SHAKESPEARE PIKE GAG (right)
A gag is used to hold open the sharp-toothed mouth of a pike or other predatory fish while it is being unhooked. The sprung arms of this model are ball-ended so that they do not damage the mouth of the fish.

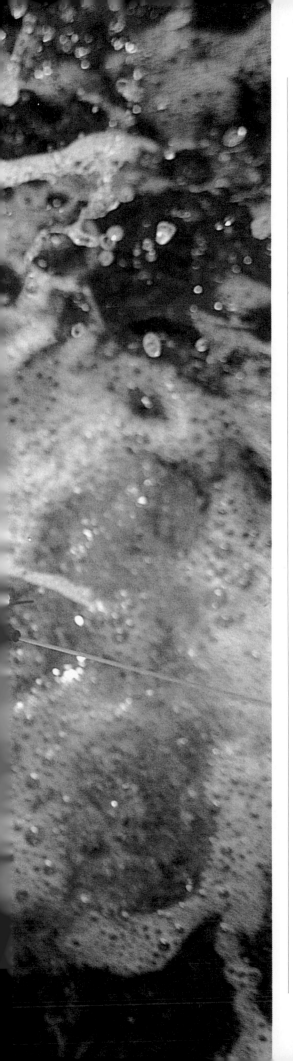

BAIT

USING A SUITABLE BAIT is one of the secrets of successful angling, whether you are fishing for carp on a small pond or marlin on a tropical ocean. But the variety of baits used by today's anglers is huge, and choosing the right one requires a good knowledge not only of the diet and feeding habits of your chosen quarry but also of the range of baits that have proved effective in luring it. Baits can be divided into naturals, artificials, and processed baits, but the essential function of all of them is to fool fish into taking the hook.

Naturals are whole or cut items of the natural diet of the quarry, and are therefore inherently attractive to it. Most can be collected easily and free of charge from the water, its banks, or the shore; some, such as worms and maggots, are available from tackle dealers. Artificials, such as plugs and spinners, either mimic natural food items, such as small fish, or are designed to incite fish to grab them out of aggression, curiosity, or hunger. Their benefits include their ease of use and the fact that they can be used time and time again. Processed baits, such as cheese and bread, although edible, are obviously not part of any wild fish's natural diet. For fish, their attraction lies in their smell and taste, and for anglers, in their convenience and proven effectiveness.

This chapter describes the most effective and widely used baits for both freshwater and saltwater species.

THE RIGHT BAIT
Using a bait that will tempt your quarry into taking the hook is one of the secrets of angling success.

Natural Baits

Most natural baits cost nothing and often have the additional benefit of being part of the diet of the fish you are seeking. For example, earthworms (usually called lobworms or nightcrawlers) will tempt almost every freshwater fish worth catching, and water-based fauna that make good baits include freshwater shrimp and caddis grubs. Never collect more naturals than you think you will need, and always return any that are unused.

Maggots & Casters

The type of maggot most often used as bait is the larva of the bluebottle fly, a proven catcher of fish of all species. Maggots are usually sold in their natural white or dyed bronze, although they can be changed to any colour with a suitable liquid dye. The main places to use these dyed maggots are waters where the fish have been subjected to a lot of angling pressure and become wary of the white or bronze varieties.

Anglers fishing for small fish will often use other varieties of maggot, such as squatts (housefly larvae) and pinkies (greenbottle fly larvae). These are smaller and lighter than bluebottle maggots and are particularly good for fishing on the drop.

Casters (pupated maggots) are an excellent bait for most species and tend to attract bigger fish. They are good where fish have become maggot-shy, and are very effective when fished as a hookbait over a bed of hempseed. They become darker in colour and lighter in weight as they age, and old, floating casters are a splendid bait for surface-feeding species such as rudd.

Casters

Maggots

Pinkies

Dyed maggots

MAGGOT

HOOKING MAGGOTS (*above*)
Hook a maggot through the blunt end and as lightly as possible to ensure that it remains livelier for longer. Use maggots singly on hook sizes 16 to 18, or in bunches on a size 12. When fish are proving wary, it can pay to hook maggots halfway along their bodies. This will make them sink horizontally, and therefore more slowly and naturally.

HOOKING CASTERS (*right*)
To hook a single caster, pierce the thick end and push the hook in, completely burying it inside. Use hook sizes 14 to 18. Casters can also be presented singly, or in twos or threes, by lightly hooking them through their blunt ends.

CASTER

Worms & Slugs

SLUGS

WORMS

Carp, tench, and chub will gulp down a whole lobworm in seconds, while smaller species find half a lob or a smaller worm, such as a brandling, more manageable. Slugs are adored by chub, carp, and roach. On mild, damp nights, lobworms can be collected from lawns, and slugs emerge from rockeries and hedgerows; brandlings and redworms can be found in compost heaps.

LOBWORM

HOOKING WORMS
When using lobworms, either thread the hook a good way through the body, or hook it twice, top and bottom, to prevent it from flying off during casting or being torn off by a lunging fish. Use hook sizes 4 to 8 for lobworms, and 10 to 14 for worm sections or brandlings. Lightly hook small worms once when fish are confident, but thread the hook some way through the body when fish are only plucking tentatively at the bait.

BRANDLING WORM

HOOKING SLUGS
Use a big hook, size 2 or 4, and nick it gently through the body. A slug's weight enables it to be cast a long way and because of its tough skin, more than one fish can be caught on it.

SLUG

82

FISH

MACKEREL

HERRING

SARDINE

Many fish species include other fish in their diet. Pike, for instance, will eat just about any fish bait offered to them, although some are undoubtedly preferred: herring, sprat, smelt, sardine, mackerel, trout, and grayling are all good pike baits, as is freshwater eel. Where pike become used to certain fish baits, try painting these baits with liquid dyes to make them different.

Other freshwater species regularly taken on fish baits include catfish, perch, zander, bass, muskellunge, and trout, and in recent years some big chub have fallen to deadbaits intended for pike.

Fish baits can be freelined or legered static, trotted beneath a float, or spun or wobbled like an artificial lure. Being relatively soft-fleshed, sea fish tend not to last too long when continually cast out and retrieved. Freshwater baits are preferable for this, and none is better than small trout.

HOOKING FISH
Fish deadbaits on a pair of semi-barbless trebles, size 8 or 10. Set the uptrace treble in the tail root and the other no more than 8 cm (3 in) from it, with both facing the tail. For spinning, set the uptrace treble in the mouth, the other in the flank.

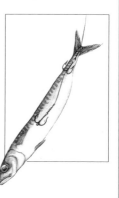

SHRIMPS & PRAWNS

These baits, when peeled, are excellent for catching just about every freshwater species. Unpeeled, they are best known as salmon baits, but they will also account for catfish, chub, bass, barbel, carp, tench, and crappies. They can be used raw or boiled, and are readily available canned, frozen, or fresh from most supermarkets.

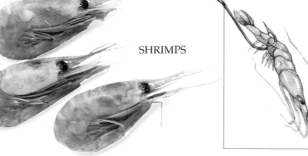

SHRIMPS

HOOKING PRAWNS
Peeled prawns are best presented singly on a size 8 or 10 hook pushed through the thick end of the tail. Mount unpeeled prawns on a size 2 or 4 hook, threaded through the tail or through and out of the underside of the body.

MUSSELS

MUSSELS

Freshwater mussels are a traditional tench bait but will also be eaten by carp, bream, eels, and catfish. They are found in the margins of muddy stillwaters and are best collected by gently raking the bed. Open the shells with a thick-bladed knife, then cut through the area of thick meat, or "foot", where the mussel is attached to its shell.

HOOKING MUSSELS
For close to medium casting, use a size 2 or 4 hook passed through the meaty foot. For fishing at a greater distance, also lash the softer part of the flesh to the hook shank with elasticated thread.

EELS

Freshwater eels are a fine pike bait and can be used whole, if small, or in sections. They are tough-skinned, which often allows several fish to be caught on the same bait, and can be cast a long way. Eels up to 30 cm (12 in) long make good baits for wobbling, while smaller eels and cut sections are generally fished on a freeline or legered.

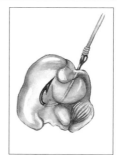

CUT EEL

HOOKING EELS
For wobbling and legering, mount an eel or eel portion on a standard snap tackle of two size 8 or 10 semi-barbless trebles on a 50 cm (20 in) wire trace. Small sections of eel can be fished on a large single hook threaded through the flesh with only part of the bend and point visible.

PROCESSED BAITS

Most of the large number of processed baits are common foodstuffs such as bread, cheese, meat, and vegetables, and while most are very unlikely to feature naturally in the diets of fish, they are nonetheless eaten when offered. In addition to these household foods, there is one group of processed baits that is produced exclusively for fishing: the high-protein (HP) baits. These were originally developed for carp fishing but are now widely used for many other non-predatory species, such as tench.

CHEESE

PROCESSED CHEESE

STRONG CHEESE

CHEDDAR CHEESE

In summer, cheese can be used straight from the pack. However, cold water hardens cheeses such as cheddar, so in winter grate these and mix them into a stiff paste with breadcrumbs and a sprinkling of water and cooking oil.

HOOKING CHEESE
For large baits, such as for carp or chub, use a size 4; for small ones use a 10. Bury the hook point inside the cheese.

HOOKING CORN
Use size 10 or 12 for a single kernel and up to a size 4 for a bunch.

SWEETCORN

SWEETCORN

Available either canned or frozen, corn is liked by many species. The kernels are relatively tough-skinned, enabling them to be cast a fair distance without flying off the hook. They are also fairly dense and sink quite quickly to the bottom, which is useful on rivers. On waters where corn has been used extensively, it can still be an effective bait if you liven it up with a tiny amount of edible flavouring such as clove oil or dye it a different colour.

BREAD

BREAD PASTE BALLS

BREAD CRUSTS

BREAD FLAKE

BREAD CUBES

Bread provides a number of different baits that can be fished in a variety of ways. The crust can be trotted, legered, or even freelined, on lakes for carp and rudd and on rivers for roach and chub. The soft flake (inner crumb) can be used both as a hookbait and as a groundbait. For the hook, the best flake to use is from a really fresh loaf as it will stay on longer. It can also be turned into a paste by mixing with water then kneading in a porous cloth.

HOOKING BREADFLAKE
Use hook sizes 4 to 14, depending on the size of fish you are after. Fold the flake right around the hook, then squeeze it together to ensure it stays on.

MEAT & BISCUITS

Canned pork and ham, cut into small cubes, are fine bait for chub and barbel. Canned cat food is liked by carp and catfish: mix it into a paste with breadcrumbs, then shape it into small balls. Dog biscuits are a good surface bait for carp, and can be turned into a paste bait by grinding them up with eggs and cornmeal.

CAT BISCUITS

LUNCHEON MEAT

HOOKING MEAT
Use a hook size 4 to 8, threaded carefully through the meat so that the point shows, and secure the bait with a piece of leaf.

CANNED CAT FOOD

POTATOES & CARROTS

POTATO CUBES

WHOLE POTATO

CARROT RINGS

WHOLE CARROTS

Small potatoes are a traditional and effective bait for carp and other cyprinids if the water is prebaited to allow the fish to become accustomed to them. (To prebait a swim, throw about a handful of bait into it at the same time every day for a few days before you fish it.) Parboil them to soften them, or use canned boiled potatoes. Carrots, boiled and sliced, are taken by many cyprinids. As with potatoes, prebaiting the swim is necessary when using carrots.

HOOKING POTATOES
Thread the line through the potato with a needle, attach the hook (size 2 to 8), and pull it inside.

PEAS, BEANS, & PASTA

DRIED PEAS

HARICOT BEANS

CHICK PEAS

BUTTER BEANS

PASTA

Fresh and dried peas, beans, and other small "particle" baits have all been used to catch carp since the early 1970s. Mass prebaiting of these baits will, in the right place, also account for chub, tench, barbel, and roach. All dried peas and beans must be boiled to soften them before use, but do not allow them to become mushy. Pasta, if boiled until soft, and prebaited, will take many fish; macaroni is a tried and tested chub bait but nowadays little used.

HOOKING PEAS AND BEANS
Use hook sizes 8 to 12. Round baits are simply threaded onto the hook; mount oval beans lengthwise.

SEEDS & GRAINS

RICE

MAIZE

RAW TARES

PROCESSED HEMP

COOKED TARES

PEANUTS

Many seeds and grains make excellent particle baits, but all must be boiled to soften them before use, because fish cannot digest them uncooked. The most widely used seed is hemp, which sends many cyprinid species into a feeding frenzy. It is often used as groundbait, with the bigger tare, a reddish brown berry, fished on the hook. Boiled peanuts have proved to be a very effective bait for carp, and maize, wheat, and barley (all boiled) are good roach baits. Boiled rice is useful for supplementing a meagre supply of maggots.

HOOKING SEEDS AND GRAINS
Most seeds and grains are simply pushed onto the hook (size 6 to 14). Boiled hemp splits, and the hook is inserted into the split.

HIGH-PROTEIN (HP) BAITS

HP baits are made of milk proteins, eggs, animal proteins, soy flour, wheatgerm, colourings, and flavourings. The mixture is either used as a paste or rolled into balls and boiled, producing "boilies". These have a thin skin that is impervious to the attentions of small nuisance fish. Most boilies produced are sinkers, but floaters are also made.

BOILIES

HOOKING BOILIES
Use a hook size 2 to 8 and ensure that the hook point and gape are not impeded, or use a hair rig or a boilie bayonet.

FRESHWATER GROUNDBAIT

Groundbait is a bait or mixture of baits introduced into the water to draw fish to the vicinity of the baited hook, and to keep them feeding in the area long enough for them to notice and take the hookbait. The key to successful groundbaiting is to use a bait that will attract the species you are after, and to use enough to hold their attention without offering them so much food that they are likely to miss or ignore the hookbait.

USING GROUNDBAIT

Groundbait can be used both in rivers and in stillwaters. In rivers with moderate or swift currents, and in waters where bottom-feeding species are the quarry, use balls of stiff, heavy, bread-based groundbait that sink quickly to the bottom before breaking up.

In still or slow-moving waters, and for fish feeding in the upper layers, use the lighter, finer type of groundbait known as cloudbait. This is made of finely crushed dried breadcrumbs, dampened with water and squeezed into small balls immediately before use. When they are thrown into the water, the balls break up into a slowly sinking cloud of tiny bread particles.

The effectiveness of cloudbait can be enhanced by mixing a little powdered milk with the crumbs before forming them into balls.

Mixing groundbait
When mixing groundbait, the first step is to prepare the base. For a fast-sinking groundbait, soak stale bread in cold water for at least half an hour (do not use warm water because it makes the bread go slimy). Then pour away the water in which it was standing, and remove some of the water it has soaked up by gently squeezing it – the more you squeeze, the firmer the mixture will be. Mash the wet bread into a smooth paste consisting of tiny particles of flake and crust with no lumps. Stiffen the paste with bran or a coarse cereal meal, such as maize meal.

This mixture can be formed into balls, preferably with the addition of hookbait samples such as maggots or cut worms, and perhaps something to enhance their flavour. For example, many members of the carp family have a sweet tooth, and find groundbait laced with small amounts of sweet flavourings highly palatable.

GROUNDBAIT BASES
The simplest bases for groundbait are soaked, mashed-up stale bread, and bread that has been heated in an oven to dry it and then crushed into crumbs. Both can be used alone or mixed with hookbaits and other additives. Many anglers consider that brown bread makes a more effective groundbait than white.

Mashed bread   Bread crumb

Commercial groundbait and additives
Commercially made groundbaits need little or no preparation, and many are formulated specifically for particular species or fishing methods. Additives, either liquid or powder, add colour, flavour, and scent to baits and groundbaits and revitalize their attractiveness when fish have become suspicious of them. These additives should be used sparingly, because too high a concentration in a bait will repel fish rather than attract them.

CATAPULTS

A good way to deliver balls of ground-bait into distant swims is to use a catapult, preferably one designed specifically for the task. To prevent the balls from breaking up in flight, form them from a stiff groundbait mixture and make the firing action as smooth as possible. For consistent accuracy when baiting a swim at long range, aim towards a feature on the far bank, such as a tree, and pull the catapult pouch back the same distance on each firing. When you are using a catapult, always hold it at arm's length and chest height. This will ensure that if the elastic breaks and flies back, it will not injure your eyes.

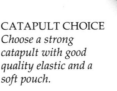

CATAPULT CHOICE
Choose a strong catapult with good quality elastic and a soft pouch.

BAIT FOR CATAPULTS
Stiffen your basic groundbait mixture with a binder such as flaked maize, and shape it into balls. Flaked maize takes time to absorb water, so the mixture will usually take an hour or so to reach its maximum stiffness.

SWIMFEEDERS

Swimfeeders, or feeders, are widely used in legering for presenting either groundbait or samples of the hookbait close to the baited hook, and are attached to the terminal tackle in place of the leger weight. Most are simple perforated plastic or wire-mesh cylinders, and are weighted to aid casting and to ensure that they remain on the bed of the lake or river after their contents have been released. This weighting can take the form of a weight or weights at the base of the feeder, or may be a metal strip running along one side.

Open-ended feeders

Open-ended feeders are plastic tubes, open at both ends and usually perforated to hasten the inflow of water, thus speeding up dispersal of the bait contained inside. They are usually weighted with strips of lead, folded over and stapled at either end. Because the weight is not adjustable, these feeders are produced in a range of different sizes with different widths of lead strip.

Open-ended feeders are generally used with groundbait, although they can also be filled with hookbait samples, held inside by a plug of groundbait at each end. They are particularly suitable for bream and other species that roam in big shoals and need large quantities of bait to hold them in a swim.

Blockend feeders

As their name suggests, these feeders are blocked (closed) at each end by caps. On some models, both caps are removable, while on others only the top cap can be taken off for the feeder to be filled with bait.

They are normally used with maggots, casters, or hempseed; the plastic tube is liberally perforated to allow the maggots to crawl out and the static casters and hemp to be washed out by the water. The release of bait can be slowed by winding insulating tape around part of the feeder to seal some of the holes.

The position of the weight on blockend feeders varies. On some, it is located below the base, on others in one of the end caps, while on others flat lead strip is used. Most blockends are tubular, but some are oval in cross-section to hold bottom in fast water.

OPEN-ENDED FEEDERS
These are used with straight or bait-laced groundbait, or samples of hookbait held in by plugs of groundbait pushed into each end.

FEEDER WEIGHT

When you are using a swimfeeder, make sure that its weight when filled with bait is not too great for the rod and line you are using.

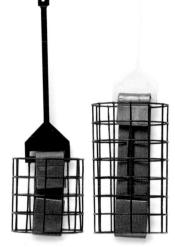

WIRE CAGE FEEDERS
These are made of wire mesh and filled quickly and easily by simply pushing them into groundbait.

SIDE VIEW

DAIWA HARRIER FEEDERS
The aerodynamic shape of these feeders permits accurate, long-range casting and helps them to rise quickly to the surface for a rapid retrieve. Slots instead of holes speed up the inflow of water and therefore groundbait release.

BAIT DROPPER
The hinged front face of the bait dropper opens to release the groundbait when the weighted plunger hits bottom. It is sometimes cast out and retrieved on a separate rod and line.

DRENNAN FLAT BLOCKEND
This feeder has a flattened shape (rather like that of a hip flask) and lead strip weight to help it stay in place on the bottom in fast-flowing water.

DRENNAN FEEDERLINK
The Feederlink has a removable top cap, and interchangeable weights that are clipped onto the base.

THAMESLEY BLOCKEND
Both end caps of this versatile feeder are removable. This facility enables it to be quickly and easily converted from a blockend to an open-ended feeder.

SPINNERS & SPOONS

Spinners and spoons are artificial baits designed to provoke a response from predatory fish as they pass through their line of vision, either because the fish are hungry or because they are defending their territory. They can be made of a variety of materials and come fitted with single or treble hooks.

SPINNERS

On a spinner, a vane or blade rotates around a central bar as the lure is retrieved. Some have lifelike worms or fish of soft rubber that encourage fish to hang on after grabbing the lure. Others, including buzz baits, have plastic skirts over their hooks that imitate swimming crayfish: the throbbing action of the blade attracts the fish, which then lunge at the plastic tassels.

LIL' HUSTLER SPOILER (*above*)
A spinner bait. Being virtually weedless, it is at its best when worked in fish-holding vegetation. Fish it shallow on a continuous retrieve or by sink and draw.

SPRAT (DEVON MINNOW)
Made in both floating and sinking versions for a variety of water conditions, this is a traditional salmon and trout lure that takes many other species.

TEASER (*above*)
An in-line spinner bait, best fished at a medium to fast pace. Its sleek, aerodynamic shape ensures that it casts well.

GOLD WING (*above*)
A buzz bait, at its best when retrieved on or just under the surface. Virtually weedless, it can be fished among lily pads where pike often lurk.

FLYING CONDOM
This unique lure produces a tremendously heavy throbbing action on the retrieve, and it has proved highly effective for many species including salmon, bass, pike, and perch.

SNAGLESS SALLY (*left*)
Fitted with a double-pronged weed guard, this lure can be cast right into and pulled through dense fish-holding weedbeds without fear of snagging.

MEPPS COMET (*left*)
A small lure with an attractive fluttering action that works well for trout, chub, pike, and perch. It fishes best in lakes or slow rivers.

BIG FISH
This variation on the Flying Condom lure is equipped with a highly natural, soft rubber fish below the spinning blade.

SPOONS

Spoons wobble through the water in a fishlike manner, and are often trolled behind boats as well as being cast and retrieved. Most are oval, and cast well due to their all-metal construction. Their action depends on the style of retrieve: winding in erratically can give the impression of a fish in distress, while twitching the rod tip when winding in gives extra "life" to the lure.

ABU ATOM
The Atom's rippled finish catches and reflects light as it is pulled through the water. It has an irregular action and is particularly good for pike in clear water.

ATLANTIC
This is a well-proven spoon for pike and other predatory fish. It is at its most effective when fished very slowly, just off the bottom, in lakes and gravel pits.

CISCO
A lure with a realistic action, designed for salmon, trout, and pike. Equally at home trolled, even up to 13 km/h (8 mph), or fished from the bank, where sink-and-draw is recommended.

HERON
A king-sized spoon designed specifically for big pike, this is perfect for distance casting on large, deep waters as well as for trolling or downrigging.

ABU TOBY SALMO
A highly effective gamefish lure that imitates the movement of a small fish as it twists and turns on its way through the water. The Salmo is a good lure to use in moving water.

HEDDON MOSS BOSS (left)
Designed to be used in well-weeded waters where other lures can foul up. Its interesting action helps it to glide over dense weed.

ABU LILL-ÖRINGEN (below)
This is a small, streamlined, and lightweight spoon, good for fishing near the surface or in shallow water.

TOBY FAT
The elliptical shape and double curve of this spoon induce a lively but undulating action. A good lure for long casts. Retrieve slowly for best results.

ABU GLIMMY
An excellent pike and salmon lure with an undulating swing produced by its double-curve profile. Surfaces rapidly when retrieved at speed.

ABU STOR-ÖRINGEN
A lively big brother to the Lill-Öringen, this is a productive lure for salmon and zander. Displaces a lot of water during the retrieve.

KILTY KERRYMAN
This Irish salmon lure has also proved to be an enticer of pike. Its fluttering action often produces hard takes.

PLUGS

Plugs are made of materials such as wood, plastic, and metal, and designed to either float, dive below the surface, or sink when retrieved. Floating plugs are fished across the surface, and they often have features that create extra fish-attracting surface disturbance, such as propellers or plastic skirts. Floating plugs that dive when cranked in are very versatile, because the speed of retrieve determines how deep they dive, allowing a great variety of depths to be explored. The diving action is produced by an angled vane or lip at the head, and some plugs contain balls that rattle to enhance their attractiveness. Sinking plugs are made in a variety of densities to fish at different depths.

FLOATING PLUGS

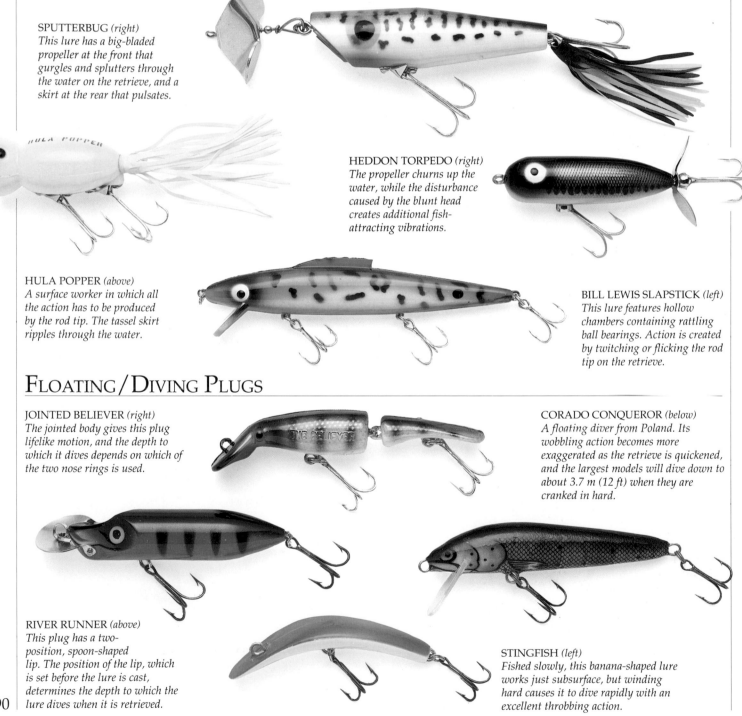

SPUTTERBUG (right)
This lure has a big-bladed propeller at the front that gurgles and splutters through the water on the retrieve, and a skirt at the rear that pulsates.

HEDDON TORPEDO (right)
The propeller churns up the water, while the disturbance caused by the blunt head creates additional fish-attracting vibrations.

HULA POPPER (above)
A surface worker in which all the action has to be produced by the rod tip. The tassel skirt ripples through the water.

BILL LEWIS SLAPSTICK (left)
This lure features hollow chambers containing rattling ball bearings. Action is created by twitching or flicking the rod tip on the retrieve.

FLOATING/DIVING PLUGS

JOINTED BELIEVER (right)
The jointed body gives this plug lifelike motion, and the depth to which it dives depends on which of the two nose rings is used.

CORADO CONQUEROR (below)
A floating diver from Poland. Its wobbling action becomes more exaggerated as the retrieve is quickened, and the largest models will dive down to about 3.7 m (12 ft) when they are cranked in hard.

RIVER RUNNER (above)
This plug has a two-position, spoon-shaped lip. The position of the lip, which is set before the lure is cast, determines the depth to which the lure dives when it is retrieved.

STINGFISH (left)
Fished slowly, this banana-shaped lure works just subsurface, but winding hard causes it to dive rapidly with an excellent throbbing action.

SINKING PLUGS

SMITHWICK DEVIL'S HORSE (right)
This wooden lure can be cast and retrieved or trolled. Its twin propellers churn up the water, creating a disturbance similar to the thrashing of an injured baitfish.

LEROY BROWN (below)
A lifelike vibrating lure with a busy, wobbling action that is a very effective fish attractor.

SHIMMY (right)
A darting lure with a built-in wriggle. This slow-sinking plug is designed to be fished sink-and-draw at varying speeds of retrieve.

CORDELL RATT'L SPOT (above)
The shiny finish of this lure makes it more easily visible in poor light, and its vibrating action is enhanced by rattling ball bearings that are housed inside the body.

JOINTED WIGGLER (left)
A heavy, fast-sinking plug from Canada that is excellent for fishing large stillwaters and deep, swift-flowing rivers.

DEEP-DIVING PLUGS

BAGLEY DIVING BANG-O-B (right)
A large, tough, hardwood trolling lure with a big lip that will take it down to depths of 6 to 9 m (20 to 30 ft). It can be used for marine species as well as for freshwater fish.

THE HUNTER (below)
A pike lure designed to be fished slowly just off the bottom, especially in winter when the fish are lying deep and torpid.

HEDDON MAGNUM HELLBENDER (above)
This classic lure will dive rapidly down to 11 m (35 ft) when trolled. Effective along deep banks, marginal ledges, and drop-offs.

BAGLEY DEEP DIVING 5 (left)
A tough lure made of balsa reinforced with hardwood. Designed for use in the deeper parts of lakes and reservoirs and in powerful rivers.

NATURAL BAITS

In addition to fish baits, such as cut or whole mackerel and herring, the saltwater angler has a wide range of natural baits to choose from. There are probably more species of fish reliant on non-fish meals than species regularly eating other fish, so the broader the range of natural baits used, the greater the chances of angling success. Fresh, good-quality bait has no equal, but it must be kept cool and moist at all times during storage, and should, if possible, be presented naturally when used.

CUTTLEFISH

SQUID

RAGWORMS

Anglers classify the various species of ragworm (*Nereis* spp.) by colour and size. Red ragworms can be dug from shellfish beds and stone patches in estuaries, and kept for up to a week if loosely wrapped in damp newspaper and refrigerated. King ragworm are the largest reds, used in portions or whole for stingrays, pollack, and similar large predators. Smaller reds are popular general-purpose baits, while tiny harbour ragworms, dug from estuarine mud, are much loved by flounders and mullet. White ragworms, the favourite bait of match anglers, are found on clean sands.

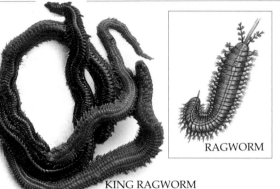

RAGWORM

KING RAGWORM

HOOKING RAGWORMS
Feed the worm up the shank until the hook is full, or push it up onto the trace leaving nothing hanging free for fish to tug at. Beware of the nippers at the head end when handling ragworm.

LUGWORMS

There are two common species of lugworm (*Arenicola* spp.), and both leave telltale heaps of debris at their burrow entrances. Brown lug can be dug from the middle shore sands. They will keep for a few days if loosely wrapped in damp newspaper and put in a refrigerator, or they can be kept in tanks. The larger black lug live beneath the lower shore and can be frozen. Many species of fish find them irresistible.

LUGWORM

HOOKING LUGWORMS
To hook a lugworm, carefully thread the hook through the head and the centre of the body, taking care not to burst the worm. Nip off any surplus tail that might give small fish a starting point for tearing the bait from the hook.

BROWN LUGWORM

SANDEELS

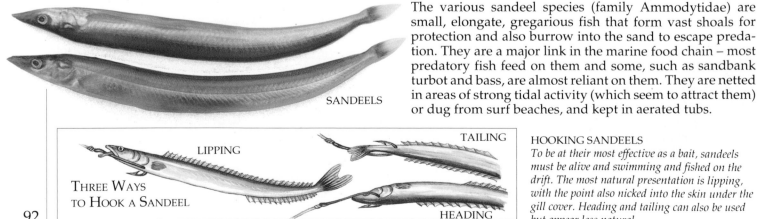

SANDEELS

The various sandeel species (family Ammodytidae) are small, elongate, gregarious fish that form vast shoals for protection and also burrow into the sand to escape predation. They are a major link in the marine food chain – most predatory fish feed on them and some, such as sandbank turbot and bass, are almost reliant on them. They are netted in areas of strong tidal activity (which seem to attract them) or dug from surf beaches, and kept in aerated tubs.

LIPPING

TAILING

THREE WAYS TO HOOK A SANDEEL

HEADING

HOOKING SANDEELS
To be at their most effective as a bait, sandeels must be alive and swimming and fished on the drift. The most natural presentation is lipping, with the point also nicked into the skin under the gill cover. Heading and tailing can also be used but appear less natural.

SQUID AND CUTTLEFISH

Squid and cuttlefish are cephalopods, tentacled molluscs with small internal shells. They are highly intelligent and active predators in their own right, but, either strip-cut or whole, they make excellent baits for a very wide range of species. If they have a fault as baits it is their lack of fish-attracting scent, but fish will take them avidly once they find them. Small squid are available from retail fish outlets, cuttle and large squid from inshore fishing boats.

CUTTLEFISH HEAD

HOOKING SQUID (left)
Cut open, remove guts and outer skin, then strip-cut the flesh. Insert the hook through twice; the flesh is tough, so bait hanging beyond the hook is not a problem.

SQUID STRIP

HOOKING CUTTLE
Prepare and hook as for squid. The head, on a big hook, is good for conger and cod. The entire body, and cut or whole tentacles, can also be used.

OCTOPUS

Octopus are more common in inshore waters than many people realize, and are taken on rod and line in some areas. Like squid and cuttlefish, they are predatory cephalopods, and as baits they are prepared and used in much the same way; small ones can be used whole. Long strips of octopus flesh, when fished fluttering in the tide, will attract fish by their visual appeal. When using long strips, give a taking fish enough time to get the whole bait down before striking to set the hook.

OCTOPUS TENTACLE

OCTOPUS

HOOKING OCTOPUS
Strips are hooked as for squid; to hook a whole tentacle, insert the hook down the centre, bringing it out a shank's length down.

RAZORSHELLS

Several species of razorshell (*Ensis* spp. and *Solen* spp.) inhabit the sands of the extreme lower shore. Razorshells move too quickly to be dug up, so are either speared or coaxed from the sand by squirting a strong salt solution into their keyhole-shaped burrow apertures. They appeal to many fish, including those usually taken on fish strips. Take care not to damage the flesh when taking it from the shell, and remove the tough foot, which fish dislike.

RAZORSHELL

HOOKING RAZORSHELLS
Cut a suitably firm section of flesh, and pass the hook through it as many times as possible because it is soft and tears easily.

Foot

RAZORSHELL

CRABS

As crabs grow, they shed their shells and grow larger ones. At such times, the crab crawls out, then takes on water to expand a soft, wrinkled outer skin that hardens in a few days to form the new shell. Crabs about to shed are called peelers; those without hard shells, softbacks. Both make excellent baits for a wide range of fish, but the peeler is the more effective.

PEELER CRABS

HOOKING CRABS
Peel fully, then cut into halves. Pile these onto the hook and bind in place with thread. Appearance is unimportant: the appeal lies in the smell.

PEELER CRAB

SALTWATER GROUNDBAIT

Saltwater groundbaiting, also known as chumming or swimfeeding, is a very effective means of attracting fish into the vicinity of a baited hook, and of delaying the passage of passing fish so that you can place baits in front of them. It can also be used to give fish a taste for whatever bait you intend to put on your hook, and to encourage them to feed when they otherwise might not. The secret lies in using measured amounts appropriate to the species and the prevailing conditions, and in using enough to tempt the fish without feeding them so much that they have no appetite for the hookbait.

RUBBY DUBBY (above)
The best rubby dubby is made from stale mackerel mixed with bran and pilchard oil. Some anglers mince the mackerel, but this produces particles of uniform size that will disperse in a uniform manner, which fails to exploit the technique's full potential. It is far better to pulp the fish in a tub or bucket with a lump of wood. This gives a variety of particle sizes, which will sink to different depths, and some of them will not wash out of the bag but stay there to draw fish right up to the boat.

RUBBY DUBBY

This is a very effective particulate groundbait, based on the flesh of oily fish, which is released into the water and carried along by the tide to create a long, continuous slick of particles, blood, and body juices. The heavier particles sink, making the slick three-dimensional, and the baits are set at appropriate depths within it. For pelagic fish, such as sharks, it is normally used when drift fishing but can also be used from an anchored boat.

When fishing at anchor for bottom-feeding fish, some anglers tie a mesh bag full of minced mackerel to the anchor in the belief that the ensuing trail will pass beneath the boat, but this will not always be the case. On a dying tide with a stiff breeze cutting across it, the boat will be pushed out of line, and fish following the slick through to its source will not pass beneath it. It is better to hang the bag over the stern on a short, weighted rope.

USING RUBBY DUBBY (left)
The mixture is packed in a mesh bag and hung over the side of the boat. It should be shaken and topped up regularly to maintain the consistency of the slick.

BAIT DROPPERS

Bait droppers are lowered on a rope, or by rod and line, to place large portions of bait on the seabed. These attract sharks and other large predators, and draw territorial species such as conger from their lairs. Because a strong tide will tend to disperse the bait portions away from the hookbaits, this technique works best on neap tides.

A bait dropper usually consists of a weighted plastic tube with a flap that opens when the dropper hits the bottom. A cheaper alternative is a plastic bag with a sinker tied inside one corner. On a fast drop, water pressure keeps the bag closed around its contents, which are released by raising the rod tip a couple of times when the sinker has touched the bottom.

LOWERING DROPPERS (left)
Lower a custom-made dropper carefully so as not to trigger the flap prematurely.

BAITS FOR DROPPERS (above)
When using a dropper, choose a bait or baits that are likely to attract the species of fish you hope to catch. Suitable baits to use in droppers include large pieces of fish or squid, whole or cut worms, whole or crushed shellfish, and broken crabs; you can also use pulped or minced fish.

Big-game Groundbaiting

CHUMMING FOR SHARKS
Cruising sharks can be attracted towards the baited hooks by chumming – dropping chopped stale fish and squid into the water. Oily fish, such as mackerel and herring, are the most effective.

Big-game groundbaiting can take a number of forms, but all are intended either to draw fish towards the hooks or to stir them into a feeding frenzy.

Rubby dubby and bait droppers are good ways of attracting fish to the baited hooks when fishing with natural baits. Another method is to drop chum (small pieces of fish) into the water, but to be effective this needs one person constantly cutting and dropping the chum.

When trolling with natural baits, one way of attracting fish up from the depths is to space twenty link swivels along a length of mono, then clip a live pilchard to each. This rig is trailed astern, and more live pilchard are thrown in loose to form a school with those on the links. If you are trolling lures, you can create the impression of a small school of fish by using multiple lures or by trailing a team of teaser lures. These are hookless lures designed simply to attract species such as marlin and sailfish into the vicinity of the hooked lures.

Shore Groundbaiting

Rock and pier anglers cannot normally reach the areas where fish are feeding, but they can draw feeding fish within casting range by groundbaiting with shirvy. When this paste is put into deep water, such as that below rock ledges, it is carried out to sea by the tide, creating a scent trail that will entice fish right up to the shore. Mullet and bass are among the species readily attracted by shirvy, and conger respond well to a bag of rubby dubby hung over a harbour wall at night.

Fish also gather to feed on bits of fish washed from the decks of trawlers, and on refuse from pier restaurants and moored boats.

USING SHIRVY
When using shirvy, it is essential to create a continuous slick to keep the fish moving inshore. You can do this by putting it into a mesh bag and lowering it into the sea, or by throwing in small amounts with an old serving spoon. The slick makes an oily line on the surface, showing where the baits should be placed. When this fades, throw in another spoonful.

SHIRVY
Shirvy is a thick paste that can be made by mixing finely minced meat and meat fat with bran and fish blood, or by mixing boiled pulped oily fish with bread and pilchard oil. Like rubby dubby, its variously sized particles and its oil and juices are carried along by the tide to form a three-dimensional slick.

LURES

Artificial lures, used alone or in conjunction with natural baits, will take most species of saltwater gamefish. As in freshwater fishing, the size and type of lure to use depends mainly on the species you intend to catch and the style of fishing you are going to employ, such as trolling or spinning. There are thousands of different lures on the market, but if you equip yourself with a small range of each of the basic patterns you will have a selection to cover most of your normal fishing requirements.

TROLLING FEATHER (*above*)
This is a loose lure, one that is threaded onto the line before the hook is attached. This allows it to be used with your personal choice of hook and trace. It can be used weightless and skipping the surface, lightly weighted with a trolling weight, or sent deeper on a downrigger.

PLASTIC SQUID (*below*)
Known informally as "muppets", these lures first proved their value in wreck fishing. They are very attractive to cod, but will take many other species, including ling and pollack, and are especially effective when baited. Like feathers, they are put onto short droppers above a sinker or pirk, but they are fished only at the bottom. The dropper is passed through a small hole in the head of the lure, then a bead is added to prevent it from sliding down over the hook.

FEATHERS (*above*)
When feathers are strung out on short droppers above a sinker, there are few fish they cannot catch. The original versions, devised for mackerel fishing, were simply bunches of feathers, sometimes dyed, whipped to the shank of a hook. These are still used, but bright synthetic materials are increasingly popular. For mackerel, they should be worked up and down repeatedly at all levels until the shoal has been located.

SALTWATER FLIES (*above*)
Small saltwater fish, such as shad, mackerel, and bass, can be taken on many freshwater fly patterns, including the Dog Nobbler. Streamers and bucktails, some based on freshwater flies and others designed specifically for saltwater species, are used for fish such as tarpon, sharks, and sailfish.

MARLIN LURE (*above*)
This large plastic lure is one of many on the market that are similar in appearance and action to the original Kona Head design. The Kona Head, which originated in Hawaii, is a big-fish trolling lure with a big reputation. It is one of the standard big-game lures and will take a wide range of species including marlin, tuna, dolphinfish, and bonito.

LARGE SQUID (*above*)
The large version of the plastic squid is often used in conjunction with a trolled deadbait, or as an additional skirt for another lure, when fishing for open-ocean gamefish such as marlin. On its own, with a big single hook, a large plastic squid is a good trolling lure for species such as sailfish.

SPOONS (*right*)
The fixed-hook spoon is designed specifically to attract fish to within detection range of a natural bait, which induces the fish to take the hook. The metal blade wobbles as it moves through the water, sending out eyecatching glints of light that attract species such as cod, snapper, and grouper.

SPINNER (*above*)
In saltwater, as in freshwater, a spinner is fished by casting and retrieving. Spinners can be used with light spinning tackle for small species such as bass, barracuda, and jack.

MACKEREL SPINNER (*above*)
This spinner has a blade that rotates like a propeller when the lure is retrieved or trolled. It is an excellent lure for mackerel and most small predatory species.

TWO-TAILED EEL (*below*)
This version of the rubber sandeel has two tails to give it a lively, attractive action when worked through the water. When fished on a flying collar rig (see page 249) it is good for pollack, bass, and cod.

ATTRACTOR SPOON (*above*)
A small attractor spoon is a useful flatfish lure when the water is clear and long drifts over clean ground are possible. When mounted just above a baited hook on a long trace, and fished along the bottom, it glints and stirs up puffs of sand as it rotates.

TROLLING LURE (*above*)
There are many variations on this basic theme, which is essentially a loose lure with a plastic skirt and a drilled head that allows it to be rigged to personal taste. Skirts are made of turkey marabou, feathers, or plastic, and coloured to imitate a particular baitfish or to trigger an aggressive response from predatory fish.

PLUGS (*below*)
In warm waters, slowly trolled plugs are very effective lures for a wide range of shallow-reef and open-ocean species. In cooler temperate waters, bass that are hunting around shallow offshore reefs will take them without hesitation.

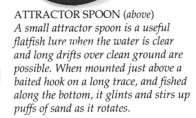

RUBBER SANDEELS (*above*)
Since Alex Ingram designed his legendary Redgill rubber sandeel, imitations, which are reputedly the sincerest form of flattery, have been legion. The trace line passes down the body via the mouth to the hook, which appears from the vent. The tail is thin, flat, and flexible, with an angled end, and provides a lifelike swimming action and enticing vibrations that few fish can resist. Most species will take rubber sandeels, and they are fished on long traces, retrieved slowly from bottom to top, for free-swimming species such as pollack and bass.

PLASTIC EELS (*above*)
These simple but effective jigging lures are made of lengths of coloured plastic tube, crimped to swivels attached to long, twisted-shanked hooks. The lures are fished on short droppers above the sinker, which is bounced along the bottom. Plastic eels are excellent lures for cod, coalfish, and shoaling reef pollack.

PIRKS (*above and right*)
These metal jigging lures were developed from cod lures used by commercial handliners. They range in size from tiny lures weighing as little as 28 g (1 oz), which are used to catch baitfish, to huge slabs of metal weighing 910 g (2 lb) or more for use in deep water with strong currents. Pirks are used unbaited for cod and pollack, and baited for ling and halibut.

THE FLY

THE CAPTURE, ON ARTIFICIAL FLY, of a fish instilled with all the cunning that evolution bestows, is to many the ultimate angling challenge. Where other methods, such as fishing with a natural bait, may be more effective, fly fishing offers an experience that has tested the angler's skill for many hundreds of years.

Today, except where local fishing rules dictate, our choice of fly is extremely wide but essentially practical. We simply choose the most effective for the prevailing conditions, be it a large streamer or a tiny dry fly. Many new materials, including man-made products, ensure that the development of the artificial fly carries on at a pace more rapid than at any time in its history.

This chapter looks at the various fly classifications, from the gaudiest of attractors to the most delicate of imitative patterns. The major fly groups, including streamers, hairwings, nymphs, wet flies, and dry flies, are all covered, and effective examples are illustrated. The groups include patterns that appeal to a wide range of species, from trout and salmon to pike, bass, and grayling. The link between artifice and nature is also covered, with a review of the main prey items and insect groups that are so important to the angler intent on an imitative approach. This craft of mimicry is further illustrated by an outline of flytying and the relevant tools and materials.

FLY PATTERNS
The earliest flies were tied to catch the brown trout, but today there are patterns designed for a wide range of freshwater and saltwater species.

NATURALS 1

For the fly fisher intent on an imitative approach, a comprehensive knowledge of the fish's prey is extremely important. Even for the less dedicated, a basic understanding of it provides an important insight into the way that a fish will respond to an artificial fly. There are seven main groups of creatures of interest to the fly fisher and imitated or suggested by artificial flies: mayflies (Ephemeroptera); caddis flies (Trichoptera); stoneflies (Plecoptera); chironomids or non-biting midges (Diptera); damselflies and dragonflies (Odonata); crustaceans and fish; and terrestrials, creatures that find their way inadvertently onto the water.

FEEDING TROUT
Brown trout will take full advantage of whatever food is available. Try to use a fly pattern that corresponds to the naturals that the fish are feeding on at the time.

MAYFLIES

The order Ephemeroptera encompasses the up-wing flies and olives that are among the most important insects to the fly fisher. They are called "up-wing" because they fold their wings vertically when at rest, as a butterfly does.

The life cycle begins with the egg hatching into a larva or nymph. This is the longest-lived stage, which (depending on the species) feeds on detritus, small organisms, or algae until fully developed. Once mature, it rises to the water's surface, emerging as the subimago, or dun. Although winged, it is not sexually mature, and it must cast its skin one more time to become the imago, or spinner. Its task then is simply to reproduce.

The largest of all the up-wings are the mayflies, genus *Ephemera*, which measure 2.5 cm (1 in) or so in body length. Although the mayflies are the largest of the group, smaller species, including the medium olive, blue-winged olive, iron blue, and spurwings, have longer seasons and are taken more often by fish. Some, such as *Caenis*, are so small that imitations are tied on hooks as tiny as size 24.

FEMALE MAYFLY SPINNER
The imago, or spinner, of the mayfly Ephemera danica *is a handsome creature with sparkling, dark-veined wings. After mating, the female returns to the water to lay her eggs. With this task accomplished, her life is over, and she falls spent upon the water's surface. The trout are quick to take advantage.*

FEMALE MAYFLY DUN
The subimago, or dun, of the mayfly emerges towards mid-day, when it may elicit a spectacular rise of fish.

GREENWELL'S GLORY
This, perhaps the most famous of all up-wing imitations, was devised in 1854 by Canon Greenwell and James Wright to tempt large brown trout on Scotland's River Tweed.

POND OLIVE NYMPH
This has the typical profile of nymphs of the family Baetidae, which also includes the medium olive and large dark olive. They are all basically olive in colour, well camouflaged to avoid detection by predators, and because of their ability to move quickly when necessary are called "agile darters".

OLIVE NYMPH
This is a simple, general tying to suggest a wide range of up-wing nymphs. It uses a pale olive fur body plus dark pheasant tail fibres to mimic the coloration of the natural close to emergence. It should be fished dead-drift or with a slow retrieve.

CADDIS FLIES

Caddis or sedge flies are to be found on both still and running water, and their life cycle includes larval, pupal, and adult stages. They are mothlike insects belonging to the order Trichoptera, which means "hairy-winged"; caddis flies have hairs on their wings, whereas the wings of moths are covered in tiny, dustlike scales.

The larva is soft bodied, and many species build protective cases from stones, sand, weed, even small snail shells. There are also caseless caddis fly larvae, however, and these include species of *Hydropsyche* and *Rhyacophila*. The larva is an active creature with a pair of specially adapted, hair-fringed legs that enable it to swim strongly.

When pupation occurs, even the caseless species build a protective case, which is usually anchored to a large rock. When fully developed, the pupa uses its strong jaws to cut itself free of its case. It then rises to the surface, at which point its skin splits along the thorax and the adult emerges. The adult has four wings, which lie along the body when at rest, and these give the caddis its typical roof-winged profile.

CADDIS LARVA CASES
The protective cases built by the larvae of many caddis species are bonded together by a tough material that is secreted by the creatures.

CADDIS PUPA
This imitation of a medium-sized caddis pupa mimics the natural's curved body and antennae.

ADULT SEDGE
The adult sedge has long antennae and four wings. Species range in size from 6 mm (¼ in) up to 38 mm (1½ in) in the case of the great red sedge Phryganea grandis.

FISH & CRUSTACEANS

The diet of trout and bass is not restricted to insects; various baitfish also make up a proportion of their diet. Many not only provide a substantial meal but are to be found in convenient, tightly packed shoals, just there for the taking. Silvery flanked species such as roach and bream are very important on stillwaters, where trout can go into a veritable feeding frenzy as they charge into the shoals. On rivers, minnows and small, bottom-dwelling species are the selected prey.

Crustaceans, too, rank high on the dietary list. Most numerous are the freshwater shrimps or scuds, such as *Gammarus*, which are bottom-dwelling creatures ranging in length from 6 mm (¼ in) to 18 mm (¾ in) and varying in colour from a pale, washed-out olive to a rusty brown. Imitations should reflect this if they are to be effective. Another common food item, the water hoglouse (*Asellus*), is similar in size to a freshwater shrimp. This crustacean is most often found in stillwaters, where it occurs in prolific numbers, living and feeding in the bottom detritus.

MILLER'S THUMB
Sculpins such as the miller's thumb are heavily preyed upon, particularly by large brown trout.

WATER HOGLOUSE
This dull, insignificant-looking creature inhabits many lakes and slow rivers in huge numbers.

FRESHWATER SHRIMP
The freshwater shrimp, Gammarus, forms an important part of the diet of both stillwater and river trout. Imitations should be well weighted, and similar in colour to the naturals.

HOGLOUSE
Hare fur, brown partridge, and dark turkey tail make an effective copy of the natural.

101

NATURALS 2

DAMSELFLIES & DRAGONFLIES

Summer would not really be the same without the sight of these large, predatory insects darting around marginal vegetation as they quarter their territories. Both belong to the order Odonata but are grouped into suborders, the damselflies being Zygoptera while the dragonflies are Anisoptera.

Both suborders have an aquatic nymphal stage, which is also predatory and feeds on tiny aquatic creatures. The adults of damselflies may be distinguished from adult dragonflies by their slimmer bodies and by the way they fold their wings along their bodies when at rest; the dragonflies hold their wings out horizontally. Both nymphs and adults are taken by fish such as bass and trout, and good imitations can prove very successful when cast around weedbeds and partly submerged timber.

DAMSELFLY NYMPH *(left)*
The damselfly nymph may be distinguished from the dragonfly nymph by its much slimmer appearance and the three leaflike gills on the tip of the abdomen. It comes in a wide range of shades of olive and brown to mimic its habitat.

COMMON BLUE DAMSELFLY *(below)*
The common blue damselfly, Enallagma cyathigerum, *is a well-known sight around lakes. When mature, the nymph climbs free of the water, its skin splits along the back, and the adult emerges.*

DAMSELFLY
A dry damselfly imitation can prove effective in summer, when trout and bass leap to take the natural insects.

STONEFLIES

Stoneflies, which are insects of the order Plecoptera, are creatures of stony or gravel-bottomed rivers. On these waters, particularly in their nymphal form, they form an important part of the diet of trout and other fish.

Most species are dark brown or black but a few are much brighter, notably the aptly named Yellow Sally. At rest, the hard, shiny, heavily veined wings are held flat along the top of the body. The aquatic nymphal stage (or creeper) of the stonefly is an active creature, scuttling over the rocks that are its habitat. When mature, it clambers free of the water, usually onto marginal rock. The skin along the back of the thorax splits and the adult emerges.

Although trout will take the female returning to lay her eggs, the nymph is the most important stage to the fly fisher. A heavily weighted nymph imitation, allowed to drift just off the bottom, can prove very effective during high water conditions.

STONEFLY NYMPH
The stonefly nymph differs from the nymphs of up-winged flies in having two tails rather than three.

DRY STONEFLY
When female stoneflies return to lay their eggs, flopping along on the water's surface, trout feeding on them will often take a dry imitation of the correct size.

ADULT STONEFLY
Stoneflies vary in length from less than 6 mm (¼ in), in the case of small species such as needle flies, to the 5 cm (2 in) of the Pteronarcys *species. Although they are capable of flight, many stoneflies are happy to crawl through bankside cover.*

CHIRONOMIDS

The various species of chironomid, or non-biting midge, belonging to the genus *Chironomus* make up a very large proportion of the stillwater trout's diet. The life cycle begins when the egg hatches into a small, wormlike larva that burrows into the bottom mud. Chironomid larvae vary in colour from pale olive and brown to the vivid blood-red of the *Chironomus plumosus* larva, known as the bloodworm. The bloodworm receives its colour from haemoglobin, a substance that enables it to thrive in the black, oxygen-poor mud of lakebeds.

When the larvae pupate, the pupae remain within their mud burrows until fully developed, a period that can be as little as 36 hours. Then they rise to the surface to transform into adults, where they are at the mercy of the trout, which take them in truly prodigious quantities. The pupae are taken not only as they rise but also at the very point of emergence as adults.

ADULT CHIRONOMID
The adults of the chironomids have slim bodies and two wings, and range in size from the merest wisp up to 12 mm (½ in) or more. They vary in colour from black and brown to bright green.

MIDGE PUPA
Imitations of chironomid pupae should mimic the bulbous-thoraxed profiles of the naturals.

CHIRONOMID PUPA
Although varying in size, all chironomid pupae have slim abdomens, bulbous thoraxes, and white breathing filaments. Black is the most common colour.

TERRESTRIALS

Not all creatures that find themselves engulfed by large predatory fish are aquatic: many are terrestrials, which are non-aquatic insects and other life forms that are carried or fall onto the water's surface. Many, such as spiders, beetles, hoverflies, ants, and aphids, are blown onto the water by the wind. On large, windswept expanses of water, it is common for winged insects to be blown out over the surface. Many of them succumb to the waves, or are simply weak fliers that have to touch down on the water.

The large, gangling-legged crane fly is one such insect. Also known as the daddy longlegs, it is usually at its most numerous during the damp days of autumn, when it can produce a confident rise of feeding fish. Earlier in the year, the hawthorn fly and related species can find their way onto rivers and lakes with similar results.

Terrestrials make up a large part of the diet of many fish, including trout, in rainfed rivers. The water in this type of river is often deficient in nutrients, resulting in a poor aquatic biomass. In such waters the trout are opportunist feeders, quick to snap up caterpillars, beetles, and indeed any unfortunate small creature that happens to fall from bankside vegetation.

HAWTHORN FLY
This large, jet-black fly is on the wing during late spring, when the long-legged males hover in small swarms around bankside vegetation.

CRANE FLY
To be effective, imitations of the crane fly, or daddy longlegs, should always include the long, trailing legs of the natural.

BLACK ANT
This pattern is useful during the sultry days of late summer, when swarms of flying ants often appear.

GUM BEETLE
The iridescent gum beetle is very popular with Australian brown and rainbow trout.

THE ARTIFICIAL FLY

The artificial fly is the link between the fly fisherman and the fish, and designing it offers the angler the challenge of creating the illusion of a delicate insect or other small creature from a handful of inanimate objects. The fly and the skill of presentation then come together to seduce the fish into taking that fly, either from aggression or from the belief that it is a living creature. It is this pitting of the angler's abilities against the natural guile of the fish that gives fly fishing its special appeal.

ORANGE BUSTARD

GOLDEN DRAKE

FLY HISTORY
The first stirrings of modern fly design began in 1676 with Charles Cotton's chapter in The Compleat Angler *listing 65 effective fly patterns. The creation of new patterns reached its peak in the late 19th and early 20th centuries.*

ATTRACTORS & DECEIVERS

Artificial flies fall into two main groups: attractors and deceivers. Attractors are usually gaudy, bright creations designed to stimulate a predatory fish's aggression; they suggest nothing edible but provoke a predatory response. Orange and yellow are favourite colours for attractor flies. Deceivers are intended to fool the fish into mistaking them for natural food items, such as nymphs, crustaceans, or small fish. This group includes dry flies, nymphs, and some wet fly patterns, particularly those that are direct imitations of a fish's food. Deceivers are usually subtle in coloration, mimicking the hues of the naturals.

DECEIVER

ATTRACTOR

TYPES OF FLY

HAIRWING

WINGED DRY FLY

NYMPH

WINGED WET FLY

Wet flies
Wet flies are effective on a wide range of water types, from rivers and streams to vast, windswept lakes, but all have one thing in common: they are fished beneath the water's surface. Some wet flies are subtly coloured deceivers, while the more gaudy types of dressing work as attractors.

Wet fly types vary from simple spider patterns, with merely a few turns of hackle at the eye, to intricate dressings with hackles both along the hook and at the throat, plus a wing. Many of the winged wet flies used for stillwater boat fishing are of this latter type.

Another type, palmers, have rough, dubbed bodies with hackles running the entire length.

Dry flies
The dry fly is designed to float on the water's surface. To prevent it sinking, water-repellent hackles are wound around the hook to distribute the weight over the surface of the water. The hackles also simulate the legs and "buzz" of an aquatic or terrestrial insect trapped on the water.

Most dry flies are deceivers, and many patterns are designed to imitate specific insects; examples include the Blue Winged Olive, Grannom, and Crane Fly. Others, such as the Wickham's Fancy and the Adams, are more general designs that are intended just to look edible.

Dry flies may be simply hackled, or tied with wings, depending on the level of imitation required.

Nymphs
A nymph is the immature stage of certain aquatic insects such as mayflies and damselflies. Imitations of this stage are likewise termed nymphs, and the term is also applied to wingless patterns that suggest the larval and pupal stages of insects. Natural nymphs have sombre hues, so the artificials are similarly coloured. Browns, olives, and greens are especially effective, as are mottled shades.
Emergers
Emergers are tied to imitate that stage of an aquatic insect's life when it actually emerges, at the water's surface, from its nymphal or pupal skin. While trapped on the surface, emerging insects are particularly vulnerable to fish predation.

Streamers and hairwings
Streamer and hairwing flies, which are generally large and tied on long-shanked hooks, include the majority of salmon and steelhead patterns. The difference between streamers and hairwings is simply that the wings of streamers are tied with feathers, such as marabou or cock hackles, while those of hairwings are tied with hair, including bucktail and squirrel tail.

Like wet flies, streamers and hairwings may be brightly coloured attractors or more subtle deceivers, and many have an imitative role. For example, some are tied to imitate the small fish that are eaten by predators such as trout and pike. These patterns often incorporate white and silver materials.

PARTS OF A FLY

The head
The head is normally the last part of the fly to be tied, and usually consists of turns of tying thread that hold in place the wing, the hackle, and the loose ends of both rib and body materials. Because it secures these other components it is the weak point of the fly, and therefore it is important that the thread is finished off correctly and that the bare turns are well protected. The head is protected by coats of cellulose varnish, which are applied with either the tip of a fine needle or a specially designed applicator. When coloured threads are used, clear varnish gives the best results, though for streamers and other large flies, two or three coats of black or red varnish produce a smooth, glossy effect.

The wing
In both dry and wet flies the wing often suggests that of a natural insect, but may be added simply to provide movement. This is particularly the case in those wet flies and streamers that use mobile wing materials, such as cock hackles, to give "life" to the fly. Many feathers and furs are used to produce fly wings, one of the most popular materials being slips taken from the primary feathers of game birds. Duck feathers are especially useful, and the smoky shades of mallard and teal closely match the wing coloration of many species of mayfly.

The tail
In dry flies the tail not only acts in an imitative way, suggesting that of the natural, but, by becoming trapped on the surface of the water, it balances the fly and helps it to float. In wet flies and streamers the tail is usually decorative rather than functional; often brightly coloured, it is added to give the fly extra fish-attracting allure.

Cock hackle fibres are often used for imitative tails, while for a brighter effect, wool, fluorescent floss, hair, and golden pheasant toppings and tippets are all very popular. Highly mobile materials are also widely used; marabou, dyed in a variety of colours, gives a wonderfully sinuous action to a wide range of large nymphs and lead-headed patterns.

The wing

The head

The rib

The tail

The hackle

The body

Hook

Hooks
Fly hooks range from the tiny midge-sized models to giant long-shanks, with single, double, or treble points, depending on their use. Worldwide, singles are by far the most popular for all types of fly.

The hackle
Hackles, in their various forms, are the basis of the vast majority of fly patterns. Although a range of feathers may be used, it is those taken from the necks or "capes" of domestic poultry that provide the hackle on over 90 per cent of artificial flies. The diversity of colours and stiffnesses, found in both male and female plumage, has shaped the whole development of wet flies and dry flies throughout their history.

In dry flies, it is inevitably the stiffer-fibred, more water-repellent cock hackles that provide the flotation. Conversely, the softer hen hackle is preferred for wet flies and streamers, where its ability to become rapidly waterlogged is a prime factor. Soft hackles also work better in the water, providing movement and a semblance of life to what is an otherwise dead object.

Where softness and mobility are the prerequisite, rather than the ability to float, other types of feather may be used. Feathers from species such as grouse, snipe, partridge, and mallard are all effective examples; their coloration mimics superbly that of many natural nymphs and pupae.

The body
The body of a fly covers the bulk of the hook and provides the substance of a pattern. A wide range of materials is used, from sombre furs to flashy metallic products. On imitative patterns, or those that merely suggest a living creature, fur (or a man-made substitute) gives a wonderful shaggy effect, especially when teased out. Smoother effects are produced by floss, flat metal tinsel, or Lurex. Mylar tubing, with its scaly appearance, is particularly good for imitations of small fish. Feather fibre also gives an interesting texture: goose, turkey, and cock pheasant tail are effective examples.

Detached body
The detached body is the only type that is not formed around the hook: it is created out of plastic, deer hair, or feather and secured to the hook at one end only, projecting back over the bend. Its advantages, even on a large fly, are that it is light and it allows the use of a much smaller hook.

The rib
The function of a rib is threefold. Firstly, it mimics the segmentation of the body of an insect or small crustacean. Secondly, if made from a sparkling material, such as metal tinsel or Lurex, it adds extra flash to a pattern, or, on more imitative dressings, it is used to suggest the gases trapped within an emerging insect's skin. Thirdly, a tough material (metal wire for example) adds to the durability of the fly, holding a delicate body in place or protecting it from the ravages of a predatory fish.

Traditionally, wire and metal twists were used to rib all types of fly. Plain wire is still very popular, and now comes in a variety of colours. While metals are fine for patterns intended to sink, their weight is a disadvantage on flies intended to sit on or in the surface. Here, lighter materials are better. Nylon monofilament is a robust alternative, while Lurex, although more delicate, works superbly on emerger-style patterns. Coloured, translucent plastic strands produce a very lifelike segmented effect on nymph and pupa imitations.

FLY TYING EQUIPMENT

Before you can begin tying your own flies, you need to obtain the basic tools and materials. For tools, a vice, scissors, hackle pliers, and a bobbin holder are all that are really necessary at first, and the other tools can be purchased as you gain experience. The most difficult decision is what to choose from the dazzling array of furs and feathers available. The best solution to this is to take a look at three or four of your favourite patterns, make a note of all the ingredients, and then use this as your shopping list.

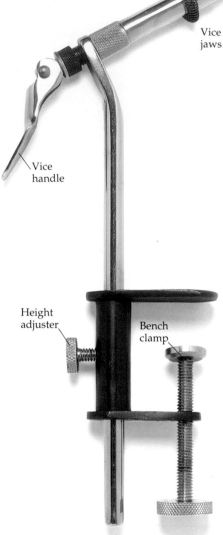

Vice jaws

Vice handle

Height adjuster

Bench clamp

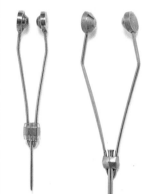

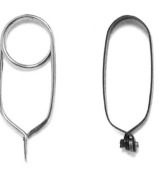

BOBBIN HOLDERS
The best bobbin holders are the spigot type, where the bobbin is held by sprung metal arms. The thread is fed off through a tube.

HACKLE PLIERS
Hackle pliers are used to wind hackles, chenille, and other materials. The simplest and best are made of sprung metal, with either smooth metal or rubber-covered jaws to prevent them cutting the hackle material.

DUBBING NEEDLE
A fine, sharp needle has many uses, such as dividing wing slips or picking out dubbed body material to create a ragged effect. You can buy a purpose-made dubbing needle or use a large sewing needle.

SHARP-NOSED SCISSORS
Scissors, with either straight or curved blades, are extremely important to the fly tier. The base of the jaws is used to cut tough materials, leaving the tips sharp enough for precise trimming.

HAIR STACKER
Producing a neat hairwing with all the tips even is not easy: all too often the hairs remain staggered. Using a hair stacker enables you to get the tips neatly aligned.

WHIP FINISH TOOL
The whip finish tool is very useful if you find the hand whip finish difficult, or when materials are very close to the eye of the hook. The standard tool has two wire arms over which the thread is looped.

VICE
Of all the tools used by the fly tier, the vice is certainly the most important. It is the means by which the hook is held stationary while all the threads and materials are added to produce the finished fly. The hook is held between a pair of metal jaws, which can be adjusted to accommodate a wide range of hook sizes and diameters of wire. Various types of vice are available. Some have simple screw-tightened jaws, while on others the jaws are spring loaded or, as in the type shown here, are operated by a single cam lever. Whichever type of mechanism is used, the mark of a good vice is that it holds the hook securely, allowing no movement.

DUBBING TWISTER
Looping the dubbing produces some interesting effects. This tool uses sprung metal arms to hold the loop open, and its weight helps you to spin the thread.

BOBBIN THREADER
Using this simple tool makes it much easier to feed thread through the thin tube of a spigot bobbin holder.

GOLDEN PHEASANT TIPPETS

PHEASANT FEATHERS
The feathers of many species of pheasant are used for tying flies, especially the centre tails of both sexes of the ring-necked pheasant. The most colourful pheasant feathers are used for salmon patterns.

SECTION OF COCK PHEASANT TAIL FEATHER

HEN PHEASANT TAIL FEATHERS

TEAL WINGS

HEN CAPE

CAPES
The hackles from the capes of domestic poultry form the basis of most flies. The soft hackles of hens are good for wet flies, while the more water-repellent cock hackles are better used for dry flies.

COCK CAPE

TEAL WINGS
The primary feathers of a number of duck species, including teal, offer pale grey shades that mimic those found in the wings of many natural up-winged flies.

DYED SQUIRREL TAIL

MARABOU

MARABOU
Once obtained from the marabou stork, this highly mobile feather now comes from the domestic white turkey.

WOOD DUCK

NATURAL SQUIRREL

MALLARD

DUCK FEATHERS
Among the most popular duck feathers used in fly tying are bronze and speckled grey mallard feathers and the barred black-and-white feathers of the teal and pintail. The striking black-and-white and speckled, lemon feathers of the wood duck are also used.

SQUIRREL TAIL
Although the grey, white, and black tail hair of the grey squirrel may be used in its natural state, bleaching it and then dyeing it with pure colours vastly increases its versatility as a fly material.

PEACOCK HERL
The herl (barbs) of the male peacock's eye feather produce sparkling, bulbous bodies and thoraxes.

PEACOCK HERL

TINSEL
Tinsel gives sparkle to the fly and protects delicate body materials.

POLYPROPYLENE FLOSS
This light, water-repellent material is ideal for both bodies and for the wings of dry flies that imitate "spent" naturals.

TYING THREAD
Fly-tying thread was originally made of natural silk, but today silk has been almost entirely superseded by man-made fibres such as nylon, which are much stronger and also rotproof. Tying threads are sold in many colours, either plain or pre-waxed.

RAYON FLOSS
Like tying thread, floss was originally made from silk. Today, fibres such as rayon are used to make multi-stranded, rotproof floss that spreads and flattens as it is wound, helping to produce a neat body.

WOOL
Natural or man-made wool is used to make tails, or wound or teased out and dubbed to form fat, "buggy" fly bodies.

VARNISH
Varnish is used to protect the bare threads at the eye of the hook. Clear or coloured cellulose varnish may be used, but for bonding materials in place an adhesive varnish with a vinyl base is much better.

MYLAR TUBING
This sparkling, metallic-finish tubing has a wonderful scale-effect surface, perfect for producing the bodies of fish fry imitations.

FLY TYING BASICS 1

The ability to tie flies is one of the fly fisher's greatest assets, and fly tying is also a source of considerable pleasure in itself. Tying flies allows the individual angler to develop new and effective patterns, or to make subtle adjustments to an established dressing to increase its fish-catching potential. To the angler-entomologist it is an indispensable skill: to watch a fish taking a particular insect, then to construct an imitation good enough to fool that fish into taking it, elicits a sense of satisfaction rarely found elsewhere in angling.

FLY TYING
The pleasures of fly fishing are greatly enhanced when you use flies that you have tied yourself.

STARTING OFF & WHIP FINISHING

There is obviously little point in beginning to tie a fly if you do not know how to start off the tying thread. What may not be so obvious is that it is equally important to learn how to finish the fly securely: without a robust finish, the fly will simply fall apart during fishing. Starting the thread off properly allows you to build a neat, strong bed to which you will attach the rest of the materials; neatness and strength are the secret of constructing a tidy, robust fly. The whip finish is the most secure way of finishing a fly. It entails winding a loop of thread over itself repeatedly then pulling it tight, and bedding the loose end beneath turns of thread produces a firm finish that will take a good deal of punishment.

Starting off

 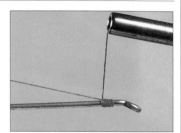

1 Fix the hook securely in a vice. Next, loop the thread beneath the hook, forming an upright V-shape.

2 Hold the loose end of thread taut and wind the bobbin end over it. Wind until the loose end is trapped.

Whip finishing by hand

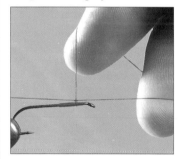 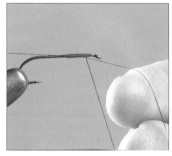 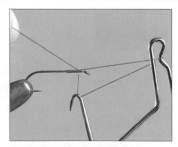 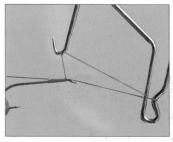

1 When the fly is complete, form a figure-4-shaped loop over the first two fingers of your right hand.

2 Flip the fingers around, bringing them beneath the hook. This takes the vertical strand over the loose end.

3 Repeat four or five times, ensuring that the loop is wound neatly over the loose end lying back along the hook.

4 Slip the thread off the fingers, draw the loop tight, and insert a dubbing needle into it to retain tension.

Using a whip finish tool

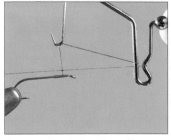 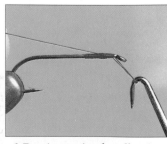

1 Loop the tying thread around the two prongs of the whip finish tool. Then bring the thread back to form a figure-4 shape.

2 Rotate the tool so that it falls beneath the hook, trapping the loose end. This movement forms the first turn of the whip finish.

3 Repeat the process four or five times. When you are happy with the number of turns, slip the thread off the lower prong of the tool.

4 Retain tension by allowing the thread to catch on the hooked prong. Steadily pull the loose end of the thread to draw the loop tight.

TAILS

A tail may represent that of a natural insect, impart movement to a fly, or just add a flash of colour. The materials used for tails range from cock hackle fibres to fluorescent floss, and on traditional wet fly patterns, the black and gold banding of the golden pheasant tippet feather produces a striking effect.

Tying a tail

1 Tie the thread to the hook shank opposite the barb. Select a well-marked golden pheasant tippet feather.

2 Remove five or six fibres from the feather. Offer the bunch up to the hook, extending it beyond the bend.

3 Catch in the tail with turns of thread, ensuring it does not twist. The tail should be about half the hook's length.

BODIES

Bodies come in many shapes and sizes, from the slimness of flat tinsel to the ragged effect of dubbed fur. In most patterns, the main task of the body is to provide the substance of the fly.

Most bodies, except those that are detached or of Mylar tubing, are actually wound around the hook shank. Take care to ensure that each turn is as close to the next one as possible, with no gaps.

Tying a tinsel body

1 Ensure that an even bed has been formed, then cut the tip of the tinsel to a thin "scallop" and catch it in.

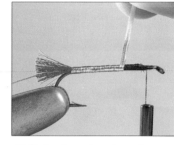

2 Take the tying thread to just short of the eye. Wind the tinsel up the body in tight, closely butted turns.

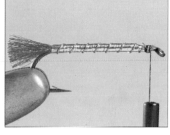

3 Secure the loose end with turns of thread; remove excess tinsel. Wind rib over the body in an open spiral.

Dubbing a body

1 With the rib caught in, offer a small pinch of dubbing up to prewaxed thread. Ensure that the spread is even.

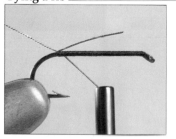

2 Gently twist the dubbing between forefinger and thumb into an even rope. Wind over hook in close turns.

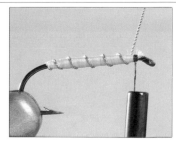

3 Finish the body just short of the eye. Wind the rib, then tease out the fibres of fur with a dubbing needle.

RIBS

The rib provides sparkle and adds strength, whether it is bedding into a soft body or protecting a delicate body or hackle. The perfect rib forms a neat, open spiral, running the length of the body. Coloured wires and tinsel are the traditional materials, but nylon monofilament is ideal for ribbing dry flies. Lurex and Crystal Hair both give a superb, non-tarnish sparkle effect.

Tying a rib

1 Run the tying thread down the hook to a point opposite the barb. There, catch in the ribbing material with several turns of thread.

2 Allow the waste end of the ribbing to lie along almost the full length of the hook shank to produce an even underbody.

3 Add the body material. Then wind the ribbing material firmly around and along the body so that it forms a neat, open spiral.

FLY TYING BASICS 2

HACKLES

The exact function of a hackle depends on the type of fly it is tied on. In wet flies, nymphs, streamers, and in fact any pattern that is fished subsurface, the hackle represents the legs of a nymph or the twitching fins of a small fish. In dry flies and emergers, the hackle is used to suggest the legs and wings of an insect and also to keep the fly afloat. Palmered flies not only have a hackle at the head but also one wound along the body. This produces a dense "bumble" effect, providing great floatability in dry flies and a superb action in wet flies.

Most hackles are made of feathers, but various types of hair may also be adapted into a hackle: rabbit, hare, and squirrel may all be spun in a dubbing loop, then wound over the hook to form a thorax-cum-hackle. It is a technique that lends itself particularly well to nymph and pupa imitations.

Wet-fly hackle

1 Catch in the hackle feather just behind the eye. Make four full turns, using hackle pliers, then secure the tip.

2 Stroke the hackle fibres beneath the hook, fastening them in place with turns of tying thread.

3 Remove any hackle fibres still above the hook or not lying back properly. Finally, add a wing and a whip finish.

Dubbing-loop hackle

1 With the body covering the rear two-thirds of the hook, insert a pinch of hare's fur into a loop of tying thread.

2 Take hold of the loop with a pair of hackle pliers and twist it until the fur spins into a fluffy rope.

3 Wind the fur over the hook up to the eye; trim the thorax top and sides, but leave some hairs beneath the hook.

Dry-fly hackle

1 With the body complete, prepare a cock hackle by stripping the butt, leaving a short, bare stem.

2 Catch in the hackle and take hold of the tip with a pair of hackle pliers. Make three or four full turns.

3 Ensure that the turns are butted together. Secure the hackle tip, remove the waste end, and tie a whip finish.

Palmered hackle

1 With body in place prepare a cock hackle by stripping the butt, leaving a short, bare stem. Catch in the hackle.

2 Using pliers, wind the hackle down the body to the bend. Ensure each turn is evenly spaced.

3 Wind the ribbing material up through the hackle in the opposite spiral. This will fix the hackle in place.

4 Remove excess hackle at the bend and ribbing at the eye. Add a second, slightly longer-fibred hackle at the eye.

WINGS

Wings can give movement to a fly or, when used in a more imitative role, suggest those of a real insect. In streamers, the traditional wing material is cock hackle, taken either from the neck or saddle of the bird, but dyed turkey marabou, with its superb, pulsating action, is now the firm favourite. Hairwings use a variety of hair types to provide their profile and to create a stiff, robust appearance well suited to fast water.

Imitative wet-fly and dry-fly wings may be tied in a variety of positions, such as paired, split, advanced, or pent, depending on the insect stage being copied. Paired slips of duck primary feather are the most widely used, but other materials, including hackle points, polypropylene yarn, feather fibre, and even hair, all have their place.

Hackle-point wing

1 With tail and body complete, select two well-marked hackle points with fibres the same length as the hook gape.

2 Remove the base fibres from the bottom of each hackle, leaving two points approximately the same length as the hook shank.

3 Catch the hackle points in by their bare stems and bring them to a vertical position with a few turns of tying thread.

Feather wing

1 With body and hackle in place, remove two equal-sized slips from duck primaries taken from opposite sides of the bird.

2 Place the slips together, curves inward, so the curves cancel each other out. Secure the wing with several turns of thread.

3 With the wing in place, remove the excess stubs of feather before building up a neat head and finally adding a whip finish.

Single wing case

1 When the tail and body are complete, catch in a slip of feather fibre at the rear of the thorax position.

2 Add the thorax (here it is dubbed fur) then stretch the fibre over the back, securing it at the eye.

Hair wing

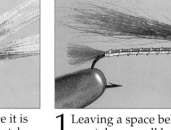

1 Leaving a space behind the eye, take a small bunch of hair, removing broken hairs before judging for length.

2 With the hair projecting slightly past the bend, fix it in position with locking turns of thread around the base.

HEADS

The head may simply be the finishing point of a fly or it may have an extra function: it can be weighted to make the fly sink, or else made buoyant to enable the fly to be "waked" through the water's surface. The Muddler, with its buoyant deer-hair head, is a famous example of this latter group.

Muddler head

1 With body and wing in place, offer up a bunch of deer hair to the hook shank, securing it in place with two loose turns of thread.

2 Pull the thread tight. This makes the hair flare and spin. Add further bunches, if required, and then carefully trim the hair to shape.

3 Using a sharp pair of scissors, clip the hair into a neat bullet shape. Allow a ruff of hair tips to remain as a sort of hackle.

SIMPLE HEAD

DRY FLIES

The term "dry fly" covers a vast and structurally diverse range of patterns, from the merest speck intended to imitate a midge right up to something as bulky as a large caddis fly, mayfly, or dragonfly imitation. The main prerequisite of all dry flies is that they should float on or in the surface, and so they are tied with various light or water-repellent materials. Cock hackles are the most often-used aid to flotation, but other materials such as deer hair and polypropylene are also used to good effect.

GREY WULFF
This is one of a series of large, well-hackled patterns, devised by the late Lee Wulff, which ride high even in fast-flowing or broken water. This version is a representation of the mayfly Ephemera danica.

IRON BLUE *(right)*
This imitates a number of small, dark, up-winged flies of the genus Baetis, *including B. muticus. This hackled pattern is effective during the naturals' main emergence periods of early summer and autumn.*

TRAUN-WING CADDIS
Traun River Products manufactures meshed, lifelike wing material, which mimics the veining of a caddis fly's wing. Used in conjunction with softer materials, it produces good imitations of many caddis species.

LETORT HOPPER
Pennsylvania's Letort River gives its name to this simple grasshopper imitation. As in many other imitations of this chunky terrestrial, deer body hair is used for the head and overwing to give the required buoyancy.

DADDY LONGLEGS
The daddy longlegs, or crane fly, is a large, gangling terrestrial and is common in late summer and early autumn. Imitations fished dry or wet often produce better-than-average fish.

GODDARD SEDGE
This highly buoyant imitation of an adult caddis, devised by John Goddard, is made almost entirely of deer hair. It works well on both stillwaters and streams.

CUT-WING GREEN DRAKE
This pattern uses shaped mallard breast feathers to imitate the wings of a mayfly dun or green drake. The realistic profile makes the fly effective even when the trout have seen everything else.

POLY-WING SPINNER
The water-repellent properties of polypropylene are put to good use here, where the material forms the wing of a small imitation of a spent spinner.

ADAMS
The Adams has gradually become the most widely used up-winged dun pattern. Its grey fur body, grizzle hackle-point wings, and mixed grizzle and brown hackle give the subtle coloration of a freshly emerged olive dun. It may be tied on hooks ranging in size from a 10 right down to a 24.

HUMPY
The Humpy uses the buoyancy of deer body hair to keep it riding high even in fast, broken water. It is an excellent general pattern that will take anything from trout in small streams to salmon on wide, powerful rivers.

IRRESISTIBLE
The Irresistible, dressed in a range of sizes, is a truly adaptable pattern that will take trout from small, broken streams and even salmon and steelhead. The key to its effectiveness is the body of spun and clipped deer hair, which produces an almost unsinkable fly.

BLACK KLINKHAMMER
Hans van Klinken, of the Netherlands, devised this novel variation on the parachute hackle theme. It is tied large on an emerger hook to give it the bent effect typical of an emerging chironomid.

COMPARA-DUN
The easily tied Compara-dun, which was devised by American fly tiers Al Caucci and Bob Nastasi, offers a very lifelike profile of a newly emerged olive dun mayfly.

TROTH CADDIS
Al Troth is the originator of this very effective imitation of an adult caddis fly. It uses a wing of bleached elk hock to create the correct silhouette and make it very buoyant, and is effective on both still and running water.

DUCK'S DUN
Cul de canard feathers, which are taken from around the preen glands of ducks such as mallard, make effective wings for up-wing imitations. The Duck's Dun suggests a wide range of species including the blue-winged olive, medium olive, and lake olive.

EPHEMERELLA SPINNER
This imitates the spent imago or spinner of up-wings of the genus Ephemerella, such as the blue-winged olive. Its hackle suggests the insect's wings trapped in the surface of the water.

HARE'S FACE MIDGE
Charles Jardine devised this fine representation of an adult chironomid midge. It uses the sandy fur from a hare's mask to suggest the shading of the natural, plus a wing of cul de canard feather for good visibility.

HAWTHORN FLY
This is a specific imitation of the hawthorn fly Bibio marci, *a terrestrial that gathers in small swarms around bankside vegetation in middle to late spring. Imitations should mimic the size, colour, and trailing legs of the natural.*

THORAX MAYFLY
The speckled, lemon feathers from wood duck are used to mimic the wing colour and markings in this imitation of the larger mayfly species such as Ephemera danica.

CLARET HOPPER
The Hopper series has taken the stillwater fishing scene by storm. Dry-fly fishing was once seldom considered an effective technique on lakes and reservoirs, but the Hopper, with its devastating effectiveness even in calm conditions, has changed all that.

GINGER QUILL
This traditional pattern imitates the dun of small to medium-sized olives or up-wings. A strand of peacock eye feather represents segmentation, and slips of grey mallard or starling primary imitate the wing coloration of the natural. Similar patterns include Olive Quill and Red Quill.

DAVE'S HOPPER
The Dave in this instance is American fly tier Dave Whitlock, an angler who has put his name to many very effective trout and bass patterns. This wonderful imitation of a grasshopper uses knotted slips of turkey feather to imitate the large jumping legs of the natural.

BEACON BEIGE
This fly, popularized by fly tier Peter Deane, is one of the best general imitations of an olive dun. It uses a mixed hackle of grizzle and brown to give a lifelike "buzz", and the body is of stripped peacock quill.

WET FLIES

The wet fly is designed to fish below the water's surface. In order to accomplish this, many wet flies are tied slim, with wing and hackle swept back to minimize water resistance. Exceptions to this include the palmers, which are dense, bushy-hackled flies created for use on large natural waters. These are designed to make an attractive disturbance in the water's surface as they are retrieved. Other winged wet-fly patterns are tied as general attractors or as the suggestion of an adult insect.

DARK CAHILL
This is the dark member of a pair of patterns created by American fly tier Dan Cahill. With its dark grey body and lemon wood-duck wing it is a fair representation of a number of darker medium-sized species of Ephemeroptera, including members of the genus Stenonema. It may be fished upstream or in the classic down-and-across style.

INVICTA
The Invicta, created back in the late 19th century by James Ogden, is as popular today as ever. With its yellow seal-fur substitute body and palmered brown hackle, it makes a fair imitation of an emerging sedge pupa.

OLIVE BUMBLE
The doyen of Irish fly tiers, T. Kingsmill Moore, created this as part of a range of bumbles designed for the wild conditions found on large Irish waters. It is a big, bushy representation of a mayfly.

PARTRIDGE AND ORANGE
The best known of the Partridge series, and an excellent fly for rough-stream trout and grayling. In this variation, the body is of fur instead of the silk of the original version.

MALLARD AND CLARET
A traditional wet-fly pattern, and the most popular and enduring of a large series with bodies and hackles of various colours. The wing of the Mallard and Claret comes from the shoulder feathers of the drake mallard, and the body is of seal-fur substitute. Good for brown trout and sea trout.

BUTCHER
A fly with a long pedigree dating back at least 150 years, when it was known as Moon's Fly. Its name was changed to Butcher in the early 19th century. A fine pattern for both stillwater and river, and good for sea trout.

DUNKELD
Originally the Dunkeld was a fully dressed salmon fly with a married wing. This much-simplified version is an effective attractor pattern for trout, and it works well when fished on the point of a three-fly cast.

BREADCRUST
Not an imitation of a piece of bread, but a general hackled wet-fly-cum-nymph. Seal-fur substitute or wool is used to build the succulent body, which is ribbed with a stripped brown cock hackle stem. It provides a fair imitation of a caddis pupa.

SOLDIER PALMER
Although this pattern should really be known as the Red Palmer, it is the dressing most stillwater trout fishers recognize as the Soldier Palmer. A superb top-dropper pattern for fishing the drift, it works well throughout the season and particularly during early summer. An indispensable pattern.

DARK WATCHETT
This version of the Dark Watchett, by T. E. Pritt, is a traditional soft-hackled fly that has proved very effective on trout streams.

OLIVE QUILL
A wet-fly member of the popular Quill series, all of which use stripped peacock quill to give the body a striking segmented effect. This version suggests a medium-sized olive such as a lake olive or a large dark olive. Good on both lakes and rivers.

TEAL, BLUE, AND SILVER
With its barred wing and silver body, this member of the Teal series is a fine representation of a small fish. Good for stillwater and river trout, and large versions (up to a size 2 hook) are excellent for night fishing for sea trout.

MARCH BROWN
An effective imitation of the natural March brown, Rhithrogena germanica, this is a very edible-looking fly that works well even on trout that have never seen the natural. It may also be tied in a silver-bodied version.

BIBIO
This highly effective pattern is a good general representation of a number of terrestrials of the Bibionidae family, especially the heather fly, whose red legs are imitated by the brighter central section.

SOOTY OLIVE
The lake olives (Cloeon simile) that hatch from the large limestone loughs of western Ireland are of a particularly dark hue. This pattern uses a dark olive seal-fur substitute body and a brown mallard wing to mimic their coloration. A great fly for early season.

ROYAL COACHMAN
This definitive American pattern is the gaudy cousin of the Coachman. This, the wet-fly version, is a derivative of John Haily's 1878 dry fly and has spawned a whole range of variants including streamers and hairwings. Although the wings may vary, all have the same red central body section, butted either side with peacock herl. It often works when nothing else will.

GOSLING (right)
The Gosling is the epitome of the Irish stillwater fly. It is tied to represent the dun of the mayfly Ephemera danica, *which is distributed throughout Europe and hatches in impressive numbers from limestone lakes. It uses an orange cock hackle, overwound with one of speckled grey mallard flank, to suggest the wings. The colour match is hardly perfect, but it certainly does work.*

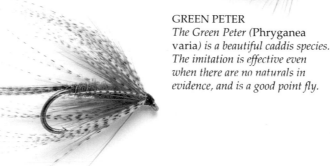

GREEN PETER
The Green Peter (Phryganea varia) is a beautiful caddis species. The imitation is effective even when there are no naturals in evidence, and is a good point fly.

OAKHAM ORANGE
During the warmer summer months, stillwater rainbows experience what can only be described as "orange madness". As the water warms they become more and more willing to chase bright flies, and little could be brighter than hot orange. This palmered fly, with its tag of fluorescent orange floss, is a very effective pattern either on a floating line or fished slightly deeper.

DOOBRY
The Scottish angler and fly tier, Stan Headley, devised the Doobry for fishing in clear water on overcast days or in coloured water in brighter conditions. It is very successful in peaty water, where its combination of black, orange, and gold not only looks very good, but also catches fish.

KATE MCLAREN
A sombre, heavily huckled pattern, this fly is named after the wife of Charles McLaren, a truly great sea-trout angler. It is a very effective pattern on large lakes, taking brown trout, sea trout, and salmon, and works well as a top-dropper fly.

NYMPHS

Although the word "nymph" refers to the larval stages of a number of aquatic insect species, to the fly fisher it has become a far more general term. Along with the true nymphs, it includes insect pupae, small crustaceans, and even general patterns used to suggest something small and edible. The diversity of flies classified as nymphs is truly astounding, ranging from tiny imitations of larval up-wings and midge pupae to the veritable giants that mimick creatures as different as dragonfly and stonefly nymphs.

SUSPENDER BUZZER
This Brian Leadbetter pattern imitates the chironomid pupa at the point of emergence. It uses a thorax of buoyant, closed-cell foam to keep the fly floating in the water's surface.

FOX-SQUIRREL NYMPH
This effective general nymph pattern was devised by Dave Whitlock and suggests a wide range of naturals such as stonefly nymphs and caddis larvae. It is constructed almost entirely from fox-squirrel fur.

GOLDEN STONE
The nymphs or creepers of the stonefly species vary widely in size and colour. This dressing mimics the medium to large, golden types, and should be heavily weighted to fish hard along the riverbed.

DISTRESSED DAMSEL
The long, mobile tail of olive marabou adds a wonderful sinuous action to this oversized imitation of a damselfly nymph. Devised by Charles Jardine, it works well on small stillwater trout, either fished blind on a slow-sinking or intermediate line, or cast to individual fish.

MARABOU NYMPH
Mobile turkey marabou works well in both tails and wings, and it may also be dubbed to produce an effect that is especially good for nymph imitations. The Marabou Nymph is one such pattern, and the buoyant back of deer hair makes it a very slow-sinking fly.

GOLD-HEAD DAMSEL
This effective pattern resembles a damselfly nymph, and has a gold bead at the head plus a tail of dyed olive arctic fox. The weighted bead and highly mobile tail impart a ducking, diving action to the fly that trout find irresistible. This olive form works particularly well when the natural damselfly nymphs are in abundance, but it will take fish throughout the season.

CASUAL DRESS
The Casual Dress, a highly effective general nymph pattern, was devised in the early Sixties by E. H. (Polly) Rosborough for fishing the Upper Big Deschutes in Oregon. It is made almost entirely from muskrat fur; even the thorax-hackle consists of spun muskrat, and the only exception is the ruff of black ostrich herl at the head. It is a very good suggestion of medium to large stonefly nymphs, and may be fished weighted.

DRAGONFLY NYMPH
Large, sluggish dragonfly nymphs form an important part of the diet of trout and bass in late summer. This pattern incorporates lead eyes to help work the pattern along the lakebed. Fish it around sunken timber and weedbeds.

GE NYMPH
This Charles Jardine pattern suggests a general range of up-wing or ephemerid nymphs, hence GE for "general ephemerid". It is tied in many sizes, from 20 to 10, mimicking the Baetidae and other nymphs of similar form.

LONGSHANK PHEASANT TAIL
A much smaller version of this fly is used on rivers and streams, but this large, heavy nymph is a useful addition to the stillwater angler's armoury. It works best when fished from midwater down, and is often weighted.

OLIVE FLASHBACK

This is part of a range of patterns that have a strip of pearl Lurex along the back to impart sparkle. The Lurex mimics the effect created by subcutaneous gases trapped within a nymph about to change into an adult.

WALKER'S MAYFLY NYMPH

Richard Walker was without doubt one of the greatest contemporary designers of trout flies, with many well-thought-out patterns to his credit. His Mayfly Nymph is one of the best; observing the natural mayfly, he noted that it was not olive, as some authorities stated, but a pale ivory.

PHEASANT TAIL NYMPH

All of the great many versions of this pattern use the glossy chestnut tail feather fibres of the cock ring-necked pheasant.

EMERGENT PUPA

This is part of a range developed by Gary LaFontaine to imitate the various stages of the caddis pupa. It uses a man-made material, Antron, to give a sparkling layer over the duller dubbed body. The Antron is added as a loose sheath so that it traps bubbles of air, giving a great impression of life. The pattern is dressed in a range of colours including brown and amber.

WOOLY WORM

The Wooly Worm is an easily dressed pattern that has the appearance of a hairy caterpillar but is used more as a general bottom-grubbing nymph. It is tied in various natural colours including olives and browns.

LARGE DARK STONE

This imitates many of the largest stonefly nymphs, particularly the darker types such as Pteronarcys californica. Since it is fished in fast water it should be tied with a heavily weighted underbody.

THE GOLDHEAD

Hans van Klinken originated this novel but highly effective bottom-grubbing pattern. It is a very good suggestion of a cased caddis fly, and uses a combination of a weighted underbody and a gold bead at the head to allow it to be bumped along the riverbed.

CASED CADDIS

This Bob Carnill dressing is a great early-season fly, imitating the cased caddis larva as it trundles along the bottom. Its weighted underbody helps it fish deep and slow.

SHRIMP

This is a specific imitation of the freshwater shrimp Gammarus pulex. The natural tends to skulk along the bottom among stones and weeds, so the imitation should be fished similarly.

JORGENSEN'S FUR THORAX PUPA

The Fur Thorax Pupa is Poul Jorgensen's superb caddis pupa imitation. The interesting part of this fly is that, by spinning in a dubbing loop, hare, rabbit, or squirrel fur is used to form a very lifelike combined thorax and hackle.

TRUE-TO-LIFE MIDGE PUPA

This is a highly lifelike imitation of the pupal stage of the non-biting midge, or chironomid. It includes the most important features of the natural, including the bulbous thorax, slim body, and breathing filaments.

FOUR WATER FAVOURITE

This variation of the Hare's Ear nymph is a specific stillwater pattern developed by Gordon Fraser, and uses a small tuft of rabbit fur in the tail to provide extra movement. It should be tied weighted, using either a weighted underbody or a gold bead.

BIRD'S STONEFLY NYMPH

This very good suggestion of the larger species of stonefly nymph was created by Calvert T. Bird. It is not as obviously lifelike as some imitations, but Bird's philosophy of producing a fly that is suggestive of something for the trout to eat, rather than an exact imitation of a natural, has produced a classic pattern.

SALMON & STEELHEAD FLIES

With a few exceptions, migratory salmonids cease feeding as they return to freshwater to spawn, but salmon and steelhead can be tempted or provoked into taking a general attractor pattern or an impression of something that they were feeding upon in the open ocean. Shrimp or prawn patterns are very effective, but curiously few dressings are produced to imitate sandeels or other baitfish. Often, however, a salmon will succumb to something as nondescript as a tiny black hairwing, having totally ignored a whole procession of larger, more colourful patterns.

SILVER RAT
The Rat series of patterns has proved extremely effective for Atlantic salmon throughout their range. The silver version uses grey fox guard hairs for the wing and has a soft grizzle hackle. It is a truly universal fly and a great favourite on Canadian rivers such as the Restigouche and Matapedia.

SILVER DOCTOR *(right)*
The Silver Doctor is one of the fully dressed patterns much loved by salmon anglers of the 19th and early 20th centuries. The dressings of these patterns are extremely complicated, and the original dressings included strips of dyed swan feather, married together, plus exotic plumage such as Indian crow, blue chatterer, and toucan, many of which materials are no longer available.

EGG-SUCKING LEECH
This large, dark pattern suggests the big leeches that feed on the eggs of Pacific salmon. The weighted head and the pulsating body and tail of dyed black rabbit fur give this pattern a superb action, and salmon, steelhead, and rainbows find it very attractive, attacking it with gusto.

BLACK BRAHAN
This fly is ideal for salmon in early summer, when the water is at a reasonable level. A good fly at both dawn and dusk, its only sparkle comes from the red (or sometimes green) Lurex body.

ALLY'S SHRIMP
Alistair Gowans created this pattern to simulate the translucent, shrimplike crustaceans he had observed in a trawler catch. The pattern has proved successful for salmon on large rivers.

TEENY NYMPH
Jim Teeny rates among the very best of salmon and steelhead anglers, and any pattern of his design is worth a second look. The Teeny Nymph is not really a nymph at all, but it is a very effective pattern. It uses natural or dyed pheasant tail for the body.

GENERAL PRACTITIONER
This was developed in the early Fifties by Esmond Drury as an imitation of a prawn, for use where the natural is banned. It consists of golden-pheasant body feathers and orange fur, and has proved effective on a wide range of waters in Britain, Canada, and Iceland.

SPARKLE SHRIMP
A direct imitation of a shrimp, the Sparkle Shrimp uses a strip of pearl Lurex tied as a shell back to add extra fish attraction. It has proved a good fly for Pacific salmon.

118

CHARTREUSE STREAMER
Steelhead and Pacific salmon find chartreuse a very attractive colour, and this pattern works well in coloured water even when fished near the bottom. Its mobile tail and weighted bead chain eyes give a superb action.

PURPLE ZONKER

The strip of rabbit fur used for the wing gives the Purple Zonker great movement, which is attractive to steelhead and salmon. However, although purple is a good colour to use during dull conditions or when light levels are low, it can either prove very effective or actually spook the fish.

COMET
During the early season, when the water is cold, tube flies offer the fly fisher a lure large enough to tempt what can be very dour fish. The Comet is a dark fly that has a wing of black bucktail, and may be tied up to 8 cm (3 in) long on plastic or brass tubes, depending on how deep it is to be fished.

GREEN HIGHLANDER

This is the hairwing version of the famous fully dressed Green Highlander pattern, and mixes various colours of bucktail to form the wing, rather than feathers as in the original. This method is used to update many traditional patterns.

WILLIE GUNN (right)

The Willie Gunn is named after the Sutherland Estate's head keeper on the River Brora in Scotland, and its wing is a mixture of yellow, red, and black bucktail. This tube-fly version may be tied on plastic or metal tubing, and works well in high or cold water.

TWO-EGG SPERM FLY (below)
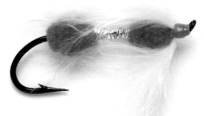
Egg flies are effective patterns for steelhead and salmon, and this fly develops the idea by imitating two salmon eggs in tandem. Fluorescent orange chenille mimics the roe being shed, and a white turkey marabou wing imitates the flow of sperm over them.

SPRUCE

The Spruce was originally designed for sea-run cutthroat trout and rainbows, but it has also proved to be very successful for steelhead. It has become one of the most popular West Coast streamer patterns.

UMPQUA SPECIAL
This classic pattern was developed by Don Hunter in the Thirties to tempt the steelhead of Oregon's Umpqua River. It is a bright fly, ideal for coloured water where the red-and-white combination of the hair wing is particularly deadly for steelhead. It is tied in a range of sizes, most commonly on up-eyed salmon hooks sizes 2 to 8.

EGG FLY

This is one of the simplest of all flies, being formed from a clipped ball of Glo-Bug yarn. It is extremely effective for steelhead, Pacific salmon, and rainbow trout, and it should be weighted and fished dead-drift to imitate the movement of real eggs.

STREAMERS & HAIRWINGS

Streamers and hairwings differ in one obvious way: the wing of the streamer is made of feather, while that of the hairwing is made of hair. Most streamers and hairwings are large and usually dressed on long-shank hooks, and tend to be attractors or suggestive of something alive and edible for a predatory fish. The major exceptions are the imitations of coarse fish or baitfish, which include representations of species such as miller's thumbs, sculpins, or more active shoaling fish such as perch or roach.

ORANGE BOOBY
This is the lure version of Gordon Fraser's original Booby nymph. All Boobies have buoyant eyes of closed-cell foam, and this buoyancy plus a turkey marabou tail gives a tremendous action. Fish it on a fast-sinking line and an ultra-short leader.

GOLDIE
Black, gold, and yellow is an effective colour combination where brown trout are concerned, and Bob Church used it when he devised this pattern to tempt big stillwater browns. It may be tied on a single hook or as a tandem, and is a good fly for sea trout as well as browns.

BLACK GHOST
This is a typical streamer, using pairs of white cock hackle back-to-back for the wing. A good general pattern for trout and steelhead on both rivers and stillwaters, and an effective fry imitation.

DAHLBERG DIVER
This Muddler variation, created by Larry Dahlberg of Minnesota, is designed to dive by means of an angled vane trimmed from the collar of the head. It has terrific action, popping along the surface as well as diving at each pull of the retrieve. A great pattern for big trout and bass.

JAFFA
This orange mini-lure, tied with dyed turkey marabou, is very effective for stillwater rainbows in high summer, and is tied to fall within the size limit for international-rules fly-fishing competitions.

THUNDER CREEK MINNOW
This was designed by Keith Fulsher as a specific imitation of a range of small baitfish species. It offers a slim profile using brown and white bucktail, tied forward and then drawn back and secured along the hook, to provide it with the all-important countershading.

FLOATING FRY
When small baitfish are dying off, trout often take them rather than chase a more elusive meal, and an imitation designed to float can prove extremely effective. Deer hair is the perfect material for this type of buoyant pattern.

MUDDLER MINNOW
This is the original Don Gapen dressing, tied with a wing and tail of oak turkey and a head of deer body hair to imitate a small sculpin. From this pattern has developed the vast range of Muddlers we have today.

RABBIT
This effective Australian pattern uses a small strip of rabbit fur to produce a highly mobile wing. The body colour may be varied to give a wide range of patterns of an impressionistic nature.

WOOLLY BUGGER
Tied in a variety of sizes and colours, this big streamer is used as a general bottom-grubbing pattern, as an imitation of a leech, and as a general representation of large nymphs such as those of stoneflies and dragonflies.

TIN HEAD

Flies with weighted heads and long, mobile tails are much in vogue on the British stillwater scene. The Tin Heads come in a variety of tail, body, and head colour combinations. These include olive with a silver head, and black with a grizzle hackle and either a red or a fluorescent green head.

ZONKER
Rabbit fur on the skin provides a robust wing for a large range of Zonker variations, not least those that imitate small baitfish. This example has a weighted keel that keeps the hook inverted, allowing the fly to be fished around sunken timber and weedbeds without snagging.

MINKIE

This pattern is similar to the Zonker, but uses mink fur rather than the more mundane rabbit. It is tied weighted or plain and with or without a Muddler head, and is excellent as a fry imitation fished in slow draws or with a figure-of-eight retrieve.

WHITE TANDEM
Trout will at times concentrate on quite large fish fry, sometimes as large as 15 cm (6 in), to the exclusion of all other food forms. It is then important to use a pattern similar in size to the prey fish, and by joining two long-shank hooks together in tandem, a large, lightweight, and easily cast streamer is created.

PINK NASTY
Pink is a curious colour, sometimes proving almost totally ineffective, but often triggering a response in the fish that no other colour will. Gordon Fraser is responsible for this garish pattern, which combines striking fluorescent pink with a mobile tail.

BADGER MATUKA
The idea of binding the hackle wing of a streamer along the top of the hook shank originated in New Zealand. It is a technique that makes for a very robust wing resembling an elongated dorsal fin.

SOFT HACKLE STREAMER
American fly tier Jack Gartside came up with the idea of using a marabou feather as a hackle rather than as a bunched wing or tail. This simple but very effective turkey marabou tying works as a general attractor or fry imitation.

VIVA
Black and green is a very effective colour combination for a stillwater trout fly, especially when fished slowly in the early season. This Viva is a compact hairwing version of the Victor Furse original.

121

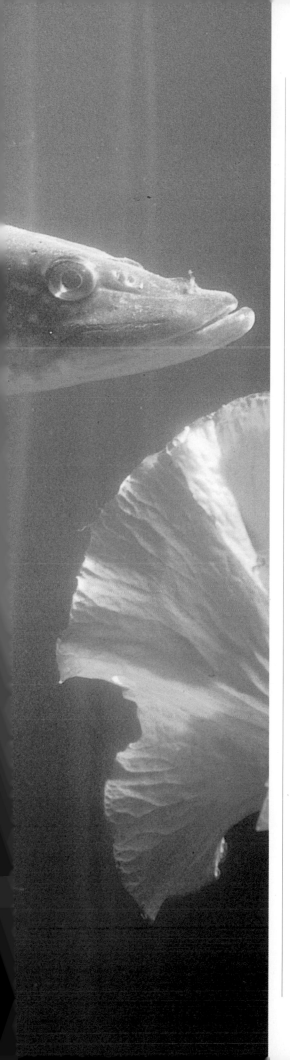

SPECIES

A SPECIES OF FISH (or any other organism) is a genetically distinct group, consisting of related individuals that resemble each other in appearance and behaviour, and can breed among themselves but not – with some exceptions – with other species. Closely related species are grouped together into genera (or genuses), and related genera are grouped into families.

Because the common names of fish can vary greatly from one region or country to another, biologists refer to them by their scientific names to avoid confusion. The scientific name of a species consists of two words, usually derived from Latin; the first of these defines the genus, and the second identifies the species. The brown trout, *Salmo trutta*, is thus the species *trutta* of the genus *Salmo*. It is also described as a salmonid, because it belongs to the Salmonidae family, which includes the salmon, trout, and char.

There are about 22,000 known species of fish, of which relatively few are of interest to anglers. This chapter gives brief descriptions of major sporting species, together with notes on the sort of techniques, tackle, and bait that may be used to catch them. They are grouped, as far as is practicable, into freshwater and saltwater species, and arranged within these groups alphabetically by family name.

THE ANGLER'S QUARRY
The fish pursued by anglers range from small species that feed mainly on insects to voracious predators such as pike and shark.

ANATOMY

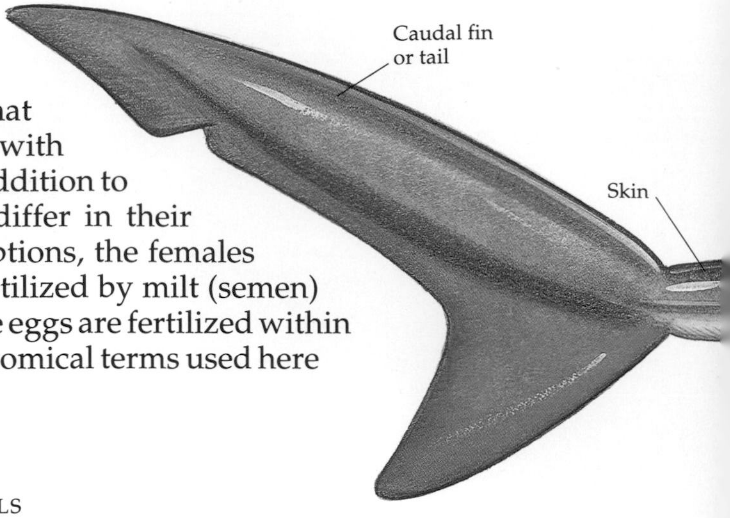

Fish can be divided broadly into two groups: those that have skeletons made of bone (the bony fish) and those with skeletons made of cartilage (the cartilaginous fish). In addition to having different skeletal materials, the two groups differ in their means of reproduction. In bony fish, with a few exceptions, the females discharge their eggs into the water, where they are fertilized by milt (semen) from the males. In cartilaginous fish, as in mammals, the eggs are fertilized within the bodies of the females. (Brief explanations of the anatomical terms used here are given in the glossary on pages 280–281.)

Caudal fin or tail

Skin

BONY FISH (OSTEICHTHYES)

A typical bony fish has two sets of paired fins (pectoral and pelvic) and a set of vertical fins (dorsal, anal, and tail). The four gill openings on each side of the head are covered by flattened bones, of which the operculum is the largest, and most species possess a gas-filled swim bladder. By altering the amount of gas (usually oxygen) in this bladder, a bony fish can adjust its buoyancy and maintain its chosen depth in the water without constantly swimming. Cartilaginous fish (*see opposite*) lack swim bladders and must keep swimming or sink to the bottom.

GILLS
A fish "breathes" by drawing water into its mouth, then forcing it through its gill chambers and out via the gill slits. Inside the gill chambers, delicate filaments absorb oxygen from the water and pass it into the blood, and remove carbon dioxide from the blood and then discharge it into the water.

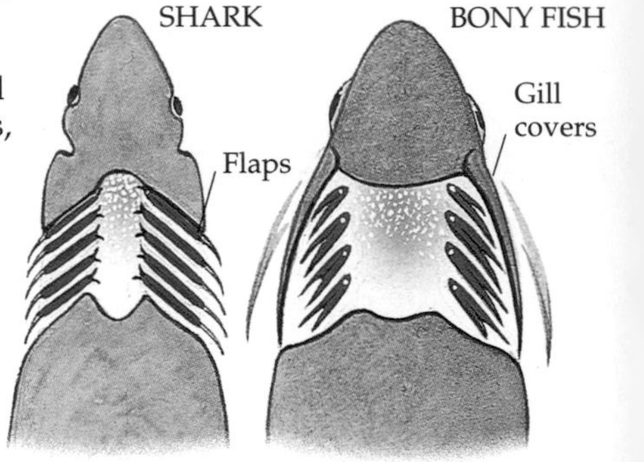

SHARK

BONY FISH

Flaps

Gill covers

ANATOMY OF A BONY FISH

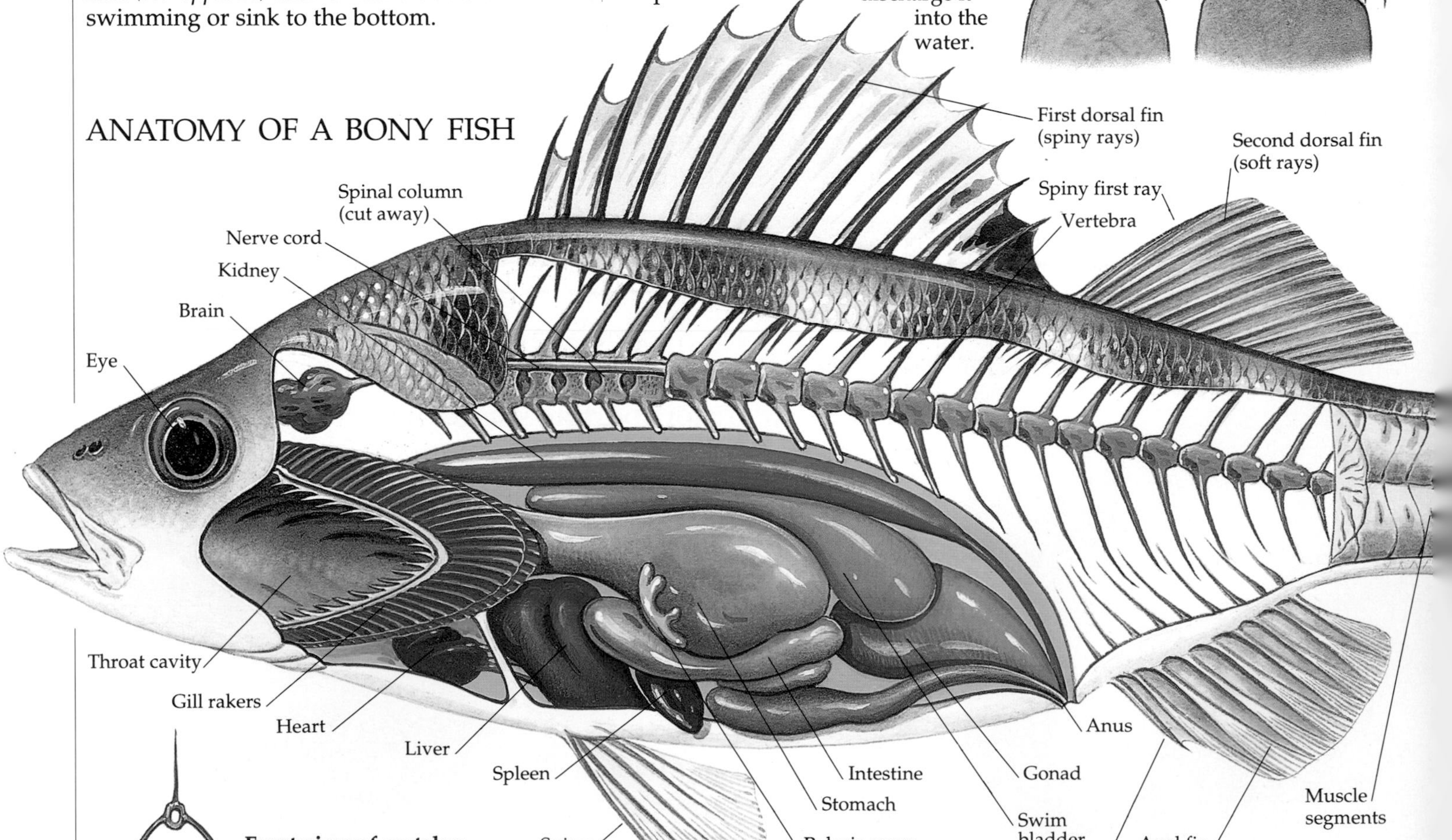

First dorsal fin (spiny rays)

Second dorsal fin (soft rays)

Spinal column (cut away)

Spiny first ray

Nerve cord

Vertebra

Kidney

Brain

Eye

Throat cavity

Gill rakers

Heart

Liver

Spleen

Spiny first ray

Pelvic fin

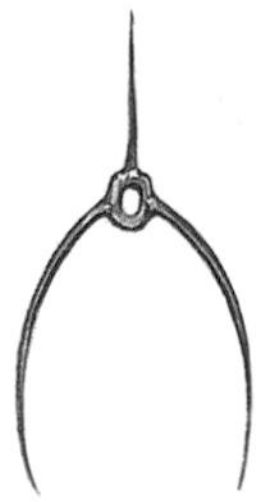

Intestine

Stomach

Pyloric caeca

Anus

Gonad

Swim bladder

Anal fin (soft rays)

Spiny first ray

Muscle segments

Front view of vertebra
Each segment, or vertebra, of the flexible backbone is hollow, with a plug of gristle at its centre.

ANATOMY OF A CARTILAGINOUS FISH

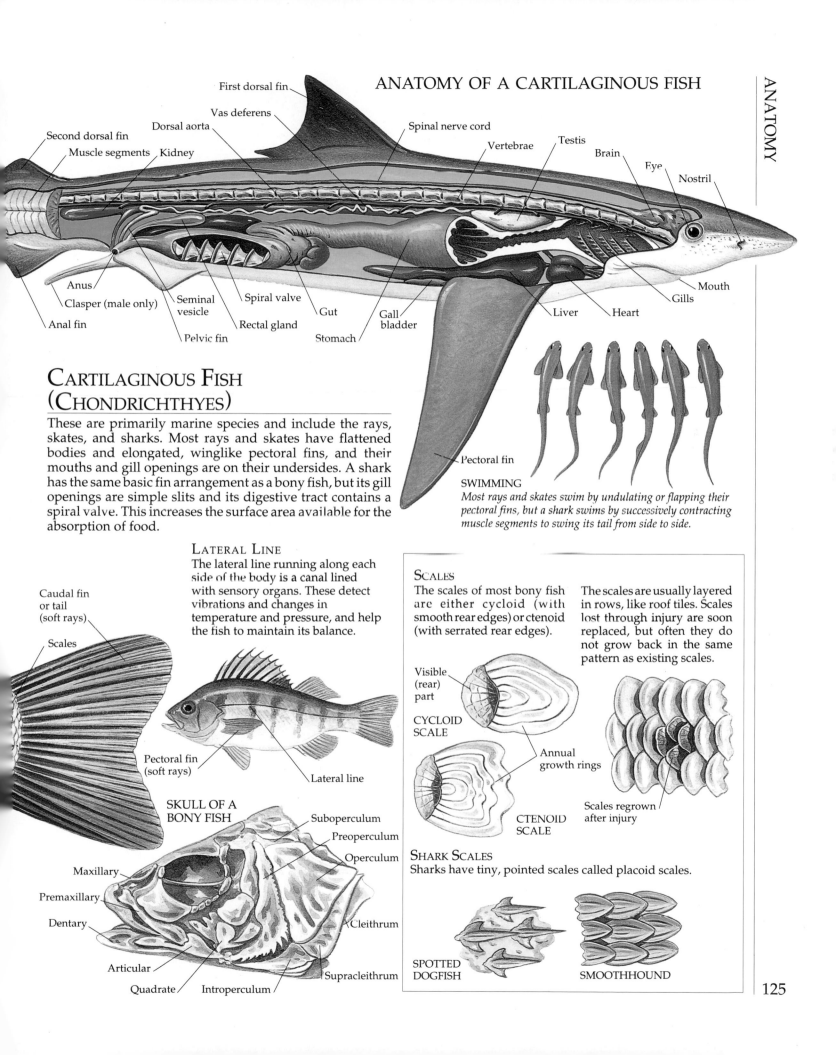

First dorsal fin

Vas deferens

Dorsal aorta

Spinal nerve cord

Second dorsal fin

Vertebrae

Testis

Muscle segments · Kidney

Brain

Eye

Nostril

Anus

Clasper (male only)

Seminal vesicle

Spiral valve

Mouth

Gills

Anal fin

Rectal gland

Gut

Liver · Heart

Pelvic fin

Stomach

Gall bladder

Pectoral fin

SWIMMING

CARTILAGINOUS FISH (CHONDRICHTHYES)

These are primarily marine species and include the rays, skates, and sharks. Most rays and skates have flattened bodies and elongated, winglike pectoral fins, and their mouths and gill openings are on their undersides. A shark has the same basic fin arrangement as a bony fish, but its gill openings are simple slits and its digestive tract contains a spiral valve. This increases the surface area available for the absorption of food.

Most rays and skates swim by undulating or flapping their pectoral fins, but a shark swims by successively contracting muscle segments to swing its tail from side to side.

LATERAL LINE

The lateral line running along each side of the body is a canal lined with sensory organs. These detect vibrations and changes in temperature and pressure, and help the fish to maintain its balance.

Caudal fin or tail (soft rays)

Scales

Pectoral fin (soft rays)

Lateral line

SKULL OF A BONY FISH

Maxillary

Premaxillary

Dentary

Articular

Quadrate · Introperculum

Suboperculum

Preoperculum

Operculum

Cleithrum

Supracleithrum

SCALES

The scales of most bony fish are either cycloid (with smooth rear edges) or ctenoid (with serrated rear edges).

The scales are usually layered in rows, like roof tiles. Scales lost through injury are soon replaced, but often they do not grow back in the same pattern as existing scales.

Visible (rear) part

CYCLOID SCALE

Annual growth rings

CTENOID SCALE

Scales regrown after injury

SHARK SCALES

Sharks have tiny, pointed scales called placoid scales.

SPOTTED DOGFISH

SMOOTHHOUND

125

Freshwater SPECIES

BLACK BASS

The species collectively known as black bass include two of the most important sporting species in North America: the smallmouth bass and the largemouth bass. Black bass are the largest members of the Centrarchidae family, which also includes the bluegill, the crappies, and the sunfish (*see page 128*).

SPOTTED BASS
This bass gets its name from the rows of small, dark spots on its pale flanks and belly. It is found mainly in the Ohio and Mississippi river systems and has two localized subspecies, the Alabama spotted bass and the Wichita spotted bass, *Micropterus punctulatus henshalli* and *M. p. wichitae*. It grows to about 2.27 kg (5 lb).

GUADALUPE BASS
The Guadalupe bass is similar to the spotted bass, but has distinctive dark bars along each side and is smaller, seldom reaching 454 g (1 lb). Its range is restricted to the Guadalupe, Colorado, Brazos, San Antonio, and Nueces river systems of central Texas.

SUWANNEE BASS
This small bass, which rarely exceeds 340 g (12 oz), is found in the Suwannee and Ochlockonee river drainages of Florida and Georgia. Its overall coloration is brownish, with dark markings along the back and sides; the adult male has blue cheeks, breast, and belly.

SUWANNEE BASS
Micropterus notius

Male has blue cheeks, breast, and belly

GUADALUPE BASS
Micropterus treculi

LARGEMOUTH BASS
The largemouth bass is so named because its upper jaw extends to behind its eye; that of the smallmouth bass does not extend beyond the eye. The northern largemouth seldom exceeds 4.54 kg (10 lb), but the southern subspecies, the Florida largemouth (*M. s. floridanus*), can reach more than 9.1 kg (20 lb).

SPOTTED BASS
Micropterus punctulatus

REDEYE BASS
The red eyes and white-tipped orange caudal (tail) fin of the redeye bass make it easy to distinguish from other bass; young redeyes also have brick-red dorsal and anal fins. The redeye is one of the smaller bass species, and although it can exceed 3.6 kg (8 lb) it usually does not grow to more than about 454 g (1 lb).

REDEYE BASS
Micropterus coosae

White tip to caudal fin

FISHING NOTES

Techniques
Spinning or baitcasting with artificial lures, fly fishing, and trolling with livebaits will all prove successful.

Tackle
For lure fishing, try a 1.7 m to 2.1 m (5½ to 7 ft) spinning or baitcasting rod and a fixed-spool or multiplier reel with 2.7 to 4.54 kg (6 to 10 lb) mono line. A good rod to use for fly fishing is a 2.1 to 2.7 m (7 to 9 ft) bass fly rod with a fast taper, fitted with a single-action fly reel carrying a floating #7 to #9 line with a 2.7 to 3.6 kg (6 to 8 lb) leader. For trolling, use a 2.7 or 3 m (9 or 10 ft) stiff-action rod with a 1.1 kg (2½ lb) test curve, and a multiplier reel with 4.5 to 9.1 kg (10 to 20 lb) mono line, a nylon or Dacron trace, and hook sizes 2/0 to 5/0.

Bait
Black bass, being active predators that feed on a wide variety of creatures, can be tempted to strike at practically any kind of bait, either artificial or natural. Artificials such as spinners, spoons, crankbaits, surface plugs, and plastic worms are particularly effective. For fly fishing, bass bugs, streamers, and bucktails have all proved their worth; for trolling, try worms, crayfish, leeches, and minnows.

SMALLMOUTH BASS

The hard-fighting smallmouth is the most highly regarded black bass. It is slightly larger than the northern largemouth, reaching a maximum of about 5.4 kg (12 lb), and it prefers clear lakes and streams with rocky or gravel bottoms. The largemouth favours weedy, mud-bottomed waters.

SMALLMOUTH BASS
Micropterus dolomieui

DISTRIBUTION

Smallmouth: from North Dakota to Quebec, Oklahoma, and Alabama; also widely introduced elsewhere.
Largemouth: from Minnesota to Quebec and south to the Gulf; widely introduced elsewhere.
Spotted: Mississippi basin from southern Ohio to the Gulf; introduced elsewhere.
Guadalupe: central Texas.
Suwanee: Florida and Georgia.
Redeye: Alabama, Georgia, South Carolina; introduced elsewhere.

LARGEMOUTH BASS
Micropterus salmoides

Feeding

All the black bass are active predators. When young, they feed at first on tiny crustaceans, insects and their larvae, worms, and tadpoles, but they soon progress to larger prey such as fish, crayfish, and frogs. The largest bass will even take small waterfowl.

LARGEMOUTH BASS

SMALLMOUTH BASS

Dorsal fins

In addition to the different lengths of their upper jaws, largemouth and smallmouth bass have different dorsal fin structures. The spiny first dorsal fin of the largemouth bass is highest at its midpoint and is almost separated from the soft-rayed second dorsal. The smallmouth bass has a somewhat flatter first dorsal fin, which is connected to the second dorsal, and the second dorsal has a patch of scales at its base.

Size comparison

Largemouth bass   Smallmouth bass   Spotted bass   Redeye bass   Guadalupe bass   Suwanee bass

127

BLUEGILL, CRAPPIES, PUMPKINSEED, & SUNFISH

These small relatives of the black bass are among the most popular American panfish, which are fish that are too small to be considered true gamefish but still provide considerable angling (and eating) pleasure. The range of each of these species has been considerably extended by widespread stocking programmes.

Sharply arched back and dip above eye

PUMPKINSEED
This attractive little fish lives among the weeds in lakes, ponds, and quiet river pools. Its maximum weight is about 482 g (1 lb 1 oz), but most individuals are much smaller.

BLUEGILL
This the most widely distributed panfish, and probably the most fished-for species in North America. It prefers quiet, weedy waters and averages about 113g (4 oz), although it can grow to over 1.8 kg (4 lb).

Dark spot on dorsal fin

BLUEGILL
Lepomis macrochirus

PUMPKINSEED
Lepomis gibbosus

REDBREAST SUNFISH
The redbreast sunfish, which reaches a maximum weight of about 454 g (1 lb), is most abundant in the creeks and small to medium-sized rivers of the Atlantic Slope. It is also sometimes found in ponds and lake margins.

Gill covers
Sunfish of the genus Lepomis *can be identified by examining the shape and markings of their gill covers.*

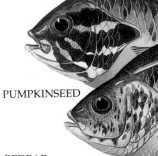

REDBREAST SUNFISH

PUMPKINSEED

REDEAR SUNFISH

REDBREAST SUNFISH
Lepomis auritus

GREEN SUNFISH
The green sunfish has a more elongated body than most other sunfish, and the upper jaw of its large mouth extends back to below the midpoint of the eye. Like the redbreast sunfish, it is primarily a stream fish but is also found in stillwaters. It can attain a weight of over 910 g (2 lb).

GREEN SUNFISH
Lepomis cyanellus

REDEAR SUNFISH
Lepomis microlophus

REDEAR SUNFISH
The plump redear sunfish is also called the "shellcracker", because its diet includes snails and clams, which it crushes up with powerful grinding teeth. It can grow to over 2.15 kg (4 lb 12 oz).

128

WHITE CRAPPIE
Pomoxis annularis

WHITE CRAPPIE

The white crappie is generally a little larger than the closely related black crappie, and its overall coloration is usually paler. The most reliable way to distinguish between the two is to count the spines in the first dorsal fin: the white crappie has six, while the black crappie has seven or eight. The white crappie usually reaches 454 to 680 g (1 lb to 1 lb 8 oz), but it can grow to over 2.27 kg (5 lb).

DISTRIBUTION

Pumpkinseed: the Dakotas and Iowa to the Atlantic drainages.
Bluegill: from the Great Lakes to the Gulf and New Mexico; widely introduced elsewhere.
Redbreast sunfish: the Atlantic drainages.
Green sunfish: From the Great Lakes to Texas.
Redear sunfish: Indiana to the Gulf; introduced elsewhere.
Crappies: eastern North America from southern Canada to the Gulf; widely introduced.
Rock bass: From Manitoba to New England and northern Alabama.

BLACK CRAPPIE
Pomoxis nigromaculatus

BLACK CRAPPIE

The black crappie is often found together with the white, and both species are widely distributed in ponds, lakes, and rivers, although the black tends to prefer larger, clearer waters than those tolerated by the white. Its average weight is in the 340 to 680 g (12 oz to 1 lb 8 oz) range, with a maximum of up to 2.27 kg (5 lb).

ROCK BASS
Ambloplites rupestris

FISHING NOTES

Techniques
Float fishing, fly fishing, and baitcasting, all with light tackle.

Tackle
For float fishing, a 3 to 4.3 m (10 to 14 ft) pole, 2.7 to 6.8 kg (6 to 15 lb) mono line, and a small jig or livebait fished below a small float; or a 1.8 to 2.1 m (6 to 7 ft) ultralight spinning rod with a fixed-spool reel, 1.36 kg (3 lb) mono line, and a small float. Use hook sizes 10 to 14, and weight the rig with split shot about 30 cm (12 in) from the hook. For fly fishing, use a fly rod up to 113 g (4 oz) in weight, with matching reel and line. When baitcasting, use a 1.4 to 1.8 m (4½ to 6 ft) rod, a baitcasting reel, and 910 g to 1.8 kg (2 to 4 lb) line.

Bait
Small minnows, worms, maggots, and jigs for float fishing; tiny wet flies, nymphs, and dry flies for fly fishing; miniature spinners and crankbaits for baitcasting.

ROCK BASS

The mottled, dark olive rock bass has distinctive red eyes and a large mouth, and there is usually a white or gold margin to the dark spot on its gill cover. It is most common in clear, rocky streams and is also found in lake margins where the bottom is rocky and there is ample vegetation. Its maximum weight is about 1.36 kg (3 lb), but it typically weighs around 227 g (8 oz).

Size comparison

White crappie

Black crappie

Rock bass

Bluegill

Pumpkinseed

Green sunfish

Redear sunfish

Redbreast sunfish

BARBEL, TENCH, & ASP

The tench is a very popular angling species in its native Eurasian waters and has been introduced into North America and Australia. It is mainly a stillwater species, although it also inhabits the lower reaches of rivers. The asp is found in large lakes and, like barbel, in the middle reaches of clean rivers where the current is relatively fast and the water well oxygenated. Asp and barbel are often found together in those areas of Europe where their ranges overlap, asp in midwater and barbel on the bottom.

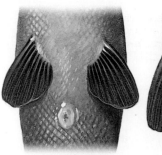

FEMALE   MALE

Male and female tench
The sex of a tench can be determined from its pelvic fins. Those of the male are much longer and broader than those of the female, and they extend to beyond the anal vent.

TENCH

The tiny scales of the tench are covered with a layer of protective slime and set flat against its thick-set body, making it appear almost scaleless. The fins are smoothly rounded, and the wrist of the barely forked tail is distinctively thick. Large individuals of up to 8.5 kg (18 lb 12 oz) have been reported, but the tench is slow-growing, and the usual maximum is about 1.8 kg (4 lb).

TENCH
Tinca tinca

GOLDEN TENCH
Tinca tinca

Golden Tench
The rare golden variety of tench is stocked as an ornamental fish in private ponds and park lakes. It has an orange or yellow body with scattered black markings, and its pink-tinged fins are less rounded than those of the common tench.

Spawning male asp
At spawning time the male asp develops numerous tough, wartlike lumps (tubercles) on its head, which help it to fend off rivals. Asp spawn in spring over gravel beds.

ASP

The slender, streamlined body of the predatory asp gives it the speed and agility it needs to capture its food, which is primarily small midwater and near-surface fish. A popular angling species that fights strongly when hooked, it favours deep water and is often found in weir pools. Asp average about 3.5 kg (7 lb 11 oz), but can reach a maximum of around 12 kg (26 lb 7 oz).

Natural food
Tench and barbel have a varied diet that includes plants, insects, molluscs, and crustaceans. When young, the asp eats insects and small crustaceans, but as an adult it preys on small fish such as bleak.

ASP
Aspius aspius

Size comparison

Asp   Barbel   Tench   Southern barbel

SOUTHERN BARBEL

The southern or Mediterranean barbel inhabits fast-flowing upland rivers and streams in southern Europe. It is much smaller than the common barbel, averaging only about 250 g (9 oz).

SOUTHERN BARBEL
Barbus meridionalis

DISTRIBUTION

Tench: throughout Europe with the exception of northern Scandinavia; introduced into North America and Australia.
Barbel: from southern England and Wales to southern Europe.
Southern barbel: northern Spain, southern France, and northern Italy; Danube basin.
Asp: from eastern Holland east through northern and central Europe to the Caspian Sea.

BARBEL

In the fast-flowing water that it prefers, the barbel's streamlined, flat-bellied body helps it to stay close to the river bed, where it feeds. When hooked, it will use its considerable strength and stamina to the full and fight hard until it is exhausted, and its power is comparable with that of a salmon of similar weight. It usually grows to about 2.27 kg (5 lb), but it can reach a maximum of around 7.3 kg (16 lb).

BARBEL
Barbus barbus

Mouth and barbels
The barbel's downturned mouth and fleshy lips are beautifully adapted for bottom feeding. The four barbels (or barbules) that give the fish its name carry a large number of taste and touch cells, and act like external tongues with which the fish can examine potential food items.

Young barbel
Up to a weight of around 227 to 340 g (8 to 12 oz) and a length of 15 to 20 cm (6 to 8 in), young barbel often have speckled flanks, and their overall coloration tends to be more olive-green than that of their parents.

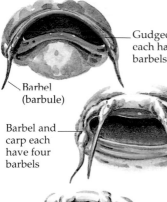

Gudgeon and tench each have two barbels

Barbel (barbule)

Barbel and carp each have four barbels

A stone loach has six barbels

Identification
Count the barbels to distinguish young barbel and carp from similar fish.

FISHING NOTES

Techniques
Float fishing, legering, and freelining for tench; lure fishing and deadbaiting for asp; for barbel, float fishing and legering, especially legering with a swimfeeder.

Tackle
When float fishing for tench, use a 3.7 m (12 ft) medium-action rod, with a fixed-spool reel, 4.54 kg (10 lb) line, and hook sizes 6 or 8. To leger for tench, try a 3.7 m (12 ft) Avon rod with a fixed spool reel, 3.2 kg (7 lb) line, size 6 to 12 hook, and a swimfeeder. For asp, try a 2.7 m (9 ft) medium-action spinning rod with a fixed-spool reel, 6.8 kg (15 lb) line, and a small spoon. To leger for barbel, use a 3.7 m (12 ft) rod with quivertip, a fixed-spool reel, 3.6 kg (8 lb) line, hook sizes 8 to 12, and a swimfeeder.

Bait
Good tench baits include bread, maggots, corn, worms, meat, and small boilies. Asp can be taken on spoons, especially if a small piece of red wool is tied to the hook to provide extra attraction, and on small fish baits such as bleak. For barbel, try maggots, meat, tares, hempseed, corn, worms, bread, and cheese.

BREAM, NASE, & VIMBA

Freshwater SPECIES

These European members of the carp family are all primarily bottom-feeders. Bream are widely distributed in stillwaters, canals, and deep, slow-flowing rivers, the nase prefers the faster-flowing waters of the middle reaches of rivers, and the vimba is found in the middle and lower reaches of large, slow rivers. The most widespread of these species, and the most popular with anglers, is the bronze bream.

YOUNG BREAM

Young bream
When young, bronze bream are silvery with black fins. In Britain, these little fish are known as tinplate bream or skimmers.

NASE
Chondrostoma nasus

NASE
The silvery, slender-bodied nase has red-tinged fins and a smallish head with a noticeably protuberant snout. It feeds on algae and diatoms, which it scrapes from rocks and stones with its hard, horny lower lip, and can reach a maximum weight of about 1.8 kg (4 lb). The toxostome, or soiffe (*Chondrostoma toxostoma*), is similar to the nase, but smaller.

Roach/bream hybrids
Where spawning schools of bream and roach (see page 137) occur in the same waters, roach/bream hybrids are common. To identify a hybrid, count the number of rays in the anal fin: a roach has 9 to 12, a bream has 23 to 29, and a hybrid 14 to 19.

VIMBA *Vimba vimba*

ROACH/BREAM HYBRID

Bream anal fin

VIMBA
For most of the year, the vimba (known in Germany as the Zährte) has silvery sides and a blue-grey back, but at spawning time (in early summer) the male becomes very dark on the back with an orange-red belly. The vimba's staple diet consists of worms, molluscs, and crustaceans, and its weight ranges from around 910 g (2 lb) to 3 kg (6 lb 10 oz).

Feeding bream
When feeding, a bream upends itself and its mouth protrudes down to suck in worms, molluscs, crustaceans, and insect larvae. A school of feeding bream will betray its presence by stirring up clouds of silt from the bottom.

SILVER BREAM
Blicca bjoerkna

Size comparison

Bronze bream   Vimba   Nase   Silver bream   Danubian bream

BRONZE BREAM
Abramis brama

BRONZE BREAM

The bronze, or common, bream, a very popular angling species, has a scaleless head and a deep, flat-sided body with small scales and a generous covering of slime. The body is predominantly golden brown, and the pectoral and pelvic fins are tinged with red. Typical adult weights range from about 1.8 kg (4 lb) to 3.2 kg (7 lb), with a rare maximum of 9 kg (19 lb 13 oz).

DISTRIBUTION

Bronze bream: from Ireland east through most of northern, central, and southern Europe to the Urals and into parts of central Asia.
Silver bream: from eastern England to the Caspian, except northern Scandinavia, Spain, Portugal, and Italy.
Danubian bream: Danube and Volga basins.
Nase: from France to western Russia and the Caspian.
Vimba: from the Baltic Sea through northern, central, and eastern Europe.

IRISH BREAM

Many bronze bream from Ireland's Shannon system, where bream tend to reach a good size, have unusual striped sides and reach weights of more than 4.54 kg (10 lb).

IRISH BREAM
Abramis brama

DANUBIAN BREAM
Abramis sapa

Blunt snout

Long anal fin

DANUBIAN BREAM

The Danubian, or whiteye, bream is a small, silvery fish, weighing only some 800 g (1 lb 12 oz), with a blunt snout and long anal fin. It is found in the Danube basin and rivers feeding the Black, Caspian, and Aral Seas.

FISHING NOTES

Techniques

The nase and vimba are bottom feeders, so use a float rig that works the bait just above the bottom. For bream, whether you are float fishing or legering, heavy and frequent ground-baiting is recommended because they will not stay long in a swim where there is no readily available food: use large lumps of bread containing hempseed, maggots, casters, or worms.

Tackle

When fishing for nase and vimba, try a 3.7 to 4m (12 to 13 ft) float rod with a light tip action, a fixed-spool reel, 910 g (2 lb) line, and hook sizes 16 to 20. For bream float fishing, use a 4 to 4.3 m (13 to 14 ft) light-action float rod with a fixed-spool reel, 3.2 to 4.1 kg (7 to 9 lb) line, and hook sizes 10 to 14. To leger for bream, try a 3.4 to 3.7 m (11 to 12 ft) rod with a built-in quivertip, and a fixed-spool reel, 1.8 to 2.7 kg (4 to 6 lb) line, and hook sizes 6 to 12.

Bait

Try small pieces of bread flake for nase, and boiled barley, maggots, small pieces of worm, and bread flake for vimba. For bream, bread flake, maggots, casters, worms, and corn are all effective float-fishing baits, and maggots or small worms enclosed in bread paste are good for legering.

SILVER BREAM

The small size, more slender body, and brilliant silvery flanks of the silver or white bream help to distinguish it from the bronze bream. Its habitat and feeding habits are the same as those of the bronze, but it is much smaller, its usual maximum weight being only 454 g (1 lb).

133

CYPRINIDAE

CARP

The wild carp was being farmed for food in Asia by about 400 BC. Since then, selective breeding on eastern European fish farms has produced a number of variants such as the common, leather, and mirror forms. These and the wild carp have spread throughout Europe both naturally and by introduction, and have been introduced elsewhere, including North America and Australia.

FISHING NOTES

Techniques
Float fishing, legering, and freelining for common carp; float fishing for crucian.

Tackle
For common carp float fishing, use a 3.7 m (12 ft), 680 g (1½ lb) test curve rod with a fixed-spool reel, 3.6 kg (8 lb) line, and hook sizes 8 to 12. Legering calls for heavier tackle, for instance a 3.7 m (12 ft), 910 g (2 lb) test curve rod, fixed-spool reel, 5.4 kg (12 lb) line, and hook sizes 6 to 10. For crucian carp, use a 4 m (13 ft) light-action rod with a fixed-spool reel, 680 g to 1.1 kg (1½ to 2½ lb) line, and hook sizes 12 to 18.

Bait
The range of baits used by carp fishermen is enormous and constantly growing. It extends from simple, traditional baits, such as bread, worms, and maggots, through luncheon meat, sweetcorn, and potatoes, to the numerous commercially prepared baits such as boilies, and bait additives such as aromatic meat-, spice-, and fruit-flavoured oils.

WILD CARP
The wild carp is a strong, slow-growing fish with a scaleless head and a fully scaled body. Smaller and less deep-bodied than the common carp, its average weight is 910 g to 2.27 kg (2 to 5 lb) and it seldom exceeds 9.1 kg (20 lb).

WILD CARP
Cyprinus carpio

Breeding
Wild and common carp spawn in late spring and early summer, when the water temperature exceeds 18°C (64°F). The eggs are laid in shallow water that has abundant dense vegetation and good exposure to sunlight, and are attached to the leaves and stems of water plants. They hatch in five to eight days, the hatchlings initially remaining attached to the plants. The young fish grow very quickly.

Eggs

Hatchling

Larva

Feeding
The common carp feeds at the surface, on the bottom, or in midwater on plants, algae, snails, worms, insect larvae, shrimps, mussels, and many other organisms. It opens its mouth wide and sucks its food in like a vacuum cleaner, and often rummages through the bottom detritus, sending up clouds of silt and uprooting plants.

CRUCIAN CARP
Carassius carassius

CRUCIAN CARP
This small, deep-bodied carp is more closely related to the goldfish than to the wild carp, but will interbreed with both species. It averages about 255 g (9 oz), but can exceed 2.5 kg (5 lb 8 oz), and it will tolerate a wide range of temperatures, low oxygen levels, acidity, and dense vegetation.

Size comparison

Grass carp   Common carp   Mirror carp   Leather carp   Wild carp   Crucian carp   Goldfish

GRASS CARP

The wide mouth of the grass carp is superbly adapted for feeding on plants, and because of its huge appetite it has been introduced into many canals, ponds, and drains in Europe and North America for weed clearance. Its growth rate is very rapid, and in warm waters it can reach 35 kg (77 lb).

GRASS CARP
Ctenopharyngodon idella

DISTRIBUTION
Common carp: through most of Eurasia; North America, South Africa, India, Australia, and New Zealand.
Crucian, grass, and goldfish: native to Eurasia and widely introduced elsewhere.

GOLDFISH
Carassius auratus

GOLDFISH

Within a few generations of release into the wild, the domestic goldfish reverts to its natural carplike coloration and can grow to a weight of about 3 kg (6lb 10 oz).

COMMON (OR KING) CARP

The heavy, deep-bodied common, or king, carp, together with its leather and mirror varieties, is the result of centuries of selective breeding by fish farms. Like the wild carp from which it derives, the common carp has a scaleless head and a fully scaled body, and its coloration is variable. It can reach a weight of 36 kg (80 lb) and a length of about 1.5 m (5 ft).

Mirror carp scale
The scales of the mirror carp are much larger than those of the common carp. A typical mirror carp scale might be 5 cm (2 in) long and 3 cm (1.2 in) wide, compared with a length of 3 cm (1.2 in) and a width of 2.5 cm (1 in) for a scale of a similar-sized common carp.

COMMON (OR KING) CARP
Cyprinus carpio

MIRROR CARP
Cyprinus carpio

LEATHER CARP

The scaleless or almost-scaleless leather carp is a variety of common carp. Any scales that are present are large and few in number, and usually near the fins and tail. Like the common and mirror varieties, it has been introduced around the world.

LEATHER CARP
Cyprinus carpio

MIRROR CARP

The mirror variety of common carp occurs in a number of forms. The fully scaled is covered in large, irregular scales; the scattered has individual, randomly sited scales; the linear has a continuous line of scales along the lateral line; and the plated has just a few, very large, scales along the lateral line.

135

CYPRINIDAE

CHUB, DACE, ROACH, & RUDD

These popular angling species are widespread in the rivers and stillwaters of Europe. Chub and dace prefer moderate to fast flows of clean water, but they are also found in slow lowland rivers and sometimes in lakes. Roach and rudd thrive in canals, slow-flowing rivers, and stillwaters where there is plenty of vegetation. The roach has been introduced into Australia, where it is found in Victoria and southern New South Wales, and the rudd has been introduced into the northeastern United States, where there are breeding populations in Maine and in the lower Hudson basin in New York.

Chub food
Young chub eat mostly insect larvae and aquatic invertebrates. Adults will take anything edible that comes their way, opening their large, wide mouths to engulf small fish, frogs, crayfish, and small water voles, and snapping up berries that fall from overhanging trees and bushes.

Convex dorsal fin

CHUB
Leuciscus cephalus

Convex anal fin is pink, becoming darker with age

Concave dorsal fin

DACE
Leuciscus leuciscus

Pink pelvic fin

Slim body

CHUB
The body of the chub is thickset, with rounded fins and a blunt snout, and the dark edges of its scales give its back and sides an attractive, latticed appearance. In British waters the maximum weight is probably about 5.4 kg (12 lb), but in mainland Europe it can reach 7.26 kg (16 lb).

Concave anal fin

Protruding lower jaw

Large eye

DACE
The slim, silvery dace is one of the smallest species to be of serious angling interest: its maximum weight is only about 600 g (1 lb 5 oz), and a fish of 170 to 227 g (6 to 8 oz) would be a good catch. It feeds on insects, crustaceans, and plants.

BLEAK
Alburnus alburnus

Long anal fin

FISHING NOTES

Techniques
Float fishing and legering are the most usual techniques for these species, but fly fishing is an enjoyable alternative.

Tackle
To leger for chub, use a 3.7 m (12 ft) rod with a built-in quivertip, a fixed-spool reel, 2.27 kg (5 lb) line, hook sizes 8 to 16, and a suitable blockend

feeder. For float fishing, try a 3.7 to 4 m (12 to 13 ft) rod with fixed-spool reel, 1.36 kg (3 lb) line, and hook sizes 14 to 20. To float fish for dace, use a 3.7 m (12 ft) rod with a light tip action, a fixed-spool reel, 910 g (2 lb) line, and hook sizes 16 to 20. To float fish for roach or rudd, try a 3.7 m (12 ft) rod with a light tip action, a fixed-spool reel, 1.1 kg (2½ lb) line, and hook sizes 14 to 20. When legering for roach or rudd, use

a 3 to 3.7 m (10 to 12 ft) rod with quivertip, a fixed-spool reel, 1.36 to 1.8 kg (2½ to 4 lb) line, and hook sizes 10 to 16.

Bait
For all these species, good float fishing or legering baits include maggots, casters, bread flake, and worms, and large slugs are especially effective for chub. These species can also be taken on fly tackle, using either wet or dry flies.

Chub, dace, or bleak?
Young chub are similar in size and general appearance to dace and bleak, but each has its own distinguishing features. The chub has convex dorsal and anal fins, and its pelvic and anal fins are pink. In comparison, the greyish dorsal fin and pale, yellowish anal fins of the dace are concave, and the greyish, concave anal fin of the bleak is much longer than that of either the chub or the dace. The bleak also has a protruding lower jaw and large, prominent eyes.

136

DANUBIAN ROACH

This relatively slender-bodied roach has a small head and large, silvery scales, and occurs as two subspecies: *Rutilus pigus pigus* of the Po basin in northern Italy, and *R. p. virgo* of the Danube basin. It can reach a weight of 1 kg (2 lb 3 oz) or more, but most are much smaller.

DANUBIAN ROACH
Rutilus pigus

DISTRIBUTION
Chub: Europe, except Ireland, the snowbelt of Scandinavia, and southern Italy.
Dace: from Ireland to Siberia, but not south of the Pyrenees and the Alps.
Roach: Europe from Ireland to the Urals, but not found in the Scandinavian snowbelt or south of the Pyrenees and the Alps; has been introduced into Australia.
Rudd: Europe from Ireland to the Urals and from southern Sweden to northern Italy and Greece; introduced into the northeastern United States.

ROACH
Rutilus rutilus

ROACH

The silvery, deep-bodied roach has red eyes, reddish pectoral fins, red pelvic and anal fins, and dusky dorsal and tail fins. It is the most popular angling species in Europe, mainly because it is extremely common and catching it requires skill. It reaches about 1.8 kg (4 lb), and often hybridizes with bream *(see page 132)*.

RUDD
Scardinius erythrophthalmus

Upturned mouth

Orange pectoral fins

Golden flanks

Bright red or orange anal fin

RUDD

The deep-bodied rudd grows to a maximum weight of about 2 kg (4 lb 7 oz), slightly more than that of the roach. Because it takes much of its food at or near the surface, it is more easily located than the deeper-feeding roach, and this makes it somewhat easier to catch. However, the older, larger individuals often lie deep and feed at the bottom, so bottom fishing may catch bigger (if fewer) rudd than fishing near the surface.

Feeding rudd and roach
The rudd's upturned mouth is adapted for surface feeding on food such as insects, plants, and fish fry. The roach has a similar diet but is less of a surface feeder.

Fry

Egg

Breeding rudd and roach
Rudd and roach spawn in late spring and early summer, laying sticky yellow eggs on the stems and leaves of aquatic plants. Rudd eggs hatch in 8 to 15 days and roach eggs in 9 to 12 days; on average, fish of both species take nine or ten years to reach a weight of 500 g (1 lb 2 oz).

Size comparison

Chub · Roach · Rudd · Danubian roach · Dace · Bleak

137

ESOCIDAE

PIKE, PICKEREL, & MUSKELLUNGE

The members of the pike family are voracious predators, disliked and even feared by some anglers but greatly admired by others because of their size and the tenacious fight they put up when hooked. They inhabit rivers, streams, and stillwaters with clear water but with plenty of vegetation in which to lurk in wait for their prey. The pike itself, known in North America as the northern pike, is one of the few freshwater species to be native to both Eurasia and North America. Pickerel and muskellunge are purely North American species.

REDFIN PICKEREL
Esox americanus americanus

GRASS PICKEREL
Esox americanus vermiculatus

PICKEREL

The chain pickerel averages only 910 g (2 lb) but has been known to reach 4.25 kg (9 lb 6 oz). Despite being relatively small, it provides good sport on light tackle, as do the even smaller grass and redfin pickerels, which are less than half its size. Apart from the difference in their sizes, the chain pickerel can be distinguished from the grass and redfin by its markings. The chain pickerel has a distinctive dark, chainlike pattern on its sides, while the grass and redfin are both marked with dark bars; the redfin, as its name implies, also has red fins.

CHAIN PICKEREL
Esox niger

MUSKELLUNGE

The mighty muskellunge is a powerful, fast-growing fish that can reach a length of 30 cm (12 in) in only four months and grows to 1.83 m (6 ft) or more. Its maximum weight is at least 31.75 kg (70 lb), and weights in excess of 45 kg (100 lb) have been reported. The most visible difference between the muskellunge and the northern pike is in their markings: the "muskie" has dark bars or blotches on its sides, while the pike has a series of pale bars and spots.

MUSKELLUNGE
Esox masquinongy

FEEDING

The principal food of the pike family is fish, including smaller fish of their own kind. They are, however, great opportunists and will take any available small prey including frogs, snakes, crayfish, rodents, and ducklings. Their markings provide excellent camouflage as they hide among the weeds, waiting to pounce on passing fish, which they swallow head first.

FISHING NOTES

Techniques

These active predators are usually caught by spinning, baitcasting, and trolling, using lures, deadbaits, and livebaits. Fish for them from the bank, or use a boat to reach weedbeds that are otherwise inaccessible.

Tackle

For pickerel, try a 1.7 m (5½ ft) baitcaster with a multiplier reel or a 1.8 to 2.1 m (6 to 7 ft) spinning rod with a fixed-spool reel; use 2.7 to 3.6 kg (6 to 8 lb) line with a short wire trace. When lure fishing from the bank or a boat for pike or muskellunge, try a 1.8 to 2.7 m (6 to 9 ft) spinning or baitcasting rod with a multiplier or a fixed-spool reel, 4.54 to 6.8 kg (10 to 15 lb) line, and a 9.1 kg (20 lb) wire trace. When you are downrigger trolling for pike or muskellunge, use a 1.8 to 2.1 m (6 to 7 ft) fast-taper rod with a multiplier reel, 6.8 to 9.1 kg (15 to 20 lb) line, and a 11.3 kg (25 lb) wire trace.

Bait

Small spinners and spoons are ideal baits for pickerel. For pike and muskellunge, use large spinners, spoons, and plugs, cut fish baits (especially herring, mackerel, and eel), and whole minnows.

DISTRIBUTION

Pike: northern Europe south to the Pyrenees, east to Siberia; Labrador west to Alaska, south to Pennsylvania, Missouri, and Nebraska.
Muskellunge: Great Lakes region, Mississippi basin, Atlantic drainages south to Georgia and Virginia.
Chain pickerel: Atlantic drainages from Nova Scotia to Florida, Mississippi basin from Missouri south.
Redfin pickerel: Atlantic drainages.
Grass pickerel: Mississippi basin and Great Lakes.

Jaws

The members of the pike family have abundant sharp teeth and very complex skull and jaw structures. These enable them to seize and swallow relatively large fish and other prey; the pike, for example, tends to select prey that is 10 to 25 per cent of its own body weight.

PIKE
Esox lucius

PIKE

Like the other members of the family, the pike is an aggressive, solitary hunter, and its torpedo-shaped body is built for short bursts of acceleration rather than sustained speed. It is usually found in or near weedbeds that provide it with cover, but in large lakes it ventures into open water to feed on salmon, trout, or other fish. Growth rates for pike vary enormously and are directly dependent on the available food supply, but an annual weight gain of 910 g to 1.4 kg (2 to 3 lb) is fairly typical. The maximum weight is thought to be about 34 kg (75 lb), but most are much smaller and a pike of 4.54 to 9.1 kg (10–20 lb) is a worthwhile catch.

Size comparison

| Muskellunge | Pike | Chain pickerel | Grass pickerel | Redfin pickerel |

BULLHEAD

The North American bullhead and freshwater catfish (*see page 142*) are members of the Ictaluridae, which, with some 40 species, is the largest family of freshwater fish native to North America; some have been introduced into Europe and elsewhere. Bullhead are omnivorous, bottom-feeding fish, found mostly in still and slow-flowing waters and characterized by a scaleless body, four pairs of barbels, an adipose fin, and stiff, sharp spines at the leading edges of the pectoral and dorsal fins.

PECTORAL SPINES

Black bullhead

Brown bullhead

Pectoral spine comparison
The teeth on the black bullhead's pectoral spines are much smaller than those of the brown bullhead.

YELLOW BULLHEAD
(Viewed from above)

Body shape
Viewed from above, a bullhead has a large, bulbous head and broad "shoulders", and its body tapers sharply from the pectoral fins back to the tail.

YELLOW BULLHEAD
The yellow bullhead has a yellowish brown body and white or yellow barbels. It is found in waters where the bottom is soft, and will eat almost any available food, including plants, snails, insect larvae, small fish, and crayfish. It grows to a maximum weight of about 1.9 kg (4 lb 4 oz).

SNAIL
BULLHEAD
Ameiurus brunneus

YELLOW BULLHEAD
Ameiurus natalis

SPOTTED BULLHEAD
Ameiurus serracanthus

SPOTTED BULLHEAD
The pale spots on the dark body of the spotted bullhead make it easy to recognize. A small fish, its maximum weight is only about 454 g (1 lb).

SNAIL BULLHEAD
The snail bullhead prefers the rocky runs and flowing pools of swift streams to muddy-bottomed stillwaters and sluggish streams. Its weight ranges from around 113 g (4 oz) up to about 454 g (1 lb).

Size comparison

Black bullhead   Brown bullhead   Yellow bullhead   Snail bullhead   Flat bullhead   Spotted bullhead

BLACK BULLHEAD
Ameiurus melas

BROWN BULLHEAD
Ameiurus nebulosus

BLACK BULLHEAD
Also known as the horned pout, the black bullhead is a popular angling species that will tolerate very poor water quality. It is broadly similar in appearance to the brown bullhead, but lacks the mottled coloration and large pectoral spine teeth of that species. The black is the largest of the bullheads, but although it can grow to about 3.6 kg (8 lb) it seldom exceeds 910g (2 lb).

DISTRIBUTION
Black: from Montana east to the Great Lakes and south to the Gulf Slope drainages; introduced into Europe.
Brown: the Great Lakes and Maine south to Mexico and Florida; introduced into Europe and New Zealand.
Yellow: Dakotas to Atlantic and Gulf Slope drainages.
Spotted: Florida, Georgia, and Alabama.
Snail: southern Virginia to eastern Alabama and northern Florida.
Flat: Virginia to Georgia.

FLAT BULLHEAD
In profile, the flat bullhead has a flattened head and relatively straight snout. Its coloration is a mottled yellow to dark brown, with a light belly, and it averages about 454 g (1 lb) with a maximum of 910 g (2 lb).

Fins edged with black

BROWN BULLHEAD
The brown bullhead has a mottled coloration, and sharp teeth on its pectoral spines. Its maximum weight of around 2.5 kg (5 lb 8 oz) is less than that of the black, but its average of about 1.36 kg (3 lb) is slightly more. Both have been introduced into many European waters, with the brown now common in Holland and Germany and the black thriving in southern France.

FLAT BULLHEAD
Ameiurus platycephalus

Spawning bullhead
Bullhead spawn in spring and early summer, laying their eggs in depressions in the mud or among stones or other cover. One or both parents will then guard the eggs until they hatch.

FISHING NOTES

Techniques
Bullhead can be caught on most natural or processed baits by float fishing or legering, and also on small artificial lures by spinning or baitcasting.

Tackle
For float fishing, try a 3.7 m (12 ft) rod with a tip action, a fixed-spool reel, 1.1 kg (2½ lb) line, and hook sizes 10 to 16. For legering, use a 3 to 3.7m (10 to 12 ft) rod with a quivertip, a fixed-spool reel, 1.1 to 1.8 kg (2½ to 4 lb) line, and hook sizes 10 to 16. For spinning or baitcasting, try a 1.5 to 2.1 m (5 to 7 ft) medium-action rod with a multiplier or small closed-face fixed-spool reel, and 1.36 or 1.8 kg (3 or 4 lb) line.

Bait
Like their larger relatives the freshwater catfish, bullhead will take a wide range of natural and processed baits. These include worms, meat, bread, cheese, cut fish, tiny minnows, mussels, snails, shrimps, and freshwater clams. Adding small amounts of flavourings, such as spice oils, helps to make bread and other relatively bland baits more attractive. When baitcasting or spinning, try lightweight spinners and spoons, plastic worms, tiny jigs, and small wet flies.

141

FRESHWATER CATFISH

Worldwide, there are over 30 families of freshwater and marine catfish, containing about 2,250 species. These families include the Ictaluridae of North America (*see also page 140*), the Siluridae of Europe, and the Plotosidae of Australasia, all of which have scaleless bodies, broad heads, and "whiskers" around their mouths. They generally inhabit still or slow-flowing waters, and are most active at night and on cloudy days.

Head shows distinctive flattening

CHANNEL CATFISH
The channel catfish, one of the larger North American catfish species, is the only one to have both spots and a deeply forked tail; the spots tend to fade in old, large fish. Its maximum size is about 27 kg (60 lb).

YOUNG ADULT FISH

CHANNEL CATFISH
Ictalurus punctatus

WHITE CATFISH
The coloration of the white catfish varies from white to silvery beige or blue, with a white belly. It is very popular as an angling and food fish, and usually grows to about 1.36 kg (3 lb) although it has been known to reach weights of over 7.7 kg (17 lb).

WELS
Also known as the Danubian catfish, the wels is native to central and eastern Europe but has been widely introduced into western European waters. The reason for these introductions is that the wels is one of the largest of all freshwater fish, reliably known to reach a length of 3 m (9 ft 10 in) and a weight of 200 kg (441 lb); individuals weighing over 320 kg (700 lb) have been reported.

WELS
Silurus glanis

WHITE CATFISH
Ameiurus catus

TANDAN
Tandanus tandanus

TANDAN
The tandan is a member of the Plotosidae family, which comprises about 30 marine and freshwater species that are widely distributed throughout Australasia and the Indo-Pacific. It inhabits stillwaters and slow-flowing streams, typically reaching a weight of up to 2 kg (4 lb 7 oz) with a maximum of about 6 kg (13 lb 4 oz).

FISHING NOTES

Techniques
Freshwater catfish are usually taken on natural or processed baits by float fishing, legering, or freelining, but spinning with artificial lures is also effective, particularly for channel and blue catfish.

Tackle
Use a 2.7 to 3m (9 to 10 ft) rod, such as a heavy bass rod, with a fixed-spool reel, 2.7 to 5.4 kg (6 to 12 lb) line, and hook sizes 6 to 1/0. To freeline for the larger species, such as the wels, use a 3 to 3.7 m (10 to 12 ft) rod with a powerful all-through action, a fixed-spool reel, 6.8 kg (15 lb) line, 9.1 kg (20 lb) Dacron trace, and hook sizes 4 to 2/0.

Bait
Freshwater catfish can be taken on practically any type of bait or lure, even a bare, shiny hook. Every catfish angler has a personal preference when it comes to a choice of bait, but the best results are said to come with "stink" baits. These baits include soured clams and ripened chicken entrails, beef liver, pig liver, and rabbit liver, coagulated blood, and even pieces of scented soap.

FLATHEAD CATFISH
Pylodictis olivaris

FLATHEAD CATFISH
The preferred habitat of the flathead is the deep, sluggish pools of large rivers, but it is also found in smaller streams and stillwaters. It averages about 1.8 kg (4 lb) but may reach 45 kg (100 lb).

Front view of a wels showing its very wide and flattened head

Whiskers
The barbels or "whiskers" around the mouth of a catfish are highly sensitive organs with which the fish can taste, smell, and feel its food. The wels has six whiskers, and the American catfish and the tandan have eight.

DISTRIBUTION
Wels: southern Sweden to the Danube basin and Amu Darya; introduced into England, France, Spain, Italy.
Channel: Great Lakes to Gulf Slope drainages.
White: Atlantic and Gulf Slope drainages.
Flathead: lower Great Lakes, Mississippi basin, Gulf Slope drainages.
Blue: Mississippi basin, Gulf Slope drainages.
Tandan: Queensland, New South Wales, Victoria, and South Australia.

BLUE CATFISH
Ictalurus furcatus

BLUE CATFISH
The blue catfish is the largest North American catfish, averaging up to 22.7 kg (50 lb) and capable of exceeding 45 kg (100 lb). Unlike most catfish it prefers swift-flowing and relatively clear streams to slow, turbid waters, and is found over rock, sand, or gravel bottoms rather than mud or silt.

Feeding
Blue catfish feed mainly at night, when they move from deep water into shallow, swift-flowing rapids and chutes to hunt for fish and crayfish.

Size comparison

Wels

Blue catfish

Channel catfish

Flathead catfish

White catfish   Tandan

BASS & MURRAY COD

Until recently, these perchlike species were all classified as members of the Percichthyidae family, but those of the genus *Morone* are now considered to be a separate family, the Moronidae. Both families are widely distributed in temperate and tropical waters, some being exclusively freshwater fish, others exclusively marine, and some migrating from the sea into freshwater to spawn. They feed mainly on small fish, crustaceans, worms, and insects.

AUSTRALIAN BASS

This is one of the most important gamefish of the coastal rivers, estuaries, and lakes of southeastern Australia. It grows to a weight of 1 kg (2 lb 3 oz) or more, and spawns in estuaries during the winter. The eggs hatch in about three days, and by around three months of age the young fish resemble small adults but are marked with faint vertical bars on the back and sides.

AUSTRALIAN BASS
Macquaria novemaculeata

YELLOW BASS
Morone mississippiensis

WHITE PERCH
Morone americana

WHITE PERCH

The white perch can reach a weight of about 2.2 kg (4 lb 12 oz), but averages only about 454 g (1 lb). It is found in the Atlantic Slope drainages of northeastern North America, primarily in brackish water near the mouths of rivers. It is also found in the quiet pools of medium to large rivers, and close inshore in shallow coastal waters.

YELLOW BASS

This little freshwater bass has silvery yellow sides, and the lower stripes along them are broken and offset. It rarely exceeds 1 kg (2 lb 3 oz) and usually weighs only 113 to 340 g (4 to 12 oz), but despite its small size it offers good sport on light tackle.

WHITE BASS
Morone chrysops

WHITE BASS

The white bass is very similar to the yellow bass, but its coloration is silvery white, the stripes along its sides are not broken and offset, and its lower jaw is more protuberant. It is found mainly in large, relatively clear waters, and although it grows to over 3 kg (6 lb 10 oz) most of those caught are in the 227 to 910 g (8 oz to 2 lb) range.

Size comparison

Striped bass   Murray cod   European sea bass   Spotted sea bass   Australian bass   Yellow bass   White bass   White per

MURRAY COD

With a maximum length of 1.8 m (6 ft) and a weight of up to 113.5 kg (250 lb), the Murray cod is the largest Australian freshwater fish. Its preferred habitat is deep holes in muddy, slow-flowing water, and it is fished for commercially as well as for sport. It is widely distributed through the Murray-Darling River system, and has been introduced into many lakes in New South Wales and Victoria.

MURRAY COD
Maccullochella peeli

SPOTTED SEA BASS
Dicentrarchus punctatus

EUROPEAN SEA BASS
Dicentrarchus labrax

STRIPED BASS
Morone saxatilis

DISTRIBUTION

Australian bass, Murray cod: Queensland to Victoria.
White perch: from Quebec to South Carolina.
Yellow bass: from Montana and Wisconsin south to the Gulf of Mexico.
White bass: Manitoba and Quebec to the Gulf.
Spotted sea bass: western France to North Africa.
European sea bass: southern Norway to the Black Sea.

SPOTTED SEA BASS

The spotted sea bass is similar in size and habits to the European sea bass, from which it may be distinguished by its spotted sides. Its range overlaps that of the European sea bass, but it is not found as far north.

EUROPEAN SEA BASS

The European sea bass is found in coastal waters and the brackish water of estuaries, and reaches a weight of about 8.6 kg (19 lb). It spawns in the sea in spring and early summer, and young fish often have spots on their sides like those of the spotted bass; these spots fade and disappear as the fish mature.

STRIPED BASS

This large bass, which can grow to 2 m (6 ft 7 in) long and a weight of 57 kg (126 lb), is found along the Atlantic and Gulf coasts of North America, and was introduced into the Pacific coastal waters in 1886. It migrates into freshwater to spawn during late spring and early summer, and there are a number of landlocked, lake-dwelling populations. It will readily take baits such as mullet, sandeels, squid, crabs, clams, worms, and lures, and is fished for commercially as well as for sport.

FISHING NOTES

Techniques
In freshwater, try spinning or trolling for striped bass and Murray cod, and spinning or fly fishing for the smaller species. In saltwater, try surfcasting, trolling, or uptide fishing.

Tackle
For freshwater striped bass and Murray cod, use a heavy spinning rod with 9.1 to 18.1 kg (20 to 40 lb) line. For the smaller freshwater fish, use a 2.1 to 2.7 m (7 to 9 ft) light spinning or fly rod. For striped bass in saltwater, try a 13.6 kg (30 lb) class boat rod for trolling and a 3.7 m (12 ft) rod for surfcasting; when fishing for the smaller species in saltwater, use a 3.4 m (11 ft) light surfcasting rod or a 5.4 kg (12 lb) class uptide rod.

Bait
These fish are all active predators, and will therefore take most suitably sized natural baits or artificial lures.

145

Freshwater SPECIES

AUSTRALIAN PERCH & GRUNTERS

The Macquarie, golden, and estuary perches are members of the Perchichthyidae family *(see page 144)*, while the jungle perch belongs to the Kuhliidae, a small family of fish that are similar to the Centrarchidae of North America *(see pages 126–9)*. The silver perch and sooty grunter are members of the Teraponidae (grunter) family, which consists of about 45 Indo-Pacific marine and freshwater species.

SILVER PERCH
Bidyanus bidyanus

SILVER PERCH
The silver perch, or bidyan, is found in the rivers and lakes of southeastern Australia. Its overall coloration is silver-grey with a paler belly, and the dark edges of its scales create an attractive, latticed effect. It feeds mainly on insects, worms, and molluscs and grows to a maximum weight of about 1.5 kg (3 lb 5 oz). Its flesh is tasty, so it is fished for commercially as well as being a popular angling species.

MACQUARIE PERCH
Macquaria australasica

SOOTY GRUNTER
Hephaestus fuliginosus

Dark patch on anal fin

SOOTY GRUNTER
The sooty grunter, also known as the black bream, has a dusky overall coloration, sometimes with a golden sheen or patches of gold on its sides. It is primarily a river fish, and grows to about 4 kg (8 lb 13 oz) on a varied diet that includes insects, worms, shrimps, frogs, and berries.

Elongated rays

MACQUARIE PERCH
The colour of the Macquarie perch varies from greenish brown to almost black, with a pale, sometimes yellowish, belly. It occurs in cool rivers and deep lakes, and has been introduced into reservoirs. Its diet consists mainly of insects, molluscs, and crustaceans, and it reaches a weight of around 1.5 kg (3 lb 5 oz). It spawns in spring and early summer.

FISHING NOTES

Techniques
Spinning or baitcasting with artificial lures, fly fishing, and trolling with livebaits will all prove successful.

Tackle
For lure fishing, try a 2.1 m (7 ft) spinning or baitcasting rod, a fixed-spool or multiplier reel and 2.7 kg (6 lb) mono line. For fly fishing, use a 2.7 m (9 ft) rod with a fast taper, a fly reel, and a floating #7 to #9 line with a 2.7 kg (6 lb) leader. For trolling, use a 2.7 m (9 ft) stiff-action rod with a 1.1 kg (2½ lb) test curve, and a multiplier reel with 4.54 to 9.1 kg (10 to 20 lb) mono line, a nylon or Dacron leader attached by a swivel, and hook sizes 2/0 to 5/0.

Bait
These fish will take a wide range of lures and flies, and trolled natural baits such as worms, minnows, and crayfish.

JUNGLE PERCH
Kuhlia rupestris

Black patch on second dorsal fin

Black patches on tail

DISTRIBUTION
Silver perch: Victoria, New South Wales, Queensland.
Sooty grunter: Northern Territory and Queensland.
Macquarie perch: New South Wales and Victoria.
Jungle perch: Queensland.
Golden perch: South Australia, Victoria, New South Wales, Queensland, and Northern Territory.
Estuary perch: New South Wales, Victoria, and South Australia.

JUNGLE PERCH
The jungle perch is silvery with distinctive reddish-brown markings, and there are black patches on the second dorsal fin and each lobe of the tail fin. It lives in clear, fast-flowing streams, feeding on insects, fish, and crayfish, and its maximum weight is about 3 kg (6 lb 10 oz). It is found in the coastal streams of eastern Queensland, and occurs widely elsewhere in the tropical Indo-Pacific region.

GOLDEN PERCH
Macquaria ambigua

Young golden perch
The juvenile golden perch has a slender body and is heavily spotted.

Elongated first and second rays

JUVENILE GOLDEN PERCH

ESTUARY PERCH
Macquaria colonorum

GOLDEN PERCH
This is one of the largest Australian perch, having a maximum weight of around 23 kg (50 lb 11 oz). It is widely distributed through the Murray-Darling system and elsewhere, and its preferred habitat is muddy, slow-moving water. It feeds on shrimps and crayfish, and its coloration varies from olive green to yellow, with a pale, yellowish belly.

ESTUARY PERCH
The silvery-grey estuary perch is found in the coastal streams and estuaries, and some lakes, of southeastern Australia. It feeds on fish, crustaceans, molluscs, and worms, and can grow to a weight of 10 kg (22 lb). Spawning takes place in the saltwater reaches of estuaries, and occurs in winter in New South Wales but not until early summer in Victoria. The eggs float on the surface, and hatch within three days.

Estuary perch spawning
Each female lays many hundreds of thousands of eggs, which float to the surface and are eaten by fish and other marine predators. Only a tiny number become adults.

Size comparison

Golden perch   Estuary perch   Sooty grunter   Jungle perch   Macquarie perch   Silver perch

147

PERCIDAE

PERCH, SAUGER, WALLEYE, & ZANDER

The Percidae is a large and diverse family of fish comprising perch and related species. These are characterized by their long, slender bodies and their two dorsal fins, separate in some species but joined in others, with the first dorsal having spines and the second having soft rays. The members of the Percidae are found both in streams and in stillwaters. The small species and the young of the large ones feed on insect larvae and other invertebrates; the adults of the large species are fish-eaters.

Perch scales
Perch feel rough to the touch because they have ctenoid scales – scales that have fine teeth on their exposed edges. Smooth scales with no teeth, such as those of the carp family, are called cycloid scales.

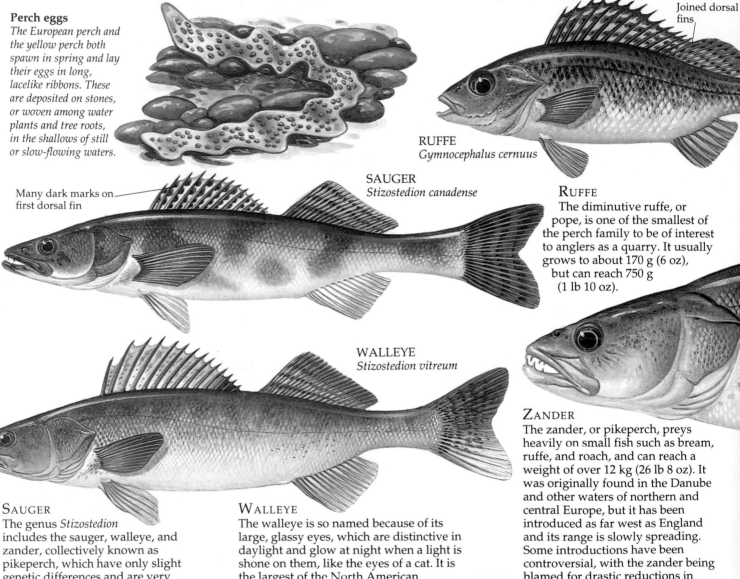

Perch eggs
The European perch and the yellow perch both spawn in spring and lay their eggs in long, lacelike ribbons. These are deposited on stones, or woven among water plants and tree roots, in the shallows of still or slow-flowing waters.

Joined dorsal fins

RUFFE
Gymnocephalus cernuus

SAUGER
Stizostedion canadense

Many dark marks on first dorsal fin

RUFFE
The diminutive ruffe, or pope, is one of the smallest of the perch family to be of interest to anglers as a quarry. It usually grows to about 170 g (6 oz), but can reach 750 g (1 lb 10 oz).

WALLEYE
Stizostedion vitreum

ZANDER
The zander, or pikeperch, preys heavily on small fish such as bream, ruffe, and roach, and can reach a weight of over 12 kg (26 lb 8 oz). It was originally found in the Danube and other waters of northern and central Europe, but it has been introduced as far west as England and its range is slowly spreading. Some introductions have been controversial, with the zander being blamed for drastic reductions in local fish populations, but in many waters the introductions seem to have caused no major problems.

SAUGER
The genus *Stizostedion* includes the sauger, walleye, and zander, collectively known as pikeperch, which have only slight genetic differences and are very similar in appearance and habits. Like all pikeperch, the sauger is a predator; it can reach a maximum weight of more than 3.6 kg (8 lb).

WALLEYE
The walleye is so named because of its large, glassy eyes, which are distinctive in daylight and glow at night when a light is shone on them, like the eyes of a cat. It is the largest of the North American perches, typically reaching 1.36 kg (3 lb) with a maximum of 11.3 kg (25 lb), and is a prized food fish as well as being a favourite quarry of anglers.

Size comparison

Zander   Walleye   Sauger   European perch   Volga zander   Yellow perch   Ruffe

YELLOW PERCH
Perca flavescens

YELLOW PERCH
The North American yellow perch is very similar to the European perch in appearance and habits, and the two species are closely related. Like all the large members of the Percidae, they make excellent eating and are among the tastiest of freshwater fish.

EUROPEAN PERCH
Perca fluviatilis

EUROPEAN PERCH
This perch is widespread in stillwaters and slow-flowing lowland rivers throughout Europe. It is a shoaling fish that feeds on insects and small fish, including perch fry, and in some waters of the European mainland it can attain a weight of up to 6.5 kg (14 lb).

DISTRIBUTION
Sauger, walleye: Northwest Territories east to Quebec, southeast to Alabama.
Zander: northern and central Europe; also introduced into western Europe and England.
Volga zander: river systems entering the northern Black and Caspian Seas.
Ruffe: eastern England to Asia; introduced into Scotland and the Great Lakes.
European perch: from Ireland to Siberia; has been introduced into Australia.
Yellow perch: found from the Northwest Territories to the Atlantic drainages as far south as South Carolina.

ZANDER
Stizostedion lucioperca

Eggs

Spawning zander
Zander spawn in spring and early summer, laying clumps of pale yellow eggs on plants or on sand and stones. The larvae hatch after a few days and live on their yolk sacs until their teeth develop and they can feed themselves. Young zander feed on small prey, such as insect larvae and fish fry.

VOLGA ZANDER
Stizostedion volgensis

VOLGA ZANDER
The appearance of the Volga zander is similar to that of the zander, but the dark markings on its back are much more well defined. It is also generally smaller, and lacks the long fangs of the zander, although its mouth is well equipped with small, sharp teeth. The Volga zander is found in rivers flowing into the Caspian and Black seas, including the Volga itself and the Danube as far upstream as Vienna. It prefers open, deep water to vegetated areas, and grows to about 2 kg (4 lb 6 oz).

FISHING NOTES

Techniques
Legering, float fishing, and spinning are all effective.

Tackle
For legering and float fishing, try a 3 to 3.7 m (10 to 12 ft) slow or medium-action rod with a fixed-spool reel. Use 2.27 kg (5 lb) mono line and hook sizes 4 to 10 for ruffe and perch, and 2.7 to 4.45 kg (6 to 10 lb) mono with a 50 cm (20 in) wire trace and size 10 treble hook for walleye, sauger, and zander. When spinning, for perch use a 2.1 to 2.7 m (7 to 9 ft) light spinning rod with a fixed-spool reel, 2.27 or 2.7 kg (5 or 6 lb) mono line, and a swivelled trace; for walleye, sauger, and zander, use a 2.4 m (8 ft) medium-action spinning rod, fixed-spool reel, 2.7 to 3.6 kg (6 to 8 lb) mono line, and a short, fine-wire trace.

Bait
Worms and maggots for perch, small fish for walleye, sauger, and zander. Spinning: spinners, spoons, jigs, plugs.

149

SALMONIDAE

CHAR

The most obvious difference between char (salmonids of the genus *Salvelinus*) and salmon and trout (genera *Salmo* and *Oncorhynchus*) lies in their coloration: char have light markings on a darker background; salmon and trout have dark markings on a lighter background. Char feed on invertebrates and small fish, and they are native to the cool waters of the northern parts of the Northern Hemisphere; they are all excellent angling species. Lake and brook trout have been widely introduced elsewhere.

ARCTIC CHAR
Salvelinus alpinus

BREEDING MALE

Breeding male char
In the breeding season the coloration of both sexes deepens, but that of the male becomes especially vibrant, with rich orange fins and a bright orange-red belly.

ARCTIC CHAR
Above latitude 64°N, all arctic char winter in coastal waters and move into rivers to spawn. Below that latitude, they also inhabit cold, deep lakes, and many of these lake populations have evolved into distinct varieties that vary greatly in size and coloration. The sea-run char, silver with reddish spots, grows to about 12 kg (26 lb); the lake char, typically greenish with red and white spots and an orange belly, reaches about 3.6 kg (8 lb).

NON-BREEDING CHAR

Parr marks
In the parr stage of its life cycle, from a few months up to about two years of age, a char has the banded markings on its sides that are typical of young salmonids.

CHAR PARR

Hybrids
Hybridization among members of the Salmonidae family occurs both naturally and as a result of selective breeding by fish farms. Natural hybrids include Atlantic salmon × sea trout and rainbow × cutthroat; farmed crossbreeds include the splake (brook trout × lake trout), the tiger trout (brook × brown), and the cheetah trout (brook × rainbow).

SPLAKE (HYBRID)

FISHING NOTES

Techniques
Fly fishing, spinning, and trolling for arctic char and lake trout; fly fishing and spinning for brook trout and Dolly Varden.

Tackle
For fly fishing use a 2.4 to 3.4 m (8 to 11 ft) fly rod with a fly reel, floating or sinking line as appropriate, and flies dressed on hook sizes 10 to 14. For spinning and for shallow trolling try a 2.7 m (9 ft), medium spinning rod with a fixed-spool reel, and use 1.8 to 2.7 kg (4 to 6 lb) line for spinning and 4.54 to 6.8 kg (10 to 15 lb) line for shallow trolling.

For deep trolling, use a 1.8m (6ft), fast-taper trolling rod with braided wire line; the rod should have hardened rings or roller guides to resist the abrasive action of the wire line.

Bait
For arctic char, use small, bright spinners or spoons, or wet fly patterns that incorporate a flashy material such as gold or silver tinsel, for example Butcher or Mallard and Claret. Use large, trolled spoons or livebait for lake trout in deep water, and spoons, spinners, plugs, or streamer flies when the fish are close inshore. Brook trout and Dolly Varden may be taken on lures, dry flies, wet flies, and nymphs.

LAKE TROUT
Salvelinus namaycush

DISTRIBUTION
Arctic char: Alaska, northern Canada, and New England; Greenland, Iceland, northern Eurasia; cold lakes in Russia, Britain, Ireland, Scandinavia, and the Alps.
Lake trout: Alaska through Canada to New England; introduced into western USA, South America, Europe, and New Zealand.
Brook trout: northeastern North America; introduced elsewhere in North America and in South America, Europe, Asia, southern Africa, and Australasia.
Dolly Varden: western North America, eastern Asia.
Bull trout: southern Yukon to northern California.

LAKE TROUT
The fast-swimming lake trout is an aggressive predator that is found in lakes and streams (both shallow and deep) in the north of its range, and in deep lakes in the south. It has a relatively slender, streamlined body with a deeply forked tail, and usually reaches a maximum of about 18 kg (40 lb), although it can grow to over 45 kg (100 lb).

The male brook trout has a white throat during the winter

BROOK TROUT
Salvelinus fontinalis

BROOK TROUT
The distinguishing features of the brook trout include pale blotches and wavy lines on the back, pinkish spots with blue halos on the sides, and a square or slightly forked tail. It inhabits cool, well-oxygenated streams and lakes, and some northern populations are migratory. It has been known to reach 6.58 kg (14 lb 8 oz) but the usual maximum is about 4.54 kg (10 lb) and it rarely exceeds 2.27 kg (5 lb).

BULL TROUT
Salvelinus confluentus

BULL TROUT
The bull trout is almost identical to the Dolly Varden, but its head is slightly longer and flatter. It lives in deep, cold rivers and lakes, and rarely migrates to the sea.

DOLLY VARDEN
In freshwater, the Dolly Varden is similar in appearance to the arctic char, and can reach a weight of 3.6 kg (8 lb). Its migratory form, when in the sea, is silvery and steel blue with cream and pink spots.

DOLLY VARDEN (migratory form)
Salvelinus malma

Size comparison

Lake trout   Arctic char   Bull trout   Splake   Brook trout   Dolly Varden

SALMON

Salmon are some of the most important commercial and sport fish in the world. All begin their lives in freshwater and most migrate to the sea to mature, returning to freshwater to spawn. The principal exceptions are the landlocked varieties of the Atlantic and sockeye salmon, and two Eurasian landlocked species, the huchen (*Hucho hucho*) and the taimen (*Hucho taimen*). The huchen, a fish of the Danube basin, is now a protected species in many of its native waters but has been introduced successfully into some French rivers; the taimen is common in the Volga basin and Siberia.

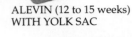

ATLANTIC SALMON
LIFE CYCLE

ALEVIN (12 to 15 weeks)
WITH YOLK SAC

EGG

Life cycles
The life cycles of all the salmon species are broadly similar. The main differences are that the Pacific species die after spawning but many Atlantic salmon spawn more than once; the landlocked species do not migrate to the sea but mature in freshwater; and there are some differences in timing. The eggs are laid in redds (nests) scooped out of gravel by the female, and take from 70 to 200 days to hatch.

BREEDING MALE
(3 to 8 years)

BREEDING
MALE

ATLANTIC SALMON
Salmo salar

COHO SALMON
Oncorhynchus kisutch

Spots on
upper lobe
only

Coloration
The coloration of a salmon changes when it is ready to breed, and the male develops a hook (kype) on its lower jaw.

BREEDING
MALE CHINOOK

COHO SALMON
The coho or silver salmon is an important sport fish both in its native waters and those to which it has been introduced, such as the Great Lakes. It is similar to the chinook, but has white gums rather than black, less extensive spotting on the tail, and is smaller, reaching a maximum of around 15 kg (33 lb).

MASU SALMON
The relatively small and stocky masu, or cherry salmon, is an Asian species with both migratory and freshwater forms. It reaches maturity in three or four years, growing to about 4.54 kg (10 lb), and is fished for commercially as well as for sport.

MASU SALMON
Oncorhynchus masou

PINK SALMON
Oncorhynchus gorbuscha

BREEDING
MALE PINK

PINK SALMON
Because of the distinctively humped back of the spawning male, the pink salmon is also known as the humpback or humpy. It is the most abundant of the Pacific species and is of considerable commercial importance, but it is a small fish, usually averaging 1.36 to 2.27 kg (3 to 5lb) with a maximum of 5.4 kg (12 lb).

FISHING NOTES

Techniques
The Atlantic salmon is fished for in freshwater. The most usual technique is fly fishing, but it is also taken on spoons, plugs, and natural baits on waters (and at times of the year) where these methods are permitted. Pacific salmon, of which the chinook and coho are the most important species for the sport fisherman, are usually taken by trolling just offshore and in estuaries, but they are also caught by fly fishing and spinning (as are the landlocked varieties) when they move into freshwater to spawn.

Tackle
Fly tackle for freshwater salmon fishing is typically a 3.7 to 4.9 m (12 to 16 ft) rod, a fly reel, and weight-forward fly line. For spinning and bait fishing, try a heavy 3 m (10 ft) spinning rod with a multiplier reel and 6.8 to 9.1 kg (15 to 20 lb) line. The usual saltwater rig for chinook and coho is a boat or trolling rod with a star-drag multiplier reel and 9.1 to 20.4 kg (20 to 45 lb) line.

Bait
In freshwater, use flies, lures, worms, or prawns. In saltwater, use streamers, lures, or fish baits.

PARR
(6 months to 2 years)

SMOLT
(2 to 3 years)

FRESH-RUN FISH (3 years)

Atlantic salmon has a shorter-based anal fin with fewer rays than the Pacific species

ATLANTIC SALMON
The Atlantic salmon is highly prized because of its size, its tasty flesh, and the expertise needed to catch it: it does not feed when it returns to freshwater, so inducing it to take a fly, lure, or bait calls for great skill. At sea, it feeds mainly on crustaceans, and the size it reaches depends on how long it stays in the sea. A fish that has spent one winter at sea, known as a grilse or jack, will weigh up to 4.1 kg (9 lb), while a three-sea-winter fish can exceed 31.75 kg (70 lb).

DISTRIBUTION
Atlantic salmon: Europe from the Arctic to Portugal, and North America from Quebec to Connecticut; landlocked form (the ouananiche or Sebago salmon): northeast United States, eastern Canada. Also introduced into Australia, New Zealand and Argentina.
Coho, chinook, pink, chum, sockeye, kokanee: Alaska to California; northeast Asia; introduced elsewhere.
Masu: northeast Asia.

CHINOOK SALMON
Oncorhynchus tshawytscha

Both lobes spotted

CHINOOK SALMON
The largest Pacific salmon is the chinook or king salmon, which averages 4.54 to 6.8 kg (10 to 15 lb) with a maximum of 54 kg (120 lb) or more. Like most salmon, it does not feed when it runs upriver to spawn but relies on stored energy reserves to sustain it during what may be a long and arduous journey. For example, chinook that spawn in Teslin Lake, Yukon, travel over 3,860 km (2,400 miles) up the Yukon and Teslin Rivers to get there.

Very fine speckles

SOCKEYE SALMON
Oncorhynchus nerka

SOCKEYE SALMON
The migratory sockeye or red salmon will rarely take a lure or bait and so is of only minor interest to anglers. The landlocked form, however, which is known as the kokanee, is a very popular angling species that readily takes lures, flies, and baits. The sockeye can reach 6.8 kg (15 lb), but the kokanee seldom exceeds 2.27 kg (5 lb).

BREEDING MALE SOCKEYE

CHUM SALMON
Although it is not highly regarded as a gamefish, the chum salmon can provide good sport on light saltwater tackle. Sea-run chum and sockeye are very similar, but the chum is generally larger, averaging about 4.54 to 6.8 kg (10 to 15 lb) with a maximum of 15 kg (33 lb), and has white-tipped lower fins.

BREEDING MALE MASU

CHUM SALMON
Oncorhynchus keta

Dark tip to caudal fin

Size comparison

| Chinook | Atlantic | Coho | Chum | Sockeye | Pink | Masu |

SALMONIDAE

TROUT

The brown trout and the rainbow trout are two of the world's most important gamefish species, and because of the high-quality sport they offer their distribution has been increased by extensive introduction schemes. The cutthroat trout, despite its qualities as a gamefish, has not been widely introduced beyond its natural range for a number of reasons, such as its tendency to hybridize with the rainbow trout. Trout thrive in cool, clean streams and lakes and feed mainly on insects, insect larvae, crustaceans, and fish. When at sea, the migratory forms eat fish and crustaceans.

RAINBOW TROUT
The rainbow trout varies greatly in appearance and size, and there are many different races and subspecies such as the Kamloops, Shasta, and Kern River rainbows. Most, however, have a pink stripe along the lateral line and small black speckles on the sides, back, upper fins, and tail. In North America, rainbows weighing more than 22.7 kg (50 lb) have been recorded, but the usual maximum in European waters is only around 11 kg (24 lb).

STEELHEAD
Steelhead are rainbow trout that migrate to sea before returning to rivers to spawn, or live in lakes and move into streams to spawn. Fresh-run steelhead are silvery, but their coloration soon changes to resemble that of non-migratory rainbows.

SEA TROUT
Migratory form of brown trout

Sharply squared-off tail

BROWN TROUT
Salmo trutta

SEA TROUT
The sea trout, the silvery migratory form of the brown trout, enters the sea at about two years old but returns to rivers to spawn. A large sea trout resembles an Atlantic salmon (*see page 152*), but its tail has a thicker "wrist" and is more squared-off.

BROWN TROUT
The brown trout is highly variable in appearance and size, and these variations are caused by environmental and genetic factors. In general, the body is brownish and sprinkled with black and red spots, and its weight ranges from under 454 g (1 lb) in small streams to over 13.6 kg (30 lb) in large waters.

FISHING NOTES

Techniques
Trout are taken on natural baits and on spinners, but fly fishing is without any doubt the pre-eminent trout-fishing technique.

Tackle
For fly fishing, use a 1.8 to 3.4 m (6 to 11 ft) fly rod, a fly reel, and floating or sinking line as appropriate. To fish for trout with naturals such as worms, use a 2.1 to 3 m (7 to 10 ft) medium-action rod

with a fixed spool reel, 1.8 to 3.6 kg (4 to 8 lb) line, and hook sizes 6 to 14. For spinning with artificial lures, try a 2.1 to 2.7 m (7 to 9 ft) spinning rod with a fixed-spool reel and 1.8 to 3.6 kg (4 to 8 lb) line.

Bait
For fly fishing, use whichever pattern is appropriate for the water, the style of fishing, and the prevailing conditions. For spinning, use small spinners, spoons, and plugs. Suitable naturals for trout include larvae and worms.

Hooked jaw

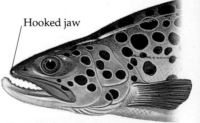

Cannibal trout
Although all brown trout are carnivorous, large individuals will even eat smaller members of their own species. These cannibal trout, which develop a distinctly hooked lower jaw, lurk in deep water waiting to pounce on their prey as it swims past.

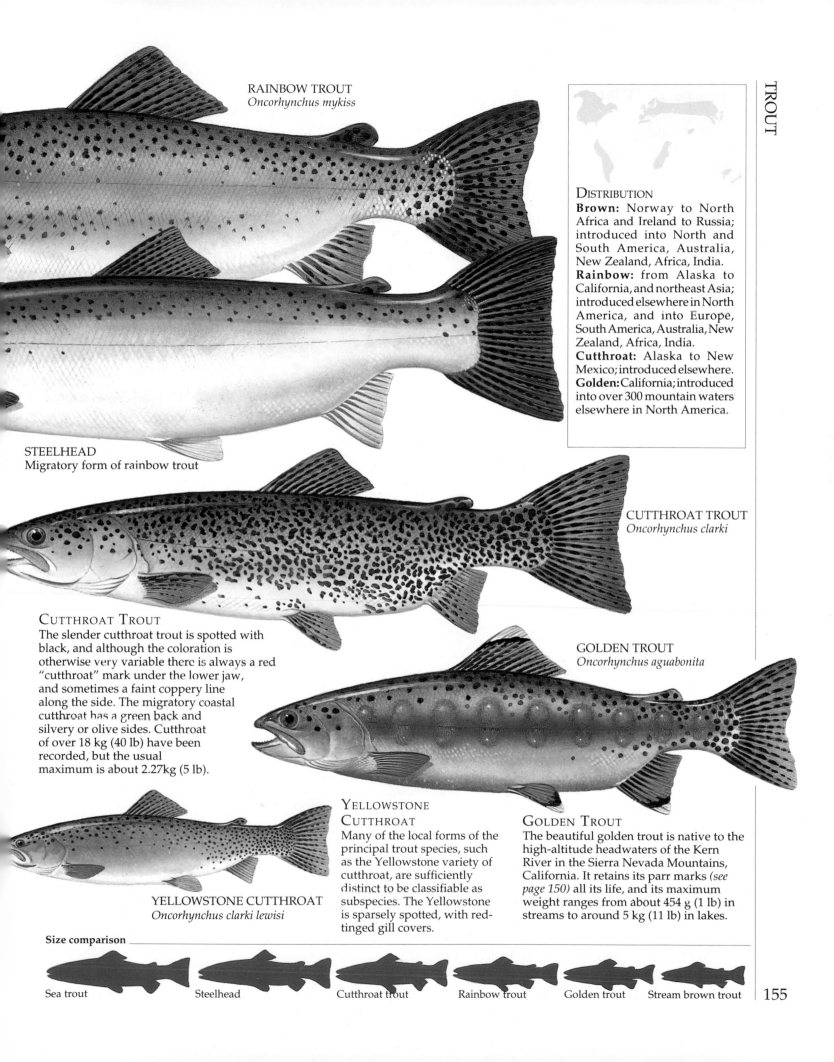

RAINBOW TROUT
Oncorhynchus mykiss

STEELHEAD
Migratory form of rainbow trout

CUTTHROAT TROUT
Oncorhynchus clarki

GOLDEN TROUT
Oncorhynchus aguabonita

YELLOWSTONE CUTTHROAT
Oncorhynchus clarki lewisi

DISTRIBUTION

Brown: Norway to North Africa and Ireland to Russia; introduced into North and South America, Australia, New Zealand, Africa, India.
Rainbow: from Alaska to California, and northeast Asia; introduced elsewhere in North America, and into Europe, South America, Australia, New Zealand, Africa, India.
Cutthroat: Alaska to New Mexico; introduced elsewhere.
Golden: California; introduced into over 300 mountain waters elsewhere in North America.

CUTTHROAT TROUT

The slender cutthroat trout is spotted with black, and although the coloration is otherwise very variable there is always a red "cutthroat" mark under the lower jaw, and sometimes a faint coppery line along the side. The migratory coastal cutthroat has a green back and silvery or olive sides. Cutthroat of over 18 kg (40 lb) have been recorded, but the usual maximum is about 2.27kg (5 lb).

YELLOWSTONE CUTTHROAT

Many of the local forms of the principal trout species, such as the Yellowstone variety of cutthroat, are sufficiently distinct to be classifiable as subspecies. The Yellowstone is sparsely spotted, with red-tinged gill covers.

GOLDEN TROUT

The beautiful golden trout is native to the high-altitude headwaters of the Kern River in the Sierra Nevada Mountains, California. It retains its parr marks (*see page 150*) all its life, and its maximum weight ranges from about 454 g (1 lb) in streams to around 5 kg (11 lb) in lakes.

Size comparison

Sea trout   Steelhead   Cutthroat trout   Rainbow trout   Golden trout   Stream brown trout

WHITEFISH & GRAYLING

Whitefish and grayling are widely distributed in the colder lakes and streams of the Northern Hemisphere. Grayling are popular angling species, as are several of the whitefish, but many whitefish species are threatened with extinction (see page 279) and it is illegal to fish for them in many countries and on certain waters. Grayling feed mainly on bottom-dwelling creatures such as insect larvae, crustaceans, and worms, but will also take insects at the surface. The whitefish's diet ranges from plankton to fish.

INCONNU

The large, powerful inconnu, or sheefish, is the only predatory whitefish in North America. Its average weight is about 2.27 kg (5 lb), but it can live for over 20 years and has been known to reach weights of up to 25 kg (55 lb). Most inconnu live in the estuaries and lower reaches of rivers and migrate upstream to spawn, but there are some non-migratory lake populations. The young fish feed on plankton at first, and then on small, bottom-dwelling creatures before becoming predatory during their second year.

INCONNU
Stenodus leucichthys

Protruding
lower jaw

EUROPEAN WHITEFISH
Coregonus sp.

EUROPEAN WHITEFISH

In Europe, the many whitefish species, subspecies, races, and local variants have yet to be classified definitively. In general, they are at best of minor interest to anglers, but many are netted commercially because of their tasty flesh. Common names include vendace, houting, powan, and schelly; they are slender, silvery fish that range in size from about 454 g (1 lb) (*Coregonus albula*) to around 5 kg (11 lb) (*C. pallasi*).

CISCO

Because of its herringlike size, shape, and general appearance, the cisco is also known as the lake herring. Despite being a small fish, rarely exceeding 910 g (2 lb), it is popular with anglers because it will readily take a wide range of lures and baits, including flies.

CISCO
Coregonus artedi

Size comparison

Inconnu　　　　　Lake whitefish　　　Grayling　　　　Cisco　　　European whitefish

LAKE WHITEFISH
Coregonus clupeaformis

LAKE WHITEFISH
Although it is primarily a lake-dwelling species, the lake whitefish also enters rivers. It feeds mainly on insects and crustaceans, and averages about 1.4 kg (3 lb); larger specimens, of up to 9.1 kg (20 lb), are now rare. The lake whitefish, together with the cisco, the round whitefish *(Prosopium cylindraceum)*, and the mountain whitefish *(P. williamsoni)*, is commercially important as well as being a popular angling species.

DISTRIBUTION
Lake whitefish: throughout Alaska, Canada, and northern United States.
Inconnu: Alaska, northwest Canada, northeast Asia.
Cisco: northern Canada to the Great Lakes and upper Mississippi basins.
European whitefish: a few lakes in Britain and Ireland; cool lakes, rivers, and coastal waters of mainland Europe and northern Asia.
European grayling: England and Wales to the Black Sea.
American grayling: Alaska to Hudson Bay; Montana; the northeast of Asia.

GRAYLING
Thymallus thymallus (European)
Thymallus arcticus (American)

Grayling dorsal fin
The huge, rounded, and sail-like dorsal fin of the grayling develops a more intense coloration in the breeding season. When a pair of grayling are spawning, the male curls his dorsal fin over the female.

Dwarfing
In overstocked grayling waters, the amount of food available to each fish is limited, and small, deep-bodied individuals are common.

GRAYLING
The European grayling and the American, or arctic, grayling are very similar, and nowadays are usually classified separately from the Salmonidae in a family of their own, the Thymallidae. Like the brown trout, grayling are found in cool, clean, well-oxygenated streams, and they also occur in lakes, especially in North America. Grayling are relatively small, with a maximum weight of about 2.7 kg (6 lb).

Breeding grayling
Grayling spawn in gravelly shallows in spring and early summer, lake fish entering streams to spawn. The hatchlings lurk among stones, living off their yolk sacs.

FISHING NOTES

Techniques
Whitefish and grayling are taken by fly fishing, by spinning with artificial baits, and also by float fishing or legering with natural baits.

Tackle
For fly fishing, try an a 2.4 to 2.7 m (8 to 9 ft) medium-action fly rod with a fly reel and #5 to #7 line. For float fishing or legering, try a 3.4 to 4 m (11 to 13 ft) rod with a fixed-spool reel, 910 g to 1.36 kg (2 to 3 lb) line, and hook sizes 10 to 16. For spinning, use an ultralight rod for grayling and cisco, and a medium-action rod for inconnu and lake whitefish.

Bait
Use imitative dry flies, wet flies, and nymphs for grayling, streamers for inconnu, and dry flies for cisco and lake whitefish. When spinning, use small, bright spinners and spoons. Natural baits for grayling include maggots and small worms; lake whitefish can be taken on cut fish.

BONEFISH, BLUEFISH, & TARPON

Saltwater SPECIES

These fish haunt the shallow coastal waters of the tropical and warm-temperate regions of the world, and are among the most exciting and popular marine sports species. The food of bonefish (the Albulidae) and tarpon (the Elopidae) consists mainly of crustaceans and small fish, but the bluefish (a member of the Pomatomidae) is a savage predator that will eat virtually anything edible that crosses its path.

BONEFISH

The bonefish is a bottom feeder that grubs in the mud or sand for food such as shrimps and crabs. In very shallow water, the tails of feeding bonefish often break the surface, betraying their presence to stalking anglers who wade the mudflats in pursuit of them. Adult bonefish typically weigh up to 4.54 kg (10 lb) but can reach 8.6 kg (19 lb).

Vertical bars fade with age

BONEFISH
Albula vulpes

TARPON
Megalops atlanticus

BLUEFISH
Pomatomus saltatrix

BLUEFISH

The highly migratory bluefish can grow to over 23 kg (50 lb), and travels in huge schools that go into a feeding frenzy when they encounter shoals of prey fish such as herring or menhaden. They have been known to come close inshore and attack bathers, and their sharp, prominent, triangular teeth can inflict painful wounds. They should be handled with care when caught, especially when they are being unhooked.

TARPON

The large, silvery tarpon is usually caught in tidal creeks, estuaries, mangrove swamps, and lagoons, and can sometimes be taken offshore. Its scales are large and tough, with a bright, metallic sheen, and the last ray of the dorsal fin is greatly elongated. Most tarpon landed by anglers weigh between 9.1 and 36.3 kg (20 and 80 lb), but the maximum weight is much higher and individuals of over 136 kg (300 lb) have been reported.

FISHING NOTES

Techniques

The usual techniques are trolling for bluefish, and spinning and fly fishing for bonefish and tarpon.

Tackle

For bluefish, use a 9.1 kg (20 lb) class boat rod with a 4/0 multiplier, 9.1 kg (20 lb) nylon or Dacron line, a trolling weight, a wire terminal trace, and hook sizes 4/0 to 6/0. When spinning for bonefish and tarpon, try a 2 to 2.1 m (6½ to 7 ft) medium-action rod and fixed-spool reel. Use 3.6 kg (8 lb) mono line with a mono leader for bonefish, and 6.8 kg (15 lb) mono line with

a short wire trace for tarpon. Suitable fly tackle for bonefish and tarpon would be a 2.7 to 3 m (9 to 10 ft) saltwater fly rod and a 10 cm (4 in) reel, with 3.6 kg (8 lb) backing for bonefish and 12.2 kg (27 lb) backing for tarpon; hook sizes are 6 to 1/0 for bonefish, 2 to 5/0 for tarpon.

Bait

Bluefish are usually taken on plugs or baitfish. For bonefish, spin with small leadhead lures and use shrimp imitator patterns, bucktails, and small imitation marabou streamers for fly fishing. For tarpon, spin with medium-sized plugs, and use yellow or orange splayed-wing streamers for fly fishing.

Hard fighter
The hard-fighting tarpon is justifiably regarded as one of the world's most exciting gamefish. As soon as it feels the hook being set, it begins a series of spectacular, twisting leaps in an effort to free itself, and it very often succeeds in doing so.

LADYFISH

This slender, fine-scaled fish is usually found in shallow, warm-temperate or tropical waters with mud or sand bottoms. It is generally fished for on light tackle, and despite also being commonly known as the tenpounder it usually weighs no more than about 2.27 kg (5 lb), although it can occasionally reach around 6.8 kg (15 lb).

LADYFISH
Elops saurus

Bonefish larva
The larva of the bonefish is similar to that of an eel, with a small head and a transparent body. As it matures it shrinks in size and begins to resemble a tiny adult bonefish, and then grows to its full size.

BONEFISH LARVA

SHAFTED BONEFISH
Albula nemoptera

Elongated rays

SHAFTED BONEFISH

The shafted, or longfin, bonefish resembles the bonefish (to which it is closely related) but grows to only half its size, and has distinctively elongated last rays in its dorsal and anal fins. Its habits are generally similar to those of the bonefish.

DISTRIBUTION

Bonefish: worldwide in tropical coastal waters.
Shafted bonefish: tropical coastal waters of Central and South America.
Bluefish: temperate to tropical coastal waters of the Atlantic and Indian Oceans; absent from European waters.
Tarpon: western Atlantic, Gulf of Mexico, the Caribbean, the west coast of Central America, and coast of northwest Africa.
Ladyfish: mainly Florida and the Caribbean.
Oxeye tarpon: Indo-Pacific.

The oxeye tarpon, like its Atlantic cousin, has an elongated dorsal fin ray

Caudal peduncle ends in double V shape

Lower fins lighter than those of larger tarpon

OXEYE TARPON

Also known as the oxeye herring, this Indo-Pacific fish is very like its Atlantic relative, the tarpon, but is smaller and rarely grows to more than 18 kg (40 lb). Like the tarpon, it ventures into creeks and estuaries and it fights hard when hooked.

OXEYE TARPON
Megalops cyprinoides

Size comparison

Tarpon   Oxeye tarpon   Bluefish   Bonefish   Ladyfish   Shafted bonefish

159

EELS

There are more than 20 families of eel, including the Muraenidae (morays) and Congridae (congers), and all but one of them comprise exclusively saltwater fish. The exception is the family Anguillidae, which includes the American, European, and longfinned eels, all of which mature in freshwater and travel to the sea to spawn. The American and European eels travel to the Sargasso Sea, an area in the North Atlantic; the longfinned eel and the other Australasian species of Anguillidae migrate to the Indian Ocean.

CONGER
Conger conger

MORAY

The European moray *Muraena helena*, found in the eastern Atlantic and the Mediterranean, is one of the more than 80 species of moray. All are notoriously short-tempered and quick to use their razor-sharp teeth when they feel threatened. They are rarely fished for, but are sometimes hooked when other species are being sought. *M. helena* can reach 1.3 m (4 ft 3 in) but is usually much smaller.

MORAY
Muraena helena

CALIFORNIA MORAY

This moray is found in shallow water along the coasts of California and Baja California, from Point Conception south. It attains a maximum length of about 1.5 m (5 ft).

CALIFORNIA MORAY
Gymnothorax mordax

AMERICAN EEL
Anguilla rostrata

AMERICAN EEL

Adult American eels usually spend several years in freshwater, the males staying near the mouths of rivers and the females travelling far upstream. The females grow to 1 m (3 ft 3 in) or more and a weight of over 5 kg (11 lb), but the males are much smaller, generally around 30 cm (1 ft) in length.

EUROPEAN EEL
Anguilla anguilla

EUROPEAN EEL

The European eel is very similar to its American counterpart, and the two may be a single species. After spawning, the adults die; the journey to freshwater takes young American eels about a year, and young European eels three or four years.

LONG-FINNED EEL
Anguilla reinhardtii

LONGFINNED EEL

This is one of a number of freshwater eels found in Australasia. Like the American and European eels, it migrates to the sea to spawn, possibly in the Coral Sea. It grows to 14 kg (31 lb).

Eel larvae
In the early stages of their development, eel larvae are strange, transparent, leaflike creatures called leptocephali. Later, they become elvers, miniature versions of their parents, and it is as elvers that freshwater eels arrive in rivers.

EARLY STAGE

LATER STAGE

Size comparison

Conger   California moray   Moray   Longfinned eel   American eel   European eel

CONGERS

The various species of conger differ from morays in having pectoral fins (morays have none) and from freshwater eels in being scaleless (freshwater eels have minute, embedded scales). A conger may also have a dark fringe to its dorsal and anal fins.
Conger conger, found in the Atlantic, Mediterranean and Baltic, grows to about 2.7 m (9 ft) and 65 kg (143 lb).

DISTRIBUTION

Morays: worldwide in subtropical and tropical waters; some species found in warm-temperate waters.
California moray: southern California and Baja California.
American eel: eastern North America, the Caribbean, and northeastern South America.
European eel: from Iceland and Norway to the Mediterranean.
Longfinned eel: Tasmania and eastern Australia.
Congers: most temperate and tropical waters.

Marine dwellings
Morays and congers anchor themselves in crevices in rocks or coral, or in wrecks or pier pilings, and wait with gaping mouths to seize any passing prey such as a fish, squid, or octopus. They tend to be more active at night than during the day.

FISHING NOTES

Techniques
The migratory eels are usually fished for in freshwater, by legering. Marine eels (conger and moray) are taken by fishing with natural baits from rocky shores, piers, jetties, and sea walls, and from boats over rocks and wrecks.

Tackle
For migratory eels, use a 3 to 3.7 m (10 to 12 ft), 910 g (2 lb) test curve, carp or pike rod, with a fixed-spool reel, and 2.27 kg (5 lb) monofilament line. For terminal tackle, use a running leger or fish the bait freelined, with a size 4 to 8 hook tied direct to the line. When fishing from the shore for marine eels, use a 9.1 to 22.7 kg (20 to 50 lb) class surfcasting rod with a 4/0 multiplier reel, 13.6 to 15.9 kg (30 to 35 lb) line, a running leger wire trace, a pear- or pyramid-shaped weight, and a 6/0 hook. To fish from a boat for marine eels, try a 22.7 kg (50 lb) boat rod, 8/0 multiplier reel, and 22.7 to 27.2 kg (50 to 60 lb) line. Use a wire trace, a size 8/0 hook, and a pear- or pyramid-shaped weight.

Bait
Worms are good bait for freshwater eels, as are small, dead fish. Fish baits are very effective for large eels, and they should be whole, about 13 cm (5 in) long, and punctured so that they sink. Pungent baits such as fish liver and smoked fish are also effective, and it is worth using an oily, smelly, non-floating groundbait to attract eels into the swim you are going to fish.

The marine eels can be caught on large natural baits, such as whole or cut fish, squid, and cuttlefish, and these baits should be fished on the bottom.

SEA CATFISH & BARRACUDA

The Ariidae family of sea catfish consists of about 80 species, widely distributed around the world in warm coastal waters and estuaries, and also (in the tropics) in freshwater. When caught, a sea catfish must be handled carefully, because the dorsal and pectoral fins have sharp spines that can inflict painful wounds. Barracuda belong to the Sphyraenidae family, which contains about 20 species. They are all fierce predators that feed voraciously on small, schooling species, and because they are attracted to their quarry by sight rather than smell they tend to concentrate on bright, silvery coloured prey.

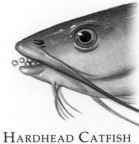

Mouth brooding
In most species of sea catfish, the male keeps the marble-sized fertilized eggs in his mouth until they hatch, which can take up to a month.

HARDHEAD CATFISH
The hardhead catfish, also called the sea catfish, is common in coastal and brackish waters from Massachusetts to Mexico. It has four barbels on its chin and two on its upper jaw, and can reach a weight of 5.4 kg (12 lb) although it usually does not exceed 910 g (2 lb). Several related species are found in the coastal waters, rivers, and lakes of northern Australia, including the blue catfish or salmon catfish (*Arius graeffei*).

GUAGUANCHE
Like other barracuda, the guaguanche has a slender, cigar-shaped body, two widely separated dorsal fins, and a protruding lower jaw; it is identifiable by the yellow stripe along its lateral line. It is found on both sides of the Atlantic, and grows to a length of about 60 cm (2 ft).

HARDHEAD CATFISH
Arius felis

GUAGUANCHE
Sphyraena guachancho

NORTHERN SENNET
Sphyraena borealis

SENNETS
The northern sennet and southern sennet are almost identical, and may in fact be a single species.
These little barracuda have the same overall coloration and both grow to about 45 cm (18 in), but the southern sennet has fewer scales on its lateral line (107 to 116 as opposed to 118 to 135) and its eyes are larger. The northern sennet is found from New England to Florida and the Gulf of Mexico, and the southern sennet from Florida to Uruguay. In the eastern Atlantic and the Mediterranean, barracuda are represented by the European barracuda (*Sphyraena sphyraena*).

GREAT BARRACUDA
Sphyraena barracuda

Large eye

SOUTHERN SENNET
Sphyraena picudilla

PACIFIC BARRACUDA
Sphyraena argentea

FISHING NOTES

Techniques
Catfish are caught by bottom fishing from the shore or piers. For barracuda fishing try trolling, or spinning from a boat or from the shore.

Tackle
For catfish, try a 3.4 or 3.7 m (11 or 12 ft) medium-action rod, with a fixed-spool reel, 3.2 to 6.8 kg (7 to 15 lb) mono line, size 4 to 6/0 hook, and a 28 g (1 oz) weight. To troll for barracuda, use a 5.4 to 13.6 kg (12 to 30 lb) class boat rod with a multiplier reel, 5.4 to 13.6 kg (12 to 30 lb) nylon line with a wire trace, a size 4/0 to 8/0 hook, and a banana-shaped trolling weight. Spinning calls for a medium spinning rod with a fixed-spool reel, 5.4 to 13.6 kg (12 to 30 lb) nylon line with a wire trace, and hook sizes 4/0 to 8/0.

Bait
Cut fish and livebaits such as sandworms are ideal for catfish, which can also be taken on jigs and plugs. For barracuda, use bright, flashy spinners, wooden plugs, strips of fish, and whole fish such as sardines, anchovies, and queenfish.

Barracuda in shallows
Barracuda are often found in shallow water, where their natural curiosity leads them to follow (and sometimes attack) swimmers.

GAFFTOPSAIL CATFISH
Bagre marinus

Very long barbel

GAFFTOPSAIL CATFISH
This catfish is recognizable by its greatly elongated dorsal spine, its two chin barbels, and the long, flattened barbel at each corner of its mouth. Its range overlaps that of the hardhead catfish, but it is less common, and its maximum weight is around 2.5 kg (5 lb 8 oz). The gafftopsail and the hardhead are both bottom feeders, taking a variety of small prey including blue crab, and are commonly caught from piers and jetties.

DISTRIBUTION
Hardhead catfish: western Atlantic and Gulf of Mexico.
Gafftopsail catfish: from Massachusetts to Venezuela.
Guaguanche: warm-temperate and tropical Atlantic waters.
Northern sennet: from New England to Florida and the Gulf of Mexico.
Southern sennet: Florida to Uruguay; Bermuda, Bahamas.
Great barracuda: tropical and temperate Atlantic waters, and the Mediterranean and Black Seas.
Pacific barracuda: Pacific coast of North America.

Dark spots below lateral line

Dark lateral stripe

GREAT BARRACUDA
This is one of the largest barracuda, growing to a length of 2 m (6 ft 6 in) and a weight of 48 kg (106 lb) or more. It is an important gamefish and puts up a hard fight when hooked, making extremely fast runs and often leaping from the water, but it has little stamina and soon tires. Small individuals are found close inshore, where they may be taken on light tackle fished from the shore or a boat, but larger fish usually stay in deeper water and are fished for by trolling with medium-heavy tackle.

PACIFIC BARRACUDA
This barracuda is found from the Gulf of Alaska to Baja California, but it is not common north of Point Conception, California. Also known as the California barracuda, it has a distinctive black stripe along its lateral line and grows to about 8.2 kg (18 lb). The Mexican barracuda (*Sphyraena ensis*) is similar, but has dark bars along its sides. Other barracudas of the Indo-Pacific region include the shortfin barracuda (*S. novae-hollandiae*), the golden barracuda (*S. flavicauda*), and the striped barracuda (*S. obtustata*).

Barracuda jaws
The powerful jaws of a barracuda are equipped with large canine teeth that seize and grip its prey, and small, very sharp teeth that cut it to ribbons.

Size comparison

Great barracuda   Pacific barracuda   Guaguanche   Hardhead catfish   Gafftopsail catfish   Northern sennet   Southern sennet

AMBERJACK & JACK

The Carangidae is a large family of predatory marine fish, and has over 200 members including amberjack, jack, and pompano (*see page 166*). They have streamlined bodies with deeply forked tails, the spiny and soft parts of their dorsal fins are separate, and they feed on fish and invertebrates such as squid. Their flesh is tasty, but you should seek local advice before eating any you catch because they can be a source of ciguatera, a distressing type of food poisoning that can be fatal.

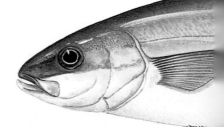

Dark band

ALMACO JACK

The almaco jack is distributed worldwide in warm waters and grows to a weight of 57 kg (126 lb) or more. It is similar to the greater amberjack and the yellowtail, but the dark bands through its eyes are more pronounced, and the front lobe of its soft dorsal fin is longer and sickle-shaped. The almaco jack of the eastern Pacific is sometimes classified as a separate species, the Pacific amberjack (*Seriola colburni*).

Dark band more pronounced than in amberjack

ALMACO JACK
Seriola rivoliana

Schooling fish
Young fish of the Carangidae family often form small schools beneath floating objects such as jellyfish. Older fish of most species roam the seas in large, fast-swimming schools, but the oldest, largest fish tend to be solitary. The carangids are widely distributed in temperate and tropical seas, and are usually at their most abundant in inshore waters.

BLUE RUNNER
Caranx crysos

Large pectoral fin

BLUE RUNNER

The blue runner is a small Atlantic jack, very closely related to the Pacific green jack (*Caranx caballus*). It grows to over 3.6 kg (8 lb) but averages less than 454 g (1 lb); like most carangids, its flesh is tasty and it is fished for commercially. It is a popular angling species, and makes a very good bait for big-game fish.

Size comparison

| Greater amberjack | Almaco jack | California yellowtail | Crevalle jack | Blue runner | Lesser amberjack |

GREATER AMBERJACK
Seriola dumerili

GREATER AMBERJACK
This fish is widely distributed in warm waters and is the largest amberjack in the Atlantic, averaging about 6.8 kg (15 lb) but capable of exceeding 80 kg (176 lb). Its overall coloration is silvery, and there is often a broad, yellow or coppery stripe along each side. The dark bands that run from its upper jaw through its eyes meet at the point where the dorsal fin begins, forming an inverted V-shape.

LESSER AMBERJACK
Seriola fasciata

LESSER AMBERJACK
The adult lesser amberjack is similar in appearance to the greater amberjack, but the dark bands on its head converge well in front of the first dorsal fin. The lesser amberjack is a relatively small fish, reaching a maximum weight of only about 4.54 kg (10 lb). It is found in the warm waters of the western Atlantic.

YOUNG FISH

Young lesser amberjack
The young of the lesser amberjack are distinctively marked with several broad, dark brown bands, usually separated by paler areas. These dark bands fade as the fish mature.

DISTRIBUTION
Almaco jack: most tropical and warm-temperate waters.
Blue runner: tropical and warm-temperate Atlantic.
Greater amberjack: most tropical and warm-temperate waters.
Lesser amberjack: western Atlantic from Massachusetts south to Brazil.
Crevalle jack: most tropical and warm-temperate waters.
California yellowtail: eastern Pacific from British Columbia south to Chile.

CREVALLE JACK
The hard-fighting crevalle jack is widely distributed in warm waters, and is found both inshore and in the open ocean. It averages under 910 g (2 lb), but can reach 25 kg (55 lb). The crevalle jack found in the Pacific is often regarded as a separate species, *Caranx caninus*; other Pacific and Indo-Pacific members of the genus *Caranx* include the trevally (*Caranx georgianus*), the ulua (*C. stellatus*), and the pauu'u (*C. ignobilis*).

Large, domed head

Dark blotches

Faint yellow stripe

CREVALLE JACK
Caranx hippos

CALIFORNIA YELLOWTAIL
Seriola lalandi dorsalis

CALIFORNIA YELLOWTAIL
This subspecies of the yellowtail (*Seriola lalandi*) has a maximum weight of about 36 kg (80 lb), and is one of the most highly prized gamefish of the Pacific coast of North America. The closely related southern yellowtail, *S. grandis*, which is abundant in Australian and New Zealand waters, can reach a weight of 52 kg (114 lb 10 oz).

FISHING NOTES

Techniques
Trolling, drifting, and spinning are the usual methods of fishing employed for amberjack and jack.

Tackle
For trolling and drifting, use a 13.6 kg (30 lb) class rod with a 4/0 multiplier reel, 13.6 kg (30 lb) mono line, a wire or heavy mono leader, and a 6/0 or 8/0 single hook. For spinning, use a heavy spinning rod with a large fixed-spool reel, 6.8 to 9.1 kg (15 to 20 lb) mono line, a wire leader, and a 4/0 or 6/0 single hook.

Bait
Chumming (groundbaiting) will attract and hold schools of fish near the boat. When trolling or drifting, use artificial lures, such as plugs and spinners, or natural baits such as squid and cut or whole fish. Good fish baits for these species include mullet, pinfish, sardines, and anchovies. For spinning, use plugs, spinners, or spoons.

Saltwater SPECIES

POMPANO, JACKMACKEREL, & ROOSTERFISH

The jackmackerel and the four species of pompano shown here (including the permit) are members of the Carangidae family, which also includes the amberjack and jack *(see page 164)*. The roosterfish is sometimes classified as a member of the Carangidae, but is usually placed in a separate family, the Nematistiidae. Pompano have deep, almost diamond-shaped bodies, while the jackmackerel and roosterfish are more elongated and streamlined. All except the African pompano venture close inshore, often into very shallow water within easy reach of shore anglers, and they offer good sport on light tackle.

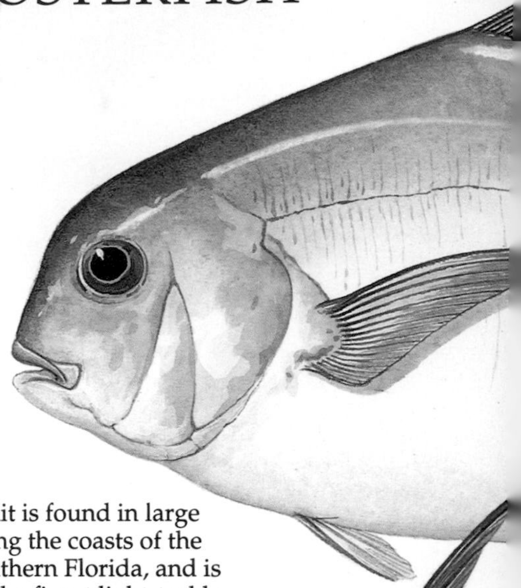

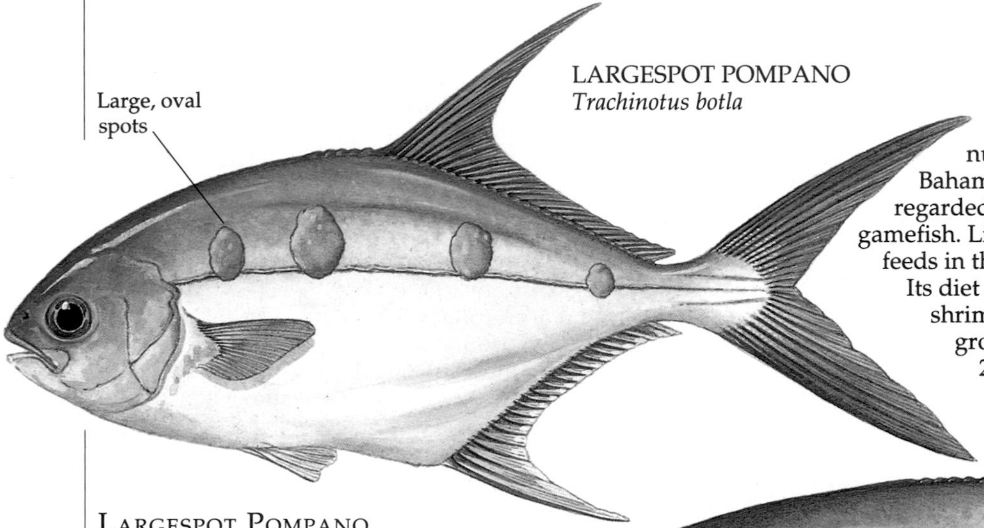

Large, oval spots

LARGESPOT POMPANO
Trachinotus botla

PERMIT
The permit is found in large numbers along the coasts of the Bahamas and southern Florida, and is regarded as one of the finest light-tackle gamefish. Like the bonefish *(see page 158)*, it feeds in the shallow waters of coral flats. Its diet includes crabs, molluscs, shrimps, and sea urchins, and it grows to a weight of over 23 kg (51 lb).

JUVENILE PERMIT

LARGESPOT POMPANO
The largespot pompano is widely distributed in coastal waters of the Indian Ocean from Africa to Australia. It is found in the surf zones of sandy beaches, and when feeding it will often swim on its side so that it can move into very shallow water. It grows to a weight of more than 2 kg (4 lb 6 oz).

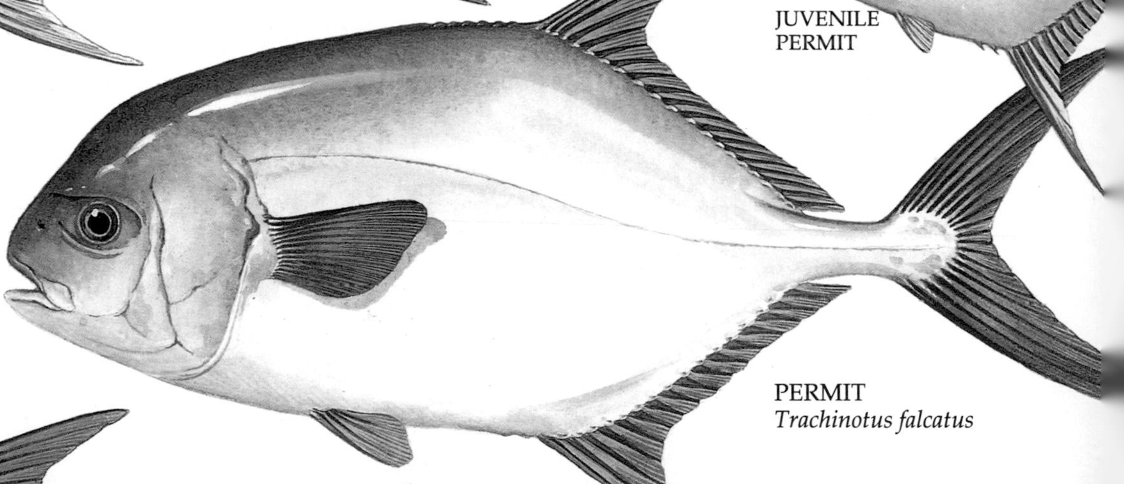

PERMIT
Trachinotus falcatus

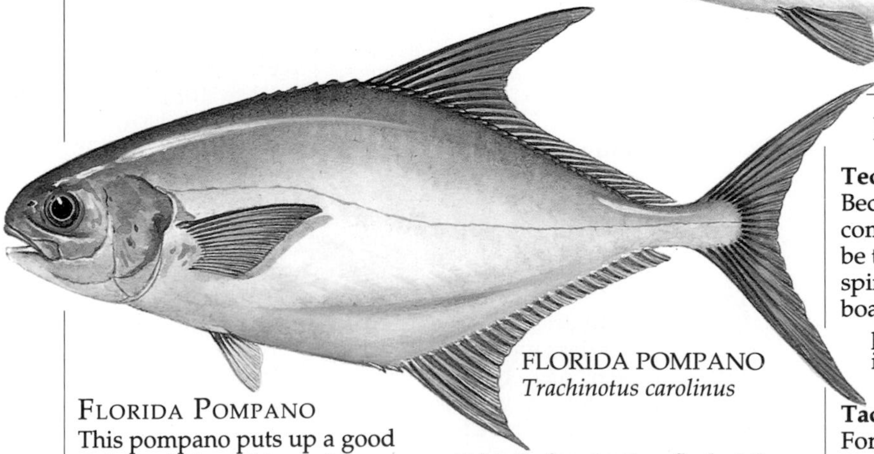

FISHING NOTES

Techniques
Because most of these species come close inshore, they can be taken by surfcasting or by spinning from the shore or a boat. The African pompano prefers deeper water and is caught by trolling.

Tackle
For surfcasting, try a 3.7 m (12 ft) rod that is capable of handling 85 to 142 g (3 to 5 oz) sinkers. For spinning and

trolling, try a 2 to 2.4 m (6½ to 8 ft) medium spinning rod with 2.7 to 5.4 kg (6 to 12 lb) mono line, a short, 9.1 kg (20 lb) mono leader, and hook sizes 2 to 2/0.

Bait
The usual baits are crabs, clams, sand fleas, small bucktails, and jigs; anchovies are an excellent bait for jackmackerel.

FLORIDA POMPANO
Trachinotus carolinus

FLORIDA POMPANO
This pompano puts up a good fight on light tackle, and is renowned for its fine-tasting flesh. Like the permit, it enters very shallow water, and is taken from beaches, piers, jetties, bridges, and drifting or anchored boats. It averages 910 g (2 lb), with a maximum weight of 3.6 kg (8 lb).

166

JUVENILE
AFRICAN
POMPANO

AFRICAN POMPANO
The African pompano is found in many warm-temperate waters, and is distributed worldwide in tropical seas. Its preferred habitat is around rocky reefs in deep water, and it can grow to a weight of around 18 kg (40 lb). Young African pompano, known as threadfish, have very deep bodies and long, threadlike dorsal and anal fin rays.

DISTRIBUTION
Permit, Florida pompano: warm-temperate and tropical western Atlantic.
African pompano: worldwide in tropical waters; warm-temperate Atlantic.
Largespot: Indian Ocean.
Roosterfish: Pacific from southern California to Peru.
Jackmackerel: Pacific from Alaska to Mexico.

Scutes
(bony scales)

AFRICAN POMPANO
Alectis ciliaris

Long filaments on
first dorsal fin

Dark body
lines

ROOSTERFISH
This fish is so named because the seven long spines of its first dorsal fin, which taper into threadlike filaments, resemble the comb of a rooster. These spines are normally folded into a groove on the fish's back, but are raised when it becomes excited. The roosterfish frequents shallow water over sandy ground, and grows to about 45 kg (100 lb). It is a fine gamefish, and is fished for commercially along the Pacific coast of Central America.

ROOSTERFISH
Nematistius pectoralis

Scutes (bony scales)
along lateral line

In large adults, second dorsal and
anal fins end in finlets with
connecting membranes

JACKMACKEREL
The slender, streamlined jackmackerel is found in the eastern Pacific and is often abundant along the coast of California, where it is an important light-tackle gamefish. It often has a dark spot at the rear of the gill cover, and the lateral line is covered in bony scales called scutes. It is found both inshore and offshore, and reaches a maximum weight of about 2.27 kg (5 lb).

JACKMACKEREL
Trachurus symmetricus

Size comparison

Roosterfish   Permit   African pompano   Jackmackerel   Florida pompano   Largespot pompano

167

COBIA, SNOOK, & BARRAMUNDI

The cobia, the only member of the Rachycentridae family, is a prized gamefish. It is also fished for commercially for its fine flesh, which is often sold smoked. Snook and barramundi belong to the Centropomidae family, which contains about 30 species. Some of the Centropomidae are exclusively marine, others are marine but move into brackish water and even into rivers; some live in rivers and spawn in brackish estuaries, while a few are found only in freshwater.

TARPON SNOOK
Centropomus pectinatus

Dark-tipped pelvic fin

COBIA

This long, slim-bodied fish occurs in most warm seas, from coastal waters to the open ocean, but is not found along the Pacific coast of North America. It has a flat head, a large mouth with a slightly protruding lower jaw, and a first dorsal fin that consists of eight separate spines. Fish and crustaceans make up the bulk of its diet, and it grows to a weight of about 68 kg (150 lb). It is usually solitary but sometimes forms small schools.

FAT SNOOK

The fat snook is a small, rather deep-bodied fish that rarely exceeds about 1.36 kg (3 lb). The most reliable way to distinguish it from other small snook is to count the number of scales along the lateral line: the fat snook has 80 to 90, the tarpon snook 65 to 70, and the black about 60.

FAT SNOOK
Centropomus parallelus

First dorsal fin reduced to eight spines

COBIA
Rachycentron canadum

FISHING NOTES

Techniques
Cobia are usually taken by bottom fishing with lures or natural baits. Lure fishing is an effective technique for barramundi and for snook, which can also be taken on fly tackle.

Tackle
For cobia, use a heavy spinning rod with 6.8 to 9.1 kg (15 to 20 lb) mono line and a 90 cm (3 ft) leader of wire or 27.2 to 36.3 kg (60 to 80 lb) mono, and hook sizes 2/0 to 4/0. Try a 1.8 m (6 ft) surfcaster with 4.54 to 5.4 kg (10 to 12 lb) mono when lure

fishing for snook, and a fast, 2.7 m (9 ft) tip-action rod for fly fishing. For barramundi, use a 2.7 to 3 m (9 to 10 ft) spinning rod with 9.1 to 13.6 kg (20 to 30 lb) mono line.

Bait
Good baits for cobia include natural baits such as fish, crabs, and shrimps, and artificials including large plugs with bright blue or silver finishes, and 42 to 85 g (1½ to 3 oz) jigs with yellow or white skirts. Try plugs, spoons, jigs, shrimps, streamer flies, and fish (especially mullet) for snook, and jointed, 15 cm (6 in) shallow-diving plugs for barramundi.

Cobia habitat
Cobia like to lurk in the cover of pilings and wrecks, and beneath buoys, floating wreckage, and other flotsam. They are also often found in the company of cruising sharks.

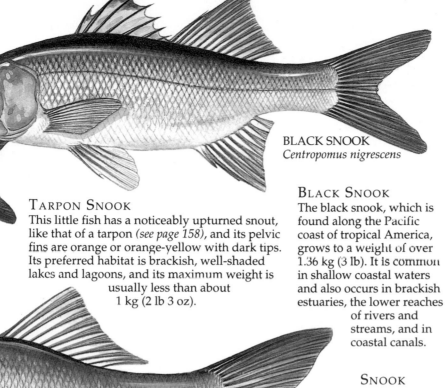

BLACK SNOOK
Centropomus nigrescens

TARPON SNOOK

This little fish has a noticeably upturned snout, like that of a tarpon *(see page 158)*, and its pelvic fins are orange or orange-yellow with dark tips. Its preferred habitat is brackish, well-shaded lakes and lagoons, and its maximum weight is usually less than about 1 kg (2 lb 3 oz).

BLACK SNOOK

The black snook, which is found along the Pacific coast of tropical America, grows to a weight of over 1.36 kg (3 lb). It is common in shallow coastal waters and also occurs in brackish estuaries, the lower reaches of rivers and streams, and in coastal canals.

DISTRIBUTION

Cobia: most warm seas, but not along the Pacific coast of North America.
Fat snook, tarpon snook: southern Florida and West Indies to Brazil.
Black snook: eastern Pacific from Baja California to Peru.
Snook: western Atlantic from South Carolina to Brazil.
Barramundi: Asian coastal regions and islands from the Persian Gulf to China, and around the northern half of the Australian coast.

SNOOK

This large, pikelike fish has a protruding lower jaw and a distinctive black lateral stripe that extends into its tail. It is an active predator, feeding on fish, shrimps, and crabs, and averages 2.27 to 3.6 kg (5 to 8 lb) with a maximum of over 24 kg (53 lb). Although it is usually found in shallow coastal waters, it also explores estuaries, mangrove swamps, and creeks, and sometimes travels well inland along rivers and canals. It should be handled with care when caught, because the edges of its gill covers are very sharp.

SNOOK
Centropomus undecimalis

BARRAMUNDI (GIANT PERCH)
Lates calcarifer

Large pelvic fin

BARRAMUNDI

The barramundi, or giant perch, lives in rivers, creeks, and mangrove swamps, and spawns in estuaries and coastal waters. It feeds on fish, crayfish, crabs, shrimps, and insects, and grows to a weight of 60 kg (132 lb); the closely related Nile perch (*Lates niloticus*), an African freshwater fish, can reach 91 kg (200 lb).

Size comparison

Barramundi   Cobia   Snook   Black snook   Fat snook   Tarpon snook

169

SURFPERCH

The Embiotocidae family consists of 21 species, of which two occur in Japan and Korea; the rest are found along the Pacific coast of North America, and all but one are marine species. The exception is the tule perch (*Hysterocarpus traski*), a freshwater fish that has a limited distribution in central California. Surfperch males use their anal fins to transfer sperm to the females, which give birth to live young. Their food includes algae, invertebrates, and fish, and they range in length from 10 to 45 cm (4 to 18 in).

Thick lips

RUBBERLIP SEAPERCH
Rhacochilus toxotes

RUBBERLIP SEAPERCH
In common usage, the term "surfperch" usually applies to members of the Embiotocidae that live in the surf zone. Those that do not primarily inhabit this zone, including the rubberlip, are called "seaperch", and species with no distinct habitat are simply "perch". The rubberlip, which is found in rocky areas and around pilings, is the largest of the Embiotocidae and reaches a length of around 45 cm (18 in).

Large eye

WALLEYE SURFPERCH
Hyperprosopon argenteum

WALLEYE SURFPERCH
The walleye surfperch is recognizable by its large eyes and its black-tipped pelvic fins, and its anal and tail fins often have dark edges. Its maximum length is about 30 cm (12 in), and it inhabits the surf zones of sandy beaches and is often found around piers. It is a very popular angling species and is of commercial importance.

Black tip to pelvic fin

Breeding female has dark anal fin

FISHING NOTES

Techniques
Surfperch are usually caught by light surfcasting or by bottom fishing.

Tackle
For surfcasting, use a light surfcaster with a small multiplier reel, 4.54 to 6.8 kg (10 to 15 lb) monofilament line, a size 1/0 hook (or smaller, depending on species sought),

and a grip or bomb-shaped sinker. For bottom fishing, try a spinning rod or a 5.4 kg (12 lb) class boat rod, fitted with a fixed-spool reel or small multiplier reel, 4.54 to 6.8 kg (10 to 15 lb) monofilament line, a size 1/0 hook (or smaller), and a bomb-shaped sinker.

Bait
Surfperch baits include cut fish and crab, ghost shrimps, clams, and mussels.

SHINER PERCH
This little surfperch, which grows to about 18 cm (7 in), is abundant and easily caught from piers, which makes it very popular with young anglers. Its habitat ranges from shallow water, where it frequents weedbeds, pilings, and piers, to depths of about 146 m (480 ft), and it will also venture into brackish areas and sometimes into freshwater. There is often a dark spot above its upper lip.

REDTAIL SURFPERCH
Amphistichus rhodoterus

REDTAIL SURFPERCH
This is one of the most common surfperch species. It grows to a length of around 41 cm (16 in), and is recognizable by its red fins and the brownish bars on its sides. The calico surfperch (*Amphistichus koelzi*) has a similar coloration, but is smaller, and its dorsal fin spines are not longer than the soft rays, as they are in the redtail.

STRIPED SEAPERCH
This beautiful fish grows to 38 cm (15 in) and is found over rocky ground and kelp beds from shallow water out to depths of about 21 m (70 ft). Although it occurs as far south as Baja California, it is most common in the cooler waters north of Point Conception.

DISTRIBUTION
Rubberlip seaperch: from northern California to central Baja California.
Walleye surfperch: from Vancouver Island to Baja California.
Shiner perch: southeast Alaska to Baja California.
Redtail surfperch: Vancouver Island to Monterey Bay.
Striped seaperch: southeast Alaska to Baja California.
Barred surfperch: northern California to Baja California.

BARRED SURFPERCH
The barred surfperch is usually silvery or brassy, with eight to ten brownish bars on each side, but in some individuals these bars are absent. It is found in the surf zones of sandy beaches and also further out, to depths of 70 m (230 ft) or more. It is an important angling species, and can reach 43 cm (17 in) and 2 kg (4 lb 6 oz), but most of those caught are less than 30 cm (12 in) and 454 g (1 lb).

STRIPED SEAPERCH
Embiotoca lateralis

BARRED SURFPERCH
Amphistichus argenteus

Males lose yellow bars in summer

SHINER PERCH
Cymatogaster aggregata

All species give birth to live young, usually 3 to 10 per litter

Size comparison

Rubberlip seaperch   Barred surfperch   Redtail surfperch   Striped seaperch   Walleye surfperch   Shiner perch

GADIDAE

COD, HAKE, LING, & BURBOT

The members of the Gadidae, the codfish family, are distributed widely around the world, especially in the colder waters of the Northern Hemisphere. Most live at or near the bottom, feeding on fish and invertebrates, and many of them have great commercial importance as well as being popular quarry for sea anglers. Unfortunately, the commercial value of many species has led to serious overfishing in some areas, particularly the North Atlantic. As a result, there has been a serious decline in the numbers and sizes of these species.

Dark spot on flank behind gill cover

Heavily toothed jaw

POLLACK

Like many other members of the Gadidae, such as the Atlantic cod, the pollack has three dorsal and two anal fins. It is most easily identified by its protruding lower jaw and the distinct curve of its lateral line. Small pollack are found over sandy bottoms, but the larger ones, which can reach a weight of about 13 kg (29 lb), prefer rocky ground.

SAITHE

The saithe is similar to the pollack, but its upper and lower jaws are approximately the same size, and its lateral line is only slightly curved. Its maximum size is about 32 kg (71 lb), and the largest individuals are usually found in the vicinity of reefs.

POLLACK
Pollachius pollachius

Downward-curving lateral line

SAITHE
Pollachius virens

Protruding lower jaw

BURBOT

This is the only member of the codfish family that lives exclusively in freshwater. It is widely distributed in deep, cold waters in northern latitudes, and although it averages about 910 g (2 lb) it can grow much larger, and specimens weighing in at around 32 kg (71 lb) have been taken from European waters. It is probably now extinct in the British Isles.

BURBOT
Lota lota

FISHING NOTES

Techniques
The marine codfish may be fished for from the shore by surfcasting or by fishing from rocks, piers, and jetties with natural baits, and from a boat with natural baits or by feathering, jigging (pirking), or using attractor spoons in conjunction with baited hooks. The burbot, the freshwater member of the codfish family, is a slow-moving fish that feeds mostly at night and may be caught by static legering in shallow water.

Tackle
When shore fishing for the marine species, try a 3.7 m (12 ft) surfcasting rod with a multiplier reel, 13.6 kg (30 lb) nylon line, hook sizes 2/0 to 8/0, and a bomb-shaped or grip weight. To fish for the marine species from a boat, use a 13.6 kg (30 lb) class boat rod with a 4/0 to 6/0 multiplier reel, 13.6 kg (30 lb) wire or nylon line, and hook sizes 2/0 to 8/0. When using natural baits and when feathering, use a bomb-shaped weight. For burbot, try a 3 to 3.7 m (10 to 12 ft) leger rod with a fixed-spool reel, 2.7 kg (6 lb) mono line, and size 10 to 14 hook.

Bait
The wide range of effective natural baits for the marine species includes many invertebrates, such as mussels, lugworms, ragworms, clams, razorshells, and squid. Fish baits, either cut or whole, are also worth trying, especially the oily fish such as herring, mackerel, sprat, and pilchard. Among the artificial baits, leadhead jigs, metal pirks, and plastic sandeels will get results, and a bunch of orange or white feather hackles on a 5/0 hook is excellent as a boat fishing lure. Burbot will take a bunch of large worms or a small fish.

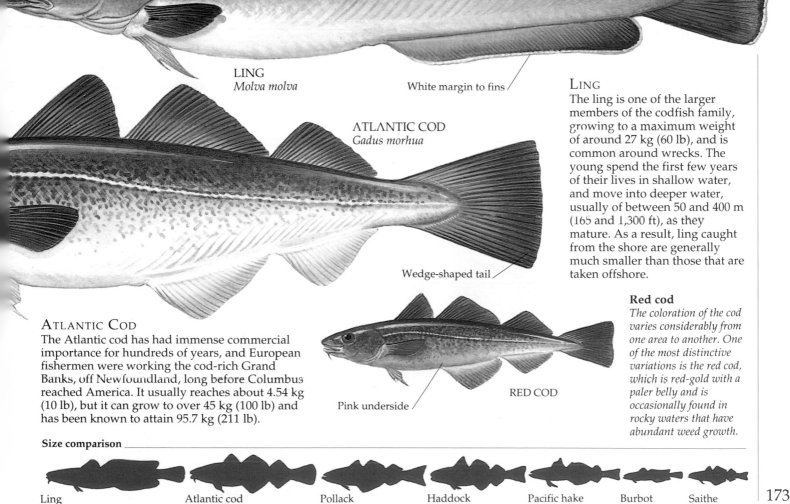

HADDOCK
Melanogrammus aeglefinus

PACIFIC HAKE
Merluccius productus

Spiny rays in dorsal and anal fins

LING
Molva molva

White margin to fins

ATLANTIC COD
Gadus morhua

Wedge-shaped tail

Pink underside

RED COD

HADDOCK
The features that help to distinguish the haddock from other codfish are its high, pointed first dorsal fin, its black lateral line, and a dark "thumbprint" above its pectoral fin. In addition, its lower jaw, which carries a small barbel, is shorter than the upper. It travels in large schools, usually near the bottom at depths of 40 m (130 ft) or more, and averages less than 2.27 kg (5 lb) with a usual maximum of around 6 kg (13 lb).

PACIFIC HAKE
In all the many species of hake, the second and third dorsal fins are joined to form one long fin, as are the anal fins; in several species, such as the Pacific hake, these fins are notched or indented. The Pacific hake and its Atlantic cousin *(Merluccius merluccius)* reach weights of over 11 kg (25 lb).

DISTRIBUTION
Pollack: northeastern Atlantic and northwest Mediterranean.
Saithe: North Atlantic.
Burbot: northern Eurasia, Alaska, Canada, the northern United States.
Haddock: North Atlantic.
Pacific hake: North Pacific; other hake occur elsewhere in the Pacific and the Atlantic.
Ling: northeast Atlantic.
Atlantic cod: North Atlantic; other varieties occur elsewhere in the Atlantic and the Pacific.

LING
The ling is one of the larger members of the codfish family, growing to a maximum weight of around 27 kg (60 lb), and is common around wrecks. The young spend the first few years of their lives in shallow water, and move into deeper water, usually of between 50 and 400 m (165 and 1,300 ft), as they mature. As a result, ling caught from the shore are generally much smaller than those that are taken offshore.

Red cod
The coloration of the cod varies considerably from one area to another. One of the most distinctive variations is the red cod, which is red-gold with a paler belly and is occasionally found in rocky waters that have abundant weed growth.

ATLANTIC COD
The Atlantic cod has had immense commercial importance for hundreds of years, and European fishermen were working the cod-rich Grand Banks, off Newfoundland, long before Columbus reached America. It usually reaches about 4.54 kg (10 lb), but it can grow to over 45 kg (100 lb) and has been known to attain 95.7 kg (211 lb).

Size comparison

Ling   Atlantic cod   Pollack   Haddock   Pacific hake   Burbot   Saithe

BILLFISH & SWORDFISH

Highly prized by big-game anglers, the spectacularly hard-fighting billfish and swordfish roam widely through the world's tropical and warm-temperate seas, occasionally venturing into higher latitudes in summer. In all of these huge, fast-swimming fish – marlin, spearfish, sailfish, and swordfish – the upper jaw is elongated into a "bill" or "sword".

SHORTBILL SPEARFISH
Tetrapturus angustirostris

SPEARFISH

Spearfish are the smallest of the billfish, reaching 2.1 to 2.4 m (7 to 8 ft) and a weight of 40 to 52 kg (90 to 115 lb). The upper jaw of the shortbill (a Pacific species) is only about 50 per cent longer than the lower, whereas in the longbill (an Atlantic fish) the upper jaw is at least twice the length of the lower. A third species of spearfish, *Tetrapturus belone*, is found in the Mediterranean. Spearfish are seldom found in coastal waters, except in areas that have steep drop-offs.

LONGBILL SPEARFISH
Tetrapturus pfluegeri

SAILFISH

The Atlantic and Pacific sailfish are classified as the same species, but the Pacific variety is much the heavier of the two, growing to about 110 kg (240 lb) and 3.3 m (10 ft 10 in) as opposed to the 58 kg (128 lb) and 2.4 m (8 ft) of the Atlantic fish. A sailfish is easily recognizable by its long bill and huge, sail-like dorsal fin; the length of the longest ray of this fin is some 150 per cent or more of the maximum depth of the body.

SAILFISH
Istiophorus platypterus

STRIPED MARLIN
Tetrapturus audax

SWORDFISH
Xiphias gladius

SWORDFISH

The swordfish is the only member of the Xiphiidae family. Like the billfish, it has a greatly elongated upper jaw, but unlike that of a billfish the swordfish's upper jaw is flat in cross-section rather than round. Other features distinguishing the swordfish from the billfish are body shape and scales. A billfish has a body that is compressed in cross-section and has narrow, pointed scales; the body of a swordfish is nearly round, and the adult fish has no scales. In size, the swordfish is comparable to the largest billfish, reaching 4.6 m (15 ft) and weighing up to 590 kg (1,300 lb).

Natural food
Billfish and swordfish feed on fish (particularly tuna and herring), crustaceans, and squid. Once pursued, the quarry has little chance of escaping these powerful, fast-swimming predators.

FISHING NOTES

Techniques

Trolling at or close to the surface is the usual technique for these species, but swordfish and blue marlin may also be taken by deep still-fishing using live or dead natural baits. In addition, the sailfish offers exciting sport to the saltwater fly fisherman. A billfish must be handled carefully when it is brought to the boat to be hauled on board or cut free, because the bill can inflict nasty wounds, and it is wise to wear gloves to protect your hands because the bill is very rough.

Tackle

For the smaller species, use a 9.1 to 22.7 kg (20 to 50 lb) class boat rod with a 20- to 50-class lever drag reel or a 6/0- or 7-class star drag reel. For larger fish use a 36.3 to 59 kg (80 to 130 lb) class rod with an 80- to 130-class lever drag or 12/0 or 14/0 star drag. Use 9.1 to 59 kg (20 to 130 lb) nylon or Dacron line with a heavy wire or nylon trace. Hooks should be flat forged, 8/0 to 14/0. When fly fishing for sailfish, use a heavy fly rod with a suitable saltwater fly reel, a weight-forward #10 line with a 9.1 kg (20 lb) leader, and a streamer fly on a 2/0 to 5/0 hook.

Bait

Live or dead fish, such as mullet, mackerel, herring, and squid, and lures such as Kona Heads, feathered jigs, and plastic squids.

DISTRIBUTION

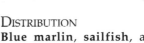

Blue marlin, **sailfish**, and **swordfish**: worldwide.
Black and **striped marlins**: Pacific and Indian Oceans.
Shortbill spearfish: Pacific.
White marlin, **longbill spearfish**: Atlantic.

BLUE MARLIN
Makaira nigricans

BLUE MARLIN

The blue marlin, the biggest of the billfish, may exceed 4.6 m (15 ft) and 910 kg (2,000 lb). It is rivalled in size by the black marlin (*Makaira indicus*), and fish of both species weighing over 455 kg (1,000 lb) have been taken on rod and line. Once hooked, a marlin of any size will put up a tremendous fight.

Marlinsuckers

Marlins are often accompanied by remoras (suckers), which cling to their hosts with suction discs on the tops of their heads. They feed on scraps of the marlins' food.

STRIPED MARLIN

The striped marlin is an important sport fish of the Pacific and Indian Oceans. It grows to more than 4 m (13 ft) and about 313 kg (690 lb), but in the waters accessible to anglers those caught are usually 91 to 113 kg (200 to 250 lb). Some of the best striped marlin fishing is to be found off the coasts of Chile and New Zealand, where fish in the 180 to 227 kg (400 to 500 lb) range have been taken.

Size

The billfish and the swordfish range in maximum size from the 2.4 m (8 ft) of the shortbill spearfish to the 4.6 m (15 ft) of the blue marlin.

0   Blue marlin   5 m (16 ft 5 in)

Size comparison

Blue marlin   Swordfish   Striped marlin   Sailfish   Longbill spearfish   Shortbill spearfish

WRASSE & DOLPHINFISH

Wrasse belong to the Labridae family, which has more than 400 members distributed widely in coastal tropical and temperate waters. A typical wrasse has thick lips and strong teeth, which it uses to crush shellfish, and swims by flapping its pectoral fins rather than by using its tail. Wrasse range in size from small species about 10 cm (4 in) long up to the 2.3 m (7 ft 6 in) giant maori wrasse (*Cheilinus undulatus*) of Indo-Pacific waters. The dolphinfish is one of the two members of the Coryphaenidae family.

CALIFORNIA SHEEPHEAD

The coloration of the California sheephead varies with age and sex. Adult males are typically a striking black and red, but females are usually pinkish overall; both sexes have white throats. Young fish are red, with a dark spot on each fin. This wrasse is found along the coast of southern California, usually over rocky ground and kelp beds, at depths of about 3 to 55 m (10 to 180 ft). It grows to a maximum of around 90 cm (3 ft) and 16.4 kg (36 lb 4 oz).

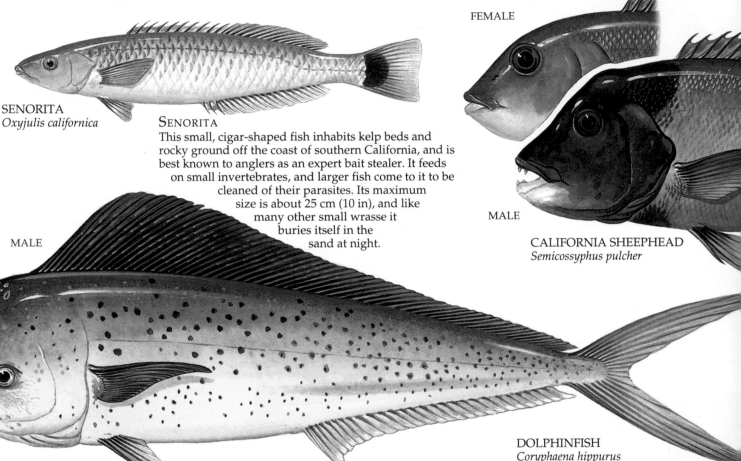

SENORITA
Oxyjulis californica

FEMALE

MALE

SENORITA

This small, cigar-shaped fish inhabits kelp beds and rocky ground off the coast of southern California, and is best known to anglers as an expert bait stealer. It feeds on small invertebrates, and larger fish come to it to be cleaned of their parasites. Its maximum size is about 25 cm (10 in), and like many other small wrasse it buries itself in the sand at night.

MALE

CALIFORNIA SHEEPHEAD
Semicossyphus pulcher

DOLPHINFISH
Coryphaena hippurus

DOLPHINFISH

The dolphinfish, also known as the dolphin or dorado, grows to about 40 kg (88 lb). Its diet consists mainly of fish (especially flying fish) plus squid and crustaceans, and it puts up a tremendous fight when hooked, making fast, powerful runs and leaping and tailwalking over the surface. The flesh of the dolphinfish is delicious, and is often sold under its Hawaiian name, *mahi mahi*. The much smaller pompano dolphin (*Coryphaena equisetis*), which resembles the female dolphinfish, reaches a weight of about 2.27 kg (5 lb).

FISHING NOTES

Techniques
Most wrasse are taken by bottom fishing from the shore or cliffs. The usual techniques for dolphinfish are drift fishing, trolling, and spinning.

Tackle
For wrasse, try a 3 to 3.7 m (10 to 12 ft) light surfcasting or heavy spinning rod with 5.4 to 6.8 kg (12 to 15 lb) mono line. Terminal tackle should be a size 1/0 or 2/0

hook on a paternoster or running leger, with the sinker attached by a sacrificial weak link. For dolphinfish, try a heavy spinning rod or a 9.1 kg (20 lb) class boat rod, with 9.1 kg (20 lb) mono line and a 4/0 hook.

Bait
Wrasse will take a wide range of natural baits, including worms, crabs, molluscs, and crustaceans, and dolphinfish take fish, plugs, and spoons.

FEMALE

Head shape
The heads of female dolphinfish, and of young of both sexes, are more rounded than those of adult males.

FEMALE

MALE

TAUTOG
Tautoga onitis

Concave tail

TAUTOG

The tautog is a large, western Atlantic wrasse, found over rocky ground and around wrecks and pilings. Females and young fish are a pale olive or brownish grey, with dark mottles and blotches, but adult males are darker, with much less blotching. The tautog feeds mainly on mussels and other shellfish, and its average weight is about 1.36 kg (3 lb), with a maximum of around 10.9 kg (24 lb).

BALLAN WRASSE
Labrus bergylta

BALLAN WRASSE

The overall coloration of the ballan wrasse varies from reddish brown to dark green, with an abundant covering of small, pale spots. It inhabits kelp beds, rocky ground, and wrecks, in waters up to 20 m (66 ft) deep, and its maximum weight is about 4.25 kg (9 lb 6 oz).

Pointed snout

CUNNER
Tautogolabrus adspersus

CUNNER

Like the tautog, the cunner is a western Atlantic species, and where their ranges overlap (from Maine to New Jersey) they are often found together. They are similar in overall appearance and habits, but the cunner is smaller and slimmer than the tautog, averaging only about 113 g (4 oz) with a maximum of 910 g (2 lb), and has a noticeably pointed snout.

Wrasse mouth
When feeding, a wrasse extends its lips to expose its large, strong teeth.

WRASSE & DOLPHINFISH

DISTRIBUTION
California sheephead: eastern Pacific from Monterey Bay to the Gulf of California.
Senorita: eastern Pacific from northern California to central Baja California.
Dolphinfish: worldwide in open waters of tropical and warm-temperate seas.
Tautog: western Atlantic from Nova Scotia to South Carolina.
Cunner: western Atlantic from Newfoundland and Gulf of St. Lawrence to Chesapeake Bay.
Ballan wrasse: northeastern Atlantic from Scotland and southern Norway to Morocco.

Size comparison

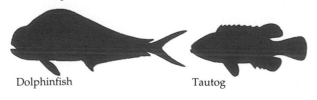  

Dolphinfish   Tautog   California sheephead   Ballan wrasse   Cunner   Senorita

177

SNAPPER

Most of the 230 or so species of snapper that make up the Lutjanidae family are found in tropical seas, but a few also occur in warm-temperate waters. They are predatory fish, with sharp, conical teeth, including one or two large canine teeth on either side of the front of each jaw. These canine teeth help to distinguish the snappers from the groupers *(see page 200)*, many species of which are similar in overall appearance. Large numbers of snapper are taken in shallow coastal waters and over reefs by anglers and spearfishers, and some species are fished for commercially.

Long canine teeth

MUTTON SNAPPER

This is one of the most common snappers in the Caribbean and the waters off southern Florida, and is found near coral heads, in shallow channels and tidal creeks, on coral flats, and in blue holes – deep, circular holes or pits in the seabed. Its coloration is variable, but there is a blue stripe beneath each eye and a small dark spot on each side. Adults usually weigh from 2.27 to 4.54 kg (5 to 10 lb), and the maximum weight is about 11.3 kg (25 lb).

Blue stripe

MUTTON SNAPPER
Lutjanus analis

GRAY SNAPPER

The gray snapper, also known as the mangrove snapper, is found in the same waters as the mutton snapper and also occurs along the coast of tropical western Africa. It is most common along mangrove shores, but also lives over reefs, and grows to about 4.54 kg (10 lb). The overall coloration is greyish, sometimes tinged with red or copper, and there is often a dark stripe running from the snout through each eye.

GRAY SNAPPER
Lutjanus griseus

LANE SNAPPER

This little snapper is identifiable by its pink and yellow stripes, the black edge of its tail fin, and the large dark spot on each side between the dorsal fin and the lateral line. It is found in shallow water throughout the tropical west Atlantic, and although it usually weighs less than 454 g (1 lb) it is popular with anglers because it can be caught from piers and the shore and is good to eat.

LANE SNAPPER
Lutjanus synagris

FISHING NOTES

Techniques
Cubera, mutton snapper, and red snapper are taken by slow bottom trolling. Cubera and mutton snapper are also brought to the surface by chumming, and then taken by spinning with artificial lures. Spinning, with either artificial lures or natural baits, will take gray snapper, lane snapper, and mangrove jack.

Tackle
For trolling, try a medium spinning rod with a fixed-spool reel, 6.8 to 9.1 kg (15 to 20 lb) mono line, a 30 cm (12 in) wire or heavy mono leader, and a size 2/0 hook. For spinning, use a light or medium spinning rod with a multiplier reel, 6.8 to 9.1 kg (15 to 20 lb) mono line, a 30 cm (12 in) wire or heavy mono leader (use transparent mono for gray snapper), and a size 2/0 treble hook.

Bait
Good natural baits for cubera, mutton, red, and lane snapper include shrimp and cut fish such as mullet. Artificial lures used for cubera snapper, mutton snapper, and mangrove jack include bucktails, feathers, and jigs, and plugs with a flashy, silvery finish. These often work best when fished with a jerky retrieve. The best bait to use when fishing for gray snapper is live shrimp.

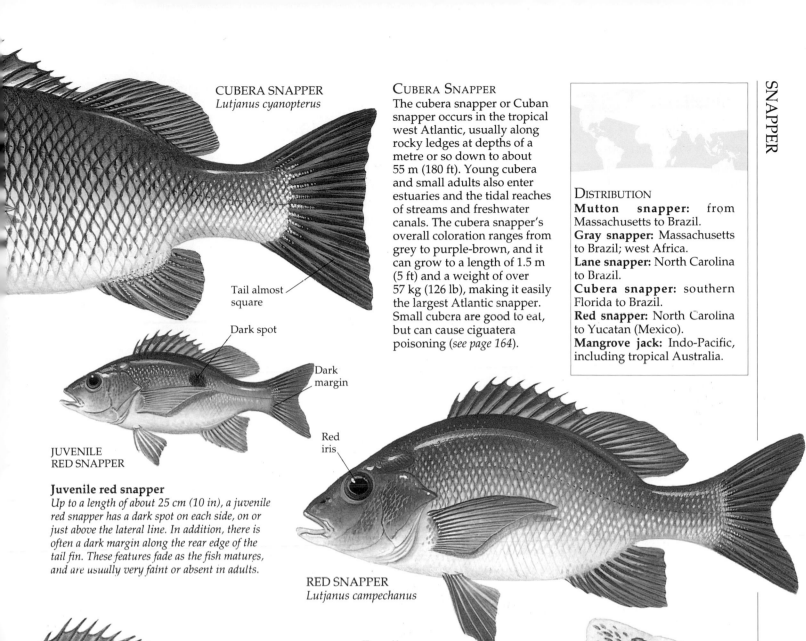

CUBERA SNAPPER
Lutjanus cyanopterus

Tail almost square

Dark spot

Dark margin

Red iris

JUVENILE RED SNAPPER

Juvenile red snapper
Up to a length of about 25 cm (10 in), a juvenile red snapper has a dark spot on each side, on or just above the lateral line. In addition, there is often a dark margin along the rear edge of the tail fin. These features fade as the fish matures, and are usually very faint or absent in adults.

RED SNAPPER
Lutjanus campechanus

MANGROVE JACK
Lutjanus argentimaculatus

CUBERA SNAPPER
The cubera snapper or Cuban snapper occurs in the tropical west Atlantic, usually along rocky ledges at depths of a metre or so down to about 55 m (180 ft). Young cubera and small adults also enter estuaries and the tidal reaches of streams and freshwater canals. The cubera snapper's overall coloration ranges from grey to purple-brown, and it can grow to a length of 1.5 m (5 ft) and a weight of over 57 kg (126 lb), making it easily the largest Atlantic snapper. Small cubera are good to eat, but can cause ciguatera poisoning (*see page 164*).

RED SNAPPER
This snapper occurs at depths of about 37 to 183 m (120 to 600 ft), and its maximum weight is about 16 kg (35 lb). It is found from North Carolina to Mexico, and in the south its range overlaps that of the similar Caribbean red snapper (*Lutjanus purpureus*).

MANGROVE JACK
The mangrove jack, also known as the silver jack, is an Indo-Pacific species. It inhabits coral reefs as an adult but spawns, and matures to a weight of about 4 kg (8 lb 13 oz), in mangrove estuaries. Like most snappers, its coloration tends to vary with age, size, and habitat.

DISTRIBUTION
Mutton snapper: from Massachusetts to Brazil.
Gray snapper: Massachusetts to Brazil; west Africa.
Lane snapper: North Carolina to Brazil.
Cubera snapper: southern Florida to Brazil.
Red snapper: North Carolina to Yucatan (Mexico).
Mangrove jack: Indo-Pacific, including tropical Australia.

Red snapper schools
The red snapper forms large schools that swim close to the bottom over rocky ground. These schools are easily detected by sonar.

Size comparison

Cubera snapper   Red snapper   Mangrove jack   Mutton snapper   Gray snapper   Lane snapper

Saltwater SPECIES

MULLET

There are about 70 species of mullet in the Mugilidae family, distributed worldwide in temperate and tropical waters. Most live close to the shore and often move into estuaries and rivers, and some, including the Australian mullet, inhabit freshwater. They are primarily bottom-feeders, living on algae, organic detritus, and small, mud-dwelling organisms, and are fished for commercially as well as by anglers. The red mullet belongs to the Mullidae family (the goatfish), which consists of over 50 species widely distributed in warm waters.

STRIPED MULLET

This is one of the largest and most widely distributed of the mullet family, reaching a weight of about 6.8 kg (15 lb) and occurring in most warm seas. It is the only species of mullet found along the Pacific coast of North America. Its stripes are formed by horizontal rows of small dark spots, and there is a dark patch at the base of each pectoral fin. The origin of the second dorsal fin is in line with that of the anal fin.

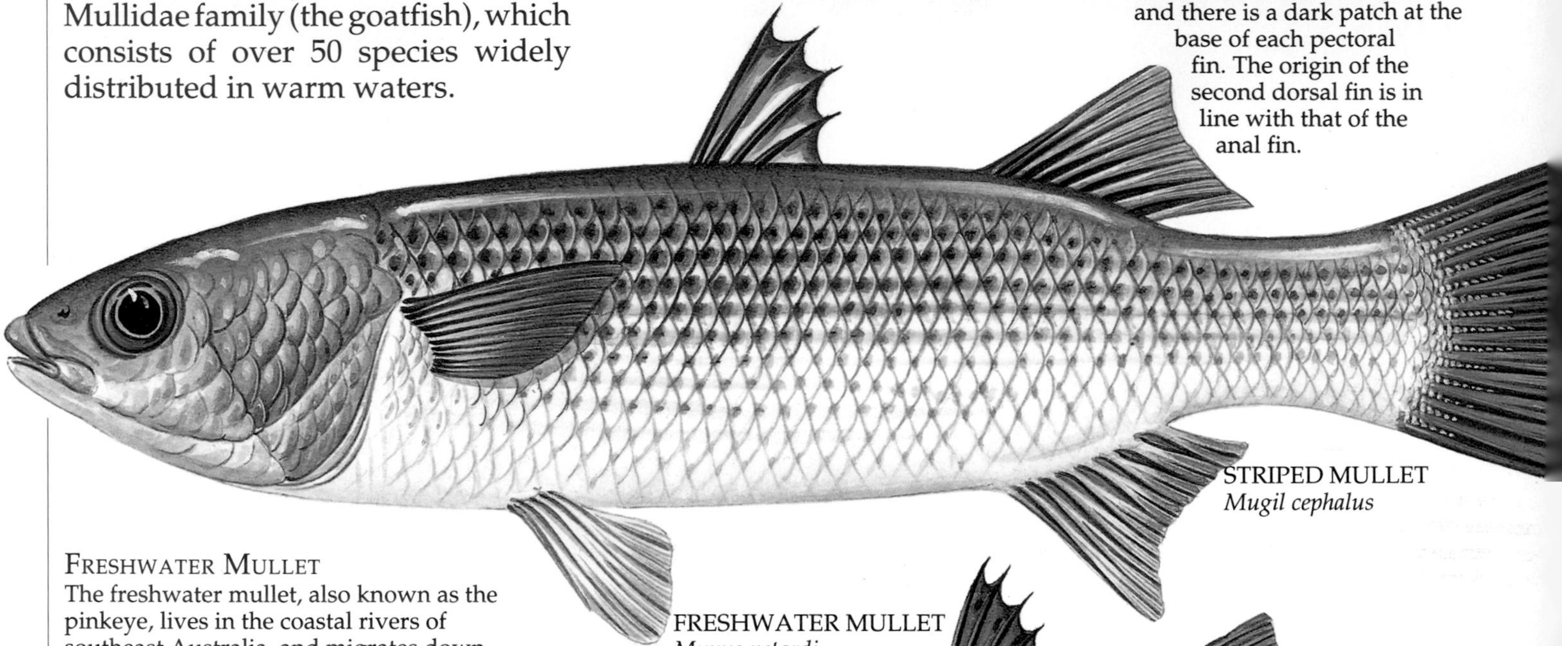

STRIPED MULLET
Mugil cephalus

FRESHWATER MULLET

The freshwater mullet, also known as the pinkeye, lives in the coastal rivers of southeast Australia, and migrates downstream to estuaries to spawn. It usually grows to about 40 cm (16 in), but can reach twice that length and a weight of 7.5 kg (16 lb 8 oz). Like marine mullet, it feeds mainly on algae and detritus.

FRESHWATER MULLET
Myxus petardi

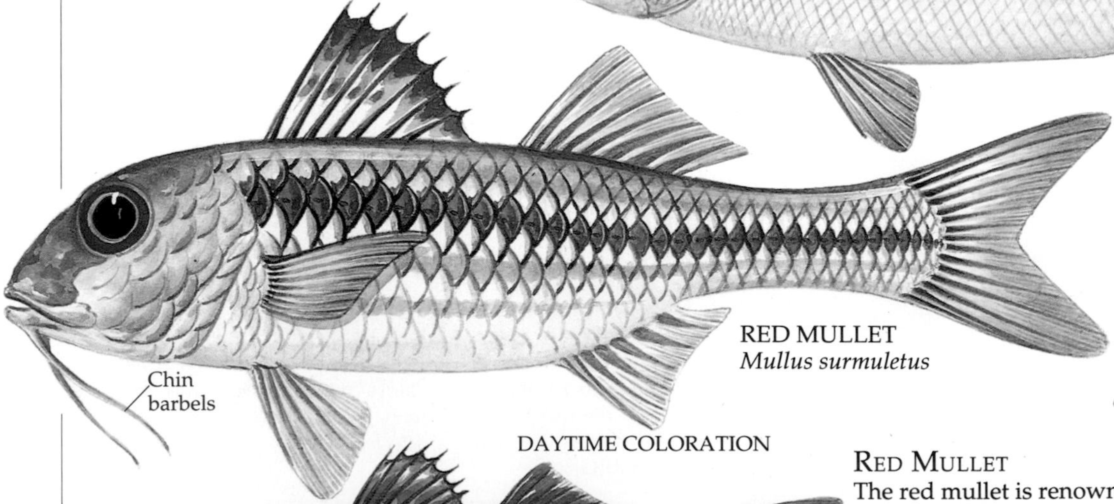

Dark fins

Chin barbels

RED MULLET
Mullus surmuletus

DAYTIME COLORATION

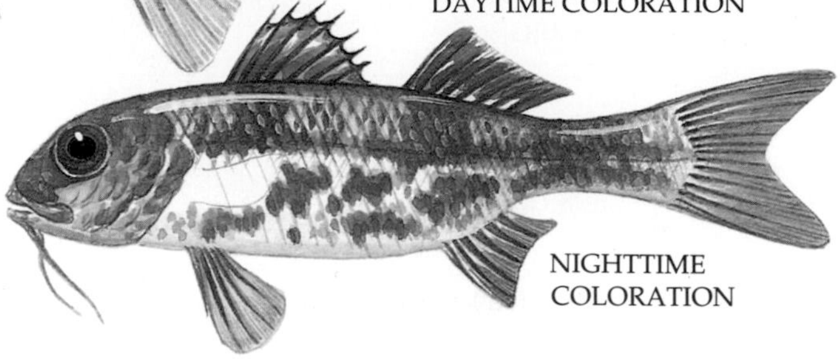

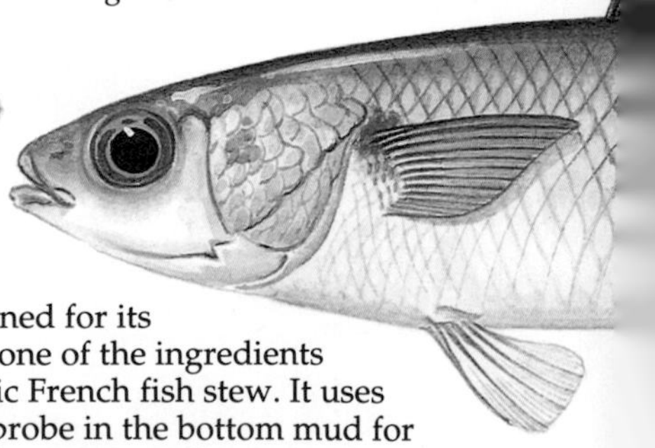

WHITE MULLET
Mugil curema

RED MULLET

The red mullet is renowned for its fine-tasting flesh and is one of the ingredients of *bouillabaisse*, the classic French fish stew. It uses its long chin barbels to probe in the bottom mud for its food, which is mainly worms, molluscs, and crustaceans, and at night its coloration changes from striped to mottled and barred. Its maximum weight is about 1.64 kg (3 lb 10 oz).

NIGHTTIME COLORATION

ery broad
ps

**THICK-LIPPED
GREY MULLET**
Chelon labrosus

First dorsal
fin set well back

Narrow
lips

Dark spot

**THIN-LIPPED
GREY MULLET**
Liza ramada

DISTRIBUTION
Striped: almost worldwide in warm waters.
Freshwater: Burnett River, Queensland, to Georges River, New South Wales.
Red: Mediterranean; eastern Atlantic from southern Norway to the Canary Islands.
Thick-lipped, thin-lipped, golden: Mediterranean; eastern Atlantic from southern Norway to the Canary Islands.
White: warm-temperate and tropical Atlantic; eastern Pacific from Mexico to Chile.

THICK-LIPPED GREY MULLET

The large lips of this European mullet help to distinguish it from the very similar thin-lipped grey mullet, which is found in the same waters where their ranges overlap. The thick-lipped grey mullet, which forms small schools that cruise near the surface, is found close inshore and enters harbours and estuaries. Its maximum weight is around 6.4 kg (14 lb).

THIN-LIPPED GREY MULLET

In addition to having thinner lips than the thick-lipped grey mullet, this fish has a dark spot at the base of each pectoral fin and its first dorsal fin is set further back. Its habits are similar to those of the thick-lipped grey, but it is more likely to enter freshwater and is the most abundant mullet in European estuaries. It grows to a maximum of about 3.2 kg (7 lb).

GOLDEN MULLET

The golden mullet, sometimes called the golden grey mullet, resembles the thin-lipped grey but has an overall bronze hue and golden blotches on its cheeks. It is also smaller, with a maximum weight of under 1.36 kg (3 lb).

GOLDEN MULLET
Liza aurata

WHITE MULLET

This mullet is found in warm Atlantic waters and in the tropical eastern Pacific. It has a dark spot at the base of each pectoral fin, and often one or two gold patches on each side of its head. It usually grows to a weight of about 1.36 kg (3 lb).

FISHING NOTES

Techniques
Float fishing, spinning, or freelining. These fish have soft, relatively small mouths and are easily spooked, so light tackle, delicate bait presentation, and a careful approach are required.

Tackle
Use a 3 to 3.7 m (10 to 12 ft) float rod for float fishing and freelining, with a fixed-spool reel, 2.27 kg (5 lb) mono line, and hook sizes 6 to 16; for float fishing, use a peacock, Avon, or slider float and split shot. For spinning, try a 2.1 to 3 m (7 to 10 ft) light spinning rod with a fixed-spool reel, 2.27 kg (5 lb) mono line, and size 10 treble hook.

Bait
Mullet will take a wide range of small, soft, natural and processed baits, including small or cut worms, maggots, banana, corn, cut fish, bread, cheese, peas, minced meat, and pasta. For spinning, use tiny spoons and spinners, baited with small or cut ragworm.

Size comparison

Striped mullet   Freshwater mullet   Thick-lipped grey mullet   Thin-lipped grey mullet   Golden mullet   Red mullet   White mullet

FLATFISH

For a few days after hatching from the egg, the larva of a flatfish resembles that of any other fish, but then it begins to change into the compressed, asymmetrical shape that makes flatfish superbly adapted to a bottom-hugging life. There are over 500 species, the main families being the Pleuronectidae or righteyed flatfish, in which both eyes are on the right side of the body; the Bothidae or lefteyed flatfish, in which both eyes are on the left; and the Soleidae or sole family, which contains mostly righteyed species.

PACIFIC HALIBUT
This huge, righteyed flatfish and its Atlantic counterpart (*Hippoglossus hippoglossus*) are among the largest fish in the sea, probably capable of exceeding 360 kg (800 lb). However, most caught by anglers are young fish weighing less than 4.54 kg (10 lb), the largest adults being found in very deep water.

SUMMER FLOUNDER
Paralichthys dentatus

Five prominent spots near tail

Black and yellow bands on fins

SUMMER FLOUNDER
This lefteyed flatfish reaches a weight of 12 kg (26 lb) and is usually marked with numerous ocelli (rimmed spots), of which five near the tail are large and prominent. It is found along the Atlantic coast of the United States, and from the Carolinas south its range overlaps that of the southern flounder (*Paralichthys lethostigma*), which is often marked with spots but not with ocelli.

SOLE
The sole, a common flatfish of the eastern Atlantic and the Mediterranean, is brown with dark patches on its upper side and creamy white below. It spends the day buried in the sand, feeding at night in midwater, and grows to 3 kg (6 lb 10 oz).

EUROPEAN PLAICE
Pleuronectes platessa

STARRY FLOUNDER
Platichthys stellatus

STARRY FLOUNDER
This flatfish, which can be righteyed or lefteyed, is common on the Pacific coast of North America. Its fins are marked with black and yellow bands, and the upper side of its body has patches of shiny, star-shaped scales. It grows to 9.1 kg (20 lb), and hybridizes with the English sole (*Parophrys vetulus*) to produce the "hybrid sole."

Eggs and larvae
Female flatfish lay up to 500,000 eggs. These float in the water, as do the symmetrically shaped larvae.

EUROPEAN PLAICE
The righteyed European plaice is found in the eastern Atlantic from the tidal shallows out to depths of about 200 m (650 ft). It is marked with bold red or orange spots and grows to a weight of over 4.54 kg (10 lb). The American plaice (*Hippoglossoides platessoides*) is similar, but lacks the red spotting and reaches 6.4 kg (14 lb).

SOLE
Solea solea

Size comparison

Pacific halibut | Turbot | Summer flounder | Starry flounder | Winter flounder | Plaice | Sole

PACIFIC HALIBUT
Hippoglossus stenolepis

DISTRIBUTION
Pacific halibut: North Pacific.
Starry flounder: North Pacific.
Summer flounder: western Atlantic from about Maine to northern Florida.
Plaice: North Atlantic and western Mediterranean.
Sole: Norway to Morocco and the Mediterranean.
Turbot: from Norway to the Black Sea.
Winter flounder: western Atlantic from Labrador south to Georgia.

TURBOT
Scophthalmus maximus

Straight lateral line

WINTER FLOUNDER
Pseudopleuronectes americanus

WINTER FLOUNDER

The winter flounder is one of the most common flatfish of the western Atlantic. It is a valuable commercial species and a popular gamefish, capable of reaching 3.6 kg (8 lb) and occurring from the tidal shallows out to depths of about 120 m (400 ft) or more. Its coloration and markings are very variable.

TURBOT

This large, lefteyed flatfish is widely distributed in European waters and occurs from near the shoreline to depths of up to 80 m (260 ft). The coloration of its upper side is typically light brown with dark speckles and blotches, and generally matches the colour of the bottom on which it lives. Its maximum weight is about 15 kg (33 lb).

Development
The eyes of the growing fish move to one side of its body.

FISHING NOTES

Techniques
Most flatfish can be caught by bottom fishing, surfcasting, and spinning. For large halibut, try trolling, drifting, and bottom fishing.

Tackle
For most species, bottom fishing and surfcasting call for a 5.4 to 13.6 kg (12 to 30 lb) class rod with a multiplier reel, 5.4 to 13.6 kg (12 to 30 lb) line, and hook sizes 1 to 5/0; for spinning for fish such as plaice and flounder, try a 2.1 to 2.4 m (7 to 8 ft) medium spinning rod, fixed-spool reel, 4.54 to 6.8 kg (10 to 15 lb) line, and hook sizes 2 to 6. For halibut, use a 13.6 to 36.3 kg (30 to 80 lb) class boat rod, with a 4/0 to 9/0 multiplier, 13.6 to 36.3 kg (30 to 80 lb) mono line, a wire trace, and hook sizes 4/0 to 8/0.

Bait
Fish, squid, crab, worms, metal lures.

RAYS

The order Rajiformes consists of eight families of cartilaginous fish and includes the rays, mantas, sawfish, and skates *(see page 186)*. These fish are characterized by flattened bodies and wide, often winglike, pectoral fins; their mouths and gill openings are on the undersides and their eyes on the upper. In most families, the eggs are fertilized and hatch within the body of the female; the exception is the Rajidae, in which the internally fertilized eggs are laid before hatching.

MANTA

The mantas or devil rays belong to the Mobulidae family, which contains about a dozen species. These range in size from the Australian mobula *(Mobula diabola)*, which measures about 60 cm (2 ft) across its wings, to the manta *(Manta birostris)*, which reaches 6.7 m (22 ft) across the wings and a weight of 1,820 kg (4,000 lb). Despite its tremendous size, the manta is a generally harmless fish that feeds on small fish and crustaceans, which it steers into its mouth with its cephalic fins, the pair of "horns" on its head. Mantas cruise between midwater and the surface, and frequently leap into the air, perhaps to rid themselves of parasites or maybe just for fun.

THORNBACK RAY

The thornback is the most common ray in European waters. A member of the Rajidae family, it is a bottom-dweller found at depths of 10 to 60 m (about 30 to 200 ft), and gets its name from the numerous thorny spines on its tail, back, and pectoral fins. Young thornbacks live in shallow water and feed on small crustaceans, and as they grow they move into deeper water and begin feeding on larger prey including crabs and fish. They grow to about 18 kg (40 lb).

SPOTTED RAY
Raja montagui

THORNBACK RAY
Raja clavata

Colour variation
The colour of the thornback is very variable, but most individuals are a mottled brown.

SPOTTED RAY

Like the thornback, the spotted ray is a European member of the Rajidae family. It lives in deeper water than the thornback, preferring depths of 60 to 120 m (about 200 to 400 ft), and is a smaller fish, with a maximum weight of around 3.8 kg (8 lb 6 oz). Its diet consists mainly of crustaceans but it will also take small fish.

Spines
The thorny spines of the thornback and many other species have a strong, buttonlike base.

Egg cases
The eggs laid by members of the Rajidae family are each enclosed in a tough case known as a "mermaid's purse".

MANTA
Manta birostris

Size comparison

Manta   Sawfish   Bat ray   Thornback ray   Round stingray   Spotted ray

ROUND STINGRAY

The stingrays, members of the Dasyatidae family, have one or more venomous spines on their whiplike tails. Any wounds inflicted by the spines must get prompt medical attention because they can be fatal. The round stingray, measuring about 56 cm (1 ft 10 in) across the wings, is one of the smaller species; the Atlantic roughtail stingray *(Dasyatis centroura)* can be 2.1 m (7 ft) across.

Sharp spine can inflict painful wounds

ROUND STINGRAY
Urolophus halleri

DISTRIBUTION

Manta: worldwide in warm-temperate and tropical waters.
Thornback ray: from Iceland to the Black Sea.
Spotted ray: from Scotland to the western Mediterranean.
Round stingray: from northern California to Panama.
Smalltooth sawfish: Mediterranean and warm-temperate and tropical Atlantic.
Bat ray: from Oregon to the Gulf of California.

LONGTOOTH SAWFISH
20 or fewer teeth

24 or more teeth
SMALLTOOTH SAWFISH

SAWFISH

Sawfish (the Pristidae) are sharklike rays with elongated, flattened snouts that are equipped with rows of strong, sharp teeth along each side. The largetooth sawfish *(Pristis pristis)* and the smalltooth sawfish *(P. pectinata)* are Atlantic species that can reach weights of up to 360 kg (800 lb). Sawfish are also found in freshwater; for example, the largetooth sawfish is found 750 km (470 miles) up the Amazon.

SMALLTOOTH SAWFISH
Pristis pectinata

BAT RAY

The bat ray is a member of the Myliobatidae, the eagle ray family, which consists of about 30 species. They are large, free-swimming rays with distinct heads and very long tails, and feed on the bottom on shellfish and crustaceans. The bat ray grows to about 1.8 m (6 ft) across the wings.

BAT RAY
Myliobatis californica

FISHING NOTES

Techniques
Most rays live or feed on the bottom, so bottom fishing is the best technique. Manta usually feed at midwater or close to the surface, and are sometimes taken by trolling; they can be very dangerous and difficult to handle when hooked.

Tackle
For the thornback and spotted rays and the round stingray, use a heavy shore rod or a 9.1 kg (20 lb) class boat rod, with a 4/0 to 6/0 multiplier, 11.3 kg (25 lb) mono line and a 13.6 kg (30 lb) mono trace, size 2/0 to 4/0 hook, and a bomb-shaped weight. For sawfish and manta, try a 36.3 to 59 kg (80 to 130 lb) class rod with 36.3 to 59 kg (80 to 130 lb) mono line and a heavy wire or nylon trace, and size 8/0 to 14/0 hook.

Bait
Peeler crab, ragworm, and strips of fish such as mackerel.

Saltwater SPECIES

SKATES

The skates are members of the Rajidae *(see also page 184)*, which contains over a hundred species and is the largest family within the order Rajiformes. Most skates are a mottled brownish colour with whitish undersides, and their tails are relatively thick, rather than whiplike. Skates usually rest on the bottom during the day, lying partly buried in sand or mud, and become active at night to feed on shellfish, crustaceans, and sometimes small fish. They swim by making smooth undulations of their pectoral fins.

BIG SKATE
Raja binoculata

BARNDOOR SKATE
Raja laevis

BARNDOOR SKATE
This large, aggressive skate of the northwestern Atlantic grows to a length of around 1.5 m (5 ft) and a weight of 18 kg (40 lb). It is found from the tidal shallows out to depths of 430 m (1,410 ft), and will sometimes enter brackish water. It has a noticeably pointed snout, large, black pores on its underside, and a smooth skin. Its wings (pectoral fins) have concave leading edges and sharply angled corners. It feeds mainly on large crustaceans, molluscs, and fish such as herring, and it will readily take a baited hook.

Eye spot

BIG SKATE
The big skate, as its name indicates, is a large fish and can reach a length of 2.4 m (8 ft) and weigh over 91 kg (200 lb). It has a triangular snout, and there is a large eyespot on the upper surface of each wing. The big skate is found at depths of 3 to 110 m (10 to 360 ft) along the Pacific coast of North America, and the southern part of its range overlaps that of the California skate *(Raja inornata)*. This skate is much smaller, about 76 cm (2 ft 6 in) long, with a sharply pointed snout and usually no eyespots.

Mouth

Gill slits

Dark bars and streaks

Sharp-angled corner of wing

CLEARNOSE SKATE
Raja eglanteria

Pale area each side of snout

CLEARNOSE SKATE
The clearnose skate, which grows to a length of about 90 cm (3 ft), gets its name from the pale, translucent areas at either side of its snout. The overall coloration of its upper side is light brown to reddish brown, marked with dark bars, streaks, and spots. It migrates inshore to breed during the spring, and in summer it is the most abundant skate in the western Atlantic from Long Island to the Carolinas.

Skate underside
The underside of a skate is usually a pale, whitish colour. The mouth is just below the snout, and just above the two sets of five gill slits.

Size comparison

Common skate

Big skate

Barndoor skate

Winter skate

Clearnose skate

COMMON SKATE
Raja batis

COMMON SKATE

The huge common skate of the eastern Atlantic and western Mediterranean is an active predator and feeds mainly on fish, such as cod and haddock, and crustaceans. Large females, which are bigger than the males, can reach a length of 2.8 m (9 ft 2 in) and a weight of about 103 kg (227 lb). The skate's upper side is dark olive with light blotches, and the colour of the underside is usually a pale blue-grey. Other skates found in European waters include the long-nosed skate (*Raja oxyrinchus*) and the white skate (*R. alba*). The long-nosed skate is similar in colour to the common skate, but has a long, thin snout and the leading edges of its wings are more concave.

DISTRIBUTION
Barndoor skate, winter skate: from Newfoundland south to North Carolina.
Big skate: from the Bering Sea to Baja California.
Clearnose skate: from New England to the Gulf of Mexico.
Common skate: Iceland to Madeira; the Mediterranean.

Blunt nose

WINTER SKATE
Raja ocellata

WINTER SKATE

The winter skate usually has one to four eyespots on each wing, but these are sometimes absent. A winter skate with no eyespots closely resembles the little skate (*Raja erinacea*), and the only reliable way to distinguish between the two is to count the rows of teeth in the upper jaw: the winter skate has at least 72, the little skate fewer than 66. The winter skate is so named because it migrates into inshore waters, principally between New England and New Jersey, in winter. It grows to a length of 1.1 m (3 ft 7 in).

Clasper (male sex organ)

FISHING NOTES

Techniques
Bottom fishing from a boat is the usual method for skate.

Tackle
Use a 2 to 2.1 m (6½ to 7 ft), 22.7 kg (50 lb) class boat rod with a 4/0 to 6/0 multiplier reel, 22.7 kg (50 lb) mono line and a 45.4 kg (100 lb) wire trace, size 6/0 to 8/0 brazed eye hooks, and a bomb- or pyramid-shaped weight. Use a butt socket or full harness to help you exert maximum leverage on the rod when fighting the

fish, and to make the fight less tiring for you: it can take a lot of effort to dislodge a skate from the bottom, and big skate have been known to fight hard for up to an hour.

Bait
Most skate are caught on fresh fish. Mackerel is particularly effective, but almost any common fish will do, and large strips of cuttlefish and squid are also good skate baits. Small fish can be used whole, because skate have big mouths and readily gulp them down.

Mating
Skates breed by internal fertilization. The male has a pair of modified pelvic fin extensions, called claspers, with which he inserts sperm into the female.

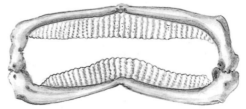

Skate jaws
The teeth of a skate, arranged in rows in its powerful jaws, are well adapted to crushing and grinding up the fish, lobsters, crabs, and molluscs that it feeds on.

187

DRUM & KAHAWAI

The widely distributed Sciaenidae (drum) family consists of over 200 tropical and warm-temperate marine species – including drum, croaker, seatrout, seabass, and weakfish – plus the freshwater drum (*Aplodinotus grunniens*) of North America. Many species can make drumming sounds by contracting muscles on the walls of their swim bladders (gas-filled bladders that help to give them buoyancy). The kahawai, one of the two members of the Arripidae family, is also known as the Australian salmon because its juveniles bear a superficial resemblance to the Atlantic salmon.

BLACK DRUM

The black drum grows to a weight of over 52 kg (115 lb), and its deep body is marked with four or five dark bars on each side. It is a bottom feeder, and uses the barbels on its chin to help it locate the crustaceans and molluscs that make up the bulk of its diet. It is an important gamefish, commonly caught from the shore and piers.

Large chin barbels

RED DRUM

This large drum, also known as the redfish or channel bass, has a reddish overall coloration and one or more dark spots at the base of the tail. Its body is not as deep as that of the black drum, and it lacks chin barbels. It feeds at the bottom on crustaceans and molluscs and also takes small fish, especially mullet. The usual adult weight is under 18 kg (40 lb) but it can reach about 43 kg (95 lb).

RED DRUM
Sciaenops ocellatus

WHITE SEABASS
Atractoscion nobilis

Black bars

JUVENILE WHITE SEABASS

WHITE SEABASS

The white seabass is one of a number of important gamefish of the drum family found along the Pacific coast of North America. Others include the white croaker (*see opposite page*), the California corbina (*Menticirrhus undulatus*), the spotfin croaker (*Roncador stearnsii*), and the yellowfin croaker (*Umbrina roncador*). The white seabass is found over rocks, near kelp, and in the surf zone, feeding on fish and squid and growing to about 41 kg (90 lb).

KAHAWAI
Arripis trutta

KAHAWAI

The two members of the Arripidae family, the kahawai and the ruff (*Arripis georgianus*), are related to the Sciaenidae and resemble them in overall appearance. During the summer, kahawai form huge schools that cruise inshore near the surface, feeding on small fish and krill. Its average weight is 1.36 to 4.54 kg (3 to 10 lb), with a maximum of around 7.3 kg (16 lb).

Size comparison

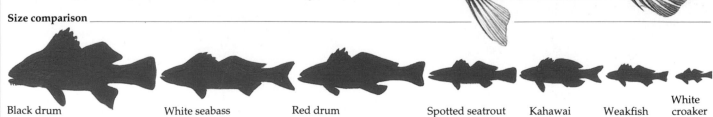

| Black drum | White seabass | Red drum | Spotted seatrout | Kahawai | Weakfish | White croaker |

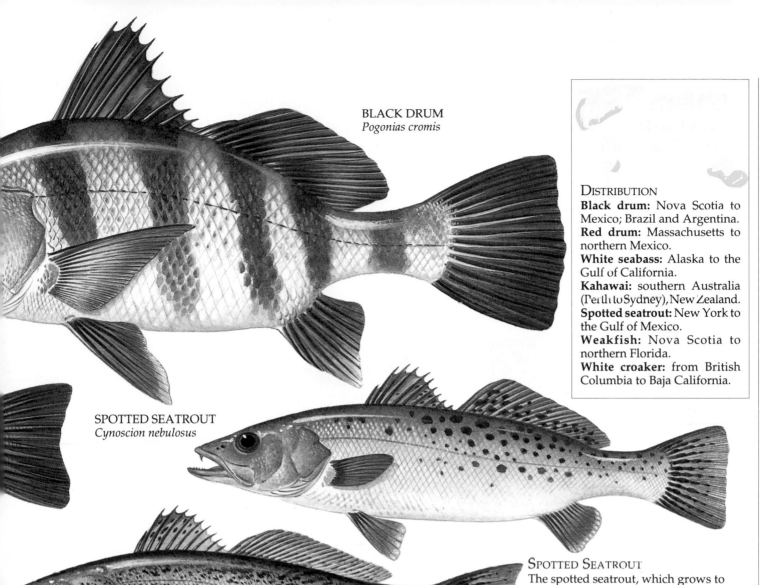

BLACK DRUM
Pogonias cromis

SPOTTED SEATROUT
Cynoscion nebulosus

WEAKFISH
Cynoscion regalis

WHITE CROAKER
Genyonemus lineatus

DISTRIBUTION
Black drum: Nova Scotia to Mexico; Brazil and Argentina.
Red drum: Massachusetts to northern Mexico.
White seabass: Alaska to the Gulf of California.
Kahawai: southern Australia (Perth to Sydney), New Zealand.
Spotted seatrout: New York to the Gulf of Mexico.
Weakfish: Nova Scotia to northern Florida.
White croaker: from British Columbia to Baja California.

SPOTTED SEATROUT
The spotted seatrout, which grows to about 7.3 kg (16 lb), is a very popular western Atlantic gamefish and, because of its delicate flesh, it is an important commercial species. It is attractively marked with numerous small black spots, which make it easily distinguishable from the unspotted, and smaller, sand seatrout (*Cynoscion arenarius*) and silver seatrout (*Cynoscion nothus*).

WEAKFISH
The weakfish is so named because its mouth is soft and tears easily when hooked. It forms small schools in shallow water over sandy ground, and feeds at the bottom on worms, crustaceans, and molluscs, and in midwater and at the surface on small fish. Weakfish weighing over 8.6 kg (19 lb) have been caught, but the average size is declining and a weight of over 2.7 kg (6 lb) is rare.

WHITE CROAKER
The white croaker is most reliably distinguished from other species of drum found along the Pacific coast of North America by the number of spines in its first dorsal fin: the white croaker has 12 to 16, the others 11 or fewer. It is found from close inshore to depths of 183 m (600 ft), and grows to about 454 g (1 lb).

FISHING NOTES

Techniques
These fish are taken by a number of methods, the most usual being bottom fishing, surfcasting, and spinning.

Tackle
For bottom fishing, try a 13.6 kg (30 lb) class boat rod with a size 4/0 multiplier reel, 13.6 kg (30 lb) mono line, size 4/0 hook, and a bomb-shaped sinker. When surfcasting, use a 3.7 m (12 ft) surfcasting rod with a fixed-spool or multiplier reel, 9.1 kg (20 lb) mono line, size 4/0 hook, and a grip sinker. For spinning, use a 2.4 to 2.7 m (8 to 9 ft) spinning rod with a fixed-spool reel, 6.8 to 9.1 kg (15 to 20 lb) mono line, and size 1/0 to 4/0 hook.

Bait
Good baits include shrimp, fish, crab, clams, mussels, worms, and most types of artificial lure.

189

SCOMBRIDAE

MACKEREL

The Scombridae family consists of about 45 species and includes the many species of mackerel plus tuna, bonito, and wahoo. The typical scombrid is a fast-swimming predator with a beautifully stream-lined, spindle-shaped body and a large, deeply forked or lunate (crescent-shaped) tail. Many scombrids are able to fold some of their fins into slots in their bodies to make them more streamlined and enable them to swim faster. The bluefin tuna, for example *(see page 193)*, withdraws its pectoral, pelvic, and first dorsal fins in this way when travelling at speed.

CHUB MACKEREL

The chub mackerel or Pacific mackerel can reach a weight of 2.9 kg (6 lb 5 oz) but usually does not exceed 1 kg (2 lb 3 oz). It occurs in temperate and subtropical waters worldwide but its distribution is uneven, and there are minor differences between the Atlantic and Pacific varieties. Both, however, have widely separated first and second dorsal fins and about 30 wavy, dark bars on the back. This species is a very important commercial fish, especially in the Pacific region, and is found in large schools in inshore waters.

ATLANTIC MACKEREL
Scomber scombrus

Orange and yellow stripes and spots

ATLANTIC MACKEREL

The Atlantic mackerel is very similar to the chub mackerel, but has fewer (20 to 23) dark bars on its back and lacks the dusky spotting on the flanks that is present in the Atlantic form of the chub mackerel. Some individuals, known as "scribble" mackerel, have dark, wormlike markings on their backs instead of bars. The Atlantic mackerel forms large schools, which can often be seen close inshore, feeding voraciously on small fish, and although it can grow to around 3.4 kg (7 lb 8 oz) the usual adult weight is about 680 g (1 lb 8 oz).

Horse mackerel
The horse mackerel or scad (Trachurus trachurus) *is not a mackerel but a member of the* Carangidae *(see page 164). It has a distinctive row of scutes (bony scales) along its lateral line.*

HORSE MACKEREL

CERO

The orange and yellow stripes and spots along its side help to distinguish the cero from the somewhat similar king and Spanish mackerel. The species is found in the warmer parts of the western Atlantic and in the Caribbean, and although most of those caught are in the 2.27 to 4.54 kg (5 to 10 lb) range its maximum weight is thought to be about 16 kg (35 lb).

Black leading edge to first dorsal fin

Dull, glazed appearance

Bony scales on lateral line

EYELIDS
Fish of the genus Scomber, *including the Atlantic and chub mackerels, are easily identified by their unusual eyelids. These are translucent membranes covering the front and rear margins of each eye, giving the eyes a dull appearance. These fish also have only five dorsal and anal finlets.*

ATLANTIC SPANISH MACKEREL
Scomberomorus maculatus

Size comparison

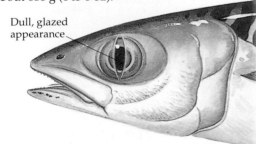

King mackerel   Cero   Spanish mackerel   Atlantic mackerel   Chub mackerel

CHUB MACKEREL
Scomber japonicus

Pacific fish have clear bellies,
Atlantic fish have spotting
below the lateral line

CERO
Scomberomorus regalis

DISTRIBUTION
Chub mackerel: worldwide in temperate and tropical seas.
Atlantic mackerel: Atlantic, Mediterranean, Black Sea.
Horse mackerel: Atlantic, Mediterranean.
Cero and king mackerel: the western Atlantic from about Massachusetts to Brazil.
Atlantic Spanish mackerel: warm-temperate and tropical Atlantic waters; related species found in the Atlantic, Pacific, and Indian Oceans.

KING MACKEREL
This is one of the largest mackerel and perhaps the most popular with anglers, who appreciate it for its size, the strong fight it puts up, and its tasty flesh. It averages only about 4.54 kg (10 lb), but it can grow much larger and individuals weighing around 45.4 kg (100 lb) have been netted by commercial fishermen. Huge schools of king mackerel gather in the Caribbean in the spring and migrate northwards to the Gulf of Mexico. The fish in these schools are in the 3 to 11 kg (7 to 25 lb) range; larger fish tend to be more solitary.

KING MACKEREL
Scomberomorus cavalla

Lateral line falls suddenly, and
young fish sometimes have bronze
spots on flanks

Orange spots on flanks
fade quickly after death

ATLANTIC SPANISH MACKEREL
This mackerel is found in the warmer parts of both the eastern and western Atlantic, and reaches a weight of about 5 kg (11 lb). Like the cero and the king mackerel, it is a member of the genus *Scomberomorus*, which also includes the Atlantic sierra (*S. brasiliensis*), the Pacific sierra (*S. sierra*) and the Gulf Sierra or Monterey Spanish mackerel (*S. concolor*), both of which are Pacific species; and the Indo-Pacific mackerels *S. commerson* and *S. guttatus*, which are very common in Australian waters.

FISHING NOTES

Techniques
Fish for the small species, such as the Atlantic and chub, from the shore or a boat, using feathered lures. The larger species are usually taken on artificial or natural baits, fished from a drifting boat or trolled.

Tackle
For the small mackerels, try a 3.4 m (11 ft) spinning rod with a fixed-spool reel, 4.54 kg (10 lb) line, a team of four lures with 1/0 hooks, and a 57 g (2 oz) bomb sinker. For the larger mackerel species, use a medium spinning rod with fixed-spool reel or a 5.4 kg (12 lb) class boat rod with a 4/0 multiplier, 5.4 kg (12 lb) mono line with a wire leader, and size 2/0 hooks.

Bait
For small fish, use feather or plastic mackerel lures. For larger species, try jigs, spinners, and plugs (fished either alone or in conjunction with a shrimp or a thin strip of any common baitfish), and cut or whole baitfish such as mullet and balao.

191

SCOMBRIDAE

TUNA & WAHOO

These members of the Scombridae family are widespread in temperate and tropical waters, and have considerable commercial importance as well as being important gamefish. The commercial value of tuna led to them being fished for with enormous driftnets, especially in the Pacific, but use of these nets has been restricted by international agreements because they took a heavy toll not only of tuna but also of unsought-for species including dolphins, sunfish, billfish, and Ray's bream.

ALBACORE
Because of its very long pectoral fins, which extend beyond the front of the anal fin, the albacore is also known as the longfin tuna. These fins help to distinguish the albacore from other tuna such as the bluefin. The Atlantic and the Pacific albacore were once considered to be separate species but are now known to be identical, and reach weights of around 43 kg (95 lb).

BLACKFIN TUNA
The blackfin of the western Atlantic is one of the smaller tuna, averaging less than 4.54 kg (10 lb) with a maximum of about 19 kg (42 lb). It is renowned more for its delicious flesh than for its sporting qualities, and large numbers are taken by blue marlin as well as by commercial fishermen.

BLACKFIN TUNA
Thunnus atlanticus

Dark finlets edged with white

Large and fast
The bluefin can grow to 4.3 m (14 ft) and 680 kg (1,500 lb) and is capable of speeds of up to 104 km/h (64 mph).

LITTLE TUNNY
The little tunny of the Atlantic and the Mediterranean is a popular gamefish, occurring in large schools close to the shore. It is very similar to the skipjack tuna and the other species of *Euthynnus* found in the Pacific, and grows to a maximum of about 12 kg (26 lb); most of those caught are, however, much smaller.

LITTLE TUNNY
Euthynnus alletteratus

Dark spots below pectoral fin

SKIPJACK TUNA
The skipjack tuna is found in most temperate and tropical oceans and can reach a weight of 35 kg (77 lb). Two very similar species occur in the Pacific: the wavyback skipjack or kawakawa (*Euthynnus affinis*) and the black skipjack (*E. lineatus*).

SKIPJACK TUNA
Euthynnus pelamis

Stripes on flank and belly

Double-pointed flap of skin between pelvic fins

Size comparison

| Bluefin tuna | Wahoo | Albacore | Skipjack tuna | Little tunny | Blackfin tuna |

ALBACORE
Thunnus alalunga

Very long
pectoral fin

BLUEFIN TUNA
Thunnus thynnus

BLUEFIN TUNA
The bluefin is a highly
migratory fish, which is found
in subtropical seas during
winter and moves into cooler
waters in summer. Bluefin of
up to about 45 kg (100 lb)
travel in huge schools, but
larger fish form smaller schools
and the biggest individuals are
often solitary. North Atlantic
bluefin and those found in the
Pacific and Indian Oceans are
sometimes classified as
separate species or subspecies,
but the differences between
them are very slight.

DISTRIBUTION
Albacore: in most temperate
and tropical waters; more
abundant in the Pacific than
in the Atlantic.
Blackfin tuna: Atlantic from
Massachusetts to Brazil.
Little tunny: warm-temperate
and tropical Atlantic waters
and the Mediterranean.
Skipjack tuna, bluefin tuna:
worldwide in temperate and
tropical waters.
Wahoo: most warm-temperate
and tropical waters.

Finlets
*One of the distinctive features of the
members of the Scombridae, including
the wahoo, is the presence of delicate,
soft-rayed finlets between the tail,
dorsal, and
anal fins.*

Long dorsal fin

Long, torpedo-shaped body

WAHOO
Acanthocybium solanderi

WAHOO
The long, slender-bodied wahoo makes tremendous runs with
abrupt changes of direction when hooked, sometimes leaping
from the water, and this makes it one of the most exciting fish
to catch. Its long, heavily toothed jaws form a beaklike snout,
and its first dorsal fin is long, low, and spiny. The average
weight is about 6.8 to 9 kg (15 to 20 lb), but it can grow to 83 kg
(183 lb) and a length of 2.1 m (6 ft 11 in).

HEAD OF WAHOO

FISHING NOTES

Techniques
Trolling with lures and drift
fishing with natural baits are
the usual methods of fishing
for tuna, little tunny, and
albacore. When fishing for
wahoo, try trolling with lures
and natural baits, and drift
fishing with natural baits.
Wahoo are usually taken on
flatlines that are fished quite
near to the boat, rather than
lines on outriggers.

Tackle
For tuna, use a 36.3 to 59 kg (80
to 130 lb) class rod with full
roller rings, a lever drag multiplier, and 36.3 to 59 kg (80 to
130 lb) nylon line with a 181 to
272 kg (400 to 600 lb) nylon

leader. Use hook sizes 10/0 to
12/0, flat for trolling and offset for drifting. For wahoo, use
a 13.6 to 22.7 kg (30 to 50 lb)
class rod with a 6/0 star drag
or 30- to 50-class multiplier
reel, 13.6 to 22.7 kg (30 to 50 lb)
nylon line with a heavy wire
leader, and a flat hook size
5/0 to 10/0.

Bait
Use a Kona Head lure when
trolling for tuna, and try live
mackerel or dead herring
when drifting. When trolling
for wahoo, use a Kona Head or
other large artificial, or try a
natural bait, such as a whole
mullet or balao, mounted for
trolling. For drift fishing, use
a live baitfish on hook sizes
5/0 to 8/0.

Wahoo jaws
*The wahoo is a predatory fish (as are tuna), and its jaws
contain rows of flat-sided, razor-sharp teeth that enable it to
rip into squid and shoals of baitfish. An unusual feature of the
wahoo is that both its jaws are movable.*

193

BONITO & SHAD

Bonito, like mackerel and tuna (*see pages 190–193*), belong to the Scombridae family. They are fast-swimming predators that feed on squid and small schooling fish, including mackerel, taken just below the surface. Shad, fish of the genus *Alosa*, are members of the herring family, the Clupeidae. They are marine fish that spawn in freshwater (some species also have landlocked populations), and differ from most other herring species in having a "keel" or "sawbelly", a ridge of sharp-edged scales along the belly.

PACIFIC BONITO
The Pacific bonito is a medium-sized fish that averages less than 5.4 kg (12 lb) but can grow to over 11 kg (24 lb). The northern and southern populations of the eastern Pacific are regarded as separate subspecies. Those north of Baja California are classified as *Sarda chiliensis lineolata*, and those off Peru and Chile as *S. c. chiliensis*. The striped bonito, *S. orientalis*, occurs from Baja to Peru, and in the western Pacific.

TWAITE SHAD
Alosa fallax

TWAITE SHAD
This shad differs from the Atlantic herring (*Clupea harengus*) in having a notch in its upper jaw, into which the lower jaw fits, a keel of sharp scales along its belly, and often has dark blotches along each side. Its maximum weight is about 1.4 kg (3 lb 2 oz).

ALLIS SHAD
Alosa alosa

ALLIS SHAD
The allis shad is similar to the twaite shad, but its keel is more pronounced and there may be a single dark blotch on each side, just behind the gill cover. It is also larger, reaching a weight of 2.7 kg (6 lb). Populations of both species have been severely depleted, mainly by pollution and damming of their spawning rivers.

AMERICAN SHAD
The American shad, which is capable of reaching a weight of over 5.5 kg (12 lb), has a large, dark spot behind each gill cover and usually one or two rows of dark spots along each side. It feeds almost entirely on plankton, and the adults have no jaw teeth.

Two rows of spots

AMERICAN SHAD
Alosa sapidissima

Shad diet
The diet of shad consists mainly of plankton, both animal and plant, plus insect larvae and copepods (tiny crustaceans). Skipjack herring and twaite, allis, and hickory shad also feed on small fish.

SKIPJACK HERRING
Alosa chrysochloris

SKIPJACK HERRING
The skipjack herring is also known as the river herring, and when in freshwater it prefers the open water of medium to large rivers and stillwaters. It is very similar to the hickory shad, but its flanks have a brassy tinge and no dark spots. Its maximum weight is about 1.6 kg (3 lb 8 oz).

FISHING NOTES

Techniques
Trolling and spinning for bonito, spinning and fly fishing for shad.

Tackle
To troll for bonito, use a 5.4 kg (12 lb) class boat rod with a size 2/0 multiplier reel, 5.4 kg (12 lb) mono line, and a size 2/0 hook. When spinning for bonito, try a light spinning rod with a fixed-spool reel, 5.4 kg (12 lb) mono line, and size 2/0 hook.

When spinning for shad, use a light spinning rod with a fixed-spool reel, 3.6 kg (8 lb) mono line, and small lures with treble hooks. For fly fishing, try a 2.7 m (9 ft) trout rod, weight-forward floating line, and flies tied on size 6 to 8 hooks.

Bait
For bonito, good baits include plugs, spoons, plastic squid, and whole or cut squid and fish. For shad, try small spinners and bar spoons, and small, white-coloured flies.

ATLANTIC BONITO
Sarda sarda

PACIFIC BONITO
Sarda chiliensis

ATLANTIC BONITO
The Atlantic bonito is similar to the Pacific bonito, but the stripes on its sides are more oblique, and it has 20 to 23 spines in its first dorsal fin, whereas its Pacific counterpart has 17 to 19. When feeding, it develops a yellow stripe along each side of its back and a series of dark, vertical bars down each side. These fade when it stops feeding. It travels in schools at depths between about 50 m (165 ft) and the surface, and its average weight is 1.36 kg (3 lb) with a maximum of around 8.6 kg (19 lb).

DISTRIBUTION
Pacific bonito: Pacific Ocean.
Twaite shad and allis shad: western European waters.
American shad: from about Newfoundland to northern Florida; Siberia to Mexico.
Skipjack herring: Mississippi basin and Gulf Slope.
Atlantic bonito: Atlantic and Mediterranean.
Australian bonito: southwest Pacific and Tasman Sea.
Hickory shad: from Maine to Florida.
Alewife: Great Lakes; from Labrador to South Carolina.

AUSTRALIAN BONITO
This bonito is found in the southwest Pacific, in the waters off Norfolk Island, southeast Australia, and New Zealand. The stripes on its sides are almost horizontal, rather than oblique like those of the Atlantic and Pacific species, and they are also present along the belly. It grows to a maximum weight of about 10 kg (22 lb).

AUSTRALIAN BONITO
Sarda australis

Protruding lower jaw

HICKORY SHAD
Alosa mediocris

HICKORY SHAD
This large shad has a protruding lower jaw, a dark spot behind each gill cover, and a row of dusky blotches along each side. Its usual maximum weight is about 1.1 kg (2 lb 8 oz), but it can reach 2.27 kg (5 lb). Fish make up a large part of the diets of hickory shad and skipjack herring, so they will take a lure more readily than other North American shad.

Very large eye

ALEWIFE
Alosa pseudoharengus

ALEWIFE
The alewife can grow to 227 g (8 oz) in saltwater, but the landlocked form is much smaller. It has large eyes (greater in diameter than the length of its snout), a prominent keel, and a small, dark spot behind each gill cover. The blueback herring (*Alosa aestivalis*) is similar in size and overall appearance, but its back is bluish and its eyes are smaller.

Size comparison

Australian bonito | Atlantic bonito | Pacific bonito | American shad | Allis shad | Twaite shad | Skipjack herring | Hickory shad | Alewife

SUBCLASS SELACHII

SHARKS 1

The sharks are a very ancient group of fish, characterized by cartilaginous skeletons, skins covered in tiny, thornlike scales called placoid scales, five to seven gill slits, and powerful jaws equipped with rows of strong, sharp teeth. There are about 300 species, distributed widely throughout the world's seas but particularly in tropical waters, and although most are marine some enter estuaries, rivers, and creeks. They range in size from about 60 cm (2 ft) in length up to at least 18 m (60 ft); those shown here are among the smaller species, up to 3.5 m (11 ft 6 in) long.

PORBEAGLE
Lamna nasus

LEOPARD SHARK

This distinctively patterned shark occurs close inshore along the Pacific coast of the United States, and is especially common in the shallow bays of California. It is usually found in shallow, sandy-bottomed waters less than 3.7 m (12 ft) deep. Males grow to a length of 1.5 m (5 ft), and females reach 2.1 m (7 ft) and 32 kg (71 lb).

Distinctive snout

LEOPARD SHARK
Triakis semifasciata

Large second dorsal fin

TOPE

The tope is a member of the largest shark family, the Carcharhinidae or requiem sharks. It has a slender body and prominent snout, long pectoral fins, and a strong tail fin with a large lower lobe. It is found inshore in depths of about 3 m (10 ft) or more, and can attain a length of 1.68 m (5 ft 6 in) and a weight of 34 kg (75 lb). It feeds mainly on fish, such as cod, and also takes squid.

SMOOTH DOGFISH
Mustelus canis

SMOOTH DOGFISH

This very common, bottom-dwelling shark of the western Atlantic is usually found at depths of 9 to 360 m (about 30 to 1,200 ft) and will sometimes enter freshwater. It has long pectoral fins and a large second dorsal fin that is almost the same size as the first, and there is a spiracle (a round opening that is the remnant of a first gill slit) behind each eye. It grows to about 1.5 m (5 ft).

Tope eyes
The eyes of the tope and most other requiem sharks have translucent membranes (nictitating membranes) that can be drawn across for protection.

Spiracle

TOPE
Galeorhinus galeus

Dorsal spines

SPURDOG

This slender shark, which grows to 1.2 m (4 ft) and 9.5 kg (21 lb), is unusual in having a sharp spine at the leading edge of each dorsal fin. Like the tope, it has a large, strong tail, but it has no anal fin. It lives just above the bottom in depths of 10 to 200 m (about 30 to 650 ft), and it has a very varied diet consisting of schooling fish, such as herring, plus invertebrates such as squid, jellyfish, and worms.

SPURDOG
Squalus acanthias

Size comparison

| Bull shark | Sand tiger | Porbeagle | Spinner shark | Blacktip shark | Leopard shark | Smooth dogfish | Tope | Spurdog |

PORBEAGLE

The porbeagle is a heavy, thickset shark with a rounded snout, a large tail fin, and five prominent gill slits just ahead of each pectoral fin. It is found in the Atlantic and Mediterranean and belongs to the Lamnidae or mackerel shark family, which also includes the salmon shark *(Lamna ditropis)*, found in the Pacific, and the shortfin mako and white shark *(see page 198)*. The porbeagle lives near the surface and usually prefers deep, open water, but it will venture into water of less than 6 m (20 ft) and shore anglers have landed porbeagles weighing over 45 kg (100 lb). The maximum length of the porbeagle is about 3 m (10 ft), and it can weigh up to 227 kg (500 lb).

Porbeagle tooth
A porbeagle tooth has an additional point, or cusp, on each side of the main shaft.

Equal-sized dorsal fins

SAND TIGER
Odontaspis taurus

DISTRIBUTION
Leopard shark: from Oregon to the Gulf of California.
Smooth dogfish: from the Bay of Fundy to Uruguay.
Tope: from Iceland to Morocco and the Mediterranean.
Spurdog: worldwide in cold and temperate waters.
Porbeagle: North Atlantic and the Mediterranean.
Sand tiger: most warm Atlantic waters.
Bull shark: worldwide in warm-temperate and tropical waters.
Spinner shark: subtropical and tropical Atlantic waters.

SAND TIGER

The sand tiger is found in warm-temperate coastal waters on both sides of the Atlantic, and grows to 3.2 m (10 ft 6 in) and 135 kg (300 lb). The larger but closely related grey nurse shark *(Odontaspis arenarius)* is abundant along the coasts of Australia and southern Africa. It grows to about 4.6 m (15 ft), and will readily attack swimmers and skindivers.

BULL SHARK
Carcharhinus leucas

SPINNER SHARK
Carcharhinus brevipinna

BULL SHARK

The large and dangerous bull shark is distributed worldwide in warm-temperate and tropical coastal waters. It rarely strays far from the coast and often enters rivers; there are even some lake-dwelling populations, most notably that in Lake Nicaragua. The bull shark grows to 3.5 m (11 ft 6 in) and 180 kg (400 lb), and has been known to attack swimmers.

Blacktip/spinner
These are almost identical, the main difference being that the dorsal fin of the blacktip is set further forward.

Dorsal fin

BLACKTIP

SPINNER

Inside view of pectoral fin

SPINNER SHARK

The spinner shark gets its name from its habit of making spectacular, twisting leaps from the water. It grows to a length of 3 m (10 ft), making it slightly larger than the very similar and closely related blacktip shark *(Carcharhinus limbatus)*, which reaches about 2.5 m (8 ft 2 in). The spinner and the blacktip are both dark bluish grey above, with a pale belly and a whitish flank stripe, and with a conspicuous black tip to the inside of each pectoral fin.

SHARKS 2

The sharks shown here are representative of the larger species, and range in length from just under 4 m (13 ft) up to about 9 m (30 ft) or more. Not shown, because they are too big to be fished for, are the basking shark *(Cetorhinus maximus)* and whale shark *(Rhincodon typus)*, huge but generally placid sharks that feed mainly on plankton. The basking shark is the largest shark in temperate waters, possibly growing to 13.7 m (45 ft) and 20,000 kg (44,000 lb); the whale shark, found in tropical seas, is the world's largest fish and may exceed 15.2 m (50 ft) and 35,000 kg (77,000 lb). The largest verified specimens of these two sharks were a 12.27 m (40 ft 3 in) basking shark and a 12.65 m (41 ft 6 in) whale shark.

Eye

Blunt, very short snout

Very long tail

THRESHER SHARK

This warmwater shark is immediately recognizable by the exceptionally long upper lobe of its tail, which may be longer than its body. Threshers are found in the open ocean at depths from the surface down to 100 m (330 ft), and they grow to about 6.1 m (20 ft) and 450 kg (1,000 lb). They hunt in packs, using their tails to stun their prey.

THRESHER SHARK
Alopias vulpinus

SHORTFIN MAKO
Isurus oxyrinchus

SHORTFIN MAKO

The shortfin mako, also known as the mako or bonito shark, is probably the fastest-swimming shark, capable of speed bursts of up to 74 km/h (46 mph). Its maximum size is about 3.8 m (12 ft 6 in) and 506 kg (1,115 lb), and it makes spectacular leaps when hooked.

White shark bite
When a white shark bites, it opens its huge jaws wide to expose its razor-sharp, serrated teeth, which can be up to 7.6 cm (3 in) long.

SIXGILL SHARK

This large, bulky shark is identifiable by its single dorsal fin, which is set near the tail, and the six gill slits just ahead of each pectoral fin. The sixgill is found in temperate waters and lives at or near the bottom, the young in shallow water but the adults preferring depths of 75 m (250 ft) or more. It attains a size of at least 4.9 m (16 ft) and 590 kg (1,300 lb).

FISHING NOTES

Techniques
Trolling and drift fishing are the usual forms of shark fishing, but small sharks that venture into the inshore shallows are also taken by shore anglers, including saltwater fly fishers. Take care to avoid injury when handling sharks.

Tackle
When shore fishing for shark, try a 3.4 to 3.7 m (11 to 12 ft) rod with a multiplier reel, 8.2 kg (18 lb) mono line with a wire leader, a 113 to 170 g (4 to 6 oz) weight, and hook sizes 4/0 to 6/0, or a medium to heavy saltwater fly outfit with a 30 cm (12 in) wire trace at the end of the tippet, and flies tied on 5/0 or 6/0 hooks. For trolling and drift fishing, the tackle depends on the size of shark you expect to catch. For example, a 9.1 kg (20 lb) class outfit should suffice for small species such as spurdog, but larger fish such as blue shark, porbeagle and mako require 22.7 to 36.3 kg (50 to 80 lb) class tackle.

Bait
Strips of fresh fish (such as mackerel or pollack) for small species, whole fish for the larger ones. For fly fishing, try white streamer flies.

SMOOTH HAMMERHEAD
Sphyrna zygaena

SMOOTH HAMMERHEAD

The odd-looking head of a hammerhead shark is flattened and extended to form a pair of hammerlike lobes with an eye at the tip of each lobe. There are about eight species of hammerhead, most of which are found in tropical and subtropical waters; the smooth hammerhead, however, is a fish of temperate to subtropical coastal waters. It is a large fish, with a maximum size of about 4 m (13 ft) and 408 kg (900 lb), and it can be a danger to swimmers and skindivers.

TIGER SHARK
Galeocerdo cuvieri

Tail fin
In requiem sharks, such as the tiger, the upper tail lobe is two or three times the size of the lower lobe.

TIGER SHARK

This is a large and very dangerous shark, capable of reaching a length of 7.3 m (24 ft) and a weight of 3,084 kg (6,800 lb), that will attack just about anything that moves. It is abundant in warm seas, and is found in the shallow waters of bays and estuaries (where it often feeds at night) as well as offshore. It is a dark greyish colour above with pale underparts, and younger fish have prominent, black, tigerlike markings that gradually fade with age and are sometimes absent from large adults.

WHITE SHARK
Carcharodon carcharias

DISTRIBUTION

Thresher shark, shortfin mako: worldwide in temperate and tropical waters.
Sixgill shark: worldwide in warm-temperate waters.
Smooth hammerhead: almost worldwide in subtropical and warm-temperate waters.
Tiger shark: almost worldwide in warm-temperate seas and tropical waters.
White shark, blue shark: worldwide in temperate and tropical waters.

WHITE SHARK

This huge shark, also known as the great white shark or maneater, has been known to attack swimmers, skindivers, and even boats, but has itself been so mercilessly hunted that it is becoming endangered. It is primarily a fish of the deep ocean, but it sometimes enters shallow water in search of food such as seals. It also eats fish, shellfish, turtles, and seabirds, and averages 4.3 m (14 ft) but may reach over 11 m (36 ft). The largest fish ever caught by an angler was a 1,208 kg (2,664 lb) white shark, taken by Alf Dean at Denial Bay, South Australia, in 1959.

New teeth

Shark teeth
Teeth are constantly breaking and falling out, only to be replaced by whole rows growing behind them in the gums.

Broken tooth

Blue shark teeth
The teeth of the blue shark are pointed, with serrated edges.

Claspers
Male sharks are identifiable by their claspers, modified pectoral fin extensions that function as sex organs.

Claspers

BLUE SHARK
Prionace glauca

BLUE SHARK

This beautifully coloured and very streamlined shark is found in nearly all temperate and tropical waters, but rarely comes within about 24 km (15 miles) of the shore. It is a fast swimmer, capable of speed bursts of 39.5 km/h (24½ mph), and travels great distances: two that were tagged off southwest England were later caught by anglers off Long Island, New York, about 5,630 km (3,500 miles) away. The blue shark grows to around 3.8 m (12 ft 6 in) and 151 kg (333 lb).

Only one dorsal fin

Very long pectoral fin

SIXGILL SHARK
Hexanchus griseus

Size comparison

White shark   Tiger shark   Smooth hammerhead   Thresher shark   Sixgill shark   Shortfin mako   Blue shark

GROUPER

The Serranidae is a large and important family of fish, consisting of more than 375 species. These are mostly temperate and tropical marine fish, ranging in size from less than 30 cm (12 in) to about 3.7 m (12 ft), and are found near rocks, reefs, wrecks, and piers in coastal waters. The larger members of the family are robust, sharp-toothed, basslike fish, which live near the bottom and feed on fish, crustaceans, and shellfish. They tend to be solitary rather than schooling, except at spawning time, and the individuals of many species change sex as they grow: they mature and breed as females, and become males when they grow older and larger.

NASSAU GROUPER
Epinephelus striatus

YELLOWFIN GROUPER
This grouper has distinctive yellow tips to its pectoral fins, dark oval blotches on its head and body, and is speckled with small black spots. Its coloration is otherwise highly variable, but those in shallow water tend to be yellowish or green (yellow phase) and those in deep water red (red phase). Maximum weight is about 9.1 kg (20 lb).

RED PHASE

NASSAU GROUPER

The Nassau grouper is found over rocks, coral reefs, and weedbeds from shallow inshore waters out to depths of around 30 m (100 ft). Its maximum weight is about 25 kg (55 lb), and it is one of the most attractive groupers, having a variable, pale overall coloration marked with dark bars and light spots. It is an important commercial species, as are the red grouper, black grouper, and black seabass, and it fights hard when hooked.

YELLOWFIN GROUPER
Mycteroperca venenosa

FEMALE

YELLOW PHASE

MALE

Three-lobed tail fin

BLACK SEABASS
Centropristis striata

BLACK SEABASS

The black seabass has an average weight of around 680 g (1 lb 8 oz) and a maximum of 3.6 kg (8 lb), but despite its relatively small size it is one of the most popular marine gamefish along the Atlantic coast of the United States. It winters offshore and moves to inshore waters in spring and summer, when it enters sounds and bays where the bottom is hard and there are abundant shellfish. It is caught by bottom fishing from anchored boats, and from piers and docks.

Size comparison

Jewfish | Black grouper | Red grouper | Yellowfin grouper | Nassau grouper | Black seabass

RED GROUPER
Epinephelus morio

RED GROUPER
The red grouper inhabits rocky reefs at depths of 24 to 120 m (80 to 400 ft), but small individuals are sometimes found near the shore in shallow water. This grouper is recognizable by its blotched, reddish coloration, its squared-off tail, and the even top edge of its first dorsal fin; the lining of its mouth is orange or deep red. It can attain a weight of 23 kg (50 lb) or more, and fights hard when hooked on light tackle.

DISTRIBUTION
Yellowfin grouper: Bermuda and Florida to Brazil.
Nassau grouper: Bermuda and North Carolina to Brazil.
Black seabass: from Maine to northeast Florida; eastern Gulf of Mexico.
Red grouper: Bermuda and Massachusetts to Brazil.
Black grouper: Bermuda and Massachusetts to Brazil.
Jewfish: Bermuda; Florida to Brazil; Pacific from the Gulf of California to Panama.

BLACK GROUPER
Mycteroperca bonaci

BLACK GROUPER
The black grouper, which can weigh over 82 kg (180 lb), has a variable overall coloration marked with dark, rectangular blotches. The name "black grouper" is sometimes also used for the warsaw grouper (*Epinephelus nigritus*), which has a uniform dark brown coloration and grows to 263 kg (580 lb).

Rounded tail fin

JEWFISH
Epinephelus itajara

JEWFISH
This huge grouper is known to reach a length of 2.4 m (8 ft) and a weight of 310 kg (680 lb), and may grow to 454 kg (1,000 lb) or more. Despite its size, it lives in shallow water – usually no deeper than 30 m (100 ft) – and is found around rocky ledges, wrecks, and pilings. It is not a hard fighter, but its size and weight, and its habit of bolting into a hole when hooked, make it difficult to land. The Queensland grouper (*Promicrops lanceolatus*), an Indo-Pacific species, is even larger and can grow to 3.7 m (12 ft) and over 500 kg (1,100 lb).

FISHING NOTES

Techniques
Bottom fishing and trolling, using natural or artificial baits, are effective methods for these species. Black seabass are also taken from jetties, docks, breakwaters, and piers on saltwater spinning gear and light, general-purpose tackle.

Tackle
For bottom fishing, use a 13.6 to 22.7 kg (30 to 50 lb) class boat rod with a 4/0 to 6/0 multiplier reel and 13.6 to 22.7 kg (30 to 50 lb) mono line; terminal tackle should be a running leger with an 85 to 227 g (3 to 8 oz) pyramid- or bomb-shaped sinker and 2/0 to 6/0 hook. For trolling, try a 36.3 kg (80 lb) class rod with a 9/0 multiplier reel, 36.3 kg (80 lb) mono line, a heavy wire leader and 10/0 hook.

Bait
Fish, squid, worms, shrimps, clams, and crab are good baits for bottom fishing. These natural baits can also be used for trolling, as can plugs, spinners, spoons, and feathers.

SPARIDAE

PORGY & SEABREAM

Porgy and seabream are among the 120 species that make up the Sparidae family. The Sparidae have a worldwide distribution in temperate and tropical waters, but are most abundant in warm coastal seas. Most are small to medium-sized fish but some are quite large; in African waters, some species of steenbras (or musselcracker), such as *Pagrus nasutus* and *Petrus repuestris*, can grow to well over 54 kg (120 lb).

RED SEABREAM
The red seabream has red fins and a reddish tinge to its silvery body, and there is a large dark spot behind each gill cover. It is found in depths of 50 to 300 m (160 to 1,000 ft), particularly near reefs and wrecks, and feeds mainly on fish but also takes shrimps, crabs, and squid. Its maximum weight is about 4.54 kg (10 lb).

BLACK SEABREAM
This seabream is silvery grey overall, with a darker back, and usually has six or seven dark vertical bars on each side. Its maximum weight is around 3.2 kg (7 lb). The gilthead (*Sparus aurata*) is somewhat similar, but has a golden stripe across its forehead.

Dark spot

BLACK SEABREAM
Spondyliosoma cantharus

RED SEABREAM
Pagellus bogaraveo

Natural food
Fish make up the bulk of the red seabream's diet, but black seabream and most species of porgy feed mainly on molluscs and crustaceans.

SCUP
This small porgy, which grows to about 1.8 kg (4 lb), is a dull silvery grey overall, often with faint dark bars on its sides and sometimes a blue stripe at the base of its dorsal fin. The front teeth are sharp and incisorlike. The closely related longspine porgy (*Stenotomus caprinus*) is found from North Carolina to Florida and in the Gulf of Mexico.

SCUP
Stenotomus chrysops

Size comparison

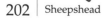

| Sheepshead | Jolthead porgy | Red seabream | Black seabream | Whitebone porgy | Scup |

Blue lines
above and
below eye

WHITEBONE PORGY
Calamus leucosteus

JOLTHEAD PORGY
Calamus bajonado

Blue line
below
eye

DISTRIBUTION
Red seabream: from Norway to the Mediterranean and the Canary Islands.
Black seabream: Norway to the Mediterranean and Angola.
Scup: Nova Scotia to Florida.
Whitebone porgy: North Carolina to southern Florida; Gulf of Mexico.
Sheepshead: mainland coastal waters from Nova Scotia to the Gulf of Mexico and Brazil.
Jolthead porgy: New England and Bermuda to Brazil.

WHITEBONE PORGY
The overall coloration of the whitebone porgy is a blotched, bluish silver, with small blue lines above and below each eye; its maximum weight is about 1.8 kg (4 lb). Like the jolthead porgy, the whitebone porgy is one of a number of fish of the genus *Calamus* found in western Atlantic and Caribbean waters. Others include the sheepshead porgy (*C. penna*), grass porgy (*C. arctifrons*), and saucereye porgy (*C. calamus*). The Pacific porgy (*C. brachysomus*) occurs from Baja California to Peru, and sometimes along the coast of southern California.

SHEEPSHEAD
This large porgy is silvery to yellowish white, with an olive-brown back, a dark bar across its nape, and five or six dark, slightly diagonal bars on each side. It is found close inshore, often in the brackish zones of estuaries, and uses its strong, flat teeth to crush molluscs and crabs and scrape barnacles from rocks and pilings. Its maximum weight is about 9.1 kg (20 lb). The red porgy (*Pagrus pagrus*) reaches a similar size and is found in relatively deep waters from New York to Argentina.

JOLTHEAD PORGY
The jolthead porgy gets its name from its habit of using its head to dislodge molluscs from rocks. Its body is a metallic, silvery yellow with bluish overtones; there is a blue line below each eye, and an orange patch at each corner of the mouth. The maximum weight of the jolthead porgy is about 3.6 kg (8 lb), and its flesh is good to eat but may cause ciguatera poisoning (*see page 164*).

SHEEPSHEAD
Archosargus probatocephalus

FISHING NOTES

Techniques
These species are taken by bottom fishing and wreck fishing.

Tackle
Use a 5.4 to 9.1 kg (12 to 20 lb) class boat rod with a multiplier reel, 5.4 to 9.1 kg (12 to 20 lb) mono line, a 2.4 m (8 ft) single-hook leader or a two-hook paternoster rig, and hook sizes from 6 to 2/0.

Bait
In general, porgy do not readily take artificial lures. Black and red seabream can be taken on mackerel feathers lowered to the bottom and retrieved in a jerky fashion, but, like porgy, they are best fished for with cut or whole natural baits. These include crab, shrimps, mussels, clams, worms, and sandeels, and strips of mackerel, cuttlefish, squid or octopus.

203

TECHNIQUES

THE BASIC TECHNIQUES of angling are easy to learn, but you could spend a lifetime and more mastering all the subtleties of any particular style. As a result, many experienced anglers tend to concentrate on one type of fishing, for example fly fishing, or on fishing for one particular species, such as bass or carp. While undoubtedly deriving great pleasure and satisfaction from their specialization, such anglers also deny themselves the variety and enjoyment offered by other kinds of fishing.

The predominant techniques used in a particular area depend as much, if not more, on the fish species sought after as on local custom and practice. For example, where the major freshwater quarry fish are predatory species, as is the case in much of North America, most fishing will be with artificial lures. But in parts of the world where non-predatory species provide the bulk of freshwater sport, as they do in Europe, the emphasis will be on fishing with hookbaits. This chapter covers the basic techniques of freshwater and saltwater angling, from pole fishing and legering to spinning and fly fishing, and from surfcasting and inshore boat fishing to big-game fishing. It also gives advice on setting up your tackle, and shows you how to tie the basic knots that join lines to reels, hooks and swivels to lines, and leaders to fly lines.

DEVELOPING SKILLS
Making the transition from hesitant beginner to skilled, confident, successful angler takes dedication and practice.

SETTING UP REELS

For a reel to work at its optimum efficiency, the line must be wound onto it properly and the spool must be neither underfilled nor overfilled. When loading a reel with line, it is also worth giving some thought to how you are going to use it. For example, many fixed-spool reel spools are deep with a big line capacity, but your style of fishing might require only a small proportion of the line to leave the reel. So instead of loading the spool with many hundreds of metres of high-quality and expensive mono, and actually using only, say, about a third of it, half-fill the spool with cheap nylon or even string and then attach a suitable length of "working line" on top.

FIXED-SPOOL & MULTIPLIER REELS

When loading these, it is important to wind the line on correctly and fill the spool to the correct level and line profile (the shape the wound line forms on the spool). Incorrect winding twists the line, which can reduce casting distance and cause line tangles. To load a fixed-spool reel, mount the spool of line in a spool holder and position it at right-angles to the front of the reel. The coils of line should leave the spool in the same direction as the bale arm of the reel rotates. When loading a multiplier, align the spool and reel so that the line runs straight from one to the other.

Spool

Overhand knot

REEL KNOT
Wet both knots to avoid damage and improve binding before pulling tight.

FIXED-SPOOL REEL
Position the reel and line spool as shown, so that coils of line unwind from the spool and wind onto the reel in the same direction, without twisting.

MULTIPLIER REEL
Position the line spool in front of the reel and in the same plane, so that the line runs straight off the spool onto the reel.

Filling a multiplier reel

In general, the spool of a multiplier should be filled with line to within around 2 mm (about $\frac{1}{16}$ in) of the flanges. However, some multipliers run better when slightly underfilled, but the only way to determine the optimum line level of a particular reel is by trial and error.

A level spread of line across the spool is vital if good casting distance is to be achieved, and to avoid problems such as rough running and vibration during casting. Although level wind mechanisms lay line evenly across the spool, they tend to feed the line on in a criss-cross fashion rather than in tight, closely packed turns. This can be a disadvantage in long-range fishing because it reduces the line capacity of the spool.

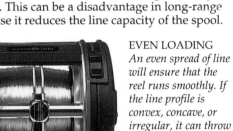

EVEN LOADING
An even spread of line will ensure that the reel runs smoothly. If the line profile is convex, concave, or irregular, it can throw the spool out of balance and cause wobbling or vibration during casting.

CORRECT LEVEL
When you find the line level that best suits your reel, mark it on the spool with a small dab of white enamel paint. This mark will show you how far to fill the spool when you load a new line.

Filling a fixed-spool reel

The line profile of a correctly filled fixed-spool reel is a smooth cone, tapering gently from the back of the spool to the front. The spool is full when the line at the front is around 2 mm (about $\frac{1}{16}$ in) below the lip. This ensures that the line will flow freely over the lip during casting, but will not fall off in coils and tangle.

Poor line profile

Overfilling the spool will produce a convex line profile, and create terrible problems during casting because coils of line will fall off and tangle. Underfilling limits casting distance by increasing the angle (and thus the friction) between line and the lip of the spool.

Profile correction

A poor line profile, such as this concave shape, can be corrected by winding on some of the line by hand in the opposite profile to that produced by the reel. Then, when the reel is about a third filled by this manner, wind on the rest of the line by turning the reel handle.

CORRECT PROFILE

CONVEX PROFILE

CONCAVE PROFILE

LOADING A FLY REEL

The best way to load a fly reel is to use a linewinder, but if you do not have one, you will need a second, similarly sized reel. Wind the fly line onto the second reel, join the backing line to it, wind the backing onto the reel until it is full, and cut it to length. Then take the first reel, tie the free end of the backing line to it, and wind on the backing and fly line.

1 When using a linewinder, first wind the fly line onto the empty reel.

2 Next, wind on backing until reel is full. Cut to length, then wind the backing from the reel onto one side of the linewinder, and the fly line onto the other.

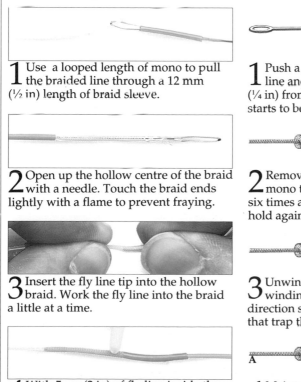

1

2

3

3 Tie the end of the backing to the reel, wind it on, and join the fly line to it. Wind the fly line on top of the backing.

4 Slightly underfill the reel: when in use the line will not wind on as tightly as it does when you load it on at home.

4

JOINING BACKING TO FLY LINE

Backing is made of materials such as braided Terylene, braided monofilament, and solid monofilament, both round and flattened. Joining braided backing to a fly line is easy, because it is hollow and the fly line is pushed up inside it and held in position with a sleeve. Solid mono should be tied to the fly line, using a knot such as the needle knot shown here. The flattened type must first be tapered to make it thin enough to go through the needle hole.

Braided mono to fly line

1 Use a looped length of mono to pull the braided line through a 12 mm (½ in) length of braid sleeve.

2 Open up the hollow centre of the braid with a needle. Touch the braid ends lightly with a flame to prevent fraying.

3 Insert the fly line tip into the hollow braid. Work the fly line into the braid a little at a time.

4 With 5 cm (2 in) of fly line inside the braid, slide the sleeve up the line to just overlap the braid; glue it in place.

Solid mono to fly line

1 Push a needle into the end of the fly line and out through the side 6 mm (¼ in) from the tip. Heat needle until line starts to bend.

2 Remove needle when cool. Thread the mono through the fly line and five or six times around it. Bring end back and hold against line.

3 Unwind all the mono turns by winding the long loops in the direction shown, creating new, tight turns that trap the loose end.

B

A

4 Maintain grip on knot. Gently tighten by pulling alternately at points A and B. When knot is firm, pull mono tight.

LEADER TO FLY LINE

Some fly lines are fitted with braided loops at their tips to which leaders can be attached quickly and easily. You can also buy ready-made loops for fixing to lines, or you can make your own from short lengths of braided mono.

Forming a braid loop

1 Push a large-eyed needle 2.5 cm (1 in) into the braid. Thread the braid through the needle eye.

2 Pull needle through braid until loose end emerges. Use a matchstick to keep the loop from closing completely.

3 Adjust the loop to the required size and trim the loose end flush. Pull the loose end back inside the braid.

4 Secure the loop with a few drops of a waterproof superglue such as Permabond 102 or Minocon.

BASIC KNOTS

All anglers should learn how to tie secure knots. This is because there will usually be at least two knots in a fishing rig (one joining the line to the reel or pole, the other joining the hook or lure to the line) and every knot is a potential weak point. Before tightening a knot, wet it with water to reduce the friction that can damage the line, and when attaching a hook, lure, or fly to a line be careful not to impale a finger on the hook point. Trim all loose ends so that they do not snag in the rod rings.

KNOTS FOR JOINING LINE TO TACKLE

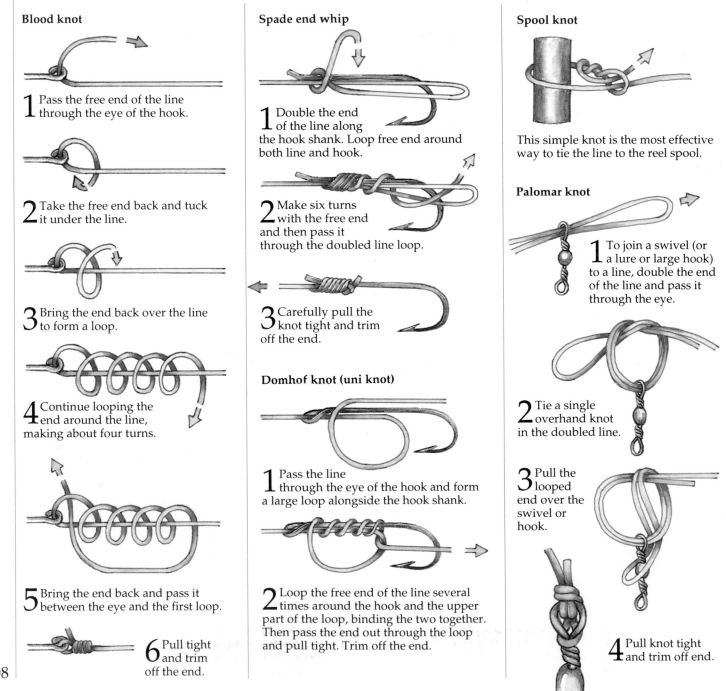

Blood knot

1 Pass the free end of the line through the eye of the hook.

2 Take the free end back and tuck it under the line.

3 Bring the end back over the line to form a loop.

4 Continue looping the end around the line, making about four turns.

5 Bring the end back and pass it between the eye and the first loop.

6 Pull tight and trim off the end.

Spade end whip

1 Double the end of the line along the hook shank. Loop free end around both line and hook.

2 Make six turns with the free end and then pass it through the doubled line loop.

3 Carefully pull the knot tight and trim off the end.

Domhof knot (uni knot)

1 Pass the line through the eye of the hook and form a large loop alongside the hook shank.

2 Loop the free end of the line several times around the hook and the upper part of the loop, binding the two together. Then pass the end out through the loop and pull tight. Trim off the end.

Spool knot

This simple knot is the most effective way to tie the line to the reel spool.

Palomar knot

1 To join a swivel (or a lure or large hook) to a line, double the end of the line and pass it through the eye.

2 Tie a single overhand knot in the doubled line.

3 Pull the looped end over the swivel or hook.

4 Pull knot tight and trim off end.

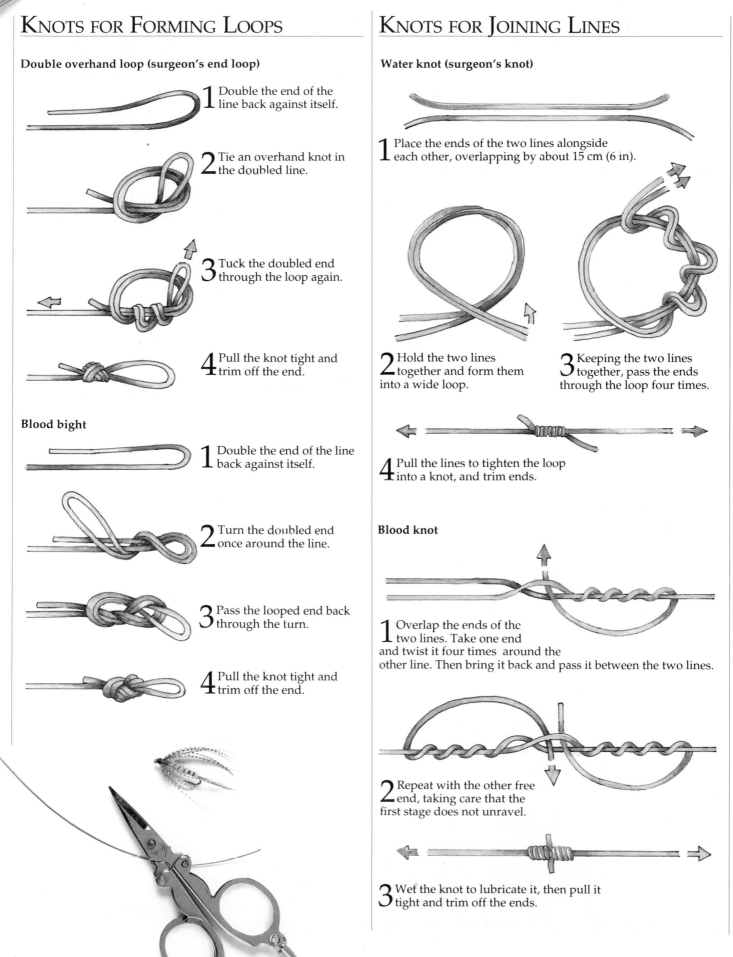

KNOTS FOR FORMING LOOPS

Double overhand loop (surgeon's end loop)

1 Double the end of the line back against itself.

2 Tie an overhand knot in the doubled line.

3 Tuck the doubled end through the loop again.

4 Pull the knot tight and trim off the end.

Blood bight

1 Double the end of the line back against itself.

2 Turn the doubled end once around the line.

3 Pass the looped end back through the turn.

4 Pull the knot tight and trim off the end.

KNOTS FOR JOINING LINES

Water knot (surgeon's knot)

1 Place the ends of the two lines alongside each other, overlapping by about 15 cm (6 in).

2 Hold the two lines together and form them into a wide loop.

3 Keeping the two lines together, pass the ends through the loop four times.

4 Pull the lines to tighten the loop into a knot, and trim ends.

Blood knot

1 Overlap the ends of the two lines. Take one end and twist it four times around the other line. Then bring it back and pass it between the two lines.

2 Repeat with the other free end, taking care that the first stage does not unravel.

3 Wet the knot to lubricate it, then pull it tight and trim off the ends.

PLAYING & LANDING

Playing a hooked fish successfully requires sound knowledge of your tackle, which must be well balanced in all respects. Before you start, set the reel clutch to slip when the rod has reached its "fighting curve", and check the setting occasionally through the day because use and temperature changes can affect the setting. The techniques shown here can be adapted directly for boat and seashore fishing, but fly fishing employs a different style of line control. When playing a fish on a fly reel, either use your free hand to pay out line under tension and to recover it, allowing it to fall in loose coils, or release line from the reel against the check mechanism or finger pressure on the spool rim, and recover it by winding in.

REEL CONTROL

When using a fixed-spool reel, engage the anti-reverse and brake the spool with your finger, or, on reels that allow it, let the handle backwind against pressure on the pick-up carrier base. With a multiplier, control the spool with your thumb.

Control with anti-reverse "on"

Backwinding (anti-reverse "off")

Thumb pressure control

PLAYING

When a fish runs, apply firm pressure by keeping the rod well up, and if necessary increase drag by using one of the reel control methods. When the rod is in this position it is well placed to absorb any lunges the fish may make. Never allow the rod to point down the line, or a break is almost certain. Do not be afraid to let a fish run, because that is what tires it.

Keep the rod well up to exert maximum pressure on a running fish

Increase the pressure by slowing the spool with your finger

TIRING THE FISH
If you play the fish until it is completely exhausted, it is less likely that you will lose it during landing.

Using sidestrain
To turn a fish away from snags, lower the rod so that it is parallel to the surface and pointing in the direction of the run (but not down the line). In one firm movement, sweep the rod around hard in the opposite direction. This knocks the fish off balance, forcing it to turn towards the pull. Repeat until under control.

REPEATING SIDESTRAIN (*left*)
Sidestrain must be applied repeatedly because a hooked fish will make many runs.

Lay the rod hard over to turn the fish

Stop the spool with finger pressure

Fish is knocked off balance and turned from snags

GAINING LINE
Each time you pump the rod you wind in more line, bringing the fish progressively closer to the net.

Pumping
When the fish reaches the end of a run and is tiring, lower the rod tip while reeling in line to maintain tension. With the rod at about 30°, clamp the spool to prevent line being drawn off and raise the rod smoothly to about 70°. This is "pumping". Hold the rod in this position to see if the fish will run again, and if it does not, repeat.

Keep the rod bent under tension and do not allow slack line between rod and fish

Alternately lower and raise the rod

Take your finger off the spool as you lower the rod and recover line. Stop the spool with finger pressure again when you raise the rod to "pump"

Draw the fish nearer with each successive pump

LANDING

Beaching, tailing, lipping, netting, and even gaffing are all methods of landing fish, but not all are equally suitable. Tailing is an ideal method for Atlantic salmon but will end in disaster with sea trout. Lipping is suitable for the less "toothy" species. Beaching removes mucus from the scales, leaving a fish vulnerable to infection, so is not suitable if the fish is to be released. Gaffing is banned in many areas, because a mistimed stroke can allow a fish to escape but leave it badly injured and doomed to a painful death.

LIPPING A FISH
Grip the lower lip gently between your thumb and forefinger.

Lipping
A played-out fish can be lifted from the water to be unhooked, or held in the water for unhooking, by gripping its lower lip firmly but gently between thumb and forefinger. This is not suitable for fish with sharp teeth, such as pike. For these, gently slip the fingers of a gloved hand into one gill casing, clamp down with your thumb, and carefully lift the fish out or unhook it in the water.

NETTING FROM THE BANK
Keep the net low in the water so that you do not drag the fish against the rim. If the fish is heavy, lift the net out of the water by grasping the rim; lifting it by the handle could bend the rim.

NETTING
Never attempt to net a lively fish by lunging wildly at it. When the fish is played out, it should be drawn over a fully submerged net with a single, smooth action of the rod.

Fish is alarmed by the obvious landing net

INCORRECT

A played-out fish will turn on its side

CORRECT

Do not take the rod too far back or you will lose tension on the line

Stop the spool with finger pressure as you raise the rod to draw the fish in; release the spool if the fish makes a sudden lunge

Net rim is well submerged

Draw the played-out fish to the net

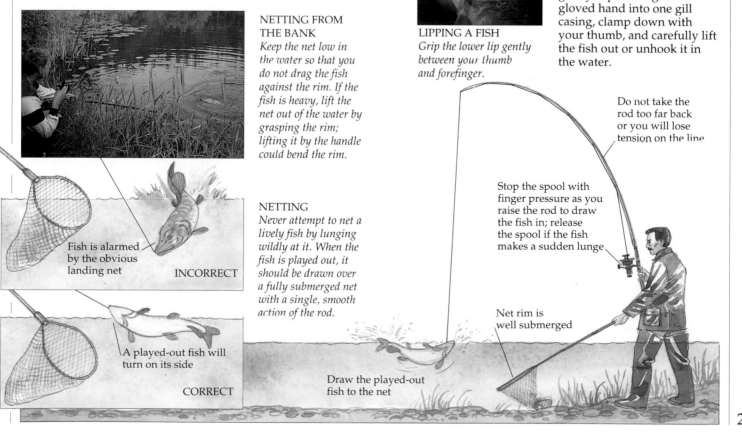

BASIC CASTING

Over the years, the design and construction of both fixed-spool and multiplier reels have been greatly improved to provide trouble-free casting and fishing for everyone. However, to get the best from any reel, you must learn how to cast properly, and practise your casting until you have eliminated any faults in your technique. Skill is more important than strength, and when you acquire it, you will be able to place your baits where you want them with consistent accuracy. The basic technique shown here is that of casting a lure with a fixed-spool reel, but it can also be used for casting float and leger rigs and, with the appropriate reel and line control methods, with multiplier and closed-face reels. The techniques of fly casting and surfcasting are different, and details of these are given on pages 232–35 and 250–51 respectively.

REEL CONTROL

FIXED-SPOOL REEL

First open the bale arm. Then hook the line over the pad of the index finger of your rod hand, to take the weight of the terminal tackle and prevent it from stripping line from the reel. For extra support, press the line against the rod handle.

MULTIPLIER/BAITCASTER

With a multiplier, clamp the thumb of your rod hand hard on the spool to stop it turning, and put the reel into free-spool mode. With most baitcasters, clamping your thumb onto the spool depresses a bar that disengages it.

CLOSED-FACE/SPINCASTER

On these reels, the line passes through a hole or slot in the front casing and is guided onto the fixed spool by a steel pin. When you want to release the line at the end of a cast, you simply press a button on the reel to retract the pin.

THE OVERHEAD CAST

With the bale arm open, support the line on your index finger with the lure about 30 to 45 cm (12 to 18 in) below the rod tip. Hold the rod at the 2.00 position and in line with the spot at which you want the lure to land (**A**).

Lift the rod briskly but smoothly towards the 12.00 position by raising your forearm and cocking your wrist back (**B**). At the start of the lift, the inertia of the rod tip and the weight of the lure will cause the tip to droop.

Stop the rod at the 12.00 position (**C**). The tip will straighten, and then bend behind you as it is pulled back by the still-travelling lure. You will feel a pull on the rod tip as the lure reaches the limit of its travel.

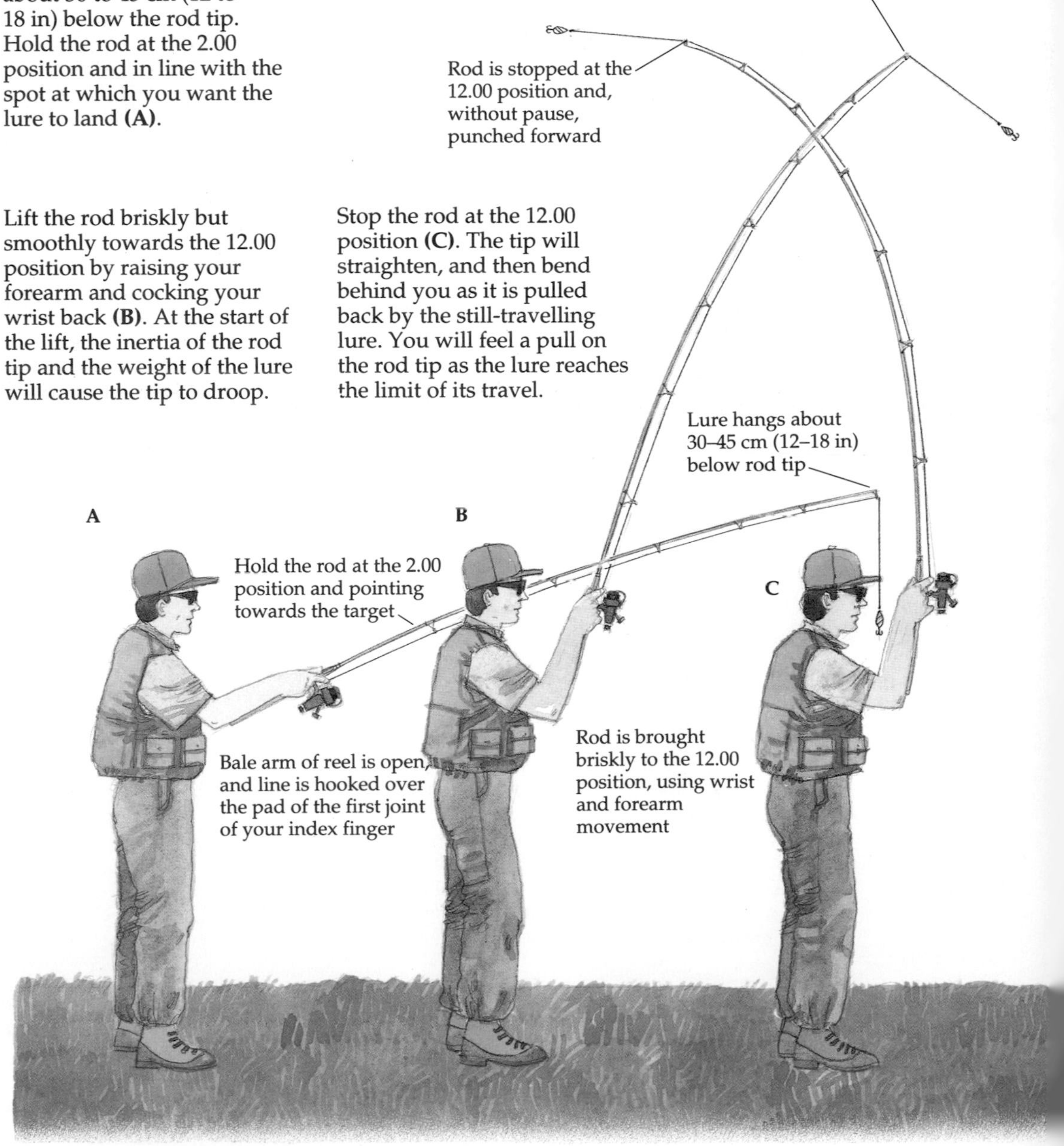

Rod tip flexes under its own inertia and the weight of the lure

Rod is stopped at the 12.00 position and, without pause, punched forward

Lure hangs about 30–45 cm (12–18 in) below rod tip

A

Hold the rod at the 2.00 position and pointing towards the target

B

Bale arm of reel is open, and line is hooked over the pad of the first joint of your index finger

Rod is brought briskly to the 12.00 position, using wrist and forearm movement

C

212

LURE FLIGHT
When casting, always pick a target spot in the swim and aim to land your lure (or other terminal tackle) in it. After releasing the line, follow the path of the lure with the rod tip so that the line flows freely through the tip ring. The lure should travel in a gentle arc towards the water.

COMMON CASTING FAULTS

The lure overshoots
• Too much power in the cast
• Line release not slowed by feathering the spool

The lure falls short
• Lure too light
• Line was released too early during the cast
• Rod held too high after line was released

The lure lands too hard
• Lure was released with the rod at too low an angle and failed to describe a gentle arc through the air

The cast is inaccurate
• The lure went off course because rod was allowed to move from side to side as the forward cast was made

THE CLOCK FACE
Clock face positions are used to describe the rod movements during casting, and make it easy to remember the position of the rod at various stages of the cast.

Rod under maximum load

When you feel the pull on the tip, the rod is under maximum load and storing energy like a spring **(D)**. Immediately punch the rod forward. This action, plus the energy released by the rod as it straightens, will throw the lure rapidly forward.

Stop the movement of the rod at about the 2.00 position, and at the same time straighten your index finger to release the line **(E)**. The lure will shoot forward in an arc towards the water, stripping line from the reel.

As the lure falls, follow its descent with the rod tip **(F)**. When it lands, put your index finger on the spool rim to stop the line, and turn the reel handle to close the bale arm and keep a tight line between the lure and the rod.

D

Line held by index finger as the rod is driven forward to the line release point

E

Index finger releases the line at the same time as the rod is stopped

Stop the rod at about the 2.00 position

F

Rod is lowered as lure drops to the water

Wind to close bale arm

Line can be slowed by "feathering" with the index finger

LINE CONTROL

FIXED-SPOOL REEL

To prevent the lure from overshooting the target, and to achieve a gentle landing, slow its flight by gently dabbing or touching the lip of the spool with the tip of your index finger. This "feathering" acts as a brake on the line.

MULTIPLIER/BAITCASTER

To slow down a bait fished on a multiplier or baitcaster, apply gentle thumb pressure to the revolving spool (but beware of friction burns). Overruns are rare with modern reels because they have magnetic braking systems.

CLOSED-FACE/SPINCASTER

Line control with these reels can be difficult, because the spool is shrouded and finger pressure on the lip is not possible. Slow the line by gently squeezing it between the index finger and thumb of your free hand as it emerges from the casing.

213

LURE FISHING – SPINNING

The relative ease of use of spinning tackle accounts for spinning being one of the most popular forms of fishing worldwide. When correctly loaded with a full spool of line, spinning reels allow long, effortless casts to be made and the angler often has to do no more than crank the handle to make the lure fish attractively. Obviously, the skilled practitioner will outfish the tyro, but spinning offers the beginner the best chance of comparatively easy success. Spinners are so termed because at least part of the lure revolves. Usually, there is a rotating blade that is separate from the body, as in standard spinners, spinnerbaits, and buzzbaits, but sometimes the whole lure rotates, as is the case in the Devon minnow and similar lures. Spinners attract fish by visual stimulus and by creating vibrations that act on the fish's lateral lines; if used correctly, they will appeal to any predatory fish.

ANTI-KINK DEVICES

The keel effect of an anti-kink vane or weight between the main line and trace helps to reduce line twist. An anti-kink weight should be fitted immediately above the swivel for maximum effect, but weights should not be used if they interfere with the action of a lure.

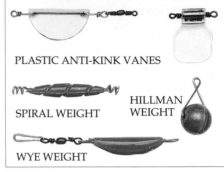

PLASTIC ANTI-KINK VANES

SPIRAL WEIGHT

HILLMAN WEIGHT

WYE WEIGHT

STANDARD SPINNERS

The most common type, the clevis, has a blade mounted on a shaft via a clevis (link). Another type, the sonic, has a blade mounted directly over the shaft. A standard spinner must be retrieved to make the blade rotate in stillwater, but in running water the current works the blade. Fish upstream in fast water, because fishing downstream makes the lure swim too shallow. In slow water, fish downstream because casting upstream allows the lure to sink too quickly.

CLEVIS TYPE

SONIC TYPE

Blade shapes and actions
The shape and thickness of a spinner blade affects the action of the lure. The high water resistance of a broad blade makes it ideal for stillwaters and slow streams, but in fast water it will rise to the surface. A thin blade has less resistance and can be fished in fast water without skating on the surface.

KEY TO BLADES
1 Indiana; 2 French;
3 Colorado; 4 Fluted;
5 In-line; 6 Willowleaf;
7 Ripple; 8 June Bug.

1

2

3

4

5

6

7

8

UPSTREAM SPINNING

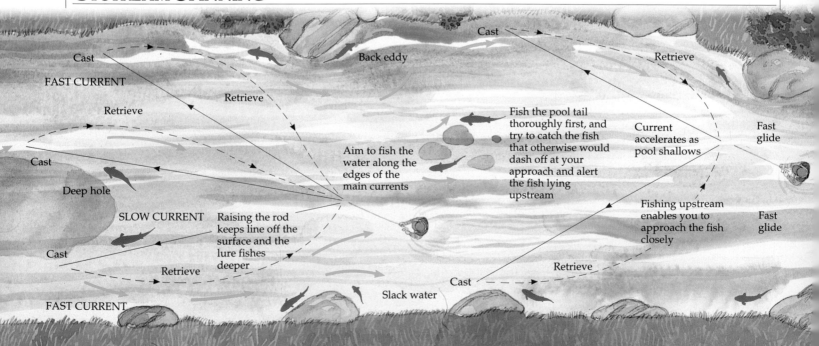

Cast

Back eddy

Cast

Retrieve

Cast

FAST CURRENT

Retrieve

Retrieve

Fish the pool tail thoroughly first, and try to catch the fish that otherwise would dash off at your approach and alert the fish lying upstream

Current accelerates as pool shallows

Fast glide

Cast

Deep hole

Aim to fish the water along the edges of the main currents

SLOW CURRENT

Raising the rod keeps line off the surface and the lure fishes deeper

Fishing upstream enables you to approach the fish closely

Fast glide

Cast

Retrieve

Retrieve

Cast

FAST CURRENT

Slack water

BUOYANT SPINNERS

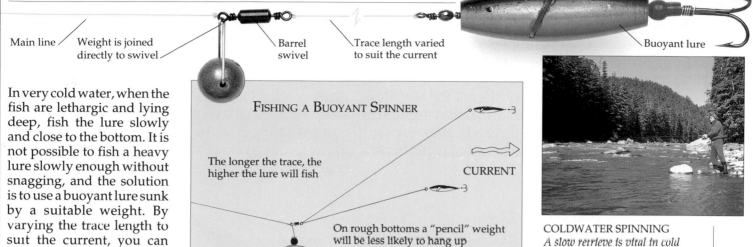

Main line / Weight is joined directly to swivel / Barrel swivel / Trace length varied to suit the current / Buoyant lure

In very cold water, when the fish are lethargic and lying deep, fish the lure slowly and close to the bottom. It is not possible to fish a heavy lure slowly enough without snagging, and the solution is to use a buoyant lure sunk by a suitable weight. By varying the trace length to suit the current, you can work the lure at the fish's eye level.

FISHING A BUOYANT SPINNER

The longer the trace, the higher the lure will fish

CURRENT

On rough bottoms a "pencil" weight will be less likely to hang up

COLDWATER SPINNING
A slow retrieve is vital in cold water, and a sunk buoyant lure fishes slowly without snagging.

SPINNERBAITS & BUZZBAITS

The most obvious difference between a spinnerbait and a buzzbait is in the blade. A spinnerbait has a fluttering blade – such as a broad, teardrop-shaped Colorado or Indiana, or a narrow, elliptical willowleaf – while the buzzbait has a single or double buzzblade rotating on a shaft. The buzzbait is designed solely for surface fishing, where its blade causes noisy, splashy disturbance. This makes it an excellent lure for weedy shallows or turbid water; vary the retrieve until successful. Twin-bladed lures, which create even more disturbance, are ideal for slow retrieves. Spinnerbaits are more versatile and can be fished at all speeds and from the surface to the bottom, or even jigged vertically around cover. Tipping the hooks of Indiana and willowleaf spinners with worms, minnows, or strips of pork rind can improve their success rate.

SUMMER SPINNING
In hot, sunny weather, when fish seek the shade of weedbeds and brush, buzzbaits are excellent lures for drawing them from their cover.

DOWNSTREAM SPINNING

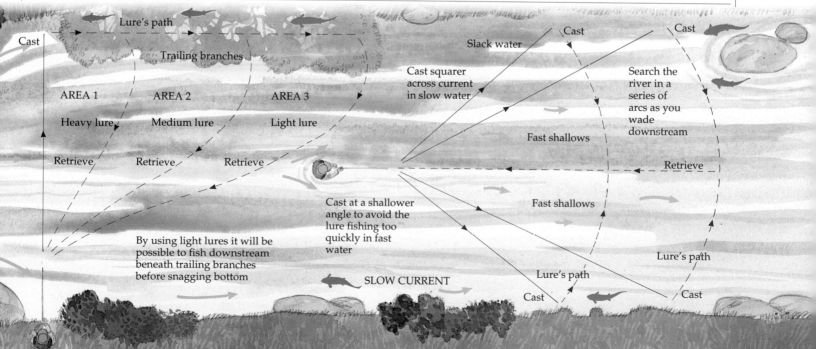

Cast / Lure's path / Trailing branches

AREA 1 / AREA 2 / AREA 3

Heavy lure / Medium lure / Light lure

Retrieve / Retrieve / Retrieve

By using light lures it will be possible to fish downstream beneath trailing branches before snagging bottom

Cast at a shallower angle to avoid the lure fishing too quickly in fast water

SLOW CURRENT

Slack water

Cast squarer across current in slow water

Fast shallows

Fast shallows

Lure's path

Cast

Cast / Cast

Search the river in a series of arcs as you wade downstream

Retrieve

Lure's path

Cast

LURE FISHING – SPOONS

Spoons can be divided into the broad categories of trolling spoons and casting spoons. The trolling spoons are generally too thin to be cast far and their use is restricted to trolling from a moving boat. Casting spoons can be either of the weedless or non-weedless types, the former having hooks with nylon or metal weedguards that prevent them from snagging on weeds, submerged brush, or other aquatic debris.

A spoon's action depends on its shape, weight, and the speed of the retrieval. Deeply concave spoons wobble more than shallow ones, while light spoons have more action than heavy ones of similar size. Use light, thin spoons in shallow water or the top layers of a lake, and heavy, thick models in deep water. Each spoon has an optimum retrieve rate that imparts the most enticing action, and this can be found by trial and error.

SPOON-FISHING TACKLE

The most suitable tackle for spoon fishing is a light spinning rod and a fixed-spool reel, or a medium baitcasting rod and a multiplier reel, plus mono line with a short wire trace if necessary. There is no need for a sensitive rod, because bite indication is never a problem when fishing artificial lures. Always attach the spoon to the line or trace with a good swivel, because tying the line direct to the attachment hole of the spoon can interfere with its action, as can adding weight to the rig. In addition, line twist can be severe with some types of spoon. Fit a rounded snap swivel into the attachment hole and join the line to it.

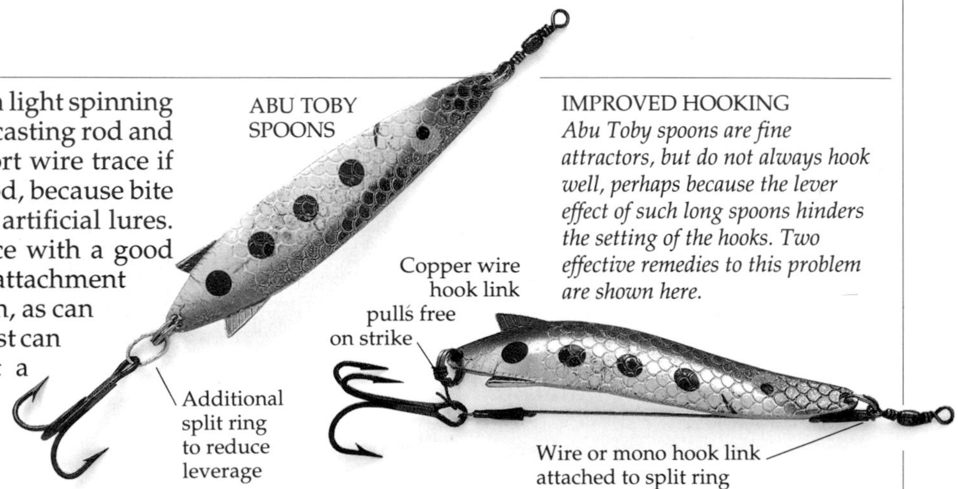

ABU TOBY SPOONS

Additional split ring to reduce leverage

IMPROVED HOOKING
Abu Toby spoons are fine attractors, but do not always hook well, perhaps because the lever effect of such long spoons hinders the setting of the hooks. Two effective remedies to this problem are shown here.

Copper wire hook link pulls free on strike

Wire or mono hook link attached to split ring

TANDEM SWIVELS

Ball-bearing swivels

Split-ring connection

Swivels 45 cm (18 in) above lure

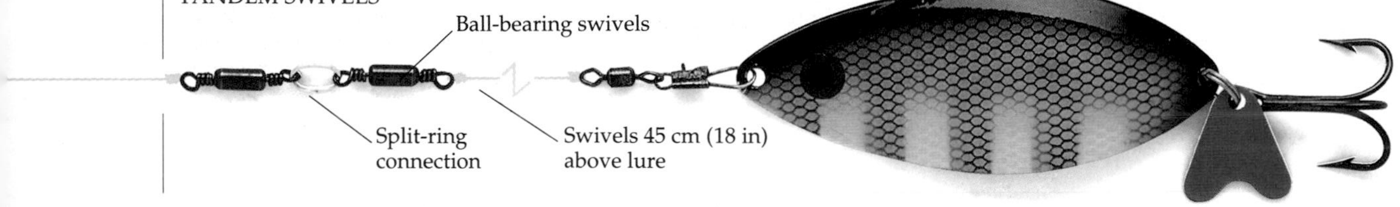

TANDEM SWIVELS
Two ball-bearing swivels joined by a split ring, about 45 cm (18 in) from the spoon, will virtually eliminate line twist.

CASTING PATTERNS

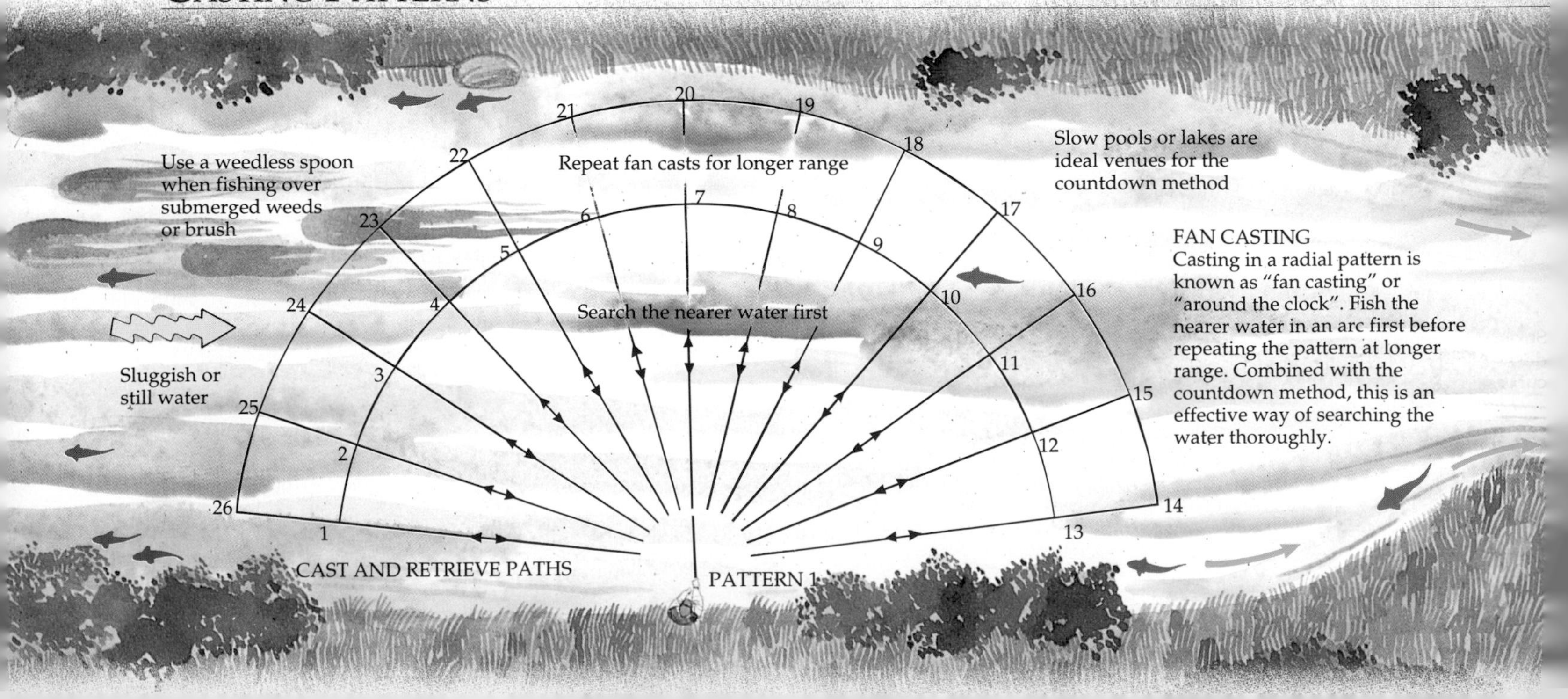

Use a weedless spoon when fishing over submerged weeds or brush

Repeat fan casts for longer range

Search the nearer water first

Sluggish or still water

Slow pools or lakes are ideal venues for the countdown method

FAN CASTING
Casting in a radial pattern is known as "fan casting" or "around the clock". Fish the nearer water in an arc first before repeating the pattern at longer range. Combined with the countdown method, this is an effective way of searching the water thoroughly.

CAST AND RETRIEVE PATHS

PATTERN 1

SPOON-FISHING TECHNIQUES

In lakes, the countdown method gives consistent fishing depth if the retrieve rate is constant, but rivers currents will affect the spoon's depth. Retrieve a spoon cast upstream quicker than one cast downstream because it will sink deeper, travelling with the flow. Use light spoons for upstream casting and for shallow or slowly retrieved downstream work. Heavy spoons are good when cast downstream in fast water or upstream in slow pools.

The countdown method

This helps you to find, and fish at, the feeding depth of your quarry. Cast the spoon out, allow it to sink, and count the number of seconds that pass until it hits bottom. Then retrieve steadily. If it reaches bottom on a count of, say, 10, and you get no strikes on the retrieve, on the next cast retrieve after a count of 8. Reduce the count by 2 on each subsequent cast until a fish strikes. Repeat the successful count to fish the taking zone.

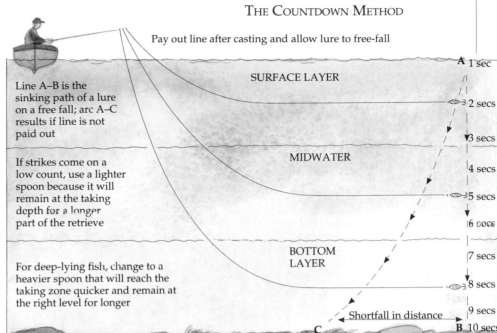

THE COUNTDOWN METHOD

Pay out line after casting and allow lure to free-fall

Line A–B is the sinking path of a lure on a free fall; arc A–C results if line is not paid out

SURFACE LAYER

If strikes come on a low count, use a lighter spoon because it will remain at the taking depth for a longer part of the retrieve

MIDWATER

For deep-lying fish, change to a heavier spoon that will reach the taking zone quicker and remain at the right level for longer

BOTTOM LAYER

Shortfall in distance

A 1 sec
2 secs
3 secs
4 secs
5 secs
6 secs
7 secs
8 secs
9 secs
B 10 secs

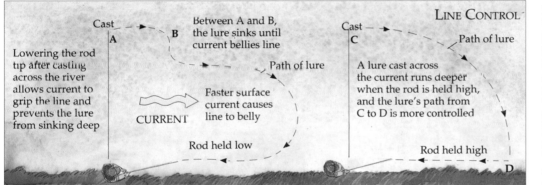

LINE CONTROL

Lowering the rod tip after casting across the river allows current to grip the line and prevents the lure from sinking deep

Between A and B, the lure sinks until current bellies line

Path of lure

Faster surface current causes line to belly

CURRENT

Rod held low

A lure cast across the current runs deeper when the rod is held high, and the lure's path from C to D is more controlled

Path of lure

Rod held high

Line control

When fishing upstream, holding the rod tip high lifts the spoon in the water, while keeping it low allows the spoon to sink. This is most obvious with a short line. When casting across the flow, however, current drag on the line holds the spoon up while a high rod allows it to sink. This effect decreases the more downstream you cast, until the upstream rule applies.

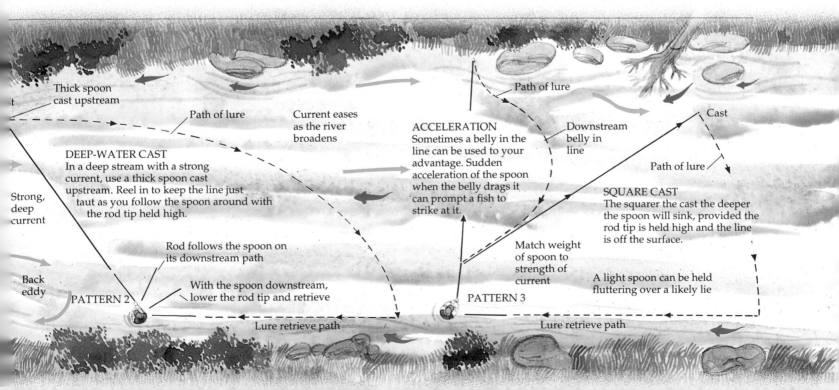

Thick spoon cast upstream

Path of lure

Current eases as the river broadens

Path of lure

Cast

Downstream belly in line

Path of lure

DEEP-WATER CAST
In a deep stream with a strong current, use a thick spoon cast upstream. Reel in to keep the line just taut as you follow the spoon around with the rod tip held high.

ACCELERATION
Sometimes a belly in the line can be used to your advantage. Sudden acceleration of the spoon when the belly drags it can prompt a fish to strike at it.

SQUARE CAST
The squarer the cast the deeper the spoon will sink, provided the rod tip is held high and the line is off the surface.

Strong, deep current

Rod follows the spoon on its downstream path

Match weight of spoon to strength of current

A light spoon can be held fluttering over a likely lie

Back eddy

PATTERN 2

With the spoon downstream, lower the rod tip and retrieve

PATTERN 3

Lure retrieve path

Lure retrieve path

LURE FISHING – PLUGS

Within the ranks of what we term "plugs" are lures for fishing at all levels, from the surface to the bottom, and at all speeds. As with all artificial lure fishing, matching the lure to the quarry and the conditions is vital. In general, the smaller the quarry is, the smaller the lure should be: a 30 cm (12 in) lure might be none too large for a pike but it would not be effective for trout. Fishing cold or muddy water necessitates getting the lure down to eyeball level, and in such conditions the first choice of lure would be a vibrating plug or a deep diver, whereas in warmer water, where predatory fish are more alert, a quickly retrieved, shallow-diving crankbait or surface lure is called for.

THE OPEN LOOP

Open-looped knot

A split ring, link swivel, or tight knot can adversely affect a lure's action. Tying the lure to the line with an open-looped knot allows it to swing freely.

SURFACE LURE TECHNIQUES

Surface lures are at their most effective in shallow water, where fish lying near the bottom are not too far away to be attracted by them. The water should also be calm, because surface choppiness can affect their action. A propbait can be cast into small gaps in surface weed and then twitched back on a slack line or retrieved steadily, in which case the action of the propeller will cause more disturbance than is achieved by most surface plugs. To prevent the nose dipping below the surface and spoiling the action, tie the lure direct to the line or trace without a snap or swivel. Crawler-type lures with projecting arms or wide, scooped faceplates fish best over shallow water on a moderate retrieve: vary the retrieve until the best action is achieved. The popper or chugger surface lures have a concave face that makes a popping sound on a short, twitched retrieve, although when fished into small openings in weedbeds they are often taken when stationary. Stickbaits are the best surface lures for bringing fish up from the depths, and the basic method of retrieve for these is known as "walking the dog".

Minnow plugs

Drifting a floating minnow plug downstream allows you to fish at far greater range than you could cast such a light lure. For bankside lies, drift the lure down past the fish. When you stop the line, the lure will dive to about 30 cm (12 in), depending on the speed of the current, and you can then bring it back upstream through the lie. From midriver, fish the lure back in a series of arcs by swinging the rod from side to side during the retrieve.

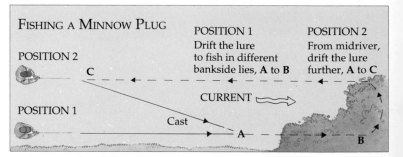

FISHING A MINNOW PLUG

POSITION 2

POSITION 1

POSITION 1
Drift the lure to fish in different bankside lies, **A** to **B**

POSITION 2
From midriver, drift the lure further, **A** to **C**

CURRENT

Cast

Stickbaits

Cast out a stickbait, jerk the rod tip vertically, then let the line go slack, and the lure will slip to one side. Repeat the action and the lure will dodge to the other side. This is known as "walking the dog". Fast jerks without letting the line go slack result in the lure moving to one side only. A fast, tip-actioned rod is best for this technique, and because stickbaits float it is an ideal method over submerged weeds or brush.

STICKBAITS
These are effective lures for most gamefish.

WALKING THE DOG

Cast

For a zigzag retrieve path alternate left and right jerks

Consecutive jerks make the lure veer off to one side

Jerk rod alternately left and right

PLUG FISHING METHODS

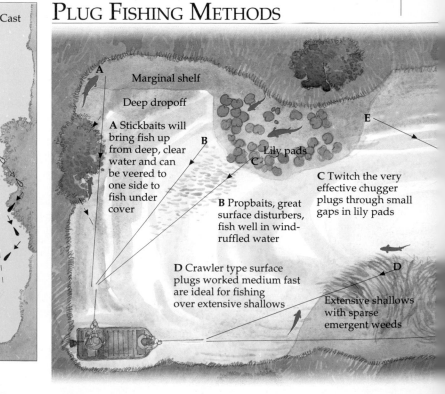

Marginal shelf

Deep dropoff

Lily pads

A Stickbaits will bring fish up from deep, clear water and can be veered to one side to fish under cover

B Propbaits, great surface disturbers, fish well in wind-ruffled water

C Twitch the very effective chugger plugs through small gaps in lily pads

D Crawler type surface plugs worked medium fast are ideal for fishing over extensive shallows

Extensive shallows with sparse emergent weeds

CRANKBAIT TECHNIQUES

Crankbaits, which are plugs with lips that cause them to dive to a greater or lesser degree, are a very useful group of lures. Some are sinking plugs, made in a variety of densities to fish at different depths, while others float at rest and dive when retrieved. Try out your crankbaits in deep, clear water to find their approximate maximum working depths, and use an indelible felt-tip pen to mark each lure with its depth. When fishing, choose the lure to suit the water. Fishing shallow water calls for a shallow-diving lure, while a sinking deep-diver is needed to fish deep

holes. To attain maximum depth, make a long cast and keep the rod tip low on the retrieve. Raising the tip lifts the lure in the water, as does using too thick a line. Generally, in water temperatures above about 16°C (60°F), predators are more active and willing to hit a lure fished quickly, while in cold or dirty water they are lethargic and more likely to be tempted by a slowly moving crankbait. In cold water, bumping bottom is a good tactic, and the crankbait's tendency to fish nose-down means that the lip often bounces the lure clear of any potential snags.

DIVING LIPS
To tell whether a crankbait is a shallow or deep diver, look at the front of the lure. A small, steeply angled lip signifies a shallow diver, but a deep-running bait will have a long, fairly shallow-angled lip.

SHALLOW DIVER

DEEP DIVER

Floating divers

For prospecting the water layers with a floating diver, choose one that will dive to a depth of about 3.7 m (12 ft) on a fast retrieve. With this type of lure, it is possible to follow the bottom contours quite closely by varying the speed of retrieve and thus the depth of the lure. However, to fish the surface or deeper holes effectively, choose a lure designed specifically for those purposes. Fishing the lure on the shady side of a bottom feature such as a sunken tree, and parallel to it, keeps it in the likeliest water for the longest period.

THE VERSATILE FLOATING DIVER

To reach maximum depth, cast as far as possible and keep rod tip low on retrieve

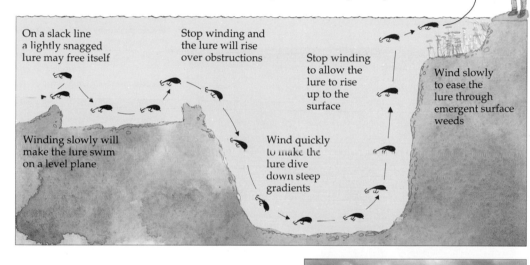

On a slack line a lightly snagged lure may free itself

Stop winding and the lure will rise over obstructions

Stop winding to allow the lure to rise up to the surface

Wind slowly to ease the lure through emergent surface weeds

Winding slowly will make the lure swim on a level plane

Wind quickly to make the lure dive down steep gradients

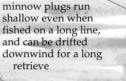

Shallow reef

E Thin-bodied minnow plugs run shallow even when fished on a long line, and can be drifted downwind for a long retrieve

F Vibrating plugs can be fished at all levels, in open water or along the edge of weeds, but snag easily

H Jerkbaits are excellent for the larger fish, and should be worked with vertical jerks of the rod while winding the reel

Deep, open water

G A buoyant/diving crankbait allows a wide variety of water to be fished from weedy shallows to depths of 3.7 m (12 ft)

Work the shaded side of cover

DEEP-DIVING PLUGS
This pike was taken on a deep-diving plug. These plugs, which have a lot of water resistance, should be used with multiplier reels.

LEGERING

Legering is a versatile technique that allows the bait to be cast a long way and presented at or near the bottom to attract fish that feed there. Although it lacks the finesse of float fishing, it does allow the bait to be presented effectively in situations where a float rig would be working at its limits. These include fishing at long range, on fast rivers, under weed rafts, and in deep water or rough weather on big lakes and pits. Apart from when fishing with a bolt rig, legering generally involves using the minimum practicable amount of weight in a given set of circumstances, in order to produce the lowest level of resistance to a taking fish. The lowest possible resistance is achieved by freelining, a variant of legering in which the only weight on the line is that of the baited hook.

ROD RESTS
A legered bait does not need constant manipulation, so the rod can be left on rod rests until the bite indicator shows that it is time to strike.

BITE INDICATORS

Because there is no float on a leger rig, bites are detected either by touch (holding the line over a finger or between finger and thumb so that the tiniest pull on the line can be felt) or by using a bite indicator. The simplest indicator is the rod tip itself, but other methods are preferable when more sensitivity is required. Quivertips, springtips, and swingtips, fitted into the tip ring, show up taps that would be missed on a rod tip, while a bobbin clipped on the line between reel and butt ring allows some slack line to be taken before the strike is made. Monkey climbers are used either alone or in conjunction with electronic indicators that sound when there is a pull on the line.

SWINGTIP
A swingtip is sensitive, but limits casting distance. Add lead wire in strong winds or undertows.

QUIVERTIP
A quivertip will "soften" close-range bites and is sensitive enough to show bites developing.

MONKEY CLIMBER
This is connected to the line to indicate any pull on it. Add a light stick for night fishing.

TOUCH LEGERING
Point rod at the bait. Crook a finger over the line, or hold it between thumb and finger.

THE RUNNING LEGER

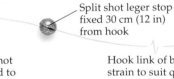

Main line of suitable strength

Swivel

Loop of heavy nylon

Split shot clipped to nylon loop

Split shot leger stop fixed 30 cm (12 in) from hook

Hook link of breaking strain to suit quarry

Hook size and bait to suit quarry

This is a simple but effective rig for close-range work. If split shot are used for weight and pinched on to the loop of nylon (the link), the rig will not snag since the shot will pull off when put under tension. If the shot on the link are butted up against one another, the rig can be made to roll along the bottom to make the bait run through the swim, which is often a highly effective method of fishing for chub and barbel. Conversely, if the shot is spaced apart, the rig will hold bottom firmly in fast water. The link on the running leger should be stopped about 30 cm (12 in) from the hook by a plastic leger stop or a BB shot. Use thick nylon for the link to ensure that it stands clear of the main line.

RUNNING LEGER IN ACTION

THE FIXED PATERNOSTER

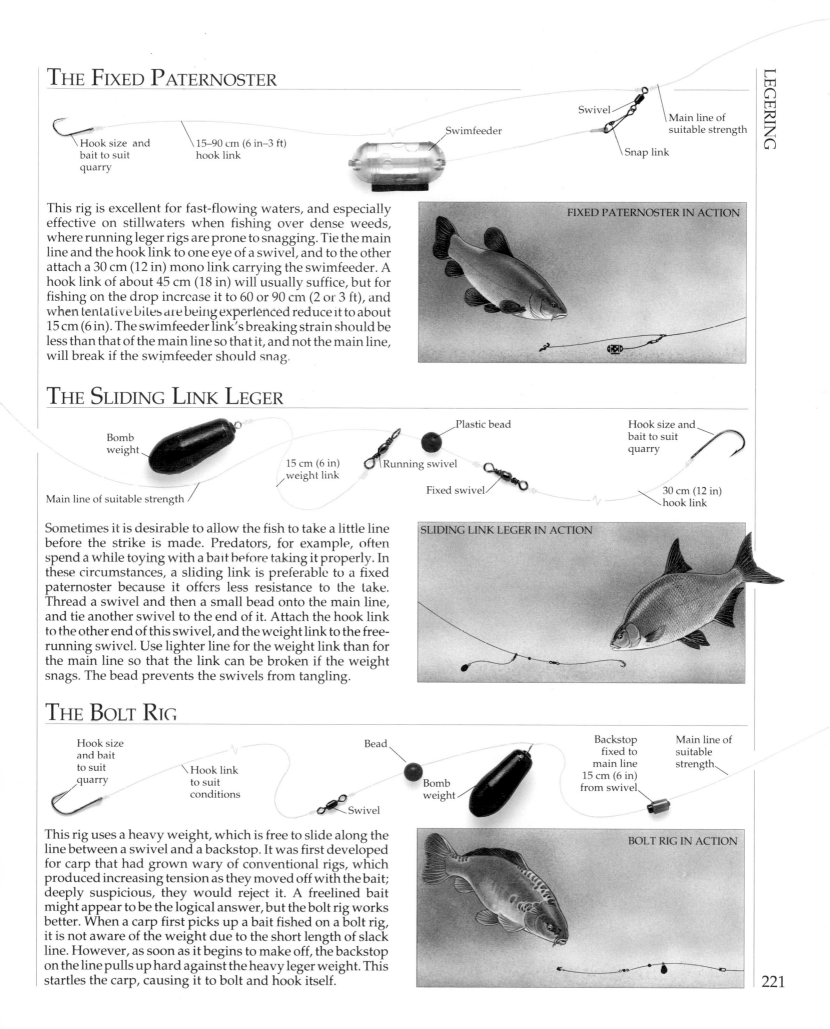

Hook size and bait to suit quarry

15–90 cm (6 in–3 ft) hook link

Swimfeeder

Swivel

Main line of suitable strength

Snap link

This rig is excellent for fast-flowing waters, and especially effective on stillwaters when fishing over dense weeds, where running leger rigs are prone to snagging. Tie the main line and the hook link to one eye of a swivel, and to the other attach a 30 cm (12 in) mono link carrying the swimfeeder. A hook link of about 45 cm (18 in) will usually suffice, but for fishing on the drop increase it to 60 or 90 cm (2 or 3 ft), and when tentative bites are being experienced reduce it to about 15 cm (6 in). The swimfeeder link's breaking strain should be less than that of the main line so that it, and not the main line, will break if the swimfeeder should snag.

FIXED PATERNOSTER IN ACTION

THE SLIDING LINK LEGER

Bomb weight

15 cm (6 in) weight link

Running swivel

Plastic bead

Fixed swivel

Hook size and bait to suit quarry

30 cm (12 in) hook link

Main line of suitable strength

Sometimes it is desirable to allow the fish to take a little line before the strike is made. Predators, for example, often spend a while toying with a bait before taking it properly. In these circumstances, a sliding link is preferable to a fixed paternoster because it offers less resistance to the take. Thread a swivel and then a small bead onto the main line, and tie another swivel to the end of it. Attach the hook link to the other end of this swivel, and the weight link to the free-running swivel. Use lighter line for the weight link than for the main line so that the link can be broken if the weight snags. The bead prevents the swivels from tangling.

SLIDING LINK LEGER IN ACTION

THE BOLT RIG

Hook size and bait to suit quarry

Hook link to suit conditions

Swivel

Bead

Bomb weight

Backstop fixed to main line 15 cm (6 in) from swivel

Main line of suitable strength

This rig uses a heavy weight, which is free to slide along the line between a swivel and a backstop. It was first developed for carp that had grown wary of conventional rigs, which produced increasing tension as they moved off with the bait; deeply suspicious, they would reject it. A freelined bait might appear to be the logical answer, but the bolt rig works better. When a carp first picks up a bait fished on a bolt rig, it is not aware of the weight due to the short length of slack line. However, as soon as it begins to make off, the backstop on the line pulls up hard against the heavy leger weight. This startles the carp, causing it to bolt and hook itself.

BOLT RIG IN ACTION

FLOAT FISHING – RUNNING WATER

Floats attached bottom-end only, such as the waggler, come into their own on slow-flowing rivers, and a waggler really scores when the wind is blowing. Because it is attached bottom-end only, most of the line between the waggler and the rod is under water and thus impervious to the wind or surface movement. On fast-flowing waters, floats attached top and bottom (by a pair of float rubbers) are the order of the day. Loafers, sticks, and Avons all fall into this group.

CASTING A WAGGLER
For fishing at long range, let the float swing smartly behind you when you begin the cast and then push hard forward with the rod to achieve distance. A more relaxed version of this cast will achieve less distance, but with less risk of the hook rig catching in bankside vegetation.

SPLIT SHOT

Split shot do more than just add weight to the line. Positioned in particular ways on the line, shot can present a bait in various fashions, ensure that different types of bite register on the float, and prevent tangling of the rig in casting. Split shot are available in a variety of sizes from the biggest, termed SSG or swan shot, down to the so-called dust shot that is often used near to the hook to produce a slow descent of the bait through the water.

Shot size	Weight (grams)
SSG	1.89
AAA	0.81
BB	0.4
No. 1	0.28
No. 4	0.17
No. 6	0.105
No. 8	0.063
No. 10	0.034
No. 12	0.02
No. 13	0.012

PLUMBING THE DEPTH

When using a float, it is important to know the depth of the swim you are fishing, and you can find it by using a plummet. Fit the plummet onto the hook and gently lower it to the bottom, then reposition the float so that it just protrudes from the surface. The distance between the float and the hook will be the approximate depth of the water. Plumb various other points around the swim to build up a mental picture of the bottom.

BASIC WAGGLER RIGS

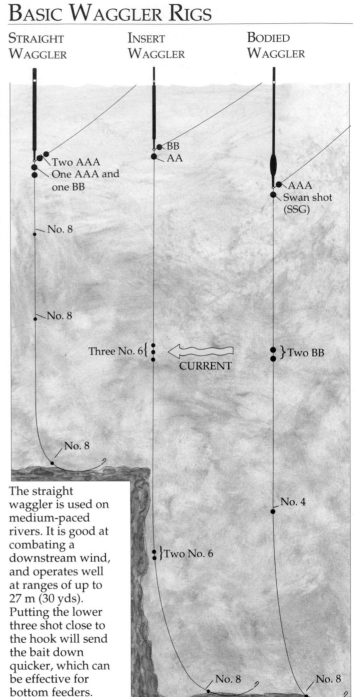

STRAIGHT WAGGLER — Two AAA / One AAA and one BB — No. 8 — No. 8 — Three No. 6 — No. 8

INSERT WAGGLER — BB / AA — Two No. 6 — No. 8

BODIED WAGGLER — AAA / Swan shot (SSG) — Two BB — No. 4 — No. 8

CURRENT

The straight waggler is used on medium-paced rivers. It is good at combating a downstream wind, and operates well at ranges of up to 27 m (30 yds). Putting the lower three shot close to the hook will send the bait down quicker, which can be effective for bottom feeders.

LOCKING SHOT
These lock a float attached bottom-end only to the required point on the line.

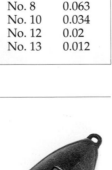

Float stem

Float adapter

Locking shot

THE PLUMMET
A plummet, a small weight, fits over or clamps onto the hook.

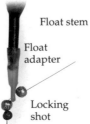

The insert waggler float is ideal on wide, slow-flowing rivers when fish are feeding on the drop (the thin insert gives good bite indication). This rig can be used in quite deep swims, but because of the sensitivity of the float, it cannot be held back and must be allowed to drift freely.

Use a bodied waggler for fishing big, slow rivers at medium to long range. The buoyant bulb enables the rig to be heavily shotted for good casting distance. The shotting pattern can be modified for fish taking on the drop or to get the bait down quickly to bottom feeders.

BASIC STICK FLOAT RIGS

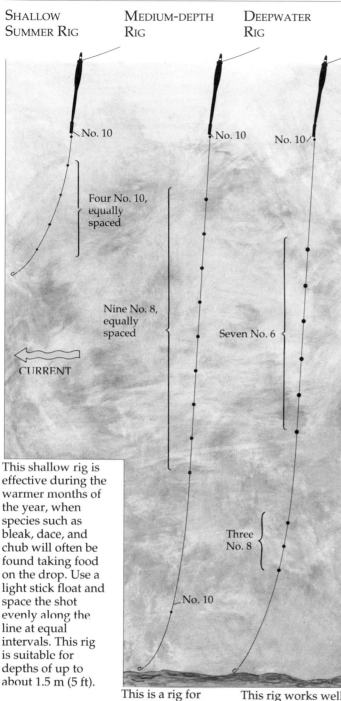

SHALLOW SUMMER RIG

No. 10

Four No. 10, equally spaced

CURRENT

MEDIUM-DEPTH RIG

No. 10

Nine No. 8, equally spaced

No. 10

DEEPWATER RIG

No. 10

Seven No. 6

Three No. 8

This shallow rig is effective during the warmer months of the year, when species such as bleak, dace, and chub will often be found taking food on the drop. Use a light stick float and space the shot evenly along the line at equal intervals. This rig is suitable for depths of up to about 1.5 m (5 ft).

DEPTH MARKER
Pinch a shot onto the line to mark the minimum depth you want to fish.

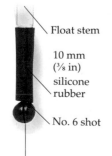

Float stem

10 mm (⅜ in) silicone rubber

No. 6 shot

This is a rig for medium depths and moderate currents. In depths of 1 to 1.8 m (3 to 6 ft), use a float with a wire stem or heavy cane base; use a light float in shallower water. In fast water, group some of the No. 8 shot just above the hook length. This rig is effective for chub and barbel.

This rig works well in depths of up to about 3 m (10 ft). Use a float with a heavy base to ensure that the bait gets down quickly to where the intended quarry is lying. This is a good rig to use for species such as barbel, roach, chub, and bream, when they are feeding on or near the bottom.

TROTTING A STICK FLOAT

Trotting a stick float involves letting it drift downstream with the current and holding back on it at intervals so that the bait swings upwards, enticing fish to take it. Set the float slightly overdepth, that is, so that the distance from the float to the hook is slightly greater than the depth of the water. Cast a little downstream of you, leave the bale arm open, and allow the float to "trot" along with the current. Press the tip of your forefinger lightly against the spool rim so that you can control the amount of line pulled from the reel as the float travels downstream. Holding back gently on the drifting float will make the bait trip along just off the bottom; holding back hard on it will swing the bait upwards.

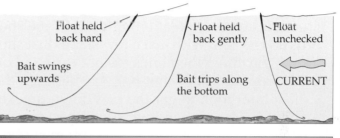

Float held back hard

Bait swings upwards

Float held back gently

Bait trips along the bottom

Float unchecked

CURRENT

TACKLE CONTROL
When you are trotting a float, you may find it easier to control your tackle if you are standing rather than sitting on the bank.

BACKSHOTTING

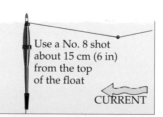

Use a No. 8 shot about 15 cm (6 in) from the top of the float

CURRENT

Backshotting
To minimize the effects of the wind on a stick float, sink the line for a short distance behind it by backshotting. In most situations, a single No. 8 shot pinched onto the line between the float and the rod, about 15 cm (6 in) from the float, will be sufficient.

FEEDING
To attract fish and get them feeding, use a catapult to throw small pieces of hookbait into the swim just before you cast. The loose bait will slowly sink or drift with the current, and fish that are feeding on it will not be unduly wary of your hookbait when it arrives.

Float Fishing – Stillwaters

For stillwater fishing, the float is usually attached bottom-end only. The line passes through a ring inserted into the base of the float, and the float is held in position on the line by split shot (known as locking shot) fixed either side of it. During the summer months, stillwater fish will often be found in the upper layers of the water and can be caught by fishing "on the drop" (fishing a bait that sinks slowly through the water). The setup in this situation involves positioning most of the shot around the float with just a few small dust shot down the line. When bites are not expected on the drop, use bulk shot halfway between the float and hook to get the bait down quickly through the upper layers. If bites are not forthcoming, try moving the bottom shot on the rig to anywhere from 10 to 45 cm (4 to 18 in) from the hook.

Casting

For long-range work on large stillwaters, it is best to use an overhead cast. Wind the float to about a metre from the rod tip. Next, open the bale arm with your free hand (or, on a closed-face, reel, press the line release button) and as you do so press the line against the spool with the index or middle finger of your rod hand. With the line still trapped against the side of the spool, bring the rod back smartly over the shoulder of your rod arm. Punch the rod forward over your head, removing your finger from the spool to release the line. Allow the float to shoot out over the water, climbing as it does so. As the float describes an arc through the air, follow its path with the rod tip until the rod is horizontal. As the float nears the water, slow its flight and ensure a gentle touchdown by putting the index or middle finger of your rod hand on the side of the spool to slow the speed of the line as it leaves the reel.

Feathering
Slowing the speed of the line to make the float land gently on the water is known as "feathering" the cast. Feathering also reduces the risk of the terminal tackle becoming tangled. This is because when the line is slowed, the momentum of the terminal tackle pulls the whole rig out straight.

CONTROLLED LANDINGS
Feather the cast to make the float touch down gently on the water, and close the bale arm when it lands.

Basic Techniques

The two basic stillwater techniques are the lift method and fishing on the drop. For the lift method, wind the line in so that only the tip of the float is above the water. If a fish takes the bait, the float will lift.

When fishing on the drop, first count the number of seconds it takes for the shot to cock the float (to pull it upright) after it has hit the water. On subsequent casts, if the float does not cock properly in the usual time, strike immediately: a fish has taken the bait.

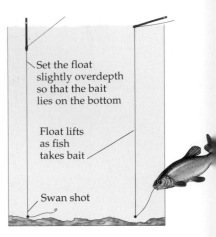

THE LIFT METHOD

Set the float slightly overdepth so that the bait lies on the bottom

Float lifts as fish takes bait

Swan shot

Basic Stillwater Rigs

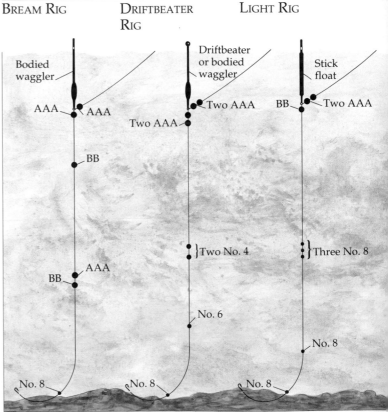

BREAM RIG   DRIFTBEATER RIG   LIGHT RIG

Bodied waggler

AAA   AAA

BB

BB   AAA

No. 8

Driftbeater or bodied waggler

Two AAA

Two AAA

Two No. 4

No. 6

No. 8

Stick float

BB   Two AAA

Three No. 8

No. 8

No. 8

The ideal rig for catching bream. The bodied waggler's buoyancy allows it to carry plenty of weight, in the form of locking shot, to eliminate tangling and make distance casting easier. The bulk shotting near the hook takes the bait down quickly.

Driftbeaters fish well in rough, windy conditions and are best fished overdepth. Plenty of weight in the locking shot keeps the float steady, and progressively lighter shot pinched on down the rig allow the bait to be fished on the drop.

This rig is ideal for fishing at a range of about 14 m (15 yds), but can be used at distances up to 23 m (25 yds). It is at its best in light winds when there is minimal surface drift. Always feather the line when casting, to prevent tangling.

FISHING ON THE DROP

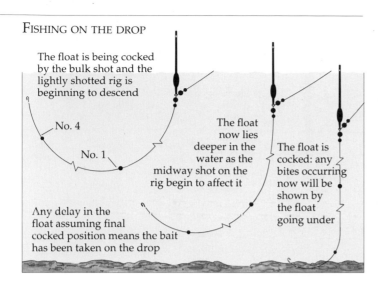

The float is being cocked by the bulk shot and the lightly shotted rig is beginning to descend

No. 4

No. 1

The float now lies deeper in the water as the midway shot on the rig begin to affect it

The float is cocked: any bites occurring now will be shown by the float going under

Any delay in the float assuming final cocked position means the bait has been taken on the drop

FISHING THE SLIDING FLOAT

Sliding floats come into their own when swims are significantly deeper than the length of the rod. Bodied wagglers, preferably loaded to some degree, are the best floats to use. This loading ensures that the float does not slide up the line during casting, while the buoyant body allows plenty of shot to be used along the rig to get the bait down to the bottom quickly. A stop knot is tied in above the float and its position is adjusted until the correct setting (which is the depth of the swim) has been found. The float runs freely up the line until it reaches the knot, which will not pass through the ring at the base of the float because of the bead.

SLIDING FLOAT RIG

Bodied waggler (peacock quill or sarcandas reed stem)

Sliding stop knot

Bead

Three AAA

No. 8

THE SLIDING STOP KNOT
The sliding stop knot is easy to tie in fine mono. To ensure it does not catch on the rod rings during casting, either leave the ends about 10 mm (³⁄₈ in) long or tie the knot in soft cotton.

Fine mono

Reel line

BANKSIDE VEGETATION
A sliding rig has only a short length of line beyond the float when casting. This is useful when bankside vegetation limits casting space.

SLIDING CONTROLLER FLOAT RIG

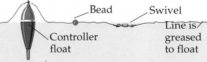

Bead   Swivel

Controller float

Line is greased to float

Sliding controller floats are excellent for presenting surface baits such as crust or air-injected lobworms for carp and chub, or floating casters for roach and rudd. The float acts basically as a casting weight, and when the bait is taken the controller is not pulled under the surface. Instead, the line runs freely through a ring attached to the top of the float. The line between the swivel and the hook should be well greased to reduce resistance to a taking fish. The sliding controller float can also act as a bite indicator: strike when it begins to slide across the surface.

SHALLOW-WATER RIG	LONG-RANGE RIG	CANAL RIG

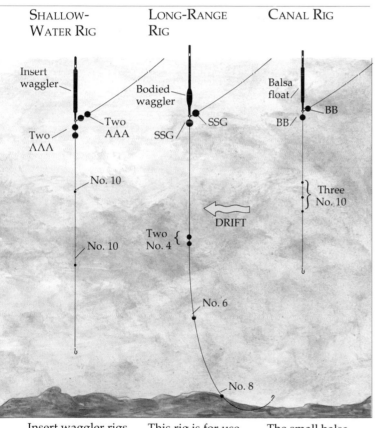

Insert waggler

Two AAA

Two AAA

No. 10

No. 10

Bodied waggler

SSG

SSG

Two No. 4

DRIFT

No. 6

No. 8

Balsa float

BB

BB

Three No. 10

Insert waggler rigs such as this are best used with small shot spaced out between float and hook. They are not designed for use with heavy bulk shotting down the rig. In shallow swims, the shot on the rig need be no bigger than No. 10.

This rig is for use on big lakes and on gravel pits. The basic shotting pattern shown here could be altered for fishing on the drop, in which case slightly heavier shotting, such as a few well-spaced No. 8s, will give better bite registration.

The small balsa float ensures a quiet touchdown on casting, and most of the cocking weight is concentrated around the float. The rest of the shot are small and allow the bait to fall slowly and naturally through the water.

POLE FISHING – STILLWATERS & CANALS

When fishing a stillwater, the first task is to use a plummet *(see page 222)* to find the shelf or dropoff where fish are likely to be. Start searching at about 5 m (16 ft) out, and shorten or lengthen the pole until it is found. On a canal, start by fishing just off the bank, and if you get no results, fish further out: if the canal is not too wide, fish the middle channel and then along the far bank. Most canals can be fished comfortably with a 10 m (33 ft) pole.

POLE TIPS

On waters where big fish are a distinct possibility, it is essential to use a pole with an elasticated tip. The tip elastic *(see page 228)* acts as a shock absorber and helps to prevent the hook being torn free. You can convert a flick tip to an elasticated tip by using one of the many conversion kits on the market. Alternatively, the components (tensioner, bung, elastic, PTFE bush, and line connector) can be bought individually.

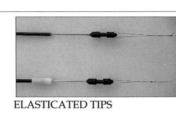
ELASTICATED TIPS

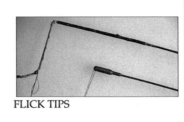
FLICK TIPS

CASTING

Set up the top three sections, attach the line and terminal rig, and cast underhand or overhand to get the terminal rig out. Then add more sections to the pole (or extend it, if it is telescopic) until the required length is reached.

Always keep well away from overhead power lines when fishing with a pole, especially if it is made of carbon fibre, and do not use one during a thunderstorm.

UNDERHAND CAST
Hold the pole in one hand and the terminal rig in the other. Swing the pole up and out, and at the same time release the terminal rig.

OVERHAND CAST
This is similar to the underhand cast, but the pole is held and cast vertically, instead of from a nearly horizontal position.

BASIC STILLWATER RIGS

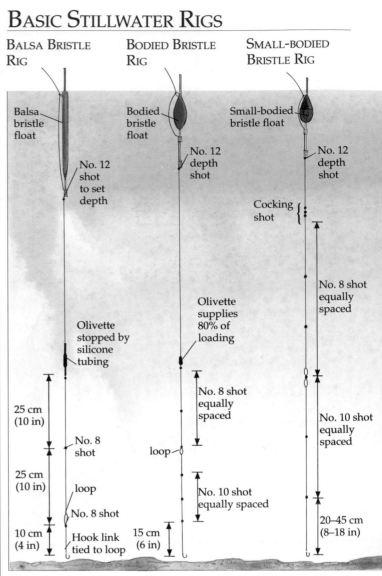

BALSA BRISTLE RIG
Balsa bristle float
No. 12 shot to set depth
Olivette stopped by silicone tubing
25 cm (10 in)
No. 8 shot
25 cm (10 in)
loop
No. 8 shot
10 cm (4 in)
Hook link tied to loop

BODIED BRISTLE RIG
Bodied bristle float
No. 12 depth shot
Olivette supplies 80% of loading
No. 8 shot equally spaced
loop
No. 10 shot equally spaced
15 cm (6 in)

SMALL-BODIED BRISTLE RIG
Small-bodied bristle float
No. 12 depth shot
Cocking shot
No. 8 shot equally spaced
No. 10 shot equally spaced
20–45 cm (8–18 in)

This float is designed for fishing baits near or on the bottom in a flat calm or slight ripple. It is a good float for detecting bites from roach and small bream, and when it is correctly shotted, only the bristle should show above the water. The shotting pattern gets the whole rig quickly down to mid-depth, after which the small shot sink the bait more slowly to the lake bed. This can produce bites on the drop as well as on the bottom.

The bodied bristle float has a cane stem and is used for fishing on the drop. It can be used in conditions from flat calm to choppy, and only the bristle should be visible above the surface, for bite detection. On this rig the shotting is evenly spaced to take the bait down at a steady rate. To get the bait down quickly to fish on the bottom, move the shot nearer the hook, and when fish are near the surface, place the shot directly under the float.

This is a good rig to use in deep water, and it is usually fished about 15 to 30 cm (6 to 12 in) overdepth. It is especially suitable for bottom-feeding species such as bream, because it gets the bait down quickly to them. The rig is set to depth with a No. 12 shot, and cocked by three closely grouped No. 8s. Below these are three equally spaced No. 10s, the lower of which is placed 20 to 45 cm (8 to 18 in) from the hook.

BASIC CANAL RIGS

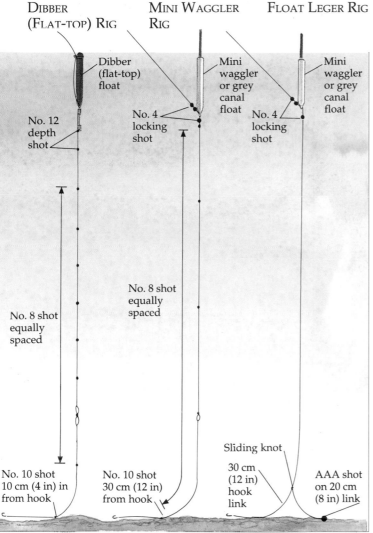

DIBBER (FLAT-TOP) RIG

Dibber (flat-top) float

No. 12 depth shot

No. 8 shot equally spaced

No. 10 shot 10 cm (4 in) in from hook

MINI WAGGLER RIG

Mini waggler or grey canal float

No. 4 locking shot

No. 8 shot equally spaced

No. 10 shot 30 cm (12 in) from hook

FLOAT LEGER RIG

Mini waggler or grey canal float

No. 4 locking shot

Sliding knot

30 cm (12 in) hook link

AAA shot on 20 cm (8 in) link

The dibber rig can be used for fishing the far shelf of a canal in very choppy conditions, and it is also useful on a lake when an undertow is occurring. It is designed to take fish on the drop, and is a good rig for bream fishing. The shotting consists of a No. 12 depth shot, with eight No. 8 shot evenly spaced below it. A single No. 10 shot is positioned 10 cm (4 in) from the hook, and the top of the float should only just protrude above the surface, for bite detection.

This rig can be used on lakes and canals, and it is a good choice for bream, tench, or large roach. The float is attached bottom-end only, with locking shot pinched on at either side of the base ring, and the pole tip is usually sunk to keep the line under water. This prevents line drift, which can adversely affect bait presentation. Back shotting might also be required in a wind: pinch on a No. 8 shot about 20 cm (8 in) above the float to sink the line.

This version of the mini waggler rig is designed for use in rough conditions, when the bait needs to be firmly anchored on the bottom. A small bomb weight or an AAA shot is carried on a 20 cm (8 in) length of line attached to the main line by a sliding knot, which should be about 30 cm (12 in) from the hook. Reduce this distance if bites are not registering on the float but the bait is being sucked, and lengthen it if the undertow and wind increase.

HANDLING THE POLE

Take-apart poles are shipped (lengthened) by adding more sections, and unshipped (shortened) by removing sections. Telescopic poles and whips are shipped by pulling sections out, and unshipped by pushing them back in. Always keep pole sections free of dirt to prevent wear and ensure easy shipping and unshipping.

HOLDING A POLE
Fish from a sitting position. Hold the pole across one thigh or put the butt against your pelvis and hold it with one or both hands.

POLE RESTS
Pole rests keep the pole off the ground while you are changing the terminal tackle, unhooking fish, or groundbaiting.

UNSHIPPING
To land a fish caught on a long pole, unship the pole until it is short enough to allow the fish to be brought to the net or hand.

SWINGING TO HAND
When the pole has been unshipped to about two or three sections long, small or medium-sized fish can be swung to hand.

FISHING DISTANCE
A long pole allows you to place baits with great accuracy into distant swims, and to fish in areas that may be inaccessible with running tackle.

POLE FISHING – RUNNING WATER

Pole fishing on fast-flowing water requires small round-bodied floats, such as bung floats, that can be held back or allowed to run at the speed of the current. The bodied bristle float can be used on slow-flowing rivers. There are two basic styles of pole fishing for running water. The first involves using a long pole and a short line for holding back and slowing the bait's passage. The second style employs a long pole and long line – such as a 10 m (33 ft) pole and 9 m (30 ft) of line – for running the float and bait at the speed of the current and fishing the full length of the swim.

FEEDING METHODS

To attract fish to the swim when you are fishing on the bottom, throw in small balls of bread-based groundbait containing hookbait samples. When fishing on the drop, throw or catapult loose feed, such as maggots, into the water below the pole tip, or use a pole pot. This is clipped to the top section of the pole and filled with feed, then the pole is extended and swung out over the swim, and the pot is inverted to empty its contents into the water.

USING A CATAPULT
A good way to get groundbait or loose feed out to the vicinity of the hookbait is to use a catapult. When using one, either put the pole on the bank or on pole rests, or place it across your lap and hold it down with the forearm of the arm holding the catapult.

POLE ELASTIC

ELASTICS
Three sizes of elastic (No. 4, No. 5, and No. 6) on winders.

Elastic for use on elasticated pole tips *(see page 226)* is available in eight sizes (numbered 1 to 8), each of a different breaking strain. It is supplied on carriers or winders that can be used when empty for holding pre-assembled float rigs. Pole elastic is usually coated with a lubricant to ensure that it runs freely through the PTFE bung in the pole tip, and periodic applications of lubricant are advisable to keep a pole's elastic in good condition. Many anglers carry a number of additional pole top sections rigged up with elastics of various strengths for different species.

RIGS FOR RUNNING WATER

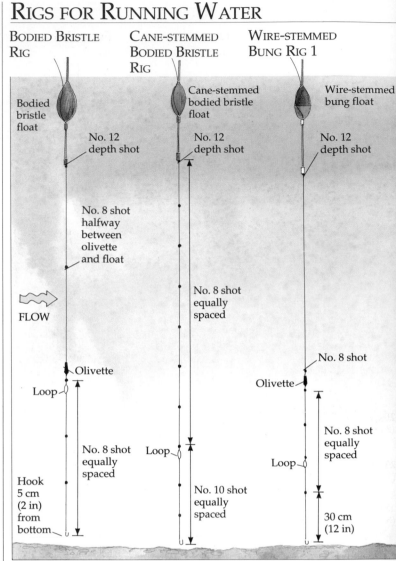

BODIED BRISTLE RIG

CANE-STEMMED BODIED BRISTLE RIG

WIRE-STEMMED BUNG RIG 1

This rig is used for catching fish near the bottom in slow to medium-paced water between 1.5 and 2.1 m (5 and 7 ft) deep. The swim should be groundbaited and the float, attached top and bottom, run through at the speed of the current. The rig is weighted by an olivette with a single No. 8 shot above it and three No. 8s below it. The baited hook should fish just off bottom, and the bristle of the float should show above the water for bite indication.

A short version of this rig will catch surface and midwater feeders in the top 60 to 90 cm (2 to 3 ft) of medium-paced water, but it can be made longer to fish the full depth of the river, as shown here. It should be run through the swim at the speed of the current, with just the bristle of the float, which is attached top and bottom, showing above the surface. The shotting consists of eight equally spaced No. 8 shot above two equally spaced No. 10s.

With this versatile rig, you can fish a bait on the bottom below the pole tip, hold back in deep, fast water over groundbait, or run the bait through at the speed of the current. Position the bulk shot or an olivette at about 75 cm (30 in) from the hook, with three No. 8 shot spaced equally below it. Attach the float top and bottom, with the tip of the bristle showing above the water for bite indication. This rig gives excellent bait control, even in fast-flowing rivers.

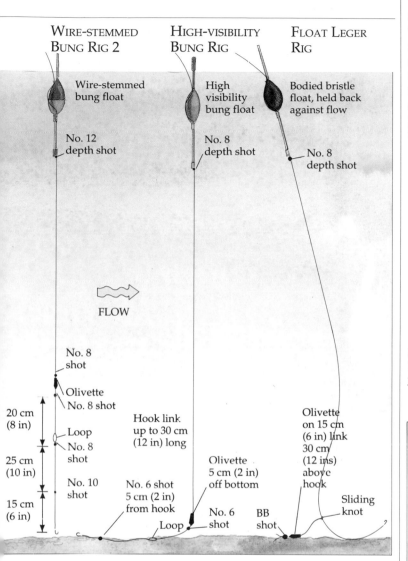

WIRE-STEMMED BUNG RIG 2

Wire-stemmed bung float

No. 12 depth shot

FLOW

No. 8 shot

Olivette
No. 8 shot

20 cm (8 in)

Loop
No. 8 shot

25 cm (10 in)

No. 10 shot

15 cm (6 in)

HIGH-VISIBILITY BUNG RIG

High visibility bung float

No. 8 depth shot

Hook link up to 30 cm (12 in) long

Olivette 5 cm (2 in) off bottom

No. 6 shot 5 cm (2 in) from hook

Loop

No. 6 shot

FLOAT LEGER RIG

Bodied bristle float, held back against flow

No. 8 depth shot

Olivette on 15 cm (6 in) link 30 cm (12 ins) above hook

BB shot

Sliding knot

Use this rig to present baits just off the bed for fish that feed in the bottom third of the water, and run it through at the speed of the current. Position bulk shot or an olivette 60 cm (2 ft) from the hook, or at one-third of the distance from the hook to the float. Fix a No. 8 shot just above the bulk shot or olivette, another just below it, with a No. 8 and a No. 10 spaced below that. Set the float so that the bristle just shows above the surface.

This rig is suitable for fishing close-in for small, bottom-feeding fish of up to 227 g (8 oz). Set the float so that the bristle is above the surface, and fish the rig through the margins, no more than about 1.8 to 3 m (6 to 10 ft) out and held back slightly. The simple shotting pattern consists of bulk shot or an olivette set 30 cm (12 in) from the hook, and a No. 6 shot just below it, and another No. 6 near the hook. The olivette takes the bait down quickly through the layers.

This rig can be used for presenting a static bait on the bottom. It will also allow you to make a bait move slowly along the bottom towards the bank, and to hold it back hard to inch the bait slowly through the swim. The float is well overshotted by a small bomb weight attached to the line 30 cm (12 in) from the hook by a short link of about 15 cm (6 in) of mono. Attach the float top and bottom, and set it so that only the bristle is protruding above the water.

POLE FISHING WEIGHTS

The weights most widely used in pole fishing are split shot and olivettes, plus small bomb weights for float leger rigs. Olivettes thread onto the line and are used in place of bulk shot; barrel leads can also be used, but they are more prone to tangling. Lead wire is better than split shot when using seed baits.

BARRELS

OLIVETTES

SPLIT SHOT

LEAD WIRE

FLOAT RIGS
With pre-assembled float rigs you can change your tackle quickly and easily.

OLIVETTE AND SPLIT SHOT SIZES

Olivette size (Paquita)	Weight (grams)	Olivette size (Torpille)	Weight (grams)	Shot size	Weight (grams)
12	3.0				
11	2.45	11	2.5		
10	2.1	10	2.0		
				SSG	1.89
9	1.85	9	1.5		
8	1.56	8	1.2		
7	1.36	7	1.0		
6	1.16				
5	0.82				
				AAA	0.81
		6	0.8		
4	0.67				
		5	0.6		
		4	0.5		
3	0.44				
		3	0.4	BB	0.4
2	0.37	2	0.3		
				No. 1	0.28
				No. 2	0.24
1	0.25			No. 3	0.20
		1	0.2	No. 4	0.17
0	0.17			No. 5	0.13
2/0	0.13	0	0.13	No. 6	0.105
3/0	0.105			No. 7	0.083
				No. 8	0.063
4/0	0.081			No. 9	0.049
				No. 10	0.034
				No. 11	0.026
				No. 12	0.020
				No. 13	0.012

TROLLING

Trolling is a method by which a bait, either natural or artificial, is pulled along through the water behind a moving boat. It is used on stillwaters and rivers for fish such as trout and walleye, and is also used on saltwater, for example in big-game fishing *(see page 258)*. The boat can be powered either by oars or by a motor, and the trailed bait, which can be fished at practically any depth, is intended to resemble a live fish to any predators it passes. Trolled spoons, plugs, and even flies can be made to fish deep by the addition of weights or by using lead-cored line, while natural baits are often fished below a sliding float, set overdepth, to give an early indication that a predator has taken hold.

READING A LAKE

Deep lakes can be divided into separate layers, the epilimnion, thermocline, and hypolimnion. During summer and autumn the epilimnion will be warmer than the hypolimnion, and the reverse is true in winter. The water temperatures within each of these two layers are fairly uniform, but there is a sharp change in temperature within the thermocline. Strong winds will cause the layers to tilt, resulting in the epilimnion becoming "thicker" on the lee shore. Fish that show a marked preference for cold water, such as lake trout, will move deeper as the summer progresses, and the best way to locate these deep-swimming fish is to use an echo sounder.

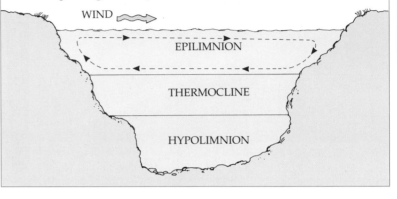

TROLLING THE LAYERS

A wet fly can be trolled just under the surface by using a medium sinking fly line and a standard leader. To fish deeper, the same pattern can be trailed behind the boat on a lead-cored line, or alternatively a heavy tube fly can be employed. Small plugs, too, can be fished relatively deep on a lead-cored line, or on a small-diameter wire line that cuts easily through the water. To fish even deeper, it is necessary to move on to a heavy, vaned trolling weight attached well up the line above the lure. Alternatively, a downrigger can be used for really deep work, its great advantage being that the lure can be fished at a constant, preset depth.

BOATS
Trolling is best done from a motor-powered boat, but a rowing boat may also be used.

Trolling with multiple rods
A trio of anglers can fish together, with minimal risk of their lines tangling, by fishing at different depths and distances. The angler in the stern should fish his lure or bait shallow and closest to the boat, so that if a take occurs on one of the other rods he can get his bait in quickly and operate the motor.

TROLLING WITH MULTIPLE RODS

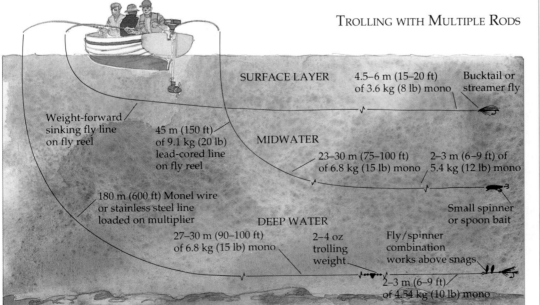

SURFACE LAYER — 4.5–6 m (15–20 ft) of 3.6 kg (8 lb) mono — Bucktail or streamer fly

Weight-forward sinking fly line on fly reel

45 m (150 ft) of 9.1 kg (20 lb) lead-cored line on fly reel

MIDWATER — 23–30 m (75–100 ft) of 6.8 kg (15 lb) mono — 2–3 m (6–9 ft) of 5.4 kg (12 lb) mono

180 m (600 ft) Monel wire or stainless steel line loaded on multiplier

Small spinner or spoon bait

DEEP WATER — 27–30 m (90–100 ft) of 6.8 kg (15 lb) mono — 2–4 oz trolling weight — Fly/spinner combination works above snags

2–3 m (6–9 ft) of 4.54 kg (10 lb) mono

ROD LAYOUT

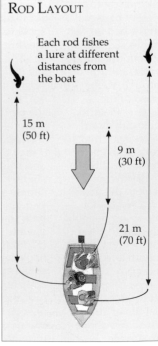

Each rod fishes a lure at different distances from the boat

15 m (50 ft)

9 m (30 ft)

21 m (70 ft)

USING A DOWNRIGGER

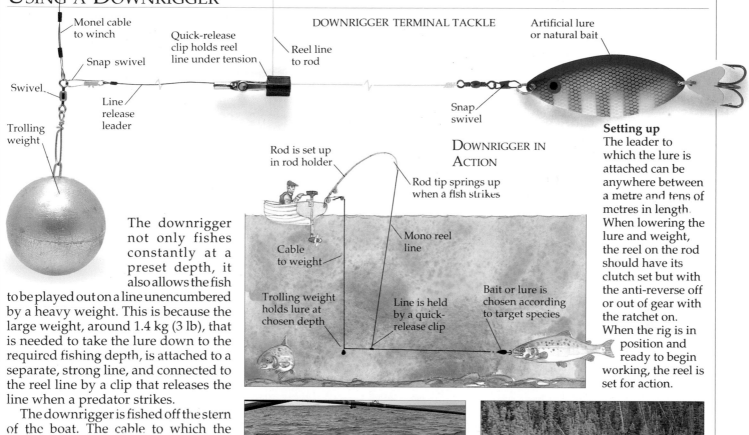

DOWNRIGGER TERMINAL TACKLE

Monel cable to winch

Quick-release clip holds reel line under tension

Reel line to rod

Artificial lure or natural bait

Snap swivel

Swivel

Line release leader

Trolling weight

Snap swivel

DOWNRIGGER IN ACTION

Rod is set up in rod holder

Rod tip springs up when a fish strikes

Mono reel line

Cable to weight

Trolling weight holds lure at chosen depth

Line is held by a quick-release clip

Bait or lure is chosen according to target species

Setting up
The leader to which the lure is attached can be anywhere between a metre and tens of metres in length. When lowering the lure and weight, the reel on the rod should have its clutch set but with the anti-reverse off or out of gear with the ratchet on. When the rig is in position and ready to begin working, the reel is set for action.

The downrigger not only fishes constantly at a preset depth, it also allows the fish to be played out on a line unencumbered by a heavy weight. This is because the large weight, around 1.4 kg (3 lb), that is needed to take the lure down to the required fishing depth, is attached to a separate, strong line, and connected to the reel line by a clip that releases the line when a predator strikes.

The downrigger is fished off the stern of the boat. The cable to which the weight is attached is normally run off a winch and marked at intervals with a waterproof marker pen so that the depth the lure is sent down to can be gauged. (Using an echo sounder makes this marking unnecessary.) After the rig has been sent down to the prescribed depth, the reel line is tightened right up to put a good bend in the rod. When a fish grabs hold of the lure, the clip releases the line and the rod tip springs back straight, indicating the take and often setting the hooks.

DOWNRIGGER WINCH
The cable that carries the trolling weight is run off a winch secured near the stern of the boat.

DEEPWATER FISHING
Using a downrigger enables you to fish at depths of 150 m (500 ft) or more.

BAITWALKING

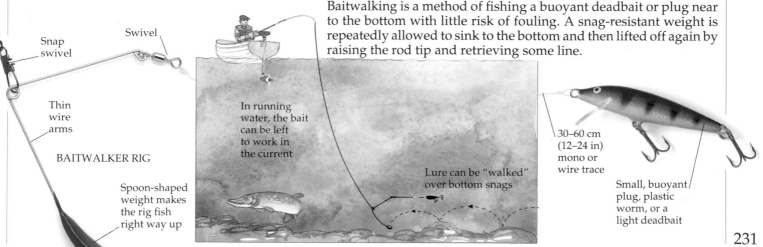

Baitwalking is a method of fishing a buoyant deadbait or plug near to the bottom with little risk of fouling. A snag-resistant weight is repeatedly allowed to sink to the bottom and then lifted off again by raising the rod tip and retrieving some line.

Snap swivel

Swivel

Thin wire arms

BAITWALKER RIG

Spoon-shaped weight makes the rig fish right way up

In running water, the bait can be left to work in the current

Lure can be "walked" over bottom snags

30–60 cm (12–24 in) mono or wire trace

Small, buoyant plug, plastic worm, or a light deadbait

231

THE OVERHEAD CAST

The overhead cast is an important part of all fly fishing. It is essential for anyone taking up fly fishing that they master it, and the better their technique, the more successful an angler they will be. The main elements of the basic overhead cast are the back cast and forward cast, plus the false cast, and these are described here together with suggestions on how to improve your technique and correct common casting faults. The way in which you hold the rod for casting is also important, but it depends largely on your personal preference and the distance you wish to cast. Try the grips shown here, then choose the one that most suits your casting requirements.

The momentum of the line bends the rod back

Stop the rod when it is at the 11.30 position

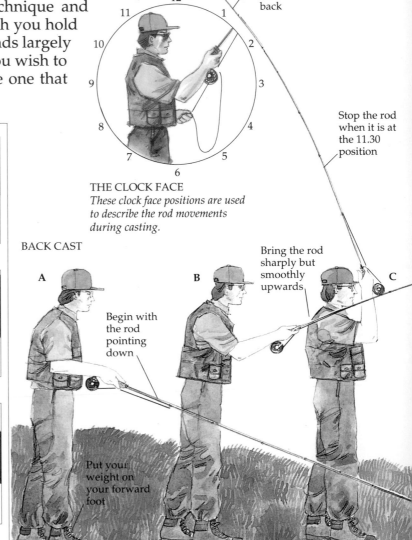

THE CLOCK FACE
These clock face positions are used to describe the rod movements during casting.

THE GRIP

Continental grip
In this grip, the forefinger points along the rod. This style is best for short, accurate casts with dry flies or nymphs on rivers and small stillwaters.

Continental grip

Standard grip
The style preferred by many all-round anglers who fish a variety of different methods and waters. Fine both for short, accurate work and for long-distance casting on large rivers and lakes. With the thumb running along the top of the handle, the strain on the wrist is not too great when a long line is aerialized.

Standard grip

Tournament grip
A strong but relaxed grip, ideal for long-distance work with weight-forward or shooting-head lines. Lacks the fine control needed for short, accurate casting.

Tournament grip

BACK CAST

A Begin with the rod pointing down

Put your weight on your forward foot

B Bring the rod sharply but smoothly upwards

C

BALANCED TACKLE
Good casting depends on balanced tackle. Fly size, line weight, and rod rating must match.

Back cast
A good back cast is the prerequisite for a good forward delivery, and neglecting this essential movement results in a poor casting technique. Before you begin, stand with the foot on your rod side forward, with the rod tip in the 4.00 position, about 6 m (20 ft) of line extended beyond the rod tip (**A**). Trap the line between your index finger and the rod handle.

To begin the back cast, bend your elbow to raise your forearm (**B**), accelerating the rod smoothly and progressively from the 4.00 position to the 11.30 position and lifting the line from the water (**C**). Stop the rod at this point and

pause briefly, allowing the line to extend fully behind you, before commencing the forward cast; momentum will flex the rod tip back a little to 11.00. This pause is vital, and practice will teach you how long it should be, but if it is too long the line will lose momentum and drop low behind you. If it is too brief it will result in a whiplash effect that can crack and thus weaken the fly line, or even cause the fly to snap off.

Keep your wrist straight during the back cast, because bending it allows the rod to drift too far back. This will make your forward cast more of a throwing action than a smooth, controlled delivery.

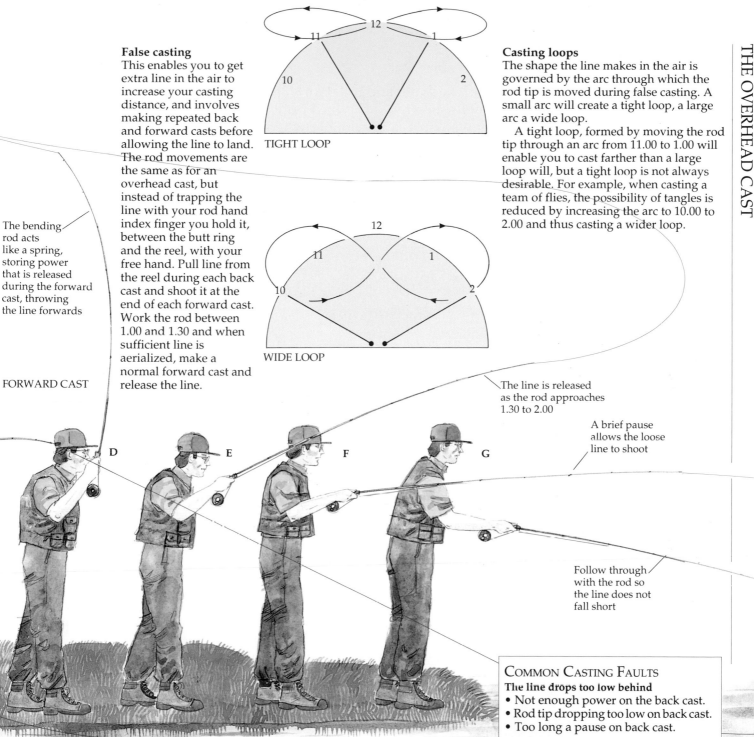

False casting

This enables you to get extra line in the air to increase your casting distance, and involves making repeated back and forward casts before allowing the line to land. The rod movements are the same as for an overhead cast, but instead of trapping the line with your rod hand index finger you hold it, between the butt ring and the reel, with your free hand. Pull line from the reel during each back cast and shoot it at the end of each forward cast. Work the rod between 1.00 and 1.30 and when sufficient line is aerialized, make a normal forward cast and release the line.

The bending rod acts like a spring, storing power that is released during the forward cast, throwing the line forwards

FORWARD CAST

TIGHT LOOP

WIDE LOOP

Casting loops

The shape the line makes in the air is governed by the arc through which the rod tip is moved during false casting. A small arc will create a tight loop, a large arc a wide loop.

A tight loop, formed by moving the rod tip through an arc from 11.00 to 1.00 will enable you to cast farther than a large loop will, but a tight loop is not always desirable. For example, when casting a team of flies, the possibility of tangles is reduced by increasing the arc to 10.00 to 2.00 and thus casting a wider loop.

The line is released as the rod approaches 1.30 to 2.00

A brief pause allows the loose line to shoot

Follow through with the rod so the line does not fall short

The forward cast

With the rod flexed under compression and the line at full extension, accelerate the rod smoothly forward (**D**) to about the 2.00 position. Stop it there abruptly (**E**) and with a slight forward flick of your wrist. This wrist action is similar to the one you would use when lightly tapping a nail with a hammer, and when you do it you should aim your rod hand at an imaginary point about 1 m (3 ft) above the surface of the water.

Allow the rod to follow through as the line extends fully in front of you and falls gently to the water (**F**, **G**). The tapping motion and follow-through should be made in one continuous action.

Shooting line

There is an optimum length of line that any particular rod can aerialize, and to make a longer cast it is necessary to "shoot" line. This is achieved by pulling extra line from the reel, and allowing it to lie on the ground during the back cast.

When the rod reaches the 2.00 position (**E**) on the forward cast, lift the index finger of your rod hand to release the line. The momentum of the line extending in front of you will pull the loose line through the rings, adding extra distance to the cast. Aim high enough to allow all the extra line to straighten fully before it lands on the water.

COMMON CASTING FAULTS

The line drops too low behind
• Not enough power on the back cast.
• Rod tip dropping too low on back cast.
• Too long a pause on back cast.

The line will not shoot or straighten
• Line released too early.
• Failure to follow through.
• Insufficient power on forward punch.
• Slack line between false casts.

The line lands in a heap
• Too short a pause on back cast.
• Aiming too low.
• Aiming too high in a facing wind.

The flies snap off
• Too short a pause on back cast.
• Leader point too fine for the size and weight of the fly.

THE ROLL CAST

To make a roll cast, you lift the line off the water and roll it forward, without first making a back cast, by using a rapid forward punch that swings over and curves downwards. It is invaluable where there are obstructions behind you that prevent a normal overhead cast, and in many other situations, for example when you want to lift a sunk line and roll it onto the surface, prior to lifting it off for an overhead cast. The roll cast is a very versatile technique that should be part of every fly fisher's repertoire.

Making a roll cast
Begin by taking up a suitable stance, with one foot slightly in front of the other and the rod pointing down the line (**A**). Then begin a smooth, steady draw (**B**), raising your rod hand to just above shoulder height and lifting the rod to the 10.30 or 11.00 position (*see page 232*). This steady draw allows a loop of line to form between the rod top and the water. While the line is still moving, raise the rod slightly (**C**), then punch it rapidly forward and down (**D**). The rod is now flexed and under maximum compression, and the line follows its path, bellying out slightly behind you and coming off the water close to your feet. As you power the rod down through the 3.00 position, the belly of line will roll forward (**E**). Follow through smoothly (**F**) so that the line unfolds and straightens above the water.

STANCE
With any cast, the starting position is important if you are to achieve controlled turnover and make a smooth delivery, so take up position and stand with your best foot forward. For most right-handed anglers, this will mean the right foot, but it can pay to make the left foot the front foot, since this will open up the cast during the forward roll.

If necessary, take up any loose line with your free hand and hold on to it, as in the overhead cast, until late in the forward movement of the cast.

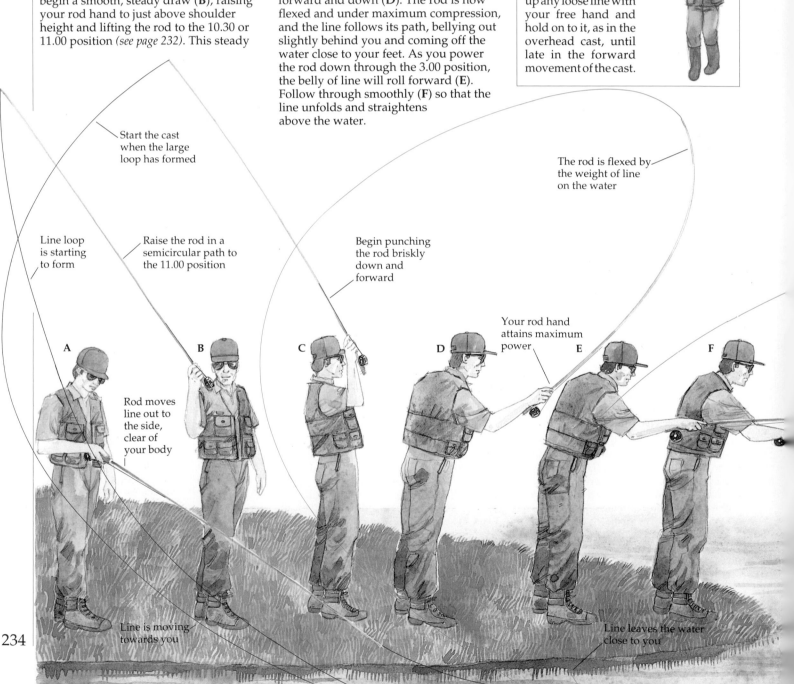

Start the cast when the large loop has formed

The rod is flexed by the weight of line on the water

Line loop is starting to form

Raise the rod in a semicircular path to the 11.00 position

Begin punching the rod briskly down and forward

Your rod hand attains maximum power

Rod moves line out to the side, clear of your body

A   B   C   D   E   F

Line is moving towards you

Line leaves the water close to you

CASTING ON A RIVER (*right*)
When you are fishing on a river, the roll cast is useful if you want to change direction quickly or where obstructions prevent an overhead cast. Salmon anglers fishing large rivers with long rods find that the roll cast is also invaluable for lifting a sunk line to the surface before making an overhead cast.

CASTING FROM A BOAT (*left*)
Anglers fishing on the drift use the roll cast when short-lining with a team of three flies, or for lifting off a short line to cover fish that rise close to the boat. The roll cast, being one continuous movement, enables you to cover fish much faster than with an overhead cast, in which there is a delay while you make the back cast.

COMMON ROLL-CASTING FAULTS

Fly gets caught up behind
• When the rod is lifted too quickly, the bow from rod tip to water will not form properly, because the tension on the line is too great. The line will consequently lift and come through low, and then go behind you.
• If you hold your rod hand too low during the lift and roll, the line will come through too low and flat.

The line fails to roll out in front
• A lack of power during the forward movement, which should be a smooth but punchy action.
• The line is not straight or under tension before beginning the cast.
• Poor timing. If the lift and roll are hurried, the rod cannot build up power against the drag of the line as it comes off the water through the bow.

Line tangles on forward roll-down
• The rod has been brought up and over in the same vertical plane, causing the line to hang up. To remedy this, tilt the rod away from your body during the lift and roll.
• The line has not been kept tight by your line hand, causing a loss of power.
• A lack of power during the forward movement of the rod.

The belly of line travels forward in a rolling loop

The line loop is tightened by the full force of the rod

The line unfolds and straightens above the water

Follow through for a smooth line turnover

WET-FLY FISHING

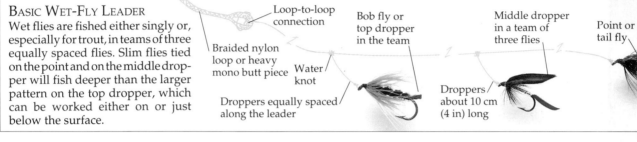

Wet-fly, because it encompasses so many different styles, is one of the most universal methods of catching gamefish, best suited to streamy water but also effective on slower, canal-like stretches and stillwaters if the fly is worked properly. Styles and tactics have evolved to suit different conditions, seasons, and species of fish. One thing never changes: whether using willowy rods and sparse Clyde-style fly dressings in northern England, or tip-actioned, single-handed wands and bucktail streamers in North America, devotees of wet-fly enjoy their sport in some of the most wild and beautiful areas of the world.

BASIC WET-FLY LEADER

Wet flies are fished either singly or, especially for trout, in teams of three equally spaced flies. Slim flies tied on the point and on the middle dropper will fish deeper than the larger pattern on the top dropper, which can be worked either on or just below the surface.

Loop-to-loop connection

Bob fly or top dropper in the team

Middle dropper in a team of three flies

Point or tail fly

Braided nylon loop or heavy mono butt piece

Water knot

Droppers equally spaced along the leader

Droppers about 10 cm (4 in) long

UPSTREAM FISHING

The upstream method uses the speed of the current to present a fly on smooth glides and steady streams, or on the flat pockets in broken water. Because you approach from downstream there is less chance of being detected by the fish, so takes can be very positive. If the fish can be seen and are on the move looking for food, allow enough lead with the cast for the fly to sink to the correct depth. For trout lying deep, use a leaded fly to get down to the holding depth. Watch for movement of the leader or the fish as the fly passes by.

APPROACHING UNSEEN

Stalking your quarry from behind, so that you are within its blind spot, allows you to approach much closer and to use a shorter cast than if you approached from another angle. A short line is less vulnerable to drag induced by the current, so it allows a faster response to a take.

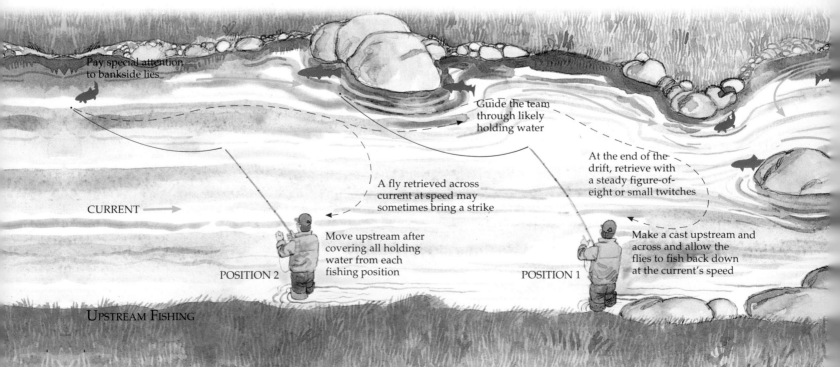

Pay special attention to bankside lies

Guide the team through likely holding water

At the end of the drift, retrieve with a steady figure-of-eight or small twitches

CURRENT

A fly retrieved across current at speed may sometimes bring a strike

Move upstream after covering all holding water from each fishing position

POSITION 2

Make a cast upstream and across and allow the flies to fish back down at the current's speed

POSITION 1

UPSTREAM FISHING

DOWNSTREAM FISHING

A wet fly fished downstream and across follows the path of the fly line in a sweeping curve, and as the fly swings through this arc, gamefish find its movement irresistible. Controlling the speed of the fly is the key to consistent success. As the fly line sweeps around, keep the rod in line with it, because this produces a more controlled swing and improves take detection. A square cast produces a fast sweep and is a good tactic when using a team of three wet flies for trout. A long cast downstream and across makes a shallower angle and a slower swing, which is more effective for salmon.

FISHING DOWNSTREAM AND ACROSS
When you are fishing downstream and across, search all the possible fish-holding water, especially the areas between the main current and slack water.

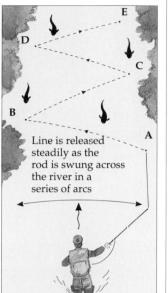

Line is released steadily as the rod is swung across the river in a series of arcs

Mending line

When a fish rises in a streamy run but comes short, the reason can often be poor presentation: if the fly is fishing too fast, the fish will miss it. "Mending" the fly line slows the fly as it swings across the fish, and is achieved by throwing an upstream bow into the line immediately after the cast. This gives a slower, more controlled swing over the path **A** to **D**. If a fish is holding at **B** or **C**, but the swing is still too quick, several mends might be needed before the fly passes over it.

Deep wading

Even with upstream mending, the fly will fish too quickly over its path from position 1. Fishing from position 2 eases the problem because the angle is more acute, but the wading angler at 3 can cover the fish at the same speed but with a much shorter cast.

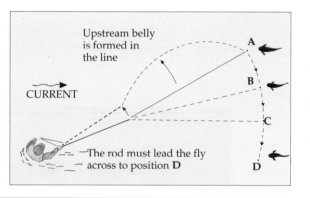

Upstream belly is formed in the line

CURRENT

A

B

C

The rod must lead the fly across to position **D**

D

Position 3

CURRENT

Position 2

Position 1

Leading the fly

This is a method for fishing down water too deep to wade or where overgrown banks obstruct casting. Cast to **A**, then swing the rod across your body while releasing line to slow the fly. This makes the fly follow the path **A** to **B**. Repeating, by swinging the rod back to the start position and releasing more line, will drop the fly down to **C**. This can be repeated (to **D**, **E**, and beyond) until as long a line as practical has been fished. Takes will usually come on the swing across, so do not feed the line too quickly once the fly begins to move across.

Flies quarter the river in a series of sweeping arcs

Holding as much line as possible off the water allows the fly to sink deeper

Mend the line as necessary to slow the fly's drift

Make a cast downstream and across on a slack line

Take a pace or two downstream after each cast to slow the fly's drift

Work bucktails and streamers with the rod tip to imitate small baitfish

POSITION 1

POSITION 2

DRY-FLY FISHING

Dry-fly fishing becomes an obvious choice for the angler when trout are feeding on surface flies. Immortalized in the 19th century by experts such as Frederic M. Halford and Theodore Gordon, who placed great emphasis on exact imitation, dry-fly fishing has now become one of the most widely used methods for catching trout. It will also take many other species, including grayling, carp, and pike, and even salmon and sea trout can be caught on dry flies. The dry fly is fished on waters ranging from fast, rocky streams to large stillwaters, but the basic principle is always the same: to catch a fish on an artificial fly worked on or in the surface.

THE TROUT'S VISION

Because light bends when it enters water, a trout can only see objects on the surface that are (from its point of view) within an angle of about 48° each side of the vertical. This gives it a total "window" of vision of surface objects of about 96°, extended by a further 32° each side of the vertical for objects beyond the surface (including near-by anglers). Beyond the boundary of the window, light striking the surface at angles of less than 10° does not penetrate the water; all the trout sees is a reflection of its underwater surroundings.

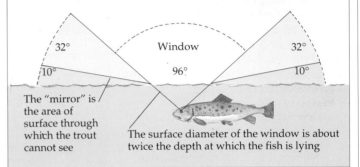

The "mirror" is the area of surface through which the trout cannot see

The surface diameter of the window is about twice the depth at which the fish is lying

UPSTREAM FISHING

In rivers, fish prefer to lie facing the current. By approaching them from downstream you increase your chances of remaining unobserved, and by casting just upstream of your target fish you can get your fly to drift gently downstream into its field of vision. Good watercraft is essential. Keep a low profile, learn how to identify likely lies, and cover the water carefully. Travel light for free mobility, and wear polarized sunglasses and a wide-brimmed hat or visor to cut out the reflected glare that makes it difficult to see into the water.

FISH FINDING
Back eddies and areas behind bridge buttresses are good places to look for feeding trout. Watch out for fish facing downstream into the reverse current of a back eddy: if you approach them from downstream they may spot you. Present the fly downstream of the target fish to avoid the line entering its window of vision.

Fish face downstream in a back eddy

CURRENT

Current divides

WINDOW
Try to place your fly just inside the trout's window, with as little leader as possible showing within it.

Fish lying tight into a steep bank will often only accept a fly hard into the bank

Cast a slack line to defeat drag caused by midstream current

Unless there are especially attractive features in midstream, fish are likely to be found near the banks

UPSTREAM FISHING

BLIND SPOT
A trout cannot see you when you are behind it, so upstream casting allows you to approach unseen.

STILLWATER FISHING

In stillwaters, trout tend to cruise the water, taking their food in a series of rises. By observing several successive rises you can anticipate the direction of travel of a fish, and cast your fly 1 to 3 m (3 to 10 ft) ahead of it so that there is time for the fly to settle before the fish reaches it. Let the fly drift naturally, and try to avoid drag: if drag occurs, your fly and leader will create a wake that will inevitably spook the fish. Use a fine, pale-coloured, double-strength or super-strong monofil for leaders when surface fishing, and avoid the darker sort that tend to scare the fish.

SURFACE FEEDING
Dry flies and emergers come into their own during light winds or flat calms, when fish feed on insects at the surface.

Dealing with a flat calm
Fish are easily spooked by a floating leader when dry flies are fished in a flat calm. Ensure that your leader sinks quickly by degreasing it with a mixture of fuller's earth and detergent or with a commercial degreaser. Keeping the line tight to the fly helps the leader to cut through the surface, as will a small nymph tied on a dropper above the dry fly or, as here, tied New Zealand style. The nymph sinks the leader but not the dry fly.

Dry fly or emerger pattern

Length and strength of leader between flies to suit conditions

Small, streamlined nymph

DOWNSTREAM FISHING

Fishing downstream is a good way to present a dry fly to fish in lies that are impossible to cover with upstream tactics. If a downstream trout is taking sedges, surface drag can be used to advantage by skating a fly across its nose to induce a take. This is achieved by making the line draw tight as the fly reaches the fish. The drifted fly can also be fished drag-free by feeding out line as it drifts downstream. The disadvantage with this method is that the fish is directly downstream of the angler, and this gives a poor hooking angle.

WADING
Unlike upstream dry-fly anglers, those fishing downstream usually wade. Wading gives you a better angle of presentation, better coverage of the water, and keeps your profile lower. When wading do not lift your feet too high: it can be dangerous in faster flows. Always wear a buoyancy aid.

The tightened line straightens and the fly begins to skate

Cast a slack line across and downstream

SKATING THE FLY
To skate the fly across the stream in front of a feeding fish, tighten the line as the fly reaches it. The drag of the current will then pull the fly towards midstream.

CURRENT

PROHIBITED!
Downstream fishing is not allowed on many streams because it is thought to give an unfair advantage to the angler. Check the local rules.

THE DRIFTED FLY
To drift a fly to a fish, pay out line so that the current carries it downstream without drag. The fish will see the fly before the line appears in its window of vision, so there is less chance of spooking the fish and more chance of a take.

DOWNSTREAM FISHING

Feed out loose line at a speed to match the current

NYMPH FISHING

Nymph fishing has progressed in many ways since the early 20th century, when G. E. M. Skues wrote his classic books on the subject. It no longer means just the subsurface fishing of an exact imitation of the trout's food, because today there are many different patterns, tied on hooks of various lengths, shapes, and sizes, that are classified as nymphs. For example, the use of fluorescents and bright synthetic fibres has led to a vast range of modern nymph dressings that arguably look more like lures than representations of the trout's food. In addition, there are now many tactics for fishing up to three patterns on a cast for both river and stillwater, so nymph fishing is no longer even restricted to using a single fly.

SIGHT INDICATORS

A sight indicator or bob is a visual aid, attached to the leader, that gives early warning of a taking fish. There are several different types available commercially, and most have a fluorescent finish that provides maximum visibility.

The Orvis Never-Miss foam ball can be slid to any position on the leader depending on water depth, and is reusable, unlike the self-adhesive Orvis Stay-On indicator. Moser's Butterfly Loop is an integral part of the leader system, being a length of braided nylon looped at each end for connection between the fly line and the leader butt. Visibility is enhanced by fluorescent wool incorporated into the braid.

Orvis Never-Miss

Orvis Stay-On

Moser's Butterfly Loop

RIVER NYMPHING

A nymph will often take trout that are on the move, either bulging below the surface or rooting about in the bottom weeds, and refusing to rise to a dry fly. This refusal to take a dry fly is often associated with preoccupied feeding on shrimps or ascending nymphs. It is essential to get the fly down to the feeding fish, so a weighted pattern is often required. Cast with enough lead to allow the fly time to sink to the required depth.

THE INDUCED TAKE
The clear waters of a chalkstream are ideal places to practise the induced take.

Inducing a take
Trout find flies that rise in front of their noses hard to resist. To induce a take in this way, you must be able to see the fish and make the fly rise at the right time. Allow a weighted fly to sink to the trout's holding depth, and then lift it, by raising the rod, as it nears the fish.

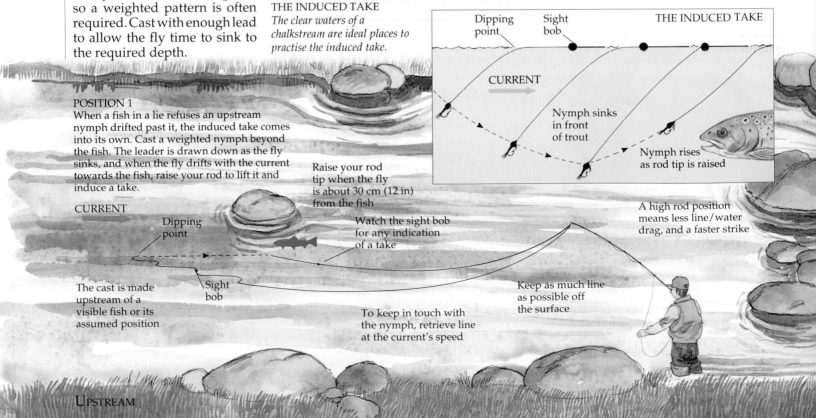

POSITION 1
When a fish in a lie refuses an upstream nymph drifted past it, the induced take comes into its own. Cast a weighted nymph beyond the fish. The leader is drawn down as the fly sinks, and when the fly drifts with the current towards the fish, raise your rod to lift it and induce a take.

CURRENT

Dipping point

The cast is made upstream of a visible fish or its assumed position

Sight bob

Raise your rod tip when the fly is about 30 cm (12 in) from the fish

Watch the sight bob for any indication of a take

To keep in touch with the nymph, retrieve line at the current's speed

THE INDUCED TAKE

Dipping point

Sight bob

CURRENT

Nymph sinks in front of trout

Nymph rises as rod tip is raised

A high rod position means less line/water drag, and a faster strike

Keep as much line as possible off the surface

STILLWATER NYMPHING

The larval and pupal stages of many aquatic insects are eaten by trout, as are water lice, tadpoles, snails, shrimps, daphnia, and corixids, to name just a few. Nymph fishers therefore tie flies to represent many such items of the trout's diet, creating either imitative or general patterns, and classify all of these flies as nymphs.

However, it is argued by some fly fishers that the only true nymphs are the nymphs of the Ephemeroptera (*see page 100*), and that all the other aquatic creatures represented with artificial flies are therefore misrepresentations. This is strictly true, but nymph fishing today is defined not by true imitations but by the methods used.

It is difficult to pinpoint exactly where nymph fishing ends and wet-fly and lure fishing begin, but most stillwater anglers who fish with an artificial fly that represents an aquatic lifelike presentation, consider themselves to be nymph fishers.

Stalking

This is a method for clear waters where the fish can be seen and a specific target selected, and is useful on small stillwaters for catching large, deep-cruising trout. Use a fly that has some weight and a good entry into the water, so that it gets down quickly to the cruising depth, and apply an induced take before the fish has passed by. On large waters, big fish can be ambushed in the margins.

CREATING A CURVE

Walk downwind with the drift to position 1 to allow the fly to sink deeper. Then take a few paces back upwind to position 2. This brings the flies up from deeper water as the bow forms.

WIND

POSITION 1　　　　POSITION 2

LINE COLOUR
Nymph fishermen find that pale-coloured fly lines are a great aid in detecting subtle takes.

CONCEALMENT
Study the cruising patterns of the fish when stalking, but stay hidden, keep a low profile, and wear sombre clothing.

Fishing a curve

Flies fished in a curve are always attractive to fish, in streams or in stillwaters. It is the change of speed and direction that deceives them. Wind puts a natural bow in the fly line, but it can pay to walk along the bank to create your own curve.

THE OPEN LOOP
Attach the fly to the leader with a universal or grinner knot, leaving a small loop when you tighten it. This will allow the fly to move freely and naturally.

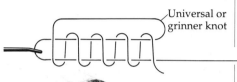

Universal or grinner knot

Open loop allows fly to move more freely

STALKING FLIES
Walker's Mayfly Nymph is an excellent example of a leaded fly for stalking. Small, weighted bug or midge patterns can be effective with choosy fish on warm days, but these flies can be hard to see, so use a sight bob to make them easier to spot.

Walker's Mayfly nymph

Lead bug

POSITION 2
When wading a river, you can drift a nymph down with the current over water too deep to wade. Check the fly at intervals during the drift to make it rise in the water, simulating the movement of the induced take. Release more line after each check so that the nymph sinks again and drifts further down the pool.

POSITION 3
The dead-drift swing uses the acceleration of a fly through the arc created by the belly formed in the fly line as it drifts down with the current. Cast slightly upstream, and make the rod follow the line as it moves with the current. At the end of the drift the fly will speed up and lift as the belly straightens.

Rod follows the nymph around

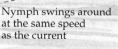

Line speeds up and lifts the nymph in the water

Cast slightly upstream

Nymph swings around at the same speed as the current

Each time the line is checked, the nymph swings invitingly upwards

Drift　　　　Check　　　　Release　Drift　　Check　　　　Release

DOWNSTREAM

BOAT FLY FISHING

The technique of "fishing the drift" is an effective tactic for catching stillwater trout. This style of fishing involves working a team of three or four flies on a short line from a drifting boat, and is especially effective on breezy days and on wild waters. It has now largely been replaced by more modern, longer-line styles that use floating or sinking lines. With all these styles, the top dropper will take a lot of fish if it is worked properly. The secret is a steady lift at the end of the retrieve, holding the fly in the water's surface for as long as possible. Long leaders are now the norm, and the traditional flies have been replaced by newer patterns such as Raiders, Mini Muddlers, and emergers. However, a team of old favourites such as a Wickham's on the top dropper, a Silver Invicta on the middle dropper, and a Gold Ribbed Hare's Ear on the point is still an effective combination, particularly in high summer.

SAFE CASTING ANGLES

When two anglers share a boat, each must fish a restricted area to avoid interfering with the other's fishing and, more importantly, to avoid injuries that can arise from careless casting. If both are right-handed, angler A can fish safely in sector 3 and, with allowance for angler B's movements and safety, in sectors 1 and 2. Angler B can fish safely in sector 4. If one angler is left-handed, he or she should take position A and can then fish sectors 1, 2, and 3. If both are left-handed, the sector pattern is the reverse of that for two right-handed anglers.

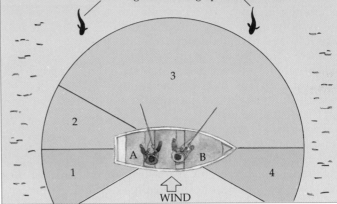

Feeding fish working upwind

WIND

FISHING THE DRIFT

A 3 to 3.4 m (10 to 11 ft) rod gives good control when lifting the flies to the surface, and casts a wide enough loop to avoiding tangling them. Using long droppers improves presentation and allows for several fly changes before a dropper has to be replaced. Always keep in touch with the flies, and strike at the slightest sign of a rise to the team. Look for unusual movements downwind of the boat, and drift windlanes (flat tracts of water that run for considerable distances down the waves) because they usually hold fish.

LOCAL KNOWLEDGE
Lake fish populations are often localized, and without the assistance of a local fisherman or guide on waters that are unfamiliar to you, you could waste much time fishing unproductive areas. Here, a guide is controlling the drift of the boat, allowing the fisherman to retrieve his team of flies through the productive shallows around a rocky outcrop.

WIND

Bob fly or top dropper

The boat is allowed to drift sideways with the wind, and the flies are cast downwind of it

In a strong breeze, the speed of the boat can be controlled by using a drift controller or drogue, which acts like a small underwater parachute to reduce the rate of drift

Feeding fish working upwind

In a strong breeze, use a large-sized or leaded pattern for the point fly so that it acts as a sea anchor to stabilize the team

The fly on the middle dropper takes fish attracted by the disturbance created by the top fly, or because it is an attractor in its own right

TOP DROPPER
Use a bushy fly in big waves and a sparser pattern in light winds. Highly visible flies such as Mini Muddlers not only catch many fish but also attract the trout onto the more sombre, imitative patterns on the other droppers.

SUNK LINE FISHING

The tactic of lift and hold with a sunk, high-density (Hi-D) line can be very effective for fish lying deep. As the flies sink through the layers, use a steady retrieve to keep in touch with them and detect takes on the drop. Draw the flies to the surface as the boat drifts down on them, but stop the draw just as the top dropper comes into view or is about to break surface, and hold it there for as long as possible. Bright attractor patterns provoke the fish into taking as the flies are held before being lifted out, and nymphs fished behind a bright top dropper catch well when the trout are feeding on midges.

TIME FOR THE HI-D
A bright day early season, when the fish are lying deep, is just the time for the fast-sinking line and a flashy attractor on the top dropper.

FISHING THE HI-D
Fast-sinking, high-density lines are a necessity when you want to reach trout lying deep; WF #7 to #8 lines with 3 m (10 ft) rods are a popular choice. To find the holding depth of the fish, try the countdown method (*see page 216*). Once the holding depth has been found, vary the retrieve rate until you find the most productive taking speed.

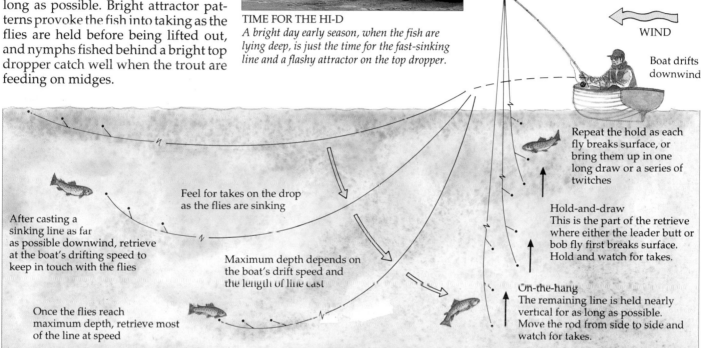

WIND

Boat drifts downwind

Repeat the hold as each fly breaks surface, or bring them up in one long draw or a series of twitches

Hold-and-draw
This is the part of the retrieve where either the leader butt or bob fly first breaks surface. Hold and watch for takes.

On-the-hang
The remaining line is held nearly vertical for as long as possible. Move the rod from side to side and watch for takes.

Feel for takes on the drop as the flies are sinking

After casting a sinking line as far as possible downwind, retrieve at the boat's drifting speed to keep in touch with the flies

Maximum depth depends on the boat's drift speed and the length of line cast

Once the flies reach maximum depth, retrieve most of the line at speed

DAPPING

Dapping, the technique of tripping a fly lightly over the surface of the water, has a reputation for producing large trout, salmon, and sea trout from large stillwaters. Long rods 4.6 to 5.2 m (15 to 17 ft) and a floss "blow line" that carries in the wind are essential. The filamentous strands of the blow line fray in use, but a knot tied every 45 cm (18 in) will prevent the line from disintegrating. Dapped natural flies are illegal on some waters.

WORKING THE FLY
The blow line is fed out to work the fly on the surface as far as possible downwind of the boat. The fly is worked by holding it just above the water and dropping it gently onto the surface at intervals, by allowing it to float, and by drawing it lightly across the surface. On windy days, a second fly adds stability.

BOAT FISHING ETIQUETTE
When drifting along a shoreline, keep clear of bank anglers and do not drift too close to the shore. At the end of the drift, motor upwind well away from other boats, do not disturb the "hot spot" area where the fish are, and never cut into another boat's drift too soon. Only stand up if it is absolutely necessary, and always wear eye protection and a lifejacket.

START OF DRIFT

WIND

HOT SPOT

Do not take short cuts to push in ahead of other boats

Motor upwind well away from line of drift

END OF DRIFT

KEY
x 90 m (100 yd) minimum gap
• Bank fisherman

INSHORE FISHING

By using an outboard-powered dinghy or a small motor cruiser, you can fish waters that are beyond the reach of the shore angler but not far enough offshore to warrant being worked by larger boats. These include not only those close to the shore, but also the quiet bays, estuaries, and saltwater creeks that are often very productive because they are seldom fished.

SAFETY AT SEA

When you are in charge of a boat, of whatever size, it is essential that you are capable of handling it properly and that you and your companions know exactly what to do in an emergency. The boat must be seaworthy and of adequate size, with a reliable motor, a full tank of fuel, and basic emergency equipment including life-jackets, compass, flares, a first-aid kit, and, if possible, a radio. Before setting out, get an up-to-date weather forecast, and let someone know where you are going and when you expect to return.

UPTIDE FISHING

During fishing from an anchored boat in shallow water, the noise from the boat and the anglers can create a "scare area" into which most fish (apart from flatfish) are reluctant to stray. This area extends not only around the boat but also below it. In shallow water, if the fish cannot go deep enough to avoid the sound they may avoid the area of the boat altogether, and then it will not be possible to take them by drop-down fishing, in which the baits are simply lowered over the side.

Uptide fishing, in which the baits are cast uptide and well away from the boat, will overcome this problem. It works best in depths to around 12 m (40 ft), but it can be used much deeper. Wired sinkers are used to anchor the baits, and the length of line cast needs to be at least three times the depth of the water being fished.

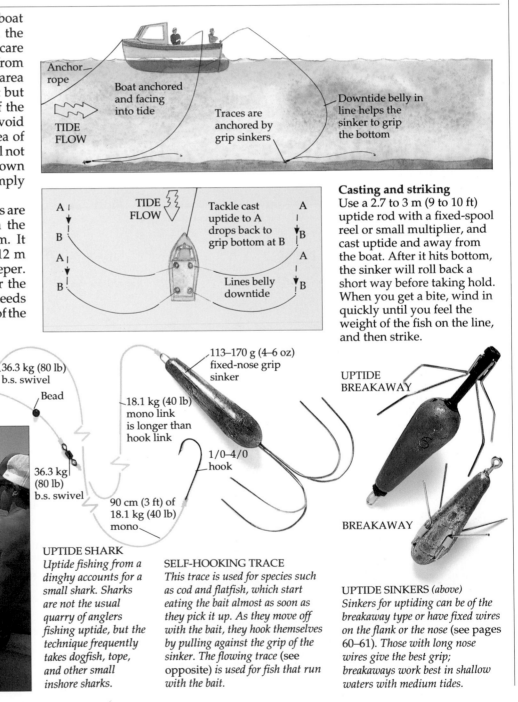

Anchor rope

Boat anchored and facing into tide

TIDE FLOW

Traces are anchored by grip sinkers

Downtide belly in line helps the sinker to grip the bottom

TIDE FLOW

A — Tackle cast uptide to A drops back to grip bottom at B — A

B — B

A — A

B — Lines belly downtide — B

Casting and striking
Use a 2.7 to 3 m (9 to 10 ft) uptide rod with a fixed-spool reel or small multiplier, and cast uptide and away from the boat. After it hits bottom, the sinker will roll back a short way before taking hold. When you get a bite, wind in quickly until you feel the weight of the fish on the line, and then strike.

SELF-HOOKING TRACE

Reel line 5.4–8.2 kg (12–18 lb) mono

36.3 kg (80 lb) b.s. swivel

Bead

113–170 g (4–6 oz) fixed-nose grip sinker

18.1 kg (40 lb) mono link is longer than hook link

36.3 kg (80 lb) b.s. swivel

1/0–4/0 hook

90 cm (3 ft) of 18.1 kg (40 lb) mono

UPTIDE BREAKAWAY

BREAKAWAY

UPTIDE SHARK
Uptide fishing from a dinghy accounts for a small shark. Sharks are not the usual quarry of anglers fishing uptide, but the technique frequently takes dogfish, tope, and other small inshore sharks.

SELF-HOOKING TRACE
This trace is used for species such as cod and flatfish, which start eating the bait almost as soon as they pick it up. As they move off with the bait, they hook themselves by pulling against the grip of the sinker. The flowing trace (see opposite) is used for fish that run with the bait.

UPTIDE SINKERS (*above*)
Sinkers for uptiding can be of the breakaway type or have fixed wires on the flank or the nose (see pages 60–61). Those with long nose wires give the best grip; breakaways work best in shallow waters with medium tides.

DOWNTIDE FISHING

Not all boat-angling situations either suit or demand the technique of uptide fishing, nor do they require specialized rods. Downtide, drop-down bottom fishing in waters that are deeper than about 9 m (30 ft), particularly reef and general drift fishing, can be done perfectly well with standard boat tackle. Rods are generally around 2.1 m (7 ft) long, reels do not need to have good casting ability, and a wide variety of traces can be used.

The sinkers do not have to hold bottom securely, so need not be wired. They must, however, be able to maintain bottom contact, and so they must be matched to the strength of the tide and of the line – the lower each of these is, the less weight will be required. In addition, the weight of sinker being used should be changed as the strength of the tide increases or decreases.

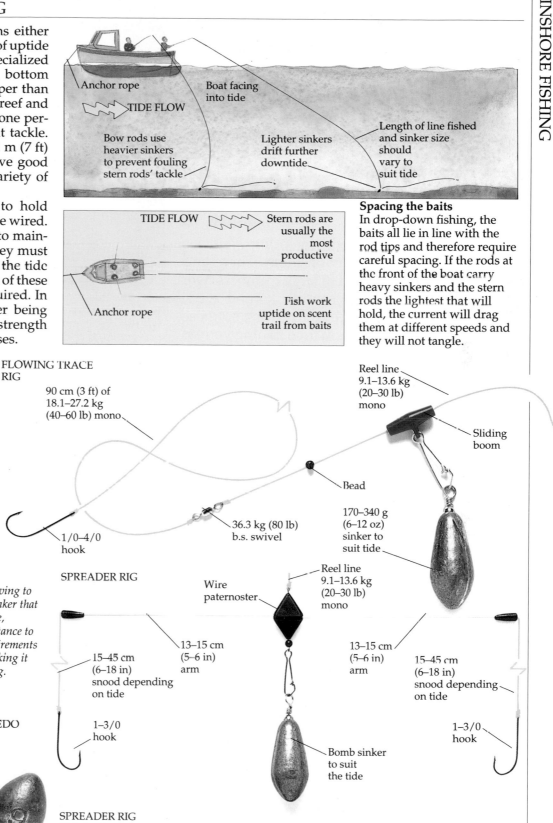

Spacing the baits
In drop-down fishing, the baits all lie in line with the rod tips and therefore require careful spacing. If the rods at the front of the boat carry heavy sinkers and the stern rods the lightest that will hold, the current will drag them at different speeds and they will not tangle.

FLOWING TRACE
Fish such as bass, which run with a bait before eating it, will drop it if they feel any resistance from the sinker. The flowing trace allows unhindered feeding movement, so that the angler can wait until the fish has the bait inside its mouth before striking. When using a flowing trace, the reel is set on free spool to allow the line to be taken through the boom without moving the sinker.

DOWNTIDE SINKERS *(below)*
To maintain bottom contact without having to pay out an excessive line, you need a sinker that combines adequate weight with a simple, streamlined shape that offers little resistance to the current. The bomb meets these requirements and is the shape least likely to snag, making it the best choice for most downtide fishing.

BELL   TORPEDO   FLAT BOMB

SPREADER RIG
This is a type of paternoster, a rig that presents baits on short lengths of mono, called snoods or droppers, above a sinker. The snoods are attached to the trace or to booms, and spaced so that they do not tangle with each other. This spreader rig has two wire booms, each carrying a short snood, allowing two baits to be fished at the bottom as a team. The snood lengths should be varied with changes in the tide: use snoods of 45 cm (18 in) in a fast-flowing tide, but shorten them to about 15 cm (6 in) at slack water to help minimize tangling. Flatfish, whiting, and codling are among the species that are highly susceptible to this type of bait presentation.

OFFSHORE FISHING

Fish tend to increase in numbers, size, and variety of species with greater water depth and distance from shore. But this does not mean that you will always have to sail a long way out to find large fish: they move to wherever their instincts tell them to be at any given time, which may be not far from the shore. For example, the biggest examples of cod, conger, and turbot are usually to be found well offshore at depth, but they could just as easily be within a few minutes' sailing time of port. One of the factors that determines the location of large fish is the availability of food, including sandeels and the mackerel that prey on them. These and other food items are found in large numbers over features such as offshore sandbanks and reefs, regardless of their distance from shore, so these features are often very productive fishing venues for the offshore angler.

DRIFT FISHING
Fishing on the drift over rough ground is no place for light tackle, because fierce tides demand heavy sinkers to take the terminal tackle down to where the largest fish feed. In addition, big fish have to be bullied to prevent them from gaining the sanctuary that rough ground affords.

FISHING OVER SANDBANKS

Sandbanks are exciting places to fish, because they are one of the few types of offshore feature likely to concentrate clean-ground species of fish in the way that wrecks attract rough-ground species. Moreover, the fish likely to be feeding in good numbers around a large, steep bank include prized angling species such as bass, turbot, brill, and cod. The supporting cast can include numerous species of ray, plus plaice, dab, whiting, and even pollack.

Bank-fishing rigs
Bank-rig design depends on whether you are fishing at anchor or on the drift. For anchored-boat fishing, use a standard flowing trace *(see page 245)*, made of 1.2 m (4 ft) of heavy mono and armed with a 4/0 Aberdeen hook. When drift fishing, increase the trace length to 3 to 6 m (10 to 20 ft) and attach the sinker via a long, tubular boom.

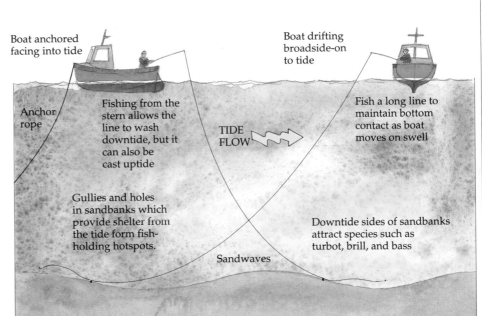

Boat anchored facing into tide

Boat drifting broadside-on to tide

Anchor rope

Fishing from the stern allows the line to wash downtide, but it can also be cast uptide

TIDE FLOW

Fish a long line to maintain bottom contact as boat moves on swell

Gullies and holes in sandbanks which provide shelter from the tide form fish-holding hotspots.

Downtide sides of sandbanks attract species such as turbot, brill, and bass

Sandwaves

BANK-FISHING SINKERS
Because a sandbank is a maze of ridges and gullies, end tackle often wanders from its intended path and this can lead to tangles. A studded watch weight is less prone to wandering and tangling than other types of sinker.

WATCH WEIGHT

Fishing on the drift
Drifting is by far the easiest way to fish a large bank, because it requires no prior knowledge of where the gullies and sandwaves are. If you start the drift well uptide of the lip of the bank, and pay out enough line to cope with variations in depth, your baits will cover every nook and cranny along the boat's line of travel. Bites show as a slow pulling-over of the rod tip (and of the rod itself, if unattended). Bass, turbot, and brill are typical bank species.

Fishing at anchor
When fishing from an anchored boat, you cannot cover as much ground with your baits as when fishing on the drift. As a result, you need to place your baits in the areas most likely to hold feeding fish, which are gullies and the downtide slopes of sandwaves. Free-swimming fish, such as bass, are usually found near the lip of the bank, skate and rays near the base, and flatfish over the middle section. The most reliable way to find these features is to use an echo sounder.

FISHING OFFSHORE REEFS

A reef attracts a rich variety of marine creatures, including fish, because it offers abundant cover, and the varying bottom topography provides a wide range of habitats. Because of the large number of species likely to be present, the reef angler is often faced with the question of which one to fish for, and having decided, may well find the baits being taken by other species anyway. For example, fishing specifically for conger does not rule out other species taking the bait, although the size of the baits and hooks will have a limiting effect. One of the most effective rigs for general reef fishing is baited mackerel feathers, and this fact is reflected in the alternative rigs shown here. Like feather rigs, they present the baits above the sinker so that they flutter enticingly and are clear of bottom snags. They avoid many of the common problems with shop-bought feathers, including short snoods and poor hooks.

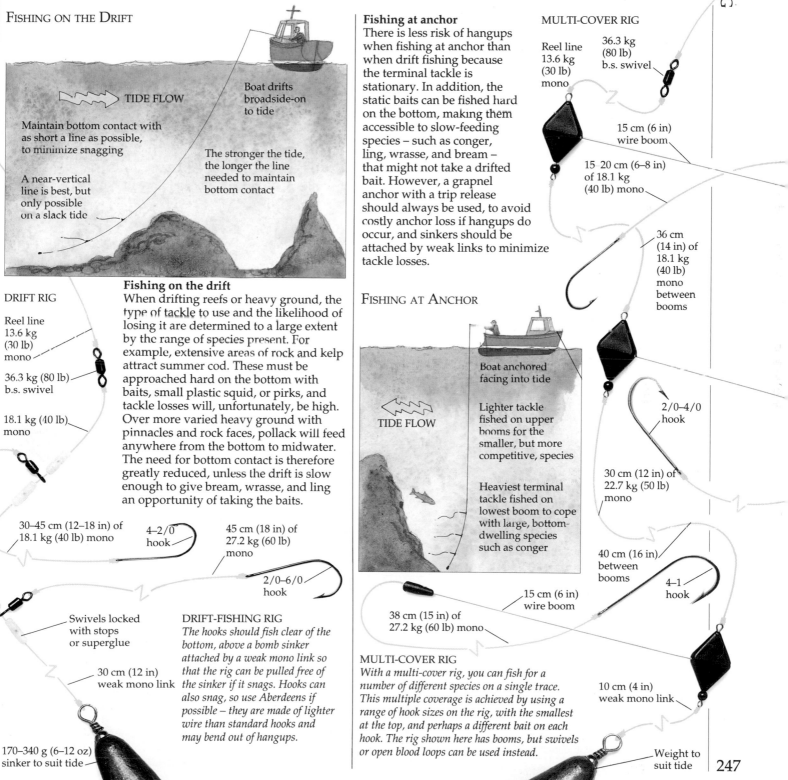

FISHING ON THE DRIFT

TIDE FLOW

Boat drifts broadside-on to tide

Maintain bottom contact with as short a line as possible, to minimize snagging

A near-vertical line is best, but only possible on a slack tide

The stronger the tide, the longer the line needed to maintain bottom contact

Fishing on the drift

When drifting reefs or heavy ground, the type of tackle to use and the likelihood of losing it are determined to a large extent by the range of species present. For example, extensive areas of rock and kelp attract summer cod. These must be approached hard on the bottom with baits, small plastic squid, or pirks, and tackle losses will, unfortunately, be high. Over more varied heavy ground with pinnacles and rock faces, pollack will feed anywhere from the bottom to midwater. The need for bottom contact is therefore greatly reduced, unless the drift is slow enough to give bream, wrasse, and ling an opportunity of taking the baits.

DRIFT RIG

Reel line 13.6 kg (30 lb) mono

36.3 kg (80 lb) b.s. swivel

18.1 kg (40 lb) mono

30–45 cm (12–18 in) of 18.1 kg (40 lb) mono

4–2/0 hook

45 cm (18 in) of 27.2 kg (60 lb) mono

2/0–6/0 hook

Swivels locked with stops or superglue

DRIFT-FISHING RIG
The hooks should fish clear of the bottom, above a bomb sinker attached by a weak mono link so that the rig can be pulled free of the sinker if it snags. Hooks can also snag, so use Aberdeens if possible – they are made of lighter wire than standard hooks and may bend out of hangups.

30 cm (12 in) weak mono link

170–340 g (6–12 oz) sinker to suit tide

Fishing at anchor

There is less risk of hangups when fishing at anchor than when drift fishing because the terminal tackle is stationary. In addition, the static baits can be fished hard on the bottom, making them accessible to slow-feeding species – such as conger, ling, wrasse, and bream – that might not take a drifted bait. However, a grapnel anchor with a trip release should always be used, to avoid costly anchor loss if hangups do occur, and sinkers should be attached by weak links to minimize tackle losses.

FISHING AT ANCHOR

Boat anchored facing into tide

TIDE FLOW

Lighter tackle fished on upper booms for the smaller, but more competitive, species

Heaviest terminal tackle fished on lowest boom to cope with large, bottom-dwelling species such as conger

38 cm (15 in) of 27.2 kg (60 lb) mono

15 cm (6 in) wire boom

MULTI-COVER RIG
With a multi-cover rig, you can fish for a number of different species on a single trace. This multiple coverage is achieved by using a range of hook sizes on the rig, with the smallest at the top, and perhaps a different bait on each hook. The rig shown here has booms, but swivels or open blood loops can be used instead.

MULTI-COVER RIG

Reel line 13.6 kg (30 lb) mono

36.3 kg (80 lb) b.s. swivel

15 cm (6 in) wire boom

15–20 cm (6–8 in) of 18.1 kg (40 lb) mono

36 cm (14 in) of 18.1 kg (40 lb) mono between booms

2/0–4/0 hook

30 cm (12 in) of 22.7 kg (50 lb) mono

40 cm (16 in) between booms

4–1 hook

10 cm (4 in) weak mono link

Weight to suit tide

247

WRECK FISHING

Ships can be wrecked anywhere from the shore to mid-ocean, but the best angling wrecks will be in water deeper than 60 m (200 ft), and the greatest concentrations are usually found in the vicinity of major ports. Wrecks can end up on virtually any type of ground, and from an angling point of view it does not matter where they settle out. In time, algae begins to grow on a wreck, followed by encrusting animals such as barnacles; eventually, a complete food chain is established. For fish, a wreck on sandy ground is like an oasis in a desert, and in rocky areas it provides more food and even better cover, for both predators and prey, than the surrounding rocks. A broken-up wreck will offer more cover than one that is relatively intact, so it will attract larger numbers of fish. The more broken-up a wreck becomes, the better its angling potential will be.

FISHING AT ANCHOR

Working a wreck from an anchored boat is a very specialized affair that makes great demands on the skills of both skipper and anglers. The skipper must make allowances for wind and tide, both of which can vary greatly over very short periods of time, and make continual fine adjustments to keep the stern of the boat just uptide of the edge of the wreck. Anchoring is always done at the slacker periods of neap tides and requires good sea conditions. At best, anglers will get 2 to 2½ hours of anchored fishing before the new tide starts to swing the boat out of position and it is time to switch to fishing on the drift. However, as the boat starts to swing, baits missing target can land on the sandwaves that build around some wrecks and are caused by the tide. Clean-ground species, including large anglerfish and turbot, often frequent these sandwaves and sometimes feed tight up to the hulk.

Fishing into the hulk
When fishing into a hulk for fish such as large conger and ling, you need very heavy tackle and wire traces, and big baits placed right into the main wreckage, where they feed. Conger live in holes, and you need to drop the baits almost onto their heads to get them to show any interest. They take incredibly lightly and must be given time to do so, but they must be dragged quickly from their retreats the instant the hook is driven home, otherwise they will not be moved. Ling are quicker onto the baits than conger, so the best conger wrecks are those where the ling population has been thinned.

Boat anchored facing into tide

Anchor chain

TIDE FLOW

The long periods of slack water at neap tides are ideal for fishing at anchor

To ensure that all rods are fishing over the wreck, all lines should be of similar diameters and all sinkers of equal weight

Water pressure on thick lines will push them too far downtide of the wreck

Wreck

RUNNING LEGER FOR CONGER
The strong, simple running leger is the best rig to use for big-fish work over snaggy terrain. Provided you follow the basic design, you can vary the lengths and components to suit your personal preferences, but for conger fishing it is better to use wire rather than mono for the terminal trace.

RUNNING LEGER – CONGER RIG

Bead

22.7 kg (50 lb) b.s. swivel

1.2 m (4 ft) of 45.4 kg (100 lb) mono

22.7 kg (50 lb) b.s. swivel

30 or 45 cm (12 or 18 in) of 45.4 kg (100 lb) wire or 68 kg (150 lb) longliner's mono

Crimp

10/0 hook or larger

Sliding boom

Reel line 22.7 kg (50 lb) mono

Streamlined sinker to suit tide

FISHING ON THE DRIFT

Drift fishing over wrecks is far easier on both skipper and anglers than fishing at anchor. A buoy is dropped to mark the starting position, and after each drift over the wreck the boat is taken back uptide for another pass.

Fish on most wrecks divide into two main categories: those feeding at or near the bottom, such as conger, ling, and cod, and higher-level feeders, such as pollack and coalfish, which hunt prey fish all around the pressure wave caused by water forced up over the wreck by the tide. Conger, and more particularly ling, can be taken on a slow drift but are better approached at anchor. The rest are best fished for by drifting with rubber eels and pirks.

TACKLE LOSSES
Most wrecks offer excellent fishing, but tackle losses due to snagging can be high, even in calm weather and a placid sea.

Boat drifts broadside-on to the tide

Work the pirk by dropping it to the bottom and then repeat every raising and lowering the rod tip.

TIDE FLOW

Work pirks as close to the wreck as possible

Wreck

Bottom fishing
Baited pirks, and small plastic squid rigged above a pirk, are excellent lures for cod and ling, and will occasionally take deep-feeding pollack. Both are fished right on the bottom, so tackle losses can be high, and it is essential to use pirks of the correct weight for the strength of tide. Plastic squid should be rigged on short, heavy mono standoff droppers, as close to the pirk as practicable.

Fishing the flying collar
This rig is effective for pollack and other species feeding above the wreck, but cod and ling might also grab at it in the initial stages of the retrieve. Flick the rig away from the boat to avoid tangles on the drop, and count the number of turns of the reel handle you make on the retrieve to get an idea of where fish might take. Set the drag light, or the hook will tear free as a taking fish kicks for bottom in one continuous, powerful run.

FISHING THE FLYING COLLAR

TIDE FLOW

Flying collar rig lowered to wreck or seabed

Boat drifts broadside-on to the tide

When the rig touches bottom, wind in 50 to 60 turns of the reel handle; if no bites occur, lower the rig and repeat

Wreck

FLYING COLLAR RIG

Boom (flying collar)

Bead

Swivel

At least 3 m (10 ft) of 18.1 kg (40 lb) mono

170–227 g (6–8 oz) sinker

10–20 cm (4–8 in) rubber eel

8/0 hook

PIRK/PLASTIC SQUID RIG

27.2 kg (60 lb) b.s. swivel

15 cm (6 in) to first dropper

Reel line 13.6–22.7 kg (30–50 lb) mono

27.2 kg (60 lb) mono

30 cm (12 in) between droppers

Droppers formed from open blood loops

30 cm (12 in) to pirk

Plastic squid (or rubber eels) on droppers

Pirk size and weight according to tide

249

SURFCASTING

Casting a bait from the beach into the surf is one of the most enjoyable styles of shore angling. It is also one of the most physical forms of angling, using more body movement than any other. However, in surf fishing it is not brute force that produces a good cast but correct technique. The first step is to master the basic casting action, which you can do quite quickly, but to develop good casting rhythm and movement you must practise until they become automatic; distance will come naturally once the rhythm is perfected. The off-the-ground cast is easy to learn, but it cannot be learned properly from books alone; a few lessons from a skilled surfcaster or a qualified casting coach will amply repay the time invested.

LOADING A SHOCK LEADER

MULTIPLIER REEL

FIXED-SPOOL REEL

To load a shock leader (see page 253) onto a multiplier, start with the knot near the right-hand flange. Lay it in open coils to the left and then to the right, stopping short of the knot. Open coils prevent the leader from biting into the main line, and if the knot is on the right it will not cut your thumb during the cast.

It is not necessary to load the leader manually onto a fixed-spool reel because the reel will cross-lay it automatically. However, starting with the knot at the rear of the spool and winding a minimum of six evenly spaced turns forward reduces the chance of the knot stripping bunches of line on the cast.

The grip
The reel-up position is more commonly used than the reel-down, and feels more natural. The reel-down position is favoured by many distance casters because the stronger hand supplies the power, leaving the weaker to control the spool.

REEL-UP POSITION

REEL-DOWN POSITION

THE OFF-THE-GROUND CAST

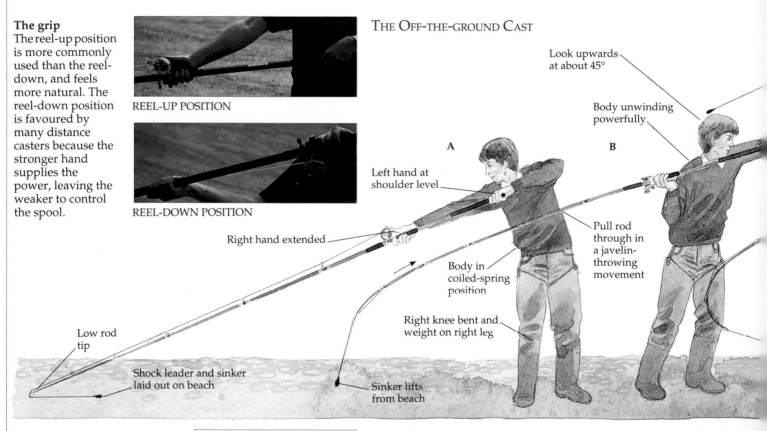

Look upwards at about 45°

Body unwinding powerfully

A

Left hand at shoulder level

Right hand extended

Body in coiled-spring position

Right knee bent and weight on right leg

Low rod tip

Shock leader and sinker laid out on beach

Sinker lifts from beach

B

Pull rod through in a javelin-throwing movement

The stance
Scrape a line in the sand or shingle to mark out the direction of the cast. Then stand with your right foot on the line and your left foot 15 cm (6 in) back, with both feet angled slightly forward. With the reel set ready to cast, swivel your waist and shoulders to position the sinker on the beach with the rod tip just off the ground.

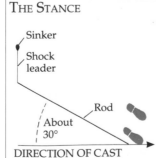

THE STANCE

Sinker

Shock leader

Rod

About 30°

DIRECTION OF CAST

The Cast
Set the reel for casting (see page 212), with the sinker hanging at 90 cm to 1.2 m (3 to 4 ft) from the tip ring. Brake the line with your thumb or finger, depending on the type of reel you are using. Then adopt the correct stance, taking your weight on your right leg (A). Your left hand should be next to your right shoulder, your left elbow raised, and your

right arm extended. Turn your head to face the cast direction, looking upwards at about 45° (B). Start to uncoil your body powerfully but smoothly to the left, simultaneously pulling the rod forward like a javelin along its own axis, not in a side sweep. Your left hand starts to rise while your right arm moves in close to your chest

COMMON CASTING FAULTS

Laying out the tackle on the beach before setting your feet in position reduces the "feel" through the muscles of your legs, back, and waist. Set your feet first, then swivel your waist and shoulders to lay out the sinker on the beach.

A second fault is to push the rod too soon in the initial stages of the cast (steps **A** to **C**). The rod should follow you rather than be pushed ahead of you. Concentrate on getting your head turned in the casting direction and "unwinding" your body like a spring, and the arm movement should then follow naturally.

SUITABLE TERRAIN
Off-the-ground casting is a technique for fairly clean, smooth beaches. It cannot be used on very rough ground, or when wading in the surf.

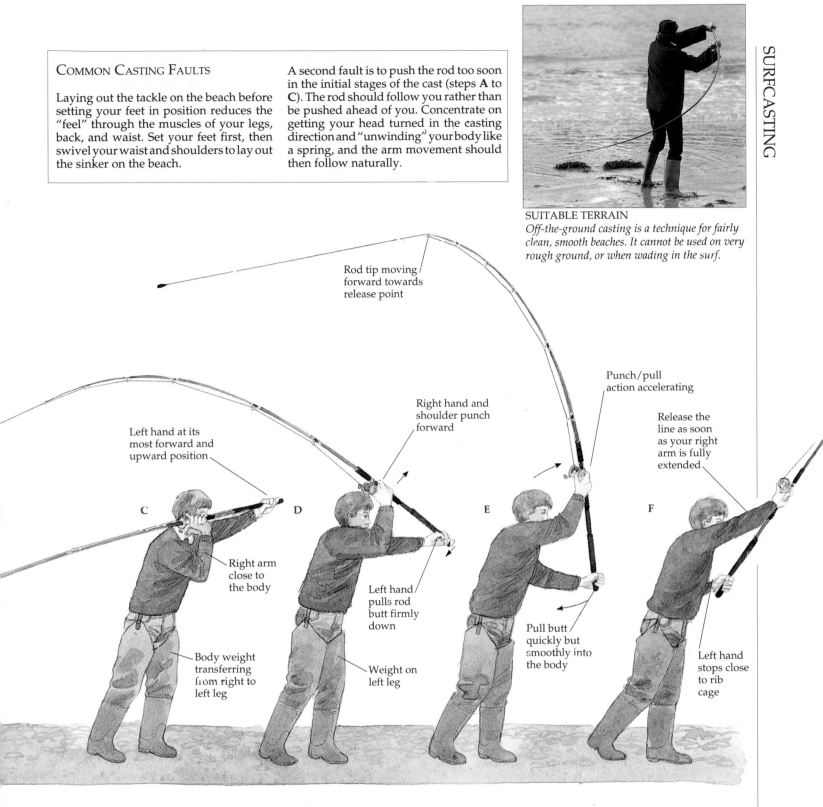

Rod tip moving forward towards release point

Left hand at its most forward and upward position

Right hand and shoulder punch forward

Punch/pull action accelerating

Release the line as soon as your right arm is fully extended

C

Right arm close to the body

Body weight transferring from right to left leg

D

Left hand pulls rod butt firmly down

Weight on left leg

E

Pull butt quickly but smoothly into the body

F

Left hand stops close to rib cage

as its elbow flexes. With your left arm now at its fullest extension, and your right hand at eye level, transfer your body weight to your left leg (**C**). The extra power that comes into the cast from the transfer of body weight translates into increased casting speed, which can be felt through the rod because the butt seems to tighten up in your hands.

As your left arm reaches maximum extension, start to punch your right hand upwards and at the same time pull the rod butt down sharply towards your ribcage with your left hand (**D**). This casting action should be one smooth, continuous movement, with no break between the initial "javelin throw" and the punch/pull sequence.

Continue the punch/pull sequence, accelerating the rod smoothly towards the release point (**F**). Your left hand should be pulling the rod butt towards your ribcage and your right arm should begin to straighten from the elbow. Your chest should be pointing in the direction of the cast with most of your body weight transferred to your left leg.

The powerful but smooth punch/pull action results in a fast, smooth turnover of the top tip. Release the line, when your right arm is at full extension and your left hand is tucked in against your ribcage (**F**). Stop the reel as soon as the sinker hits the water, to prevent the line from overrunning under its own momentum and tangling.

SHORE FISHING 1

When fished at distance from a low vantage point, such as a beach, all traces present baits hard on the bottom regardless of where the sinker (weight) is positioned. Most traces are variations on the simple themes of the running leger and the paternoster, and the exact type of terminal rig to use at any particular time depends on local geography, sea conditions, and the way in which the target species is known to feed. To perform at their best, terminal rigs need to be as simple and free from self-snagging as possible. Use booms (*see page 60*) to keep sinkers and snoods (short lengths of line that carry the hooks) clear of each other and of the reel line.

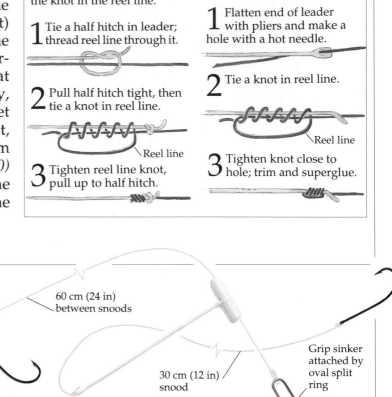

LEADER KNOTS

Basic knot
A leader knot must be strong, reliable, and have a slim profile for safe passage through the rings. Tighten the half hitch with pliers before tying the knot in the reel line.

1 Tie a half hitch in leader; thread reel line through it.

2 Pull half hitch tight, then tie a knot in reel line.

3 Tighten reel line knot, pull up to half hitch.

High-performance knot
Tie the reel line through a hole in the leader for a strong but very slim knot. This works best when the reel line is much thinner than the leader.

1 Flatten end of leader with pliers and make a hole with a hot needle.

2 Tie a knot in reel line.

Reel line

3 Tighten knot close to hole; trim and superglue.

BASIC TWO-HOOK PATERNOSTER

Split ring

30 cm (12 in) snood

Plastic boom

60 cm (24 in) between snoods

30 cm (12 in) snood

Grip sinker attached by oval split ring

Slow-moving fish, and those unlikely to run with or drop a bait at any hint of resistance, are best approached with a simple two-hook paternoster rig. In this one, each snood is tied to a loop dropper, formed by knotting a loop in the reel line and supported by plastic tubing to reduce tangles, but booms and swivels are effective alternatives to droppers. The wired grip sinker, besides anchoring the bait, will encourage fish to hook themselves as they pull the bait against its resistance. This is without equal as an all-round rig for a wide range of fish including flatfish and codling.

TIDE FLOW

A different bait can be fished on each hook

90 cm (36 in) between snood and sinker

BASIC RUNNING LEGER

Split ring

Sliding boom

Bead

Swivel

90 cm (36 in) snood

Wired grip sinker

Some fish, such as bass, like to run with a bait and might eject it should they sense something is wrong. Others, such as tope, make long runs before swallowing baits properly. All these fish must be allowed to take line freely before the strike is made, and the basic running leger rig allows them to do so. It is not a rig that lends itself to distance work, but it is excellent for medium-distance casting and for backing up the beach on a flooding tide. It is also a very good big-bait trace for fish such as conger, dogfish, and rays, although no fish will have any qualms about picking it up.

TIDE FLOW

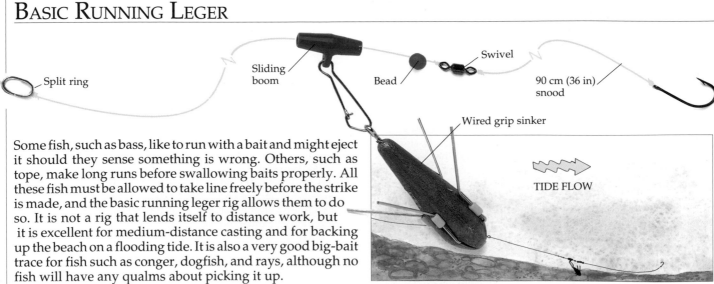

BASIC RUNNING PATERNOSTER

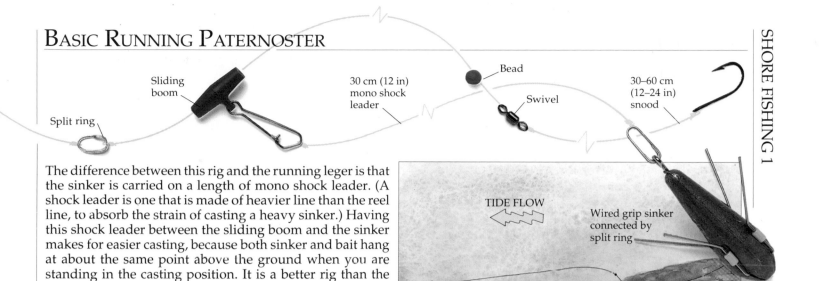

Split ring

Sliding
boom

30 cm (12 in)
mono shock
leader

Bead

Swivel

30–60 cm
(12–24 in)
snood

The difference between this rig and the running leger is that the sinker is carried on a length of mono shock leader. (A shock leader is one that is made of heavier line than the reel line, to absorb the strain of casting a heavy sinker.) Having this shock leader between the sliding boom and the sinker makes for easier casting, because both sinker and bait hang at about the same point above the ground when you are standing in the casting position. It is a better rig than the running leger for slow or finicky fish that do not have to be allowed lots of line before the strike can be made.

TIDE FLOW

Wired grip sinker
connected by
split ring

ANCHORING THE BAIT

Uptide casting
Although tides appear to move up and down a beach, the direction of flow is often parallel to the shore. When such lateral currents are strong, bottom-holding and bite-detection problems can make the shore angler's life extremely difficult. The way to get around these problems is to use a wired grip sinker. These are available in a variety of sizes and wiring styles to offer differing

degrees of hold to suit a wide range of conditions. When fishing a grip sinker uptide, cast well uptide of your rod rest and allow the sinker to fall freely. Before re-engaging the reel gearing, walk back to the rest, free-spooling line to create a bow. The force of the tide on the bow will help the grip wires to dig in well. A taking fish will dislodge the sinker, and the line will fall slack as the fish drops away downtide.

ROD POSITION
In heavy surf it is not only the strength of the tide that can cause difficulty in anchoring the bait: seaweed brought in by the breakers can foul the line and drag the sinker free. Holding the rod high, while feeling for bites, helps the line to clear the breakers.

CASTING A GRIP SINKER

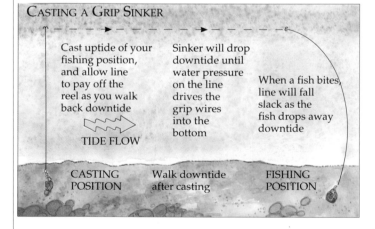

Cast uptide of your fishing position, and allow line to pay off the reel as you walk back downtide

Sinker will drop downtide until water pressure on the line drives the grip wires into the bottom

When a fish bites, line will fall slack as the fish drops away downtide

TIDE FLOW

CASTING
POSITION

Walk downtide
after casting

FISHING
POSITION

Avoiding snags
Typical snags that can cause tackle "hangups" include flotsam, weed, and heavy ground. When fishing heavy ground close in, and when there is heavy ground between you and cleaner, snagfree ground, sinker shape is important. All sinkers can snag, but the bomb-shaped type is less likely to than the rest. Where hangups are inevitable, attach the sinker by means of a sacrificial weak link.

WEIGHT LIFTER
Hangups can be a problem when shore fishing, because it is often difficult to lift the terminal tackle clear of any snags. A vaned device, known as a weight lifter, helps lift the sinker clear of snags when the tackle is retrieved rapidly with the rod held high.

Searching the bottom
There are times when using the rolling leger technique with a plain bomb sinker offers a distinct advantage over using an anchored bait, especially when fish are reluctant to move about or when they gather in isolated pockets, which are not always easy to locate. By casting the bomb well uptide and allowing it to roll slowly back down, you can search and cover large areas of ground with the bait or baits. However, if the tidal currents are strong, the bomb will travel too quickly to present the bait effectively, and it is prone to hangups on snaggy ground.

When retrieved quickly, the weight lifter rises in the water, carrying the sinker along path **A** instead of path **B**

A

B

SHORE FISHING 2

Not all shore fishing is done from the gradually shelving vantage point of a beach, nor do all coastal species of fish feed on or near to the bottom at all times. The sea is a three-dimensional world, with its unseen downward dimension assuming increasingly greater importance for anglers where deep water touches land. This could be beneath rock ledges, below harbour walls, or alongside piers and breakwaters. To get the best out of shore fishing in deep water, you must position your baits at the most appropriate depth. This could mean, for example, suspending a lugworm or a strip of fish beneath a float, or working a suitably heavy or weighted lure through the feeding zone. Spinning and float fishing have much to commend them as techniques for shore fishing, but it is important to use suitable tackle. The range of saltwater spinning and float tackle is increasing, but you may have to turn to the heavier end of the freshwater tackle stand to find what you need.

THINK FIRST
A dropnet, which can be lowered on a rope, is the only feasible means of landing fish from such a precarious position. Plan how to land your catch before starting to fish – not after.

FLOAT FISHING

Float fishing is regarded by many sea anglers as a sort of extension of freshwater fishing, and indeed, much of the tackle used is freshwater gear. Its use is limited, however, but not so much by the range of species that can be caught on it as by the conditions often prevailing where those fish live and feed. Fishing for mullet in quiet harbours, for example, presents no problems to standard freshwater tackle, but other situations call for a heavier approach. For instance, heavy tackle is needed when fishing baits just above kelp for wrasse, because these powerful fish will dive for cover the moment they take a bait. Fishing for pollack from rocky headlands, when they are feeding at some distance from the shore, also requires heavy tackle to get the baits out far enough and to control the situation at long range. Freshwater rods suitable for light float fishing include 3 to 4 m (10 to 13 ft) float and leger rods and 2.1 to 3 m (7 to 10 ft) spinning rods. Use a surfcaster for the really heavy work.

Sliding float fishing

Always use a sliding rather than a fixed float when fishing at depths greater than the length of the rod. With any float rig, you can wind in line only until the float reaches the top rod ring, and if the float is fixed for fishing at, say, 6 m (20 ft), you will still have 6 m (20 ft) of line paid out. This will make it difficult to retrieve the terminal tackle or to play or land a hooked fish. A sliding float rig is also preferable where casting room is limited, such as on a cramped rock ledge: with only the float and hook length hanging free, casting control and accuracy are much improved. A small sliding stop knot tied on the line above the float controls the depth at which the hook will fish, but winds easily through the rod rings.

HEAVYWEIGHT FLOAT RIG

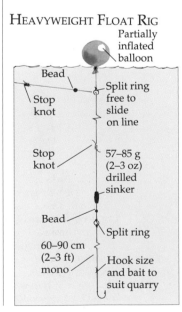

- Partially inflated balloon
- Bead
- Stop knot
- Split ring free to slide on line
- Stop knot
- 57–85 g (2–3 oz) drilled sinker
- Bead
- Split ring
- 60–90 cm (2–3 ft) mono
- Hook size and bait to suit quarry

Heavyweight float fishing
This rig is designed for situations where standard sea float tackle cannot cope. These include fishing in a fast current, where as much as 142 g (5 oz) of weight may be required to maintain depth, or when a big bait is to be drifted out to predators such as small sharks *(see page 256).* It is based on the sliding float principle, and uses a very large float, such as a balloon. This is tied to a swivel or split ring, running freely on the line below a bead and stop knot. Below the swivel or split ring are a drilled barrel sinker, a bead, and then a mono or wire hook length.

HARBOUR FISHING
This garfish was taken from the deep water off a harbour wall, an ideal venue for float fishing.

SLIDING FLOAT RIG

- Stop knot
- Bead
- Sliding float
- Stop knot 5–7.5 cm (2–3 in) above split ring
- 28–42 g (1–1½ oz) drilled sinker
- Bead
- Split ring
- 60–90 cm (2–3 ft) mono
- Hook size and bait to suit quarry

BOTTOM FISHING

Bottom fishing over heavy ground is always difficult, and losses of both tackle and fish will probably be high. These problems must be accepted as unavoidable if you are to have any reasonable hope of success, but there are ways of minimizing them. The most important of these is to keep your rigs as simple as possible. Basic single-hook terminal tackle is not only less likely to snag than a more complicated rig, but is also cheaper and therefore more expendable. Hangups usually occur either at the hook or the sinker, so these should be attached by weak links so that the rest of the rig can be pulled free of them if they snag (but do not use a weak link for the hook length if you are after sharp-toothed species). Alternatively, you can use a buoyant leger rig to float the bait clear of the bottom and thus of potential snags.

Supported-line fishing
This technique employs a balloon to support the line, so that the terminal tackle rises clear of snags when it is retrieved: it has no effect on bait presentation. Using a supported line, you can cast onto clean ground to the seaward side of snags and be reasonably sure that the tackle will make it back for another throw. You can use whichever bottom-fishing rig you prefer: simply slide a swivel or split ring, attached to a balloon, onto the reel line before attaching the terminal tackle.

Buoyant leger fishing
Using a buoyant leger rig, it is possible to float a bait at a fixed distance above the bottom. This offers improved bait presentation as well as reducing the risk of snagging. For example, it can help to prevent the bait from becoming "lost" between rocks and therefore inaccessible to fish, and reduces the risk of crab damage that can render a bait worthless within minutes of it touching bottom. The rig is simply a balsa float slipped onto the hook length of a leger rig, and the height to which the bait rises is determined by the position of a stop knot.

BUOYANT LEGER RIG

Reel line

Bomb sinker

Bead

Split ring or swivel 60 cm (2 ft) from stop knot

Fluorescent green balsa float 7.5 cm (3 in) long, 12 mm (½ in) thick

Stop knot 15–30 cm (6–12 in) from hook

Hook size and bait to suit quarry

SUPPORTED-LINE FISHING

The line supported by balloon retrieves clear of inshore snags

Split ring

Balloon free to slide up reel line

Stop knot

Bead

Unsupported line snags on retrieve

Leger tackle on clean seabed

SPINNING

SHALLOW SPINNING RIG

90 cm (3 ft) trace

21 g (¾ oz) anti-kink weight

Small rubber sandeel

SHALLOW SPINNING RIG
Cast this rig with a gentle lobbing action. If you cast too vigorously, the uptrace sinker will travel ahead of the lure, causing tangles.

Spinning offers certain advantages over bait fishing, one being that with only a small box of lures and a light rod and reel to carry, you can easily cover long stretches of coastline in a day's fishing. Rocky shores provide some of the best saltwater spinning venues, because they usually attract a wide variety of the predatory species, such as mackerel, bass, and pollack, which strike readily at artificial lures. When spinning, search the water as thoroughly as possible by varying the lure depth and using a radial casting pattern *(see page 216)*. Suitable lures include plugs, spinners, wobbling spoons, and bar spoons, and you should carry a selection of different types so that you can use whichever is most suitable for the species you are seeking and for the prevailing conditions. Fish usually attack from below, so use dark-coloured lures when the sky is bright and switch to lures with light or reflective finishes when fishing in poor light conditions.

LANDA LUKKI TURBO SPOON
Use a heavy lure like this for deep spinning.

Lure weight
The greater the distance you can cast a lure, the more water you can cover with it. For this reason, and to fish deep in strong tides, a heavy lure (fished on tackle that can handle it) is often preferable to a light one. Ideally, the lure should be self-weighted, but this is not always possible, and you may need to add a streamlined anti-kink weight to the line *(see page 214)*. To minimize the risk of tangling, straighten the line by checking its flow from the reel just before the lure hits the water, or start winding in the moment it touches down.

SAFETY FIRST
Rocky shores usually have deep water close inshore. This makes them suitable venues for spinning, which generally works best in waters more than 1.8 m (6 ft) deep. However, deep water and spray-soaked rocks are a dangerous combination: wear suitable shoes with good grip and always fish with a companion.

255

SHARK FISHING

Sharks can be caught by a number of techniques, including drift fishing, bottom fishing from an anchored boat, shore fishing, and trolling with natural baits, either live or dead (*see page 258*). They can also be taken on fly tackle. The basic techniques shown here are suitable for sharks that feed in the middle and upper layers, such as blue shark, mako, and porbeagle, and for tope and other small sharks that feed near or at the bottom.

Because sharks have abrasive skins and very sharp, strong teeth, it is essential to use a wire trace at the end of the terminal tackle. One end of this trace is attached to the hook by a crimped loop, and crimped loop at the opposite end joins it to the main line (or to an intermediate length of heavy mono trace) via a swivel.

CRIMPING A WIRE TRACE

1 Slide the crimp onto the wire. Pass the wire through the hook or swivel eye, then tie a single loop knot and pull it tight with pliers.

2 Slide the crimp over the loose end of wire. Leave a short length of the loose end protruding beyond the crimp.

3 Loop the loose end, and tuck it back inside the crimp. This will prevent the sharp end of the wire from causing any damage.

4 Squeeze the crimp tightly closed with the pliers. Squeeze it at as many points as possible along its length.

DRIFT FISHING

Blue sharks and makos are mainly open-water species, feeding on pelagic shoal fish such as mackerel and pilchard, while porbeagle hunt closer to the shore over shallow-lying reefs. All can be caught from a drifting boat on 13.6 to 36.3 kg (30 to 80 lb) class boat rods, using baits suspended by floats (balloons) over a slick of rubby dubby. Sharks have a keen sense of smell and can lock onto very low concentrations of scents, so the slick will attract their attention. Moving their heads from side to side to detect the greatest concentration of scent, they will follow it to its source.

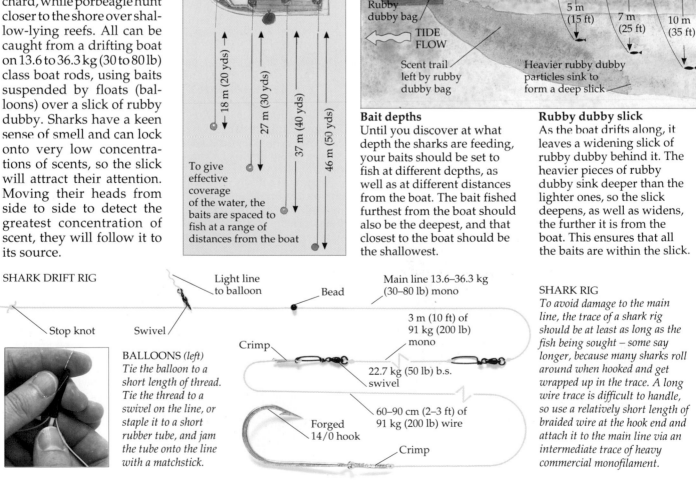

SPACING THE BAITS

To give effective coverage of the water, the baits are spaced to fish at a range of distances from the boat

18 m (20 yds)
27 m (30 yds)
37 m (40 yds)
46 m (50 yds)

Boat drifts with the tide

USING RUBBY DUBBY

Balloons

Rubby dubby bag

TIDE FLOW

5 m (15 ft)
7 m (25 ft)
10 m (35 ft)

Scent trail left by rubby dubby bag

Heavier rubby dubby particles sink to form a deep slick

Bait depths
Until you discover at what depth the sharks are feeding, your baits should be set to fish at different depths, as well as at different distances from the boat. The bait fished furthest from the boat should also be the deepest, and that closest to the boat should be the shallowest.

Rubby dubby slick
As the boat drifts along, it leaves a widening slick of rubby dubby behind it. The heavier pieces of rubby dubby sink deeper than the lighter ones, so the slick deepens, as well as widens, the further it is from the boat. This ensures that all the baits are within the slick.

SHARK DRIFT RIG

Light line to balloon

Bead

Main line 13.6–36.3 kg (30–80 lb) mono

Stop knot   Swivel

3 m (10 ft) of 91 kg (200 lb) mono

Crimp

22.7 kg (50 lb) b.s. swivel

60–90 cm (2–3 ft) of 91 kg (200 lb) wire

Forged 14/0 hook

Crimp

BALLOONS (*left*)
Tie the balloon to a short length of thread. Tie the thread to a swivel on the line, or staple it to a short rubber tube, and jam the tube onto the line with a matchstick.

SHARK RIG
To avoid damage to the main line, the trace of a shark rig should be at least as long as the fish being sought – some say longer, because many sharks roll around when hooked and get wrapped up in the trace. A long wire trace is difficult to handle, so use a relatively short length of braided wire at the hook end and attach it to the main line via an intermediate trace of heavy commercial monofilament.

BOAT FISHING FOR TOPE

The tope is one of the many small and medium-sized shark species that hunt near or at the bottom, feeding on fish such as cod, whiting, and flatfish over clean or mixed ground close inshore. Tope seem to hunt either as loners, or in single-sex groups that gather over feeding grounds. They can be caught by bottom fishing from an anchored boat or from the shore, and the best bait is cut or whole fish.

When fishing from an anchored boat, you can use either uptide or downtide casting techniques *(see page 244)*. For uptide fishing, use a soft-tipped uptide rod around 3 m (10 ft) long, and a wired grip sinker that will hold bottom in the prevailing tide. Pay out enough line to allow a belly to form in it when the sinker has taken hold. For downtide work, use a 13.6 kg (30 lb) class boat rod and a suitable plain bomb sinker.

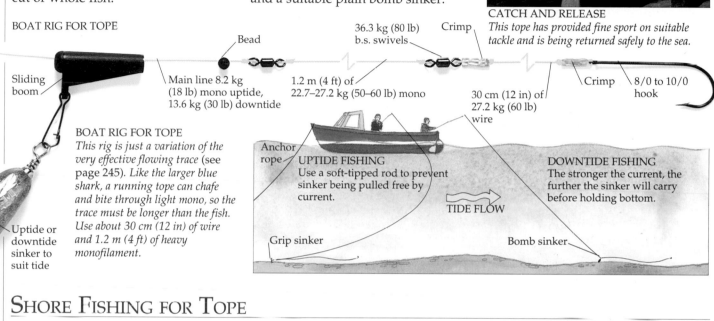

CATCH AND RELEASE
This tope has provided fine sport on suitable tackle and is being returned safely to the sea.

BOAT RIG FOR TOPE

Bead — Main line 8.2 kg (18 lb) mono uptide, 13.6 kg (30 lb) downtide

Sliding boom

36.3 kg (80 lb) b.s. swivels — Crimp

1.2 m (4 ft) of 22.7–27.2 kg (50–60 lb) mono

30 cm (12 in) of 27.2 kg (60 lb) wire

Crimp — 8/0 to 10/0 hook

BOAT RIG FOR TOPE
This rig is just a variation of the very effective flowing trace (see page 245). Like the larger blue shark, a running tope can chafe and bite through light mono, so the trace must be longer than the fish. Use about 30 cm (12 in) of wire and 1.2 m (4 ft) of heavy monofilament.

Uptide or downtide sinker to suit tide

Anchor rope

UPTIDE FISHING
Use a soft-tipped rod to prevent sinker being pulled free by current.

TIDE FLOW

Grip sinker

DOWNTIDE FISHING
The stronger the current, the further the sinker will carry before holding bottom.

Bomb sinker

SHORE FISHING FOR TOPE

Stop knot — Bead — Balloon tied to swivel (or matchstick method)

BALLOON FLOAT RIG
Bead

Bead — Main line 9.1–11.3 kg (20–25 lb) mono

113 g (4 oz) drilled sinker

1.2 m (4 ft) of 22.7 kg (50 lb) mono

36.3 kg (80 lb) b.s. swivels

30 cm (12 in) of 27.2 kg (60 lb) wire — Crimp

Crimp

6/0 to 8/0 hook

Tope are often found within casting range of the shore. Rock ledges and headlands looking out onto sand can attract them, as do steep beaches of sand, shingle, or mixed ground. Use a good-quality shore rod that can cast weights of up to 170 g (6 oz). The reel should be loaded with about 275 m (300 yds) of 9.1 to 11.3 kg (20 to 25 lb) mono, because a tope can run a long way when hooked.

Shore rigs
Use either a simple flowing trace rig, or one with a balloon float and weighted by a drilled barrel sinker. A long flowing trace prevents damage to the main line, and also allows the fish to pick up the bait and make a run before the hook is set. Casting a long trace with a big bait is difficult, but you should use one made up of at least 1.2 m (4 ft) of heavy monofilament and 30 cm (12 in) of wire.

FISHING FOR DOGFISH

Smoothhounds and most of the small sharks collectively known as dogfish, including the smooth dogfish, are shallow-water species that feed mainly on crabs and molluscs. These sharks have flattened teeth that crush rather than cut, and are commonly caught by casting from the shore and by boat fishing over shallow offshore banks. When hooked they are capable of putting up a hard fight.

PENNEL-RIGGED HOOKS

4/0 hook

Rubber sleeve over hook shank holds hook in place on line

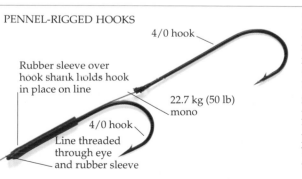

22.7 kg (50 lb) mono

4/0 hook — Line threaded through eye and rubber sleeve

Dogfish rigs
For sharks with crushing rather than cutting teeth, you need a heavy mono flowing trace about 1.2 m (4 ft) long. Use a single hook or a pennel rig, baited with peeler crab portions. The advantage of the pennel rig over a single hook is that you can present a bigger bunch of crab portions, with a hook at each end.

BIG-GAME FISHING

Big-game fishing is the pursuit, with rod-and-line tackle, of a wide range of large fish, including billfish, sailfish, wahoo, tarpon, the larger species of tuna, and large, active sharks, such as the mako and tiger. Most big-game fishing is done from charter boats, many of which provide tackle, bait, and instruction if required. The species sought depends partly on the preferences of the anglers and partly on what is available in the waters being fished, as do the techniques and tackle employed. Some big-game fishers prefer fly tackle, but the majority use boat tackle in the 5.4 to 59 kg (12 to 130 lb) IGFA classes, and methods such as lure trolling, deadbait trolling, and even livebaiting. All have their advantages and drawbacks, all catch plenty of fish, and on its day, each one can outfish the others. It all depends on the circumstances and conditions prevailing at the time, and no technique is good enough to warrant the neglect of the others. An open mind is just as important for success in big-game fishing as it is in any other form of angling.

LURE TROLLING

There are a great many species of fish that will take a trolled lure, so it is difficult to predict what you are going to catch when trolling, but there is a hard core of species that will regularly respond to the technique. These include marlin, sailfish, tuna, and similar large pelagic feeders favouring deep, open water, often where the ocean floor is quite literally miles below the surface. Middleweight gamefish such as wahoo, dolphinfish, and bonito will also hit a moving lure in open water. Whether these fish are truly big-game species is arguable, but large specimens occur, and at any size all of them are hard to subdue. Lure trolling is especially useful in open water where the fish are not concentrated in any particular area, because it allows the coverage of a lot of ground. The lures work as a spread at the surface, and are chosen so that each has a slightly different action. Together they create noise and leave a trail of bubbles behind them, which draws large predatory fish up from below. These then attack the lures.

Lure-fishing pattern
Big-game boats typically fish four rods at a time: one from each side, held clear of the boat on outriggers up to 14 m (45 ft) long, and two from the stern. Between them they usually fish a combination of submerged lures and lures that skip the surface. Each rod fishes with a different length of line paid out, for example 37 m (120 ft) and 43 m (140 ft) for the outrigger lines, and 21 m (70 ft) and 27 m (90 ft) for the stern lines. This spread of lures is designed to create the impression of a small school of baitfish, but when a fish gives chase, it will not necessarily go for the outermost lures. The stern lines often produce the most strikes, perhaps because fish are attracted towards them by the wake of the boat.

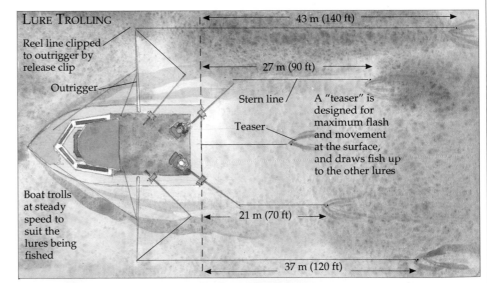

LURE TROLLING

Reel line clipped to outrigger by release clip

Outrigger

43 m (140 ft)

27 m (90 ft)

Stern line

A "teaser" is designed for maximum flash and movement at the surface, and draws fish up to the other lures

Teaser

Boat trolls at steady speed to suit the lures being fished

21 m (70 ft)

37 m (120 ft)

LURE SELECTION
Although manufacturers often label their lures as being for particular species, such as marlin or tuna, the fact is that any lure can take any species in the right circumstances. Select a range of lures, including Kona Heads and plastic squid, that will give you a good choice of colours, sizes, and actions to suit the quarry you happen to be after and the prevailing conditions.

KONA HEAD LURES

BIG-GAME SPECIES
In addition to billfish and other very large species, many smaller fish – such as this barracuda – are often grouped under the general heading of big-game fish. Other such species include dolphinfish, albacore, king mackerel, and amberjack.

BAIT FISHING

There is nothing more stimulating to the aggressive instincts of most predatory fish than the natural scent or movement of a prey fish. This makes natural baits generally more effective than artificial lures, but there are some drawbacks to using them. For example, wahoo are very adept at chopping baits off just astern of the hook, and some species take livebaits more readily than others: black marlin are more susceptible to a slowly trolled tuna or dolphinfish than to a lure, but sometimes the reverse is true of blue marlin. Livebaits also attract sharks, which are only rarely willing to strike at a lure. This can be a problem if other species are your quarry, and it does not diminish when dead or cut baits are used, because the sharks home in on the scent instead of the vibration. However, there is more chance of a dead or cut bait being grabbed by one of the highly prized species than by a shark if it is trolled rather than fished static.

Deadbait trolling

The appearance and smell of a deadbait make it potentially more attractive to predators than an artificial lure, but the presentation should allow it to "swim" in a natural manner or this advantage will be lost. With mullet, balao, and other small baitfish, rigging is fairly simple, but larger baits such as bonito and dolphinfish need to have their mouths stitched shut to reduce water resistance, and their pectoral and dorsal fins stitched erect to keep them upright. Large baits should be trolled at a much slower speed than small baits and lures.

DEADBAIT RIGS

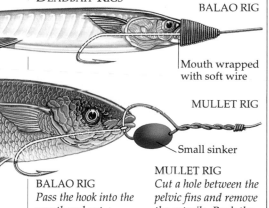

BALAO RIG

Mouth wrapped with soft wire

MULLET RIG

Small sinker

BALAO RIG
Pass the hook into the mouth and out through the body cavity, then close the mouth over it. To close the mouth, bind it with soft wire.

MULLET RIG
Cut a hole between the pelvic fins and remove the entrails. Push the hook shank through the hole into the mouth, and attach it to the line via a wire loop through the lips.

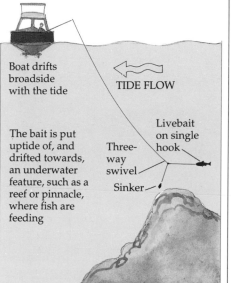

Boat drifts broadside with the tide

TIDE FLOW

The bait is put uptide of, and drifted towards, an underwater feature, such as a reef or pinnacle, where fish are feeding

Livebait on single hook

Three-way swivel

Sinker

Livebait drifting

This technique is used mainly to catch amberjack and other species when they are feeding over small targets such as pinnacles and reefs. The main drawback with the technique is interference from other species, particularly sharks, although when amberjack are present in large numbers they usually monopolize the feeding. Small baitfish, such as grunts, are hooked through the nostrils or lips, sent down with a heavy sinker uptide of the holding area, and drifted along the bottom towards the target.

Livebait trolling

Livebaits must be treated with care if they are to remain alive, and trolled slowly to prevent them from drowning. Use only those fish that have suffered minimal hook damage during catching, and rig them in the least injurious way possible. The best approach for large baits such as bonito and dolphinfish is to use the bridle rig, which involves tying the bait to the hook instead of impaling it on it, and thus minimizes bleeding. Small baits can also be rigged this way, but are are more effective when put onto a wide-gape livebait hook via their nostrils.

FISHING VENUES
Mid-ocean islands, such as the Azores, offer deepwater fishing for species such as marlin within a short sailing time from harbour.

TROLLING AND DRIFTING

SLOW TROLLING

FAST TROLLING

DRIFTING
This is a good way to present natural baits over localized fish-holding areas such as reefs, pinnacles, and wrecks.

DRIFTING

TIDE FLOW

FAST TROLLING
This allows you to fish for the faster-swimming species, such as wahoo and bluefin tuna. Use lures with shallowly angled faces.

SLOW TROLLING
For trolling at about 5 to 8 knots, use long, lightweight, softhead or rubber lures with steeply angled faces.

LIVEBAIT TROLLING
When trolling livebaits, two rods only are fished to prevent crossover tangles. Four deadbaits can be worked over the surface by slow trolling.

THE WATER

THE OBSERVANT ANGLER WHO LEARNS how to "read" the water, whether it be a small pond or a stretch of ocean, will be able to deduce what fish might be present, whereabouts in the water they are likely to be, what they are feeding on, and where and how to present the lure or bait to catch them. Acquiring and using this knowledge does not guarantee a catch, but it makes one much more likely than guesswork or relying on luck will.

If you fish a particular water regularly, spend time studying it at different times of the day and watching the movements and feeding habits of the fish. This will help you to locate and catch fish on that water, and also provide you with knowledge of fish and their habitat that you can put to good use on other waters.

Binoculars and polarized sunglasses are a great help when you are studying the activities of fish. Binoculars enable you to watch for small, distant clues to fish movements, such as slight surface disturbances. They are especially useful at sea, for spotting changes in water colour that might indicate fish-holding areas, for instance, or shoals of baitfish rising to the surface to escape attacking predators.

In this chapter, you will find the signs to look out for on a variety of different waters, including streams, stillwaters, and the open sea.

LOOKING FOR CLUES
Time spent studying the water to find out where the fish are likely to be is never wasted.

STREAMS & RIVERS 1

Streams and rivers can be divided into two basic types: chalk (or limestone) streams, fed by springs and containing high levels of calcium carbonate and other mineral nutrients; and rainfed (or freestone) streams, fed mainly by surface runoff and generally low in minerals. They can be further subdivided into three zones: the rushing upland stream; the moderately paced middle reaches; and the wide, deep, lower reaches.

CHARACTERISTICS OF STREAMS

Streams generally originate up in the hills or mountains, where rainfall is at its highest. Their tumbling upper reaches tend to be rich in oxygen but cold and rock-strewn, offering little in the way of either comfortable habitats or food for fish. As these young waterways begin to flow through less rugged countryside and are joined by tributaries, they grow in size and slow in pace, allowing vegetation to gain a foothold. Aquatic weeds begin to establish themselves, while earthy, rather than rocky, banks play host to trees, bushes, and plants. When the river becomes old, winding slowly across a wide flood plain, the types of aquatic weed and the species of fish present change, with those able to tolerate lower oxygen levels in the water and greater turbidity (muddiness) becoming dominant.

MOUNTAIN STREAMS
The fast-flowing trout streams of mountainous areas are fed by surface runoff and melting snow. The water provides little in the way of food, so the fish they contain tend to be small.

Types of stream
Some streams have as their source a bubbling spring, created by rainwater that has percolated through a porous rock, such as chalk, until it has reached a material that it is less able to permeate, such as clay. Because the water cannot filter through the clay, it emerges as a spring at the base of the chalk. Other streams result from water seeping out of bogland, which is able to retain water and continue releasing it long into dry spells.

Rivers that begin their lives in rain-soaked hills are much more at the mercy of the weather than those that are springfed. Long dry spells can see a rainfed river reduced to the merest trickle, making life very difficult for the fish that inhabit it; in drought years, some rivers dry up completely. At the other extreme, sudden heavy rain can transform them into boiling torrents, sometimes in a matter of hours.

Snowfed rivers tend to be at their best in summer. During the spring months, snow on the mountains melts, creating a rise in the levels of the rivers that drain them. Sometimes, the thaw can be rapid, turning these streams and rivers into torrents. This meltwater is freezing cold, and not much good for fishing in. It is better to wait until towards the end of the snow melt, when air and water temperatures are rising, the flow has eased, and water levels are on the decline. A winter of low snowfall followed by a dry spring and summer will see the flow of snowfed rivers drastically reduced.

Streams and rivers emerging from reservoirs and managed lakes tend to enjoy steadier levels of flow, because it is possible to vary the amount of water passing through or over the exit sluice gates or weir. In times of low rainfall, compensation water can be released to keep up river flows, and because a stillwater acts as the source, the river may well never become too muddy, even after very wet weather.

The zones of a river
The species of fish present in a river vary from one zone to another. In the upper reaches, where the water is flowing at its fastest and clearest, and carrying the greatest amount of dissolved oxygen (caused by its being "broken up" by the mass of stones and boulders which make up the riverbed), trout and grayling will be found. Food is normally in limited supply, being restricted to the larvae of a few species of insect and shrimps (plus whatever terrestrials fall in), so the fish tend to remain small.

Further downstream, where the river becomes deeper and the flow steadier, weedbeds provide cover for fish and attract the animal life on which they feed. This, combined with the less turbulent flow, results in more species being present, including barbel, chub, dace, and roach. Trout and grayling may also be found, if the water is clean.

In the latter part of most rivers' lives, flow is slow, particularly in summer. The riverbed usually consists of soft mud and silt, and weed growth may be profuse. The mud and silt are often in suspension, which results in reduced visibility and an unsuitable environment for the species found further upstream. Instead, bottom-loving fish, more tolerant of water with lower dissolved oxygen levels, are present. These include bream and tench.

CHALKSTREAMS
The gin-clear water of a chalkstream has a high mineral content, enabling it to support abundant vegetation and thriving fish populations.

VEGETATION

Vegetation in and along streams and rivers provides many benefits to both anglers and fish. Trees and other plants growing at the water's edge can help to bind and stabilize the bank, protecting it from erosion, and aquatic weeds can help to filter pollution from the water as well as hold up water levels during times of low rainfall. Weedbeds of all kinds also provide protective cover for fish and a home for the many different species of invertebrate on which they feed, and provide predators, such as pike, with concealment while they lie in wait for their prey. Overhanging trees also give cover, and terrestrials such as beetles and caterpillars often fall from their branches into the water, as do berries (elderberries, for instance, are taken by roach and chub).

WEEDBEDS
Lush beds of weed are home to large populations of aquatic invertebrates, which attract feeding fish. Weeds protruding above the surface are easy to spot, but submerged weedbeds may not be so obvious: look for the slack water they create.

BANKSIDE VEGETATION
Fish like to lie beneath undercut banks and overhanging bankside trees and plants, which offer them shade from the sun, cover from predators such as herons (and anglers), and a source of insects and other foods.

SURFACE INDICATIONS

An ability to read the water can greatly improve an angler's success rate. Surface flow is rarely uniform, and patches of disturbance or areas of slack can provide clues as to what is happening under the water.

Underwater obstructions
Swirls and whorls in an otherwise uniform stretch of fast-flowing river reveal the presence of an underwater obstruction, such as a large boulder or an outcrop of rock. It is likely that an area of slacker water will exist behind it, and possibly on either side as the flow is deflected. Many fish, including trout and salmon, like to lie up and rest in such areas of slack water. In winter, a similar surface disturbance, or even a small patch of slack water, may betray the existence of a bed of true bulrush that has died back but is still big enough to obstruct the flow and create an area of sheltered water immediately behind it.

Fallen, sunken trees, often carried down the river on a flood before coming to rest, also create areas of slack water behind them and are much loved by roach, particularly where a sandbank is built up by the deflected flow.

Water flow
Where bends occur on rivers, the main flow is deflected by the outer bank and a visible "crease" develops between it and

WATER FLOW
By studying the flow patterns of a stream you can learn a lot about its underwater features. For example, rocks and weeds create ripples and patches of slack water, while deep holes, containing slack water that offers fish respite from the current, appear to be slightly darker than the surrounding areas of water.

the slacker inside water. When the stream or river is running at normal level, species such as chub tend to lie right on the crease. They swim slowly or just hold a position in the slacker water, but are always ready to move out into the main flow to inspect items brought down by the main current.

As river levels rise after rain, or temperatures plummet, the fish will move progressively into the slacker water. At such times, slack water and gentle eddies can be full of fish, because they offer a comfortable environment in which to escape the raging current.

Where a river or stream consists of a series of pools and rapids or glides, fish are often to be found right at the necks or tails of the pools. At spawning time, migratory fish frequently rest in these spots while making their way upstream to their spawning grounds.

STREAMS & RIVERS 2

UPLAND STREAMS & RIVERS

The bed of an upland stream usually consists of rocks, boulders, and stones, over and between which races fast, and generally shallow, water. In the highest reaches, trout are the only gamefish likely to be present, and these never grow to any size on their thin diet of insect larvae, freshwater shrimps, and the occasional worm.

These little trout, often still carrying their parr markings, spend their lives hiding in slacks behind stones and boulders, ever ready to dart out into the current to grab a passing morsel. In these small pockets of slack water they also grub about in the bed for the few invertebrates present.

Lower down, where the water is less turbulent, the trout are often joined by grayling and salmon. The salmon will be both immature parrs (this is where they were born) and adults that have returned to spawn in the headwaters from which they originated.

In this lower part of an upland stream, the water gradually deepens and there will be depressions in the bed gouged out by floodwater. It is in these depressions or holes and behind boulders and rocks that the trout and grayling are found. The returning salmon also rest behind rocks during their upstream journey, before seeking patches of smooth gravel on which to spawn.

LOWLAND STREAMS & RIVERS

Lowland streams contrast strongly with their upland counterparts. As the speed of the current slows, deposition of suspended material begins, resulting in a riverbed that changes downstream from rocks and boulders, through beds of gravel and sand, to silt banks. Each attracts its own varieties of fauna and flora and, as a rule, invertebrate life is plentiful. Because of this abundant food supply there are many varieties of fish present, including predators such as pike and perch.

Slacks and eddies

The calmer water behind submerged rocks and boulders provides comfortable living quarters for many fish. These underwater obstacles may not be visible in normal conditions, so a visit to a river during a dry spell, when the water level is low and the rocks are exposed, is well worth while. Draw a map or make a mental note of the positions of the rocks and the adjacent lies, so that you know where to find them when the stream returns to its normal height.

Other areas likely to hold fish include the slack water around and behind bridge supports, the eddies that often form where a river meets a smaller or slower flowing stream, and deep holes. These holes are scoured into the riverbed by the force of the flow during high water conditions. When the flow returns to normal, they often act as natural larders, collecting many invertebrate food items brought down on the current. Bottom-feeding fish such as barbel find such holes highly appealing.

LOWLAND RIVERS
Many lowland rivers are fast flowing, although not as fast as upland streams, and submerged rocks can cause considerable surface turbulence. Stretches that contain submerged rocks are usually best fished from the bank rather than from a boat, especially if you are unfamiliar with them.

BRIDGES
A bridge supported on piers built on the riverbed creates a variety of water conditions. Water channelled between the pier bases speeds up, while areas of slack water form behind the piers, and if the bridge is low it will provide the fish with plenty of shade on sunny days. Barbel and bream are among the species that are attracted to this shaded water.

UPLAND STREAMS
(left)
The lower parts of an upland stream are good places to fish for trout, salmon, and grayling. Too fast, shallow, and rocky for boat fishing, they can be fished from the bank or by wading. Wading is especially effective when the river is wide or one bank is inaccessible because of vegetation.

UPLAND TROUT
(right)
The little trout in the high reaches of upland streams often retain their parr markings throughout their lives.

Confluences and islands

At the confluence of two streams of similar size and pace, a "crease", a small area of slack water between the two, is created. Fish like to lie in this slack, as it requires them to expend little energy yet allows them to move quickly into the stream on either side of them to intercept food drifting down with the current.

When two streams flowing at different speeds or of disparate size join up, the secondary (lesser) stream in both cases tends to be "held up". This results in the final length of the secondary stream running more slowly and even a little deeper. Fish are attracted to this steadier water, particularly during times of high water when the speed of the major stream increases to the point where it becomes uncomfortable for them.

Islands also hold great attraction for fish. This is because they deflect the flow, creating numerous areas of slack water,

and are often thickly covered with trees and undergrowth. Much of this vegetation overhangs the river, producing cover and a canopy from which terrestrial creatures often fall.

Weirpools and millpools

These turbulent spots, with their oxygen-rich water, are a great attraction to many species. Trout (if the river is clean) are found up in the fastest, white water of a pool, while lower down the pool species such as chub, barbel, and grayling will be in evidence. Species such as perch, bream, and roach, which have a preference for calmer water, lie in the steadier flow at the tail of the pool, and in the slacks and eddies created to the sides. Pike are not far away, either, often tucked in close to the bank and using the marginal weed for camouflage.

In some weirpools, the actual weir sill is quite deeply undercut, and a light leger

rig cast into the white water will be caught by the undertow and pulled underneath. Bites tend to be very positive, and sometimes the fish responsible for them can be very surprising. For as well as the expected chub and barbel, fish such as perch and bream will, remarkably, also take up residence below an undercut sill.

Dams

Dams are built across rivers to create reservoirs for drinking water or for driving hydroelectric turbines. A dam can help to maintain the flow of the river that runs out of the reservoir, keeping the levels topped up in times of low rainfall, but the effect on the fish in the river depends on how the water is released. Water released from spillways at the top of the dam is relatively warm, but water released from the base of the dam is often extremely cold. At hydroelectric dams in regions where the summers are hot, cold water released via the turbines often provides an ideal habitat for trout, but elsewhere a sudden introduction of cold water into a river normally fed from the spillways can have a severe dampening effect on sport, which only picks up again after the effects of the artificial flood have passed through.

Where water is constantly being released from the lake via the spillways in times of normal rainfall, it sometimes falls with such force that deep holes are formed below the dam. Fish are attracted to these and will only move out during times of heavy flow, finding refuge downstream and often behind the structures built to prevent bank erosion.

WEIRPOOLS

Weirs are built across rivers to raise the upstream water level or to control the downstream flow. The water tumbling over a weir mixes with air as it falls, and so becomes well oxygenated. In hot weather, when oxygen levels in the rest of the river are low, the dissolved oxygen in a weirpool makes it very attractive to fish.

STILLWATERS 1

The term "stillwaters" covers a broad spectrum of waters. At one end of this spectrum is the tiny, springfed farm pond, either a natural feature or created in a shady corner of a field to provide a source of cool drinking water for livestock on hot summer days. At the other end are enormous natural and man-made expanses of water, some of which (such as the Great Lakes of North America) are much bigger than many of the world's smaller countries.

CHARACTERISTICS OF STILLWATERS

Each type of stillwater presents the angler with a unique set of problems that must be solved if success is to be achieved. Different types also have many features in common, however, and the knowledge and experience gained when fishing one can be used to advantage on others. For example, while lakes may vary enormously in size and topography, all of them will usually have features such as bays, promontories (points), and shallow margins. In addition, the weeds found in the bays and shallows of big lakes and reservoirs are very often the same varieties seen in little ponds and medium-sized lakes, and in many cases the invertebrate life living among the weeds, and the species of fish in close proximity to them, are also the same. Your chances of angling success on any stillwater will be greatly increased if you learn what goes on beneath the surface.

Types of stillwater
The vast majority of stillwaters are natural features, fed by springs, streams, or rivers, and usually with one or more rivers draining them. A great many ponds and lakes are artificial, however, having been formed by the damming of a stream or river or by excavation. Most of those formed by damming are shallow where the watercourse enters and are at their deepest at the dam end.

Many of the small artificial stillwaters were created to form ornamental lakes, but most large waters were dammed to provide reservoirs of drinking or irrigation water, or for hydroelectric schemes. These waters vary greatly in size, from relatively small reservoirs that you could walk around in a couple of hours or less, to massive and deep expanses of water with shorelines measured in thousands of kilometres.

Another important group of stillwaters are those created by the flooding of worked-out pits and quarries, such as the gravel and clay pits resulting from the extraction of materials for use in the construction industry. The bottoms of flooded clay and gravel pits are often highly irregular, and the water can be very deep with few shallow areas. The water is also usually very clear, and weed growth is often profuse in less deep areas. The invertebrate life can be prolific, but often there are very few suitable spawning sites for fish. This situation leads to a food-rich environment containing a low population of fish, and because these fish have little competition, their growth rates are usually rapid.

GRAVEL PITS (*above*)
A flooded gravel pit can acquire a fish population naturally by the introduction of fish eggs by birds, but many pits are artificially stocked.

PONDS (*left*)
Small ponds often hold surprisingly large fish, especially when managed as fisheries, but overstocking can result in stunted fish.

FISHING LARGE WATERS
The shores and shallow margins of large waters are in most respects similar to the edges of small waters, and are fished in much the same way. But if you are going to fish offshore on a really large water, it pays to obtain a chart of it so that you can locate likely fish-holding areas such as bars, underwater plateaux, shallows, and deepwater dropoffs. A sonar will help you to search the bottom and, together with a water temperature probe, to detect the colder layers that may hold species such as arctic char and lake trout.

Water colour

As stillwaters begin to warm up each spring, minute plant organisms known as phytoplankton begin to multiply. The extent to which their population expands depends on a number of factors, including the depth and temperature of the water, the amount of weed growth, and the quantity of nitrates and phosphates present in solution (washed in from farmland treated with fertilizer). In hot summers, shallow, fertilizer-polluted stillwaters turn green as the phytoplankton population explodes.

Phytoplankton are eaten by zooplankton, which is the animal constituent of plankton and includes fish larvae and simple animal organisms such as daphnia (water fleas). Great clouds of orange-red daphnia can often be seen in the warmer shallows of clear stillwaters, rising and falling through the water layers and drifting with the wind.

If zooplankton occur in sufficient numbers, they help to keep a water clear of phytoplankton, and this encourages the growth of weeds, which need clear water and sunlight to thrive. As well as helping stillwaters to remain clear, zooplankton are an important food item for many species of freshwater fish, and they are particularly loved by reservoir rainbow trout.

Shallow waters usually warm up more quickly than deeper ones, encouraging the rapid growth of weeds and phytoplankton. Exceptions to this include springfed pools, with their constant supply of cold water, and small pools surrounded by thick tree growth, which reduces the amount of sunlight that can reach the water.

WATER COLOUR
Many small stillwaters are turned green in summer by the presence of huge numbers of phytoplankton. A large population of zooplankton, which eat phytoplankton, plus a good growth of aquatic weeds, which consume nutrients that would otherwise be taken up by phytoplankton, can help to keep the water clear.

UNDERWATER FEATURES

When fishing stillwaters, try to locate underwater features that attract fish. Inflowing streams, for example, prove attractive to fish because their water often contains food, and may be cooler and contain more oxygen than the stillwater, particularly during long spells of warm weather.

Fish also gather around rocks and fallen or submerged trees, and feed on the algae, snails, and other invertebrates that take up residence on them. Shoals of baitfish feel secure alongside or even among submerged branches, and predators lie in wait for them, close by and well camouflaged in the same branches. Another place to look for predatory fish is near the dropoff line between the marginal shallows and deep water, where they lie in wait for baitfish shoals patrolling the dropoff in search of food.

SUBMERGED TREES
Trees that have fallen into the water, for instance when a riverbank is eroded and collapses, become gathering places for fish that find cover and food among the trunks and branches. Submerged trees are often also found in flooded pits and in lakes formed by damming, and may be in deep water a long way from the shore.

STILLWATERS 2
VEGETATION

Vegetation in stillwaters is usually restricted to the margins and shallows, and takes the form of weeds, rushes, beds of sedge, and water lilies. Weeds, rushes, and sedge provide many benefits, from helping to keep the water clear (by taking in nutrients to the detriment of phytoplankton), to giving sanctuary to various species of fish and the creatures on which they feed. Floating plants can also help to keep water clear of excessive phytoplankton. On ponds and small lakes where the surface is almost covered by such plants, the amount of sunlight entering the water is greatly reduced. Phytoplankton, being plants, cannot survive without any sunlight, so the water stays clear.

Reedbeds

Beds of reed line the margins of many stillwaters, and are as common on recently created waters as on well-established lakes. Their stems play host to a wide variety of animal life, including many invertebrates such as snails and the larvae of damselflies and dragonflies. Normally too dense for fish to swim in and out of, they are nonetheless attractive to some species. Pike and perch, for example, lurk alongside reed stems waiting for passing prey, beautifully camouflaged by their markings.

REEDBEDS *(above)*
Reeds are tall grasses that can reach a height of about 3 m (10 ft). When there is no wind, any movement of reed stems may be caused by fish.

WATER LILIES
(right)
Most species of water lily normally grow in depths of no more than about 1.8 m (6 ft). The presence of these plants in an area of water thus gives a rough indication of its maximum depth.

Water lilies

Fish love to lie under the broad leaves of water lilies on hot days, and can often be heard making distinctive kissing sounds as they suck small animals from the undersides of the pads.

Although the pads themselves are often tightly packed on the surface, sometimes even riding up over one another, the stems below the water never seem to form an impenetrable barrier. Predatory fish lie in ambush among them, and slim fish such as rudd and roach can swim between lily stems with ease.

Bigger, more rounded species such as carp can make their way through, but they tend to set the stems and pads rocking as they go – a phenomenon well worth looking out for when wandering the banks of a stillwater in search of fish.

Bankside plants

Trees, bushes, and other plants overhanging the banks of stillwaters provide cover for fish and are also a source of food, because terrestrial creatures such as spiders, beetles, and caterpillars frequently fall from their branches and leaves into the water. Fish also find a plentiful supply of food where the roots of marginal plants extend into the water, creating a habitat for insect larvae and snails.

OVERHANGING PLANTS
The water beneath overhanging vegetation is a good place to fish for the many species, including trout, that feed on terrestrials. Trees and bushes offer concealment for you as well as cover for the fish, but can make casting difficult, so fishing from a boat is often a better option than bank fishing.

FISHING A SMALL POND (*above*)
On this small pond, good places to seek out fish include the lily beds (where a fish snatching a food item from beneath a pad has created ripples) and the water below the overhanging trees that line the banks.

Brush piles

Fishery managers responsible for lakes and reservoirs with virtually featureless beds often create artificial fish-holding areas. One common way of doing this is by anchoring large piles of tree branches or cut trees to the bottom.

These brush piles, whose positions are usually marked by buoys or indicated by signs on the shore, offer fish the same sort of cover and feeding opportunities that they get from submerged or sunken trees (*see page 267*).

SURFACE INDICATIONS

In the flowing water of streams and rivers, underwater obstructions and other features create surface disturbances that can indicate areas likely to hold fish (*see pages 262–65*). Surface indications of this type seldom occur on stillwaters, but the fish often betray their presence by creating their own surface disturbances.

Bubbles and ripples

Bottom-feeding fish such as tench and carp send up clouds of silt while searching the bed for food. And, as their noses disturb the silt, pockets of gas that are released from it bubble up to the surface. Patches of bubbles indicate one or more fish foraging in one particular area, and lines of bubbles reveal the presence of fish working along the bottom. Trout and other fish that feed at the surface create ripples that reveal their

position, and big fish foraging in shallow water for food often set up bow-waves that can ripple the surface.

Wind lanes and scumlanes

On big waters in windy weather, lines of calm water may appear on the otherwise wind-ruffled surface. These "wind lanes" are often caused by obstructions on the bank, such as trees, that deflect the wind, creating a long, narrow slick of calm water. In strong winds, foam spray caused by breaking waves collects in the smooth water, creating "scumlanes".

During the summer months, hatching insects are blown into wind lanes and become trapped, unable to escape because of the greater surface tension of the unbroken strip of smooth water. Many species of fish, but particularly trout, will take advantage of this harvest and can be seen working their way upwind along the lanes.

SCUMLANES
In addition to the scumlanes formed by foam blown into wind lanes, there are those made up of pollen, leaves, twigs, and other pieces of debris that collect against a shore when the wind blows from the same direction for several days. These scumlanes attract fish because they often include items of food such as insects and daphnia.

269

SHORELINES

Unlike offshore waters, which can usually be read only by studying charts and by echo sounding, it is normally possible to make a direct survey of all the fishable stretches of a shore. Select the lowest spring tide available in daylight and walk the shoreline, making notes about landmarks and other features of the lower, middle, and upper shore, and perhaps using a camera or camcorder to record the scene for later reference.

TYPES OF SHORELINE

Shores vary in many ways, the most obvious being in the type of substrate (seabed material), which may be sand, shingle, rocks, or a mixture of these. Different species of fish often prefer different substrates, but the amount of shelter, the gradient of the shore, the presence of freshwater inflows, and food availability also play a part in determining the numbers and species of fish found along a shore. For the angler, the important thing is to understand what motivates fish movements.

Shingle beaches
Shingle beaches tend to give the impression of being devoid of life, but this is far from true. The shingle, which may be stacked high by wave action, is often just the visible part of a complex, multi-substrate mix, sometimes including clays and old peat beds, at or beyond the low water mark. Cod, bass, rays, conger, and even flatfish are regularly caught from shingle beaches.

Watch for signs of submerged banks causing variations in the wave pattern beyond the low-water mark. At low water, aim to drop baits on their seaward sides; as they deepen on the flood, drop the baits into the gullies in front. It is also worth putting baits close to boulders, groynes, and anything else that breaks the normal pattern of the shingle.

Sandy shores
The size of the sand particles on a sandy shore influences the types of fish-food organisms, and thus the species of fish, that will be present. Fine particles with high amounts of organic matter are good for lugworms, cockles, and shrimps, and therefore for the fish that feed on them. They also become stirred up and colour the water with the least bit of wave action, and the low light levels in the coloured water tempt species such as cod, which normally feed along the shore only at night, to feed during daylight.

Coarser sands, which settle out very quickly, are often associated with surf beaches, where bass, flounders, and small turbot are taken when a surf is running. A gentle gradient assists the wind in bringing good surf conditions, because friction between the seabed and the water slows the bottom of a wave, causing the top to overtake it and turn. This happens more readily in shallow water than in deep, and a line of breaking waves can be a sign of banks and gullies beyond the low-water line.

Any undulation on an otherwise featureless beach will be of interest to fish. They travel along channels, and are attracted to banks, which enhance wave movements, evicting concealed food items from the bed. Fish also gather at scour holes at the ends of breakwaters, picking up food items that have been washed into them.

SHINGLE BEACHES
On a shingle beach, the most productive water is usually out beyond the low-water mark, where the pebbles give way to grit and fine sand.

Cliffs
The main attractions of cliff-lined shores are almost-permanent water, very often with good depth, and the presence of a wide range of features including kelp jungles for wrasse, broken rock for conger, pinnacles for pollack, and clean ground for rays, tope, and flatfish.

However, cliffs must be fished with care. Every year, anglers are plucked from low ledges by large swells, and spray and rain make rocks dangerously slippery. Good climbing boots, a safety rope, a minimum of tackle, and reliable company are essential, as is a safe retreat route for when the tide floods in.

SANDY SHORES
In temperate waters, sandy shores attract species such as bass and flatfish. These are also found over sand in warmer waters, along with rays (such as this eagle ray), bonefish, and many species of shark, some of them large and dangerous.

SURF BEACHES (*left*)
The typical surf beach is a broad expanse of sand, facing the open ocean, where waves whipped up by the wind come crashing ashore. Fishing a gently shelving surf beach requires fairly long casting, but a steep beach should be fished with short- to medium-distance casts. When wading a surf beach, beware of the undertow, which can pull your feet from under you.

ROCKY BEACHES (*below*)
Some of the most productive shores are those with rocky, bouldery ground. Deepwater rock ledges with rough and clean ground within casting range also fish well.

PIER FISHING (*above*)
Long casting is usually unnecessary when fishing from piers, because many species, including bass, pollack, mullet, and conger, feed close to the underwater structure.

WEEDBEDS (*above*)
Despite the frustrations of snagged tackle, fishing weedbeds can be very productive because many species of fish are attracted to them by the cover and food they find there. Here, an angler is landing a large mullet that was hooked in a dense mat of weed.

Rocks, gullies, and kelp beds

Variations in shoreline geography, unless pronounced, are less important on rocky shores than on sand. This is because the numerous nooks and crannies offer fish a wide range of sheltered spots and feeding areas. As on sandy shores, however, the larger features such as gullies and holes still provide shelter from the tide, areas into which food might settle, and ambush points for picking off victims passing overhead. Shell-crunching wrasse and night-stalking conger take maximum advantage of the available cover, while pollack, bass, and cod often move in to hunt over patchy, broken ground.

Beds of kelp, a common type of seaweed, tend to show only along the extreme lower shore at the lowest tides. Some anglers curse them because tackle snags in them, but they provide good cover for baitfish, and large kelp "jungles" hold lots of big fish.

Piers, jetties, and sea walls

Man-made structures frequently offer deep water at their bases and the chance for anglers to hit different or even deeper water by casting from them. Casting can, however, place the bait beyond fish that have been attracted to a structure because of the food that is available there. An open-framed pier standing on sand offers fish and their food a degree of shelter in an otherwise featureless world. Food collects in the scour holes, crabs thrive around the supports, and food is dumped in from facilities on the pier.

Most stone piers and harbour arms are built on deposited rock, which attracts a wide range of food types and fish. The bases of walls built on natural rock butting onto sand are usually rich in crabs, prawns, and small fish using the weed fringes for cover. Mullet browse microscopic organisms on the stonework, and predators such as bass may move in on the tide to feed after dusk.

ESTUARIES

Estuaries are dynamic environments, changing uniformly as the predictable freshwater inflow makes its effect felt, and changing unpredictably when heavy rains, often a long way inland, result in larger than normal amounts of freshwater flowing down the river. Even fish able to tolerate some degree of freshwater need time to acclimatize during sudden spates, which force them to move downstream or out into the sea to a point where they can find the salinity (saltiness) that they are accustomed to.

ESTUARINE FLOUNDER
In temperate waters, most estuaries are home to large numbers of flounder.

TYPES OF ESTUARY

In a typical estuary, the river creates a plume of freshwater that extends into the saltwater of the sea. An area of brackish water is created where the two meet and mix. The size of this brackish zone at any one time depends on the size of the estuary, the tide, and the amount of freshwater that is entering from the river.

Estuaries vary greatly in size and topography. Some rivers enter the sea through narrow, rocky channels, others carve their way through wide expanses of mudflats or marshland, and others create huge deltas. They also differ in the quality of the freshwater flowing downstream into the sea, but despite all their differences the same basic rules governing species diversity and distribution apply.

Estuarine species
The main factor limiting the species of inshore marine fish that enter a particular part of an estuary is salinity. Fish that can tolerate low salinity, such as mullet, move readily into the brackish water of an estuary, or even into the freshwater zone, in search of food. Other species, such as cod, cannot cope with low salinity and are found only in those parts of an estuary where the level of salinity is relatively high.

Migratory fish, such as salmon and sea trout, travel down estuaries to mature at sea, and return as adults to run upstream to spawn. As they run through estuaries, they adjust their body chemistry to cope with the changes in salinity.

Upper reaches
The species in the upper reaches of an estuary are invariably limited, often to immature flounder, an occasional bass, and mullet where the flow is slack. Channel geography and food availability are the main factors determining where fish are likely to be found. Look for them where bends in channels create slow spots, obstacles create still eddies, and shallow bays onto which a rising tide spills offer quiet areas. Dips and holes within these quiet areas have the added attraction of being gathering points for food carried along by the flow.

Lower reaches
The lower reaches of an estuary often contain the same sort of fish-holding areas as the upper reaches. In addition, larger estuaries may have extensive banks of deposited silt that attract fish because they are rich in food items such as worms, molluscs, and crabs. In small estuaries with fast-flowing, channelled outlets, bars of deposited silt often form where the easing of the flow allows suspended material to fall. Such bars have all the attractive qualities of large banks, but on a very localized scale, making fish very much easier to locate. Wind throws up a tell-tale surf over a bar, and this rough water also churns food out of hiding. This is carried to the downtide edge of the bar, where fish gather to feed.

Creeks, lagoons, and stream outfalls

Large estuaries can form a number of special geographical features at or near their mouths, of which creeks are perhaps the most common. Mullet and flounder enter these muddy openings on the tide, and sole will push into them if they are adjacent to the open shore.

Lagoons formed by deposited silt trapping large expanses of water can quickly become food-rich because water movement is greatly reduced, allowing the contained area to warm more than adjacent areas. Access for fish may well be restricted, but once they are inside, the attractions of the relatively warm water and abundant food supply ensure continued patronage and, very often, good rates of growth. Mullet and flounder are typical of the species found in lagoons.

Stream outfalls, whether dissecting beaches or discharging over rocks, are themselves usually too small to contain fish. Their importance comes from the very localized changes in salinity that they create, which fish such as bass and flounder are seemingly unable to resist. For anglers, the water around any discharge of freshwater into the sea, however small, is worth investigating.

Mangrove creeks

Coastal creeks lined with mangrove trees are common in the subtropics and tropics in areas of organic enrichment, particularly where shallow banks and flats have been formed by the deposition of organic debris from rivers.

The trees grow on these banks and flats, supported by cagelike root structures that hold their trunks above the water. When submerged at high tide, these root structures offer an ideal sanctuary for small fish and are important nursery areas for a number of estuarine and coastal species.

Wherever small fish gather, they attract larger predators, and barracuda, tarpon, crevalle jack, guitarfish, and stringray are typical of the many predatory species found in mangrove creeks. Look for them in the deep holes scoured out on bends, in the areas of slack water downtide of sharp bends, and lying in ambush among the roots of the mangroves.

MANGROVE CREEKS (above)
Tarpon love to explore mangrove creeks and, like this one, are not deterred by shallow water. Channels and creeks in mangrove swamps contain many good places for fish to lie up in. For example, a twisting creek scours deep holes on its bends into which food will settle, and which provide fish with respite from the strong flow. The downtide corner of a sharp bend also provides shelter from the flow, and is a convenient point for a big fish to lie in wait for a passing meal.

ESTUARY MUD (left)
Most broad estuaries have large expanses of mud. This mud can support very large populations of the marine creatures, such as molluscs and worms, that many fish species feed on.

OFFSHORE TEMPERATE WATERS

To the uninitiated, the sea appears to be a vast and featureless expanse of water, offering no clues as to where within it the fish might be. But, beneath the surface, it contains many features that attract a rich diversity of life, including fish that gather at them for cover and to feed. The location of many features, such as wrecks and outcrops of rock, can be read directly from charts and checked from a boat by echo sounding. At times, fish can also be found by reading surface indications, usually in shallow water or close to the shore. These indications include swirls and eddies created by rocks, and the activities of seabirds.

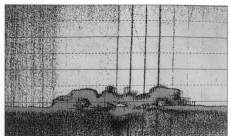

TAKING SOUNDINGS
An echo sounder provides you with a profile of the seabed beneath your boat, enabling you to locate features that might hold fish. This monochrome echo sounder trace shows the outline of a large wreck lying in deep water.

TYPES OF WATER

The nature of any stretch of sea plays an important part in determining the numbers and species of fish that are present. For example, a featureless seabed of sand results in low fish diversity and angling productivity, while rocks and wrecks are good places to fish because they attract large numbers of many different species. Deep water has better temperature stability than shallow water, so its fish population remains more stable throughout the year. If it is too deep or too turbid (coloured by silt), however, there may be insufficient light penetration for weed growth, which provides fish with cover. Inflowing freshwater reduces salinity *(see page 272)*, and pollution by sewage attracts species that feed on it, such as mackerel, but deters those that need the high levels of dissolved oxygen found in unpolluted water.

Banks and gullies
On otherwise featureless ground, such as sand or mud, banks and gullies are the best places to look for fish. Banks are usually found near islands and headlands, where fierce tidal currents carry sand and silt in suspension. Where the tidal flow eases, material settles out into huge, ever-changing mounds, crisscrossed by gullies and sand waves. Baitfish, especially sandeels, swarm over such areas, attracting bass, turbot, brill, and other predators.

Gullies cut into banks by tidal action provide predatory flatfish with excellent ambush points, and bass hunt sandeels taking refuge there from the tidal flow. Away from banks, gullies accumulate creatures such as crabs, worms, and small fish, which are carried across the shallows by the tide until they drop into the deeper water of the gullies. This abundant food supply attracts many species including flatfish, bass, cod, ray, and shark.

BOAT FISHING
(above)
Fishing from an anchored or drifting boat over a good fish-holding area, such as a gully, wreck, or reef, is usually very productive.

SANDBANKS *(left)*
The presence of a sandbank, a good place to fish, is often indicated by surface "boils" where the tidal flow is forced up over the bank.

Dropoffs

Large dropoffs, where the depth of the water increases sharply, are invariably areas of intermediate ground linking either fairly featureless areas or more productive ground. Unless they have attractive features of their own, such as fish-holding weedbeds, most of those that link featureless areas hold few fish and thus have little value to the angler. Dropoff edges linking productive areas, however, attract many species of fish.

Predatory flatfish gather along downtide slopes, breaking from cover to intercept sandeels passing overhead, and rays gather there to shelter from the current. Tope and other sharks hunt dropoffs between reefs and banks, picking off fish carried away from the edges by the tide, and reef conger may take refuge in convenient lairs.

Dropoffs should be fished from a drifting boat, starting well uptide of the area where fish are expected to be and going well beyond it.

Islands

The value of islands as concentrators of fish depends on a combination of layout and size. Groups of islands are more useful than single islands because they have a far greater effect on the surrounding waters. By deflecting, channelling, increasing, or suppressing the tidal flow, they create a broad range of habitats likely to draw in good numbers of many different fish species.

Areas of disturbed tidal flow aid the formation of banks and sand waves. Fast water attracts sandeels and mackerel, which in turn draw in tope, bass, pollack, and even porbeagle. Wrasse and conger feed in the quieter corners of bays and coves, and slack areas along the edges of strong flows allow sedentary species such as skates and rays to choose the degree of flow that suits them best.

ISLANDS
Islands tend to attract large numbers of fish because their interaction with the tidal flow creates a variety of different habitats. For example, where two islands are close together, the water rushing between them can scour out a deep hole in the seabed. Big skate often take up residence in such holes, feeding on the large numbers of food items that get swept into them by the tide. Skate will also congregate in the deep water on the downtide sides of islands.

Pinnacles and ledges

Submerged rock pinnacles are often found on deepwater reefs, and their peaks, reaching up towards the surface, may attract species that normally favour shallower water. The pinnacle base will be much the same as any other reef, attracting a wide variety of organisms, small fish, and their predators.

The peaks of submerged pinnacles can present a hazard to boats, and ledges are usually more hospitable places to fish, particularly on the drift. A lack of features can bring a certain uniformity of fish food items, and of the fish themselves, but small reef species are common, and larger predators will be nearby.

Wrecks and reefs

Wrecks are, in effect, man-made reefs, and they attract and hold the same kinds of fish as natural reefs. What these fish are depends on the depth. Shallow wrecks and reefs could have a good number of bass, plus wrasse, conger, and small pollack, which give way to cod, coalfish, ling, better pollack, and bigger conger as the depth increases.

On a wreck or a reef, the fish usually concentrate where cover and food availability are greatest, but some lie just off or along one side. It can take several drifts or some very skilful anchoring to present the bait where feeding fish are holed up.

SURFACE INDICATIONS

Away from the shore, areas likely to hold fish can be located by looking for surface indications, some man-made, others natural. Cardinal buoys and isolated danger marks indicate hazards to shipping, and many of these hazards, such as rocks, attract fish. Port and starboard navigation buoys mark channel edges, and sometimes areas of deep-lying, rocky ground – good places to fish – are dotted with crab pot markers.

Man-made markers are generally more reliable than natural surface indications. For instance, the edge of a steep bank is often betrayed by lines of white water, but these will not lie above the lip. The deeper the water, the further

CRAB POT MARKERS
Ground that supports a large population of crabs also attracts good numbers of fish. Crab pot markers are a reliable indication of such ground.

downtide they appear, and in rough weather they may merge with existing waves. Swirls, erupting boils, overfalls, and eddies all denote seabed obstructions, such as reefs and wrecks, that are deflecting water upwards in the tidal flow. These signs may also appear at varying distances downtide of the obstructions that cause them.

Diving gannets are good indicators of mackerel near the surface; more general seabird activity may indicate that predators are driving small fish to the surface. The predators will usually be mackerel but could be something more highly prized, such as bass.

275

OFFSHORE TROPICAL WATERS

Tropical coastal waters support large numbers of many different species of fish, occupying every available niche from the seabed to the surface, and the upper layers of the water remain rich in fish well beyond the continental shelf. This makes tropical waters much more productive for anglers than their temperate counterparts. In addition to wreck, reef, and bank fishing *(see page 274)*, tropical waters offer bottom and midwater fishing from small boats and the shore, fly fishing, inshore trolling, poling the flats, and big-game fishing in the deep, blue water beyond the edge of the shelf.

TYPES OF WATER

The upper layers of tropical waters contain more fish than those of cooler seas, and some tropical species are unrestricted in their ability to roam the open ocean in search of food. Most species, however, must stay close to the areas that provide them with suitable food; upwellings, coastal shallows, and the sunlit reaches close to the surface are just such places. Over fishable seabed, much the same rules apply as in temperate waters, with wrecks, pinnacles, banks, gullies, and other features having concentrations of food and fish. In addition, large inshore gamefish like to patrol specific contours along the upper continental slope or the outer edges of fringing reefs.

Gullies, dropoffs, and banks
Tropical gullies, like those elsewhere, act as out-of-the-tide resting places and areas into which food carried on the tide can settle. Large predators, such as tarpon, love to hunt in shallow gullies, and the downtide edges of gullies, banks, and dropoffs make excellent ambush points for the slower bottom-living species.

Baitfish feeding over banks always draw predators, and the depth of the water determines just which predators these might be. There are almost invariably stingray and shark, and possibly amberjack, dolphinfish, crevalle jack, and striped marlin. Large sand-loving species, including jack, bass, and roosterfish, move into very shallow water, venturing almost onto the beaches.

Coral flats
Bonefish, small shark, barracuda, and stingray are the principal coral flat species. Stingray happily lie in wait for food, but the more free-swimming species both browse and hunt and so are easily spooked by an approaching boat. For this reason, angers use light, shallow-drafted skiffs that are poled within casting distance of the fish.

FEEDING TARPON *(above)*
Tarpon often gather to feed at the surface, where they can be caught by casting to them from a drifting or anchored boat.

REEF FISHING *(left)*
Boats have gathered to fish just outside the reef to the right of this small island.

CORAL FLATS *(below)*
Coral flats, extensive areas of coral sand in very shallow water, are prime areas for bonefish and stingray.

Coral reefs

Small to medium-sized fish such as porgies, snappers, and groupers congregate in large numbers over the offshore coral reefs. Their distribution over a reef depends to some degree on its depth, and the biggest groupers are often found on the deepest parts.

Sunken coral heads are important features of the shallow parts of reefs. These huge, mushroom-shaped growths of coral are home to a wide variety of small marine creatures and the fish that feed on them. These fish in turn attract predators, including small sharks.

Gullies sculpted into reefs or between sections of reef present slow-moving predators with good ambush points, while faster-swimming species hunt along the gullies and around the reef slopes. Barracuda patrol the upper edges of the dropoffs, while hammerhead and possibly larger reef shark species are the main predators further down. Where gullies are particularly deep, otherwise offshore species will move into them, even where they are close inshore.

Huge pinnacles lunging skywards from deep water are where the very largest groupers and other reef creatures are to be found. Like the deeper gullies, areas of pinnacle rock and pinnacle coral (where the water is shallow enough for coral to grow) provide some of the best hunting and ambush points on the reef. Efficient predators grow fat on the easy pickings, and this is where the best fishing is likely to be found.

Deep water and dropoffs

The blue water of the deep sea is about as featureless as the ocean gets, but variations in the uniformity of the sea are created by upwellings of cold, nutrient-rich water. This water contains multitudes of tiny organisms, which attract baitfish shoals; small predators congregate to hunt the baitfish, and are themselves taken by large gamefish. Upwellings are thus good places to fish, and their locations are often revealed by flocks of seabirds that gather to feed on the baitfish.

Fishing dropoffs, which are easily located by means of charts and an echo sounder, is a different matter. Baitfish concentrate more predictably, for example in midwater at the outer edges of deep reefs or deep rock pinnacles. The upper edges of drops are patrolled by sharks, particularly hammerhead, and barracuda hunt along the shallowest edges of a reef. Close to the surface and along shallow edges, the higher water temperatures suit fast-swimming game species such as wahoo and sailfish.

All these fish respond to lures and slowly trolled livebaits. Where the water is at its deepest, a spread of lures and additional teasers will tempt fish such as marlin and sailfish up from depth. Other fish may not strike at surface lures and will require baits set perhaps 10 to 12 m (about 30 to 40 ft) down on downriggers.

Floating weed rafts

Floating weed rafts are a regular phenomenon in areas touched by major oceanic currents. The North Atlantic Drift, for example, brings attendant circulating clumps of algae known as sargassum. These can combine to form quite large rafts, which make a very important contribution to the biology of an area. They are also extremely valuable from an angling point of view, acting as a surface signpost on an otherwise featureless sea.

Dolphinfish and some smaller species have a habit of taking refuge beneath floating objects. These need not be weed rafts – they could be boxes, oildrums, tree roots, or other flotsam – but sargassum is the most abundant. Alongside any sizable floating object is a good place to stop a boat and start chumming with handfuls of cut fish. Very soon, the dolphinfish shoals will gather off the stern where some truly exciting light-tackle sport is virtually assured.

Dolphinfish may well be gamefish in their own right, but they are also a source of food for larger predators such as marlin. Trolling Kona Heads along the outer edges of long sargassum rafts, as opposed to more aimless quartering of areas likely to be patrolled by marlin, can thus be very productive.

TROLLING (*above*)
The best way to fish for fast-swimming big game species, such as marlin, wahoo, tuna, and sailfish, is by trolling with lures or natural baits.

TEASERS (*left*)
Trolling a string of brightly coloured teasers in addition to lures or baits will tempt marlin, tuna, and sailfish up from the depths.

CONSERVATION

The origins of all vertebrates, including ourselves, can be traced back to the primitive fish that evolved in the waters and swamps of the late Cambrian period, which ended over 500 million years ago. Some of the descendants of these early fish left the water to colonize the land, while others remained aquatic and evolved into the 22,000 or more species of fish alive today. These fish, like most living creatures, live in harmony with their environment, their numbers rising or falling according to the availability of food.

Some, however, are theatened with extinction. This may be a slow, natural process, caused for instance by changes in weather patterns to which a species cannot adapt, but many immediate and avoidable threats are posed by human activities.

POLLUTION

One of the most visible and widespread threats to fish, particularly freshwater species, is pollution of the water in which they live. This pollution takes many forms, including the discharge of inadequately treated sewage into rivers, lakes, and seas; the poisoning of waters by industrial waste products, agricultural chemicals, and oil spills; acidification of lakes and streams by acid rain; and contamination of the groundwaters that feed springs. Anglers, by the very nature of their sport, are often the first to become aware of changes in water quality caused by pollution. If you suspect that a stretch of water is becoming polluted, report it immediately to the relevant authorities and to local conservation groups.

Another threat to fish comes not from the quality of the water but from its quantity. Increasing demands for water, brought about by population growth, industrialization, and irrigation, have seriously depleted many rivers and lakes.

Eutrophication
The process of eutrophication is something of a paradox, in that it is the enrichment of water by the inflow of nutrients, which might appear beneficial but is actually a serious problem. The nutrients involved are nitrates and phosphates. Nitrates enter rivers, lakes, and the sea when rain washes nitrate-based fertilizers from farmland soil; phosphates also come from fertilizers, but their main sources are industrial and domestic effluents (phosphates are widely used in detergents).

When these nutrients enter water in excessive amounts, they promote the rapid growth of algae. These algae cover the surface of the water, preventing sunlight from reaching submerged plants. This sets up a chain reaction in which the submerged plants die, the bacteria that decompose the remains use up oxygen dissolved in the water, and this reduction in available oxygen causes the death of more plants and subsequently of the animal life inhabiting the water, including the fish.

WEED CUTTING
Good fishery management often involves some degree of intervention, such as cutting away excess weed growth, in order to keep the water in prime condition.

Acidification
Over the past few decades, thousands of lakes and many rivers in the Northern Hemisphere have become devoid of fish because of the effects of acid rain. Scandinavia and Canada are two of the worst-affected areas. This rain is created when sulphur dioxide, nitrogen dioxide, and nitrogen oxide – released into the air when fossil fuels are burned – react with moisture in the air to form sulphuric and nitric acids.

Acid rain makes the water in rivers and lakes acidic, and also frees large amounts of aluminium from the soil. The acidity of the water kills fish eggs and fry, and the aluminium affects the gills of fish, making them clog up with mucus. The combination of acidity and aluminium also kills off most plant life and the small creatures that fish feed on.

AGROCHEMICALS
Many of the chemicals used in modern intensive farming can prove very harmful if washed into streams, lakes, or the sea. These chemicals include fertilizers, which promote excessive algae growth, and herbicides and pesticides that can damage aquatic plant, insect, and animal life.

Fish Stocks

One of the most serious threats to many species of fish is that of overfishing. This is a particular problem for marine species that are fished for commercially, because of the huge numbers that are caught and the difficulty of enforcing size limits and catch quotas.

Freshwater fish are generally easier to protect from serious overfishing. For example, in most developed countries, freshwater fishing is largely for sport and is successfully regulated by licenses, permits, closed seasons, minimum size limits, and, in some cases, catch limits. In addition, most freshwater fish are relatively easy to breed for stocking depleted waters and for maintaining population levels.

Sea anglers can contribute to the maintenance of fish stocks by imposing personal minimum size limits and releasing, unharmed, any fish they do not intend to eat.

Catch-and-release fishing
Releasing fish after capture is an excellent way to help maintain fish stocks, and on some fisheries it is mandatory. However, fish must always be handled carefully if they are not to die from injury caused by rough treatment.

Use barbless hooks, or flatten barbs with pliers to make hooks easier to remove. If possible, leave the fish in the water and hold it gently while you unhook it, so that you cause as little damage as possible to its scales and its protective coating of slime. If the fish has swallowed the hook, carefully cut the leader as close to the hook as possible and leave the hook in place rather than try to remove it; the fish's digestive juices will soon break it down.

After unhooking, support the fish in the water with both hands and turn it to face into the current, if there is one. If it is exhausted, continue supporting it until it has recovered its strength and is ready to swim away.

SHARK CONSERVATION
Releasing sharks after capture, as this angler is doing, will help to ensure their survival. Many shark species have declined alarmingly in numbers, partly because of angling but also because so many are being taken for their fins. Shark finning is a particularly nasty form of commercial fishing: the sharks' fins are cut off, and the still-alive but fatally maimed fish are dumped back into the sea to die.

Several hundred species of fish have been classified by international and national agencies as actually or potentially in danger of extinction. Those listed here are some of the threatened, endangered, or vulnerable species that anglers might encounter. They should not be fished for in the areas named (in most cases it is illegal to do so), and if one is caught by accident it should be carefully unhooked and released.

Acipenseridae

Shortnose sturgeon (*Acipenser brevirostrum*)	USA, Canada
Lake sturgeon (*Acipenser fulvescens*)	USA, Canada
Adriatic sturgeon (*Acipenser naccarii*)	Italy
Atlantic sturgeon (*Acipenser oxyrhynchus*)	USA, Canada
Common sturgeon (*Acipenser sturio*)	Europe
Pallid sturgeon (*Scaphirhynchus albus*)	USA

Clupeidae

Allis shad (*Alosa alosa*)	Europe

Lamnidae

Great white shark (*Carcharodon carcharias*)	South Africa

Percichthyidae

Eastern freshwater cod (*Maccullochella ikei*)	Australia
Trout cod (*Maccullochella macquariensis*)	Australia
Clarence River cod (*Maccullochella* sp.)	Australia
Mary River cod (*Maccullochella* sp.)	Australia

Retropinnidae

Australian grayling (*Prototroctes maraena*)	Australia

Salmonidae

Atlantic whitefish (*Coregonus canadensis*)	Canada
Kiyi (*Coregonus kiyi*)	USA, Canada
Whitefish (*Coregonus lavaretus, C. albula,* and *C. oxyrhynchus*)	Europe
Blackfin cisco (*Coregonus nigripinnis*)	USA, Canada
Shortnose cisco (*Coregonus reighardi*)	USA, Canada
Shortjaw cisco (*Coregonus zenithicus*)	USA, Canada
Huchen (*Hucho hucho*)	Eastern Europe
Apache trout (*Oncorhynchus apache*)	USA
Gila trout (*Oncorhynchus gilae*)	USA
Adriatic trout (*Salmothymus obtusirastris*)	Balkans

GLOSSARY

A

Adipose fin A small, fatty fin between the dorsal fin and the tail fin.

AFTMA The American Fishing Tackle Manufacturers Association. Its activities include setting technical standards for fishing tackle, and its fly tackle specifications have become the world standard.

Alevin A recently hatched salmon or trout (*see also* **Grilse, Kelt, Parr, Smolt**).

Algae Any of a number of groups of simple plants that contain chlorophyll but lack true roots, stems, and leaves. They live in water or moist ground, and include diatoms, seaweeds, and spirogyra.

Amphidromous fish Fish that regularly migrate between freshwater and saltwater for reasons other than spawning, for example to feed or to overwinter (*see also* **Anadromous fish, Catadromous fish, Potamodromous fish**).

Anadromous fish Fish that spend most of their lives in the sea but ascend rivers to spawn (*see also* **Amphidromous fish, Catadromous fish, Potamodromous fish**).

Anal fin The fin behind the anus of a fish.

Aorta The main artery carrying blood from the heart.

Articular The rear bone of the lower jaw of a fish. It is hinged to the upper jaw and the quadrate (*see also* **Dentary, Maxillary, Premaxillary, Quadrate**).

B

Bag limit The maximum permissible number or weight of fish that can be taken from a particular water: always check local regulations before fishing.

Baitfish Any small fish, such as minnows and sandeels, that are preyed on by larger species and commonly used as angling bait.

Baiting needle A long needle used for mounting dead fish and other large baits onto terminal tackle.

Banks The right bank of a river is on your right when you are facing downstream, and the left bank is on your left.

Basin A depression in the Earth's surface; the drainage basin of a river system; a very large depression in the Earth's surface, containing an ocean and the rivers that drain into it, for example the Pacific Basin (*see also* **Drainage basin**).

Benthic A term describing anything living at or near the bottom of a lake or the sea.

Biomass The total mass of all the living organisms in a given area or (aquatic biomass) in a given body of water.

Bowfishing Fishing with a bow and arrow. It is permitted on many American waters, and the quarry is usually "trash" fish (such as carp) that are competing with more highly prized species such as bass. The arrow is tied to the end of the line, and the reel is mounted on the bow.

Brackish water Water that is slightly salty (*see also* **Salinity**).

Breaking strain The maximum load or weight that a line, swivel, or other piece of tackle can sustain without breaking.

B.s. The abbreviation for breaking strain.

Bulk shot A number of split shot grouped together on a line to concentrate weight at a particular point.

Butt pad A leather or rubber pad, strapped around the waist, into which the butt of a rod is placed so that greater leverage can be exerted when fighting large, powerful fish. It is also known as a rod socket (*see also* **Fighting chair**).

C

Caeca See **Pyloric caeca**

Catadromous fish Freshwater fish that move to the lower river or sea to spawn (*see also* **Amphidromous fish, Anadromous fish, Potamodromous fish**).

Caudal peduncle The relatively slender part of a fish's body between the last dorsal and anal fins and the base of the tail fin (the caudal fin). It is also known as the "wrist" of the fish.

Cleithrum A bone at the rear of the skull of a fish. It is the main bone supporting the pectoral fin (*see also* **Pectoral fin, Supracleithrum**).

Coarse fish Any freshwater fish of angling interest other than trout, salmon, char, grayling, and whitefish (*see also* **Gamefish, Panfish**).

D

Deadbait Dead fish or other creatures used as bait for predators (*see also* **Livebait**).

Dead drift A fly-fishing technique in which the fly (dry or wet) is allowed to drift freely along in the current.

Demersal fish Fish that live in deep water or on the sea floor (*see also* **Pelagic fish**).

Dentary The front bone of the lower jaw of a fish (*see also* **Articular, Maxillary, Premaxillary, Quadrate**).

Deoxygenation Reduction in the dissolved oxygen content of a water, caused by hot weather or the introduction of pollutants such as sewage. Excessive deoxygenation is fatal to fish.

Detritus Accumulated silt and organic debris on the bed of a river or stillwater.

Disturbance pattern A wet- or dry-fly pattern that creates a fish-attracting disturbance when retrieved or worked across the current (*see also* **Wake fly**).

Dorsal fin The fin on the back of a fish, sometimes divided into two or three partly or entirely separate sections.

Drainage A drainage basin or a drainage system; the process of draining.

Drainage basin The catchment area of a river system (*see also* **Basin**).

Drainage system A river and its tributaries.

Drogue A cone-shaped bag, usually made of canvas, which can be trailed behind a drifting boat to slow it.

E

Eddy A patch of water that is less disturbed than the surrounding water, found for instance on the edge of a current or where two streams converge (*see also* **Pool, Riffle, Run, Scour, Slack**).

Electrofishing Passing an electric current through the water to stun the fish, so that they can be collected unharmed for tagging or scientific examination or for relocation to another water.

Euryhaline fish Fish, such as most species of salmon and trout, that can live in both freshwater and saltwater.

F

Fighting chair A swivel chair bolted to the deck of a boat, from which a big-game angler can fight marlin and other large, powerful fish that can take a long time to subdue. The angler is strapped in by a harness, and either the harness or the chair is equipped with a butt pad or rod socket (*see also* **Butt pad**).

Filter feeder A fish that feeds by filtering plankton from the water.

Fingerling A small, immature fish, such as a juvenile trout.

Fish ladder A series of interconnected pools created up the side of a river obstruction, such as a weir, to allow salmon and other fish to pass upstream.

Foul-hook To hook a fish anywhere but in the mouth.

Fresh-run fish A migratory fish, such as a salmon, that has just left the sea and is travelling up a river to spawn.

Freshwater The water of rivers and most stillwaters, containing little or no dissolved salts (*see also* **pH, Salinity**).

Fry Very young fish, especially those that have only recently hatched.

G

Gall bladder A small pouch, on or near the liver of a fish, which stores bile. Bile is a fluid produced by the liver, and aids the absorption of food by the gut.

Gamefish Any fish valued for its sporting qualities (*see also* **Coarse fish, Panfish**).

Gill arch The structure behind the gill covers of a bony fish (or within the gill slits of a cartilaginous fish) that supports the gill filaments and gill rakers.

Gill filaments The parts of a fish's gills that absorb oxygen from the water.

Gill rakers Toothlike projections on the gill arches. They can be used to trap food items, such as plankton, carried in the water flowing through the gills.

Gonads The reproductive organs that are responsible for the production of sperm or eggs (*see also* **Testes, Ovaries**).

Grain A unit of weight, used for instance in the classification of fly lines. 1 gram = 15.4 grains, 1 oz = 437.6 grains.

Greenheart A tropical American tree, *Ocotea rodiae*; its wood was once used for making fishing rods.

Grilse A young Atlantic salmon making its first spawning run, usually after one and a half to two years in the sea (*see also* **Alevin, Kelt, Parr, Smolt**).

H

Handline A simple tackle rig often used by youngsters fishing from piers and harbour walls. It consists of a sinker and a hook attached to a line that is wound on a wooden or plastic frame.

Hatch The simultaneous surfacing of large numbers of insect nymphs of the same species. At the surface, the adult insects (or duns) emerge from the nymphal cases and usually rest for a while before flying off (*see also* **Rise**).

I

Ice fishing A specialized form of angling, developed in North America, for fishing through holes cut in the ice of frozen-over waters. The species sought include crappies, walleye, northern pike, pickerel, and perch, and the principal techniques are jigging and tilt (or tip-up) fishing. Jigging involves working a natural bait with a short stick, which has a specially shaped handle around which the line is wound. In tilt fishing, the bait is fished static from a rig incorporating an arm or flag that tilts up to signal a bite.

Ichthyology The scientific study of fish and their habits.

IGFA The International Game Fish Association, based in Fort Lauderdale, Florida. It maintains lists of record fish and also sets technical standards for fishing tackle.

Introperculum In bony fish, the front lower bone of the gill cover (*see also* **Operculum, Preoperculum, Suboperculum**).

Invertebrate A creature that has no backbone, for instance an insect or a worm (*see also* **Vertebrate**).

J

Jig A small artificial lure with a metal head, often dressed with feathers.

Jigging Fishing by jerking a jig or other bait up and down in the water; an ice-fishing technique (*see also* **Ice fishing**).

K

Keeper ring A small ring just above the handle of a fly rod, to which the fly can be hooked when not in use.

Kelt A salmon or trout that has spawned (*see also* **Alevin, Grilse, Parr, Smolt**).

Krill Tiny, shrimplike crustaceans, of the family Euphausiidae, that form an essential part of the marine food chain.

L

Lacustrine A term that describes anything of, relating to, or living in lakes.

Ladder See **Fish ladder**

Left bank See **Banks**

Lie A quiet or sheltered spot in the water where a fish can rest, hide from predators, or wait for food to come by.

Limnology The scientific study of lakes and ponds and the plant and animal organisms that live in them.

Livebait Any natural bait, such as a worm, maggot, or small fish, that is used live (*see also* **Deadbait**).

Loch-style fishing Stillwater flyfishing with teams of wet flies cast a short distance downwind from a drifting boat.

Low-water fly A sparsely dressed fly on a small hook, used mostly for salmon fishing in shallow water.

M

Mark An area of the sea that offers good fishing, usually one that can be located by taking the bearings of shore features.

Marrow spoon A long, slender spoon that can be passed down the gullet of a dead fish to remove its stomach contents. It is used mainly by trout anglers to find out what the fish are actually feeding on at a given time.

Maxillary The rear bone of the upper jaw of a fish (*see also* **Articular, Dentary, Premaxillary, Quadrate**).

Milt The semen of a male fish; a term for the semen-filled testes and sperm ducts of a male fish, also known as soft roe (*see also* **Ova, Roe, Testes**).

N

Neap tides The tides that occur midway between spring tides. They have smaller rises and falls than those at other times of the month (*see also* **Spring tides**).

Nictitating membrane A thin membrane that can be drawn across the eyeball to protect and clean it. Found on many fish species, including some sharks.

O

Oesophagus The gullet of a fish.

Operculum In bony fish, the uppermost and largest of the gill cover bones (*see also* **Introperculum, Preoperculum, Suboperculum**).

Osmosis The process by which a fish takes in or excretes water through its skin in order to maintain the correct balance of salts and fluids within its body tissues.

Otoliths Oval, stonelike structures within the ears of a fish or other vertebrate, which help it to maintain its balance; they are also known as ear stones.

Ova The eggs of a fish or other creature. The mass of eggs within the ovarian membranes of a female fish is termed hard roe (*see also* **Milt, Roe, Ovaries**).

Ovaries The reproductive glands (gonads) of a female fish, which are responsible for the production of eggs (*see also* **Testes**).

Oviducts The ducts between the ovaries and vent in most female fish, along which the ripe eggs pass during spawning.

Oviparous fish Fish that lay eggs from which the young later hatch. All skates, some sharks and rays, and most bony fish are oviparous (*see also* **Ovoviviparous fish, Viviparous fish**).

Ovoviviparous fish Fish whose eggs are fertilized and hatched within the female's body. The eggs are enclosed in separate membranes and the embryos within them receive no nourishment from the mother. Most sharks and rays are ovoviviparous (*see also* **Oviparous fish, Viviparous fish**).

P

Panfish Any small American freshwater food fish, such as a sunfish or perch, that is fished for by anglers but is too small to be considered a true gamefish (*see also* **Coarse fish, Gamefish**).

Parabolic-action rod Another term for a through-action rod.

Parr Young salmon and trout up to two years old, distinguishable from smolts by the dark bars (parr marks) on their sides (*see also* **Alevin, Grilse, Kelt, Smolt**).

Pectoral fins The pair of fins just behind the head of a fish.

Pelagic fish Fish that live at the surface, in the upper waters, of the open ocean (*see also* **Demersal fish**).

Pelvic fins The pair of fins on the lower body of a fish; also called ventral fins.

pH The pH number of a liquid, such as water, indicates its acidity or alkalinity. Pure water has a pH of 7; water with a pH of less than 7 is acidic, and water with a pH of more than 7 is alkaline. Acid rain typically has a pH of less than 5.

Pharyngeal teeth Teeth at the back of the throat, found in many fish species such as the members of the carp family. These teeth crush food as it is swallowed (*see also* **Vomerine teeth**).

Pisciculture The breeding and rearing of fish, for example in hatcheries and fish farms.

Pool A relatively wide, rounded area of a river, usually found just downstream of fast, narrow run (*see also* **Eddy, Riffle, Run, Scour, Slack**).

Potamodromous fish Fish that migrate regularly within large freshwater systems (*see also* **Amphidromous fish, Anadromous fish, Catadromous fish**).

Predatory fish Any fish that prey on other living creatures, particularly other fish.

Premaxillary The front bone of the upper jaw of a fish (*see also* **Articular, Dentary, Maxillary, Quadrate**).

Preoperculum In bony fish, the bone at the rear of the cheek, just in front of the gill cover (*see also* **Introperculum, Operculum, Suboperculum**).

Pyloric caeca Fleshy, fingerlike tubes at the junction between the stomach and intestine of a fish. They produce enzymes that play a part in the digestive process.

Q

Quadrate The bone that joins the upper jaw of a fish to its skull (*see also* **Articular, Dentary, Maxillary, Premaxillary**).

R

Rays The soft or spiny supporting elements of fish fins.

Redd A hollow scooped in the sand or gravel of a riverbed by breeding trout or salmon as a spawning area.

Reversed-taper handle A rod handle that tapers towards the butt end.

Riffle A small rapid in a river or stream (*see also* **Eddy, Pool, Run, Scour, Slack**).

Right bank See **Banks**

Riparian A term that describes anything of, inhabiting, or situated on a riverbank; often used in connection with ownership and fishing rights.

Rip-rap Broken rock, deposited loosely on a riverbed or on the banks to help prevent erosion. It is also used to form breakwaters and embankments.

Rise The action of a fish coming to the surface to take an insect; the taking to the air of a large hatch of mayflies or other insects on which trout feed (*see also* **Hatch**).

Rod socket See **Butt pad**

Roe A collective term for fish milt and ova (*see also* **Milt, Ova**).

Run A fast-flowing stretch of river; the movement of fish inshore or upstream for spawning; the flight of a hooked fish trying to escape; a small stream or brook. (*See also* **Eddy, Pool, Riffle, Scour, Slack**.)

S

Salinity The level of dissolved salts in the water. Freshwater normally contains less than 0.2% salts, brackish water contains up to 3% salts, and saltwater (such as seawater) more than 3%. Normal seawater contains 3.433% salts – 2.3% sodium chloride (common salt), 0.5% magnesium chloride, 0.4% sodium sulphate, 0.1% calcium chloride, 0.07% potassium chloride, and 0.063% other salts.

Saltwater Water containing a high level of dissolved salts (*see also* **Salinity**).

Scour Erosion caused by flowing water; a shallow, fast-flowing, gravel-bottomed stretch of river (*see also* **Eddy, Pool, Riffle, Run, Slack**).

Seminal vesicle A small gland that adds nutrient fluid to the milt of a male fish during spawning (*see also* **Milt**).

Sink-and-draw A method of fishing in which the lure, fly, or bait is made to rise and fall alternately during the retrieve by raising and lowering the rod tip.

Sink-tip A floating fly line with a sinking tip, used to fish flies just below the surface.

Slack Tidal water where there is little surface movement during the interval between the ebbing and flowing tides; a stretch of river with very little current, for instance above a weir (*see also* **Eddy, Pool, Riffle, Run, Scour**).

Slip A narrow strip of feather. Slips are widely used in fly tying.

Smolt A young salmon or sea trout, silver in colour, on its first journey to the sea (*see also* **Alevin, Grilse, Kelt, Parr**).

Spring tides The tides that occur around the time of full and new moons. They have larger rises and falls than those at other times of the month (*see also* **Neap tides**).

Strike To tighten the line to set the hook when a fish bites, usually by raising the rod tip or lifting the rod.

Suboperculum In bony fish, the rear lower bone of the gill cover (*see also* **Interpreculum, Operculum, Preoperculum**).

Supracleithrum A bone at the upper rear of the skull of a fish. It is one of the bones that support the pectoral fin (*see also* **Cleithrum, Pectoral fin**).

Surface film The apparent elasticlike film on the surface of water, which is created by surface tension.

Surface tension The natural tendency of the surface of water (and other liquids) to behave like an elastic sheet. It is caused by forces acting between the water molecules: the molecules at the surface are much more strongly attracted to each other, and to the molecules below them, than they are to the molecules of air above them.

Swim The stretch of a river, or the part of a pond or lake, that is being fished in at a particular time.

T

Take The action of a fish in picking up or grabbing a bait or lure.

Taper The narrowing in diameter, from butt to tip, of a rod, and the narrowing of the end section of a fly line. The rate of taper determines the action of the rod or line.

Terminal tackle The tackle, including the hook or lure, attached to the end of the reel line (main line).

Testes (singular: testis) The reproductive glands (gonads) of a male fish, which are responsible for the production of sperm (*see also* **Ovaries**).

Tilt fishing A technique used in ice fishing; is also known as tip-up fishing (*see also* **Ice fishing**).

Tippet The thin end section of a fly leader, to which the fly is tied.

Tube fly An artificial fly consisting of a metal or plastic tube, dressed with feathers, hair, or other materials and threaded onto the line. The hook, usually a treble, is then attached to the end of the line.

V

Vas deferens The duct that carries sperm from the testis of a spawning male fish (*see also* **Milt, Testes**).

Vent The anus of a fish. It is also the orifice through which a spawning female fish lays her eggs (or, in the case of a viviparous fish, gives birth) and through which a male fish discharges his milt during spawning (*see also* **Viviparous fish, Milt**).

Ventral fins See **Pelvic fins**

Vertebra An individual segment of the backbone of a fish.

Vertebrate A creature that has a backbone, for instance a fish or a mammal (*see also* **Invertebrate**).

Viviparous fish Fish whose ripe eggs are fertilized and hatched within the female's body; they give birth to live young. Unlike those of ovoviviparous fish, the developing embryos receive nourishment from the mother. Some sharks and some bony fish, such as surfperch, are viviparous (*see also* **Oviparous fish, Ovoviviparous fish**).

Vomerine teeth Teeth on the vomer, a bone at the front of the roof of the mouth of bony fish (*see also* **Pharyngeal teeth**).

W

Wake fly A dry fly that creates a splashy, fish-attracting wake when pulled across or through the surface of the water (*see also* **Disturbance pattern**).

Wobbling A freshwater spinning technique using a lure, or a small, dead fish mounted on treble hooks, for bait. The bait is cast a long way out, and retrieved in an erratic fashion by making side-to-side movements of the rod tip and at the same time varying the speed of the retrieve.

Wrist See **Caudal peduncle**

Y

Yolk sac The membrane-covered food pouch found on the belly of a newly hatched fish. It nourishes the growing fish until it is able to feed itself.

INDEX

A

Accessories 78
Acidification 278
Adriatic
    sturgeon 279
    trout 279
African pompano 167
AFTM
    fly line profiles 52
    fly line symbols 53
    fly line weights 52
    scale 15
Alabama spotted bass 126
Albacore 192
Alevin 152
Alewife 195
Allis shad
    description 194
    threatened species 279
Almaco jack 164
Amberjack
    description 164
    distribution 165
    fishing 165
    schooling 164
    young lesser 165
American
    eel 160
    grayling 157
    plaice 182
    shad 194
Anatomy 124
Anchored-boat fishing (sea)
    downtide 245
    for sharks 257
    reef 247
    sandbank 246
    uptide 244
    wreck 248
Anti-kink devices 214
Anti-reverse 32
Ants 103
Apache trout 279
Aphids 103
Arctic
    char 150
    grayling 157
Asp
    description 130
    distribution 131
    fishing 131
    spawning 130
Atlantic
    bonito 195
    cod 173
    hake 173
    halibut 182
    herring 194
    mackerel 190
    salmon 152
    sierra 191
    Spanish mackerel 191
    sturgeon 279
    whitefish 279
Attractor flies 104
Australian
    bass 144
    blue catfish 162
    bonito 195
    grayling 279
    mobula 184
    perch 146
    salmon 188
Avon rods 19

B

Backing line
    braided 207
    joining 207
    solid 207
    types of 52
Bait
    freshwater
        naturals 82
        processed 84
    saltwater 92
Bait droppers
    freshwater 87
    saltwater 94
Bait fishing
    basic tackle 13
    big-game 259
Baitcasting reels
    casting control 212
    components 33
    examples of 40
    line control 213
Baitwalking 231
Bale arm 32
Ballan wrasse 177
Bankside plants 269
Barbel
    barbels of 131
    description 131
    distribution 131
    fishing 131
    food 130
    mouth of 131
    young 131
Barbels (barbules) 131
Barley 85
Barndoor skate 186
Barracuda
    description 162
    distribution 163
    fishing 162
    in shallows 162
    jaws 163
Barramundi
    description 169
    distribution 169
    fishing 168
Barred surfperch 171
Basic tackle
    freshwater 13
    saltwater 12
Basking shark 198
Bass
    description 144
    distribution 145
    fishing 145
Bass, black see Black bass
Bat ray 185
Beach fishing
    basic tackle 12
    techniques 252
Beads 51
Beans 85
Beetles 103
Bidyan 146
Big-game fishing
    bait fishing 259
    basic tackle 12
    deadbait trolling 259
    groundbaiting 95
    livebait drifting 259
    livebait trolling 259
    lure patterns 258
    lure trolling 258
Big skate 186
Billfish
    description 174
    distribution 175
    fishing 175
    food 174
Biscuits 84
Bite indicators
    examples of 64
    in legering 220
Black
    bream 146
    bullhead 141
    crappie 129
    drum 188
    grouper 201
    marlin 175
    seabass 200
    seabream 202
    snook 169
Black bass
    description 126
    distribution 127
    dorsal fins 127
    fishing 126
    food 127
Blackfin
    cisco 279
    tuna 192
Blacktip shark 197
Blank 15
Bleak 136
Bloodworms 103
Blue
    catfish 143
    marlin 175
    runner 164
    shark 199
Blueback herring 195
Bluebottle fly larvae 82
Bluefin tuna 193
Bluefish
    description 158
    distribution 159
    fishing 158
Bluegill
    description 128
    distribution 129
    fishing 129
Boat fishing (sea)
    basic tackle 12
    big-game 258
    groundbaiting 94
    inshore 244
    offshore 246
    shark fishing 256
    wreck fishing 248
Boat-fishing rigs (sea)
    balloon float 256
    bank-fishing 246
    conger 248
    dogfish 257
    drift-fishing 247
    flowing trace 245
    flying collar 249
    heavyweight float 254
    pennel 257
    running leger 248
    self-hooking trace 244
    shark drift 256
    sliding float 254
    spreader 245
    tope 257
Boat fly fishing
    dapping 243
    etiquette 243
    fishing the drift 242
    high-density lines 243
    safe casting angles 242
    sunk-line fishing 243
Boat reels 46
Boat rods
    standup 29
    uptide 28
Body
    detached 105
    dubbing 109
    of a fly 105
    tying 109
Boilies 85
Bolognese method 20
Bolt rig 221
Bonefish
    description 158
    distribution 159
    fishing 158
    larva 159
Bonito
    description 194
    distribution 195
    fishing 194
Bonito shark 198
Bony fish 124
Booms 60
Boots 70
Braided line 50
Brandlings 82
Bread 84
Bream
    description 132
    distribution 133
    fishing 133
    food 132
    roach/bream hybrids 132
    young 132
Bronze bream 133
Brook trout 151
Brown
    bullhead 141
    trout 154
Brush piles 269
Bubbles 269
Bull
    shark 197
    trout 151
Bullhead
    body shape 140
    description 140
    distribution 141
    fishing 141
    pectoral spines 140
    spawning 141
Buoyant spinners 215
Burbot
    description 172
    distribution 173
    fishing 172
Butt 15
Buzzbaits 215

C

Caddis 101
Calico surfperch 171
California
    barracuda 163
    corbina 188
    moray 160
    sheephead 176
    skate 186
    yellowtail 165
Cannibal trout 154
Caribbean red snapper 179
Carp
    barbels of 131
    breeding 134
    description 134
    distribution 135
    fishing 134
    food 134
    scales 135
Carrots 85
Cartilaginous fish 124
Casters 82
Casting
    overhead, basic 212
    overhead, fly 232
    pole 226
    roll 234
    stillwater float rigs 224
    surfcasting 250
    uptide
        boat 244
        shore 253
Cat food 84
Catapults
    for groundbaiting 86
    in pole fishing 228
Catch-and-release 279
Caterpillars 103
Catfish, freshwater
    barbels of 143
    channel 142
    description 142
    distribution 143
    fishing 142
    food 143
    whiskers of 143
Catfish, sea
    description 162
    distribution 163
    fishing 162
    mouth brooding 162
Centrepin reels 32
Cero 190
Chain pickerel 138
Channel catfish 142
Char
    breeding coloration 150
    description 150
    distribution 151
    fishing 150
    hybrids 150
    parr marks 150
Check mechanism 32
Cheese 84
Cheetah trout 150
Cherry salmon 152
Chinook salmon 153
Chironomids 103
Chub
    dace/bleak comparison 136
    description 136
    distribution 137
    fishing 136
    food 136
Chub mackerel 190
Chum 95
Chum salmon 153
Ciguatera 164
Cisco 156
Clarence River cod 279
Clearnose skate 186
Cliffs 270
Closed-face reels
    casting control 212
    components 33
    examples of 38
    line control 213
Cobia
    description 168
    distribution 169
    fishing 168
    habitat 168
Cod
    description 173
    distribution 173
    fishing 172
    red 173
Coho salmon 152
Common
    carp 135
    skate 187
    sturgeon 279
Confluences 265
Conger 161
Conservation 278
Coral
    flats 276
    reefs 277
Corn 84
Crabs 93
Crane fly 103
Crankbait fishing 219
Crappies
    description 129
    distribution 129
    fishing 129
Creeks
    estuarine 273
    mangrove 273
Crevalle jack 165
Crimping 256
Crimps 51
Crucian carp 134
Crustaceans 101
Cuban snapper 179
Cubera snapper 179
Cunner 177
Cutthroat trout 155
Cuttlefish 93

D

Dace
    chub/bleak comparison 136
    description 136
    distribution 137
    fishing 136
Daddy longlegs 103
Dams 265
Damselflies 102
Danubian
    bream 133
    catfish 142
    roach 137
Dapping 243
Deadbait trolling 259
Deceiver flies 104
Detached body 105
Devil rays 184
Dog biscuits 84
Dogfish fishing 257
Dolly Varden 151
Dolphinfish
    description 176
    distribution 177
    fishing 176
    head shape 176
Dorado 176
Downrigger 231
Drag mechanism
    function 32
    lever 46
    star 46
Dragonflies 102
Drift fishing (sea)
    big-game 259
    reef 247
    sandbank 246
    shark 256
    wreck 249
Dropoffs
    offshore temperate 275
    offshore tropical 276
Drum
    description 188
    distribution 189
    fishing 189
Dry flies
    design of 104
    patterns 112
Dry-fly fishing
    downstream 239

in flat calm 239
stillwater 239
upstream 238
wading 239
Dun 100

E

Eagle rays 185
Earthworms 82
Eastern freshwater cod 279
Eddies 264
Eels
description 160
distribution 161
fishing 161
larvae 160
marine habitat 161
Emerger flies 104
English sole 182
Epilimnion 230
Estuaries 272
Estuarine species 272
Estuary perch 147
European
barracuda 162
eel 160
grayling 157
plaice 182
sea bass 145
whitefish 156
Eutrophication 278

F

Family 123
Fat snook 168
Feathering a cast 224
Ferrules 15
Fish baits 83
Fish stocks 279
Fixed paternoster 221
Fixed-spool reels
casting control 212
closed-face 38
components 33
general-purpose 34
invention of 32
line control 213
loading 206
loading shock leader 250
match 35
shore 49
specialist 36
spincaster 33
Flat bullhead 141
Flatfish
description 182
development 183
distribution 183
eggs 182
fishing 183
hybrids 182
larvae 182
Flathead catfish 143
Flies, artificial
attractors 104
deceivers 104
dry 112
emergers 104
hairwings 120
nymphs 116
parts of 105
salmon 118
steelhead 118
streamers 120
types of 104
wet 114
Flies, natural
caddis 101
crane fly 103
damselflies 102
dragonflies 102
hawthorn fly 103
mayflies 100
midges 103

olives 100
sedges 101
stoneflies 102
terrestrials 103
Float fishing
backshotting 223
lift method 224
on the drop 224
plumbing the depth 222
pole
canal 227
running water 228
stillwater 226
running water 222
saltwater 254
sliding controller float 225
sliding float 225
split shot 222
stick float 223
stillwater 224
stillwater casting 224
trotting 223
Float rigs
balloon
boat 254
shore 255
heavyweight saltwater 254
pole
canal 227
running water 228
stillwater 226
sliding freshwater 225
saltwater 254
sliding controller 225
stick 223
stillwater 224
waggler 225
Float rods 20
Floating divers 219
Floats 62
Florida
largemouth bass 126
pompano 166
Flounder 182
Fly fishing
basic tackle 13
boat 242
dry-fly 238
fishing the drift 242
nymph 240
overhead casting 232
roll casting 234
wet-fly 236
Fly hooks 105
Fly leaders
joining to line 207
types of 53
Fly lines
densities 53
high-density 243
joining to backing 207
joining to leader 207
loading onto reels 207
profiles 52
symbols 53
tapers 52
weights 52
Fly reels
automatic 32
components 32
large-capacity 44
loading 207
multiplier 32
single-action 32
small-capacity 42
Fly rods
light/medium 22
medium/heavy 24
Fly tying
basics 108, 110

bodies 109
equipment 106
hackles 110
heads 111
materials 107
ribs 109
starting off 108
tails 109
whip finishing 108
wings 111
Footwear 70
Freelining 220
Freshwater
catfish 142
drum 188
mullet 180

G

Gaffs 66
Gafftopsail catfish 163
Gear ratio 32
Genus 123
Giant perch 169
Gila trout 279
Gills 124
Gilthead 202
Gloves 76
Golden
barracuda 163
mullet 181
perch 147
tench 130
trout 155
Goldfish 135
Grains 85
Grass
carp 135
pickerel 138
porgy 203
Gray snapper 178
Grayling
breeding 157
description 157
distribution 157
dorsal fin 157
dwarfing 157
Great
barracuda 163
white shark 199
threatened species 279
Greater amberjack 165
Green
jack 164
sunfish 128
Greenbottle fly larvae 82
Grey nurse shark 197
Grilse 153
Groundbait
freshwater
additives 86
bases 86
mixing 86
saltwater
big-game 95
chum 95
rubby dubby 94
shark fishing 256
shirvy 95
shore 95
Grouper
description 200
distribution 201
fishing 201
Grunters
description 146
distribution 147
fishing 146
Guadalupe bass 126
Guaguanche 162
Gudgeon 131
Gulf sierra 191
Gullies
offshore temperate 274

offshore tropical 276
shoreline 271
Gum beetle 103

H

Hackle
of a fly 105
tying 110
Haddock 173
Hairwing flies
design of 104
patterns 120
Hake
Atlantic 173
description 173
fishing 173
Pacific 173
Halibut 182
Hammerhead shark 199
Hardhead catfish 162
Hats 76
Hawthorn fly 103
Head
of a fly 105
tying 111
Hempseed 85
Herring
Atlantic 194
blueback 195
lake 156
oxeye 159
river 194
skipjack 194
Hickory shad 195
High-protein (HP) baits 85
Hoglouse, water 101
Hooks
bends 56
faults 57
finishes 57
fly 105
parts of 54
pennel-rigged 257
points 57
shanks 55
shapes 56
sizes 54
types of 54
wire gauges 54
Horned pout 141
Horse mackerel 190
Housefly larvae 82
Houting 156
Hoverflies 103
Huchen
range 152
threatened species 279
Humpback salmon 152
Hybrids
Atlantic salmon × sea trout 150
brook trout × brown trout 150
brook trout × lake trout 150
brook trout × rainbow trout 150
rainbow trout × cutthroat 150
roach × bream 132
starry flounder × English sole 182
Hybrid sole 182
Hypolimnion 230

I

Imago 100
Inconnu 156
Inshore fishing
downtide 245
bait spacing 245
uptide 244
casting 244

striking 244
Irish bream 133
Islands
offshore 275
river 265

J

Jack
description 164
distribution 165
fishing 165
schooling 164
Jack (young salmon) 153
Jackets 72
Jackmackerel
description 167
distribution 167
fishing 166
Jetties 271
Jewfish 201
Jolthead porgy 203
Jungle perch 147

K

Kahawai
description 188
distribution 189
fishing 189
Kamloops rainbow 154
Kawakawa 192
Kelp beds 271
Kern river rainbow 154
King
carp 135
mackerel 191
salmon 153
Kiyi 279
Knots
basic leader 252
blood 209
blood bight 209
domhof 208
double overhand loop 209
high-performance leader 252
needle 207
Palomar 208
reel 206
spade end whip 208
spool 208
surgeon's 209
surgeon's end loop 209
uni 208
water 209
Kokanee 153
Kype 152

L

Ladyfish 159
Lagoons 273
Lake
herring 156
sturgeon 279
trout 151
whitefish 157
Lakes see **Stillwaters**
Landing
lipping 211
netting 211
tackle 66
Landlocked salmon 152
Lane snapper 178
Largemouth bass 126
Largespot pompano 166
Largetooth sawfish 185
Lateral line 125
Leader line
fly 53
types of 51
Leather carp 135
Ledges 275
Leger rigs

freshwater
bolt rig 221
fixed paternoster 221
running leger 220
sliding link 221
saltwater
conger rig 248
running leger 252
running paternoster 253
two-hook paternoster 252
Leger rods 18
Legering 220
Leopard shark 196
Lesser amberjack 165
Level wind 32
Lever drag 46
Line
class 15
guard 32
memory 44
Lines
backing 52
braided 50
fly 52
fly leader 53
leader 51
monofilament 50
wire 50
Linewinder 207
Ling
description 173
distribution 173
fishing 172
Little
skate 187
tunny 192
Livebait
drifting 259
trolling 259
Lobworms 82
Longbill spearfish 174
Longfin
bonefish 159
tuna 192
Longfinned eel 160
Long-nosed skate 187
Longspine porgy 202
Lowland streams 264
Lugworms 92
Luncheon meat 84
Lure fishing
basic tackle 13
big-game trolling 258
plug fishing 218
surface techniques 218
spinning
freshwater 214
saltwater 255
spoon fishing 216
Lures
freshwater
plugs 90
spinners 88
spoons 89
saltwater
big-game 258
plugs 97
spinners 97
spoons 96

M

Mackerel
description 190
distribution 191
eyelids 190
fishing 191
horse 190
Mackerel sharks 197
Macquarie perch 146
Maggots 82
Mahi mahi 176
Maize 85

Mako 198
Mangrove
  creeks 273
  jack 179
  snapper 178
Manta 184
Maori wrasse 176
Marlin 175
Marlinsucker 175
Mary River cod 279
Masu salmon 152
Mayflies 100
Meat baits 84
Mediterranean barbel 131
Mermaid's purse 184
Mexican barracuda 163
Midges 103
Miller's thumb 101
Millpools 265
Minnow plugs 218
Minnows 101
Mirror carp 135
Monofilament 50
Monterey Spanish mackerel 191
Moray 160
Mountain whitefish 157
Mullet
  description 180
  distribution 181
  fishing 181
Multiplier reels
  baitcasting 40
  casting control 212
  components 33
  invention of 32
  line control 213
  loading 206
  loading shock leader 250
  shore 48
Murray cod
  description 145
  distribution 145
  fishing 145
Muskellunge
  description 138
  distribution 139
  fishing 139
  food 138
  jaws 139
Musselcracker 202
Mussels, freshwater 83
Mutton snapper 178

N
Nase
  description 132
  distribution 133
  fishing 133
Nassau grouper 200
Natural baits
  freshwater 82
  saltwater 92
Naturals see Flies, natural
Nightcrawlers 82
Nile perch 169
Northern
  pike 138
  sennet 162
Nymph fishing
  fishing a curve 241
  inducing a take 240
  river 240
  stalking 241
  stillwater 241
Nymphs
  design of 104
  natural 100
  patterns 116

O
Octopus 93

Offshore
  banks
    temperate 275
    tropical 276
  fishing
    reefs 247
    sandbanks 246
  waters
    temperate 274
    tropical 276
Off-the-ground cast 250
Olives (flies) 100
Olivettes
  sizes 229
  types of 58
Ouananiche
  distribution 153
Overhead cast
  basic 212
    action 212
    common faults 213
    line control 213
    reel control 212
  fly 232
    action 232
    back cast 232
    casting loops 233
    common faults 233
    false casting 233
    forward cast 233
    grips 232
    shooting line 233
Oxeye herring (oxeye tarpon) 159

P
Pacific
  amberjack 161
  barracuda 163
  bonito 194
  hake 173
  halibut 182
  porgy 203
  salmon 152
  sierra 191
Pallid sturgeon 279
Palmered
  flies 104
  hackles 110
Parr 153
Parr marks 150
Particle baits 85
Pasta 85
Pauu'u 165
Peanuts 85
Peas 85
Pennel rig 257
Perch
  description 148
  distribution 149
  eggs 148
  fishing 149
  scales 148
Perch, Australian
  description 146
  distribution 147
  fishing 146
  spawning estuary perch 147
  young golden perch 147
Permit 166
Pickerel
  description 138
  distribution 139
  fishing 139
  food 138
  jaws 139
Piers 271
Pike
  description 139
  distribution 139
  fishing 139
  food 138
  jaws 139

Pikeperch 148
Pink salmon 152
Pinkeye 180
Pinkies 82
Pinnacles 275
Plaice 182
Playing
  pumping 211
  reel control 210
  using sidestrain 210
Plug fishing
  crankbaits 219
  floating divers 219
  minnows 218
  stickbaits 218
  surface lures 218
  walking the dog 218
Plugs
  crankbaits 219
  floating divers 219
  freshwater 90
  minnows 218
  saltwater 97
  stickbaits 218
  surface lures 218
Plumbing the depth 222
Plummets 222
Pole fishing
  basic tackle 13
  canal fishing 226
  casting 226
  danger warning 26
  feeding 227
  pole elastic 228
  pole handling 227
  pole tips 226
  running-water fishing 228
  stillwater fishing 226
  weights 229
Pole rigs
  canal 227
  running-water 228
  stillwater 226
Poles 26
Pollack 172
Pollution 278
Pompano
  description 166
  distribution 167
  fishing 166
Pompano dolphin 176
Ponds see Stillwaters
Pope 148
Porbeagle 197
Porgy
  description 202
  distribution 203
  fishing 203
  food 202
Potatoes 85
Powan 156
Prawns 83
Processed baits 84
Pumpkinseed
  description 128
  distribution 129
  fishing 129
  gill covers 128

Q
Queensland grouper 201

R
Ragworms 92
Rainbow trout 154
Ratchet 32
Rays
  description 184
  distribution 185
  egg cases 184
  fishing 185
Razorshells 93
Reading a lake 230

Red
  cod 173
  drum 188
  grouper 201
  mullet 180
  porgy 203
  salmon 153
  seabream 202
  snapper 179
Redbreast sunfish 128
Redear sunfish 128
Redeye bass 126
Redfin pickerel 138
Redtail surfperch 171
Redworms 82
Reedbeds 268
Reef fishing 247
Reefs
  coral 277
  offshore temperate 275
Reel
  foot 32
  seats 15
Reels
  baitcasting 40
  basic 12
  big-game 12
  boat 46
  centrepin 32
  closed-face 38
  components 32
  evolution of 32
  filling 206
  fixed-spool 34, 36
  fly 42, 44
  loading 206
  multiplier 40, 48
  setting up 206
  sidecast 49
  spincaster 33
  types of 32
Remora 175
Requiem sharks 196
Rib
  of a fly 105
  tying 109
Rice 85
Ripples 269
River herring 194
Rivers 262, 264
Roach
  breeding 137
  description 137
  distribution 137
  fishing 136
  food 137
  roach/bream hybrids 132
Rock bass 129
Rocks 271
Rod rests 64
Rods
  actions 15
  Avon 19
  basic 12
  big-game 12
  blanks 15
  boat 28
  components 14
  development 14
  ferrules 15
  float 20
  fly 22, 24
  guides 14
  leger 18
  poles 26
  reel seats 15
  rings 14
  shore 30
  spinning 16
  standup 29
  test curve 15
  uptide 28
  whips 26
Roll cast

action 234
  common faults 235
  from a boat 235
  on a river 235
  stance 234
Roosterfish
  description 167
  distribution 167
  fishing 166
Rotor 32
Roughtail stingray 185
Round
  stingray 185
  whitefish 157
Rubberlip seaperch 170
Rubby dubby
  basic mixture 94
  in shark fishing 256
Rudd
  breeding 137
  description 137
  fishing 136
  food 137
Ruff 188
Ruffe
  description 148
  distribution 149
  fishing 149
Running leger
  for conger 248
  freshwater 220

S
Safety at sea 244
Sailfish 174
Saithe 172
Salmon
  alevin 152
  breeding coloration 152
  description 152
  distribution 153
  fishing 152
  grilse 153
  hybrids 150
  kype 152
  landlocked 152
  life cycle 152
  migration 152
  parr 153
  smolt 153
  spawning 152
Salmon catfish 162
Salmon flies 118
Salmon shark 197
Sand
  seatrout 189
  tiger 197
Sandbank fishing 246
Sandeels 92
Sandy shores 270
Sardines 83
Saucereye porgy 203
Sauger
  description 148
  distribution 149
  fishing 149
Sawfish 185
Scad 190
Scales 125
Schelly 156
Scientific names 123
Scuds 101
Sculpins 101
Scumlanes 269
Scup 202
Sea
  catfish 162
  trout 154
  walls 271
Seabream
  description 202
  distribution 203
  fishing 203
Seaperch 170

Sebago salmon
  distribution 153
Sedge flies 101
Seeds 85
Sennets 162
Senorita 176
Setting up reels 206
Shad
  description 194
  distribution 195
  fishing 194
  food 194
Shafted bonefish 159
Shark fishing
  bait depths 256
  boat fishing 257
  dogfish 257
  drift fishing 256
  general 198
  shore fishing 257
  tope
    boat fishing 257
    shore fishing 257
  wire traces 256
Sharks
  anatomy 125
  blue shark teeth 199
  claspers 199
  description 196, 198
  distribution 197, 199
  fishing 198, 256
  porbeagle teeth 197
  requiem shark tails 199
  swimming 125
  teeth 197, 199
  tope eyes 196
  white shark bite 198
Shasta rainbow 154
Sheefish 156
Sheepshead 203
Sheepshead porgy 203
Shiner perch 170
Shingle beaches 270
Shirvy 95
Shock leader
  function 253
  loading 250
Shore fishing
  anchoring the bait 253
  avoiding snags 253
  basic tackle 12
  beach fishing 252
  bottom fishing 255
  buoyant leger fishing 255
  float fishing 254
  groundbaiting 95
  leader knots 252
  rock fishing 254
  searching the bottom 253
  spinning 255
    lure weights 255
  supported-line fishing 255
  uptide casting 253
Shore-fishing rigs
  balloon float 257
  buoyant leger 255
  dogfish rig 257
  heavyweight float 254
  pennel 257
  running leger 252
  running paternoster 253
  shallow spinning 255
  sliding float 254
  tope rig 257
  two-hook paternoster 252
Shore rods 30
Shorelines 270
Shortbill spearfish 174

Shortfin
  barracuda 163
  mako 198
Shortjaw cisco 279
Shortnose
  cisco 279
  sturgeon 279
Shrimps
  as bait 83
  freshwater 101
Sidecast reel 49
Sierra 191
Sight indicators 240
Silver
  bream 133
  jack 179
  perch 146
  salmon 152
  seatrout 189
Sinkers
  freshwater 58
    pole fishing 229
    split shot 222
  saltwater 60
    bank-fishing 246
    downtide 245
    uptide 244
Sixgill shark 198
Skates
  description 186
  distribution 187
  fishing 187
  jaws 187
  mating 187
  undersides of 186
Skimmer bream 132
Skipjack
  herring 194
  tuna 192
  wavyback 192
Slacks 264
Sliding link leger 221
Slipping clutch 32
Slugs 82
Smallmouth bass 127
Smalltooth sawfish 185
Smelt 83
Smolt 153
Smooth
  dogfish 196
  hammerhead 199
Snail bullhead 140
Snapper
  description 178
  distribution 179
  fishing 178
  juvenile red 179
  schooling red 179
Snook
  description 168
  distribution 169
  fishing 168
Sockeye salmon 153
Soiffe 132
Sole 182
Sooty grunter 146
Southern
  barbel 131
  flounder 182
  sennet 162
  yellowtail 165
Spanish mackerel 191
Species 123
Spiders 103
Spincaster reels
  casting control 212
  components 33
  line control 213
Spinner (mayfly) 100
Spinnerbaits 215
Spinner shark 197
Spinners
  actions 214
  blades 215
  buoyant 215
  buzzbaits 215

  freshwater 88
  saltwater 97
  spinnerbaits 215
  standard 214
Spinning
  freshwater
    coldwater 215
    downstream 215
    upstream 214
  saltwater 255
Spinning rods 16
Splake 150
Split shot
  and olivettes 229
  sizes 222
Spoon-fishing
  around-the-clock 216
  casting patterns 216
  countdown method
    217
  fan casting 216
  line control 217
  tackle 216
  techniques 217
Spoons
  casting 216
  freshwater 89
  saltwater 96
  trolling 216
Spotfin croaker 188
Spotted
  bass 126
  bullhead 140
  ray 184
  sea bass 145
  seatrout 189
Spurdog 196
Squatts 82
Squid 93
Standup rods 29
Star drag 46
Starry flounder 182
Steelhead 154
Steelhead flies 118
Steenbras 202
Stickbaits 218
Stillwaters 266, 268
Stingrays 185
Stone loach 131
Stoneflies 102
Stream outfalls 273
Streamer flies
  design of 104
  patterns 120
Streams 262, 264
Striped
  barracuda 163
  bass 145
  bonito 194
  marlin 175
  mullet 180
  seaperch 171
Sturgeon 279
Subimago 100
Sucker (remora) 175
Sunfish
  description 128
  distribution 129
  fishing 129
  gill covers 128
Sunglasses 76
Supported-line fishing
  255
Surface indications
  offshore temperate
    275
  rivers 263
  stillwaters 269
Surface lure fishing
  218
Surfcasting
  action 250
  common faults 251
  grip 250
  loading shock leaders
    250

  stance 250
Surfperch
  description 170
  distribution 171
  fishing 170
Suwannee bass 126
Sweetcorn 84
Swim bladder 124
Swimfeeders
  bait droppers
    freshwater 87
    saltwater 94
  blockend 87
  open-ended 87
Swivels 51
Swordfish
  description 174
  distribution 175
  fishing 175
  food 174

T_____
Tackle boxes 68
Tail
  of a fly 105
  tying 109
Tailers 66
Taimen 152
Tandan 142
Taper 15
Tares 85
Tarpon
  description 158
  distribution 159
  fighting ability 158
  fishing 158
Tarpon snook 169
Tautog 177
Tench
  barbels of 131
  description 130
  distribution 131
  fishing 131
  food 130
  sex of 130
Tenpounder 159
Terrestrials 103
Test curve 15
Thermocline 230
Thick-lipped grey
  mullet 181
Thin-lipped grey
  mullet 181
Thornback ray 184
Threadfish 167
Threatened species 279
Thresher shark 198
Tiger
  shark 199
  trout 150
Tinplate bream 132
Tope 196
Tope fishing 257
Toxostome 132
Trevally 165
Trolling
  big-game
    deadbait 259
    groundbaiting 95
    livebait 259
    lure 258
  freshwater
    baitwalking 231
    downrigger 230
    layers 230
    multiple rods 230
Trout
  cannibal 154
  description 150, 154
  distribution 151, 155
  fishing 150, 154
  hybrids 150
  vision 238
Trout cod 279
Trout flies
  dry 112

  hairwing 120
  nymphs 116
  steelhead 118
  streamer 120
  wet 114
Tule perch 170
Tuna
  description 192
  distribution 193
  fishing 193
  finlets 193
Tunny 192
Turbot 183
Twaite shad 194

U_____
Ulua 165
Underwater
  obstructions 263
  features 267
Upland streams 264
Uptide
  casting
    boat 244
    shore 253
  rods 28
Upwing flies 100

V_____
Vegetation
  bankside plants 269
  kelp beds 271
  mangroves 273
  reedbeds 268
  river 263
  stillwater 268
  water lilies 268
  weed rafts 277
Vendace 156
Vests 72
Vimba
  description 132
  distribution 133
  fishing 133
Volga zander 149

W_____
Waders 70
Wahoo
  description 193
  distribution 193
  finlets 193
  fishing 193
  jaws 193
Walking the dog 218
Walleye
  description 148
  distribution 149
  fishing 149
Walleye surfperch 170
Warsaw grouper 201
Water
  colour 267
  flow 263
  hoglouse 101
  lilies 268
Waterproofs 74
Wavyback skipjack 192
Weakfish 189
Weed rafts 277
Weights
  freshwater 58
    pole fishing 229
    split shot 222
  saltwater 60
    bank-fishing 246
    downtide 245
    uptide 244
Weirpools 265
Wels 142
Wet flies
  design of 104
  patterns 114
Wet-fly fishing
  basic leader 236
  downstream 237

  leading the fly 237
  mending line 237
  upstream 236
  wading 237
Whale shark 198
Wheat 85
Whips 26
White
  bass 144
  catfish 142
  crappie 129
  croaker 189
  mullet 181
  perch 144
  seabass 188
  shark 199
  skate 187
Whitebone porgy 203
Whitefish
  description 156
  distribution 157
  fishing 157
Whiteye bream 133
Wichita spotted bass
  126
Wild carp 134
Winch fitting 15
Wind lanes 269
Wing
  of a fly 105
  tying 111
Winter
  flounder 183
  skate 187
Wire
  line 50
  traces 256
Worms 82
Wrasse
  description 176
  distribution 177
  fishing 176
  mouth of 177
Wreck fishing
  at anchor 248
  bottom fishing 249
  flying-collar fishing
    249
  into the hulk 248
  on the drift 249
Wreck-fishing rigs
  flying collar 249
  running leger 248
Wrecks 275

Y_____
Yellow
  bass 144
  bullhead 140
Yellow Sally (stonefly)
  102
Yellowfin
  croaker 188
  grouper 200
Yellowstone cutthroat
  155
Yellowtail 165

Z_____
Zährte 132
Zander
  description 148
  distribution 149
  fishing 149
  spawning 149
Zones of a river 262

INDEX OF SCIENTIFIC NAMES

A

Abramis
brama 133
sapa 133
Acanthocybium solanderi 193
Acipenser
brevirostrum 279
fulvescens 279
naccarii 279
oxyrhynchus 279
sturio 279
Albula
nemoptera 159
vulpes 158
Albulidae 158
Alburnus alburnus 136
Alectis ciliaris 167
Alopias vulpinus 198
Alosa
aestivalis 195
alosa 194, 279
chrysochloris 194
fallax 194
mediocris 195
pseudoharengus 195
sapidissima 194
Ambloplites rupestris 129
Ameiurus
brunneus 140
catus 142
melas 141
natalis 140
nebulosus 141
platycephalus 141
serracanthus 140
Ammodytidae 92
Amphistichus
argenteus 171
koelzi 171
rhodoterus 171
Anguilla
anguilla 160
reinhardtii 160
rostrata 160
Anguillidae 160
Anisoptera 102
Aplodinotus grunniens 188
Archosargus
probatocephalus 203
Arenicola spp. 92
Ariidae 162
Arius
felis 162
graeffei 162
Arripidae 188
Arripis
georgianus 188
trutta 188
Asellus 101
Aspius aspius 130
Atractoscion nobilis 188

B

Baetidae 100, 116
Baetis muticus 112
Bagre marinus 163
Barbus
barbus 131
meridionalis 131
Bibio marci 113
Bibionidae 115
Bidyanus bidyanus 146
Blicca bjoerkna 132
Bothidae 182

C

Caenis 100
Calamus
arctifrons 203
bajonado 203
bruchysomus 203
calamus 203
leucosteus 203
penna 203
Carangidae 164, 166
Caranx
caballus 164
caninus 164
crysos 164
georgianus 165
hippos 165
ignobilis 165

stellatus 165
Carassius
auratus 135
carassius 134
Carcharhinidae 196
Carcharhinus
brevipinna 197
leucas 197
limbatus 197
Carcharodon carcharias 199, 279
Centrarchidae 126, 128
Centropomidae 168
Centropomus
nigrescens 169
parallelus 168
pectinatus 168
undecimalis 169
Centropristis striata 200
Cetorhinus maximus 198
Cheilinus undulatus 176
Chelon labrosus 181
Chironomus 103
plumosus 103
Chondrichthyes 125
Chondrostoma
nasus 132
toxostoma 132
Cloeon simile 115
Clupea harengus 194
Clupeidae 194
Conger conger 161
Congridae 160
Coregonus
albula 156, 279
artedi 156
canadensis 279
clupeaformis 157
kiyi 279
lavaretus 279
nigripinnis 279
oxyrhynchus 279
pallasi 156
reighardi 279
zenthicus 279
Coryphaena
equisetis 176
hippurus 176
Coryphaenidae 176
Ctenopharyngodon idella 135
Cymatogaster aggregata 171
Cynoscion
arenarius 189
nebulosus 189
nothus 189
regalis 189
Cyprinidae 130, 132, 134, 136
Cyprinus carpio 134, 135

D

Dasyatidae 184
Dasyatis centroura 185
Dicentrarchus
labrax 145
punctatus 145
Diptera 100

E

Elopidae 158
Elops saurus 159
Embiotoca lateralis 171
Embiotocidae 170
Enallagma cyathigerum 102
Ensis spp. 93
Ephemera 100
Ephemera danica 100, 112, 113, 115
Ephemerella 113
Ephemeroptera 100, 114
Epinephelus
itajara 201
morio 201
nigritus 201
striatus 200
Esocidae 138
Esox
americanus americanus 138
americanus vermiculatus 138

lucius 139
masquinongy 138
niger 138
Euthynnus
affinis 192
alletteratus 192
pelamis 192
lineatus 192

G

Gadidae 172
Gadus morhua 173
Galeocerdo cuvieri 199
Galeorhinus galeus 196
Gammarus 101
pulex 117
Genyonemus lineatus 189
Gymnocephalus cernuus 148
Gymnothorax mordax 160

H

Hephaestus fuliginosus 146
Hexanchus griseus 199
Hippoglossoides
platessoides 182
Hippoglossus
hippoglossus 182
stenolepis 183
Hucho
hucho 152, 279
taimen 152
Hydropsyche 101
Hyperprosopon argenteum 170
Hysterocarpus traski 170

I

Ictaluridae 140, 142
Ictalurus
furcatus 143
punctatus 142
Istiophoridae 174
Istiophorus platypterus 174
Isurus oxyrinchus 198

K

Kuhlia rupestris 147
Kuhliidae 146

L

Labridae 176
Labrus bergylta 177
Lamna
ditropis 197
nasus 196
Lamnidae 197
Lates
calcarifer 169
niloticus 169
Lepomis 128
auritus 128
cyanellus 128
gibbosus 128
macrochirus 128
microlophus 128
Leuciscus
cephalus 136
leuciscus 136
Liza
aurata 181
ramada 181
Lota lota 172
Lutjanidae 178
Lutjanus
analis 178
argentimaculatus 179
campechanus 179
cyanopterus 179
griseus 178
purpureus 179
synagris 178

M

Maccullochella
ikei 279
macquariensis 279
peeli 279
Maccullochella sp. 279
Macquaria
ambigua 147
australasica 146

colonorum 147
novemaculeata 144
Makaira
indicus 175
nigricans 175
Manta birostris 184
Megalops
atlanticus 158
cyprinoides 159
Melanogrammus
aeglefinus 173
Menticirrhus undulatus 188
Merluccius
merluccius 173
productus 173
Micropterus
coosae 126
dolomieui 127
notius 126
punctulatus 126
punctulatus henshalli 126
punctulatus wichitae 126
salmoides 127
salmoides floridanus 126
treculi 126
Mobula diabola 184
Mobulidae 184
Molva molva 173
Morone
americana 144
chrysops 144
mississippiensis 144
saxatilis 145
Moronidae 144
Mugil
cephalus 180
curema 180
Mugilidae 180
Mullidae 180
Mullus surmuletus 180
Muraena helena 180
Muraenidae 160
Mycteroperca
bonaci 201
venenosa 200
Myliobatidae 184
Myliobatis californica 185
Myxus petardi 180

N

Nematistiidae 166
Nematistius pectoralis 167
Nereis spp. 92

O

Odonata 100, 102
Odontaspis
arenarius 197
taurus 197
Oncorhynchus 150
aguabonita 155
apache 279
clarki 155
clarki lewisi 155
gilae 279
gorbuscha 152
keta 153
kisutch 152
masou 152
mykiss 155
nerka 153
tshawytscha 153
Osteichthyes 124
Oxyjulis californica 176

P

Pagellus bogaraveo 202
Pagrus
nasutus 202
pagrus 203
Paralichthys
dentatus 182
lethostigma 182
Parophrys vetulus 182
Perca
flavescens 149
fluviatilis 149
Percichthyidae 144, 146
Percidae 148
Petrus repuestris 202
Phryganea

grandis 101
varia 115
Platichthys stellatus 182
Plecoptera 100, 102
Pleuronectes platessa 182
Pleuronectidae 182
Plotosidae 142
Pogonias cromis 189
Pollachius
pollachius 172
virens 172
Pomatomidae 158
Pomatomus saltatrix 158
Pomoxis
annularis 129
nigromaculatus 129
Prionace glauca 199
Pristidae 184
Pristis
pectinata 185
pristis 185
Promicrops lanceolatus 201
Prosopium
cylindraceum 157
williamsoni 157
Prototroctes maraena 279
Pseudopleuronectes
americanus 183
Pteronarcys
californica 117
Pylodictis olivaris 143

R

Rachycentridae 168
Rachycentron canadum 168
Raja
alba 187
batis 187
binoculata 186
clavata 184
eglanteria 186
erinacea 187
inornata 186
laevis 186
montagui 184
ocellata 187
oxyrinchus 187
Rajidae 184, 186
Rajiformes 184, 186
Rhacochilus toxotes 170
Rhincodon typus 198
Rhyacophila 101
Rhithrogena germanica 115
Roncador stearnsii 188
Rutilis
pigus pigus 137
pigus virgo 137
rutilus 137

S

Salmo 123, 150
salar 152
trutta 123, 154
Salmonidae 123, 150, 152, 154, 156
Salmothymus obtusirastris 279
Salvelinus 150
alpinus 150
confluentus 151
fontinalis 151
malma 151
namaycush 151
Sarda
australis 195
chiliensis 195
chiliensis chiliensis 194
chiliensis lineolata 194
orientalis 194
sarda 195
Scaphirhynchus albus 279
Scardinius
erythrophthalmus 137
Sciaenidae 188
Sciaenops ocellatus 188
Scomber
japonicus 191
scombrus 190
Scomberomorus
brasiliensis 191
cavalla 191
commerson 191

concolor 191
guttatus 191
maculatus 190
regalis 191
sierra 191
Scombridae 190, 192, 194
Scophthalmus maximus 183
Selachii 196, 198
Semicossyphus pulcher 176
Seriola
colburni 164
dumerili 165
fasciata 165
grandis 165
lalandi 165
lalandi dorsalis 165
rivoliana 164
Serranidae 200
Siluridae 142
Siluris glanis 142
Soleidae 182
Solen spp. 93
Sparidae 202
Sparus aurata 202
Sphyraena
argentea 162
barracuda 162
borealis 162
ensis 163
guachancho 162
novae-hollandiae 163
obtustata 163
picudilla 162
sphyraena 162
Sphyraenidae 162
Sphyrna zygaena 199
Spondyliosoma cantharus 202
Squalus acanthius 196
Stenodus leucichthys 156
Stenonema 114
Stenotomus
caprinus 202
chrysops 202
Stizostedion
canadense 148
lucioperca 149
vitreum 148
volgensis 149

T

Tandanus tandanus 142
Tautoga onitis 177
Tautogolabrus adspersus 177
Teraponidae 146
Tetrapturus
angustirostris 174
audax 174
belone 174
pfluegeri 174
Thunnus
alalunga 193
atlanticus 192
thynnus 193
Thymallidae 156
Thymallus
arcticus 157
thymallus 157
Tinca tinca 130
Trachinotus
botla 166
carolinus 166
falcatus 166
Trachurus
symmetricus 167
trachurus 190
Triakis semifasciata 196
Trichoptera 100, 101

U

Umbrina roncador 188
Urolophus halleri 185

V

Vimba vimba 132

X

Xiphias gladius 174
Xiphiidae 174

Z

Zygoptera 102

ACKNOWLEDGMENTS

This book was the work of a dedicated team of authors, photographers, and illustrators, plus a huge network of specialists and suppliers, to whom we would like to express our gratitude.

First, thanks to Martin at Photo Summit, whose coffee and excellent prints helped to get the book started; to John Wilson for his time, hospitality, and advice; to Mike Millman for his help and his willingness to try the impossible at short notice; to Ron Worsfold for the loan of his pole rigs; and to the late and much-missed Trevor Housby for his advice and encouragement.

Of all our suppliers, special mention must be made of Don Neish and Peter Morley at Don's of Edmonton, for supplying tackle at ludicrously short notice. Other individuals and companies whose contributions were especially valuable were Simon Bond (Shimano); Alan Bramley and Fiona Hemus (Partridge of Redditch); Bob Brownsdon (Shakespeare); Peter Drennan and daughter Sally (Drennan International); Sue and Chris Harris (Harris Angling Company); Chris Leibbrandt (Ryobi Masterline); David McGinlay (Daiwa); and John Rawle (Cox & Rawle).

We would also like to thank Richard Banbury (Orvis); Breakaway Tackle; Browning; Paul Burgess (Airflo); Jeremy Buxton (Asset Optics); Pat Byrne (D.A.M); Alan Caulfield (Penn); Darren Cox (DCD); Roy Eskins (HUFFishing); Brendan Fitzgerald (House of Hardy); Michael McManus (Carroll McManus); Nick Page (Nican Enterprises); Graeme Pullen (Blue Water Tackle); Andrew Reade (Keenets); Nicholas Stafford-Deitsch (Edington Sporting Co.); Mike Stratton (Thomas Turner & Sons); B. W. Wright (Nomad); Val and Chris (Vanguard Tackle, Boston); Bruce Vaughan and Dennis Moss (Wychwood Tackle); Clive Young (Young's of Harrow); and Nick Young (Leeda).

Finally, special thanks to Barbara, Hilary, and Jane for their support in difficult times; to the unflappable Janet at Ace; to Steve, Andy, Tim, Nick, Sara, and Gary at the studio; to Krystyna and Derek at Dorling Kindersley for their patience; and to Peter Kindersley, whose confidence allowed it to happen.

CREDITS

Illustrators
Colin Newman *pages 124–203*
Ian Heard *pages 210–219, 226–259*
Lyn Cawley *pages 82–87, 92–93, 208–209*
Alan Suttie *pages 15, 52, 206, 223–225, 259*
Maurice Pledger *pages 220–221*

Photographers
Key: *t* top, *c* centre, *b* bottom, *l* left, *r* right.
2 Peter Gathercole
3 Steve Gorton
6 Trevor Housby
7 *t* Mansell Collection, *c* Tim Heywood, *b* Mike Millman
8 *t* Trevor Housby, *c*, *b* Peter Gathercole
9 *t*, *c* Mike Millman, *b* John Wilson
10 John Wilson
12 Mike Millman
14–31 Steve Gorton and Andy Crawford
32–33 Steve Gorton; *antique reel by* Rodney Coldron
34–53 Steve Gorton and Andy Crawford
54–57 Peter Gathercole
58–79 Steve Gorton and Andy Crawford
80 John Wilson
82–87 Steve Gorton
88–91 Steve Gorton and Andy Crawford
92–93 Steve Gorton; *worms, sandeel by* Mike Millman
94–95 Mike Millman
96–97 Steve Gorton
98–121 Peter Gathercole, *with additional photos 100 t, 102 b by* Heather Angel
122 Oxford Scientific Films/Richard Davis
123 Oxford Scientific Films/Rudolf Ingo Riepl
204 Peter Gathercole
206–209 Steve Gorton
210 *t* Andy Crawford, *c* John Wilson, *b* Mike Millman
211 *t and b* John Wilson, *c* Peter Gathercole
212 Jim Tyree
213 Jim Tyree, *b* John Wilson
214 Steve Gorton
215 *t* Steve Gorton, *tl and c* John Wilson
216–218 Steve Gorton
219 *t* Steve Gorton, *b* John Wilson
220–221 Steve Gorton
222 *t and b* Steve Gorton, *c* Jim Tyree
223 *c and br* Jim Tyree, *bl* Steve Gorton
224 *t* Steve Gorton, *b* Jim Tyree
225 *t* Steve Gorton, *c* Jim Tyree
226–227 Jim Tyree
227 *b* Rodney Coldron
228 Jim Tyree, Andy Crawford
229 Mike Millman, Andy Crawford
230 John Wilson
231 *t and b* Steve Gorton, *cl and cr* John Wilson
232 *c* Steve Gorton, *b* Peter Gathercole
235 *tl and tr* Peter Gathercole
236 *c* Steve Gorton, *t and b* Peter Gathercole
237 Peter Gathercole
238–243 Peter Gathercole
244 John Darling
246 Mike Millman
249 Mike Millman
250–251 Jim Tyree
251 *tr* John Darling
252–253 Steve Gorton

253 *c* John Darling
254–255 Mike Millman
257 John Darling
258–259 Trevor Housby
261 Heather Angel
262 *t* Peter Gathercole, *b* John Wilson
263 John Wilson
264 *t* John Darling, *c* Jim Tyree, *b* John Wilson
265 *tr* Peter Gathercole, *b* Rodney Coldron
266 *t* Peter Gathercole, *c* Jim Tyree, *b* John Wilson
267 *c* John Wilson, *b* Mike Millman
268–269 John Wilson
270 *c* Jim Tyree, *b* Mike Millman
271–273 Mike Millman
274 *t and b* Phill Williams, *c* Mike Millman
275 *t* Mike Millman, *b* Phill Williams
276 Mike Millman
277 *c* John Wilson, *b* Mike Millman
278 Peter Gathercole
279 *t* Oxford Scientific Films, *b* Mike Millman

Manufacturers and Suppliers
The tackle was supplied by the manufacturers named in the main body of the book, except the Abu tackle, which was supplied by Don's of Edmonton. The floats, pages 62–63, were supplied by Drennan, and the Milo pole floats by Keenets. The lures, pages 88–91, were provided by Harris Angling Company. The flies were tied by Peter Gathercole. Other suppliers who have provided equipment for this book include:

Airflo, Fly Fishing Technology Ltd., Powys;
Asset Optics, Oxfordshire;
Blue Water Tackle, Hampshire;
Breakaway Tackle, Suffolk;
Browning, Bedfordshire;
Carroll McManus Ltd., East Sussex;
Cox & Rawle, Essex;
Daiwa Sports Ltd., Strathclyde;
D.A.M. (UK) Ltd., Worcestershire;
DCD, Warwickshire;
Don's of Edmonton, London;
Drennan International Ltd., Oxford;
Edington Sporting Co., Wiltshire;
Harris Angling Company, Norfolk;
House of Hardy, London;
HUFFishing, Bedfordshire;
Keenets (UK) Ltd., Wiltshire;
Leeda Group, Worcestershire;
Nican Enterprises, Hampshire;
Nomad UK, Lancashire;
Orvis, Hampshire;
Partridge of Redditch, Worcestershire;
Penn UK, Strathclyde;
Ryobi Masterline Ltd., Gloucestershire;
Shakespeare Company (UK) Ltd., Worcestershire;
Shimano Europe, Swansea;
Thomas Turner & Sons, Berkshire;
Vanguard Tackle, Lincolnshire;
Wychwood Tackle, Oxfordshire;
Youngs of Harrow, Middlesex.

40-512-3